THE PUBLIC POLICY
OF CRIME AND CRIMINAL JUSTICE

Association between behaviour at age 3 years
and adult criminality

n http:// bjp.rcpsych.org /content /179/ 3/ 197. full

College of Education - University of
Washington -

Re

http:// education.washington.edu / research/
rtm_08 /emotional_lit.html

Second Edition

THE PUBLIC POLICY OF CRIME AND CRIMINAL JUSTICE

Nancy E. Marion

University of Akron

Willard M. Oliver

Sam Houston State University

Prentice Hall

Boston   Columbus   Indianapolis   New York   San Francisco   Upper Saddle River
Amsterdam   Cape Town   Dubai   London   Madrid   Milan   Munich   Paris   Montreal   Toronto
Delhi   Mexico City   Sao Paulo   Sydney   Hong Kong   Seoul   Singapore   Taipei   Tokyo

Editor in Chief: Vernon R. Anthony
Acquisitions Editor: Eric Krassow
Editorial Assistant: Lynda Cramer
Director of Marketing: David Gesell
Marketing Manager: Adam Kloza
Senior Marketing Coordinator: Alicia Wozniak
Marketing Assistant: Les Roberts
Production Editor: Steve Robb
Project Manager: Susan Hannahs

Senior Art Director: Jayne Conte
Cover Designer: Suzanne Behnke
Cover Art: Fotolia
Full-Service Project Management: Sudeshna Nandy/ Aptara®, Inc.
Composition: Aptara®, Inc.
Text and Cover Printer/Bindery: R.R. Donnelley/ Harrisonburg
Text Font: 10/12 Minion

Credits and acknowledgments borrowed from other sources and reproduced, with permission, in this textbook appear on the appropriate page within the text.

Chapter Photos: p. 3: Ramin Talaie/CORBIS- NY; p.35: Marc Anderson/Pearson Education/PH College; p. 61: EyeWire Collection/Getty Images–Photodis; p. 89: Paul J. Richards/Getty Images Inc.; p. 135: Lawrence Jackson/The White House Photo Office; p. 174: The White House Photo Office; p. 213: S. Craig Crawford/U.S. Department of Justice; p. 241: Getty Images–Stockbyte; p. 280: Mike Derer/AP Wide World Photo; p. 303: George Dodson/Pearson Education/PH College; p. 338: David Graham/Pearson Education/PH College; p. 368: Laimute Druskis/Pearson Education/PH College; p. 395: Lawrence Jackson/AP Wide World Photos; p. 431: Ed Andrieski/AP Wide World Photos

Library of Congress Cataloging-in-Publication Data
Marion, Nancy E.
   The public policy of crime and criminal justice / Nancy E. Marion, Willard M. Oliver. — 2nd ed.
      p. cm.
   Includes index.
   ISBN-13: 978-0-13-512098-9
   ISBN-10: 0-13-512098-5
   1. Criminal justice, Administration of—United States.   2. Crime—Government policy—
United States.   3. United States. Violent Crime Control and Law Enforcement Act of
1994—Evaluation.   I. Oliver, Willard M.   II. Title.

HV9950.M293 2012
364.973—dc22
                                                        2010045722

10 9 8 7 6 5 4 3 2

Prentice Hall
is an imprint of

www.pearsonhighered.com

ISBN 10:   0-13-512098-5
ISBN 13: 978-0-13-512098-9

This book is dedicated to my parents and the JAM-D Club.
—N.E.M.—

This book is dedicated to my son James, who can now say he
has his own book again!
God continues to smile on me when you smile, James.
—W.M.O.—

CONTENTS

PREFACE

NEW TO THIS EDITION

- Updated tables & charts
- New photos to reflect current administration
- Contemporary examples have been incorporated into the text
- Minor errors, omissions, etc. have been rectified
- Stronger focus on state and local criminal justice agencies
- Three years of research incorporated into text

Public policy is the study of the choices the government makes in dealing with a problem. Criminal justice is the study of the organization, function, and processes of the agencies that deal with the problem of crime, namely, the police, courts, and corrections. While the study of public policy is not relegated to any particular discipline or field, the study of criminal justice is in reality a discipline that pulls from many other disciplines, such as sociology/criminology, public administration, and law. Combining these two areas of study, public policy and criminal justice, we are then talking about the study of the choices that government makes in dealing with the problem of crime through policy that impacts the criminal justice system.

The study of the public policy of crime and criminal justice is important for all citizens but especially for the student of criminal justice, for it helps us understand the process by which public policy is made and why we have the crime policy we have today. Understanding the public policy process, how the various actors influence public policy, and ultimately how this comes to impact the criminal justice system serves to remind us that our democratic system of government and its policies constitute a political process. And there can be little dispute that crime has become a major political issue of our day. Recognizing that the formation of crime policy is indeed a political process not only helps us understand current criminal justice policies but also points us in the direction for how best to shape future crime policy in America.

Although there have been many criminal justice journal articles addressing the public policy of crime and criminal justice, there has been a dearth of books related to this subject. While there have been some edited readers and books that provide a scanty overview of the topic, this is the first serious attempt at a definitive textbook detailing the public policy process as it relates to crime and criminal justice. It is our hope that this book will help fill a gap in our collective knowledge and that it will serve the students of criminal justice well.

To that end, the book is divided into four parts. Part 1 deals with the criminal justice policy process by providing an overview of criminal justice and public policy in chapter 1, explaining the important role that ideology plays in chapter 2, and then conveying the policy process and the different perspectives in regard to this process in chapter 3. Part 2 then analyzes the important actors and the roles they play in the public policy process. Individual chapters are dedicated to the executive, legislative, and judicial branches of government as well as the bureaucracies, public opinion and the media (collectively in one chapter), and interest groups. Part 3 focuses on the role that the criminal justice system plays in the public policy process with chapters dedicated to the police, courts, and corrections as well as the juvenile justice system. Finally, Part 4, with only one chapter, provides an in-depth case study to walk the reader through a specific real-world example of a policy that has had a significant impact on criminal justice in America, namely, the Violent Crime Control and Law Enforcement Act of 1994, with its focus on community policing and the "100,000 Cops" program.

Nancy E. Marion

Willard M. Oliver

ACKNOWLEDGMENTS

There is no such thing as the lone author writing in a vacuum, devoid of any assistance from the outside world. Even when two authors collaborate, as we have done here, a book can never be solely the fruits of the authors' labors. Rather, writing is the culmination of lifelong learning and influence from others as well as the direct assistance by those around us. We would therefore like to acknowledge all of those who have had an influence on us and have participated directly in the production of this book. Oddly enough, we must start with each other:

> If it were not for the work of Nancy Marion, my doctoral work would not have been possible. Nancy laid the groundwork for what would become my dissertation, later published as *The Law and Order Presidency* (Prentice Hall, 2003). This led to a friendship with someone I highly respect and now the second edition of this book.

> —W.M.O.—

> And I would like to acknowledge Will Oliver for asking me to coauthor this book and without whom this book would never have happened.

> —N.E.M.—

In addition, we would like to thank our families for their patience and understanding in regard to the time it takes to write a book such as this. We both appreciate the love and support of our families.

Moreover, we both must acknowledge the people and institutions that served to shape our thinking about the public policy field. For Nancy it was the School of Justice at American University and their justice program as well as all the faculty, especially Barbara Ann Stolz and Richard Bennett. For Will it was the criminal justice program at Radford University and particularly Paul Lang's (currently of Northern Michigan University) public policy class as well as West Virginia University's Political Science Program, specifically with the tutelage of Kevin Leyden, John Kilwein, Jeff Worsham, Robert DiClerico, Bob Duval and Chris Mooney. We thank all of you for making this book possible.

The authors would like to thank Daniel Stewart, a graduate student at Sam Houston State University, for his work on many of the ancillaries and the Sam Houston State University Writing Center, especially Delma J. Talley and Dr. Diane Dowdey, for greatly improving our writing (although all mistakes are still clearly ours). We would like to thank all of the Prentice Hall editors we have worked for in regard to this book—Frank Mortimer, Tim Peyton, and Eric Krassow—their dedication and faith in this project has remained consistent through all three editors, which reflects highly not only on themselves, but on Prentice Hall as well. We would also like to thank Steve Robb for his work on this edition of the book.

We thank all reviewers for their suggestions and comments. Our personal reviewer has been Marvin Zalman of Wayne State University, who has continued to challenge us with his many e-mails and edits, so much so that we feel he is in many ways a third author on this book. We would also like to thank the reviewers of the second edition manuscript: Kevin L. Daugherty, Central New Mexico Community College; Helen T. Green, Texas Southern University; Richard M. Hough, Sr., University of West Florida; Arrick Jackson, University of North Texas; and Johnny McGaha, Florida Gulf Coast University.

ABOUT THE AUTHORS

Nancy E. Marion is professor of political science at the University of Akron, Akron, Ohio. She holds a Ph.D. in political science/public policy from the State University of New York at Binghamton. She is the author of several books and numerous scholarly articles on the public policy of crime and criminal justice. Her research interests revolve around the interplay of politics and criminal justice.

    Willard M. Oliver is professor of criminal justice in the College of Criminal Justice, Sam Houston State University, in Huntsville, Texas. He holds a Ph.D. in political science/public policy from West Virginia University. He is the author of numerous books, including *Community-Oriented Policing: A Systemic Approach to Policing, Fourth Edition* (Prentice Hall, 2004), and *The Law and Order Presidency* (Prentice Hall, 2003). He has published numerous scholarly articles in various criminal justice journals, many related to the public policy of crime and criminal justice. His research interests include the politics and policy of crime, community-oriented policing, and historical perspectives of crime and criminal justice.

THE PUBLIC POLICY
OF CRIME AND CRIMINAL JUSTICE

PART ONE

The Criminal Justice
Policy Process

Criminal Justice and Public Policy

INTRODUCTION

Criminal justice and public policy are the two disciplines of research between which, on occasion, we tend to find some commonality. Criminal justice researchers generally conduct research in the areas of police, courts, and corrections. When reporting their research, they will often mention in the concluding section that the findings have public policy implications. Public policy researchers often focus on areas such as economic policy and foreign policy, and on social policy issues, such as health care and welfare. Occasionally, a public policy researcher will conduct research in the criminal justice field but generally as an aside and not as their primary area of focus. In other words, the disciplines of criminal justice and public policy do not often intersect in their respective bodies of literature.

The reality, however, is that criminal justice and public policy intersect on a daily basis. All Americans at some level of cognition face the problem of crime. At the most simplistic level, there are those for whom the topic of crime is a part of everyday conversation. People read the newspapers, watch the evening news, or pick up various crime stories off the Internet. These topics, such as a local murder, the controversial debate over racial profiling, or the problem of teen drug use, can become topics of general conversation. Some individuals even change their behavior because of their fear of becoming a victim of crime. People are afraid to walk alone at night, they lock and bar their doors, or they entirely cease certain behaviors in the wake of a highly visible crime. Examples of this behavior include the avoidance of commercial air flight after the terrorist attacks of September 11, 2001, or pumping gas in northern Virginia gas stations in October 2002 because of the Washington, D.C., snipers. Finally, there are those who fall victim to crimes and those who work within the criminal justice system who must deal with crime on a very personal basis. In sum, whether we like it or not, crime is a problem that all Americans must deal with both directly and indirectly.

Americans, as a result, want something done about the problem of crime. They look to the criminal justice system to address these problems. Therefore, whatever the system does or fails to do helps shape crime policy in America. And, as it has been pointed out, "crime policy has perhaps taken on more importance at the beginning of the twenty-first century than at any other point in our nation's history."[1]

The criminal justice system does not, however, operate in a vacuum. It does not create the crime policies for America and then carry them out in isolation. The three components of the criminal justice system—police, courts, and corrections—work to address these problems on a daily basis and, as a result, help shape crime policy in America. However, the criminal justice system is merely one aspect of a larger social, political, and economic environment that forms our crime policy in the United States. Therefore, in order to understand the criminal justice system in America and the policies it implements, one must also understand the public policy process and all the factors that shape it.

To begin understanding the public policy of criminal justice, it is helpful to first place it within the context of politics. The political system helps shape and form the public policy of crime. The politics denoted here refers to the dichotomy between what the people want and what the politicians are willing to pass. This does not necessarily have to be rooted in reality, as, with crime, we will see it often is not. The fear of crime and the perceptions that people have of crime often shape the public policy of crime rather than crime shaping the public policy. This is because fear is something that is much more easily manipulated by politicians in order to serve their political purposes. It is much more difficult to manipulate crime, for crime is often unpredictable and not easily controlled. Therefore, it is easier to respond to the fear of crime rather than crime itself. Yet, this is why crime policy has become so highly politicized over the past forty years not only at the local level of government but at the national level as well. Understanding this history of how crime has become politicized and how crime policy in America has developed provides a foundation for understanding how the public policy of criminal justice works today.

To this end, this chapter first reviews the definitions that are used in both the public policy and the criminal justice fields. It then explores the topics of the politics of crime, fear of crime, crime reality, and the politicization of crime and provides a brief history of crime policy in America. Finally, a brief discussion for understanding how public policy is studied and its significance to the field of criminal justice is conveyed.

DEFINITIONS REGARDING CRIME POLICY IN AMERICA

Crime

As the basis of crime policy is crime itself, it is important to understand what is generally meant by the term *crime*. According to the *Dictionary of Criminal Justice, crime* is defined as "an act committed or omitted in violation of a law forbidding or commanding it, for which the possible penalties upon conviction for an adult include incarceration, for which a corporation can be penalized by fine or forfeit, or for which a juvenile can be adjudged delinquent or transferred to criminal court for prosecution."[2] The key element here is that someone has committed a behavior that has been defined by a legislative body as being against the law. Rush defines it even further when he explains that "crimes are defined as offenses against the state and are to be distinguished from violations of the civil law that involves harms done to individuals—such as torts—for which the state demands restitution rather than punishment."[3] The key element here is that crimes are violations against the state as per criminal legislation and not personal wrongs for which lawsuits are often brought. A crime, then, is a behavior defined by the legislative body to be a criminal act against the state for which a punishment is attached. For example, murder is defined as being a criminal act for which those convicted of this crime against the state may be sentenced to prison or, in those states with laws allowing for the death penalty, executed.

It should be noted that crimes are defined by the legislative bodies at the federal, state, or local level. According to Marion, "'Crimes' are behaviors that are defined as criminal acts by political actors through the political process."[4] Certain behaviors are brought to the attention of legislators, who then must debate whether to pass legislation making such behavior illegal. For example, a recent issue that has come to the attention of many is the watching of pornography in vehicles driving on the highways. Other people can see these videos from their cars driving on the same highway. The question arises as to whether this behavior should be illegal. It is the federal, state, and local legislative bodies that will have to determine if this is illegal behavior and what sanctions would go with a person exhibiting these behaviors in order to make it a crime. Therefore, it should be understood that defining what is a crime is purely a political process.

Criminal Law

Once crimes are defined through the political process, they become part of our criminal law as found in the criminal statutes or penal code. The federal government maintains its own penal code for defining those behaviors that are violations against federal law. Each state also maintains its own criminal code defining what behaviors are criminal and the punishment that one may receive when found in violation of the law. Most charges against the criminal law are made by using state penal codes. Federal violations are only for federal violations of the law, and most local jurisdictions (cities and towns) typically do not maintain a complete penal code, because they enforce the state penal code. However, local jurisdictions often do maintain city ordinances, or those behaviors that are violations against the law of the city or town, such as local noise violations.

Common Law

The sources of the criminal law in America are quite vast. The origins of American law first began with English common law. As early as A.D. 680, the English created a system of law that was based on English customs, tradition, and rules. Over time, as judges decided new cases, they based their decisions on the existing laws but modified them to reflect the current values, attitudes, and ethics of the people.[5] Common law was largely unwritten law, and it was not until Blackstone's *Commentaries on the Law*, published in four volumes between 1765 and 1769, that the concept of recording the law was advanced. The American colonists, however, unlike their English counterparts, recorded the law from the very beginning with Dale's Law in 1611 in the Virginia Colony. This practice would continue throughout the colonial era, and when America declared its independence in 1776, Americans at the federal, state, and local levels were given the opportunity to adopt the English common law as their own codified law, modify the English common law to suit their needs, or abolish the common law and start all over. Most chose to modify the common law, and one example of this is Thomas Jefferson's work from 1777 to 1779 to modify the English common law for Virginia.[6]

Constitutional Law

The second basis for our laws today was through the ratification of the Constitution in 1788 and the adoption of the Bill of Rights in 1791. The Constitution gave power to lawmakers to create or define new crimes as needed, but it also puts limits on the power of the federal government and thereby protects our freedom. While the Constitution established the framework for how government would work in the United States, the Bill of Rights was passed in 1791 to give individuals certain freedoms as a means of protection against the national government. The Bill of Rights—the first ten amendments to the Constitution—delineated these specific rights granted to America's citizens. These include the First Amendment's freedoms of speech, press, religion, and assembly. In terms of protecting people from what would clearly be the most intrusive element of government, the criminal justice system, the founders put limits on police behavior (Fourth Amendment); put a limit on the admissibility of confessions that have been obtained unfairly (Fifth Amendment); provided for the rights against self-incrimination (Fifth Amendment); provided for the right to a speedy and public trial, to an impartial jury, to confront witnesses, and to the assistance of counsel (Sixth Amendment); and protected against excessive bail, excessive fines, and cruel and unusual punishment (Eighth Amendment).[7] These rights continue to be a key element of citizen protection today against not only the federal government but state and local governments as well.

Natural Law

The third source of our law is called natural law.[8] Natural law was originally held as being derived from God; hence, these were God's law. They were encapsulated in the Ten Commandments, given to Moses by God. These laws included the commandments "thou shalt not kill," "thou shalt not steal," and "thou shall not covet thy neighbor's goods." These Ten Commandments were the basis of numerous legal systems, to include colonial America's, but as a result of the Enlightenment, the meaning dramatically shifted away from God and the Ten Commandments. The more modern definition has to do with people's inherent moral principles and values that guide their behavior. Most people understand what behaviors are "right" and "wrong," and this helps form our criminal laws.[9]

Statutory Law

Statutory law, which is generally referred to as criminal law, consists of the federal, state, and local ordinances and legislation that define the law. Statutes are the laws passed by the legislative body of government, such as the U.S. Congress for the federal government and state legislatures for state governments. City councils can also pass ordinances that define local offenses, but, as previously stated, state criminal law is commonly enforced at the local level because criminal violations are violations against the state.

Substantive Law

Statutory law can be further defined as either being substantive law or procedural law. Substantive law is defined as "the part of the law that creates, defines, and regulates rights."[10] This is generally focused on the guarantees provided to all citizens under the Constitution, specifically those rights found in the Bill of Rights. These are the protections against unreasonable searches and seizures, the right to a speedy and public trial, and the right against excessive bail and cruel and unusual punishments. Substantive law tells us under what circumstances searches and seizures are unreasonable, what specifically is meant by "speedy," and how we know what is excessive bail or cruel and unusual punishment.

Procedural law refers to the "branch of law that prescribes in detail the methods or procedures to be used in determining and enforcing the rights and duties of persons toward each other under substantive law."[11] Procedural law focuses heavily on the administrative process by which citizen's rights are ensured. A key aspect of procedural law is that no one can be deprived of their life, liberty, or property without due process of law; therefore, procedural law is focused on the administrative process for ensuring that these rights are protected. The government (e.g., the police) cannot simply enter a person's property and seize property. They must first go before a judge to secure a search warrant. The individual is also afforded the opportunity to have a lawyer defend him or her against the state's charges. All these rights are focused on procedural law.

Case Law

Case law is the "judicial precedent generated as a by-product of the decisions that courts have made to resolve unique disputes, as distinguished from statutes and constitutions. Case law concerns concrete facts; statutes and constitutions are written in the abstract."[12] In other words, case law is made by the decisions of judges in deciding cases. Prior to issuing their decisions, judges consult previous case law on the same subject matter and look to see how previous judges have decided. This is known as stare decisis. When they issue their decision, they are then contributing to the body of case law that builds over time, providing the precedents for future cases. As is often the case, many times judges arrive at different conclusions, and case law builds in different jurisdictions, different states, or different circuit courts. If the conflict is found at the district level, often the circuit courts will determine which body of case law is correct, thus again contributing to case law that will be used in future cases. In the case of a conflict between circuit courts, it is the U.S. Supreme Court that will be the final arbiter, as the Constitution deems the Supreme Court to be the highest court in the land; hence, it has the final say. Supreme Court decisions then set precedents for future cases.

Administrative Law

Administrative laws are "statutes, regulations, and orders that govern public agencies" and are essentially the "rules governing the administrative operations of the government."[13] These laws are regulatory in nature and are passed by government to control certain sectors. These sectors consist of various industries, businesses, and individuals and may include such laws aimed at regulating building codes, health codes, and environmental codes.[14] Governmental agencies, such as the Food and Drug Administration, the Environmental Protection Agency, or the Occupational Safety and Health Administration, are often developed to enforce these particular codes. All these agencies give regulatory powers to enforce their sector of administrative law, and individuals, industries, and businesses found guilty often face extensive fines. Because of the power of these regulatory agencies exercise through administrative law, this type of law has often been referred to as the fourth branch of government.

The enforcement, prosecution, and punishment of these laws are the responsibility of the American criminal justice system. Criminal justice is generally defined as consisting of three components: the police, the courts, and the corrections system. The police are responsible for detecting and apprehending people who are accused of breaking the law, the court system decides if a person is guilty of committing a crime, and the corrections system carries out the sentences imposed on a guilty defendant. Although many refer to this as the criminal justice "system," each of the components developed largely independent of one another into their own institutions. Many, therefore, argue that there are really three separate systems that exist in a network relationship, as they deal with the same subject matter: the crimes and the criminally accused. Others argue that the criminal justice system is truly a system of three working components all functioning together toward the attainment of the common goal: again, dealing with crime and the criminally accused.

Criminal Justice

The phrase *criminal justice* is actually absent throughout most of American history, and it was not until the 1968 publication of *The Challenge of Crime in a Free Society* by The President's Commission on Law Enforcement and Administration of Justice that "America's system of criminal justice" was referred as such.[15] The resulting effect was an emphasis in higher education to no longer focus on "police studies" or "penology studies" but rather look at the entire breadth of America's criminal justice system and study how it can best be configured to deal with the problem of crime. It does this largely through an interdisciplinary approach by drawing on the information and knowledge of many disciplines, such as sociology, psychology, economics, public administration, anthropology, law, and political science.

Criminology

There was, however, another discipline that preceded criminal justice: criminology. The term *criminology* was originally used largely to denote any studying of the topic of crime, whether it was why crime occurs, a study of police science, or when researchers looked at the courts and correctional systems. That largely changed in the 1960s, when the emphasis became more on studying the question of why people commit crime rather than looking at the specific administrative aspects of the criminal justice system. Therefore, criminology today revolves around the study of human behavior as it relates to crime. Criminologists want to know why people commit crimes and what society can do to prevent additional criminal behavior.

Administration of Justice

Another characteristic phrase common in this field is "administration of justice" or "administration theory," which explores the criminal justice system from an organizational perspective. Public organizations are those government agencies, like criminal justice, that are created to be agents of some unit of government (Federal, state, local, etc.) and have as their purpose the administration of law. The concepts here are firmly rooted in the public administration discipline and look to how criminal justice agencies organize, administer, and manage. The focus is often on how best to organize the criminal justice system to be most effective and efficient in the performance of its duties. Thus, it will explore individuals (personal communication, motivation, leadership), group behavior (occupational socialization, organizational conflict), and processes in criminal justice organizations (decision making, change, innovation).[16] Associated with the administration of justice is the concepts of creating policies and procedures, but the policies denoted here are written declarations for how these agencies organize, administer, and manage, not in the sense of the public policy process; although it should be noted that the administration of justice plays a significant role in public policy.

Public Policy

There are many definitions of the term *public policy*. Thomas R. Dye provides a very general definition when he defines public policy as "what governments do, why they do it, and what difference it makes."[17] The previously mentioned Harold Lasswell, however, defines public policy as "a projected program of goals, values, and practices."[18] Others, such as Cochran et al., refer to it as "the actions of government and the intentions that determine those actions,"[19] and Easton solely defines it as "the impacts of government activity."[20] James Anderson provides another good view when he states that it is "a purposive course of action followed by an actor or set of actors in dealing with a problem or matter of concern."[21] In the end, all these definitions look at the process by which problems, both real and imagined, are addressed by government activities in order to reach a decision that will impact the problem.[22] Thus, when looking at criminal justice in America, whenever a new crime problem arises, the public policy process, or the mechanism by which various political actors (those in power), works to address the problem and implement a new policy, be it a new law, added punishment to a preexisting law, or expenditures to direct benefits to a particular group.

Policy Analysis

Just as there are a number of definitions for *public policy*, so too are there a number of definitions for *policy analysis*. Again, Thomas R. Dye, a leading author in this area, defines policy analysis as the description and explanation of the causes of government activity as well as their conse-quences.[23] From this standpoint, the goal of policy analysis is to explain how the public policy process works rather than having the goal of offering solutions to specific policies. Others dis-agree with Dye. For instance, Grover Starling believes that policy analysis is a multidisciplinary process aimed at reaching solid public policy decisions.[24] Mood defines this even more defini-tively when he explains that the ultimate goal of policy analysis is "improving the behavior, regu-lations, practices, or agencies of public agencies; hence they are aimed at changing the laws, ordi-nances, or government structure under which such organizations operate."[25] Brewer and DeLeon believe that policy analysis should provide alternatives and suggestions to public policy decision makers, giving them as much information on policy solutions as possible.[26] Finally, Randall B. Ripley sees policy analysis as a method that can be employed by multiple disciplines to under-stand all these aspects of the public policy process.[27] Ripley sees policy analysis as the systematic and objective analysis of a specific policy to improve the policy process. Each of these authors and their definitions highlight the breadth and depth of policy analysis and demonstrate that it is a wide and varied area of study that can have an equally wide and varied impact.

Applying all this to the study of crime and criminal justice, then, is what this book is all about. Simply stated, it is the policy analysis of crime and criminal justice as it relates to the pub-lic policy process. This means that any policy issue related to the criminal law—those behaviors that have been defined by law as criminal—and the criminal justice system—specifically focusing on the administration of justice through the three components of police, courts, and correc-tions—is part of criminal justice policy process. Research aimed at providing explanations of how the process works and how the process can be improved is one aspect of policy analysis. The other aspect includes research aimed at providing decision makers with alternatives in the policy process and assessing the consequences of both past and future policies. Taken together, analyz-ing issues of criminal law and criminal justice as they apply to criminal justice policy in order to explain the process and to inform decision makers on alternatives and outcomes can be our working definition of criminal justice policy analysis.

THE POLITICS OF CRIME IN AMERICA

Crime in the United States—and especially violent crime—is an issue of concern for most Americans. Capturing the exact level of concern, however, has been difficult. A number of public opinion polls that have asked directly about a person's fear of crime appear to elicit high levels of responses, often translated as high levels of fear. For example, when respondents were asked in 2009, "Is there more crime in *your area* than there was a year ago, or less?" 51 percent answered

| **TABLE 1.1** | Public perception of crime in the United States, 1992–2009 | | |

Question: Is there more crime in the United States than there was a year ago or less?

	More	Less	Same	Don't Know/ Refused
1992	89	3	4	4
1993	87	4	5	4
1996	71	15	8	6
1997	64	25	6	5
1998	52	35	8	5
2000	47	41	7	5
2001	41	43	10	6
2002	62	21	11	6
2003	60	25	11	4
2004	53	28	14	5
2005	67	21	9	3
2006	68	16	8	8
2007	71	14	8	6
2008	67	15	9	9
2009	74	15	6	5

Source: *Sourcebook of Criminal Justice Statistics Online,* www.albany.edu/sourcebook/

that there was more and 29 percent that it was the same.[28] When asked that same year, "Is there more crime *in the United States* than there was a year ago, or less?" 74 percent answered that there was more and 15 percent that it was the same.[29] Taken together, Americans believed that crime was either getting worse or had not improved over the previous year—this in spite of the fact that, as we will demonstrate, throughout the time period 1992–2009, America had been experiencing a nearly two-decade-long decline in crime. (See Table 1.1.)

Other polls that ask about fear of crime more indirectly have demonstrated an on-again/off-again level of fear among the American people. In January 1994, in a Gallup Public Opinion Poll question that asked respondents, "What is the most important problem facing the country?" 37 percent of respondents answered "crime and violence."[30] This was the first time in the history of the Gallup Public Opinion Poll's question that crime was cited as the number one issue. The question was repeated in August, and the level rose to 39 percent of respondents indicating that crime was the most important problem. Five additional polls that same year supported this finding.[31] Crime was again the number one problem in 1995 and 1996. However, several years earlier, in 2003, only 2 percent responded with "crime and violence" as the most important problem, and more recently, in 2008, less than 1 percent of respondents mentioned "crime and violence."[32] Crime had peaked in 1991 and has been on a continual decline since 1992. This would seem to cast into confusion any legitimacy that crime is truly the "most important problem facing the country." (See Figure 1.1.)

What is perhaps not in doubt is that over the past forty years, the attitudes, opinions, and perceptions that the American people have toward crime have changed dramatically. Americans

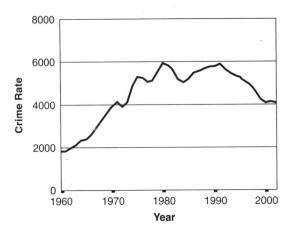

FIGURE 1.1   Crime Rate per 100,000 Population, 1960–2002.   *Source:* Federal Bureau of Investigation, Uniform Crime Reports, 2002, 1983, 1973.

have become acutely concerned with the topic of crime, and an overwhelming number have cited it as a serious threat to our rights and freedoms and argue that too little is being done to address the problem.[33] There has been a public outcry over the problem of crime (and drugs and terrorism) in our nation and politicians are only too happy to respond to these sentiments with rhetoric, legislation, and budgetary support. As a result, crime has become a political issue at all levels of government, including the national level, which traditionally has left the issue to the state and local governments.

The politicization of crime has also created a paradox. There is increased concern over crime as reported in many public opinion surveys and increased news media coverage of crime, and crime permeates our popular culture. Juxtaposed against this increased concern with crime is empirical evidence that crime over the past several decades has been steadily declining. Why, if crime rates in the United States have been falling for nearly two decades, was there such an increase in the amount of public concern over crime? The answer is essentially a paradox that pits crime perceptions against crime reality, and the results indicate that much of our crime policy is based on the former rather than on, as one would hope, the latter. To fully understand this paradox, we must first look at the empirical evidence that demonstrates that the public perception of crime has increased over the past several decades and that crime has decreased during this same time period. It is only after we establish this fact that we can later explain this crime paradox. As the perception of crime is easier to recognize, for it permeates our society on a daily basis, it is to this we now turn.

CRIME PERCEPTIONS

Public opinion polls are generally the means by which we assess the public's perception of crime in America. Polls asking respondents whether they are afraid to walk alone at night, if they believe that crime is rising, and if too little was being spent on crime have consistently, since the 1970s, been answered in the affirmative.[34] And the answers to these questions generally do not waver much in their responses for the majority, averaging around 70 percent, who have consistently responded there is a severe problem. As previously cited as well, the Gallup Poll's question of the "most important problem facing the country" has also elicited high levels of concern for crime, although far more sporadic than those polls that ask more directly about crime. Yet it is obvious that crime is of concern to the American people. The important question, however, is, Where do they derive their perceptions of crime?

The American perception of crime starts with the individual American. The perception of crime is inherently a psychological process and is therefore unique to each individual.[35] For this reason, how individuals perceive the world, the stereotypes they carry with them, and their attitudes will help shape and form their perceptions of crime. Some have articulated that there is a "mean-world" syndrome that contributes to the perception by individuals that there are always high levels of crime regardless of the reality.[36] Other empirical research has suggested that perhaps individual belief in crime is demonstrative of veiled racist attitudes and that crime is a race-coded issue.[37] Studies have shown that many Americans believe that the typical offender is African-American, and hence many believe that crime is synonymous with "black crime."[38] Americans have also demonstrated misconceptions about who goes to prison (most believe serious offenders) and how long the average prison term is (many believe twenty or more years).[39] The reality is that most people who go to jail are entering for misdemeanors, many of which are drug related, and the average stay for those convicted of felonies is only between five and seven years. Much of this may simply be ignorance of the criminal justice system. And while the origins of these beliefs are important, what is most critical to note here is that attitudes, prejudice, and stereotypes do play a role in creating the false perceptions that Americans have about crime and that, subsequently, crime policy is affected by these false perceptions.

In moving beyond the perceptions of individuals to understanding the perceptions of Americans in the aggregate, we must next look at crime itself. Crime is a very traumatic event and has the capability of being grossly distorted by everyone involved in the incident. As a crime will most likely have the greatest impact on the victim of the crime, from simple house burglaries to a robbery by gunpoint, the possibility of distorted images of crime begins at the point of the criminal incident. Research has shown that victims tend to overemphasize everything involved in the crime, including the length of the incident, the size of the weapon, and the description of the assailant.[40] This gross exaggeration is important, for often the individual's perception of the crime, the victim's narrative, and the reality of crime are very different in nature. However, as the victim is the starting point in most criminal investigations, the victim plays a critical role in establishing the initial "facts" of the case. If a victim's statements, descriptions, and recollections of the event are exaggerated, the information that friends, relatives, the police, and the media receive will be exaggerated as well. In most instances, the victim will, unless severely shamed by the crime, share his or her experiences with other people. Experience shows us that when a story or narrative is retold by others, it changes as each storyteller adds a little or cuts a little. The distortions of the crime will then be delivered to those acquaintances of the victim who will in turn relay the information to other friends, relatives, and coworkers. Because of this, the perception of crime in America can become exaggerated and distorted.

Although personal attitudes, opinions, and stereotypes—as well as the sharing of criminal events among friends, relatives, and coworkers—do help promulgate this misconception about crime in America, these contagions are limited in scope and impact because they are, after all, isolated incidents. The source of crime information that has the greatest impact on society is the mass media.[41] The various forms of mass media, including print media, television news, television real-life stories, television entertainment, and other forms of popular media, all have the capability of bringing the subject of crime to the masses. Our perception of crime is built no longer on isolated incidents or victimizations of family, friends, and coworkers but rather on crime that occurs in our towns, in neighboring towns, in other states, and indeed in other countries. A random example of this was found in the front-page section of a Charleston, West Virginia, newspaper, that reported on one criminal event in the city of Charleston; nine stories on crime across the state, including a hostage taking, a murder trial, and a mail fraud; three stories out of state, including a rape, a triple murder, and a man who killed the mayor of a Colorado town; and one out-of-country crime story.[42] Crime no longer has boundaries because the media's presentation of crime news is no longer isolated or restricted to what occurs in one's own town. In addition, research has found that the variations in the volume of local crime news being reported had little relationship to the actual changes and fluctuations in local crime rates.[43] Therefore, inflated reporting of news stories heightens awareness of crime, subsequently creating a false perception of the crime problem among the American people.

Numerous studies have shown that crime news accounts for an estimated 5 to 25 percent of all news stories in newspapers, radio, and television, confirming the adage that "if it bleeds, it leads."[44] One author has described this practice of increasing the number of crime news stories by the media as the "commodification of crime."[45] While both newspapers and radio news coverage of crime are guilty of overinflating their crime stories, the most successful perpetrator of the overinflation of crime news is television. Studies on the coverage of crime on the evening news programs of the three major networks (ABC, CBS, and NBC) have found that during the early 1990s, when crime rates were falling, the number of stories tripled from 571 stories in 1991 to 1,632 stories in 1993.[46] By 1996, there were nearly 5,000 crime stories, and news specifically about homicide increased more than 700 percent from 1991 to 1996.[47] In addition, another study has shown that 95 percent of the respondents stated that their primary source for information on crime was television.[48] Taken together, if the majority of Americans are receiving their crime news through the mass media—and particularly television—and yet the mass media have continued to distort the reality of crime by overinflating the number of stories, Americans are clearly receiving a false understanding of the crime problem.

This false reality is compounded by television shows that depict reality in the form of entertainment.[49] Television programers have found that programs often called "infotainment" and "shockumentaries" are popular with the American people for their depictions of crime and the criminal justice system. Television shows such as *Cops* and *America's Most Wanted*, as well as specials such as Fox's *World's Scariest Police Shootouts* and *World's Scariest Police Chases*, have the effect of increasing our perception of crime in the United States. In addition, television drama focuses heavily on the topic of crime, with shows such as *Law and Order: Los Angeles*, *Cold Case*, and *CSI-New York*, which feed America's fascination with crime.[50] These programs have the capability of increasing our awareness of crime. Therefore, not only do we read about crime in our newspapers, hear about it on the radio, and watch it on the evening news, but we also see it when we sit down to be entertained. While some may argue that Americans have always had a fascination for crime and that this is nothing new, one must concede that the level of graphic depiction, the passing of "real crime stories" as entertainment, and the vast amount of coverage and methods for transmitting crime stories have all increased, thus increasing the impact the media have on the public. As one researcher has pointed out, "Television's mean and dangerous world tends to cultivate a sense of relative danger, mistrust, insecurity, vulnerability, dependence, and—despite its supposedly 'entertaining' nature—alienation and gloom."[51]

Crime permeates society in a number of other ways. Crime stories are a main staple of the books, both fiction and nonfiction, that we read. Academic textbooks have also proliferated in the past several decades, including this one, which discusses and analyzes the topic of crime in a variety of ways. Children's video games are often built around some form of crime, and most are assuredly centered on the topic of violence. In addition, even children's comic books have gone the way of extreme acts of violence and a constant depiction of crime to fill their dark and somber pages.[52] We can turn to our local movie theater or video rental store and witness numerous movie titles that speak clearly of crime and violence, and now we are faced with the Internet, where crime and violence are easily accessed anywhere throughout the world via the World Wide Web. One Web site in particular is so convincing that it is a true-crime scene from the pictures, interviews, and corner reports that a specific link is titled "Reality Check" to ensure those viewers interested enough to take the time to read this link that the crime scene depicted is, in fact, fictitious.[53] It is becoming more and more difficult to discern between the reality of crime and the perceptions that we have of crime. All this has essentially led crime down the pathway to becoming part of popular culture.

It should be clear by now that the demarcation line between reality and fiction, related to crime, has become highly obfuscated. It is important to recognize and face the fact that crime perceptions are highly inflated among the American people. Otherwise, to continue encouraging these perceptions as some prejudiced people, the media, and the politicians do is to encourage a severe misunderstanding of crime and hence to contribute directly to the problem. Recognizing the perception side of this crime paradox, we must now turn to the other side of the paradox: crime reality.

CRIME REALITY

To understand the reality of crime in the United States, we must turn to those indicators that provide us with a more realistic portrait of the level of crime in the United States and how it has fluctuated from year to year. The primary indicators that are most often utilized in the field are the Uniform Crime Reports and the National Criminal Victimization Survey. Each of these provides a different perspective on the level of crime and assists us in understanding the true nature of crime in the United States since they let us measure its prevalence. Taken together, they begin to move us toward a more accurate picture of crime in the United States.

Uniform Crime Reports

The primary source for crime statistics in the United States is the Uniform Crime Reports (UCR), which are collected, maintained, and reported by the Federal Bureau of Investigation (FBI). The UCR was begun in 1930 at the behest of the International Associations of Chiefs of Police through the leadership of FBI Director J. Edgar Hoover and through a congressional mandate as a method of collecting data from every police agency in the United States in order to report on those crimes "known to the police."[54] The methodology utilized to collect these data has, for the most part, remained the same since the inception of the UCR and is based on citizens reporting crime to the police. Most law enforcement agencies in the United States then collect these crime statistics and report them to a central state location, such as state departments of justice, which then forward the collected information to the FBI, while some agencies report directly to the FBI. While there is no mandate that a law enforcement agency report its crime data to the FBI, approximately 97 percent of the more than 18,000 agencies in the United States do, yielding a data set that covers over 95 percent of the American population. Once the FBI has collected the information from the agencies, they process it for dissemination to the public through preliminary reports and a final report that is published at the end of each year for the previous year, titled *Crime in the United States: Uniform Crime Reports.*

The reports divide crime into "Part I" and "Part II" offenses. Those crimes considered by the FBI to be the most serious and most frequent in occurrence and most often to come to the

BOX 1.1
FBI Index Part 1 Crimes

Murder and Nonnegligent Homicide	The willful (nonnegligent) killing of one human being by another. Deaths caused by negligence, suicide, accident, and justifiable homicide are not included in the count for this offense. Attempt to murder or assault to murder is categorized under aggravated assaults.
Forcible rape	The carnal knowledge of a female forcibly against her will. Included are assaults or attempts to commit rape by force or the threat of force. Statutory rape (without force) and other sex offenses are excluded, however.
Robbery	The taking or attempting to take anything of value from the care, custody, or control of a person or persons by force or threat of force or violence and/or by putting the victim in fear.
Aggravated assault	An unlawful attack by one person on another for the purpose of inflicting severe or aggravated bodily injury. This type of assault is usually accompanied by the use of a weapon or by means likely to produce death or great bodily harm. Simple assaults are not included.
Burglary	The unlawful entry into a structure with the intent to commit a felony or theft. Burglary is classified into three subcategories: forcible entry, unlawful entry where force is not used, and attempted forcible entry.
Larceny/theft (excluding motor vehicle theft)	The unlawful taking, carrying, leading, or riding away of property from possession of another. Examples include shoplifting, pocket picking, thefts of bicycles, purse snatching, or the stealing of any property/article where use of force, violence, or fraud does not occur. Attempted larceny is also included.
Motor vehicle theft	The theft or attempted theft of a motor vehicle. Included in this offense is the stealing of automobiles, trucks, buses, motorcycles, and snowmobiles.
Arson	Any willful or malicious burning or attempts to burn, with or without intent to defraud, a dwelling, house, public building, motor vehicle or aircraft, personal property of another, etc.

Source: Federal Bureau of Investigation, *Crime in the United States, 2008*, www.fbi.gov/ucr/cius2008/index.html

attention of the police are known as Part I offenses, or "Index Crimes," and are broken down into violent crimes, which include homicide (murder and nonnegligent manslaughter), forcible rape, robbery, and aggravated assault, and property crimes, which include burglary, larceny, motor vehicle theft, and arson (added in 1982).[55] The Part I offense statistics include those crimes reported to the police, those crimes cleared by the police (either through arrest of the suspect or through special circumstances such as the death of the suspect), and those in which an arrest was made. It is important to note that for any given year, violent crime makes up between 10 and 20 percent of all Index Crimes, while property crimes compose the rest. The Part II offenses include such crimes as fraud and embezzlement, vandalism, prostitution, drug abuse, and gambling; however, such data are maintained only by the number of people arrested for the crime.[56] All these data are then reported both in raw numbers (the actual number of each crime per year) and as a proportion of the population to control for changing population rates each year and is reported as a certain number of crimes per 100,000 population. (See Box 1.1.)

While the UCR provides us with a measurement of how much crime exists in the United States, one must be aware that there are many problems with the use of the data.[57] The UCR data are often considered to severely underestimate the number of crimes occurring in the United States,[58] not all crimes are covered,[59] and the reporting of certain crimes may rise and fall because of increased awareness and media campaigns.[60] In addition, the amount of discretion that law enforcement personnel and agencies have in reporting crime may also have an effect on the data, such as purposeful overreporting or underreporting of crime[61]; bias and discrimination by refusing to take reports from certain categories of people, such as the poor, blacks, or immigrants[62]; the heavy enforcement of some crimes that other jurisdictions do not enforce[63]; reporting the wrong type of crime for a specific incident; changes in the way crimes are reported; or simply making a mistake in the reporting of a crime. All these make compiling accurate crime statistics more difficult.[64] However, the UCR is still the best available indicator of crime in the United States, and it has been shown that the majority of these methodological problems are rare in the case of homicides and that motor vehicle theft, burglaries involving forcible entry, and robberies generally yield more accurate data.[65] Still, while the UCR is the main indicator for assessing the reality of crime in the United States, one must remain vigilant as to the accuracy of these findings.

National Incident-Based Reporting System

To address many of these drawbacks, it should be noted that the FBI has made some effort to update the UCR program under what is known as the National Incident-Based Reporting System (NIBRS).[66] The concept for changing the way crime data are reported began in the late 1970s, and implementation began in the early 1990s. Although there was talk in the early 1990s that all states would solely use the NIBRS system by the turn of the century, slow progress did not make that happen, and little more than half the states (31 as of 2007) are in some stage of using the NIBRS program. There are some states, such as Delaware, Idaho, and Tennessee, which have every agency in the state reporting NIBRS data, while other states, such as Florida, Mississippi, and Wyoming, have not implemented the program and have no plans to do so in the future. The benefit to NIBRS is that it is a more robust collection of crime statistics. Whereas the UCR has a limited number of crime categories, NIBRS has a more expanded version. In addition, when there are multiple crimes committed at one scene, only the most serious crime is reported under the UCR. Not so with NIBRS, as it reports each individual crime. The drawback to the implementation of NIBRS has been primarily cost, as the more detailed reporting system takes more time and effort, thus costing agencies more money. One key issue is the difference in the way the UCR and NIBRS record crimes. The UCR has always taken the most serious crime in an incident and recorded that one crime. NIBRS actually records every criminal violation occurring in each incident, thus if one were to compare the number of crimes between the UCR and NIBRS, NIBRS would show significantly more crime. However, the NIBRS system still continues to see more states being certified in the system, and it is likely that eventually the NIBRS system will supersede the UCR system. (See Boxes 1.2 and 1.3.)

National Crime Victimization Survey

The second primary source of crime statistic information in the United States comes from the National Crime Victimization Survey (NCVS), formerly known as the National Crime Survey. It was first used in 1973 by the U.S. Department of Justice in cooperation with the U.S. Bureau of the Census to address the many problems cited in the UCR by creating an instrument that would obtain better and more accurate information on the number of crimes in the United States. The

BOX 1.2

National Incident-Based Reporting System—Group A Offenses

Group A offense categories are those for which extensive crime data are collected in NIBRS:

1. Arson
2. Assault offenses—aggravated assault, simple assault, intimidation
3. Bribery
4. Burglary/breaking and entering
5. Counterfeiting/forgery
6. Destruction/damage/vandalism of property
7. Drug/narcotic offenses—drug/narcotic violations, drug equipment violations
8. Embezzlement
9. Extortion/blackmail
10. Fraud offenses—false pretenses/swindle/confidence game, credit card/automatic teller machine fraud, impersonation, welfare fraud, wire fraud
11. Gambling offenses—betting/wagering, operating/promoting/assisting gambling, gambling equipment violations, sports tampering
12. Homicide offenses—murder and nonnegligent manslaughter, negligent manslaughter, justifiable homicide
13. Kidnapping/abduction
14. Larceny/theft offenses—pocket picking, purse snatching, shoplifting, theft from building, theft from coin-operated machine or device, theft from motor vehicle, theft of motor vehicle parts or accessories, all other larceny
15. Motor vehicle theft
16. Pornography/obscene material
17. Prostitution offenses—prostitution, assisting or promoting prostitution
18. Robbery
19. Sex offenses, forcible—forcible rape, forcible sodomy, sexual assault with an object, forcible fondling
20. Sex offenses, nonforcible—incest, statutory rape
21. Stolen property offenses (e.g., receiving stolen property)
22. Weapon law violations

Source: Federal Bureau of Investigation, *Crime in the United States, 2008*, www.fbi.gov/ucr/cius2008/index.html

NCVS obtains information directly from citizens and includes such things as the context in which crimes occurred, the time of day, physical setting, the extent of any injuries, the relationship between the victim and the offender, and the characteristics of the crime victim, including such variables as race, gender, and income. The data are compiled annually and published by the Bureau of Justice Statistics in a publication titled *Criminal Victimization.*

The data collection process is somewhat complex. The Census Bureau interviews approximately 110,000 residents, ages twelve and older, from some 55,000 randomly selected households in the United States every six months. In addition, once a household has been selected for the survey interviews, it remains in the sample for approximately three years, at which point it is removed from the sample and new households are selected. As the survey is concerned with measuring victimizations within a household, if individual members of a household move, the survey does not follow them but continues to focus on the household and any new occupants.

BOX 1.3
National Incident-Based Reporting System—Group B Offenses

The following eleven additional categories, known as Group B offenses, are those for which only arrest data are reported:

1. Bad checks
2. Curfew/loitering/vagrancy violations
3. Disorderly conduct
4. Driving under the influence
5. Drunkenness
6. Family offenses, nonviolent
7. Liquor law violations
8. Peeping tom
9. Runaway
10. Trespass of real property
11. All other offenses

Sources: FBI Web site; *Uniform Crime Report Handbook*, NIBRS edition, pp. 5–6.

Because the surveys are conducted through personal interviews, the response rate is more than 95 percent. The respondents are asked whether they or anyone in their household have been the victim of a crime within the past six months. The crimes are then described to the respondents, and they include aggravated and simple assault, rape and sexual assault, robbery, burglary, larceny/theft, and motor vehicle theft. For each victimization, the respondent is then asked a more detailed set of questions, including the age, race, gender, ethnicity, marital status, income, and educational level of the victim; the age, race, gender, and relationship to the victim of the offender; and the time and place of the crime, the use of weapons, the nature of any injuries, the economic impact of the crime, and whether the victimization was reported to the police. (See Figure 1.2.)

The greatest advantage of the calculation of victimization is that it allows for an understanding of the number of crimes committed in the United States rather than the number of crimes reported to the police. For example, the data collected for the year 1994 show that the UCR reported there were approximately 14 million crimes in the United States, while the NCVS estimated 42 million. More specifically, the UCR reported nearly 2 million violent crimes, but the NCVS reported nearly 11 million, and the difference among property crimes was 12 million and 31 million, respectively. These differences highlight the fact that many crimes remain unreported to the police; thus, our measurement of crime utilizing the UCR does not provide a complete understanding of the reality of crime.

While the NCVS does provide us with a better understanding of crime victimization in the United States, it, like the UCR, does have limitations.[67] And, like the UCR, its first problem is that it severely underestimates the number of crimes in the United States because it is focused on individual victimizations and not commercial victimizations, such as bank robberies and jewelry store burglaries.[68] In addition, because the NCVS asks respondents about their victimization, respondents may potentially forget a victimization,[69] they may overestimate the number of their victimizations,[70] or they may choose not to reveal their victimization to the data collector.[71] Furthermore, respondents may overreport their number of victimizations, confusing it with one that occurred outside the time frame requested by the survey,[72] while others may report their victimizations in the wrong category.

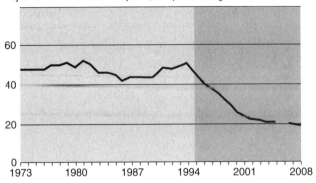

Violent crime rates
Adjusted victimization rate per 1,000 persons age 12 or older

Property crime rates
Adjusted victimization rate per 1,000 households

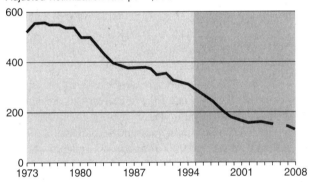

FIGURE 1.2 Victimization Trends, 1973–2003. *Source:* Bureau of Justice Statistics, *Criminal Victimization, 2003.*

While both the UCR and the NCVS do have some methodological problems, these two indicators present the best data available for assessing the reality of crime in the United States. One must recognize, however, that the two data sets are unique. Whereas the UCR is more concerned with the criminal, the NCVS is more concerned with the victim. Thus, combining the two indicators presents a more accurate understanding of crime in the United States and can reveal trends across the years. What do the data tell us about the reality of crime?

In first looking at the UCR for the offenses known to the police over time, we discover many interesting trends. First, the crime rates from the early 1930s to the late 1950s remained fairly steady when population growth is taken into account.[73] It was not until the early 1960s and into the early 1970s that crime rates began to rise dramatically among adults, being preceded by a sharp rise in juvenile offenses in the late 1950s. By the latter part of the 1970s, there was a leveling off of crime and then a decrease in the early 1980s. Then crime began to rise again slightly, with some fluctuations, and to level off in the early 1990s, followed by a steady decrease since 1991. If we break down the crimes into violent and property crimes, we find that violent crime matched the trends of "all crime" but that property crime began to level off in the early 1980s and fell in the 1990s. Finally, if one were to break the data down further, one would find violent crime, such as murder and rape, remaining fairly constant throughout the 1980s, with significant declines in the 1990s, and crimes such as aggravated assault and robbery remaining level through the early 1980s, rising a bit at the end of the 1980s, and then falling in the 1990s. Property crimes, such as motor vehicle theft and larceny/theft, remained level in the 1980s and have been dropping since the 1990s, while burglaries have been dropping steadily since the early 1980s.

The UCR provides some very interesting data in regard to the more recent trends in crime, namely, in the last decade of the twentieth century. The total crime index, controlling for population by looking at the rate per 100,000 population, has seen a decrease from the all-time highs in 1991 of 5,897 crimes per 100,000 population to 4,118 crimes per 100,000 population in 2002. We know that crime dropped by 1 percent from 1991 to 1992 and then began dropping with each following year at an increasing rate. It dropped 3.1 percent between 1992 and 1993, 5.1 percent between 1993 and 1994, 6.8 percent between 1994 and 1995, and 9.8 percent between 1995 and 1996. More important, during this same time period, violent crime was also falling with decreases of 1.4 percent from 1992 to 1993, 5.8 percent from 1993 to 1994, and 16.3 percent from 1995 to 1996. These are dramatic drops in the number of crimes in the United States and ones that would indicate a safer nation. Yet, again, public concern for crime continued to rise during this same time period, putting crime as the "most important problem facing the country" from 1994 through 1996. After crime was no longer considered such an "important problem," the crime rates continued to fall until approximately 2004. Violent crime saw a brief two year rise, then continued to fall, while property crime continued the downward trend. (See Figure 1.3.)

Recognizing some of the previously identified problems with the UCR data, perhaps it would be better to look at the most reliable crimes, such as murder, robbery, burglary, and motor vehicle theft. Each of these has fallen dramatically since the highs of 1991, such as the 24,700 murders in 1991, which fell to 14,180 murders in 2007. In the case of burglaries, there was a total of 3,157,200 in the United States in 1991. By 2007, the number had dropped to 2,222,196. Robberies also dropped from 687,730 in 1991 to 441,885 in 2007, and motor vehicle thefts dropped from 1,661,700 in 1991 to 956,846 in 2007. Even when controlling for rises in the population, we still find significant drops in crime. For example, the murder rate in 1994 was 9.6 per 100,000 population, and in 2007 it stood at 5.4 per 100,000 population. When looking to robbery

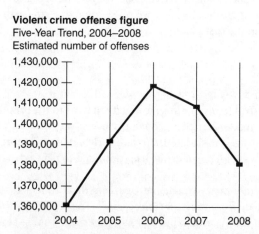

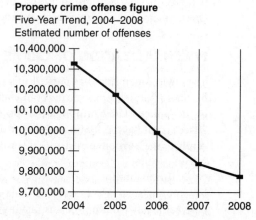

FIGURE 1.3   Crime Rate per 100,000 Population, 1989–2002.   *Source:* Federal Bureau of Investigation, Uniform Crime Reports, 2002.

data, the rate fell from a 1994 rate of 237.7 per 100,000 population to 145.3 per 100,000 population in 2007. *Regardless of how one looks at the data, according to the UCR, crime has been steadily falling for over a decade.*

Turning to the NCVS, we find very similar trend data for the time period 1973–1992.[74] Since the early 1980s, the United States has seen a steady decline in the number of victimizations, from a raw-number high of 41,454,180 victimizations in 1981 to 34,649,340 victimizations in 1992. In looking at specific crimes, a similar trend appears, including decreases in the number of rapes and robberies as well as burglaries and larcenies. Although the NCVS format was changed from the years 1992 to 1993, creating a difference in the methods of data collection and in reporting, there continued to be a downward trend in the post-1992 victimization data.[75] The year 1993 witnessed 43,547,000 victimizations, 2000 saw a decrease to 25,893,340 victimizations, and by 2008, the number of victimizations had fallen to 21,312,400. In looking at the category of personal crimes (rape, robbery, and assault), we see a decrease from 11,365,080 victimizations in 1993 to 4,856,510 in 2008. And in property crimes (burglary, motor vehicle theft, and theft), America experienced a decrease from 32,182,320 in 1993 to 16,319,180 in 2008. Overall, the trend in victimizations has continued downward with significant declines since the early 1990s, giving the lowest recorded number and rates of victimizations since the inception of the NCVS despite the methodological changes in 1992.

The overall story that the UCR and the NCVS tell is that crime rose in the late 1960s and early 1970s and began leveling off in the 1980s. Since the early 1980s, crime has been declining with some fluctuations but has been definitively declining since the early 1990s. Therefore, unlike the perception of crime that would have us believe that crime has been rising since the early 1980s and ran rampant in the 1990s, crime, in reality, has been declining. This is why we have a paradox in regard to the issue of crime, and it is this paradox that is of great concern. This is not simply semantics and numbers, for there are real consequences to this game. The belief that crime is rising creates an artificial reality, and action is based on this fiction. The consequences include such outcomes as stricter laws, a high expenditure of tax dollars on the criminal justice system, an increase in public fear, more prisons being built, stricter prisons, citizens arming themselves, the maintenance of the death penalty in many states, longer sentences for lesser crimes, an emphasis on punishment over rehabilitation, and shorter "time served" for violent crimes, all of which contribute both directly and indirectly to the crime problem. It is imperative that we recognize this paradox for what it is and the consequences it creates, but first we must come to terms with the environment that has created this paradox in the first place.

POLITICALIZATION OF CRIME

The environment that has created this paradox is most assuredly political in nature. Crime has become a hot political issue for politicians at all levels of office, from city mayors to the president of the United States. Although the subject matter has changed greatly over time, moving from "street crime" in the 1960s, to the "war on drugs" in the late 1980s and early 1990s, and more recently to the "war on terrorism," the underlying theme of crime has continued to play a dynamic role in politics.

Various authors from a variety of disciplines have made the argument that crime policy has become a particularly attractive area of policy formation for politicians.[76] The reason for this is derived largely from politicians playing on the "fear of crime" by the American public. Fear of crime can translate into a topic of discussion for politicians to talk about while in office but especially when campaigning for those offices. Topics such as street crime and drug addicts allow politicians to paint the world in black and white by having an enemy to target. As crime affects everyone and as no one, other than the criminals, is *for* crime, crime policy becomes a "safe" policy area that politicians can talk about without getting into trouble. Hence, their rhetoric toward crime becomes a focal area of their speeches.

There is also an almost symbiotic relationship as well between politicians and the media. As politicians speak out on the issue of crime, the media report this as newsworthy. In addition, whenever the media report on an issue of crime, their primary source of information typically comes from government officials, many of whom are politicians.[77] However, it has also been noted that "politicians often interpret media coverage of an issue as a sign of heightened public concern,"[78] thus creating a symbiotic relationship between the media and politicians for constructing a crime problem that may not actually exist or at least not to the degree on which it is reported. Yet the public, watching the increased media reports on the crime problem and listening to politicians' rhetoric, comes to demand that something be done about the problem. This means that political rhetoric can have real consequences, for every politician is called on to translate his or her rhetoric into action. Hence, politicians, once in office, try to translate their anticrime rhetoric into anticrime policy. This provides them something substantive to point to when arguing that they have worked hard to reduce the problem of crime. And, because there are very few politicians who would be willing to vote *against* a crime bill, as they would easily be painted as "soft on crime" and not willing to do something about the "problem," crime legislation is an easy victory for any politician. Facing this very fact of politics, U.S. Senator Joseph Biden has been quoted as saying, "If someone came to the Senate floor and said we should barbwire the ankles of everyone who jaywalks, I think it would pass."[79] Crime policy is successful policy, and one only has to look at the various legislation passed in the past several decades to realize that fact.

Good examples of legislative victories regarding crime include the Clinton administration's 1993 campaign pledge to add 100,000 more police officers to the cities and towns across America. The legislation, passed as the Violent Crime Control and Law Enforcement Act of 1994 (generally referred to as the 1994 Crime Bill), was focused on doing just that.[80] In the area of courts, the 1980s war on drugs would see numerous bills at the national and state levels that allocated additional funding to create special "drug courts" to handle the rise in drug prosecutions. In the area of corrections, since the 1970s, legislation has passed time and time again to allocate additional funds to build more prisons, generating a prison boom throughout the past two decades. The research has pointed out, however, that the 100,000 cops, the drug courts, and the prison expansion have been very effective.[81] All this has led many to believe that what has developed from this political flurry of crime legislation is the creation of a new "criminal justice–industrial complex" where the emphasis is not on dealing with the problem of crime but rather on passing legislation that plays on people's fear to generate an appearance of doing something that increases the spending on crime.[82]

The end result is crime policy that is rarely about reducing crime but policy that plays well with the public and the media. A perfect example is the "three-strikes" legislation that was touted in the 1990s as the answer to violent repeat offenders. Despite criminologists and criminal justice academics voicing their learned opinion that the policy would not work, mainly because it was a determinate sentencing formula that has not worked well in the past, they were ignored. True to form, the three-strikes legislation has not been effective, and, contrary to public belief, it has locked away not violent repeat offenders for life but rather a number of low-level offenders for very long sentences.[83]

What we are witnessing again and again in America regarding crime policy is a paradox of very large proportions. As the president of the Center for Media and Public Affairs, Bob Lichter, has explained, "The reality is going one way, the media images are going another and the public perception follows the images rather than the reality."[84] Or, as William Chambliss, one who has explored this topic in depth, has stated, "There is, in short, a huge chasm between the reality of crime, the public's perception of it, and the information being disseminated to the public by law enforcement agencies, the media, and politicians."[85] And because public opinion plays such an important role in the criminal justice policymaking process, politicians focus on the public opinion of crime. As Roberts and Stalans have explained, "All too often legislators and policy-makers and newspaper editorialists use public opinion to advance their own criminal justice policy agendas."[86] Using public opinion polls, politicians readily make the argument that "this is what the people want" when the politicians are attempting to obtain passage of their pet crime bill.[87] As a result, the realities of crime, matched up against political rhetoric, media images of crime, and crime legislation, are so divergent that it often leaves us, who study crime and criminal justice, wondering how we get the policies that we do. The answer is found in the public policy process. But before discussing this process, it is also important to understand how we got to this so-called criminal justice–industrial complex from a historical context within which to place modern-day crime policy.

HISTORY OF CRIME POLICY IN AMERICA

Crime has traditionally been a state and local issue. As crime is a local problem, crime in America has typically been handled by local communities through the local police and courts. This has its roots in the English system of "policing" dating back to the 1300s, when the watch and the ward were the mechanisms for what passed as policing.[88] As English settlers began making their way to America in the 1600s and 1700s, they naturally brought this system of policing with them. The local watch and ward (a nighttime and daytime patrol), the constables, and the sheriffs were English inventions adopted in the New World. It wasn't until the 1830s that America would establish its first bona fide police department that emulated, albeit poorly, the London Metropolitan police department, which had been created in 1829 under the leadership of Sir Robert Peel. During the Antebellum period, only a handful of police departments were created, including Boston (1838), New York (1845), and Chicago (1855). After the Civil War (1861–1865), police departments began to rapidly spread across the country, and by the turn of the twentieth century, policing was a fixed institution in America.

The same pattern is also seen in terms of prisons and jails. In early colonial America, there were no prisons or jails. Punishment was meted out immediately with some type of sanction, bodily harm, banishment, or execution. A form of jail did exist known as a "gaol" or "debtor's prison." However, inmates in these crude holding pens were either sentenced for a debt, where they would work to pay off the debt, or held for pretrial detention but never as a means of punishment. That did not come until 1790 and the conversion of the Walnut Street Jail in Philadelphia, Pennsylvania, when it went from a debtor's prison to a bona fide jail. The concept caught on, and eventually Pennsylvania, New York, and many other states began building penitentiaries to hold their criminals. The age of the prison flourished in the 1820s and 1830s and by the 1840s was a fixed institution in America.

As police departments and jails were adopted by local cities and towns, like America's English counterpart, they were placed under local control and local authority. When the framers of the U.S. Constitution began their work in 1787, they did not include any fundamental control over the enforcement of the laws. Thus, the criminal justice system was left largely to the state and local governments to create, fund, and maintain. The fact that state and local governments would have significant control over the administration of justice giving them extensive powers over the people, however, was not lost on all of the founders. Alexander Hamilton, realizing this fact, wrote about it in the Federalist Papers Number 17, when he explained,

> There is one transcendent advantage belonging to the province of the State governments, which alone suffices to place the matter in a clear and satisfactory light—I mean the ordinary administration of criminal and civil justice. This, of all others, is the most powerful, most universal, and most attractive source of popular obedience and attachment. It is this which, being the immediate and visible guardian of life and property, having its benefits and its terrors in constant activity before the public eye, regulating all those personal interests and familiar concerns to which the sensibility of individuals is more immediately awake, contributes more than any other circumstances to impressing upon the minds of the people affection, esteem, and reverence toward the government. This great cement of society, which will diffuse itself almost wholly through the channels of the particular governments, independent of all other causes of influence, would insure them so decided an empire over their respective citizens as to render them at all times a complete counterpoise, and, not unfrequently, dangerous rivals to the power of the Union.[89]

Hamilton realized that by giving the control of the criminal justice system to the states, they would have power over an area of great concern to the American public. How they performed in this public policy area would affect the relationship between the people and their government. Yet at the same time, Hamilton realized that this could pose problems for the national government, which had little authority to intervene in this arena.

Although Hamilton thought that the power of the administration of criminal and civil law was a power retained by the states, the reality was that states pushed the authority to oversee the administration of justice down to the local level. Despite such exceptions as the U.S. Marshal's Service, the Texas Rangers, or state penitentiaries, the states and territories of the eighteenth and nineteenth centuries did little in regard to the administration of criminal justice. This was abdicated to the local governments. And even when these state-level agencies did exist, they tended to be small and largely ineffectual in dealing with crime on a statewide basis. Although a number of state police agencies came into existence in the early twentieth century, they too tended to be narrow in scope and use. It really wasn't until the era of Prohibition, the Great Depression, and the New Deal that states began to assert more authority in terms of crime control. But by then, so had the federal government.

The era of Prohibition, brought on by the temperance movement and the passage of the Eighteenth Amendment to the Constitution, ushered in the first twentieth-century crime wave. Although Prohibition itself created a new class of criminals, the largest contributing factor to the rise in crime was the Mafia. As the demand for black-market alcohol increased in the early 1920s, organized crime began its rise to power as various syndicates moved to control this new and illegal sector of the economy. As they did so, the Mafia also found ample success in illegal gaming tables, prostitution, and various other crimes that were associated with liquor. As the Mafia fought over terrain, innocent people were often caught in the crossfire, and the media helped incite the public's opinion of both crime and prohibition. Public opinion led to the demand that something be done about the crime problem, and throughout the 1920s, dozens of states formed task forces and commissions to study the problem of crime. One such committee was known as the "Seabury Commission" in New York State, requested at the behest of the governor, Franklin D. Roosevelt.

Eventually, President Herbert Hoover, who was sworn into office in 1929, created the first National Commission on Law Observance and Enforcement to begin analyzing the problem of crime. The Wickersham Commission, as it was known, would begin its work in 1929 and completed it in 1932, publishing fourteen volumes on different areas of the criminal justice system and making various recommendations for its improvements. Despite the solidity of the commission's findings, America had entered the Great Depression, and there was simply no funding to implement change.

The Great Depression and America's entry into World War II would profoundly change America socially, politically, and economically. America transitioned from a reliance on local and state governments to a greater reliance on the national government during the Great Depression. As America entered World War II, the American people were very much dependent on the national government and supported the war effort while at the same time willing to be controlled more by the national government for the purposes of winning a two-theater war. Success was obtained in 1945; the war was over, and Americans attempted to return to life as it was before the war. That, however, was not possible. Economically, America was no longer in a depression; politically, America was now a world power; and socially, America had entered a whole new relationship with government that had resulted largely from the Depression and the war era. As Dilulio, Smith, and Saiger have explained,

> Since the end of World War II, virtually every major domestic policy initiative in the United States has involved state and local governments. This pattern is illustrated in the shared Social Security financing and payment arrangements under the Social Security Act (administered by the states subject to federal review for compliance with minimum standards set by the Secretary of Health and Human Services), the management for active state and local participation in land used under the Federal Land Policy and Management Act (regionally administered subject to federal review for compliance with planning criteria set by the Secretary of the Interior), and the state implementation of the Clean Air Act, under which state officials develop specific plans for environmental cleanup (subject to standards set by the Environmental Protection Agency).[90]

Policy areas as diverse as health care, welfare, transportation, housing, and economic development have all fallen under this system of American federalism.

Federalism essentially deals with the relationships between the national, state, and local level governments. Some have described federalism as a "picket fence" where the posts are the various public policies (e.g., health care, welfare, and crime) and the slats the levels of government (e.g., national, state, and local). As every slat is connected to every post, every public policy is connected to every level of government. In the post–World War II era, this has become difficult to avoid. In many public policies, the national government has used such formal means as grants, regulations, contracts, loans, and tax expenditures to influence state and local governments, while in others it has resorted to the use of arguments, threats, and manipulation.[91] In either case, the national government has become a central player in nearly every public policy, and crime is not an exception.

The national government is essentially a latecomer in terms of crime control policy. As previously stated, crime was largely a local issue until the twentieth century. States began to assert some influence and control in the 1920s, but so too had the national government. The Depression and the war put a hold on the national government's entrance into this public policy area, and so too did the tranquil and peaceful times of the 1950s. It was the rise of juvenile crime in the late 1950s and the skyrocketing crime rates of the 1960s that would bring the national government into playing a central role in crime control policy. Although President Dwight D. Eisenhower insisted that crime was a local issue and President John F. Kennedy was tentative in regard to the national government's role, it was President Lyndon B. Johnson who would bring the power of the national government to bear on the crime problem.

In 1964, after having served only a few short months as president after Kennedy's assassination, Johnson was in a race for the American presidency. The eventual Republican candidate was Barry Goldwater, who began campaigning on the issue of crime in the streets. Johnson, early on, took the stance that crime was a local issue. However, once elected to office, seeing the political benefits of focusing on the issue of crime, Johnson threw the weight of his administration behind the creation of a crime commission and the passage of numerous federal laws dealing with the issue of crime.[92] The crime commission, officially known as The President's Commission on Law Enforcement and Administration of Justice, would issue its report in 1967, detailing more than 200 recommendations for enhancing the criminal justice system in America.[93] More important, it carved out a role for the national government by articulating that "although day-to-day criminal administration is primarily a state and local responsibility, the federal government's contribution to the national effort against crime is crucial."[94] It further argued that it had "considered carefully whether or not the federal government should provide more support for such programs," and it concluded "that the federal government should."[95] It was perhaps best stated by President Johnson when writing in his memoirs, "The average American was concerned about the rising crime rate and failed to understand that under our Constitution the preservation of law and order is basically the responsibility of local government."[96] President Johnson, interviewed several times on the campaign trail in 1964, argued that crime was a local issue and not one for the federal government. However, once in office he could not ignore the reality that crime was a significant problem and people were looking to the federal government for action. He would later lament that, "Somehow, in the minds of most Americans the breakdown of local authority became the fault of the federal government."[97] The issue was no longer whether the national government should be involved in crime control policy: The new question was *how*.

This trend toward a larger federal role in crime and criminal justice policies has been referred to as the federalization of crime. Many crimes that were traditionally under the jurisdiction of state government have become federal issues. The federal government's role in the crime arena has increased dramatically since the 1960s and continues to be an important factor in many if not all areas of criminal justice.

Not everyone sees this as a positive trend. Some have argued that the federalization of crime represents a shift in power from the states to the federal government. It increases the power of Congress while decreasing the ability of the states to respond to their problems. Additionally, federalizing crime makes more demands on the federal system for funding. The federal government needs more prosecutors and judges and more federal police agencies. It increases the federal criminal caseloads, resulting in more court backlogs. Federalizing crime increases the number of people convicted of federal offenses, thus making demands for more federal correctional systems.[98]

The federal role in crime control does, however, derive its basis from the Constitution despite the fact that the framers did not specifically define a role for the government in crime control. The Constitution defines certain powers as enumerated or delegated powers that give the sole jurisdiction to the federal government. These include such powers as declaring war, printing money, and conducting foreign affairs. Reserved powers are those responsibilities that are defined clearly in the Constitution that have been reserved for the states. These include the right to conduct elections and to establish local governments. Because these are state responsibilities, the federal government does not have the right to pass laws in these areas. If a power is not an enumerated or a delegated power, then it is reserved for the states. Other powers not specified in the Constitution are implied powers. These are powers not defined by the Constitution but derived from the "necessary and proper" clause of Article 1, Section 8. This states that the federal government can perform acts "which shall be necessary and proper for carrying into execution the forgoing powers and all other powers vested by this Constitution or in the Government of the United States." The last type of power is concurrent powers, and these are when both the federal and state governments may act.

Crime control is not an enumerated or a delegated power reserved for the federal government. As previously stated, nowhere does the Constitution explicitly state that crime control is a federal responsibility. But it is also not a reserved power given to the states, as it is not defined in the Constitution as a state power. However, since crime control is not delegated to the federal government, it therefore becomes a state responsibility. For most of American history, crime control was largely a reserved power, one that was reserved for the states with little activity from the federal government. However, since the turn of the twentieth century, it has shifted more to a concurrent power in that presidential administrations, especially since the latter half of the century, have made crime a national policy issue.

All presidents since Johnson have focused on the issue of crime in some form or fashion, making crime control policy a part of their agenda.[99] Since the 1970s, the national government has greatly enhanced its expenditures on crime with a rise from $535 million in 1965 to $11.7 billion in 1992, an increase of more than 2,000 percent.[100] It has greatly expanded the number of federal criminal laws, for, as the American Bar Association has pointed out, "of all federal crime enacted since 1865, more than 40 percent have been created since 1970."[101] It has also greatly enhanced the funding for more police, courts, and prisons throughout the country. Moreover, with the recent war on terrorism, federal activity related to this crime has greatly increased. All this activity has been through various federal, state, and local partnerships, or federalism, much akin to the federalism activities witnessed in other areas of public policy. It should also be noted that while the national government has become heavily involved in the politics of crime policy, it has remained a highly political issue for state and local governments as well. Despite the encroachment of the national government in crime policy, local governments still bear the larger stake in crime control policy in America. What is most important in understanding today's public policy of crime is that crime policy, like other public policies, is an area where all levels of government are now actively involved.

WHY CRIMINAL JUSTICE POLICY STUDIES?

The importance of criminal justice policy analysis cannot be lost in the attempt at providing a working definition. Mike Israel perhaps said it best when he argued that "the criminal justice system is one of government. A democratic government, by definition, invites participation; and participation inherently means politics. Politics, to the exclusion of almost everything else, makes crime policy."[102] Studying how crime policy is made, offering alternative policies to decision makers, and assessing both descriptive (past) and prescriptive (future) outcomes are an important aspect of both the public policy and the criminal justice fields. Combining these two approaches and rooting them in the criminal justice field, however, is what is critical to our understanding of the process and moving theoretical research solutions to political substantive solutions. As Israel articulates, moving research from the field of criminal justice into the realm of public policy regarding crime and criminal justice is critical to sound crime control policy. The importance of criminal justice policy studies is, then, to generate sound scientific (theoretical), political, and practical (professional) information.[103]

Theoretical Perspective

Criminal justice policy analysis from a purely scientific or theoretical perspective provides for a better understanding of the causes and consequences of crime control policy.[104] Criminal justice academicians seek to explain the world of criminal justice. Criminal justice policy analysis would allow the criminal justice discipline to make policy recommendations that might improve the performance of national, state, and local governments in an era when the public has continued to demand "better" government. Criminal justice research could be used to suggest remedies that could alleviate the problems of crime and disorder in communities across America. While criminal justice research has been very good at pointing out what doesn't work, more research needs to focus on what does work.

Political Perspective

Criminal justice policy analysis from a political perspective, as Israel articulated, would thus allow us to analyze what programs are successful and which are not in order to reduce crime and disorder and make policy recommendations.[105] This information in the hands of future and current politicians can provide them with more competent policy ideas for addressing these problems and to make intelligent decisions. This may also help avoid the formation of policy based on sound bites, sensational images, and reactionary statements addressing the problems of crime, such as the standard political line about "getting tough on crime" or the calls in the 1990s for "three strikes and you're out." This is the stance that Israel takes when he urges the criminal justice discipline to become more involved in the policymaking process to ensure that sound crime policy is advocated and that successful policies, rather than those based on fear, move forward in the public policy process.

Practical Perspective

Finally, the last perspective is a practical one.[106] Criminal justice academicians and students of crime policy apply scientific knowledge to solve practical problems. This is the type of criminal justice policy analysis that focuses on understanding the public policy process so that one can make the process more rational and effective. Part of this is understanding the causes and consequences of public policy in order to apply criminal justice knowledge to the solution of the problems of crime and disorder. It is also to understand the process in order to know where the process breaks down or experiences roadblocks as well as understanding the entry points to the policy process for those seeking access to the criminal justice policy process.

Conclusion

Crime and criminal justice is a public policy area that is often understudied in America. Understanding the public policy process helps us understand how we get the crime control policies we have today, but it also informs us as to how the policy process works and how it can be shaped and influenced. As we have seen, crime perceptions and crime reality don't often have much relationship with each other. The politicians and media play off crime perceptions—namely, the fear of crime, disorder, or, more recently, the terrorist attacks—in order to mobilize support for a particular crime control policy. These policies may not be the most successful strategies for reducing crime and disorder, but they obtain passage because they appear as solutions to allay the fears that the public harbors. As a result, all levels of government have increasingly politicized the issue of crime control policy, with the federal government increasingly taking a larger role in shaping the process not only at the national level but at the state and local levels as well. Studying this polit-ical process by way of policy analysis, rooted in the criminal justice discipline, can help us understand the process, the determinants of crime policy, and the impact these policies have. Understanding these three factors can also help us influence and potentially shape the direction of crime policy in America.

Notes

1. B. W. Hancock and P. M. Sharp, *Public Policy, Crime, and Criminal Justice* (Upper Saddle River, N.J.: Prentice Hall, 2004).
2. G. E. Rush, *The Dictionary of Criminal Justice*, 5th ed. (New York: McGraw-Hill, 2000), p. 86.
3. Ibid.
4. N. E. Marion, *Criminal Justice in America: The Politics behind the System* (Durham, N.C.: Carolina Academic Press, 2002), p. 58.
5. Ibid., p. 59.
6. W. M. Oliver and J. F. Hilgenberg, Jr., *A History of Crime and Criminal Justice in America* (Boston: Allyn & Bacon, 2006).
7. Marion, *Criminal Justice in America.*
8. Ibid.
9. Ibid.
10. Rush, *The Dictionary of Criminal Justice*, p. 311.
11. Ibid., p. 270.
12. Ibid., p. 44.
13. Ibid., p. 193.
14. Marion, *Criminal Justice in America.*
15. The President's Commission on Law Enforcement and Administration of Justice, *The Challenge of Crime in a Free Society*, p. 70.
16. S. Stojkovic, D. Kalinch, and J. Klofas, *Criminal Justice Organizations: Administration and Management*, 4th ed. (Belmont, CA: Thomson Wadsworth, 2008).
17. T. R. Dye, *Understanding Public Policy*, 8th ed. (Englewood Cliffs, N.J.: Prentice Hall, 1995), pp. 2–3.
18. G. Starling, *The Politics and Economics of Public Policy* (Homewood, Ill.: Dorsey Press, 1979), p. 4.
19. C. E. Cochran, L. C. Mayer, T. R. Carr, and N. J. Cayer, *American Public Policy: An Introduction*, 5th ed. (New York: St. Martin's Press, 1996), p. 1.
20. D. Easton, *A Systems Analysis of Political Life* (New York: John Wiley & Sons, 1965), p. 212.
21. J. Anderson, *Public Policymaking: An Introduction* (Boston: Houghton Mifflin, 1990), p. 24.
22. J. P. Lester and J. Stewart, Jr., *Public Policy: An Evolutionary Approach* (St. Paul, Minn.: West, 1996).
23. Dye, *Understanding Public Policy*, pp. 2–3.
24. Starling, *The Politics and Economics of Public Policy.*
25. A. Mood, *Introduction to Policy Analysis* (New York: North-Holland, 1983).
26. G. D. Brewer and P. DeLeon, *The Foundations of Policy Analysis* (Homewood, Ill.: Dorsey Press, 1983).
27. R. B. Ripley, *Policy Analysis in Political Science* (Chicago: Nelson Hall, 1985).
28. Bureau of Justice Statistics, *Sourcebook of Criminal Justice Statistics 2002—Online* (2003), available online at www.albany.edu/sourcebook/index.html (see Table 2.34).
29. Ibid., see Table 2.32.
30. George H. Gallup, *The Gallup Poll Monthly*, no. 340 (Princeton, N.J.: The Gallup Poll, 1995). The poll was taken on August 15–16, 1994, and 39 percent reported "crime and violence" as the most important problem, with an additional 9 percent stating "drugs and drug abuse."
31. These surveys were conducted by CBS News, CBS News/*New York Times*, the Wirthlin Group, the Princeton Survey Research Associates, and the Harris Poll. See also Mark Warr, "The Polls—Poll Trends: Public Opinion on Crime and Punishment," *Public Opinion Quarterly* 59: 296–310.
32. Bureau of Justice Statistics, *Sourcebook of Criminal Justice Statistics 2002—Online* (2003), available online at www.albany.edu/sourcebook/index.html (see Table 2.1).
33. Kathleen Maguire and Ann L. Pastore, *Bureau of Justice Statistics Sourcebook of Criminal Justice Statistics—1994* (Washington, D.C.: U.S. Government Printing Office, 1995). In regard to Americans' attitudes in 1994, when crime was the "most important problem," 83 percent of respondents believed that crime was a "very serious threat" (p. 144), and 75 percent of respondents believed that "too little" was being spent to halt the rising crime rates (p. 162). In a more recent poll, in 2002, 56 percent of respondents answered that "too little" was being spent to

halt the rising crime rates despite the fact that crime had been falling for a decade. See Bureau of Justice Statistics, *Sourcebook of Criminal Justice Statistics 2002*, table 2.40.

34. Warr, "The Polls—Poll Trends." See also Bureau of Justice Statistics, *Sourcebook of Criminal Justice Statistics 2002*.

35. Curt R. Bartol, *Psychology and American Law* (Belmont, Calif.: Wadsworth, 1983).

36. G. Gerbner, L. Gross, M. Elley, M. Jackson-Beeck, S. Jeffries-Fox, and N. Signorelli, *Trends in Network Television Drama and Viewer Conceptions of Social Reality* (Philadelphia: University of Pennsylvania Press, 1977).

37. M. Peffley, T. Shields, and B. Williams, "The Intersection of Race and Crime in Television News Stories: An Experimental Study," *Political Communication* 13 (1996): 309–27; J. Hurwitz, and M. Peffley, "Public Perception of Race and Crime: The Role of Racial Stereotypes," *American Journal of Political Science* 41 (1997): 375–401; M. Peffley, J. Hurwitz, and P. M. Sniderman, "Racial Stereotypes and Whites' Political Views of Blacks in the Context of Welfare and Crime," *American Journal of Political Science* 41 (1997): 30–60.

38. M. J. Lynch and E. B. Patterson, *Justice with Prejudice: Race and Criminal Justice in America* (Guilderland, N.Y.: Harrow and Heston, 1996); S. Walker, C. Spohn, and M. DeLone, *The Color of Justice: Race, Ethnicity and Crime in America* (Belmont, Calif.: Wadsworth, 1996).

39. J. Austin and J. Irwin, *It's About Time: America's Imprisonment Binge* (3rd ed.) (Belmont, Calif.: Wadsworth, 2001).

40. D. J. Champion, *Measuring Offender Risk: A Criminal Justice Sourcebook* (Westport, Conn.: Greenwood Press, 1994); A. Young, *Imagining Crime* (Thousand Oaks, Calif.: Sage, 1996).

41. R. Surette, *Media, Crime, and Criminal Justice: Images and Realities* (Belmont, Calif.: Wadsworth, 1992).

42. *Charleston Gazette*, February 28, 1998.

43. J. F. Davis, "Crime News in Colorado Newspapers," *American Journal of Sociology* 57 (1992): 325–30; D. A. Graber, *Crime News and the Public* (New York: Praeger, 1980); W. G. Skogan and M. G. Maxfield, *Coping with Crime: Individual and Neighborhood Reactions* (Beverly Hills, Calif.: Sage, 1981); J. Sheley and C. Askins, "Crime, Crime News, and Crime Views," *Public Opinion Quarterly* 45 (1981): 492–506.

44. J. Garofalo, "Crime and Mass Media: A Selective Review of Research," *Journal of Research in Crime and Delinquency* 18 (1981): 319–50; Graber, *Crime News and the Public*; Julian V. Roberts and Loretta J. Stalans, *Public Opinion, Crime, and Criminal Justice* (Boulder, Colo.: Westview Press, 1997).

45. K. Tunnell, "Film at Eleven: Recent Developments in the Commodification of Crime," *Sociological Spectrum* 12 (1992): 293–313.

46. R. S. Lichter and L. S. Lichter, *Media Monitor: 1993—The Year in Review*, vol. 8, no. 1 (Washington, D.C.: Center for Media and Public Affairs, 1994).

47. "Survey Finds TV News Focusing on Violence," *New York Times*, August 13, 1997.

48. Graber, *Crime News and the Public*.

49. K. Beckett and T. Sasson, *The Politics of Injustice: Crime and Punishment in America* (Thousand Oaks, Calif.: Pine Forge Press, 2000).

50. Beckett and Sasson, *The Politics of Injustice*; Surette, *Media, Crime, and Criminal Justice*; F. Y. Bailey and D. C. Hale, eds., *Popular Culture, Crime, and Justice* (Belmont, Calif.: West/Wadsworth, 1998).

51. N. Signorelli, "Television's Mean and Dangerous World: A Continuation of the Cultural Indicator's Perspective," in *Cultivation Analysis: New Directions in Media Effects Research*, ed. M. Morgan and N. Signorelli (Newbury Park, Calif.: Sage, 1990), p. 88.

52. Bailey and Hale, *Popular Culture, Crime, and Justice*.

53. www.crimescene.com/.

54. Title 28, Section 534, of the U.S. Code.

55. Arson was added to the Uniform Crime Reports Part I offenses in 1979.

56. Part II offenses are as follows: simple assaults, forgery and counterfeiting, fraud, embezzlement, stolen property, vandalism, weapons, prostitution and commercialized vice, sex offenses, drug abuse, gambling, offenses against the family and children, driving under the influence, liquor law violations, drunkenness, disorderly conduct, and vagrancy.

57. There exists a very large set of literature that explores this particular topic. The authors suggest first and foremost that readers consult C. J. Mosher, T. D. Miethe, and D. M. Phillips, *The Mismeasure of Crime* (Thousand Oaks, CA: Sage, 2002). See also R. H. Beattie, "Problems of Criminal Statistics in the United States," *Journal of Criminal Law, Criminology, and Police Science* 46 (1955): 178–86; A. D. Bidermna and J. P. Lynch, *Understanding Crime Incidence Statistics* (New York: Springer-Verlag, 1991); D. J. Black, "Production of Crime Rates," *American Sociological Review* 35 (1970): 733–48; M. Hindelang, "The Uniform Crime Reports Revisited," *Journal of Criminal Justice* 2 (1974): 1–17; J. L. Kituse

and A. V. Cicourel, "A Note on the Use of Official Statistics," *Social Problems* 11 (1963): 131–38; D. Seidman and M. Couzens, "Getting the Crime Rate Down: Political Pressure and Crime Reporting," *Law and Society Review* 8 (1974): 457–93; C. E. Silberman, *Criminal Violence, Criminal Justice* (New York: Random House, 1978); W. G. Skogan, "The Validity of Official Crime Statistics: An Empirical Investigation," *Social Science Quarterly* 55 (1974): 25–38; S. Wheeler, "Criminal Statistics: A Reformulation of the Problem," *Journal of Criminal Law, Criminology, and Police Science* 58 (1967): 317–24.

58. R. Block and C. R. Block, "Decisions and Data: The Transformation of Robbery Incidents into Official Robbery Statistics," *Journal of Criminal Law and Criminology* 71 (1980): 622–36; W. Gove, M. Hughes, and M. Geerken, "Are Uniform Crime Reports a Valid Indicator of the Index Crimes? An Affirmative Answer with Minor Qualifications," *Criminology* 23 (1985): 451–501.

59. J. Reiman, *The Rich Get Richer and the Poor Get Prison*, 4th ed. (Boston: Allyn & Bacon, 1995); S. Simpson, A. R. Harris, and B. A. Mattson, "Measuring Corporate Crime," in *Understanding Corporate Criminality*, ed. M. R. Blakenship (New York: Garland, 1995); S. Walker, *The Police in America* (New York: McGraw-Hill, 1992), pp. 295–96.

60. G. F. Jensen and M. Karpos, "Managing Rape: Exploratory Research on the Behavior of Rape Statistics," *Criminology* 31 (1993): 363–85; J. D. Orcutt and R. Faison, "Sex-Role Attitude Change and Reporting of Rape Victimization, 1973–1985," *Sociological Quarterly* 29 (1988): 589–604.

61. See Lois B. DeFluer, "Biasing Influences on Drug Arrest Records: Implications for Deviance Research," *American Sociological Review* 40 (1975): 88–103; Joseph G. Weis, "Crime Statistics: Reporting Systems and Methods," in *Encyclopedia of Crime and Justice*, vol. 1, ed. Sanford H. Kadish (New York: Free Press, 1983), pp. 378–92; David Seidman and Michael Couzens, "Getting the Crime Rate Down: Political Pressure and Crime Reporting," *Law and Society Review* 8 (1974): 457–93.

62. See Donald J. Black, "The Production of Crime Rates," *American Sociological Review* 35 (1970): 733–48; Pamela I. Jackson and Leo Carroll, "Race and the War on Crime: The Sociopolitical Determinants of Municipal Police Expenditures in 90 Non-Southern U.S. Cities," *American Sociological Review* 46 (1981): 290–305; Allen E. Liska and Mitchell B. Chamlin, "Social Structure and Crime Control among Macrosocial Units," *American Journal of Sociology* 98 (1984): 383–95.

63. See Joseph F. Sheley and John J. Hanlon, "Unintended Consequences of Police Decisions to Actively Enforce Laws: Implications for Analysis of Crime Trends," *Contemporary Crises* 2 (1978): 265–75; Lawrence Sherman and Barry D. Glick, *The Quality of Police Arrest Statistics* (Washington, D.C.: Police Foundation, 1984); James Q. Wilson, *Varieties of Police Behavior: The Management of Law and Order in Eight Communities* (Cambridge, Mass.: Harvard University Press, 1978).

64. See Richard McCleary, Barbara C. Nienstedt, and James M. Erven, "Uniform Crime Reports as Organizational Outcomes: Three Time-Series Experiments," *Social Problems* 29 (1982): 361–72; The President's Commission on Law Enforcement and Administration of Justice, *The Challenge of Crime in a Free Society* (Washington, D.C.: U.S. Government Printing Office, 1967); Wesley Skogan, "Citizen Reporting on Crime: Some National Panel Data," *Criminology* 13 (1976): 535–49.

65. See James Q. Wilson, *Thinking about Crime* (New York: Basic Books, 1975); James Lynch, "Crime in International Perspective," in *Crime*, ed. James Q. Wilson and Joan Petersilia (San Francisco: ICS Press, 1995).

66. See Federal Bureau of Investigation home page (2004), available online at http://www.fbi.gov/, and Bureau of Justice Statistics, home page (2004), available online at http://www.ojp.usdoj.gov/.

67. Mosher, Miethe, and Phillips, *The Mismeasure of Crime*.

68. See A. D. Biderman and J. P. Lynch, *Understanding Crime Incidence Statistics: Why the UCR Diverges from the NCS* (New York: Springer-Verlag, 1991); Gove, et al., "Are Uniform Crime Reports a Valid Indicator of the Index Crimes?"; Robert G. Lehnen and Wesley G. Skogan, *The National Crime Survey: Working Papers, Volume 1: Current and Historical Perspectives* (Washington, D.C.: Bureau of Justice Statistics, 1981); Robert O'Brien, *Crime and Victimization Data* (Beverly Hills, Calif.: Sage, 1985); Anne L. Schneider, "Methodological Problems in Victim Surveys and the Implication for Research in Victimology," *Journal of Criminal Law and Criminology* 72 (1981): 818–38.

69. See Michael R. Gottfredson and Travis Hirschi, "A Consideration of Telescoping and Memory Decay

Biases in Victimization Surveys," *Journal of Criminal Justice* 5 (1977): 205–16; Panel for the Evaluation of Crime Surveys, *Surveying Crime* (Washington, D.C.: National Academy of Sciences, 1976).

70. Black, "Production of Crime Rates."

71. See Helen M. Eigenberg, "The National Crime Survey and Rape: The Case of the Missing Questions," *Justice Quarterly* 7 (1990): 655–71; Gary F. Jensen and Maryaltani Karpos, "Managing Rape: Exploratory Research on the Behavior of Rape Statistics," *Criminology* 31 (1993): 363–85; Richard F. Sparks, "Surveys of Victimization–An Optimistic Assessment," in *Crime and Justice: An Annual Review of Research*, ed. M. Tonry and N. Morris (Chicago: University of Chicago Press, 1981), p. 236.

72. See Paul Brantingham and Patricia Brantingham, *Patterns in Crime* (New York: Macmillan, 1984); Michael R. Gottfredson and Travis Hirschi, "A Consideration of Telescoping and Memory Decay Biases in Victimization Surveys," *Journal of Criminal Justice* 5 (1977): 205–16.

73. The following data were obtained from Federal Bureau of Investigation, *Uniform Crime Reports* (Washington, D.C.: U.S. Government Printing Office, various years); Kathleen Maguire and Ann L. Pastore, *Bureau of Justice Statistics Sourcebook of Criminal Justice Statistics—1995* (Washington, D.C.: U.S. Government Printing Office, 1996).

74. The following data were obtained from Bureau of Justice Statistics, *Criminal Victimization in the United States: 1973–90 Trends* (Washington, D.C.: U.S. Government Printing Office, 1992); Bureau of Justice Statistics, *Criminal Victimization in the United States, 1992* (Washington, D.C.: U.S. Government Printing Office, 1994); Bureau of Justice Statistics, *Highlights from 20 Years of Surveying Crime Victims: The National Crime Victimization Survey, 1973–92* (Washington, D.C.: U.S. Government Printing Office, 1993).

75. Data collected from Bureau of Justice Statistics, *Criminal Victimization in the United States, 1995* (Washington, D.C.: U.S. Department of Justice, 1997). Some of these recent changes in the National Crime Victimization Survey include a revised "screening" strategy, additional questions on rape and family violence as well as the use of computer-assisted telephone interviewing and computer-assisted personal interviewing systems.

76. K. Beckett, *Making Crime Pay: Law and Order in Contemporary Politics* (New York: Oxford University Press, 1997); Beckett and Sasson, *The Politics of Injustice*; W. J. Chambliss, *Power, Politics, and Crime* (Boulder, Colo.: Westview Press, 2001); S. R. Donziger, *The Real War on Crime: The Report of the National Criminal Justice Commission* (New York: HarperPerennial, 1996); T. Gest, *Crime and Politics: Big Government's Erratic Campaign for Law and Order* (New York: Oxford University Press, 2001); W. Kaminer, "Federal Offense," *Atlantic Monthly*, June 1994, pp. 102–14; S. A. Scheingold, *The Politics of Law and Order: Street Crime and Public Policy* (New York: Longman, 1984), and *The Politics of Street Crime: Criminal Process and Cultural Obsession* (Philadelphia: Temple University Press, 1991); E. Schlosser, "The Prison-Industrial Complex," *Atlantic Monthly*, December 1998, pp. 51–77; L. Windlesham, *Politics, Punishment, and Populism* (New York: Oxford University Press, 1998).

77. R. G. Lawrence, *The Politics of Force: Media and the Construction of Police Brutality* (Berkeley: University of California Press, 2000).

78. Beckett and Sasson, *The Politics of Injustice*, p. 85.

79. As quoted in Kaminer, "Federal Offense."

80. W. M. Oliver, *The Law and Order Presidency* (Upper Saddle River, N.J.: Prentice Hall, 2003).

81. Gest, *Crime and Politics*.

82. Donziger, *The Real War on Crime*; Schlosser, "The Prison-Industrial Complex"; Beth Shuster, "Living in Fear," *Los Angeles Times*, August 23, 1998, pp. A1–A9.

83. Gest, *Crime and Politics*; J. C. Harris and P. Jesilow, "It's Not the Old Ball Game: Three Strikes and the Courtroom Workgroup," *Justice Quarterly* 17 (1, 2000): 185–203.

84. Shuster, "Living in Fear."

85. Chambliss, *Power, Politics, and Crime*, p. 9.

86. Roberts and Stalans, *Public Opinion, Crime, and Criminal Justice*, p. 6.

87. Ibid.

88. Oliver and Hilgenberg, *A History of Crime and Criminal Justice in America*.

89. Hamilton quoted from C. Rossiter, *The Federalist Papers* (New York: New American Library, 1961), p. 120.

90. J. J. Dilulio, Jr., S. K. Smith, and A. J. Saiger, "The Federal Role in Crime Control," in *Crime*, ed. J. Q. Wilson and J. Petersilia (San Francisco: ICS Press, 1995), pp. 445–62, at p. 446.

91. Ibid., pp. 445–46.

92. M. W. Flamm, "'Law and Order': Street Crime, Civil Disorder, and the Crisis of Liberalism" (Ph.D. diss., Columbia University, 1998).

93. The President's Commission on Law Enforcement and Administration of Justice, *The Challenge of Crime in a Free Society* (New York: Avon, 1968), p. 630.

94. Ibid., p. 630.

95. Ibid., p. 632.

96. L. B. Johnson, *The Vantage Point: Perspectives of the Presidency, 1963–1969* (New York: Holt, Rinehart and Winston, 1971), p. 549.

97. L. B. Johnson, *The Vantage Point: Perspectives of the Presidency, 1963–1969* (New York: Holt, Rinehart and Winston, 1971), p. 549.

98. F. E. Zimring and G. Hawkins, "Toward a Principles Basis for Federal Criminal Legislation," *Annals of the American Academy of Political and Social Science* 543 (1995): 15–26.

99. N. Marion, *A History of Federal Crime Control Initiatives, 1960–1993* (Westport, Conn.: Praeger, 1994).

100. Congressional Digest, *The Federal Role in Crime Control* (Washington, D.C.: Congressional Digest Corporation, 1994).

101. Task Force on the Federalization of Criminal Law, *The Federalization of Criminal Law* (Washington, D.C.: American Bar Association, 1998), p. 2.

102. M. Israel, "'The Hope of the World': A Role for Criminologists in the Making of a Rational Crime Policy," *ACJS Today* 25 (1, 2003): 1–5.

103. Dye, *Understanding Public Policy*; Lester and Stewart, *Public Policy*; Ripley, *Policy Analysis in Political Science*.

104. Ibid.

105. Ibid.

106. Ibid.

2

Criminal Justice Ideology

Chapter Outline

INTRODUCTION

The way that we think about crime and criminal justice has a significant impact on the public policies we advocate, support, and sustain. The way that we think is called our ideology. Ideology refers to a structure of interrelated values, ideas, and beliefs that we have regarding the nature of people and how society should be ordered.[1] We carry these beliefs, which tell us the best way for people to live and what institutional arrangement best support these beliefs. Ideology is, in a sense, our image of what a good society would look like, but it also tells us how best to achieve that society. Therefore, people's ideologies help shape the policies that they believe should be put into place, what policies should be supported, and which policies should be sustained. The resulting impact is that ideology helps us organize our thoughts, evaluate policy proposals, determine the value of programs, and select which political party we support and the politicians that we will vote for. Thus, ideology becomes our policy reality.

Ideology is important to understanding the types of crime and criminal justice policies that we have and those that are advocated by various groups. Since people have different ideological perspectives about the world, they also have differing and often competing perceptions about how to best deal with crime. Many believe that we should lock up all criminals in prisons for lengthy sentences, while others believe that most criminals should remain in the community. Many believe that the death penalty is an appropriate punishment for murder, while others believe it is never justified. Many believe that an armed citizenry is the best way to control crime, while others believe that this contributes to violence and that only sanctioned officials should be authorized to carry firearms. These viewpoints are shaped by people's ideological perceptions of how society should be ordered that then help shape the policies that they support. In the first example, ideology tells people whether they believe in the policy of prison expansion. In the second example, ideology tells people whether they support the death penalty. And in the final example, ideology tells people whether they support gun control laws. The resulting impact is that ideological controversy ends up shaping policy controversy in America. This is why an understanding of ideology is important for understanding crime and criminal justice policy in America.

This chapter discusses what we will refer to as criminal justice ideology. It begins with a discussion of several models of criminal justice that have been described by leading scholars in the field to help us understand how ideology shapes the criminal justice system we have. It then discusses the various and often competing perspectives of what the ultimate goal of the criminal justice system should be. From there, we discuss more directly how ideology is formed, especially in an individual's formative years. This then leads to a discussion of the two major ideologies, liberalism and conservatism, and their general embodiment in the two political parties of Democrats and Republicans. In addition, other ideological perspectives are briefly discussed. Finally, major changes in some of the ideological perspectives over the past forty years are reviewed and the policy implications of ideology detailed.

MAJOR MODELS OF THE CRIMINAL JUSTICE SYSTEM

Packer's Models

The first major conceptual model of the criminal justice system came from Herbert Packer, who was a distinguished professor of law at Stanford University. In the 1960s, Packer published an article titled "Two Models of the Criminal Process," which was later included in a book titled *The Limits of the Criminal Sanction.*[2] In these publications, Packer presented two models of the criminal justice system: the crime control model and the due process model. His goal was to present two models that would "give operational content to a complex of values underlying the criminal law."[3] Packer achieved his goal, for these two models have come to reflect the competing ideologies and policies of the criminal justice system.

Packer did not necessarily want these two models to become an oversimplification of the values that underlie the criminal process. Rather, he wanted to be able to communicate the two competing systems of values that created an enormous amount of tension on the development of the criminal process and how it should best be ordered. He did contend that the polarity of the two models was not absolute and that there was some common ground between these competing philosophies. The primary commonality between these two competing models, Packer explained, could actually be found in their adherence to the U.S. Constitution. Both adhered to the principles found in the Constitution, but each does so in its own unique way. In addition, both agree that our system is an adversarial system, pitting the prosecution against the defense. Neither model disagrees with this basic premise, but how they react to the adversarial system of justice is quite diverse. Despite the articulation of this "common ground" between the competing models, it is the polarity of the two models that is most renowned and most discussed in terms of Packer's models. Therefore, it is to these two competing models we now turn.

CRIME CONTROL   The crime control model articulates that the repression of criminal conduct is by far the most important function of the criminal justice system. If the system and, more specifically, the police fail to keep criminal conduct under tight control, then it is believed that this will lead to the breakdown of public order, which will cause the denigration of human freedom. If people are not free to do as they choose for fear of crime, then society suffers. Thus, the criminal justice system becomes a guarantor of human freedom. And to achieve this freedom, the crime control model argues that the criminal justice system is charged with arresting suspects, determining guilt, and ensuring that criminals are properly punished. Therefore, the crime control model stresses the need for efficiency and speed to generate a high rate of apprehension while dealing with limited resources. The goal is to then process these individuals through the system by moving those who are not guilty out of the process and moving those who are toward some form of sanction. Every step in the system, however, is focused on the successful and speedy prosecution of the offender. To this end, individual constitutional rights must often be seen as secondary to the effective prosecution of offenders. This model assumes that in most cases, people who are brought into the system are in fact guilty; otherwise, they would not have been brought into the system in the first place. Thus, a presumption of guilt exists prior to a suspect becoming a defendant. Therefore, one way to achieve successful prosecution of these suspects is for lawyers from both sides to come to an agreement about the case, achieve a guilty plea, and close the case.

DUE PROCESS   The due process model is generally the polar opposite of the crime control model. The ideology behind the model is that due process is "far more deeply impressed on the formal structure of the law"[4] and that the protection of individual, and thus constitutional rights, is paramount. Every effort must be made to guarantee that an individual is not being unfairly labeled and treated as a criminal, especially before being found guilty. Hence, rather than assuming a suspect to be guilty, due process assumes the suspect to be innocent, and guilt must be proven by the criminal justice system. The purpose of the system, then, is to create a process of successive stages that is "designed to present formidable impediments to carrying the accused any further along in the process."[5] The reason it does this is to prevent and eliminate any mistakes being made in the process, at least to the greatest extent possible. Packer describes the due process model as always being skeptical of the morality and utility of the criminal sanction and is wary of the actors in the criminal justice system. Thus, at each successive stage of the system, roadblocks are created to ensure that the innocent go free and that the guilty receive equal protection under the law.

Although Packer did not desire the two models to be seen as entirely polar opposites of an ideological spectrum, it is this aspect of the model that is most attractive to the student of criminal justice. The crime control model resembles an assembly line, while the due process model resembles an obstacle course. The crime control model is oriented on being as efficient as possible, while the due process model desires to be equitable. The goal of the crime control model is to punish criminals, while the due process model aims to protect individual rights. The crime control model achieves its ends through tough legislation and strong enforcement through the administrative process. The due process model is more judicially oriented and is legalistic in nature. And, as both models are ideologically driven, they tend to be represented by the two political ideological perspectives as well. The crime control model is adhered to more often by conservatives, and the due process model is more often attributed to liberals. Although there are always exceptions to the rule and these generalizations might not always hold true, they have a strong consistency because they are ideologically based.

Feeley's Models

Taking Packer's two models a little further was Malcolm M. Feeley, a professor of criminal justice and the law, in a 1973 article titled "Two Models of the Criminal Justice System: An Organizational Approach."[6] Feeley's purpose was to create a theoretical framework for explaining the organization of criminal justice in order that research could be viewed through these two perspectives. Feeley articulated that there were two models of organization: the rational-goal model and the functional-systems model.

RATIONAL GOAL   To create his rational-goal model, Feeley combined two models that had been previously advanced and merged them into one model. The rational model argues that an organization is focused on the means of accomplishing its mission, while the goals model argues that it is not the means but rather the end that is important. Feeley advances the argument that in criminal justice these two concepts, the means and the goals (ends), are often the same thing, for in criminal justice we seek justice (means) to obtain justice (goals). The way this is accomplished is through an adherence to strict rules and procedures within the bureaucracy, much in the vein of Max Weber.

Weber is the primary scholar who speaks to the rational organization as being the primary means by which government achieves its goals. Organizations are characterized by several major components, consisting of (1) a continuous organization of official functions bound by rules, (2) a specific sphere of competence (obligations) in the division of labor to be performed by a person who is provided with the necessary means and authority to carry out their tasks, (3) the organization of offices following the principle of hierarchy, and (4) a set of technical rules and norms regulating the conduct of the offices.[7] As in the criminal justice system, the system itself is made up of various officials (police, judges, correctional officers, and so on) who are bound by formal rules, given specific responsibilities and authority to carry out their duties, must follow a chain of command (especially in policing and corrections), and are guided by policies and procedures in the performance of their duties. By ensuring that the organization is highly effective in the performance of their duties (means), they can ensure that they achieve their ends (goals). Thus, effectiveness, like in Packer's crime control model, is the overriding goal.

FUNCTIONAL SYSTEMS   The functional-systems model is a different conception of how an organization is employed. The common characteristics of this model are that criminal justice is a "system of action based primarily upon cooperation, exchange, and adaptation"[8] and that it emphasizes "these considerations over adherence to formal rules and defined 'roles' in searching for and developing explanations of behavior and discussing organizational effectiveness."[9] In fact, this model would acknowledge the viewpoint that the criminal justice system is not very effective in operating through its rules and that the actual means for obtaining these goals is the adherence to the more informal rules of the game, folkways, personal relationships, and dedicated individuals. Another way of explaining the differences between the two models is that the rational-goal model is focused on creating a rational organization, while the functional-systems model is focused on creating rational individuals, those people who work within the criminal justice system, to be better adept at pursuing goals. Hence, increased discretion is important in the functional-systems model because it allows those actors in the system to make decisions in the application of the law rather than the rules, as would be the case in the rational-goal model.

In Feeley's two models, we once again see ideology as shaping the viewpoint of how criminal justice should best be organized. Packer's models provided us two viewpoints for understanding the purpose of criminal justice, while Feeley's models provide us a perspective on how best to organize society in order for these ends to be achieved. Thus, it can be seen that those whose ideological beliefs lead them to believe that the crime control model is the proper function of our criminal justice system will also most likely believe that the rational-goal model is the best way to achieve this end. Those who believe in the due process model will most likely articulate that the functional-systems model is the best way to organize the criminal justice system. Ideology again shapes our understanding of how criminal justice should best be ordered.

If the complexity of Feeley's two models is lost on the reader, then perhaps it can be made clearer through the more recent debates over whether criminal justice is a system or a nonsystem. In the criminal justice system model, the concept that criminal justice operates as a bona fide system is advanced. A system is made up of interdependent elements that work together to perform one or more tasks or goals. This definition implies first that the component parts or subsystems are working together to reach one ultimate goal and second that the system is a sequential, orderly process similar to a factory assembly line whereby a client must be processed through each stage before entering into the next. There are component parts (the police, courts, and corrections agencies) that work together to reach the goal of reducing or preventing crime. There is also a sequential process that must be followed as one goes through the criminal justice system. When individuals enter the system, they must do so through an arrest: They cannot go straight to the courts or to the corrections components. Then, after the arrest stage, a defendant goes through the court component. They cannot go directly to the corrections area. Only after the defendant had been processed through the first two components of the system can he or she enter the corrections component. In order to get to the next level, an offender must have had contact with all the preceding ones.

Each of the components must work together to achieve a final result, meaning that they are interdependent. The work of each department, therefore, is heavily influenced by the work of every other department. When one unit changes its policies or practices, other units will be affected. For example, an increase in the number of people arrested by the police will affect the work not only of the judicial subsystem but also of the probation and correctional subsystems. Each part must make its own distinctive contribution: Each part must also have at least minimal contact with at least one other component of the system.

From this perspective, the criminal justice system is indeed a "system." However, many people see the criminal justice system as a nonsystem in which the component parts do not work together to achieve a goal. Each of the departments is independent and has its own tasks or goals. The police have a goal of bringing people into the system, while the corrections system wants to get them out. Within the courts, the prosecution wants to keep the defendant in the system, and the defense wants to get the case dismissed. Each agency acts as its own department, with its own goals and needs. In addition, each component struggles to find its own resources, sometimes competing for the same resources. This competition, added to strained relations, poor communications, and a reluctance to cooperate with each other, can generate antagonism between the departments. This, in turn, can lead to poor working relationships and resistance to working with each other and doing what is in the best interest of the client and society. Additionally, people working inside the system, as well as those observing the system, lose their respect for the system and may be more likely to seek justice in alternative ways.

Cox and Wade's Criminal Justice System

Another way of thinking about the nonsystem approach has been advanced by Cox and Wade, who argue that the traditional flowchart presentation of the criminal justice system is often misleading and inaccurate.[10] They argue that it fails to indicate the routine pursuit of different, sometimes incompatible goals by various components; the effects of feedback based on personal relationships inside and outside criminal justice; the importance of political considerations by all those involved; and the widespread use of discretion.[11] Instead, what they argue is that we really do not have a criminal justice *system* but rather a criminal justice *network*. They advance this nonsystem concept as "consisting of a web of constantly changing relationships among individuals, some of whom are directly involved in criminal justice pursuits, others who are not" and that "a network may be thought of as a net with intersecting lines of communication among components designed to function in a specific manner."[12] What Cox and Wade argue is that each criminal event can be unique and that the network will come to bear on the problem in different ways. A series of simple larcenies from auto may generate a network of police officers, detectives, and prosecutors to address the problem, while a kidnapped child who is taken across state lines will create a network of both criminal justice actors (local police, state police, Federal Bureau of Investigation, prosecutors, and so on) and non-criminal justice actors (victims' family, the media, the National Center for Missing and Exploited Children, and so on). Different actors, agencies, and resources are all brought to bear on a specific problem, but it is not a standard response, nor is it always going to be the same responders. These various criminal justice and non-criminal justice actors employ those aspects of the network that are necessary to address a specific problem. This is why they explain that the criminal justice "network" is a "web of constantly changing relationships among individuals involved more or less directly in the pursuit of criminal justice."[13]

These various models of the criminal justice system (or network) provide varying ideological approaches to criminal justice and help us understand how we perceive this system. Yet there is something more to our understanding of criminal justice that is an extension of our ideological approach to justice that tells us the purpose of the system itself. While most would agree that the ultimate goal of the criminal justice system is to seek justice, the term *justice* can have various meanings to various people. Again, these variations generally proceed from one's ideological perspective. What defines this complexity is most often the discussion of the *goals* of the criminal justice system. It is here that perhaps the greatest conflict begins to arise in policy formulation, and it is to this topic we now turn.

MAJOR GOALS OF THE CRIMINAL JUSTICE SYSTEM

Ideology plays an important role in shaping one's understanding about how the world works, and this subsequently shapes one's views of the criminal justice system. All this will then come to bear on the question: What is the goal of the criminal justice system? While preventing crime and dealing with the aftermath of crimes are clearly functions of the criminal justice system, how it achieves these ends are embodied in the goals of the system. The goals of the system are many, varied, and often conflicting, largely because of the ideological differences that people have over human behavior and how society should be ordered. Understanding these varying goals is important to our understanding of not only criminal justice policy but also the criminal justice system itself.

Deterrence

The first major goal of the criminal justice system is to deter people from committing crime.[14] There are two types of deterrence: general and specific.

GENERAL DETERRENCE General deterrence can be described as punishing an individual so severely that it makes an example of him or her in order to deter the rest of the public from committing a similar act. Deterrence theory operates on the assumption that people are rational actors and that they weigh the costs and benefits of all their actions. If they factor in the cost of committing a crime, as evidenced by the individual of whom an example was made, then their rational process would conclude that the cost far outweighs any benefit they may obtain from the crime. Thus, they will be deterred. For example, when the newspaper reports that someone was sentenced to serve a ten-year sentence in prison for theft, it is thought that this information will prevent others from committing the same or a similar offense because they too could be sentenced to ten years in prison if they commit a similar act. Another prime example of general deterrence is found in the death penalty. Many argue that the old method of public executions served as a general deterrent to the rest of the community who witnessed the executions in person in order to deter them from committing such heinous crimes that would merit similar punishment. Although some would argue that moving such executions behind prison walls and limiting the number of witnesses have decreased the effect of deterrence, many still argue that the prospect of being executed for murder will prevent future murders.[15] Another, more recent example is found in a book by Michael G. Santos titled *About Prisons*,[16] where he describes his life of drug dealing in his early twenties, being arrested, and ultimately given a 45-year sentence of which he would have to serve 27 in a federal penitentiary. The judge fully intended to make an example of Santos by giving him a very severe punishment for his crimes, most likely with the intent of deterring future drug dealers or, at a minimum, of deterring Mr. Santos from future crimes.

SPECIFIC DETERRENCE   This last case of deterrence, the judge giving Santos a lengthy sentence to prevent *him* from committing future crimes, is what is known as specific deterrence. The goal of specific deterrence is to make the punishment for committing an offense so negative that the same person doesn't commit further criminal acts. This can be equated to the common practice among parents who punish their children for bad behavior in the hopes that it will deter them from committing the same bad behavior in the future. Equally, by punishing an adult who commits a criminal act through a heavy fine, jail time, or both, it is the goal of specific deterrence that this experience will be so negative that they will never repeat those same illegal behaviors.

Incapacitation

Related to specific deterrence is the goal of incapacitation, whereby a criminal is sentenced to a lengthy time in a correctional facility.[17] In this particular goal, "the opportunity for offending again is limited (or eliminated) because the offender's freedom is restricted."[18] Many scholars have suggested that the drop in crime during the 1990s had something to do with the prison expansion of the 1980s.[19] As more prisons were built, this allowed for more criminals to be sentenced to prison and for longer sentences, thus incapacitating them in the 1990s and preventing them from committing more crime. An extreme example of incapacitation is the death penalty. An offender who is sentenced to death is virtually unable to commit more offenses while on death row and can obviously commit no other crimes once executed. Mandatory life sentences will also reduce the amount of crime offenders can commit in prison but eliminate their chances for committing more crimes on the streets. Other correctional options provide fewer restrictions on inmate behavior, including curfews, house arrest, day reporting centers, and probation. Each of these options makes it more difficult for offenders to have the opportunity to commit additional crimes, thus incapacitating them.

SELECTIVE INCAPACITATION   Like specific deterrence is to general deterrence, there is a more narrowly focused type of incapacitation known as selective incapacitation. Selective incapacitation refers to "sentencing policies that attempt to distinguish between higher-rate and lower-rate criminal offenders in determining who will be incarcerated and for how long."[20] The idea here is for the criminal justice system to target those who are considered career criminals and repeat offenders (or likely career criminals and likely repeat offenders) in order to prevent these few people from committing future crimes. Adhering to the belief that a few people cause the most problems, the goal is to take the few criminals who cause the most crime, the higher-rate offenders, and severely incapacitate them.

Punishment

Another goal of the criminal justice system is punishment, also known as "retribution," "revenge," or the "just deserts" models of criminal justice.[21] All these simply refer to punishing offenders for having committed a crime. Regardless of whether it is a biological or moral response, it is a human urge to pay back an offender for harms committed.[22] The concept of punishment is based on the idea that individuals should be held accountable for their actions. If they commit the crime, they should do the time. Thus, when someone violates the laws, they are to be held accountable for their actions through various forms of punishment. The goal of the criminal justice system is to ensure that those who commit crimes are then held accountable and, if found guilty, are punished for their crimes. Examples of the punishment orientation abound over the past three decades, such as the growing amount of criminal legislation, legislation that has increased the sentences for various crimes, an increase in the use of the death penalty, the hiring of more police officers, and the prison expansion. All this suggests an increased movement toward the goal of punishment.

Some have also argued that one aspect of punishment is to teach and enforce morality within the community. Morality, as being the understanding of what is right and what is wrong, is inherently a part of our system of criminal laws. All laws tell people what is right and what is wrong behavior. According to Marion, when the state establishes this series of punishments and offenses, citizens can get a sense of what is "right" (proper, moral) and what is "wrong" (improper, immoral) behavior.[23] For example, when the act of prostitution or gambling is deemed wrong by the government, this is teaching a certain population that those actions are inappropriate. When an individual violates society's morality and they commit a "wrong" behavior, then it is the role of the criminal justice system to enforce society's morality through the application of the criminal (moral) law.

Rehabilitation

Another goal of the criminal justice system is rehabilitation or the treatment of offenders so that they can rejoin society with the goal of no longer committing crime. This is based on the medical model that assumes that there is something wrong with offenders (or some underlying cause for their behavior) and that they can be diagnosed and treated so they won't commit more crimes, just like someone who is sick and can be treated so they are well again.[24] Many people believe that by teaching criminals a specific trade or job skills, this can give them the means to become productive citizens when they are released from confinement. In other cases, officials believe that behavior modification is the proper response in order to socialize the individual to the proper norms of society so that, once released, they will not commit further crimes. Another means of rehabilitation is to educate the offender, either through classes to help them earn their G.E.D. or to begin work toward a college degree. Finally, one other means of rehabilitation is a direct application of the medical model either by guiding the individual through a drug treatment program or providing them with the necessary medication to help control mental illnesses that may have been a contributing factor to the offender's crimes.

Reintegration

An extension of the goal of rehabilitation and treatment is reintegration. Here the goal is to continue to work with offenders as they make the transition from life in prison or jail to life back in their community. At this point, the goal is not so much to rehabilitate or treat as it is to help move offenders into a community, provide them with an alternative to criminal behavior, and help them become productive citizens. Examples of reintegration include correctional programs that slowly wean offenders from prison life by allowing them to work outside the prison but to return to the prison at night and during the weekends. Eventually, many of these offenders are moved into halfway houses where they are provided a controlled environment outside prison and are given the assistance they need to make the transition back into a community.

Restoration

Another goal, and one that recently has become a growing area of interest in criminal justice, is restorative justice, sometimes referred to as simply restoration or community justice.[25] This approach implies that crime is a disruption of the community's peace, and it aims to restore the community to its state before the crime was committed.[26] It does this to some degree by avoiding the traditional criminal justice model and pursuing a civil mediation process. Victims and offenders are brought together with a mediator to work through the violation and attempt to arrive at some form of reparation that restores order. It then moves to reintegrate the victim and offender back into the community, thus allowing them to either become or return to being full participants in their community. Through restoration, the community can attempt to repair the peace rather than punish the offender in response to a crime. Community policing, victim–offender mediation, and community-based corrections are all seen as means toward this end, along with an expansion of these concepts to create a sense of community justice, rather than criminal justice.[27]

Pragmatism

Finally, one other goal that has recently emerged is what these authors would call the pragmatic goal of criminal justice. Pragmatism is a philosophy that stresses practical consequences as being the most important criterion in determining justice. It is very utilitarian in nature and, again, practical. More recently, this has come to be found in the literature that asks, "What works?"[28] The premise here is to ignore ideology, theory, or goals by simply looking at programs that work in preventing or reducing crime regardless of the reason why. The predominant literature in this area has looked at crime prevention methods in association with different areas that have been attributed to affecting crime. For example, schools are often seen as a potential source of spawning crime but also one for preventing crime. Evaluating various programs, such as drug and alcohol education, counseling and mentoring programs, and after-school programs, and looking at what is effective at reducing crime provides us with practical solutions to the crime problem. As a result, these programs are then encouraged, replicated, and implemented in other jurisdictions. This has been done in the area of community programs, family-based programs, and risk factors associated with labor markets and in terms of police crime prevention programs and the broader criminal justice programs. The goal of pragmatism, then, is to figure out what works and to replicate these programs in other jurisdictions.

While some would argue that these goals are compatible and that all of them can be obtained simultaneously, this argument loses credibility as one begins to explore the details of each of these goals. Is it realistic to believe that one can be punished with a lengthy sentence while at the same time being treated and rehabilitated? Even more difficult are such goals as incapacitation, especially selective incapacitation, when faced with the tenets of restorative justice. Further, when faced with the reality of constrained budgets in the criminal justice system, it is highly unlikely that the system can afford long prison sentences while providing rehabilitation and treatment programs to each offender for the period of these lengthy sentences. Therefore, one must accept the fact that these goals do in reality conflict with each other. (See Box 2.1.)

BOX 2.1
Major Goals of the Criminal Justice System

Deterrence	The philosophy that crime can be prevented before it occurs through the threat of criminal sanctions. General deterrence initiatives, such as increased penalties for drunk driving, are aimed at deterring would-be law violators, whereas specific deterrence measures apply to those already convicted and are imposed to deter any further criminal conduct.
Incapacitation	The policy of incarcerating dangerous law violators to eradicate their potential for committing additional offenses. Collective incapacitation refers to locking all persons up convicted of a given crime, such as armed robbery. Selective incapacitation, on the other hand, concerns enhanced sentences for individuals who pose a high risk of recidivism.
Punishment	The philosophy of justice that holds that those who violate the law deserve to be punished.
Rehabilitation	The medical model-based philosophy of justice that emphasizes "treating" offenders to correct their behavior. Examples of rehabilitation programs include general education and drug counseling.
Reintegration	The correctional policy of facilitating the offender's return to the community.
Teach Morality	The philosophy that criminal sanctions should be imposed to determine the boundaries between moral and immoral behavior.
Restoration	An approach to administering justice that holds that the victim, the community, and the offender should be given a more active role in seeking justice and repairing the harm caused.
Pragmatism	The philosophy that emphasizes the criminal justice responses that are most effective in controlling crime.

In looking at the reason for the conflict within the criminal justice system over its intended goals, one has to return to ideology. The goals of deterrence, incapacitation, punishment, and to some degree morality all fit into Packer's crime control model. The goals of rehabilitation, reintegration, and restorative justice all intend a very different purpose of the criminal justice system, and, while not specifically Packer's due process model, they do reflect a more humanitarian approach to justice. Finally, the goal of pragmatism, while trying to divest itself of ideological constraints, generally still finds itself constrained, for the programs themselves are often implemented for very specific ideological reasons.

Perhaps the more important question is a normative one, that is, whether goal conflict is a "good" or a "bad" thing in criminal justice. Those who would argue that goal conflict is "bad" take the position that conflicting goals prevent a rational system; that they strain resources, thus making criminal justice less efficient or effective; and that they fail to send clear signals to those working within the system as to what specifically they are trying to accomplish. Those who argue that goal conflict is "good" argue that conflict allows for a wide variety of interests (ideologies) to be represented within the system. It creates a type of checks-and-balances process whereby one goal does not become too excessive in nature and in actuality creates a "smoothly operating offender-processing system" because it does not try to unify the criminal justice system, causing it to bog down in bureaucratic inertia.[29] The most likely reason, however, for this difference in perception over goal conflict is again due to ideological differences. Those who perceive goal conflict as bad prefer a neatly ordered world where there is a criminal justice *system* that has a well-ordered and agreed-on goal. Those who perceive goal conflict as good prefer a less orderly world where the criminal justice *network* allows for various goals to be applied to specific cases, depending on the circumstances of each incident or event. One desires a monolithic and unified system, while the other desires a highly fragmented system. Thus, in order to understand goal conflict, it again becomes imperative to understand ideology.

FORMATION OF IDEOLOGY

To more fully understand the varying ideological viewpoints that people have regarding how the American criminal justice system should be organized and what its primary goals should be, one must understand how ideology is formed in the first place. The basis of one's ideology is directly derived from one's values. While some may posit that values can exhibit innate qualities, stating effectively that we are born with certain values, most tend to accept the fact that values are learned. As values are learned, so too are our ideological positions on the way the world should be ordered. The sources of learning are varied and can differ from person to person, but in general the leading influences on our ideological beliefs tend to come from family, schools, religion, civic organizations, the mass media, and our participation in political activities.

Family

The most influential of these sources of our political ideology in the United States is family. Children are educated from an early age about ideology without ever knowing it. When parents talk about national events, politicians, or particular laws being passed, they will generally discuss them with the ideological perspective they adhere to. When they go to vote or participate in a campaign, they are communicating to their children their specific ideology. And when they talk to other adults, children listen and absorb the information they hear. Hence, parents, primarily through what they say and do, transmit their ideological beliefs to their children. As young children strive to be accepted and loved by their parents, they will also accept their parents' ideological beliefs without question.

Schools

The first chance that children generally have to hear other points of view on issues is in the schools. Here children learn not only from their teachers (other adults with potentially differing ideological perspectives from their parents) but also from their peers who have generally absorbed their parents' beliefs. In addition, what the children do in school can have an impact on their ideological beliefs, as young children know only what they are taught. As children grow older, they begin to think more for themselves, but what occurs in school will still have an influence on their worldviews as they participate in school elections, read school newspapers, or absorb the various values taught in history, economics, and social studies courses.

Religion

Another influencing factor for many is their religious beliefs. For many, this is where their values are either learned or put into more concrete understanding in terms of their relationship with God. Religion teaches values by teaching what is right and what is wrong behavior. And, because

America has an understanding that everyone has the right to worship in their own way without interference from government, America has many diverse religious institutions, hence many diverse ideological perspectives. In addition, religious education plays a major role in transmitting ideological beliefs, as does participation in church groups and taking on various roles during church services.

Civic Participation

Civic participation, which many have argued has been on the decline in America for the past three or four decades, is another important part of the social process when it comes to learning values and forming our ideological beliefs. There are numerous groups that children can become involved in, and each in their own ways will shape their beliefs by the values they teach. Belonging to such things as local team sports or academic clubs can have an influence as they teach the values of team participation. More important, however, those civic organizations that purposefully teach values to the young, such as the Boy Scouts, Girl Scouts, 4-H Clubs, and Future Farmers of America, all have a great influence on shaping their ideological beliefs.

Political Activities

Another source of learning our values and beliefs comes from our political activities themselves. When we actually engage in the political process, by campaigning, voting, or participating in the electoral process, we are reinforcing our ideological beliefs by putting them into action. As a result, we tend to become more adamant that our worldview is the correct one, and we become advocates for these beliefs.

Mass Media

Finally, there can be little doubt that in more modern times the mass media have had a profound impact on shaping the ideological beliefs of the young. Many have even argued that with two-parent-income families and declining religious, civic, and political participation, the mass media have become the primary source for transmitting our values and for shaping our ideological beliefs. Today, by the time most children become adults, they will have spent more time watching television, listening to the radio, or surfing the computer than any other activity in their entire lives. The impact this has on an individual is profound. The viewpoints and ideological beliefs of those who shape the mass media thus become the viewpoints and ideology conveyed by the mass media. And it is from this that a majority of Americans learn their values and ideological beliefs on how the world should be ordered.

There are a number of ideological perspectives that people often develop. One perspective is known as the libertarian ideology, which believes that the government should regulate only what is expressly specified in the Constitution of the United States and then only as a means of protections against government. If something is not expressly stated in the Constitution, then the government should have no jurisdiction. While libertarians are noted for upholding civil liberties, they are also noted for advancing the legalization of drugs. Another view is the socialist perspective, which believes that government should be involved in all aspects of our lives to ensure that everyone is provided a basic level of comfort and that no one is excluded. Other ideological views include a feminist perspective, which sees everything as a power play between men and women and calls for a perfect equality between the two genders. Despite these various ideological viewpoints, most of them tend to side with one of two perspectives: the liberal or the conservative ideological perspective. These two worldviews are the dominant ideological perspectives in the United States, and most people, even when calling themselves a libertarian, a socialist, or a feminist, tend to fit into one of these two ideological camps. Hence, it is to these two camps that we now turn.

LIBERAL IDEOLOGY

Liberalism, in modern American terms, tends to refer to the strongly held belief that government is the best entity to bring about justice, ensure equality, and create opportunities for all Americans.[30] Modern-day liberals strive to protect individual rights, but they are willing to allow government to intervene in both social and economic aspects of American life in order to rectify deficiencies. They do this to ensure that people have adequate education, housing, and medical assistance. Liberals tend, then, to believe in larger government interest in our daily lives and hence larger government to carry out these types of social programs. One other area of association with liberals is their belief in creating a minimum standard for the poor in America. By creating a certain standard of living for the poor, the goal is to bring everyone up to this standard, whether it is a certain level of income, housing, or medical care. Finally, on a philosophical level, liberals are progressives and are always seeking change to make things better in society.

Liberals, when trying to articulate the reasons for criminal behavior, tend to focus their attention on the conditions of social arrangements and environmental structures.[31] Crime is largely a product of social ills, such as poverty, unemployment, poor education, and unequal opportunities. They believe that crime is a product of social pressures rather than individual motivations and that these societal dysfunctions are to blame. Hence, the best response to the problem of crime is not to deal directly with the individual but rather to address the social conditions that cause crime in the first place. In addition, liberals believe that while these economic conditions do create the situation for crime, crime does occur among all sectors of society and all economic classes. However, liberals believe that the majority of law enforcement is directed toward the poor and disenfranchised and that this is a discriminatory application of the criminal justice system. Moreover, liberals also believe that the system has a propensity to make distinctions among individuals based on various classes of society, such as age, sex, race, social class, and criminal versus noncriminal. As a result, certain classes are treated differently from other classes, which then become labeled and stigmatized, thus further exacerbating the discrimination against these individuals. Finally, liberals tend to believe that many crimes, especially moral crimes, should not be crimes at all and that many should be removed from the focus of the criminal justice system through either legalization or decriminalization.

Liberals, because of these general assumptions about crime and criminals, tend to focus on certain problems within the criminal justice system.[32] They look at such issues as the overcriminalization of behavior, arguing that certain behaviors should not be illegal or that they should be decriminalized, such as drug use, prostitution, pornography, homosexuality, and gambling, to name a few. Liberals also believe that the system is too quick to label and stigmatize people; thus, from their perspective, designating someone a "delinquent" or a "criminal" only aggravates the problem of crime rather than resolving it. Taking this even further, liberals believe that the criminal justice system has not only a tendency to overlabel people but also an overtendency to institutionalize them. Prisons become nothing more than warehouses for offenders, and it is there that they become even more criminal as they learn from other prisoners. Liberals also contend that the criminal justice system has too much centralized control and that the community should assert more control over not only the police but also the courts and correctional systems. Finally, liberals focus on the problem of discriminatory bias in the criminal justice system, as the system is considered to be very racist and sexist and to target minorities and the poor.

When looking at how the criminal justice system should be ordered to best deal with the problem of crimes, liberals tend to believe that there should be a reduction in the use of the criminal justice system in America. There should be more communal control over the police, courts, and correctional systems, and the current institutionalization methods should be largely reduced. As liberals have argued that social conditions create the situations that lead to crime, it is therefore the social conditions that must be altered in order to reduce crime. If unemployment, poverty, and discrimination are largely reduced, then it follows that crime will be reduced as well. In other words, if children have a good education, communal life, and opportunities for employment, they will be less likely to commit crime and will become productive citizens. The criminal justice system then becomes charged with serving to protect individual rights and is based on Packer's due process model, being heavily focused on treatment and rehabilitation. The system is thus responsible for ensuring that all individuals are fairly treated, provided due process of law, and assured of their rights at all stages of the criminal justice process. If an individual is convicted and sentenced for a crime, the emphasis of the system should shift to providing the individual with a community correctional setting if possible, but regardless, it should provide them with counseling, therapy, educational opportunities, job skills, and possible employment outside the jail or prison. It should then help those incarcerated begin their transition back into society through various minimum-security and halfway house programs. Supporters of the liberal perspective argue that while this will be difficult and expensive in the short term, it will be less costly in the long run because those social conditions that cause crime will be removed, thus reducing crime in the future and providing a more humane approach to dealing with the issue of crime.

Perhaps the most noted advocate of the liberal ideology of crime and criminal justice is Elliott Currie.[33] In what has become his most widely disseminated book, *Crime and Punishment in America*,[34] Currie explains how the system should be ordered to best deal with the problems of crime. He believes that the most important investment is in the prevention of crime rather than belated responses to crimes that have already occurred. He details that the priorities should go toward preventing child abuse, expanding early intervention for children at risk, dealing with vulnerable adolescents, and then targeting those who are showing early signs of delinquency. In each of these, Currie articulates that the government should play a key role in the programs and that it should be very active in people's family life in order to prevent future crimes.

Currie then argues that the next step is to take social action to target those factors that create crime, namely, the social arrangements and social environment in society.[35] He argues that the distribution of work in the United States favors the middle and upper classes and that the support services available to the poor are lacking. He therefore argues that the government should begin reforming the system of work in America to create a system where those who are able to work can work. By ensuring a strong labor market and spreading work through a process of reducing the standard workweek, thus increasing the number of people needed to complete certain tasks, America could create more job opportunities. This would lead to a more widespread distribution of the labor market to all Americans and would reduce crime. In addition, government, where necessary, should fund and create new jobs in order to provide jobs, job training, and job skills for those who might not otherwise be able to obtain a position in the labor market. Along with this, however, he also articulates that many crucial services need to be provided for so that the labor market is not undermined by the high cost of services that will be necessary when all able-bodied Americans go to work. His key concerns are to provide child care for single-parent families and health care for the lower classes.

In terms of the criminal justice system itself, Currie makes several recommendations for its reform based on his liberal ideology.[36] He argues that the system must move away from its punishment orientation and more toward a focus on rehabilitation and treatment programs. In addition, in order to ease offenders back into society after undergoing these various programs, there must be a reintegrative approach that allows the offender to make the transition from being an inmate to being a productive member of society. Finally, in terms of policing, he makes the argument for community policing methods to be employed by police departments to enhance the police–community relationship in order to give more communal control over the police response to crime.

Several other authors also provide their liberal ideological perspective when it comes to crime and how the criminal justice system would best be organized to deal with the problems of crime. These authors, however, take a specific viewpoint regarding the discrimination of the system and from these perspectives what would best address these deficiencies. Michael Tonry, in his book *Malign Neglect: Race, Crime, and Punishment in America*,[37] argues that the criminal justice system is discriminatory toward minorities, especially blacks. He states that the criminal justice system must set up a fair system of punishments and that the least restrictive appropriate punishment should be given to an offender. He also advocates for more rehabilitation and treatment programs. Randall G. Shelden, in his book *Controlling the Dangerous Classes*,[38] places a strong viewpoint on the criminal justice system being a highly patriarchal system, one that tends to exclude and discriminate against women. This feminist perspective provides a liberal ideological viewpoint on the criminal justice system that, like Tonry, advocates for more rehabilitation and treatment programs. Finally, Jeffrey Reiman, in his book *The Rich Get Richer and the Poor Get Prison: Ideology, Class, and Criminal Justice*,[39] argues from the viewpoint that the critical issue is class differences in America. He articulates that class is the key component to the cause of crime in America and that the criminal justice system is merely a tool for maintaining class distinctions in America. Like Currie and the other authors, he argues for less classification and institutionalization of offenders and more rehabilitation and treatment. (See Box 2.2.)

CONSERVATIVE IDEOLOGY

Conservatives, in modern American terms, believe that government should be limited and that a limited government ensures order, allows for competitive markets, and creates personal opportunity.[40] Conservatives desire to keep government small. They believe that each area of social and economic interest is best dealt with at the lowest level of government (or nongovernment) possible. For example, national defense is a national function and hence should remain at the federal government level, while education should be handled at the lowest level of government, the local PTA boards, or school associations. Conservatives also believe that morality is critical to the ordering of society and that government should adhere to moral principles by legislating against those things that are considered immoral. As a result, conservatives believe that firm laws, strict moral codes, and their enforcement will do best to maintain order, thus allowing for society to ensure order. Moreover, creating a system with a free market allows personal opportunity for everyone. People are allowed to rise and fall based on their own merit. Finally, conservatives seek stability by adhering to traditions that have been in existence far longer than any individual person and think that change should come about only after serious examination and then only in moderation.

Conservative assumptions regarding crime are quite different from their liberal counterparts.[41] Conservatives believe that people are responsible for their own behavior and that they

BOX 2.2

Senator Barack Obama's Crime Platform

Drugs

- Condemned Federal raids in California for medical marijuana
- Fix the powder/crack cocaine disparities
- Eliminate mandatory minimum laws for drug crimes
- Take on Mexican drug cartels in partnership with Mexico and other nations
- Fund prevention and treatment programs

Gun Control

- Supported ban of handguns in Washington, D.C.
- Believed in individual's right to bear arms.

Death Penalty

- Claimed support for the death penalty for most heinous crimes

Law Enforcement

- Called for increased funding of the COPS Program
- Deployed more officers on the street and better technology
- Funded Bryne Grants to fund law enforcement, antigang, and antidrug programs

Illegal Immigration

- Called for increased border patrol personnel, infrastructure and technology
- Endorsed licenses for illegal immigrants
- Cracked down on employers who take advantage of undocumented workers

choose to commit crime or, conversely, choose not to commit crime. People are not merely passive entities who respond automatically to their environments; rather, they have the capacity of free will to choose between right and wrong behavior. Therefore, conservatives believe that a strong, well-communicated moral order is necessary to educate everyone about what is right and what is wrong behavior. The understanding of what is right and wrong behavior traditionally comes from shared religious Judeo-Christian values that communicate the general values of society. This can then be captured in the legal system by the laws dictating what is acceptable and what is not. Despite establishing this system, there is an acceptance that some people will commit wrong behavior; thus, public safety is paramount in order for society to function. Therefore, the legitimate authority given to the criminal justice system is to be adhered to at all times, and it is organized to provide a mechanism for public safety. Yet at the same time, people have the right to defend themselves against violence, attacks, and theft of their property.

The key issues for conservatives regarding crime consist of first the problem of excessive leniency toward lawbreakers.[42] It is believed that continually being lenient toward offenders teaches them that they are not to be held responsible for their actions, and as a result they become conditioned to commit more crime knowing that little will happen to them. In addition, conservatives believe that the system is far too permissive in that it allows for immoral behavior to flourish because of a moral breakdown in our society. Taking this even further, conservatives believe that underlying much of the crime problem in America is the erosion of discipline in society and any respect for constituted authority. The breakdown in discipline is seen in the changing practices of parenting, the ordering of our schools, and the criminal justice system itself. The lack of respect extends to all public officials, from those elected to government to schoolteachers, police officers, judges, and correctional officers. This breakdown in respect further accentuates the disrespect for authority, the law, and moral order. Finally, conservatives contend that the criminal justice system is wrongly named and that too much emphasis is placed on the offender than the victim. Conservatives believe that a well-ordered criminal justice system should focus on the rights of the victims, law enforcement officials, and law-abiding citizens, not on the people who choose to violate the law.

According to the conservative ideology, the proper means for ordering the criminal justice system, then, is to create a more efficient system where better coordination, a reduction of wasteful overlap, and avoiding the duplication of services are the best means for organizing to address the problem of crime. In addition, the system, especially the police, should be highly visible and given the necessary power and resources to enforce the law. While individuals should be given a fair hearing, they should not be able to escape criminal prosecution based on various technicalities that serve only to undermine the law. And because individuals commit their crimes out of choice, the emphasis of the criminal justice system should be focused on crime prevention in order to reduce the possibility that an individual will choose crime. By making it more difficult to commit crimes through target hardening and through harsh sanctions for those convicted of a crime, these factors will deter people from choosing crime as an option, thus lowering the prevalence of crime. These laws, according to the conservative viewpoint, should also be based on the overarching standards of morality within the country and that those crimes considered to be immoral should remain violations of the law and strictly enforced.

Perhaps the most noted author of the conservative ideology regarding crime and criminal justice is James Q. Wilson.[43] Wilson, a political scientist by trade, has spent much of his career looking at the issue of crime and morality and published what has become the seminal book regarding the conservative ideological viewpoint of crime, *Thinking about Crime.*[44] The book is essentially a compilation of essays written on the subject of crime, but there are several themes that run throughout the book. He makes the argument that the search among mainstream criminologists for "root causes" of crime is a fruitless search, as crime is committed by individuals and out of individual choice. Wilson's most significant condemnation comes when he states that these same criminologists tend to speak of the societal and environmental causes of crime from their ideological perspective, not from empirical fact, so that their perspective on crime and how best to order the criminal justice system is ideologically driven. He also addresses the fact that crime is a moral issue and that what must be adequately addressed is the problem of declining morality in America. Crime—all crime—has some moral element to it, for morality is the judgment of what is right and wrong behavior. The embodiment of this morality into the law entails defining what a crime is. Finally, Wilson articulates the belief that "wicked people exist" in the world and that the criminal justice system should deal harshly with these particular offenders. In fact, he argues that the criminal justice system should be focused primarily on these individuals.

Several other authors echo Wilson and provide a conservative perspective regarding the problem of crime and how the criminal justice system should be best ordered to address these problems. One set of authors, William J. Bennet, John J. Dilulio, Jr., and John P. Walters, in their book *Body Count,*[45] present the argument that the root cause of crime in America is a moral poverty that has been allowed to take hold over the past 40 years. Their solution is to reinforce moral standards in America, enforce these moral standards through the law, and support these moral standards through various means of crime prevention. Another book that echoes these sentiments is Robert J. Bidinotto's *Criminal Justice? The Legal System vs. Individual Responsibility*.[46] In his book, Bidinotto highlights the fact that crime is not caused by social or environmental factors but is wholly a matter of individual responsibility. As crime is committed by personal choice, no form of rehabilitation will be successful; thus, the system should be more about punishing offenders for their transgressions and should emphasize victims' rights in the process. Finally, an edited volume by Edwin Meese and Robert E. Moffit titled *Making America Safer: What Citizens and Their State and Local Officials Can Do to Combat Crime*,[47] published by the Heritage Foundation, a conservative think tank located in Washington, D.C., presents another call for how the criminal justice system should be ordered based on conservative ideology. The essays in this book articulate that the root causes of crime are a breakdown in marriage, family, and community as well as declining moral standards in America. They suggest that crime prevention, by adhering to tough moral standards, enhancing the means of disciplining juveniles, and enforcing the laws, is the key to reducing the problem of crime. They believe that the police should be made more efficient and given the tools necessary to enforce the law and that the criminal justice system should be victim centered rather than offender oriented. (See Box 2.3.)

BOX 2.3
Senator John McCain's Crime Platform

Guns
- Opposed any gun control measure
- Advocated against Brady Bill, weapons ban

Drugs
- Supported war on drugs
- Targeted borders to prevent flow of drugs into the United States
- Supported drug treatment as part of prisoner reentry program

Illegal Immigration
- Cracked down on illegal immigration
- Upheld the Federal government's responsibility to secure our borders
- Advocated for tougher sentences for illegal immigrants who commit crimes
- Deported illegal immigrants currently in jails and prisons
- Prosecuted employers who hire undocumented workers
- Built fence along the border

Death Penalty
- Advocated use of death penalty for federal crimes and called for expansion

Law Enforcement
- Enhanced funding for law enforcement based on need
- Created national law enforcement gang database

POLITICAL PARTIES AND IDEOLOGY

As people learn their core values, develop their beliefs, and create their understanding of how the world should be ordered, they tend to develop one of two schools of thought. Ideological thinking tends to embrace one of two camps: the liberal and the conservative viewpoints. While these ways of thinking do not always translate into a set political position, they are useful for understanding how a person will respond to various issues placed before them. In other words, just because someone adheres to liberal principles does not mean that his or her political party affiliation will be restricted to being a Democrat. And those who have conservative views will not always adhere to the Republican Party. What these terms do allow for is an understanding of an individual's belief system, communicated in a very short manner, in order to understand how that person views the world, how that person believes government would best be organized, and how that person perceives the role of the criminal justice in American society.[48] Hence, these two ideological camps communicate a lot about the values that people hold. (See Table 2.1.)

In the broader focus, Democrats tend to take a "civil liberties" perspective regarding crime and criminal justice, and hence they adhere to the due process model. They also tend to support programs oriented toward treatment and rehabilitation. Republicans, on the other hand, tend to take a more punitive perspective related to crime and criminal justice, and hence they support programs aimed at deterring and punishing criminals. A good example of the liberal ideology becoming Democratic crime policy and the conservative ideology becoming Republican crime policy can be found in the Johnson (1963–1968) and Nixon (1969–1974) administrations. President Johnson argued that the problem of crime was a result of social and economic decay that resulted from unemployment, poverty, and inflation. He argued that his Great Society policies, directed at eliminating or reducing the social problems, would also affect the crime rate. Hence, his crime policies were a direct result of the Great Society, which was reflected in his liberal ideology. The Johnson administration focused heavily on the issue of juvenile crime prevention, drug treatment and rehabilitation, gun control, and research in order to learn the "root causes of crime."[49]

In 1968, President Johnson declared that he would not seek the nomination of the Democratic Party to run for another term, and the 1968 presidential election became a race for a totally open seat. Richard Nixon would win the nomination of the Republican Party, and he ran on a "get tough" approach to the issue of crime, stating that he would bring an end to social unrest by passing "law and order" policies. Nixon won the election; after entering the White House, it became very clear that his approach to crime was very different from Johnson's. His was based on a conservative ideological perspective. Nixon believed that criminal behavior is a rational choice made by the offender, and because of that, the offender should be punished rather than treated. Nixon would focus heavily on legislation that would help the District of Columbia crack down on crime, target drug users and dealers, attempt to reduce the circulation of pornographic material, and streamline the criminal justice system to ensure swift and sure punishment for convicted criminals.

While this conservative/Republican and liberal/Democratic relationship would appear to hold up well with the Johnson and Nixon pairing, the reality is not so neat and simple. For example, President Johnson advocated the hiring of more police and enhancing some penalties for certain crimes, especially in Washington, D.C., President Nixon had actually advocated providing drug treatment, primarily through methadone clinics, for those addicted to heroin and especially for those soldiers returning from Vietnam addicted to drugs. This confusion has actually continued and became even more complex over the next three decades as the Republicans advocated more government control in the area of crime when generally they advocated less government

TABLE 2.1   **Perception of Crime in the United States by Demographic Characteristics, 2009**

Question: Is there more crime in the United States than there was a year ago, or less?

	More (%)	Less (%)	Same (%)	Don't Know/ Refused (%)
National	74	15	6	5
Sex				
Male	71	17	7	5
Female	78	12	5	5
Race				
White	73	16	6	6
Nonwhite	79	13	6	2
Black	79	16	5	1
Age				
18 to 29 years	70	21	7	2
30 to 49 years	76	13	3	8
50 to 64 years	77	13	6	3
50 years and older	76	14	7	3
65 years and older	75	14	8	4
Education				
College postgraduate	58	22	13	8
College graduate	73	17	5	4
Some college	74	15	6	5
High school graduate or less	83	11	2	4
Income				
$75,000 and over	71	18	7	4
$50,000 to $74,999	72	16	7	5
$30,000 to $49,999	73	14	6	7
$20,000 to $29,999	75	14	7	4
Under $20,000	83	13	2	2
Ideology				
Conservative	79	11	4	6
Moderate	75	16	6	3
Liberal	65	21	10	4
Region				
East	69	16	9	6
Midwest	72	19	4	5
South	82	11	5	3
West	71	16	6	7
Politics				
Republican	79	13	3	5
Democrat	72	17	8	4
Independent	73	15	6	6

Source: Sourcebook of Criminal Justice Statistics Online, www.albany.edu/sourcebook/index.html Table 2.34. 2009.

intervention overall. Many Republicans have advocated more treatment and rehabilitation programs for those addicted to drugs, and some have even called for the decriminalization of drugs if not all-out legalization. In other cases, Democrats have called for enhanced penalties against offenders, hiring more police officers to control crime, and adding the death penalty for certain crimes.

Many scholars today make the argument that the ideological dichotomy is gone and that both Republicans and Democrats advocate one ideology—that of crime control.[50] Others are not so quick to pass this one ideological viewpoint. Samuel Walker, a criminal justice academician who has written extensively on policy issues, has explained that the liberal/conservative "dichotomy is not quite as sharp as it was a few years ago" and that "the ideological lineup on crime control policies has become very muddled."[51] Another criminal justice academician, Stuart Scheingold, makes a similar argument in that "a troubling theme in this parade of policy perversity is the increasingly pronounced tendency to federalize crime control policy," and he explains that we have encountered "something of a role reversal between conservatives and liberals, with conservatives in the vanguard of federalization and liberals voicing, albeit weakly, reservations."[52] Finally, Dilulio, Smith, and Saiger argue that we have adopted neither side but have placated both when they state, "If experience is any guide, the national government will continue [to] do something to satisfy each of a diverse set of views on crime policy, without adopting any one, single, overarching vision of how best to combat crime."[53] Most of the evidence available tends to support this last viewpoint; the two ideological perspectives still tend to hold up under scrutiny and generally give way only to the political winds of change. Regardless, these ideological viewpoints do come to bear on the interests that politicians have regarding crime control and thus form our crime control policy in America. In short, these ideological views have serious policy implications, and it is to these implications that we now turn.

POLICY IMPLICATIONS

To understand the policy implications that are derived from one's ideology, we must turn to one of the premier political scientists, Hugh Heclo, who has managed to convey this phenomenon in relatively simplistic terms.[54] Heclo explains that there are three building blocks on which our political system is shaped and formed, including our criminal justice system. These three building blocks are ideas, interests, and institutions. Ideas are our ideological beliefs and our views of how the world should be ordered. These ideas are important for shaping not only what we believe in but also what we actually do. Hence, when we put our ideas into action, we are acting on our interests. Therefore, ideas matter because they shape our interests. Our interests are those things that we believe in and work toward obtaining. We may voice our individual interest for a particular policy, or we may join an interest group to band together with other like-minded individuals in order to shape policy in America. The ultimate goal, however, is to shape the institutions in America, to get them to conform to our interests (and hence our ideas) so that the way of life in America that we envision becomes normalized. Once something has become institutionalized, it is generally something that sticks around for a long time, providing continuity to the ordering of things in our lives. Thus, institutions give life to ideas. Heclo concludes that the formula goes something like this: Ideas tell interests what to mean, interests tell institutions what to do, and institutions tell ideas how to survive.[55]

A criminal justice example may suffice to provide an understanding of the policy implications of our ideological perspectives. An individual who is a confessed liberal and leans toward the Democratic Party may believe that the death penalty in America is abhorrent and must be abolished. He would argue that the death penalty fails to stop crime, deter crime, or reform the offender. He may also argue that the state does not have the right to take the life of a person just because he or she committed a heinous crime. Thus, liberal ideology forms his beliefs and helps shape how he views the world. In this case, he would argue that the United States should abolish all death penalty laws and that offenders should be sentenced to life in prison without the chance of parole but never to an execution. These ideas form his interests, and hence he chooses to speak out against the death penalty. Perhaps he writes a letter to the editor or attends a campus rally against the death penalty or perhaps even a vigil outside the prison where an execution is going to take place. When he engages in these activities, he comes across other people who share his worldview, making it easy to become involved in various interest groups. These groups are bands of like-minded people coming together for a common cause, in this case the abolition of the death penalty. From there, the individual may join such groups as the American Civil Liberties Union, the National Coalition to Abolish the Death Penalty, Citizens United for Alternatives to the Death Penalty, or Amnesty International. If these interest groups were to be successful and the death penalty abolished through the United States, this abolition would become an institutionalized part of the American criminal justice system. The death penalty would not likely be reinstated anytime soon after this occurred, thus bringing long-term stability to a new ordering of things. In this scenario, ideas told interests what to mean, interests told the institutions what to do, and the institutions gave life to the ideas.

Now picture another scenario, equally plausible. Another individual has grown up with a conservative ideology and is a member of the Republican Party. He believes that criminals choose to commit crimes and that criminals, especially murderers, cannot be rehabilitated. He also believes that having a tough, well-communicated criminal justice system will deter future crimes (general deterrence). He also argues that if someone commits premeditated murder, he or she should be executed by the state for the crime in order to deter future murders (specific deterrence). In addition, this individual argues that what is lost in the criminal justice system is a perspective regarding the victim in the murder. This victim will never have his or her life back, and the offender took it from him or her. Therefore, there should be little concern for the criminal's rights and more concern for seeking out "just deserts." This individual's ideas have helped shape and form his beliefs and how he believes the world should be ordered. As a result, he may write commentaries or letters to the editor in support of the death penalty, band with fellow college students at rallies supporting the death penalty, or attend vigils outside of the prisons where an individual is about to be executed in support of the policy. As this individual associates with people who believe in the same things he does, he will become more interest-group focused and may even join such groups as Justice for All, the Justice Coalition, the Criminal Justice Legal Foundation, or such state-level groups as Virginians United Against Crime, Maryland Coalition for State Executions, and Texans for Equal Justice. If these interest groups became successful, the death penalty would be legal in every state in the union and would be used on a regular basis. In addition, the system for taking an offender from conviction to execution would be streamlined and the number of appeals severely limited. As a result, the death penalty would become an institutionalized part of the American criminal justice system, and executions would be routine. The death penalty would not likely be repealed anytime soon after this occurred, thus bringing long-term stability to the new ordering of things. In this scenario, ideas told interests what to mean, interests told the institutions what to do, and the institutions gave life to the ideas.

In both scenarios, policy was derived from ideas. The two varying ideologies created two very different institutions regarding the American criminal justice system. Therefore, the point cannot be overemphasized when stating that ideas matter and that they influence the policy process. In fact, in order to understand how certain aspects of the criminal justice system have be-come institutionlized, one need only trace it back to the interests that had the greater influence on policy, which can be traced back to the ideas that the lawmakers supported when advocating a particular policy. Those living in Michigan tend to lean more liberal and Democratic and thus have no death penalty statutes. Those living in Texas tend to lean more conservative and Republican and thus have the death penalty and use it frequently. While it should be noted again that these are oversimplifications, for many liberal/Democrats support the death penalty and many conservative/Republicans are against the death penalty, for the most part these generaliza-tions (or labels) do communicate quite handily the ideas, interests, and policies that an individual will tend to subscribe to. In sum, understanding one's ideology will explain the positions and policies he or she advocates for the criminal justice system.

Conclusion

To comprehend the implications of one's ideology on the political process, it is important to under-stand the various ways in which we perceive the criminal justice system. Packer provides us with two, often competing models: the crime control model and the due process model. Those who advocate for crime control perceive the criminal justice system as enforcing the laws to punish offenders who have committed a crime. Those who advocate the due process model see the criminal justice system as being ordered to protect individual rights and to en-sure that everyone is treated equally. Feeley offers two models for how the criminal justice system should function: the rational-goal model and the functional-systems model. The rational-goal model believes that criminal justice would best be organ-ized if it were streamlined and could avoid duplica-tion by creating a rational system of justice. The functional-systems model argues that the overlap and duplication is necessary to ensure that no one entity becomes all too powerful and that in reality this type of model is actually more effective and effi-cient. Finally, Cox and Wade offer up the perspective that the criminal justice system is not a system at all but rather a network of agencies—all having the issue of crime in common. These agencies come to-gether at times to form networks, depending on the issue at hand. The argument that criminal justice is a system argues that all the components—police, courts, and corrections—are working together to process suspected criminals and deal with them in a process fashion. These models help us understand

how people perceive the justice system, much of which is derived from their ideology.

Taking this a step further, analyzing the major goals of the criminal justice system (deterrence, inca-pacitation, punishment, rehabilitation, treatment, reintegration, teaching morality, restoration, and pragmatism) demonstrates that many are compatible with each other but that many are not. Understanding that there are those who advocate for deterrence, inca-pacitation, punishment, and teaching morality differs greatly from those who advocate rehabilitation, treat-ment, reintegration, and restoration. This is because ideology helps shape the beliefs that people have to-ward what are the proper goals and the overriding purpose of the criminal justice system.

Since ideology is important to how people see the world and what they believe is the proper ordering of things, it is helpful to recognize how ideological viewpoints are formed. Ideology is formed generally in the growing years of an individual and usually starts with family and religion and expands to reli-gion, civic participation, political activities, and in-fluence through mass media. All these help shape and form our perspectives on the world and lead to our ideological viewpoints. These viewpoints typically fit into one of two camps: the liberal or the conserva-tive ideology. These ideologies then often translate into political party affiliations, either Democrat or Republican. While liberals are not always Democrats and conservatives are not always Republicans, this generalization is helpful in understanding what an individual believes in and the policies he or she will most likely advocate. These ideas then help form a person's interests and the policies he or she advocates, thus having the ultimate impact when laws, rules, and policies change to reflect these beliefs. When this occurs, the ideas and interests are said to be "institutionalized," and they become a way of life for most Americans. These institutions are important to our society because they provide a framework and stability to our world, which is why it is important that they are difficult to change. However, institutions do change, and it is through ideas and interests that this occurs. Therefore, understanding people's "criminal justice ideology" helps us understand their worldview, the policies they advocate, and how the criminal justice system would be ordered in their vision of a perfect system.

Notes

1. C. L. Cochran and E. F. Malone, *Public Policy: Perspectives and Choices*, 2nd ed. (Boston: McGraw-Hill College, 1999).
2. H. L. Packer, "Two Models of the Criminal Process," *University of Pennsylvania Law Review* 113 (1964): 113–25, and *The Limits of the Criminal Sanction* (Stanford; Calif.: Stanford University Press, 1968).
3. Packer, *The Limits of the Criminal Sanction*.
4. Ibid.
5. Ibid.
6. M. M. Feeley, "Two Models of the Criminal Justice System: An Organizational Approach," *Law and Society Review* 7 (3, 1973): 407–25.
7. Ibid.
8. Ibid.
9. Ibid.
10. S. M. Cox and J. E. Wade, *The Criminal Justice Network: An Introduction*, 3rd ed. (Boston: McGraw-Hill, 1998).
11. Ibid.
12. Ibid.
13. Ibid.
14. N. E. Marion, *Criminal Justice in America: The Politics behind the System* (Durham, N.C.: Carolina Academic Press, 2002) F. E. Zimring and G. J. Hawkins, *Deterrence: The Legal Threat in Crime Control* (Chicago: University of Chicago Press, 1973).
15. W. J. Bowers and G. L. Pierce, "Deterrence or Brutalization? What Is the Effect of Executions?" *Crime and Delinquency* 26 (1980): 453–84.
16. M. G. Santos, *About Prisons* (Belmont, Calif.: Wadsworth, 2004).
17. J. Cohen, "Incapacitation as a Strategy for Crime Control: Possibilities and Pitfalls," in *Crime and Justice: An Annual Review of Research*, ed. M. Tonry and N. Morris (Chicago: University of Chicago Press, 1983), pp. 1–48.
18. Marion, *Criminal Justice in America*, p. 25.
19. A. Blumstein and J. Wallman, *The Crime Drop in America* (Cambridge: Cambridge University Press, 2000); J. E. Conklin, *Why Crime Rates Fell* (Boston: Allyn & Bacon, 2003).
20. P. Greenwood, *Selective Incapacitation* (Santa Monica; Calif.: Rand Corporation, 1982), p. 15.
21. A. Von Hirsch, *Doing Justice: The Choice of Punishments* (New York: Hill & Wang, 1976).
22. Thanks are extended to Dr. Marvin Zalmanm of Wayne State University, for suggesting more explicit wording for the definition of punishment and retribution, and to incorporate the "teaching morality" section under the "punishment" section.
23. Ibid.
24. Marion, *Criminal Justice in America*.
25. P. H. Hahn, *Emerging Criminal Justice: Three Pillars for a Proactive Justice System* (Thousand Oaks, Calif.: Sage, 1998); D. Van Ness and K. H. Strong, *Restoring Justice* (Cincinnati: Anderson, 1977).
26. Marion, *Criminal Justice in America*.
27. T. R. Clear and E. Cadora, *Community Justice* (Belmont, Calif.: Wadsworth, 2003).
28. Examples include G. W. Cordner and D. C. Hale, *What Works in Policing?* (Cincinnati: ACJS/Anderson, 1992); A. Etzioni, *What Can the Federal Government Do to Decrease Crime and Revitalize Communities?* (Washington, D.C.: U.S. Department of Justice, 1998); L. Sherman et al., *Preventing Crime: What Works, What Doesn't, What's Promising* (Washington, D.C.: U.S. Department of Justice, 1997).
29. K. N. Wright, "The Desirability of Goal Conflict within the Criminal Justice System," *Journal of Criminal Justice* 9 (3, 1981): 209–18.
30. Cochran and Malone, *Public Policy*.
31. W. B. Miller, "Ideology and Criminal Justice Policy: Some Current Issues," *Journal of Criminal Law and Criminology* 64 (2, 1973): 1–26.

32. Ibid.

33. P. B. Kraska, *Theorizing Criminal Justice: Eight Essential Orientations* (Long Grove, Ill.: Waveland Press, 2004), p. 107.

34. E. Currie, *Crime and Punishment in America: Why the Solutions to America's Most Stubborn Social Crisis Have Not Worked—and What Will* (New York: Owl Books, 1998).

35. Ibid.

36. Ibid.

37. M. Tonry, *Malign Neglect: Race, Crime, and Punishment in America* (New York: Oxford University Press, 1995).

38. R. G. Shelden, *Controlling the Dangerous Classes* (Boston: Allyn & Bacon, 2001).

39. J. Reiman, *The Rich Get Richer and The Poor Get Prison: Ideology, Class, and Criminal Justice*, 7th ed. (Boston: Allyn & Bacon, 2003).

40. Cochran and Malone, *Public Policy*.

41. Miller, "Ideology and Criminal Justice Policy."

42. Ibid.

43. Kraska, *Theorizing Criminal Justice*, p. 107.

44. J. Q. Wilson, *Thinking about Crime*, rev. ed. (New York: Vintage, 1983).

45. W. J. Bennet, J. J. Dilulio, Jr., and J. P. Walters, *Body Count* (New York: Simon & Schuster, 1996).

46. R. J. Bidinotto, *Criminal Justice? The Legal System vs. Individual Responsibility* (New York: Foundation for Economic Education, 1996).

47. E. Meese III and R. E. Moffit, *Making America Safer: What Citizens and Their State and Local Officials Can Do to Combat Crime* (Washington, D.C.: Heritage Foundation, 1997).

48. J. R. Zaller, *The Nature and Origins of Mass Opinion* (Cambridge: Cambridge University Press, 1992).

49. N. E. Marion, *A History of Federal Crime Control Initiatives, 1960–1993* (Westport, Conn.: Praeger, 1994).

50. W. J. Chambliss, *Power, Politics, and Crime* (Boulder, Colo.: Westview Press, 2001); T. Gest, *Crime and Politics* (New York: Oxford University Press, 2001).

51. S. Walker, *Sense and Nonsense about Crime and Drugs: A Policy Guide* (Belmont; Calif.: Wadsworth, 2001).

52. S. A. Scheingold, "Politics, Public Policy, and Street Crime," *Annals of the American Academy of Political and Social Science* 539 (1995): 160.

53. J. J. Dilulio, Jr., S. K. Smith, and A. J. Saiger, "The Federal Role in Crime Control," in *Crime*, ed. James Q. Wilson and Joan Petersilia (San Francisco: ICS Press, 1995), p. 451.

54. H. Heclo, "Ideas, Interests, and Institutions," in *The Dynamics of American Politics: Approaches and Interpretations*, ed. Lawrence C. Dodd and Calvin Jillson (Boulder, Colo.: Westview Press, 1994), pp. 362–92.

55. Ibid.

3

The Criminal Justice Policy Process

Chapter Outline

INTRODUCTION

The criminal justice public policy process consists of the various steps by which an issue related to crime becomes a policy that governs the criminal justice system. There are a number of public policy participants in this process, including not only government, such as the executive and legislative branches, but interest groups, voters, and the media as well. How these various participants come together to shape and form public policy for crime and criminal justice is often varied, and many scholars have attempted to create models of how these various actors come together. Once a crime or criminal justice problem does rise to the level of being an issue, many of these actors begin to call for action or the reform of existing policies; hence, the criminal justice policy process begins. The specific steps consist of problem identification, agenda setting, policy formulation, policy implementation, and finally policy evaluation. After the evaluation process, old methods may need to be reformed or new initiatives may be taken, starting the policy process all over again. As part of the policy formulation process, there are four different types of policies, and these contain distributive, redistributive, regulatory, and morality policy. Which type of policy is employed will determine specifically how the issue is addressed. Moreover, policies can also be substantive, meaning that they actually do something, or "symbolic," meaning that they invoke the threat of doing something through rhetoric but don't actually "do" anything. In the area of crime policy, it is recognized that a policy dilemma exists where the public wants something done about crime and continually calls for more programs; however, most of these programs are inefficient and ineffective.

POLICY PARTICIPANTS

Elected political actors on the federal, state, and local levels, including the executive branches, the legislative branches, and the judicial branches, impact criminal justice in their own ways. Nonelected officials, such as the bureaucracies, the media, and public opinion and interest groups, also impact criminal justice.[1] Finally, it should be noted that the criminal justice system, which includes police, courts, and corrections, are all participants in the policy process, both as instruments to carry out policy and to shape its future. While each of these participants will be expanded on later in part 2 (Chapters 4–9) and part 3 (Chapters 10–13), they are introduced here to assist in understanding policy models and the public policy process.

Executive Branch

The executive branch at the federal level is the president, at the state level it is the fifty governors, and at the local level it is the thousands of mayors who serve in towns and cities across America. All these executives play an important role in the formation of crime control policy, for they are often seen as the representative of government who can address such problems as crime. Therefore, pressure is often placed on them to place the issue of crime on their agenda, essentially a list of things that the executive is actively engaged in addressing. It has been called the "to-do" list of our government's executives.[2] By focusing their attention on the issue of crime, they can advocate for certain policies and try to persuade, through the support of public opinion, the legislature to pass their particular crime policies.

Taken further, all three executives are also authorized the power of the veto—to nullify a bill that is sent to them from the legislature if they disagree with the legislation proposed. For example, in June of 2010, Governor Jodi Rell of Connecticut vetoed a bill passed by the State Legislature that would have created a new Sentencing Commission to review the state's sentencing statues and practices. The Governor's explanation for vetoing the bill, a bill that received a near unanimous vote, was that it would have cost the state $130,000, money not available in a recession. On the federal level, President George W. Bush vetoed House Resolution 810 in May of 2005, a bill that would have allowed for additional federal funding to go to embryonic stem-cell research. Bush vetoed the bill for ideological reasoning, arguing that the use of embryos is immoral and that additional federal funding would encourage the destruction of more embryos. Congress tried to override the bill, but fell short of the necessary votes. Congress again passed a bill in 2007, and once again the President vetoed the bill.

Executives are also given the authority to appoint certain criminal justice personnel that can influence the criminal justice system. Presidents have the power to appoint such individuals as Supreme Court justices, such as President Obama's recent appointment of Supreme Court Justice Sotomayor, as well as the attorney general (Eric Holder) and the solicitor general (Elena Kagan). The power of presidential appointment is, however, checked, for presidents require Senate approval in order for the appointment to take effect. Likewise, state governors have the power to appoint such individuals as the head of the various state divisions (departments) of criminal justice services or the divisions (departments) of corrections, those individuals who are responsible for the criminal justice administration in their respective states. At the local level, mayors are often given the power to appoint those individuals who will serve as police chiefs and wardens of the local jail, thus giving them significant powers over the local criminal justice system (see Chapter 4 for more detail).

Legislative Branch

Legislative branches of government, according to Marion, are arguably the most important players in the criminal justice realm.[3] The legislative branches are the U.S. Congress on the federal level, the various general assemblies on the state level, and the town councils or township trustees on the local level. The reason the legislative branch is so powerful is that they create the policies and, through their legislation, put them into place. They pass the laws that the criminal justice system will enforce. They can create new policy procedures or modify old procedures that will influence how the criminal justice system functions. And they can either increase or decrease the budget allocation to the criminal justice system to influence how the system will perform in addressing the problems of crime. Finally, it should be noted that legislatures can also plan an investigatory role into possible corruption and brutality within the criminal justice system, thus acting as a check on the powers given to the system.

On the federal level, Congress has become very active in its role of creating criminal justice policy. The first major anticrime legislation was made with the passage of the Omnibus Crime Control and Safe Streets Act of 1968. This was enacted in response to the high crime rates the country saw during the 1960s. It was followed in 1986 and 1988 by major federal legislation that focused on illicit drug use and violent crime. Another major piece of legislation, passed in 1994, was the Violent Crime Control and Law Enforcement Act, which put into motion the "100,000 Cops" program under President Clinton for implementing community policing across the nation's police departments (see Chapter 14). More recently, on October 28, 2009, President Obama signed into law the Matthew Shepard and James Byrd, Jr. Hate Crimes Prevention Act, a bill that expanded the 1969 United States federal hate-crime law to include crimes motivated by a victim's actual or perceived gender, sexual orientation, gender identity, or disability.

On the state level, legislatures have always been active in the area of crime legislation, and this activeness appears to have increased substantially since the latter half of the twentieth century. State legislatures have recently become active in legislating policy regarding the death penalty, and prior to the U.S. Supreme Court ruling that the execution of the mentally retarded is unconstitutional, states such as Connecticut and North Carolina had already passed legislation banning such executions. Another controversial issue that has surfaced over the past several years is whether an assault on a pregnant female, resulting in the death of her baby, is recognized as a murder. A number of state legislatures, including those of Idaho, Michigan, and Ohio, have passed laws stating that the criminal law of those states does recognize the crime as either murder or manslaughter. This crime and the associated legislation have become more highly visible in recent years with the case of Laci Peterson, who was eight-months pregnant and whose husband was convicted of murdering her and their unborn baby, Connor.

Finally, on the local level, it should be noted that city and town councils, as well as county commissions, are given the authority to determine the local ordinances that are considered violations of the law. While local police generally enforce state law, they are also given tools, such as noise ordinances, zoning laws, and parking policies, to ensure order in a community. These ordinances, laws, and policies are passed by the local body that serves the legislative function within cities, towns, and counties in the United States (see Chapter 5 for more detail).

Judicial Branch

The judicial branch of government also plays an important role in the formation of crime policy in the United States. The judicial branch, which established our court system in America, authorizes the Supreme Court, a circuit court, and district courts at the federal level. These courts handle either federal criminal cases or appeals from the lower courts, and in the case of the Supreme Court, they rule on issues of constitutionality. The judicial branch at the state level plays a similar role in that they are the courts in which state criminal violations are heard, and intermediate (appellate) courts allow for appeals with the supreme courts being the final arbiter of state cases (unless an issue of constitutionality arises, in which case it may enter the federal courts). The judicial branch at the local level consists of those courts that enforce minor offenses, such as low-level misdemeanors, local ordinances, and traffic violations.

While it would appear at the outset that the judicial branch merely handles cases based on violations of the law and provides a forum for determining if one is guilty or not guilty, the judicial branch does become a political actor in the policy process when decisions are handed down by the higher courts. Whether it is through procedural or substantive law, when the court issues a decision, it establishes not only policy for the court system underneath it but also policies by which other members of the criminal justice system must abide. Arguably, the most obvious of these cases are the Supreme Court decisions that affect police, courts, and corrections throughout the land (see Chapter 6 for more detail).

Bureaucracies

Bureaucracies are the agencies found on the federal, state, and local levels that carry out or implement the laws and policies passed by the legislatures.[4] There are dozens of bureaucracies at the federal level, hundreds at the state level, and thousands at the local level when they are all added up. For example, at the federal level, there are several bureaucracies that deal with the issue of crime, such as the Department of Justice, the Department of the Treasury, and the Department of Homeland Security. At the state level, there are the divisions of criminal justice services, departments of corrections, and state police agencies. At the local level, there are over 15,000 police departments, 3,000 sheriff's departments, and thousands of local and regional jails. Bureaucracies are pervasive in American society, but they are how policies get implemented.

When Congress passes a law, the language that it uses is usually intentionally ambiguous and vague because the legislative branch sets the policy, but the bureaucracies (administrations) must determine the specifics of carrying out the intended policies. For example, when Congress passed the Brady Bill requiring background checks on all handgun purchases in the United States, it was the bureaucracies that had to determine who would be responsible for these background checks and how the system would work.

The bureaucracies often must also determine the specifics in the case of judicial decisions, as the courts are often establishing policy but not the specifics as to how it is to be enforced. For example, when the Supreme Court issued its decision in the case of *Atkins* v. *Virginia* (2002), it ruled that executions of mentally retarded criminals are "cruel and unusual punishment" under the Eighth Amendment to the U.S. Constitution. The problem here was defining what was meant by "mentally retarded."

Still further, presidents can issue executive orders that require the bureaucracies to begin enforcing (or not enforcing) a particular policy of the executive branch. It is then up to the bureaucracy to determine specifically how they will enforce it. For example, President Ronald Reagan issued Executive Order 12564, which required mandatory drug testing of federal employees. The problem was defining who should be tested. All government workers? Contract workers? What about the president of the United States himself?

The bureaucracies at all levels of government, those responsible for the implementation of policy, have their greatest power in defining the specific terms under which a policy is to be implemented. They are given vast amounts of discretion to interpret the vague laws that are passed, judicial decisions made, and executive orders issued, and thus they are given an enormous amount of power in determining how these policies are to be carried out, if at all (see Chapter 7 for more detail).

Media

"Media" refers to all means of mass communications, including daily and weekly newspapers, television, radio, movies, newsmagazines, and so on.[5] It is largely through the media that most citizens become aware of events in their community, in their state, or across the world. Since most people are unable to spend much time in Washington, D.C., or in their state capital gathering information about what bills are being considered, they must rely on the media to provide that information. The media help inform citizens what the government is doing. In this sense, the media act as a linkage institution between the people and the government, helping to link the people with their representatives and other elected officials.[6]

It is essential that the information that is provided to citizens by the media be unbiased so that people can make accurate judgments about the people and policies involved. If citizens do not get unbiased news coverage, the opinions they form may not be accurate. This becomes especially critical in a democracy, where citizens are able to take an active role in the government process. Especially in a system where policies are meant to reflect the will of the people, the media must provide accurate information about events. Regardless of whether the media provide fair coverage, suffice it to say the media greatly influence our understanding of public policies and hence are a powerful factor in shaping criminal justice policy[7] (see Chapter 8 for more detail).

Public Opinion

Public opinion is an important part of the democratic process because of the theoretical link between public opinion and policy.[8] Government is intended to reflect the will of the people and is beholden to the people because it is comprised of elected officials. If elected officials are to retain their position in government, they must listen to their constituents and advocate policies based on their constituents' desires. If they fail to do so, they face the possibility of not being reelected. Holding politicians to this relationship reinforces the concept of democracy in American institutions. Today, however, because society has grown so large and diverse, it is generally an accepted fact that the "will of the people" is known primarily through public opinion polls. These surveys of Americans' thoughts, beliefs, and attitudes are what then often guide politicians in terms of the policies that they propose and attempt to legislate. In the case of crime policy, politicians listen to their constituents' attitudes on crime and what they think are the best solutions to resolving the problem and will attempt to create legislation that reflect these desires. It is often argued that these policies do not necessarily make for good crime policy in America but that they do reflect the will of the people. Others argue that they make poor policy and reflect only the attention paid to a particular crime issue by the media or the politicians in the first place. Regardless of which viewpoint is correct, it should be clear that public opinion influences the public policy process at all levels of government (see Chapter 8 for more detail).

Interest Groups

An interest group is a group of citizens who attempt to influence decisions made with the public policymaking system.[9] They "lobby," or act to alter the behavior of other actors. They play an important role in the system. They do this through providing money (campaign contributions), resources, campaign volunteers, or information to help a member of Congress. In addition, they provide information to like-minded people, those who have a similar interest in changing the laws to advance their cause. There are many interest groups that work to influence criminal justice policy in many realms. Some of the more well known are the National Rifle Association; Handgun Control, Inc.; and the American Civil Liberties Union. Often called pressure groups, they work toward influencing legislation so that it reflects their policy goals. Interest groups can be either specific, narrow groups or those with broad interests. Some groups are around all the time, while others come and go as issues arise and policy is changed (see Chapter 9 for more detail).

Criminal Justice System

The criminal justice system, comprised of the police, courts, and correctional agencies at the federal, state, and local levels, can also have a significant impact on the public policy process. While most see the criminal justice system as enforcing the laws made by the legislature, adhering to the decisions made by the courts, and following the directions of the executive branch, this does not mean they always agree or believe that a particular policy, as it exists, is the best course of action. Rather, the criminal justice system (essentially a bureaucracy) can influence the system by advocating for specific policies and demonstrating from their viewpoint of practical experience how changes in the law or policies would allow them to deal with crime more effectively and efficiently. Hence, criminal justice practitioners, whether police officers and correctional guards or police chiefs and wardens, can play a role in the public policy process (see Chapters 10–13 for more detail).

Intergovernmental Relations

When two levels of government have any relationship, it is called intergovernmental relations.[10] With funding programs, the federal and state governments work together to fight crime. The two basic types of funding mechanisms are "formula," or "block," grants versus "discretionary" grants. Formula grants are distributed based on a formula that may include factors such as population or crime rates. With discretionary grants, the funding agencies have more ability to choose who gets what funding amounts. Many programs in the 1960s and 1970s utilized the formula method, such as the grants dispersed by the Law Enforcement Assistance Administration, which was an agency responsible for dispersing grant money under the Omnibus Crime Control and Safe Streets Act of 1968. In the 1980s and 1990s, discretionary grants became more popular, but they usually consisted of a combination of formula and discretionary grants. The Bryne grants instituted by the Anti-Drug Abuse Act of 1988 and the Office of Community Oriented Policing Services, created by the Violent Crime Control and Law Enforcement Act of 1994, consisted of both formula and discretionary grants.

When it comes to intergovernmental relations in the United States, there is always the question about who has the power when it comes to the relationships between federal, state, and local governments. A federal government means that both national and state governments share power, but that isn't always the case. Three different models have been used to explain the relationship: coordinate, overlapping, and inclusive models.[11] The coordinate model states that the federal and state governments have complete autonomy, power, and control over themselves and therefore must coordinate between themselves when it comes to intergovernmental relations. The overlapping model argues that many areas, including crime, impact all three levels of government and therefore that each is interdependent of the other. They must bargain with each other when it comes to intergovernmental relations. Finally, the last model, the inclusive model, argues that the national government has usurped much of the power in the United States and has therefore established a hierarchy placing itself in charge of the states with the states being in charge of the local governments. While many people believe that the inclusive model is reality and nearly everyone believes that the coordinate model is obsolete, the reality is more likely that the overlapping model is the most widely used method for intergovernmental relations in the United States. What is more important to note here, however, is that intergovernmental relations can play a serious role in the development of crime policy in the United States.

POLICY MODELS

To understand how the relationships of these participants lead to the formation of public policy, many researchers have tried to create "policy models" (sometimes called "policy subsystems") to help explain how policies are created. These are generally ways of thinking about how the policy process works, and they can assist us in simplifying what can be a very complex and often distasteful process. There is some truth to the old saying that if you like politics and sausage, you should never see how either is made. But to understand how we arrive at the criminal justice policies we have, we must come to understand those factors that contribute to the formation of crime policies in America, and this is the intent behind the policy models.

Garbage Can Model

In the early 1970s, several researchers attempted to present what they saw as being the model for how policy is made and they provided what is perhaps one of the most image-filled names for a policy model—the "garbage can model." What Cohen, March, and Olsen were trying to explain with this imagery is that like a garbage can, a lot of stuff goes into the policy process and what comes out is often just as messy, if not messier, than what goes into the garbage can.[12] In addition, they wanted to relay the fact that nearly anything and everything goes into a garbage can and that the analogy works well with the development of policy. Many of the policy participants put in requests based on their beliefs and their ideologies. What gets passed by the legislatures is often difficult to understand, and this is why bureaucracies must act to define what the legislatures meant by the bills they passed.

There was, however, some method to their silliness, namely, that they tried to explain that policymaking is really a process of "organized anarchies." This comes as a result of three different factors: problematic preferences, unclear technology, and fluid participation. The first, problematic preferences, is derived from the fact that people often fail to be very clear in their desires, and this translates into muddled policy. The second issue they addressed was unclear technology, meaning that those who make the policy often don't understand how things really work and thus make policy that is not as workable as it should be. Finally, fluid participation meant that the various participants described previously come and go from the process without much consistency.

The garbage can model is perhaps best exemplified by the passage of the USA PATRIOT Act of 2001, passed in the aftermath of the attacks on New York City and the Pentagon on September 11, 2001. The USA PATRIOT Act, which actually stands for "Uniting and Strengthening America by Providing Appropriate Tools Required to Intercept and Obstruct Terrorism," was the result of some very rapid hearings, proposals, and bills being put forth on homeland security. After the September 11 attacks, Congress was trying to pass laws that would ensure that America was safe from future attacks, but it was an organized anarchy because despite the urgency of the situation, Congress still went through the machinations to pass a bill. Yet the outcome of the bill shows that there were many different thoughts about how best to protect America (problematic preferences), the makers of the policy did not consider exactly how these policies would be implemented (unclear technologies), and while many of the participants remained active throughout the bill's creation, many came and went from the process (fluid participation). The result was a very large bill that targeted many diverse security issues, ranging from money laundering by terrorists to increasing the investigatory powers of the government in terrorism-related crimes. What complicated the bill's passage was the fact that a variety of agencies could utilize the laws, but the one agency that would take the lead, the Department of Homeland Security, didn't even exist yet. It would seem that the garbage can model is a good policy model description for how much of our crime policy is created.

Iron Triangles

One of the complaints with the garbage can model is the fact that it is not very specific as to how policy is really created. It assumes that we simply get a whole bunch of people together, and they'll create something. This also makes the assumption that all these people carry equal weight, but we know that is not true. That is why the concept of "iron triangles" might make more sense as a description of the policy process. Iron triangles have often been called by a variety of names, including policy whirlpools, cozy little triangles, triple alliances, and power triads. Regardless of the name, the basics of this policy model are the same, that there are three key players in the policy process who wield the most weight and that this never changes. This is where the "iron" comes in, to denote never changing or never bending.

The three key players in the iron triangles are executive bureaus, congressional committees, and interest groups.[13] These do not appear to be the most obvious policy participants, as public opinion as a whole, the media, and the president tend to be excluded. Generally, when we think of the most visible participants, it is these three we think of, not the bureaucracies, congressional committees, or interest groups. But what the iron triangles model argues is that the reality behind policymaking is that these three wield the most influence and that they are the policy participants who create most policy.

The executive bureaucracies are the agencies that deal with the issue on a daily basis; hence, they are in the best position to create new policy that has a chance of actually working. In the case of crime, it is argued, the Department of Justice and the Federal Bureau of Investigation making crime policy makes more sense than going with the public will or what several news reporters might advocate. The congressional committees are those that actually control what bills are considered by the entire Congress, and they are the committees that actually draft the legislation. Despite the wide variety of input they may receive, their negotiations between the bureaucracies and the interest groups are really what shape the policies they create. Finally, the interest groups have influence because of time, money, and power. Since the average American does not have the time or the money to influence members of Congress, they do not have a lot of power. But when they band together under an interest group that can work full time to lobby congressional committee members to propose, draft, and push a specific policy in their committees, these interest groups come to wield a lot of power. As a result, crime policy is derived from the machinations of these three entities.

One criminal justice example of the iron triangles in action in the creation of crime policy comes in a Virginia law of 1995 that was aimed at making it easier to obtain a concealed-handgun permit in that state.[14] In early 1995, a confluence of the Virginia Department of Criminal Justice Services, under the direction of then Governor George Allen, began to look at changing state law related to the carrying of concealed weapons. At the time, judges had an enormous amount of discretion to determine who should be allowed to carry concealed, and the Allen administration wanted to make it less arbitrary and more systematic. The National Rifle Association and the Law Enforcement Alliance of America agreed with the proposed changes and worked with the legislative committees to draft a new policy. The law was passed on April 6, 1995; signed into law by Governor Allen on May 5, 1995; and went into effect on July 1, 1995. The iron triangle that formed around Virginia's concealed-handgun policy changed the law that minimized the judges' role in issuing permits, making it more open while at the same time disqualifying felons and those convicted of such crimes as driving under the influence or assault and battery as well as illegal immigrants and anyone under age twenty-one.

Issue Networks

While the iron triangles might be more specific than the garbage can policy model, many have argued that it conveys too much of a backdoor and underhanded method of creating policy and ignores the other policy participants in the process. At a minimum, the critics argue, there is a great amount of influence placed on these "three sides of the triangle" that cannot be ignored. From a larger perspective, however, these other actors do play a significant role that is just as important as the three sides of the triangle. This is why Hugh Heclo argued that the iron triangle concept is incomplete and that a more accurate model should be the "issue networks model".[15]

Issue networks simply makes the argument that when policy is being formulated, networks begin to form around the policy issue. A network is essentially a systems approach to something that consists of a number of interrelated parts. In the example of the USA PATRIOT Act cited previously, it is clear that the public was mobilized because of September 11 and demanded something be done to fight terrorism. The media were mobilized and continually reported on the issue. Congress gathered as many ideas from interest groups and the bureaucracies as possible to create the very extensive act, and there is no doubt that President Bush was energized to sign into law something that would demonstrate that the U.S. government was taking action. According to Heclo, however, these networks form around a particular issue, meaning that the networks will not be the same from issue to issue. Crime policy will tend to consist of the same congressional committees, the same interest groups, and so on, whereas another policy, such as environmental policy, will have a different network of policy actors participating in that policy network.

Issue-Attention Cycles

During approximately the same time frame that the policy model issue networks was being advocated by Hugh Heclo, another key scholar in the field of public policy, Anthony Downs, was advocating that an "issue-attention cycle" exists, explaining how issues become part of the public policy process.[16] He argued there were five stages that an issue tended to progress through. The first was the "preproblem stage." Here an issue exists, and some interest groups, experts, or both may be very alarmed by the problem, but it has not gained widespread attention among the American people. A good example is terrorism in the 1990s. Americans were not overly concerned about terrorism, but they knew of the concept. However, scholars and experts in the criminal justice and security fields were alarmed about the prospect of increased terrorism. Therefore, while the scholars and experts were concerned, the American people were not.

The second stage is then "alarmed discovery and euphoric enthusiasm." In this stage, a dramatic event or series of events brings the attention to the forefront of all the people, and they demand that something be done. In the case of terrorism, September 11 was clearly a dramatic event that galvanized the American people to demand that something be done to fight terrorism and prevent future attacks. Downs does note that while people demand that the problem be solved, they also demand that it be solved "without a fundamental reordering of society itself."[17] In other words, people do not want to change their lifestyles, nor do they want to give up any rights, but they do want terrorism stopped.

The third stage is "realizing the cost of significant progress." This stage is the point at which the euphoria over the issue is gone. It is also the point at which people realize that the various policy solutions proposed or implemented are going to cost an enormous amount of money, time, and resources and that the costs of these measures may not be realistic. In the case of the post–September 11 era, America is gradually coming to terms with the costs of fighting terrorism, and the cost in taxpayer dollars, American lives, and resources may be more than most Americans are willing to bear.

The fourth stage is the "gradual decline of intense public interest." It is here that, in absence of any additional dramatic events, people become complacent and no longer demand change. People become bored with the issue and lose interest, and therefore it is no longer at the forefront of their concerns. In addition, it is most likely that another issue has diverted their attention and that the people have entered the second stage with respect to that other problem. Although it may be too soon to argue that America has lost interest in the "war on terrorism," many have voiced this concern, stating that most Americans have become complacent as a result of no new attacks on American soil.

Finally, the fifth stage, according to Downs, is "the postproblem stage." Here the problem is reduced to something that no longer is on the public mind and is not actively being addressed. In some cases, the problem is considered no longer a problem, or there is a belief that it has been solved. In other cases, it no longer bears any relevance to most American people and therefore is no longer a problem. If it is considered a problem by the experts or interest groups, then it could be said to exist in the first stage, where it would cycle back to the preproblem stage, and if given another dramatic event, the policy would once again move through the issue-attention cycle. One thing to note, however, is that Downs did not specify a time frame on each stage. As a result, some issues may move through the issue-attention cycle very rapidly, say, over a summer, while others may move through the cycle over a generation or two.

Advocacy Coalitions

Although the policy model of issue-attention cycles tells how things become issues and the policy model of issue networks takes all the various policy participants into consideration in its model, they are not without their drawbacks. The issue-attention cycles tell us not how issues get addressed but only how they become issues. The issue networks convey the belief that the issue networks remain fixed within an issue area. In other words, the players may change from issue to issue, but the players within a specific issue remain fairly constant. Sabatier attempted to address both these issues (and more) by expanding on the issue network concept and detailing that not all issues are composed of the same participants.[18] For example, all crime policy does not always include the National Rifle Association or the Judiciary Committee. Rather, a policy on lowering the blood alcohol level at which point someone is legally intoxicated from .10 to .08 may actually consist of the interest group Mother's Against Drunk Drivers (MADD) and the Transportation Committee, which can use its power to regulate transportation in the United States and its highway funding to achieve this policy as was actually done in 2001. Therefore, the policy model that Sabatier advocates is known as the "advocacy coalition." The idea here is that each time a policy issue arises, like-minded policy actors (or policy entrepreneurs as they are often called) will come together to form a coalition to advocate change.

As Sabatier and Jenkins-Smith explain, the concept of advocacy coalitions takes a broader stance by synthesizing much of the past literature as represented in the previous models.[19] They articulate three key factors to consider when discussing advocacy coalitions: (1) there are competing advocacy coalitions, and these actors come from both public and private institutions as well as all levels of government and share a basic belief about how the world should be ordered; (2) there are changes that occur over time that lie outside the policy issue, specifically, social, political, and economic factors, that can redefine the issues; and (3) that there are some facets of the policy process that remain constant, specifically, the process by which issues are addressed, otherwise known as the public policy process (described later in this chapter).

A criminal justice example that may serve well is in the policy area of domestic violence. Police response to domestic violence prior to the 1970s was generally very limited, and any abuse within a marriage was often treated as a "family matter" and not a "police matter." A mixture of the civil rights and women's movements of the 1960s and 1970s brought this issue to the forefront of American social issues and moved it into the political realm, where a variety of advocates began demanding policy change. The changes in this particular area were outside the policy process, but it was ultimately the policy process that would began creating new laws in the area of domestic violence. By the early 1980s, most states had domestic violence laws on the books, and by the mid-1990s, all states had passed the proarrest policy where police officers may arrest when there are visible signs of abuse and file charges on behalf of the state. This alleviated the necessity of having the abused victim file the charges, which usually ended up being dropped at a later date.

Policy Streams

If the biggest criticism of the advocacy coalition model was that it was too difficult to apply to the real world, the biggest criticism of the next policy model is that it was too simplistic. Yet in a way, this is also its appeal. John Kingdon, in his award-winning book *Agendas, Alternatives, and Public Policies*, laid out his policy model, which consists of policy streams and policy windows.[20] Kingdon uses the imagery of streams flowing through the land, setting their own course, and traveling at their own pace. Eventually, streams converge and travel together for a while before eventually splitting off on their own again. According to Kingdon, it is when the three streams come together that a window of opportunity opens for policy change, and this is how policies move through the public policy process.

The three streams that Kingdon refers to are the problem stream, the political stream, and the policy stream. Kingdon argues that there are often problems that exist, but unless various political actors can mobilize the general public to get behind the problem or unless there is a major galvanizing event, the problem will remain an issue for only a select few and not become a public policy issue. In the second stream, the political stream, Kingdon explains that there are a number of political actors that are constantly addressing a variety of issues both inside and outside government. Inside the government, he argues that the key player is the president, along with his staff and political appointees. In addition, there are the bureaucrats who are tasked with addressing specific policy areas. Moreover, there is Congress, specifically Congress members, their staffs, and the committees. Outside government, he argues that there are the interest groups, academics, researchers, consultants, the media, political parties, and public opinion, all with various stakes in particular issues. Finally, the policy stream consists of the ideas that can actually become bona fide policy solutions and that, given the opportunity, can be passed by Congress and signed into law by the president.

The success of a specific issue becoming bona fide policy is the window of opportunity. Kingdon argues that when these three streams converge (the problem, political, and policy streams), there is a window of opportunity in which policy can be passed and made law. If one of these streams is missing, there is no window of opportunity. If the policy stream has a solution to terrorism and the political stream is behind it but there is no September 11, there is little chance the policy will become legislation. If, however, there is a September 11 (the problem stream), the various political actors are galvanized for action (the political stream), and there exists some solutions to the problem (the policy stream), the window of opportunity has opened up, and legislation can be passed, as we witnessed with the USA PATRIOT Act, which passed within a month of the attacks on American soil.

Punctuated Equilibrium

One last public policy model is that of punctuated equilibrium as articulated by Baumgartner and Jones in their book *Agendas and Instability in American Politics.*[21] Their concept isn't so much a new public policy model as a clarification of other models that details how items move into the public policy process. Nearly all the policy models tend to argue that issues develop over the long term and that these issues are constantly being addressed as a matter of routine. Perhaps the only one who had previously advocated something different was Downs in his issue-attention cycle, but Downs tended to suggest that policy issues surfaced through dramatic events only. Baumgartner and Jones combined the two concepts into what they called punctuated equilibrium.

The way policy change is derived, according to Baumgartner and Jones, is through the long-term process where an issue is continually addressed by a fairly constant process often consisting of the same actors. However, it is often the case that something can come along and disrupt this constant or, according to Baumgartner and Jones, punctuate the equilibrium. This can be either a serious event, as Downs described, or a redefining of the policy issue. An example of the latter type is the use of tobacco in America. From the early 1900s to the 1950s, American attitudes toward tobacco were fairly positive, and the only issue surrounding it was taxation. In the 1950s, when it was perceived as a health hazard, the positive attitudes toward tobacco rapidly declined, negative attitudes rapidly increased, and tobacco shifted from a taxation issue to a health issue. More recently, in the 1990s, it has shifted more toward a criminal justice issue, as the enforcement of tobacco bans, underage smoking, and illegal selling of tobacco has once again shifted the way in which tobacco policy is addressed. Baumgartner and Jones also cite the criminal justice issues of drug, alcohol, and child abuse as being issues that rapidly surfaced and would be redefined. Drug abuse rapidly shifted from a health issue to a law enforcement issue in the late 1960s, alcohol abuse saw a similar shift in the 1970s, and child abuse came to the forefront as a criminal issue in the 1980s. Although all these had been previously addressed, how they were addressed appeared to change almost overnight.

PUBLIC POLICY PROCESS

The previously mentioned policy models assist us in understanding how the public policy process works, but they do not tell us how things become identified as problems, become issues to be addressed, and then how they eventually become public policy or law. The public policy process, as detailed in a very complex five-step process, is what provides us with this information. The five steps, in order, are (1) problem identification, (2) agenda setting, (3) policy formulation, (4) policy implementation, and (5) policy evaluation (See Figure 3.1). It is to these five steps of the public policy process that we now turn.

Problem Identification

In the first step of the public policy process, the problem at hand must be identified and then must move from being perceived as a private issue affecting only a small group of people to a recognized public problem.[22] Prior to an issue becoming identified as a problem, it exists as a condition. It is something that is simply part of life, and when something happens as a result, we simply accept it and move on. For example, during the 1950s and 1960s, accidents caused by drunk drivers were simply that: accidents. There was no perception that this was a larger issue that needed to be addressed. When accidents, injuries, and even deaths occurred from drunk drivers, the incidents were dealt with by those involved but were not considered issues that needed addressing by the government.

Once a condition is identified by someone or a small group of individuals as a problem, there then exists, at a minimum, the perception of a problem. For example, if enough people perceive the issue of drunk driving as an issue, then it begins to move from a condition to a

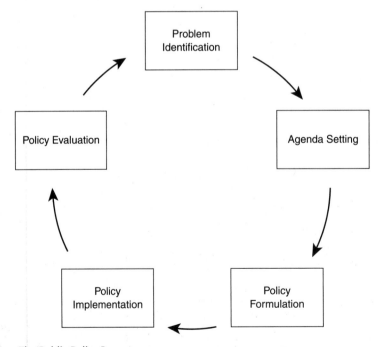

FIGURE 3.1 The Public Policy Process.

problem. Cobb and Elder talk about the "expanding public" when they detail how a p[ ] may capture the attention of one individual who voices their perception of the problem.[ ] like-minded individuals agree and unite to strengthen that voice. Eventually, this may [ ] citywide, regional, statewide, and finally nationwide impact. This is often referred t[ ] media as a "grassroots" issue, one that surfaces from the ground up. As the public expar[ ] the problem moves to the level of being an issue, much in the way that Downs spoke [ ] issue-attention cycle, then it becomes an issue for all the people, and specifically the govern-ment, to address.[24]

It has also been said that a problem becomes an issue when public disagreement exists over the best solution to the problem.[25] This is because an issue is often a "conflict between two or more identifiable groups over procedural or substantive matters relating to the distribution of positions or resources."[26] Before problems are acted on, they must be recognized by legislators as issues of concern to the voters. In other words, the problem must capture the attention of major decision makers and be recognized as a viable and significant issue. For example, the previously mentioned issue of drunk driving moved from a condition to a problem when one girl, Candy Lightner's thirteen-year-old daughter Cari, was killed by a drunk driver near her home in Fair Oaks, California.[27] On May 3, 1980, Cari was walking to a school carnival when a drunk driver struck her from behind. The driver had three prior drunk driving convictions and was out on bail from a hit-and-run arrest two days earlier. Candy Lightner, after banding together with other mothers who had similar experiences, created a local California chapter of MADD. Later that year, another chapter was created in Maryland. MADD received the attention of the Reagan ad-ministration in 1982 and began to find its place on the government agenda. By 1983, the issue of drunk driving had become a major public policy issue and one that was actively being addressed by a majority of states as well as the federal government. Drunk driving had moved from a con-dition, was recognized as a problem, and became an issue as lawmakers debated on how best to address the problem. This issue had thus proceeded from condition to problem to issue and was now on the "agenda"—the second stage of the public policy process.

Agenda Setting

In agenda setting, decision makers must select issues that will be given priority and that will be ig-nored. At any given point in time, there are thousands of issues that are constantly vying for con-sideration by government, but only some of them will find a place on the government's agenda.[28] Certain problems are recognized as needing action, while others are postponed and some simply ignored. Crime, although always on the political agenda of both federal and state officials, does have periods of greater or lesser visibility.[29] Many political actors contribute to creating the agenda: The president, members of Congress, interest group representatives, the media, and members of the general public can all help influence the final agenda.[30] However, it has been noted that many of these groups compete with one another in the agenda-setting process by competing to attract the attention of various government actors. In addition, competition can also occur within these groups because the debate may center on the specific definition of the problem, and this can then lead to "competition over which groups and views to mobilize and how to do it."[31] One example is gun control policy.[32] Many groups compete for government at-tention to their specific policies related to gun control (or no gun control) in the hopes that gov-ernment will pass (or ignore) legislation based on their views. In addition, debate can also occur within these groups about how best to deal with the problem of shootings, whether it is public education, gun locks, or gun bans.

Cobb and Elder distinguish between two types of agendas: the systemic agenda and the institutional (or government) agenda. The former "consists of all issues that are commonly perceived by members of the political community as meriting public attention and as involving matters within the legitimate jurisdiction of existing governmental authority."[33] For an issue to be placed on the systemic agenda, it must have widespread attention, a shared concern that some type of action is required, and a recognition that the matter is appropriate for the jurisdiction of a government unit. This agenda is vague and does little more than identify possible problems of concern; no alternatives or possible solutions are suggested.

Typically, gun control is on the systemic agendas of all presidential administrations. Possible problems relating to gun ownership concern most elected officials, and few officials will argue that gun control legislation is an area of concern inappropriate for federal government activity. But quite often, administrations will go no further than simply recognizing the issue as a viable one. This is the pattern that followed in the Reagan administration prior to the attempted assassination of President Reagan.

The issue of gun control moved onto the formal (or institutional) agenda after the assassination attempt of President Reagan. The formal agenda is the second type of agenda described by Cobb and Elder and refers to "that set of items explicitly up for the active and serious consideration of authoritative decision-makers."[34] In this step, an issue must be identified as a problem requiring action or as an issue involving policy alternatives. The formal agenda is more specific than the systemic agenda, as it identifies the specific aspects of the problem or alternative solutions to a problem. The formal agenda is often more significant because it is a commitment for action.

It has been noted that the formal (or institutional) agenda may have a variety of issues undergoing various levels of attention. These have been referred to as specific types of institutional agendas and may consist of (1) the problem definition agenda (those items that are receiving active and serious attention to be defined), (2) the proposal agenda (those items that have reached the proposal stage where the problem has been defined but a solution is sought after), (3) the bargaining agenda (where proposals have been defined and a specific solution selected, but how this will be developed is debated), and finally (4) the continuing agenda (consisting of those items that come up for regular review).[35]

In moving from the systemic to the formal (institutional) agenda after the attempt on Reagan's life, the issue of gun control received more serious attention from elected legislators. It was at this point that a policy alternative was suggested as a means to address (or solve) the problem of the excessive ease of availability of handguns in the United States. Here one can see that the problem is being addressed more specifically with alternative solutions suggested.

Kingdon argues that issues move from the systemic agenda to the institutional agenda as the result of two situations: the means by which officials learn about conditions and the ways in which conditions become defined as problems. In the first instance, the means, Kingdon includes indicators, focusing events, and feedback. For example, indicators can be used to assess the extent of the problem, or focusing events such as disaster can point to a problem that needs attention. Or, officials may discover problems through the feedback from an existing program. Second, according to Kingdon, conditions must become problems. He writes that we "put up with" conditions every day, but they must rise to the status of problems before they are placed on an agenda. Another way of saying this is that the first step in the public policy process largely dictates the second step.

Another way of understanding how items make it on the government's agenda is offered by Cobb, Ross, and Ross in their discussion regarding three models of the agenda-building process.[36] These three models consist of the outside initiative, the mobilization model, and the inside initiative model. The outside initiative model "accounts for the process through which issues arise in nongovernmental groups and are then expanded sufficiently to reach, first, the public agenda, and finally, the formal agenda."[37] The passage of the Prison Rape Elimination Act of 2003, interestingly, fits this particular model. In 2001, the Human Rights Watch, an interest group, released a white paper titled, "No Escape: Male Rape in U.S. Prisons."[38] From that document, numerous interest groups began to lobby Congress, including such diverse groups as the Just Detention International, Amnesty International, Focus on the Family, the NAACP, the Salvation Army, and Human Rights Watch. They were able to convince two Republicans, Senator Jeff Sessions (R-AL) and Representative Frank Wolf (R-VA) to introduce the Prison Rape Elimination Act, a zero-tolerance bill aimed at preventing and detecting incidents of sexual violence in prison and creating a National Prison Rape Reduction Commission. The bills garnered considerable bipartisan support and passed with unanimous consent in both the House and Senate. The bill was signed into law by President George W. Bush on September 4, 2003.

The mobilization model "considers issues which are initiated inside government and consequently achieve institutional agenda status almost automatically."[39] This model is almost the reverse of the outside initiative model in that, rather than something arising onto the public's agenda and then moving to the government's agenda, this will move from the government's agenda to the public's agenda. Government may generate a solution to a problem, but the bill will need the support of the people for it to pass. Clinton's "100,000 Cops" initiative in 1994 was a government-proposed policy that was intended to support police departments across the country in the implementation of community policing and to help fight crime. It was a government-created program that attempted to generate public support for its passage, which it succeeded in earning, and was subsequently passed as the Violent Crime Control and Law Enforcement Act of 1994.

The third model is the inside initiative model. This model "describes issues which arise within the governmental sphere and whose supporters do not try to expand them to the mass public."[40] A good example of this was the creation of the United States Sentencing Commission when President Reagan signed the Comprehensive Crime Control Bill into law on October 12, 1984. This comprehensive bill included the Sentencing Reform Act of 1984, which mandated that the commission create a set of sentencing guidelines to which every federal court judge would be bound. The reason for the determinate sentencing guidelines was to ensure that defendants who committed similar offenses would be treated alike and that judges would no longer be too lenient or too harsh. This was a policy created within the White House that was not intended to be moved from the government's agenda to the public's agenda for the very fact that the administration did not want interest groups to have a say in how the reforms would be made. Although it did come to the attention of many groups and there were vocal critics against the administration's proposals, the administration did not actively seek public support for its proposal, which was made into a law that took effect on November 1, 1987.

Policy Formulation

The third step in the policymaking process is policy formulation.[41] This refers to the process by which formal policies are suggested and created. There are a number of factors that go into determining exactly how a solution will be formulated into a policy. One issue is to what extent the policy will be addressed. Will it consist of a major overhaul of the existing system, such as the sweeping changes in the federal sentencing guidelines in the late 1980s or the abolishment of parole in Virginia in the early 1990s? Or will it consist of small, incremental changes, such as increasing the sentence for drug offenders from a maximum of twenty-five to thirty years in a federal penitentiary? Another factor that is often the basis for the scope of the policy is the budget. Often economic constraints will cause the solution to a policy to shift from the allocation of money to simply the reallocation of existing resources. In severe economic constraints, it may limit the bill to simply a symbolic stand on the issue, such as congressional approval of the "Just Say No to Drugs" campaign. In the worst-case scenario, budget woes may force Congress to simply do nothing, and hence policy formulation is to formulate no policy.

In addition to these constraints, Congress must also determine specifically how the policy will be formulated, what it intends, and who will be responsible for the next stage, that is, implementation. There are generally four types of policies—distributive, redistributive, regulatory, and morality (see the following discussion for more detail)—and the type of policy often dictates specifically how a policy will be implemented. A part of this is what the policy intends to do in order to alleviate or solve the problem as well as how specific Congress intends to be in determining what will be done. Often Congress is very generic in the use of its language, allowing the president and the administrative bureaucracy to determine the specifics of policy implementation. And which bureaucracy is given the responsibility for the problem often plays into how the problem will be solved. After September 11, 2001, when Congress decided to take over control of the baggage screeners in airports, it debated placing them under the Department of Justice or the Department of Transportation. Ultimately, they decided on the latter, but had they chosen the former, baggage screening would be vastly different today.

A formal process does exist for a legislative proposal to become a law in our system of government. The process is very technical and involved and has been created by Congress over its long history. It begins with the introduction of a proposed bill into either the House of Representatives or the Senate. Eventually, both chambers of Congress must agree to the proposed bill for it to become a law. After introduction into one of the two chambers, the bill is assigned to the most relevant committee, which then assigns it to a subcommittee. Here the subcommittee members go through "markup," which means that they rewrite portions of the proposal to make the bill more accurate or more politically feasible. For the members to do this, the subcommittee can hold hearings and listen to testimony from a variety of different sources in an attempt to gather information on the proposed legislation. After markup, the subcommittee members are required to vote on the proposed bill; if a majority votes in favor of the legislation, it then moves to the entire committee.

The full committee can also hold hearings and markup sessions, or it can choose not to. In either event, the members of the entire committee must then also vote on the proposal. Again, if a majority votes in favor of the legislation, then for further action the bill moves to the floor of the chamber in which it originated.

The same process must be accomplished in the opposite congressional chamber. For example, if a proposal for a federal death penalty has followed the previously described path in the House of Representatives, the same journey must be taken in the Senate. Frequently, the two versions of the bills passed by the House and Senate are not identical. In other words, as a result of the markup sessions, the House and Senate may have passed different versions of the same proposed legislation. In that case, a conference committee meets to resolve differences. This committee is composed of representatives from both the House and the Senate who attempt to iron out differences in the separate bills. It is necessary to do this because only one version of the bill can be sent to the president for approval.

After the conference committee version is agreed to by the committee members, the proposed bill (referred to as a conference bill or report) must then return to the entire floor of both the House and the Senate for another vote. If the bill is approved, the legislation is sent to the president for action. The president, at this point, has a few options. The president will either sign the bill into law or prevent its enactment by vetoing it.

The Brady Bill, after being placed on the formal government agenda and as part of a larger piece of proposed legislation, began its journey through the policy formulation process set up by Congress. The first step was a formal introduction into both houses of Congress, followed by assignments to the respective judiciary committees. A series of hearings were held in which various interested parties attempted to influence the final outcome of the proposed bill. Eventually, both the House and the Senate passed individual versions of the bill, at which point a conference committee met to resolve differences. The Brady Bill moved no further than the conference committee before Congress adjourned for the session and thus did not become law. It would take several more introductions and vetting through the process before the bill would be approved by the entire Congress and signed into law under President Bill Clinton.

Policy Implementation

The fourth step in the policy process, implementation, has often been described as "what happens after a bill becomes a law."[42] It essentially refers to "doing something" to carry out the mandate provided by Congress. Implementation consists of those activities that occur when agencies respond to the policy mandates of legislators. The agency personnel must gather necessary resources and develop a plan of action for carrying out that policy initiative in order for it to be effective.[43]

As legislators cannot foresee all the questions that might arise in implementing a program and because they often lack the expertise for creating specific programs, most of the legislation passed by Congress is vague. Thus, the legislators delegate a great deal of discretion to the various executive agencies to interpret vague policy statements produced in legislative enactments. As the agencies must fill in the gaps in the legislation, they are, in effect, making policy. This is why many have argued that policy should be clearly stated and consistent with other policy objectives and that those who are going to implement the policy should be involved in the formulation of that policy.

As a result, one can see why implementation has been described as a process, an output, or an outcome.[44] As a process, it is a combination of government decisions and actions that are directed toward putting the congressional mandate into effect. As an output, it is the way in which program goals are pursued, such as the amount of funds to be allocated to the enforcement of the Brady Bill. Finally, as an outcome, it is the impact that the policy implementation has on the problem itself: did it help reduce crime?

Policy Evaluation

The final step in the policy process is a review of the programs after they are implemented. Policy evaluations are concerned with the actual impacts of legislation or the extent to which the policy actually achieves its intended results.[45] Policy evaluation can be done by the courts, Congress, or personnel either inside or outside the agency. The purpose of program evaluation is to determine if the program is doing what it said it would do and if it is reaching the goals identified by policymakers. Another concern is whether the program is being accomplished in a cost-efficient manner.

There are two types of evaluations: process and impact. Process evaluations, often known as output evaluations, are those evaluations that look to see if an agency is meeting the mandate set forth by Congress. One example is the mandate under the Violent Crime Control and Law Enforcement Act of 1994, which mandated that the Department of Justice, through the Office of Community Oriented Policing Services (COPS), deliver grants to state and local police agencies to hire police officers under the concept of community policing. A process evaluation conducted on the COPS office found that they were in fact quite successful in moving the grants to the police agencies in a timely manner.

The second type of evaluations is known as impact evaluations and is often referred to as outcome evaluations. These consist of studies conducted on the effect that congressional policies have actually had on a specific problem. In the case of the COPS grants, they were intended to assist agencies with the hiring of additional police officers to implement community policing, which was aimed at reducing crime and improving the quality of life in the city or town receiving the grant. The outcome of the COPS grants has received mixed reviews. While some have argued that it did assist in the reduction of crime, official crime rates have been falling throughout the United States since before the implementation of the program; therefore, it is difficult to discern whether the COPS grants truly had any impact. In addition, many agencies secured the grants but then failed to implement a community policing program, or they started one up but it was limited to the officers they hired. Other agencies used the grants to start up or expand existing community policing programs that have developed far beyond the hiring of a few additional officers. Therefore, evaluating the impact of the COPS program has been more mixed.[46]

More recently, there has been a growing awareness that modifications of existing policy are possible at this step (by legislators or bureaucrats), as is identification of other problems and goals. In this sense, then, the policy process can begin again at the first step, making the development of public policy a cyclical process. What is truly at work here is policy change. If the policy is being implemented as intended, in a cost-efficient manner, and it is achieving its goals and solving problems, there is no reason to change the policy. However, this is generally the exception and not the rule. Problems associated with the policy may not have been adequately addressed or new problems arise so that policies must be changed.

The most likely scenario is change, and there are four types of policy change: linear, consolidation, splitting, and nonlinear.[47] Linear change consists of the direct replacement of a program or policy by a new program or policy. An example could be the replacement of the Drug Abuse Resistance Education (DARE) with an entirely new program to reduce drug abuse by teenagers. Consolidation is when several programs are collapsed into one program. This is essentially what President Nixon did when he collapsed the Bureau of Narcotics and Dangerous Drugs, the Office of Drug Abuse Law Enforcement, and the Special Action Office for Drug Abuse Prevention into the Drug Enforcement Agency (DEA).[48] Perhaps the best example of this is the creation of the Office of Homeland Security, which has absorbed over a dozen existing agencies or agency functions under one administrative department. Splitting a program consists of taking a preexisting agency and splitting its duties into two separate agencies. There has often been talk of splitting the two functions of the United States Secret Service, which consists of counterfeiting and presidential protection, into two agencies, but tradition and politics have prevented this from happening.[49] Finally, nonlinear change consists of a complex organizational change that doesn't follow any of the other methods intended to improve a specific program. Perhaps a good example of nonlinear change is the Bush administration's movement to keep the office of Community Oriented Policing Services, while at the same time drastically cutting its budget.

Finally, there is always the possibility that a specific policy will be terminated. In some cases, this is simply to end an old program or policy and to replace it with a new one (consolidation, as described previously). In other cases, it is to end outdated or inadequate policies that have failed to work or to continue producing results. In still more cases, Congress places a "sunset" clause into a specific bill, meaning that after a certain amount of time, the agency will be shut down. Policy termination can also mean "functional termination of a policy area, organizational termination, policy termination, and program termination."[50] Respectively, a specific policy such as drugs may be terminated through legalization of drugs, an agency such as the DEA might be terminated, a specific policy such as drug treatment may be terminated, or a specific program such as methadone treatment may be terminated. Although sometimes policies will be terminated with a dramatic suddenness, most tend to dissolve slowly over time.

PUBLIC POLICY TYPES

One more aspect of understanding public policies and how they are implemented is understanding the type of policy that is being used to resolve a problem. The type of policy employed to resolve a problem can vastly change the way in which government deals with the problem. The four types of public policies are termed distributive, redistributive, regulatory, and morality.[51] The first two are generally about how money is to be distributed within their respective policies, while the latter two are aimed at distributing values.

Distributive Policies

Distributive policies are those aimed at providing benefits to everyone. There are no qualifications on who receives the benefits, and if there are, they tend to be more administrative than anything. Distributive policies are often referred to in the media as "pork-barrel projects" because these are often add-ons to bills that bring money into a representative's or senator's state, usually through a quid pro quo—you vote for my pork project, and I will vote for yours. While generally given a negative treatment, as many pork-barrel projects are seen as wasteful spending, distributive policies can be a very powerful policy type because everyone wins. For example, with the passage of the Violent Crime Control and Law Enforcement Act of 1994 and the grants provided to state and local law enforcement agencies under the "100,000 Cops" initiative, everyone won with this program since it was nothing more than a pork-barrel project writ large. Any police agency (or city or town that wanted to start a police agency) could simply apply to the Office of Community Oriented Policing Services with a one-page form via fax, and they would be awarded a grant to hire a new police officer receiving 75 percent of that officer's pay and benefits for three years. The main reason for rejection was that the form was filled out improperly. Other than that, there were few impediments to receiving the grants. As a result, the police departments benefited, but so too did the local politicians, such as the mayor and city council members. Members of Congress could claim credit for bringing the grant into their state, and the president could claim credit for helping make America's streets safer. This credit claiming is one of the greatest benefits to distributive policies, while the biggest detractor is the cost.

Redistributive Policies

The second public policy type consists of redistributive policies. These types of policies are different from distributive policies in that they will shift benefits to specific groups by taking benefits away from other groups. Rather than everyone being a winner, as in distributive policies, here some people are winners and some losers. This type of policy is often referred to as "robin hood" politics, as it often "takes from the rich to give to the poor." For example, in the area of drug policy, when Congress allocates funds for enhancing drug treatment through behavioral modification programs and methadone treatment for convicted drug offenders, it may take away funds that could be used for other programs for nonconvicted offenders, for drug addicts, or for drug prevention in the schools. In addition, it is taking money from taxpayers who are not addicted to drugs and will not receive this benefit in order to give it to someone who is addicted. The benefits to redistributive policies are that they draw on a large amount of resources and bring them to bear on a specific problem. The drawback to redistributive policies is that they do not benefit everyone, only a select few.

Regulatory Policies

The third public policy type is regulatory policy. In regulatory policies, there is often not a tangible benefit that is distributed; rather, a policy is created to ensure that people do things in a certain way. Regulatory policies are designed to protect the public at large by establishing the conditions under which various activities can or cannot take place. What they regulate is behavior. In the criminal justice field, nearly all the policies passed are regulatory by nature. For example, dictating the blood alcohol level at which someone is legally considered intoxicated and impaired is a regulatory policy aimed at regulating behavior. Determining the amount of crack cocaine a person must have in his or her possession to be charged with the intent to distribute and the corresponding penalty associated with a conviction is also an example of a regulatory policy. Another example (discussed previously) can center on how best to regulate the selling of firearms and ammunition in America. The benefit of regulatory policies is that they are established to ensure greater order in society by attempting to control people's behavior. The drawbacks to regulatory policies are that they can become overbearing on the system, become too complex to enforce, or simply be ignored.

Morality Policies

The last public policy type is morality policy. While regulatory policies can often be complex because they are based on a variety of issues, morality policies tend to be much simpler in that they deal with what is known as "first principles."[52] These principles are based on individual morality, which determines what is right and what is wrong. Because these types of policies are rooted in people's understanding of what is right and wrong, there is usually little in terms of compromise that can be achieved; hence, they tend to become very divisive issues. And as a result of people's first principles and their highly divisive nature, the public tends to be more heavily involved in these public policy issues than most others. In criminal justice, many of the issues that we deal with are, by their very nature, morality policy issues. Examples include pornography, abortion, death penalty, drugs, homosexuality, gambling, euthanasia, gun control, and suicide. Based on their morality, people tend to have an understanding that these issues are "right" or that these issues are "wrong." As a result, we have people who favor pornography and those who do not. We have those who are in favor of abortion and those who are against it. Because such issues are based on morality and because they are two-sided issues, morality policy is often the most difficult for government to deal with. Therefore, any understanding of benefits and drawbacks are also based on individual ideology, so what may be a benefit for one group, say, legal abortion, may be a drawback for another group.

Perhaps the most important point about the four public policy types is that, however, Congress structures a specific policy will largely dictate how that policy is implemented. For example, if Congress wants to control crime, it could create a distributive policy to give every police department in the nation a certain amount of dollars to fight crime. Everyone wins. However, not every police department faces the same level of crime, and if each is given an equal share, the impact it will have on a small police department will be great, while the impact on a large metropolitan agency will be almost nonexistent. Therefore, Congress could make it a redistributive policy that uses money from all over and then redirects it only to cities that have a significantly high crime rate. A few crime-ridden cities will benefit for sure, but the majority of agencies will not. Thus, rather than formulating the policy as a redistributive policy, they could make it a regulatory policy aimed at reducing crime. For example, Congress could pass a regulatory policy aimed at reducing gun-related violence by mandating that all states increase the penalty for felonies committed with firearms to life in prison without parole or otherwise lose all Department of Justice funding. While this regulation may force states to change their laws, it may be too burdensome for states and local jurisdictions to implement. Therefore, to reduce crime, Congress could use a morality policy, perhaps still under the concept of gun control (clearly a morality policy issue), by passing a law that bans all firearms from private ownership unless the individual is in the military, police service, or security work. Certainly this last policy would be divisive, and there would be many who would support such a ban, but there would be many who would come out to protest over such a sweeping ban. All these policies are aimed at reducing crime, but the type of policy employed will determine how exactly the policy will be implemented.

SUBSTANTIVE VERSUS SYMBOLIC POLICY

One last method of looking at policy is discerning whether it is a substantive policy or symbolic policy.

Substantive Policies

Substantive policies are the types of policies that deal with a tangible and substantial problem and the policies that are formulated are created to directly deal with them in a concrete way. Substantive policy is often known as "material" policy because it provides concrete resources or very real powers to those who benefit from the policy, or they can impose a real disadvantage on those who are adversely affected by the policy.[53] Perhaps a more simplistic way of looking at these policies is that they are the ones that actually *do* something. For example, criminal justice policies that actually allocate funds to build new prisons at the federal level or funds given to police departments to purchase new crime scene collection equipment are examples of substantive and material policies. Another substantive policy that may not necessarily be tangible but is nonetheless concrete in that it gives law enforcement real power is the ability of law enforcement to conduct wiretaps on suspected terrorists in the United States via the USA PATRIOT Act of 2001.

Symbolic Policies

The other types of policies are those that are considered symbolic policies. Symbolic policies are those policies that are used to appeal to people's desires and values rather than to any form of tangible benefit.[54] Politicians will often use symbolic language in their speeches because it is language that evokes a particular response from the public but doesn't have to provide a tangible award. In other words, symbolic policies do not deliver what they appear to deliver; rather, they appeal to the cherished values of people, such as peace. For example, in criminal justice policy, politicians will often weigh-in on their desire to "fight crime" and "get tough on crime" without having to ever say what it is they will do regarding crime. Hence, their policies may be advocated not for really tangible benefits but rather to appease the public to demonstrate that they are doing something about the crime problem. A good example of a criminal justice symbolic policy resulted in the increase in carjackings during the early 1990s. Various members of Congress and the president supported getting tough on carjackings, and relevant legislation was proposed, passed, and signed into law at the federal level. Despite the very real law being passed, the law was mostly for appearances because federal law already had robbery as a violation of the law, and carjackings are nothing more than a robbery. In addition, when the law passed, there were no reported carjackings on federal property, such as federal parks, where the laws applied, and there have been few applications of the law since. The passage of the law was inherently a symbolic policy.

CRIME AND THE POLICY DILEMMA

The public policy process is an integral part of how crime is addressed in America at the federal, state, and local levels. Yet there are some problems with the outcomes of these policies that two authors, Feeley and Sarat, call the "policy dilemma."[55] The authors examined the rise of crime in the 1960s, which created a rise in public concern that resulted in the passage of the Omnibus Crime Control and Safe Streets Act of 1968. The bill, passed by Congress, created the Law Enforcement Assistance Administration (LEAA) under the Department of Justice in order to deliver grants to state planning agencies that would then disburse grants to state and local agencies in order to address the problem of crime. The authors followed the policy from its problem identification stage all the way through the implementation stage and then conducted an evaluation on both process and impact. The emphasis was more heavily on process than impact since they were analyzing only the first five years of the program. Despite this limitation to the study, their conceptualization of the policy dilemma is important, especially in the area of crime policy.

Feeley and Sarat argued that over the twentieth century, especially after the passage of the New Deal under the Roosevelt administration, people have become more demanding of government services. In the 1960s, the demand for government, especially the federal government, to do something about crime reached a critical juncture. Prior to the 1960s, most people, when it came to the issue of crime, looked to their local governments or, at most, their state governments. Yet the outcry over rising crime rates in the 1960s invoked the public policy at the federal level to become more involved in crime control policy and hence the creation of the LEAA and its grant-funding process. In addition to this increased demand, the other thing that Feeley and Sarat argued was that with the expansion comes increased inefficiency and ineffectiveness in the delivery of government goods. These two factors—high level of demand for government services and the problem of efficiency and effectiveness—"exist independently, although they are clearly interrelated."[56] The policy dilemma that results from these two factors refers "to the combined inability of government to enact and implement programs that work and to the political pressure for still more government programs."[57]

The roots of this dilemma are said to come from the way people think about public policy and what they want government to do. People want government to act and deal with the problems of crime, but at the same time people do not want the actions of government to threaten or harm their interests. A perfect example of this is with the passage of the USA PATRIOT Act in 2001. People demanded that government do something about terrorists in the immediate aftermath of September 11, 2001. However, people were also quick to demand that none of these actions should interfere with our civil liberties. Many scholars have argued that we simply cannot have it both ways, thus creating the policy dilemma. We want something done to address the problems of crime, but we do not want our liberties violated, so we propagate programs that are often ineffective and not very efficient. We then complain about these programs being inefficient and ineffective but still demand more programs. This is exactly what we continue to do with the DARE program. We want it, but we complain that it does not keep kids from doing drugs or that it is inefficient in its delivery. However, this does not lead people to fix the existing programs or reconsider their efficacy; rather, we simply demand new and improved programs.

Conclusion

The criminal justice policy process consists of a number of policy participants, ranging from the executive and legislature to criminal justice experts and practitioners in the criminal justice system. To explain how these participants contribute to the formation of crime policy in America, a number of policy models have explored this interaction. Some have explained that little sense can be made from one policy to the next (garbage can model), others have explained it in terms of relatively few participants (iron triangles), while still others point toward a confluence of factors (policy streams). All these models contribute to our understanding of how a crime problem becomes crime policy in the United States. Specifically, by looking at the public policy process, we can see how a crime problem is recognized (problem identification),

gains the attention of government (agenda setting), is created (policy formulation), and then is carried out by those in the criminal justice field (policy implementation). In addition, we also can understand why it is important to assess the success of the policy (policy evaluation) in order to determine if the policy should remain unchanged, modified, or terminated. It should also be noted that the public policy type (distributive, redistributive, regulatory, and morality) and whether it is substantive or symbolic policy will play an important role in the type of response to crime policy the public receives. And since the public continues to demand more government services, especially in the area of crime and criminal justice, it is even more imperative that we make good policy in order to avoid the pitfalls of the policy dilemma.

Notes

1. N. E. Marion, *Criminal Justice in America: The Politics behind the System* (Durham, N.C.: Carolina Academic Press, 2002).
2. P. Light, *The President's Agenda* (Baltimore: The Johns Hopkins University Press, 1982).
3. Marion, *Criminal Justice in America.*
4. Ibid.
5. Ibid.
6. Ibid.
7. Ibid.
8. Ibid.
9. B. A. Stolz, "The Roles of Interest Groups in U.S. Criminal Justice Policy Making: Who, When, and How," *Criminal Justice* 2 (1, 2002): 51–69.
10. Marion, *Criminal Justice in America.*
11. Laurence J. O'Toole, Jr., *American Intergovernmental Relations*, 2nd ed. (Washington, D.C.: Congressional Quarterly Press, 1993).
12. M. Cohen, J. March, and J. Olsen, "A Garbage Can Model of Organizational Choice," *Administrative Science Quarterly* 17 (1972): 1–25.
13. T. Lowi, *The End of Liberalism* (New York: Norton, 1969).
14. H. L. Wilson and M. J. Rozell, "Virginia: The Politics of Concealed Weapons," in *The Changing Politics of Gun Control*, ed. J. M. Bruce and C. Wilcox (Lanham, Md.: Rowman & Littlefield, 1998), pp. 125–38.
15. H. Heclo, "Issue Networks and the Executive Establishment," in *The New American Political System*, ed. A. King (Washington, D.C.: American Enterprise Institute, 1978), pp. 87–124.
16. A. Downs, "Up and Down with Ecology—The "Issue-Attention Cycle," *Public Interest* 28 (1972): 38–50.
17. Ibid., p. 39.
18. P. Sabatier, "An Advocacy Coalition Framework of Policy Change and the Role of Policy-Oriented Learning Therein," *Policy Sciences* 21 (1988): 129–68; P. A. Sabatier and H. C. Jenkins-Smith, *Policy Change and Learning: An Advocacy Coalition Approach* (Boulder, Colo.: Westview Press, 1988).
19. Sabatier and Jenkins-Smith, *Policy Change and Learning.*
20. J. C. Kingdon, *Agendas, Alternatives, and Public Policies*, 2nd ed. (New York: HarperCollins College Publishers, 1995).
21. F. R. Baumgartner and B. D. Jones, *Agendas and Instability in American Politics* (Chicago: University of Chicago Press, 1993).
22. J. E. Anderson, *Public Policymaking: An Introduction* (Boston: Houghton Mifflin, 1990), p. 8.
23. R. W. Cobb and C. D. Elder, *Participation in America Politics: The Dynamics of Agenda Building* (Baltimore: The Johns Hopkins University Press, 1975).

24. Downs, "Up and Down with Ecology."
25. R. Eyestone, *From Social Issues to Public Policy* (New York: John Wiley & Sons, 1978).
26. R. W. Cobb and C. D. Elder, "Issue Creation and Agenda Building," in *Cases in Public Policy-Making*, ed. James E. Anderson (New York: Holt, Rinehart and Winston 1982), p. 3.
27. Mother's Against Drunk Drivers (MADD) home page, available online at www.madd.org/home/.
28. R. B. Ripley, *Policy Analysis in Political Science* (Chicago: Nelson Hall, 1985).
29. E. S. Fairchild and V. J. Webb, "Crime, Justice, and Politics in the United States Today," in *The Politics of Crime and Criminal Justice*, ed. Erika S. Fairchild and Vincent J. Webb (Beverly Hills, Calif.: Sage, 1985), p. 8.
30. C. R. Wise, *The Dynamics of Legislation* (San Francisco: Jossey-Bass, 1991).
31. Ripley, *Policy Analysis in Political Science*, p. 51.
32. Bruce and Wilcox, *The Changing Politics of Gun Control*; R. J. Spitzer, *The Politics of Gun Control* (Chatham, N.J.: Chatham House, 1995).
33. Cobb and Elder, "Issue Creation and Agenda Building," p. 5.
34. Ibid., p. 6.
35. C. O. Jones, *An Introduction to the Study of Public Policy* (Belmont, Calif.: Wadsworth, 1998), p. 40–41.
36. R. Cobb, J.-K. Ross, and M. H. Ross, "Agenda Building as a Comparative Political Process," *American Political Science Review* 70 (2, 1976): 126–38.
37. Ibid., p. 127.
38. Human Rights Watch (2001). *No Escape: Male Rape in U.S. Prisons*. Washington, D.C.: Human Rights Watch.
39. Ibid., p. 128.
40. Ibid.
41. Anderson, *Public Policymaking*.
42. E. Bardach, *The Implementation Game: What Happens after a Bill Becomes a Law* (Cambridge, Mass.: MIT Press, 1977).
43. Anderson, *Public Policymaking*.
44. M. Goggin, A. Bowman, J. P. Lester, and L. O'Toole, *Implementation Theory and Practice: Toward a Third Generation* (New York: HarperCollins, 1990).
45. J. P. Lester and J. Stewart, Jr., *Public Policy: An Evolutionary Approach* (St. Paul, Minn.: West, 1996), p. 8.
46. See U.S. Department of Justice, *National Evaluation of the COPS Program—Title I of the 1994 Crime Act* (Washington, D.C.: U.S. Department of Justice, 2000); D. B. Muhlhausen, *Why the Bush Administration Is Right on COPS* (Washington, D.C.: Heritage Foundation, 2003).
47. B. G. Peters, *American Public Policy: Promise and Performance*, 4th ed. (Chatham, N.J.: Chatham House, 1996).
48. E. B. Sharp, *The Dilemma of Drug Policy in the United States* (New York: HarperCollins, 1994).
49. Reese, S. (2009). "The U.S. Secret Service: An Examination and Analysis of Its Evolving Mission." *Congressional Research Service*. March 24. Available on-line at www.fas.org/sgp/crs/homesec/RL34603.pdf
50. Lester and Stewart, *Public Policy*, p. 9.
51. See T. J. Lowi, "American Business, Public Policy, Case Studies, and Political Theory," *World Politics* 16 (1964): 677–715; C. Z. Mooney, *The Public Clash of Private Values: The Politics of Morality Policy* (New York: Chatham House, 2001).
52. Mooney, *The Public Clash of Private Values*.
53. Lester and Stewart, *Public Policy*.
54. N. E. Marion, *A History of Federal Crime Control Initiatives, 1960–1993* (Westport, Conn.: Praeger, 1994).
55. M. M. Feeley and A. D. Sarat, *The Policy Dilemma: Federal Crime Policy and the Law Enforcement Assistance Administration* (Minneapolis: University of Minnesota Press, 1980).
56. Ibid., p. 11.
57. Ibid.

PART TWO

The Criminal Justice Policy Actors

4

The Executive Branches

Chapter Outline

INTRODUCTION

The federal, state, and local executives have the basic responsibility of ensuring that the laws of the legislatures are carried out. The president, governors, and mayors do this by organizing the bureaucracy and making legislative proposals to the legislature as well as making budgetary proposals. The executive can use his or her position to advocate a particular policy or propose changes in the budget to reflect his or her policy initiatives. However, once the legislature has passed a law, it becomes the executive branch's role to honor and fulfill that law unless they choose to override it with a veto. They fulfill the law by directing the bureaucracy to adhere to and enforce the law. Each of these executives plays an important role in the policy process and can have a major impact on how the law is implemented and enforced.

U.S. PRESIDENTS AND CRIME CONTROL POLICY

For most of American history, the issue of crime, its control, and thus crime policy have been the direct responsibility largely of local governments and to some degree state governments. Many point to the Kennedy administration (1961–1963) as being the first presidential administration to become actively involved in the issue of crime control policy, although the Hoover administration was quite active in the area of "law observance."[1] Presidents, when dealing with the issue of crime, have two different types of power: those that are constitutional powers and those that are essentially institutional powers. Another way of explaining the division is simply that some of the powers of the president are "enumerated powers," those provided for by the U.S. Constitution, and others "implied powers," powers necessary for the president to perform his various roles.[2]

Constitutional Powers

The first category is deemed the constitutional powers, as they are in fact the enumerated powers derived directly from the Constitution. These consist of the power to appoint members of his cabinet and key administrators, grant pardons, deliver a message to the U.S. Congress "from time to time" on the "State of the Union," propose legislation to Congress, share with Congress the power to create and administer the federal bureaucracy, veto legislation, and respond to formal requests for assistance in cases of domestic disturbances. All these enumerated powers have been utilized by presidents to address the issue of crime at one time or another, and, as presidents' attention to crime has increased over time, so has their frequency.

The Constitution, in article II, sets forth that the "executive power shall be vested in a president of the United States of America." There are only four sections to article II, of which section 1 details how the president is to be elected, section 2 details his powers, section 3 speaks to his duties, and section 4 articulates the requirements for removal from office. While the president is granted a number of powers, such as his designation as commander in chief of the armed forces, and is given a number of duties, such as receiving ambassadors and other public ministers, there are only a few select powers and duties that are germane to the discussion at hand. In regard to the president's ability to deal with issues of crime, section 2 gives the president the power to appoint and the power to grant reprieves and pardons. Section 3 states that the president has the duty to "from time to time give to Congress information of the State of the Union," that he shall recommend to Congress "such measures as he shall judge necessary and expedient," and that "he shall take care that the laws be faithfully executed." In addition, article I, section 7, gives the president the power to veto congressional legislation, and article IV, section 4, gives the president the power to, on application by the states, intervene in cases of domestic violence.

APPOINTMENTS   One of the powers of the president, which has long been considered one of his greatest resources, found in article II, section 2, is the power to appoint key officials in the national government. These officials range from cabinet secretaries and undersecretaries to bureau and agency heads as well as the justices of the U.S. Supreme Court. As the Constitution stipulates, he

> shall nominate, and by and with the Advice and Consent of the Senate, shall appoint Ambassadors, other public Ministers and Consuls, Judges of the supreme Court, and all other Officers of the United States, whose Appointments are not herein otherwise provided for, and which shall be established by Law: but the Congress may by Law vest the Appointment of such inferior Officers, as they think proper, in the President alone, in the Courts of Law, or in the Heads of Departments.[3]

As a result, the president has the power to appoint many of the key leaders in the national government who stand in a position to exercise the will of the president or potentially either their own will or that of the agency they oversee. In terms of crime policy, the president has the power to appoint such people as the attorney general, who runs the U.S. Department of Justice; the director of the Federal Bureau of Investigation; and the solicitor general, who is the government's advocate before the Supreme Court.

One final aspect of the power to appoint comes in the form of judicial appointments by the president.[4] The president has the ability to appoint, with approval of the Senate, the nine Supreme Court justices as well as all federal judges. One only has to look to the era of the Warren court in order to understand the impact that these appointments can have on issues of crime. Under the Warren court, such cases as *Mapp* v. *Ohio* (1961),[5] *Miranda* v. *Arizona* (1966),[6] and

Gideon v. *Wainwright* (1963)[7] greatly impacted the criminal justice system and continue to have such an impact today. Therefore, presidential appointment of federal judges, although not a direct influence on crime policy, can have a significant impact in this policy area.

PARDONS   The second constitutional power granted to the president under article II, section 2, is the power to grant pardons. The president is assisted in this area by the attorney general and through the Office of the Pardon Attorney within the Department of Justice, which handles "all requests for executive clemency" and "prepares the Department's recommendation to the President for final disposition of each application."[8] The pardons may be granted in several forms, "including both conditional and unconditional pardons, commutation, remission of fine, and reprieves."[9] What is perhaps the most famous presidential pardon was the one granted to former President Nixon by President Gerald Ford for his role in the Watergate scandal.[10] Ford issued the pardon on September 8, 1974, a mere month after taking office and prior to any conviction or indictment of Nixon for his role in the scandal. In the pardon, he stated, "I, Gerald Ford, President of the United States, pursuant to the pardon power conferred upon me by article II, section 2, of the Constitution, have granted and by these presents do grant a full, free, and absolute pardon unto Richard Nixon for all offenses against the United States which he, Richard Nixon, has committed or may have committed or taken part in during the period from January 20, 1969 through August 9, 1974."[11] As a result, on Nixon's acceptance of the presidential pardon, the president had exercised his constitutional powers, and although he was accused of subverting the legal process, his power of the pardon was never disputed.[12]

It can be safely stated that the majority of presidential pardons never arise to such levels as the pardon of former President Nixon, but all presidents have granted pardons during their tenure in office. President Ford granted a number of executive warrants for clemency to citizens who evaded the draft during the Vietnam War,[13] and President Carter would pardon all "draft resisters and asked the Defense Department to consider the cases of military deserters during that war on an individual basis."[14] President Eisenhower granted the commutation of an inmate's death sentence, provided that he never be paroled, and President Nixon granted executive clemency to former labor leader James Hoffa with the strict condition that he no longer engage in union activities.[15] Perhaps the most controversial pardons came in the last few days of President Clinton's tenure in office when he pardoned 140 individuals, many for political reasons.[16] It is evident, then, that presidents are granted the constitutional power of the pardon, that they use it, and that it is generally undisputed.

STATE OF THE UNION   In article II, section 3, the Constitution states that the president "shall from time to time give to the Congress Information of the State of the Union." Although throughout most of the nineteenth century the delivery of a "State of the Union Speech" was given from "time to time," the speech would ultimately become a permanent yearly institution by the twentieth century. According to Light, the State of the Union has become a means by which presidents transmit their agenda for the following year.[17] In a sense, it has become the "must list" and a means for setting priorities.[18] As Light explains, "at least since Theodore Roosevelt, Presidents have used the message as a statement of both foreign and domestic priorities,"[19] and, as Ragsdale further comments, "since Truman, presidents have used State of the Union messages to capture congressional and national attention for their legislative programs."[20] As a result, Kessel explains that

> Cabinet members, White House aides, and others are quite aware of the significance
> of getting material included in the State of the Union message. Favorable mentions of

a policy gives visibility to it and confers presidential backing to the enterprise at one and the same time. Since there are obvious limits to the number of policies that can be thus favored, very real contests take place over control of this scarce resource.[21]

In sum, the State of the Union message has become an important constitutional power granted to the president of the United States, and when specific policy proposals or mentions are found within its pages, one can be assured that presidents and their cabinet and staff desire to make that policy issue part of the president's agenda.

LEGISLATIVE PROPOSALS   The second power granted to the president under article II, section 3, is that the president may make recommendations to Congress "such measures as he shall judge necessary and expedient." This power affords the presidents another means by which they can affect crime control, and that is through legislation on crime. Although presidents do not have direct legislative authority, they do have several means to influence the passage or nonpassage of a bill.[22] In some cases, presidents may utilize their constitutional powers to sign a bill into law or to veto the legislation. In other cases, they utilize many of their institutional powers to influence legislation through such means as the administration, the Office of Congressional Relations, or their power of speech. Although the president's relationship with Congress and his ability to influence Congress are far more complex than this, it is quite evident that the president plays a significant role in the legislative process.

EXECUTION OF THE LAW   The third power granted to the president of the United States that is related to the issue of crime and is derived from article II, section 3, is found in the clause that the president "shall take Care that the Law be faithfully executed." This clause essentially provides an imperative that it should be the president who controls the bureaucracy in order to assist him in "executing" the law. Yet it is well established that both the president and Congress share this role and that because the president is often seen as an outsider to the bureaucracy, he wields even less control despite being hierarchically superior to the bureaucracy.[23] As a result, "to a large extent, the president's influence over the bureaucracy is tied to the ability to persuade—to convince others of the rightness or political expediency of actions the president desires."[24] Presidents do in fact have multiple means by which they can influence the bureaucracy, such as those previously discussed, the power to appoint, and the power to remove key officials within the bureaucracy. Presidents have also developed a number of institutional means, such as expansion and reorganization of the bureaucracy, executive orders, and the White House staff, all of which are detailed in the next section. Suffice it to say at this point that presidents can exercise their constitutional powers of faithfully executing the laws by a "general support for law enforcement" and through the creation of, with the approval of Congress, new bureaucracies intent on dealing with crime-related issues.[25] As was seen in Chapter 1, presidents have increasingly demonstrated a strong support for law enforcement over time, and as detailed earlier in this chapter, they do have multiple bureaucratic mechanisms to address the issues of crime, primarily in the Departments of Justice and Treasury.

The president is also granted two additional constitutional powers, both of which lie outside of article II, namely, the power to veto congressional bills and the power to intervene in domestic disturbances when called on by the state legislatures or executives.

VETO   The power to veto is granted in article I, section 7, which states,

Every Order, Resolution, or Vote to which the Concurrence of the Senate and House of Representatives may be necessary shall be presented to the President of the United

States; and before the Same shall take Effect, shall be approved by him, or being disapproved by him, shall be repassed by two thirds of the Senate and House of Representatives, according to the Rules and Limitations prescribed in the Case of a Bill.

Woodrow Wilson, in his classic book *Congressional Government*, wrote of the importance of the presidential veto when he explained that "in the exercise of his power to veto, which is, of course, beyond all comparison, his most formidable prerogative, the President acts not as the executive but as a third branch of the legislature."[26] The power of the veto is a formidable one, and its use has been studied by many scholars.[27] It has been utilized for various crime legislation passed by Congress, and examples include President Ford's veto of legislation to reclassify and upgrade deputy U.S. marshals because he felt it was discriminatory against other federal law enforcement agencies,[28] President Reagan's veto of a bill concerning contract services for drug-dependent federal offenders primarily because it would have created a cabinet-level drug czar,[29] and President Clinton's veto of a Department of Justice appropriations bill because of the lack of funds to implement the president's crime-related initiatives.[30]

INTERVENTION IN DOMESTIC DISTURBANCES   Finally, the last presidential power related to crime that is drawn from the president's constitutional powers comes from article IV, section 4, which, as previously explained, details that "the United States shall guarantee to every State in this Union a Republican Form of Government, and shall protect each of them against Invasion; and on Application of the Legislature, or of the Executive (when the Legislature cannot be convened) against domestic Violence." Presidents since Washington have employed the use of this constitutional power. In most instances, these domestic disturbances are in fact state and local crimes but arise to such a level that the state is no longer effectively able to deal with the crime. As a result, governors, as has typically been the case, have applied to the president for assistance in domestic disturbances. More modern examples include President Franklin D. Roosevelt's use of federal troops to quell the Detroit race riots on June 21, 1943,[31] and what appeared to be a complete repeat on July 24, 1967, when President Johnson would send federal troops into Detroit during the race riots that summer.[32]

Institutional Powers

The other powers that presidents have in order to exert some influence over crime control policy are those that fall into the category of institutional powers. The institutional powers can be defined as the implied or informal powers that presidents obtain through broad interpretations of the Constitution, through the many roles they play in national governance, and through the requirement to ensure that the laws are "faithfully executed." According to Warshaw, "The existence of an institutional process for domestic policy is one that has been evolving for over seventy years, even before Franklin Delano Roosevelt aggressively sought to control the national agenda through the creation of the Executive Office of the President."[33] This same statement could be made regarding presidents and their domestic crime policy, for it too has greatly evolved over the past seventy years.

The institutional powers related to crime that presidents managed to build during the twentieth century are plentiful. While in many cases they resemble the same institutional powers and means by which presidents address issues other than crime, these powers have been used definitively to address the specific issue of crime. In addition, these methods of engaging in crime control policy are not relegated to only one president but demonstrate evidence of having been utilized by the office of the presidency across time. Although certain presidents may favor one means over another and some presidents may not have utilized the powers available, none of the institutional powers are relegated to only one president. Finally, it is important to also note that while presidents and their staffs often think in terms of how they can address a specific issue, in most instances the choices are not relegated to one specific response; rather, they incorporate multiple means of addressing the crime issue in crafting their administrations' response.

Although the use of executive orders, legislation, budgets, and administrative (internal) policies are most certainly key powers at the president's disposal to address the issue of crime, they are not the only means available. In fact, it would appear that presidents have at least six key methods at their disposal.[34] They can utilize the office of the presidency in a number of ways to promote crime policy, from key advisers to the White House staff and special counsels to the bureaucracy. Presidents can utilize various types of crime commissions and task forces to address crimes, executive orders, and host White House conferences. Moreover, as previously indicated, presidents have used the budget to address crime policy. Finally, presidents have used one of their primary tools to address the issue of crime, the institutional power that is granted to the office of the presidency for making speeches. It is to these six institutional powers that we now turn.

OFFICE OF THE PRESIDENCY   The first institutional power that presidents have to implement crime control policy comes from the office of the presidency. Although this power contains various components of the executive office, all these either have been or have come to be central to the institutional powers that presidents have to affect policy. As it relates to crime control policy, this consists of specific aides who deal with crime or crime-related issues or those components of the executive office that oversee aspects of crime policy (e.g., the Domestic Policy Council and the Office of National Drug Control Policy) and, through the president's ability, not only create a cabinet and the bureaucracy, as was noted under the constitutional powers, but also expand and reorganize the bureaucracy. Both of these are perhaps best understood by looking at how President Bush created the Department of Homeland Security and how a number of federal agencies were reorganized under this newly created department. It is through these entities within the executive office that presidents have come to affect crime control policy in the United States.

CRIME COMMISSIONS   The second institutional power of the president to affect crime control policy comes from his ability to create commissions to advise him on specific issues, such as crime. Smith, Leyden, and Borrelli have pointed out that "presidential commissions, known variously as 'advisory commissions,' 'blue-ribbon panels,' 'task forces,' or 'expert commissions,' have been frequent, although always temporary, additions to the office of the modern presidency."[35] They go on to explain that "officially, nearly all of these commissions carry the same presidential mandate: to study and propose alternatives in response to particularly new and/or particularly difficult problems."[36] However, they and other researchers have pointed out that commissions' reports are often ignored and that they become a political issue *because* presidents often do not follow the advice.[37] And, although these commissions are "often appointed to defuse highly sensitive issues," they "often blur critical issues," or the "commissions may make findings and suggestions that embarrass the president."[38] Despite these drawbacks, presidents still create commissions to study various issues, and crime has been no different. (See Box 4.1.)

There have been a number of crime commissions throughout the twentieth century, with the first, officially known as the President's Commission on Law Observance and Enforcement, commencing in 1929 under President Herbert Hoover.[39] Hoover would appoint George

BOX 4.1

Presidential Commissions on Crime (or Related)

Administration	Years	Commission Title
Hoover	1929–1931	President's Commission on Law Observance and Enforcement
Truman	1951–1952	President's Commission on Civil Rights (Lynchings)
Kennedy	1962–1963	President's Commission on Narcotics and Drug Abuse
Johnson	1965–1966	President's Commission on Crime in the District of Columbia
Johnson	1967–1970	Commission on Obscenity and Pornography
Johnson	1965–1967	President's Commission on Law Enforcement and Administration of Justice
Johnson	1966–1967	President's Task Force on Crime
Johnson	1967–1968	National Advisory Commission on Civil Disorders
Johnson	1968–1969	National Commission on the Causes and Prevention of Violence
Nixon	1970–1972	President's Commission on Campus Unrest
Nixon	1971–1972	National Commission on Marihuana [sic] and Drug Abuse
Nixon	1971–1973	National Advisory Commission on Criminal Justice Standards and Goals
Reagan	1983–1987	President's Commission on Organized Crime
Clinton	1996–1997	Presidential Commission on Aviation Safety and Security
Bush, G.W.	2002–2004	National Commission on Terrorist Attacks Upon the United States (9-11 Commission)

Wickersham, the former attorney general in the Taft administration, as the chairman, along with eight other members of notable reputation in various areas of criminal justice. By 1931, the so-called Wickersham Commission would publish fourteen volumes dealing with a variety of administrative and social issues, calling for a number of reforms within the criminal justice system.[40] Although both Truman and Kennedy would have commissions dealing with issues related to crime and Johnson would create the President's Commission on Crime in the District of Columbia, primarily for political purposes, it was the creation of the President's Commission on Law Enforcement and Administration of Justice by President Johnson in 1965 that would have a profound impact on the criminal justice system.[41] The attorney general, Nicholas deB Katzenbach, was appointed chairman, and the commission set out in similar fashion to the Wickersham Commission.[42] By 1967, the commission would publish its report titled *The Challenge of Crime in a Free Society*,[43] which included over 200 recommendations for changes in the criminal justice system as well as a number of additional suggestions. The recommendations themselves were not prioritized; rather, they were laid out in terms of topics, such as the police, organized crime, and research. In the end, many of the recommendations would find their way into the Omnibus Crime Control and Safe Streets Act of 1968, often in a watered-down version, and would see aspects of implementation through the Law Enforcement Assistance Administration. Although there are a variety of perspectives on the success and failure of the Katzenbach Commission, the one fact that seems to be well agreed on is that the report did have a significant impact on the criminal justice system.[44] It should also be noted that the report, like many others, encouraged a more active role for the federal government in dealing with the issue of crime.[45]

EXECUTIVE ORDERS   The third institutional power of the president is the use of executive orders. Although presidents were not given any direct legislative authority by the Constitution, many have exercised this power under article II to "take care that the laws be faithfully executed." It has been said that "most modern presidents have followed Theodore Roosevelt's 'stewardship' theory of executive power, which holds that article II confers on them inherent power to take whatever actions they deem necessary in the national interest unless prohibited from doing so by the Constitution or by law."[46] The power of executive orders has been one means by which presidents have managed to exercise some authority. During the Kennedy and Johnson administrations, many of the executive orders issued were directed toward domestic disturbances resulting from the civil rights movement,[47] and one of Reagan's executive orders brought about drug testing of federal employees.[48] Other executive orders have been used to assist the president in establishing crime control policy by the creation of crime commissions, such as the executive orders creating the President's Commission on Law Enforcement and Administration[49] and the National Advisory Commission on Civil Disorders[50]; the creation of executive offices, such as the establishment of the Special Action Office for Drug Abuse Prevention[51] and the Office of National Narcotics Intelligence,[52] both by President Nixon; or to establish mechanisms for generating crime control policy, such as the creation of the National Drug Policy Board by President Reagan.[53] In some cases, the executive orders were merely ceremonial, such as the one recognizing the death of J. Edgar Hoover[54] or the one establishing the official seal of the Office of National Drug Control Policy.[55] (See Box 4.2.)

CRIME CONFERENCES   The fourth institutional means by which presidents can focus on crime policy is largely ceremonial and symbolic in nature and operates on a more limited scale than presidential commissions; these are White House conferences. These "conferences bring together groups of experts and distinguished citizens for public forums held under presidential auspices," and "their principal function is to build support among experts, political leaders, and relevant interests for presidential leadership to deal with the problems at issue."[56] Since the Kennedy administration, one of these problems has consistently been the issue of crime. All the modern presidents have hosted a White House conference related to the topic of crime. The majority of these conferences have generally come late in the president's term in office, and none have had any significant impact on crime policy.[57] In addition, many of these conferences are simply used to highlight a policy the administration has previously addressed in order to make it appear more active in the area. However, most have made various recommendations for improving the criminal justice system, and nearly all have recommended an expansion of the national government's role in crime control. (See Box 4.3.)

BUDGET   The fifth institutional power of the president for affecting crime control policy can be found in the budgetary process, where the president proposes the annual budget and then

BOX 4.2

Examples of Presidential Executive Orders Related to Crime, 1961–2009

EO Number	President	Short Title/Description	Date
10940	Kennedy	Committee on Juvenile Delinquency and Youth Crime	May 11, 1961
11076	Kennedy	President's Commission on Narcotics	January 15, 1963
11130	Johnson	Commission to report on Kennedy assassination	November 29, 1963
11154	Johnson	Exemption of J. Edgar Hoover from retirement	May 8, 1964
11236	Johnson	President's Commission on Law Enforcement	July 23, 1965
11365	Johnson	National Commission on Civil Disorder	July 29, 1967
11403	Johnson	Restoration of law and order in D.C.	April 5, 1968
11404	Johnson	Restoration of law and order in Illinois	April 7, 1968
11405	Johnson	Restoration of law and order in Maryland	April 7, 1968
11412	Johnson	Commission on Causes/Prevention of Violence	June 10, 1968
11534	Nixon	National Council on Organized Crime	June 4, 1970
11536	Nixon	President's Commission on Campus Unrest	June 13, 1970
11599	Nixon	Special Action Office for Drug Abuse Prevention	June 17, 1971
11641	Nixon	Law enforcement activities relating to drug abuse	January 28, 1972
11676	Nixon	Office of National Narcotics Intelligence	July 27, 1972
11727	Nixon	Drug Law enforcement	July 6, 1973
11803	Ford	Clemency Board to review UCMJ convictions	September 16, 1974
12045	Carter	Relating to the Office of Drug Abuse Policy	March 27, 1978
12133	Carter	Drug policy functions	May 9, 1979
12324	Reagan	Interdiction of illegal aliens	September 29, 1981
12358	Reagan	Presidential Commission on Drunk Driving	April 14, 1982
12360	Reagan	President's Task Force on Victims of Crime	April 23, 1982
12368	Reagan	Drug Abuse Policy Function	June 24, 1982
12435	Reagan	President's Commission on Organized Crime	July 28, 1983
12564	Reagan	Drug-Free Federal Workplace	September 15, 1986
12590	Reagan	National Drug Policy Board	March 26, 1987
12696	Bush	President's Drug Advisory Council	November 13, 1989
12804	Bush	Providing for the restoration of order in L.A.	May 1, 1992
12807	Bush	Interdiction of illegal aliens	May 24, 1992
12880	Clinton	National Drug Control Program	November 16, 1993
12992	Clinton	President's Council on Counter-Narcotics	March 15, 1996
13133	Clinton	Working Group on Unlawful Conduct on Internet	August 5, 1999
13228	Bush	Establishing the Office of Homeland Security and the Homeland Security Council	October 8, 2001

BOX 4.2
(continued)

13300	Bush	Facilitating the Administration of Justice in the Federal Courts	May 9, 2003
13338	Bush	Further Strengthening the Sharing of Terrorism Information to Protect Americans	October 25, 2005
13402	Bush	Strengthening Federal Efforts to protect against Identity Theft	May 10, 2006
13481	Bush	Providing an order of Succession within the Department of Justice	December 9, 2008
13491	Obama	Ensuring Lawful Interrogation	January 22, 2009

BOX 4.3
White House Conferences Related to Crime

Year	Administration	Conference Title	Date
1930	Hoover	WH Conference on Children (Delinquents)	November 19, 1930
1934	FDR	AG's WH Crime Conference on Crime	December 10, 1934
1939	FDR	WH Parole Conference (Crime)	April 17, 1939
1939	FDR	WH Conference on Children (Crime Prevention)	April 23, 1939
1950	Truman	AG's WH Conference on Crime	February 15, 1950
1958	Eisenhower	WH Conference on Children (Delinquents)	December 16, 1958
1960	Eisenhower	WH Conference on Children (Delinquents)	March 27, 1960
1962	Kennedy	WH Conference on Narcotics (Drug Abuse)	September 27, 1962
1965	Johnson	WH Conference on Rights (Violence and Crime)	November 16, 1965
1967	Johnson	WH Conference of Governors (Crime)	March 18, 1967
1967	Johnson	National Conference on Crime Control	March 28, 1967
1972	Nixon	WH Conference on Drug Abuse	February 3, 1972
1975	Ford	WH Conference on Domestic Policy (Crime)	September 12, 1975
1988	Reagan	WH Conference on a Drug Free America	February 29, 1988
1990	Bush	WH Conference on DWI	December 11, 1990
1991	Bush	WH Conference on Crime Victims Week	April 22, 1991
1995	Clinton	WH Conference on Character Building (Crime)	May 20, 1995
1997	Clinton	WH Conference on Hate Crimes	November 10, 1997
1998	Clinton	WH Conference on School Safety	October 15, 1998
2006	Bush	WH Conference on School Safety	October 10, 2006
2009	Obama	WH Conference on Gang Violence and Crime Prevention	August 24, 2009

Source: Data collected by author from successive volumes of the *Public Papers of the Presidents of the United States* (Washington, D.C.: U.S. Government Printing Office).

delivers the budget to Congress for approval.[58] Although Congress does wield the "power of the purse" and can increase, decrease, or eliminate any of the president's proposals, as Aaron Wildavsky has explained, "the president has the first and last moves in the budget process. He can both check and use Congress, and it can both check and use him."[59] However, in the case of budget allocations for federal crime control, there appears to rarely be anything but increases in expenditures when looking at the data over time. One indication can be found in looking at the budget category "administration of justice" in the federal budget, which, "since 1965 . . . has risen from $535 million to an estimated $11.7 billion in Fiscal Year 1992, an increase of over 2,000 percent."[60] Some research has indicated that presidents have been highly responsive to rising crime rates by increasing the budget of federal law enforcement agencies,[61] and more recent research has found significant growth rates in all the agencies.[62] For example, Martinek, Meier, and Keiser have found that between 1970 and 1995 there was a 692 percent increase in the annual budget of the Bureau of Alcohol, Tobacco and Firearms; 860 percent for the Federal Bureau of Investigation; 900 percent for the Immigration and Naturalization Service; 1,389 percent for the Customs Service; 1,400 percent for the Secret Service; and 3,233 percent for the Drug Enforcement Administration.[63] Finally, when looking at the total federal expenditures on crime over time or the breakdown between direct expenditures (those to federal law enforcement agencies) and intergovernmental expenditures (those to state and local governments), it is evident that the national government has become more active in crime control at the national, state, and local levels since the last three decades of the twentieth century.

SPEECH   The sixth and last institutional power of the American president to be reviewed, which is perhaps his strongest asset, is the power of speech. Because presidents sit in a position of power and public attention, coupled with media attention focused on the president, the president has the ability to deliver speeches that will be disseminated to the American people. Therefore, they have the means by which they can deliver speeches to a largely captive audience. At a very simple level, as Marion has explained, "presidents use their speeches to communicate their agenda."[64] Shull has elaborated that it is through their use of rhetoric that "presidents set an agenda to promote and communicate their policy preferences to those inside and outside government."[65] As a result, "much of what appears on the public agenda can be traced to the rhetoric in presidential statements."[66] Finally, as one author who has extensively studied the rhetoric of American presidents, Lyn Ragsdale, explains, "Presidential speeches to the nation, even relatively mundane ones, have captured considerable attention in contemporary American politics."[67] He further states that

> through the speeches, presidents gain immediate access to the public. In preempting regular broadcasting, they receive the all-but-automatic and undivided attention of millions of radio listeners and television viewers. The forum presents presidents as sole speakers, uninterrupted by queries of newsreporters and challenged only afterwards by the rebuttals of partisan foes or the interpretations of political commentators. . . . In this solitary setting, presidents can appear as leaders of the nation; stirring public emotions and proposing solutions to national problems.[68]

Therefore, presidents have a significant power that has developed over time and has become itself an American institution. It has also become clear that this power has translated into a more focused attention on the president in American politics[69] as well as providing the president with a more refined strategy for influencing public policy.[70] (See Table 4.1.)

TABLE 4.1 Level of Crime Activity[a] by Presidential Term

President	Total Activities	Yearly Average
Hoover	119	29.75
Roosevelt, I	31	17.75
Roosevelt, II	26	6.5
Roosevelt, III/IV	9	1.8
Truman, I	25	6.25
Truman, II	59	14.75
Eisenhower, I	62	15.5
Eisenhower, II	38	9.5
Kennedy	99	33
Johnson	347	69.4
Nixon, I	193	48.25
Nixon, II	24	12
Ford	95	31.66
Carter	157	39.25
Reagan, I	378	94.5
Reagan, II	598	149.5
Bush	659	164.75
Clinton, I	1,154	288.5
Clinton, II	1,825	456.25
Bush, I	573	143.25
Bush, II	567	141.75
Obama, 1st Year	80	80

[a]Crime activity is defined as including all major and minor speeches (including mentions), news conferences, interviews, statements, messages, and letters related to crime.

Source: Coded and calculated by the author from successive volumes of the paper version of *Public Papers of the Presidents* (Washington, D.C.: U.S. Government Printing Office) and the electronic version obtained in *World Book Encyclopedia: American Reference Library* (Orem, Utah: Western Standard Publishing Company). Format of table is derived from Lyn Ragsdale, *Vital Statistics on the Presidency: Washington to Clinton,* rev. ed. (Washington, D.C.: Congressional Quarterly Press, 1998).

THE HISTORY OF PRESIDENTS AND CRIME POLICY

Prior to the 1930s, the federal government—and particularly presidents overseeing the executive branch—had focused very little effort in the area of crime control.[71] Presidents were simply relegated to a few methods for dealing with crime indirectly, including the appointment of federal judges, the nomination of Supreme Court justices, the appointment of personnel to the Department of Justice, and dealing with the constitutionally granted power of pardons.[72] It was not until the twentieth century that presidents began utilizing the issue of crime as a political issue, one in which they could take a leadership role, influence public opinion, and place crime on their agenda. (See Box 4.4.) Although several presidents spoke on the issue of crime, such as President Taft in 1905, the majority of these speeches were mostly isolated to small groups, such as the International Association of Chiefs of Police in the early twentieth century.[73]

Hoover

It was President Hoover who first articulated the need for the government—and specifically the president—to become involved in the issue of crime when he explained,

> It may be said by some that the larger responsibility for the enforcement of laws against crime rests with State and local authorities and it does not concern the Federal Government. But it does concern the President of the United States, both as a citizen and as the one upon whom rests the primary responsibility of leadership for the establishment of standards of law enforcement in this country. Respect for law and obedience to law does not distinguish between Federal and State laws—it is a common conscience.[74]

This speech was given at the height of federal concern over the increasing problem in crime due to the passage of the Volstead Act and the advent of prohibition in the United States. A dry United States created a growth industry in the underground import, manufacturing, and distribution of illegal alcohol, all contributing factors to the rising crime rates. President Hoover was not only the first to truly take up the rhetoric of crime but also the first to begin addressing the issue of crime via federal powers of office.[75]

In the same year as his speech on crime, Herbert Hoover created the National Commission on Law Observance and Enforcement to conduct the first comprehensive survey on the American Criminal Justice System.[76] The president appointed Judge Wickersham to chair what would be referred to as the "Wickersham Commission."[77] Until then, several states and local jurisdictions had conducted crime surveys, but the majority of the survey recommendations focused on state and local crime problems, meaning that the Wickersham Commission was in fact the first national survey on crime. Although the majority of citizens believed that the primary intent and focus of the commission was prohibition, the commission published fourteen reports, including *The Causes of Crime, Prosecution,* and *Police.* Each of these volumes concluded that there was a need for law observance by all citizens and the increased need for law enforcement primarily among state and local law enforcement. Although all fourteen reports would be issued throughout the years 1930 and 1931, reporting a number of findings and making a meticulous, detailed, and comprehensive agenda for criminal justice reform, the agenda was never translated into legislative policy. Given the problems the country faced with the Depression, it was not feasible to implement the required administrative bureaucratic structure, legislative authority, and a large budgetary allocation in order to implement the agenda. Therefore, the first national commission on crime created a plethora of recommendations on criminal justice reform but spurred no action.

Franklin Roosevelt

Among President Franklin D. Roosevelt's first acts in office was the repeal of the Volstead Act in 1933, and the office of the president's attention to crime began to wane. However, this did not stop the federal administration from expanding into other areas of crime, such as narcotics, thus creating the foundation for federal crime control activity in the latter half of the twentieth century.

Eisenhower and Kennedy

It was not until the Eisenhower administration that crime resurfaced as a presidential issue with a focus on the rising rate of juvenile crime in the late 1950s caused primarily by the increase in the number of teenagers in the United States of the post–World War II baby-boom generation. As these teenagers became adults, they became the concern of President Kennedy, and coupled with the awareness of a rapidly expanding crime syndicate, crime was once again on the presidential agenda.[78] It was the Kennedy administration that would begin defining and expanding the federal role in crime control for the latter half of the twentieth century despite his short tenure as president.[79] As one author stated, "The anti-crime initiatives of John Kennedy, while neither comprehensive nor politically and philosophically well integrated, were nevertheless responsible for much of the current context of federal involvement in programmatic solutions."[80] Surprisingly, however, it was the failed candidacy of the Republican nominee for president in 1964 that would receive the credit for launching crime to the forefront of not only the president's agenda but the American agenda as well.

Johnson

The 1964 presidential election campaign between Barry Goldwater and Lyndon B. Johnson has come to be considered as the watershed event that placed crime on the national agenda and moved the federal government further into the area of crime.[81] Goldwater seized on an issue that he and his strategists felt was a significant concern of the American people, as crime rates were reported to have risen over 15 percent in the first six months of 1964. In addition, it is important to note that the number of incidents over racial violence was sporadic throughout the United States at this time but was widely reported in the newspapers. That Goldwater was attempting to capitalize on the "law-and-order" issue[82] is evident in his acceptance speech before the Republican convention:

> Tonight there is violence in our streets, corruption in our highest offices, aimlessness among our youth, anxiety among our elderly. . . . The growing menace in our country tonight, to personal safety, to life, to limb and property, in homes, in churches, on the playgrounds and at places of business, particularly in our great cities, is the mounting concern of every thoughtful citizen in the United States.[83]

Despite losing the election, Goldwater's attention to the crime issue placed it on the Johnson administration's agenda and greatly expanded on what the Kennedy administration initiated. Johnson, with Robert Kennedy at the head of the Department of Justice, began focusing heavily on organized crime and the growing problems of drug abuse, gun control, and the rise in crime and racial tensions in his own backyard, Washington D.C.[84] Although Johnson's administration was focused primarily on the "war on poverty," part of his agenda was in reality a "war on crime," which was actualized through the passage of the Omnibus Crime Control and Safe Streets Act of 1968 and the creation of the Law Enforcement Assistance Administration. When passed, this federal policy was the largest, most comprehensive federal crime control package in the history of the United States and utilized a broad array of measures to address the crime problem, primarily through power, influence, and money.

President Johnson, like President Hoover, appointed a national commission to begin conducting research, generating solutions to the criminal justice system, and thereby creating an agenda for reform. The President's Commission on Law Enforcement and the Administration of Justice was appointed in 1965 and was chaired by Attorney General Katzenbach and is more commonly referred to as the "Katzenbach Commission."[85] The Katzenbach Commission differed from the Wickersham Commission in that its mandate was to study the nation's response to crime and the focus on "the administration of criminal justice."[86] In other words, this commission was concerned primarily with how the criminal justice system could be improved administratively, and the commission focused most of its recommendations on making changes in law enforcement as well as the courts and corrections components of the system. The premise behind this approach was that if the system could be improved, crime rates would decrease. The Katzenbach Commission, like the Wickersham Commission before it, published several reports with detailed agendas; however, unlike the Wickersham Commission, many of the recommendations of the President's Commission would see legislative action. For example, the Drug Abuse Control Amendment of 1965, the Narcotic Addict Rehabilitation Act of 1966, and the Juvenile Delinquency Prevention and Control Act of 1968 were all derived from recommendations by the Katzenbach Commission.[87] However, it was the final recommendations made by the commission, as reported in the general report titled *The Challenge of Crime in a Free Society*, where over 200 recommendations were made, that would formulate the first omnibus crime legislation in the history of the United States.[88] The recommendations essentially called for the federal government to expand its financial support of the criminal justice system at the state and local levels, and it was from this platform that President Johnson launched the "Safe Streets and Crime Control Act of 1967." Despite some political maneuvering on the bill and a delay of one year, a watered-down version of the bill was passed, and on June 19, 1968, President Johnson signed into law the Omnibus Crime Control and Safe Streets Act of 1968.[89]

The Omnibus Crime Control and Safe Streets Act of 1968 focused its attention on all aspects of the criminal justice system, but the majority of the legislation, the budget it fostered, and the eventual allocation of resources were geared toward the police.[90] To pursue this policy, the Law Enforcement Assistance Administration (LEAA) was created under the Department of Justice to assist state and local law enforcement agencies in a wide variety of measures, including (1) the law enforcement education program, which would promote further education and training to law enforcement personnel; (2) the National Institute of Law Enforcement and Criminal Justice, which would assist law enforcement in research and development to upgrade their crime-fighting capabilities; (3) the National Criminal Justice Information and Statistics Service to provide assistance in data collection and information sharing; (4) technical assistance and training to state and local law enforcement agencies; and, the most significant role, (5) block grants delivered to states through the establishment of state planning agencies that would allow each state to develop its own plans for improving law enforcement through the delivery of subgrants to local police.[91] As block grants were the main method by which the federal government could assist the state and local agencies, it is not surprising that the demand increased from a $25 million allocation in 1969 to a $414 million allocation in 1972, an increase of 1,600 percent in just four years.[92] In addition, Congress amended the Safe Streets Act by passing the Crime Control Act of 1973, which continued the funding to states and increased state control over the block grants.[93] While this appears to help the state and local governments, the problem was found in the details of narrowly defined grant applications, oversight into the use of grant money, and the mandates placed on the state and local governments. By 1980, the LEAA had delivered over $8 billion to state and local agencies to address the issue of crime.[94] However, in the last few years of the LEAA, the organization was left underfunded and was considered a failure because of the methods of block grant delivery through the state planning agencies.[95] The agency was quickly and quietly phased out by the Reagan administration in 1982, only to be replaced by several new and "innovative" Department of Justice agencies.

Nixon

Although Goldwater had been the first presidential candidate to campaign on the "law and order" theme, it was not until President Nixon entered the White House that crime control rhetoric would begin to translate into a more defined policy application. Nixon adopted policies and budget expenditures in the Omnibus Crime Control and Safe Streets Act of 1968 that reflected a focus on the crime control model of increasing arrests, speedy trials, and harsh punishments. The efforts to fight organized crime and drug abuse were redoubled, the criminal justice system was greatly enhanced, and the first "war on drugs" was launched.[96] While the accomplishments of the president's agenda were limited, he did manage to create what would eventually become the Drug Enforcement Agency to develop a strong tie between the federal and state governments through the allocation of monetary funds, and he dramatically increased the rhetoric on crime in regard to the institution of the presidency.[97] In essence, Nixon legitimized and institutionalized crime as an item on the president's agenda and moved the emphasis from a mixture of punishment and rehabilitation policy to one focusing strictly on "law and order."

Ford and Carter

The two presidential administrations that followed would focus on the topic of crime but through different means. President Ford, primarily because of his short tenure after the resignation of President Nixon, would merely continue to emphasize the policies of his predecessor and continue much of the law-and-order rhetoric. And President Carter spent most of his tenure attempting to deal with the "runaway" bureaucracy, particularly the LEAA, which was the most visible of the Department of Justice agencies that had become increasingly large in both budget and personnel.

Reagan

With the election of President Ronald Reagan, the law-and-order politics and the presidential rhetoric on crime reached a new level.[98] The war on drugs was renewed once again, a war on crime was launched, and a refocusing on the victim in the criminal event became a key component of President Reagan's agenda on crime.[99] In addition, renewed efforts to address organized crime, support of the right to bear arms, an effort to address pornography (especially child pornography), prison reform, juvenile crime, and criminal code revisions all found their way onto Reagan's crime control agenda.[100]

It was as a result of Ronald Reagan's restoration of law-and-order politics that Congress, because of and to some degree in spite of Reagan, began taking a very active role in crime legislation.[101] Very early in Reagan's administration, after the assassination attempt on his life, Congress began pushing for some form of gun control legislation that Reagan continued to oppose. Legislation was eventually passed in 1986 but was then rolled back by subsequent legislation in 1988.[102] In addition to gun control legislation, Reagan renewed the call for drug control legislation, and Congress passed several bills, including the Anti-Drug Abuse Act of 1986, which increased the penalties for drug use, increased authority for seizures and forfeitures, and focused heavily on expanding the federal criminal justice system to target the international drug trade, and the Anti-Drug Abuse Act of 1988, which expanded the 1986 act by increasing penalties even further and imposing the death penalty for drug trafficking and again expanded the federal budget to address the drug problem, including the creation of the cabinet-level director known as the "drug czar."[103] Congress also targeted street crime by passing the Comprehensive Crime Control Act of 1984, which overhauled the federal sentencing system, tightened the legal definition of insanity, and required minimum mandatory sentences for career criminals, and the Crime Control Act of 1990, which created new laws, new programs, and, most important, an increased budget to address the problems of crime.[104] All these legislative acts greatly expanded the federal

BOX 4.4
Presidents and Their Crime Control Policies

Kennedy	Had four primary criminal justice issues: organized crime, juvenile crime, youth delinquency, and legal counsel for indigent offenders.
Johnson	Established the Commission on Law Enforcement and the Administration of Justice to discover the causes of crime and better ways to prevent it; felt that crime control was the first duty of local law enforcement but that the federal government could help; supported outlawing all wiretapping, creating new methods to prevent juvenile delinquents from becoming criminals, adding controls on sales of firearms, and fighting illegal drug use.
Nixon	As the first "law-and-order" president, he acknowledged that crime was a local issue but that the federal government could help. He fought against unsolicited pornographic material, organized crime, street crime, narcotics, and crime in the District of Columbia. He supported juvenile delinquency prevention programs, revision of the federal criminal code, victims' rights, the war on drugs, drug treatment and rehabilitation programs, and grants to states.
Ford	Had many crime control issues on his agenda, including gun control, constitutional protections restricting the search efforts of law enforcement personnel, capital punishment for shooting a police officer, mandatory sentencing, pretrial diversion, and the prosecution of white-collar crime, political corruption, and other crimes in high places.
Carter	Did not put crime high on his agenda; supported criminal code reform, judicial reform, wiretap reform, antitrust enforcement and competition, and anticrime programs for the District of Columbia.
Reagan	Supported victims' rights, the death penalty, and the right to own handguns and fought against illicit drug use, organized crime, and pornography, especially child pornography.
George H. W. Bush	Supported mandatory sentences for drug offenders and the death penalty for drug kingpins, changes in the exclusionary rule, limiting habeas corpus appeals, limits on semiautomatic firearms and pretrial preventive detention for cases involving firearms, and adding more federal agents to help fight crime.
Clinton	Supported "three-strikes" legislation, passage of the Brady Bill, and other gun control legislation; proposed more federal agents and local peosecutors to crack down on illegal gun trafficking and dealers; and supported the Hate Crimes Prevention Act, the Violence Against Women Act, and his "100,000 Cops" plan to patrol the streets of America under the tenets of community policing.
George W. Bush	Focused early on school resource officers to prevent school shootings and after September 11, 2001, emphasized tougher antiterrorism laws, such as the USA PATRIOT Act and the creation of the Department of Homeland Security, and Drug enforcement.

Source: Adapted from the *Public Papers of the Presidents of the United States* (Washington, D.C.: U.S. Government Printing Office, 1961–2005).

involvement in crime and created a renewed war on drugs, leading Congress into a steady diet of crime-related bills throughout the 1980s that would grow into a voracious appetite in the 1990s. The issue of crime was once again at the forefront of America's agenda, the law-and-order concepts of Nixon were extended, and the politics of crime witnessed a strict adherence to the conservative ideology.

George H. W. Bush

The politics of crime and the development of a singular focus on the conservative ideology are perhaps best captured through the presidency of George H. W. Bush, ranging from his presidential campaign to his administration's policies on crime. During the 1988 presidential campaign, the law-and-order theme once again became the centerpiece of a Republican presidential nominee, and the conservative focus on punishment over rehabilitation is perhaps best articulated in one of his campaign ads. A convicted murderer, Willie Horton, had been released from a prison in Boston, Massachusetts, on a weekend furlough and raped a young woman. George Bush's opponent, Michael Dukakis, was the Democratic governor of Massachusetts at the time of Horton's crime. The political advertisement was utilized to highlight that punishment is preferred over rehabilitation and that Dukakis was soft on crime. One additional important issue centered on the ad's highlighting the fact that Willie Horton was black and the victim was white, playing not only to the criminal issue but to the racial issue as well.[105] This campaign ad set the tone for the president's agenda on crime.

President Bush's agenda on crime was as conservative as President Reagan's and was highlighted by a renewed war on drugs linking the federal and state criminal justice system through new policy and budgeting and focusing on various items related to violent crime. During his four-year tenure, President Bush expanded the criminal justice system at the federal level, increased the government's attention to crime, and entrenched the presidential rhetoric on crime even deeper. Bush was so committed to the issue of crime control that in his 1992 State of the Union Address, he went so far as to call for a "major renewed investment in fighting violent street crime," articulating that "it saps our strength and hurts our faith in our society, and in our future together."[106]

Clinton

In what is perhaps the most ironic twist of fate in regard to the politics of crime, the campaign theme of crime and violence utilized by President Bush in 1988 to win the White House was utilized by a Democrat, President-Elect Clinton, in 1992. Clinton's ability to steal the high ground on this issue may have contributed to Bush's defeat. Clinton surrounded himself with police officers, proposed adding 100,000 police officers to America's streets, spoke of increasing boot camps, and criticized the Bush administration for losing the war on crime.[107] Clinton also campaigned widely for the death penalty and went so far as to demonstrate his resolve over the issue that he interrupted his campaign to fly back to Arkansas in order to preside over two executions.[108] The politics of crime were no longer divided between liberals and conservatives or Democrats and Republicans but had become a singular ideology, namely, the conservative ideology. Now the goal was to see who could be "tougher" on crime.

President Clinton, on entering the White House, continued to make the claim that he was tough on crime, and throughout 1993 and 1994 he continued to call for legislation on crime and for a comprehensive crime control package that would adhere to many of his campaign promises. What resulted was a bipartisan Congress passing the Violent Crime Control and Law

Enforcement Act of 1994, which was signed by President Clinton in the fall of 1994. This act became the most comprehensive and expensive federal crime control package in the nation's history, at a total cost of $36 billion to be expended between the years 1994 and 2000. And it became one of the most consistently conservative crime control packages that was supported and signed into law by a Democratic president. The act provided funding to hire 100,000 new police officers, build more prisons, create new drug courts, and target crime prevention and domestic violence against women, and it increased the number of federal law enforcement officers and included funding to target both illegal immigrants and street gangs.[109] In addition, the act included numerous laws that enhanced the federal use of the death penalty, created mandatory minimum penalties for numerous crimes, created a "three-strikes" law at the federal level, and increased the punishment for illicit drugs, unlawful use of firearms, terrorism, child pornography, crimes against children, and computer crimes. Despite much talk and discussion over a few programs oriented on offender counseling, drug therapy, and the much-discussed "Midnight Basketball program,"[110] the dominant theme within the Violent Crime Control and Law Enforcement Act of 1994 was the conservative ideology. Crime was no longer (if it ever was) the dominant theme of the Republican Party, and the dichotomy of two crime ideologies had definitively dissolved into one conservative ideology.

This reality was underscored in the 1996 presidential campaign between President Clinton and the Republican presidential nominee, Bob Dole. Neither of the candidates had an upper hand on the crime issue, primarily because both candidates were espousing the same solutions. If anyone could be said to have had the advantage, it would have been President Clinton, for beyond being an incumbent, he had supported and won passage of the Violent Crime Control and Law Enforcement Act of 1994, crime rates were falling, and he was endorsed by one of the most conservative organizations in the nation, the Fraternal Order of Police. However, despite these factors, Clinton continued to call for a focus on teenage drug use and curfews and supported school uniforms while also calling for the building of more prisons, an expansion of the death penalty, and targeting violent offenders. Dole, on the other hand, was calling for tougher drug policy, prison construction, harsher penalties for juvenile offenders, and targeting violent offenders. With the win by President Clinton for a second term, the emphasis continued to be on the "100,000 Cops" initiative, which was expanded to "150,000 Cops" through congressional legislation in 2000.

George W. Bush

In the 2000 election, Governor George W. Bush of Texas was running on the Republican ticket while Vice President Al Gore received the Democratic Party's nomination to run for president. Despite the fact that crime had been falling for the previous eight years, crime policy remained an issue for both candidates during the election.[111] Both candidates attempted to capitalize on the issue of guns because of the increased public concern over the availability of weapons by students in a series of violent school shootings in the latter half of the 1990s. In addition, Marion and Farmer point out that both candidates utilized a number of symbolic statements to gain support for their campaigns' position on crime while offering only little in the way of substantive proposals.[112] In the end, the actual election itself would become the more contested issue, but once the Supreme Court issued its decision, Governor Bush was inaugurated as the forty-third president. His policies regarding crime control consisted of only minor changes related to existing policies, but after the terrorist attack of September 11 2001, his administration's emphasis, as it relates to crime, shifted to one of antiterrorism.[113]

Barack H. Obama

President Obama has engaged in no major crime initiative since taking office. His administration has continued many of the policies of past presidents and he makes appearances and speeches at what have become annual events, such as remarks at the National Peace Officers Memorial Service, and he has issued proclamations for National Child Abuse Prevention Month and National D.A.R.E. Day. Perhaps the most significant change coming from the Obama Administration was in the May 2010 shift in the National Drug Control Strategy which emphasized community treatment and prevention programs, as well as the role of health care providers in addressing the problem of drugs. The shift, however, was met with little attention and Obama has not continued to speak on the issue.

THE PRESIDENT'S AGENDA AND CRIME POLICY

The president's agenda is but one aspect of the total government agenda, but it carries significant weight in the realm of moving policies from the systemic to the institutional agenda. The old saying that "the president proposes and Congress disposes" highlights this importance in the agenda-setting process.[114] As Kingdon explains, "No other single actor in the political system has quite the capability of the president to set agendas in given policy areas for all who deal with those policies."[115] Shull also highlights the fact that presidents have "a far greater role in initiating national policies in the 20th century than they did previously,"[116] and Miroff believes that the president has come to "monopolize the public space."[117] Finally, as Bosso colorfully articulates, "the presidency is the single most powerful institutional lever for policy breakthrough," and he "is the political system's thermostat, capable of heating up or cooling down the politics of any single issue or of an entire platter of issues."[118] Bosso then further states, in relation to the process of moving issues onto the government's agenda, that "presidential intervention is a key variable."[119] Recognizing the importance of the president's agenda in relation to the total government agenda, it is important to understand what is meant by the president's agenda, why the president has so much influence, and how this relates to crime policy.

Paul Light's seminal book *The President's Agenda* has become the definitive book on understanding the president's agenda, especially as it relates to domestic policy choices.[120] Light explains that

> the President's agenda is a remarkable list. It is rarely written down. It constantly shifts and evolves. It is often in flux even for the President and the top staff. Items move onto the agenda one day and off the next. Because of its status in the policy process, the President's agenda is the subject of intense conflict. The infighting is resolved sometimes through mutual consent and 'collegial' bargaining, sometimes through marked struggle and domination.[121]

Light goes on to say that

> the President's agenda is perhaps best understood as a *signal*. It indicates what the President believes to be the most important issues facing his administration. It identifies what the President finds to be the most appropriate alternatives for solving the problems. It identifies what the President deems to be the highest priorities.[122]

In sum, the president's agenda stands as a fluid list of what the president and his top staff consider to be the most important problems, coupled with what are considered to be the best alternatives for solving these problems, to create a prioritized "list" of policy-related items. However, like understanding the process of how items find their way from the systemic agenda to the institutional agenda, which explains why the government chooses certain policies for its agenda, it is equally important to understand how certain policies, such as crime, find their way onto the president's agenda.

The key, according to Light, comes from understanding presidential power and the resources that presidents have at their disposal.[123] Light articulates that presidents have internal resources, such as time, information, expertise, and energy.[124] Kingdon adds to the list institutional resources, "including the veto and the prerogative to hire and fire"; organizational resources, such as the fact that the executive branch has a more enhanced ability for making unitary decisions than Congress; a command of public attention, "which can be converted into pressure on other government officials to adopt the president's agenda"; and, finally, like Light, the president's involvement (time and energy) in specific policy issues.[125] Light also delineates several external resources available to the president, such as party support in Congress, public approval, electoral margin, and patronage.[126] These resources must then be understood as being either increasing or diminishing resources. For example, in regard to the internal sources, presidents face the increasing resources of expertise and information. These two resources are not always readily available to a president when he enters office and must be built over his tenure in office. However, the other two internal resources are diminishing resources—time and energy—as the president moves further into his term. There is a clear conflict in these internal resources. As the president moves further into his term, he is finally in a position of having enhanced his expertise in the political arena and has the information to affect policy, but he is assuredly running out of time and, most likely, energy to affect said policies. In regard to external resources, party support in Congress often diminishes in the midterm elections, and public approval typically diminishes throughout the president's four years, leaving the president with little capital at the end of his term. Thus, all these resources, internal and external, come to bear on the president's ability to place items on his agenda and to push them through Congress to achieve a legislative victory.

Light goes on to explain the process of how items find their way onto the president's agenda by first looking at the opportunities the president has for making choices.[127] He notes that the policy cycle, often dictated by the political election cycle, influences the items a president places on his agenda.[128] Light also explains that presidents select issues not only because they are pressing systemic issues but also because the president considers his chances for reelection (establishing himself historically), and because he wants to see "good policy" pass the legislature.[129] In a sense, the president is seeking benefits from the policies he chooses. Light then further explains that the source of policy ideas plays a role in the policies the president places on his agenda.[130] The president may be influenced by external sources, such as Congress, national events and crises, bureaucrats, public opinion polls, and political parties, interest groups, and the media. In addition, he may be influenced by internal sources, such as the party platform under which he ran his campaign, the campaign promises he made along the way, and members of his staff. All these factors come to bear on the president, who must then make the decision as to what issues to address and what issues not to address.

Once the president makes the decision to have his administration move forward on a particular issue, such as crime, he must then prioritize his agenda and determine how best to address each issue.[131] This is generally done by establishing the direction he wants to take the policy issue but is then forced to make several choices along the way. He must determine whether the program will be a new one or an old one and whether he will push the policy through legislative or administrative means, and he must determine the size of the program and what type of budget the program will receive.[132] He must then weigh the political cost, economic cost, and the technical ("workability") costs of the policy proposal before moving on the policy.[133] Finally, the president must determine how committed he is to the policy as it moves through the political process.[134] This last part ultimately returns to the issue of the president's resources and how he chooses to employ them. He must determine how much support already exists for the policy (external resources) and how much time and energy he, himself, is willing to devote to the policy (internal resources).

Recognizing the importance of the president's agenda in defining the issues that the national government places on the institutional agenda, it is important then to understand the president's agenda as it relates to crime. There are a number of reasons that presidents have come to focus on the topic of crime. These reasons tend to fall into three categories: policy, political, and ideological explanations. These various explanations, as they relate to crime policy, give the president an enormous amount of power to influence both public opinion and Congress in order to obtain legislative victories, often considered the mark of a successful president.

Policy Explanations

The policy explanations for why presidents focus on crime control policy first and foremost are because of the nature of crime. This first explanation may simply lie in two realities. The first is that crime is inevitable and that many crimes will rise to the level of national awareness. Second, throughout the twentieth century, presidents have become more and more a focal point for American policy, politics, and leadership.[135]

CRISIS   When an international crisis occurs, people look to the president for guidance, direction, and leadership. Likewise, when there is a major national crisis, such as a riot, mass murder, or bombing, people look to the president. As a result, the president is naturally inclined to respond or, rather, is forced into responding to the event. This leadership role carries some political influence, and these dramatic events can have either a positive or a negative effect in that it can either unify the nation around the president or dramatize and highlight the nation's conflicts and problems.[136] Examples of presidents and national crises revolving around criminal related events include President Hoover and the Lindbergh baby kidnapping,[137] President Johnson and the series of urban riots occurring in a number of major cities across the United States,[138] President Clinton and the World Trade Center and Oklahoma City bombings, and President Bush and the terrorist attacks of September 11. In each of these cases, the public looked to the president for guidance, and the presidents responded. Perhaps President Johnson explained it best in his memoirs, which were published in 1971, when he stated, "Somehow, in the minds of most Americans the breakdown of local authority became the fault of the federal government.[139]

In the end, whether or not crime is a state or a local issue does not seem to matter much. What matters in the case of a crime that rises to the level of national attention is that presidents assume their leadership role. Most presidents, even Johnson, have not ignored this responsibility.

SUBSTANTIVE POLICY   The second explanation for why presidents focus on crime control policy may be derived from the possibility that crime is the type of issue that gives the president the ability to engage in substantive policy. The concept of substantive policy, as utilized here, is meant to denote the fact that the policy passed has a real and demonstrative nature about itself. This then allows presidents the capability of passing "good policy," for, as Light explains, "there can be little question that Presidents do engage in the search for programmatic benefits" and that

"Presidents do have notions of what constitutes good policy."[140] This can also be further explained in relation to the discussion by Theodore Lowi, who argues that "good policy" today is seen as "one which is open-ended, ambiguous, and flexible,"[141] while he argues effective policies require clarity, choice, and closure.[142] In other words, according to Lowi, policies should be more definitive. Crime lends itself to all these factors in that crime policy can often be real, demonstrative, and definitive in nature.

There are numerous examples of the substantive aspects of crime policy. One such example can be derived from President Johnson's Crime Commission in the 1960s, which published the report known as *The Challenge of Crime in a Free Society*.[143] This resulted in the legislation known as the Omnibus Crime Control and Safe Streets Act of 1968, which created the LEAA within the Department of Justice. This agency would create a program known as the Law Enforcement Education Program, designed to assist and encourage police officers to attend college and work toward furthering their education. This program would ultimately contribute to the creation and evolution of a number of criminal justice programs in institutes of higher education today.[144] Other examples include the rapid increase of federal prison facilities built across the United States during the last two decades of the twentieth century, which some have come to term the "prison-industrial complex."[145] Regardless of whether one considers prison expansion a "good" or "bad" policy, it can clearly be categorized as being a substantive policy and has a demonstrative effect. Finally, another example was President Clinton's "100,000 Cops" initiative. Although this was most certainly used for its symbolic effect, one can hardly argue that the passage of the Violent Crime Control and Law Enforcement Act of 1994 by Congress, which allocated $8.8 billion for local law enforcement and has been dispersed to police agencies across the country to hire additional officers, train them, and purchase new equipment, was merely "symbolic" in nature.

SYMBOLIC POLICY   Having stated that the second key reason for presidential involvement in crime control policy is for substantive policy reasons, it must also be stated that there is still much validity in the assertions that crime is often used extensively by presidents for purposes of symbolic politics.[146] The pioneering work by Joseph Gusfield[147] and Murray Edelman[148] provided much of our understanding about the use of symbols. Edelman explains that "every symbol stands for something other than itself, and it also evokes an attitude, a set of impressions, or a pattern of events associated through time, through space, through logic, or through imagination with the symbol."[149] He goes further in saying that "symbols become that facet of experiencing the material world that gives it a specific meaning."[150] In other words, symbols derive their meaning not from content but from the value of how people perceive them. This has clear application for politics in that politicians can utilize political symbols to convey a value, an attitude, or a sentiment without having to provide details or issue substantive policies. Political symbols can then be defined as "the communication by political actors to others for a purpose, in which the specific object referred to conveys a larger range of meaning, typically with emotional, moral, or psychological impact. This larger meaning need not be independently or factually true, but will tap ideas people want to believe in as true."[151]

Presidents have most assuredly found the use of political symbols in the area of crime policy to be of significant value.[152] Scheingold has explained that "the symbolic forms that define the politicization of street crime are more salient in national than in local politics."[153] Several other authors have explained that crime was used in the early 1960s by "presidents and would-be presidents" who "used the crime issue for a short-term political advantage."[154] They further explained that "crime in the streets as a national issue was *manufactured* and milked by presidential candidates, who began a sorry stream of symbolic politics rather than attending to practicalities and management in the war on crime."[155] As a result, presidents became engaged in the issue of street crime, but for the most part they have dealt more with symbolic politics than with substantive politics. The reason for this focus being the role of the national government in crime control policy is still somewhat limited, and presidents have succeeded more in politicizing crime policy rather than in federalizing crime policy. As Scheingold has concluded, "The policy limitations of the politics of law and order are, in part, a product of the symbolic character of politicization."[156] Despite these limitations, presidents for nearly three decades have continued to draw on the issue of crime, and a large portion of their attention has been purely symbolic.

VALENCE ISSUE   A related explanation to the argument that crime is a symbolic issue comes in the fact that crime is also a valence issue. A valence issue can be defined as one in "which the overwhelming number of voters have a single position" and in which "prevailing opinion is so strong that no opposing position seems possible."[157] The concept was actually first articulated by Butler and Stokes in their book *Political Change in Britain*.[158] The point these authors were trying to make was that most issues are position issues, where there are clearly two opposing viewpoints to the issue.[159] In sum, valence issues are those issues on which people demonstrate a consensus but may disagree as to the means by which to address the issue; politicians use these valence issues, coupled with symbolics, to make themselves appear positive, while their opponents are painted in a negative manner.

Crime is most assuredly a valence issue. As some authors have stated, "No one is for it; therefore being against it is a safe political issue."[160] As Jones has explained, "For a politician in an election to decry crime does not lead an opponent to defend it. Valence issues are important because politicians often link the raising of an issue to a policy solution; a crime wave demands harsher penalties."[161] This then feeds into the process whereby politicians utilize the positive and negative symbols by trying to paint their opponents as "soft on crime" and themselves as "tough on crime." What generally results is a consensus that crime is an important issue, but the debate then shifts to one centered on the means by which crime should be addressed. In generic terms, it falls into the punishment-versus-rehabilitation debate. Although the policy issue of crime is replete with many position issues, such as the death penalty and gun control, it is also teeming with many examples of valence issues, such as child abuse, alcohol abuse, and drug abuse as well as the issue of "street crime" itself.[162]

Presidents have also played heavily on the fact that street crime is a valence issue. As Scheingold explains, "National politicians also have a strong incentive to politicize street crime . . . for them it provides a unifying theme and thus a valence issue."[163] As a result, "in national politics, especially presidential politics, street crime has been a valence issue—and more."[164] Scheingold further highlights the fact that "not only is there overwhelming agreement that street crime should be reduced, but it has the added attraction of arousing strong emotions—something capable of gaining a firm grip on the public imagination."[165] One such example, illustrated by Jones, is the increased attention Vice President Bush paid to the issue of drug abuse during his 1988 campaign and on entering the office of the presidency despite any evidence that there was in fact a drug epidemic.[166] He was successfully able to portray his opponent, Governor Michael Dukakis (D-Mass.), as "weak on crime" while strengthening his position as being "tough on crime." President Bush, in his first major television address on September 5, 1989, would then announce his war on drugs. What occurred afterward was an eightfold increase in television coverage of the problem[167] and a thirty-six-percentage-point increase in drugs being listed as the "most important problem facing the country."[168] In the end, "a peak in awareness of the drug problem was caused primarily by presidential attention to it."[169] Bush had effectively used the valence issues of crime and drugs not only to win the office of the presidency but also to continue garnering support for addressing an issue that had little to no opposition.

RACIAL ISSUE   Finally, a more deeply related explanation for why presidents have focused their attention on the issue of crime draws on the symbolic and valence discussion to emphasize one of the most sinister but effective uses of the crime issue, and that is to link the issue of crime with racism. There is a growing body of evidence that as the civil rights movement began to take hold and public sentiment toward minorities, mainly blacks, began to change, it was no longer politically feasible to openly decry blacks.[170] Research indicates that to some degree this phenomenon had been driven underground and replaced with an emphasis on decrying those social events that are perceived to be highly associated with blacks.[171] For example, the issues of welfare and affirmative action are often associated with blacks and are decried by a large portion of Americans. What some research has begun to suggest is that negative opinions toward these policies are partly a result of masked racist sentiments.[172] In regard to crime, there is also a growing body of research that has begun to uncover this phenomenon, demonstrating that in many instances hatred for "criminals" and "drug abusers" is really a code word for hatred toward blacks and other minorities.[173] As a result, presidents, whether intentionally or not, by focusing their attention on crime policy, may in reality be connecting racist sentiments with anticrime sentiments. Hence, crime becomes a symbol for racism.

Although it is clearly difficult to disentangle the intent of the president in this regard, there is some evidence that this has been used by presidents as "a shorthand signal to a crucial group of white voters, for broader issues of social disorder, evoking powerful ideas about authority, status, morality, self-control, and race."[174] One clear example comes from the Nixon administration in comments made by Nixon's two key advisers, H. R. Haldeman and John Ehrlichman. Haldeman is quoted from an entry in his personal diary as saying, "He [President Nixon] emphasized that you have to face the fact that the whole problem is really the blacks. The key is to devise a system that recognizes this while not appearing to."[175] Ehrlichman, in describing the 1968 presidential campaign, explained, "We'll go after the racists. That subliminal appeal to the anti-black voter was always present in Nixon's statements and speeches."[176] In addition, various works by Michael Tonry have demonstrated that both Reagan and Bush were targeting issues of crime and drugs, knowing that there would be an "adverse differential effect on blacks" and that "the justification . . . [was] entirely political."[177] Finally, there is perhaps no better example of crime posited as a surrogate for race than the infamous 1988 presidential campaign commercial detailing the convicted rapist Willie Horton.[178]

In the television commercial, created by a pro-Bush political action committee, Willie Horton, a black male rapist, was granted a weekend furlough by Bush's Democratic challenger, then-Governor Michael Dukakis. During the weekend furlough, Willie Horton raped and murdered a white female victim. The commercial was designed to raise the issue of crime and make the statement that Dukakis was "soft on crime." While it succeeded in the endeavor, it also linked the issue of crime with the offender most often feared by white America, namely, a black male. As Jamieson explains, "The Horton story magnifies fear of crime, identifies that fear with Dukakis, and offers a surefire way of alleviating the anxiety—vote for Bush."[179] As a result, crime in this case became a surrogate for race hatred, and the two issues became linked. While it was not considered acceptable to voice negative attitudes toward blacks, it was perfectly acceptable to target negative attitudes toward criminals.

Political Explanations

The political reasons that presidents engage in crime control policy present an interesting laundry list of explanations. In each of these explanations, presidents at one point or another are attempting to gain politically from their engagement in crime control policy. While presidents may find themselves focused on only one of the political explanations detailed in the following sections, most likely these explanations are working in concert. Therefore, while all these are important considerations for understanding why presidents engage in crime control policy, one is not necessarily more important than the others. All can be equally important explanations.

CAMPAIGNING   The first political explanation lies in the time period before a president assumes the office of the presidency, and that is along the campaign trail. It is during this time that many future presidents first begin utilizing the issue of crime for political purposes, namely, to win votes. The use of substantive, symbolic, and valence politics is often very evident during the presidential campaigns. As presidents are making promises about how they will govern, they are seeking to get their policy views communicated to the public, and they are always looking for new and innovative policies, primarily because the media are always looking for new and interesting stories.[180] As a result, crime policy has become an attractive issue on which to campaign. As Scheingold explains, "Politicians ordinarily gain electoral success by telling the public what it wants to hear . . . when fear of street crime runs high, politicians have every reason to believe that the public is looking for promises to crack down on criminals fairly and expeditiously."[181] In fact, Milakovich and Weis go so far as to say, "Well-publicized concern about the problem of crime is often a prerequisite for a successful political campaign in which crime, either an all-out war or a brush-fire response to an increase or a promised decrease, is made a key issue."[182] As crime is always an issue in the media, providing examples on which to draw, crime has played a role in every presidential campaign since the 1964 election between Johnson and Goldwater.[183] It has also been demonstrated time and time again that crime provides a key issue on which to propose new laws[184] and policy,[185] such as Clinton's "100,000 Cops" (substantive policy); to generate photo and campaign commercial opportunities,[186] such as the candidate being surrounded by uniformed police officers (symbolic politics); and to portray themselves as being "tough on crime" (valence politics).

NATIONAL PARTIES   The second political explanation is closely related to the first, namely, that both the national parties, Republican and Democratic, have included crime as part of their party platforms since the 1960 election year.[187] In fact, while the first modern election party platforms to mention crime consisted of only a few phrases referencing "soaring crime rates," by the 1996 campaign both parties reserved several pages to address the issue of crime and drugs.[188] Although many have concluded that party platforms should not be taken seriously because candidates use them to "run on" and not to "stand on,"[189] there is some evidence that suggests presidents sometime adhere to the party platform and that in many cases presidents up for reelection essentially write the platforms.[190] While adhering to the party platform on crime can assuredly benefit the candidate in regard to the party members themselves, a unified party–president relationship on crime cannot hurt the president and may in fact, by way of communicating the candidate's views on crime, provide a political benefit with the electorate.

TYPES OF CRIME POLICY   The third political explanation deals with the type of policy in which crime can be categorized. Crime has, in one form or fashion, been categorized as all four policy types, including distributive, redistributive, regulatory, and morality. More recent crime policy initiatives have been defined as "pork" by a variety of people[191] or as distributive policies. There is some evidence to suggest that one of the earliest crime policies resulting from the Omnibus Crime Control and Safe Streets Act of 1968, which created the LEAA under the Department of Justice, was essentially a distributive policy. As Cronin, Cronin, and Milakovich explain, "Not only were LEAA funds a generous pork barrel, but everyone seemed to have a piece of the action when it came to how LEAA was to be managed and even what it was supposed to do."[192] The more recent Crime Bill of 1994, the Violent Crime Control and Law Enforcement Act, created a similar agency known as the Office of Community Oriented Policing Services within the Department of Justice and, for over six years, handed out grants for hiring, training, and equipment to any agency that applied. As of the beginning of 2000, over $8 billion in grants had been awarded to state and local agencies throughout the United States, suggesting that crime policy, at least in this case, fits the category of distributive policy.[193]

Crime, for the most part, has long been considered an area of regulatory policy. Meier has suggested that crime control efforts are obviously regulatory in nature when he stated, "At the state and local level, one major form of regulation is the legal restriction of criminal activity."[194] Spitzer has also explained that "crime control legislation, which usually includes specific prohibitions backed by firm sanctions, is classic regulatory policy."[195] Crime's relationship to regulatory policy is perhaps best explained in a historical framework, for, as Eisner has pointed out, "the history of regulation is the history of state economy relations and institutional change."[196] Crime's regulatory policy aspects are historically derived from its relationship at the federal level with the movement in the late nineteenth century to regulate interstate commerce. This would eventually lead to the creation, by President Theodore Roosevelt during the Progressive Era, of what would become the Federal Bureau of Investigation. As the Task Force on the Federalization of Criminal Law, sponsored by the American Bar Association, explains, "The last third of the nineteenth century saw a significant increase in the assertion of federal jurisdiction, marked initially by a series of Congressional statutes dealing with the misuse of the mails and asserting federal jurisdiction in connection with interstate commerce."[197] The New Deal initiatives then created a new burst of federal regulation of crime, largely coming on the heels of the prohibition movement, with a specific flurry of dozens of crime bills in 1934. Then, "almost four decades after the election of Franklin Roosevelt, the nation experienced another burst of regulatory policy-making,"[198] and crime was no exception. Again, the Task Force explained that "in the 1960s and 1970s . . . concern with organized crime, drugs, street violence, and other social ills precipitated a particularly significant rise in federal legislation tending to criminalize activity involving more local conduct, conduct previously left to state regulation."[199] Dilulio has added that the federal government's role in crime also "grew as the power to regulate interstate commerce was more broadly interpreted by the U.S. Supreme Court."[200] Finally, we have seen "in the 1980s and 1990s, the trend to federalize crime has continued dramatically, covering more conduct formerly left exclusively to state prosecution."[201] What had started initially at the end of the nineteenth century as economic regulation ultimately turned into an emphasis on social regulation in the 1960s and its expansion ever since.[202]

Another way of looking at crime policy has been by way of defining it as having the qualities of being both morality and redistributive policy. In the case of crime, these may include such specific issues as drugs, alcohol, prostitution, and gambling, crimes that are often referred to as "victimless crimes."[203] In a sense, these issues can also be defined as redistributive policies in the sense that they are redistributing values rather than income.[204] However, these issues tend to be highly salient and often leave little room for expertise because information by one side is challenged by the other side or is often simply ignored. As a result, these are not issues that presidents obviously want to be drawn into because of their divisiveness and because they tend to split the electorate, but in many cases the salience of the issue forces them into a position to either "choose a side" or attempt to find some type of "common ground" where there often isn't any.

The benefits that a president can derive from this type of policy are clear. Because the distribution of this type of policy is not a zero-sum gain, primarily because "one recipient's allocation" is not "dependent on what another receives,"[205] this creates a win-win situation for the president in that not only can he claim credit for these "particularized benefits" but so can members of Congress. As a result, there is a tendency to "distribute" these benefits universally, across all states, local governments, and, of course, throughout congressional districts. In the end, then, it becomes clear that the only means by which presidents and the federal government as a whole can address the problem of crime is either through regulatory policymaking, coupled with administrative enforcement, or through policy funding.

PUBLIC OPINION   The fourth political explanation for why presidents focus on crime results from his relationship with public opinion. It has been recognized by Brace and Hinckley that "public mobilization is critical if presidents are to succeed,"[206] and this is equally true in the area of crime policy. There is, however, a transcendent advantage to mobilizing public opinion of crime, and that is that public opinion or, rather, public fear of crime has remained relatively steady and high over time.[207] In addition, crime is always a staple of the daily media. As a result, presidents have the capability of capitalizing on these facts by attempting to influence public opinion, thereby making the president's "visibility" on crime become the public's "visibility" on crime.[208] In other words, it is believed that presidents have the ability to influence public opinion of crime.

MEDIA   The fifth political explanation is highly related to the last as well as to many of the other explanations offered, and that is the president's relationship with the media. As the president, by virtue of his office, has the full time and attention of the various forms of media, whatever issue is on the president's agenda most often becomes the media's issue of the moment.[209] Coupled with the fact that most people receive their information through the media[210] and the media report heavily on the issue of crime,[211] this combines to form a relationship that, while difficult to untangle, most certainly has an effect on the American people's perception of crime in the United States. As the president communicates to the American people mainly through the primary forms of media (e.g., television, radio, newspapers, and newsmagazines), the media and the president's access to it become a political explanation for why presidents focus on crime.

INTEREST GROUPS   The sixth and final political explanation lies in the fact that over the past thirty years, there have developed a number of interest groups related to the issue of crime, and they have become more effective in influencing criminal justice policy.[212] While there are certainly the traditional interest groups that often find themselves embroiled in issues of crime control policy, such as the National Rifle Association; Handgun Control, Inc.; and the American Civil Liberties Union, there are a number of well-established and well-organized interest groups that have specifically organized to deal with issues of crime.[213] Finally, a more recent development in this specific area is not the traditional interest group lobbying, where interest groups seek the support of the president, but rather a form of "reverse lobbying" where presidents seek the support of the interest groups.[214] This occurrence, while a relatively new method of public mobilization, was used by President Clinton in his attempts to garner support for his Crime Bill.

Ideological Explanations

One final explanation for the law-and-order presidency comes simply from the possibility that presidents, whether it is something about their character or ideological worldview, feel it is right to address the issue of crime. As Barber has explained, "Character is the way the President orients himself toward life," and a "President's world view consists of his primary, politically relevant beliefs, particularly his conceptions of social causality, human nature, and the central moral conflicts of the time."[215] Therefore, it is possible that something within the president's life may have had a profound impact to have shaped his character "not for the moment"[216] but for life regarding the issue of crime. Equally, the president's life shapes his assumptions and conceptions about how the world works, thus providing a specific worldview in regard to crime, and hence, as president, generates an ideological response to the issue.

An example of the issue of character can be seen in the life of President Ronald Reagan. There is the possibility that his character was shaped by both his parents and many of his early experiences. In regard to his parents, although he reports both as being loving and caring, it is reported that his father was an alcoholic, and this may have contributed to Reagan's profound hatred for drugs and addicts, contributing to his tough stance on drug abuse. One of his early experiences, described by Reagan in his autobiography, may also explain his future stance on crime and centers on his time as a lifeguard. As he explains, "About my second year in high school, I got one of the best jobs I ever had . . . working as a lifeguard at Lowell Park . . . one of the proudest statistics in my life is seventy-seven—the number of people I saved during those seven summers."[217] This concept of being the rescuer, the "lifesaver," can have a profound effect on an individual, and perhaps Reagan saw himself in this role. Hence, when the opportunity came to address problems of crime and drugs, he continued to see himself in this role. Finally, one has to wonder if Reagan's days as a film star, almost always playing the hero, did not have an impact on his character, hence influencing his views on law and order.

Finally, a president's worldview may influence his activity in the area of crime but, more important, may also influence how he goes about addressing the issue. Calder, who has given this a much fuller treatment,[218] explains "that ideological predispositions restrict the President's ability to effect measurable reductions in ordinary crime."[219] As he further explains, "Presidents are not unlike other people in that they arrive at their positions in life as a consequence of the actions and opportunities that they have capitalized on along the way. Their experiences and training have molded their beliefs that are subsequently incorporated in their policy positions."[220] By way of three case studies on the Kennedy, Johnson, and Nixon presidencies, Calder demonstrates that the first two, Kennedy and Johnson, had a functionalist ideology that caused them to view crime as resulting "from the inadequate socialization of the individual into the socially acceptable norms of the community."[221] Hence, their commitments to resolving the issue of crime centered on addressing the social environment, not specifically targeting criminals. Nixon, on the other hand, was demonstrated to have a mechanist ideology that viewed crime as being a result of "poor upbringing and insufficient moral guidance by the family and lack of respect for the law."[222] Hence, his commitment to resolving the crime problem was more of an enforcement of the laws and a demand for the respect of the law.

Impact

Since presidents do not engage in policy without a reason, any and all activity related to crime policy is focused on a particular end. In fact, all presidential activity is usually focused on two particular goals: influencing public opinion and influencing Congress.[223] The reason for this is simple: The office of the president is a constitutionally weak office, and the president's only means of affecting change is through his power to persuade.[224] The reason he attempts to persuade the public is to garner support in Congress. The reason he attempts to persuade Congress is to gain a legislative victory for his administration and party.

Presidents have been found to influence the public through their speeches and rhetoric related to crime.[225] As presidents speak more about the issue of crime, crime becomes more highly salient in the mind of the public and an important problem facing the nation. In fact, controlling for other factors such as media influence and crime rates, the president still has the capability of raising concern over crime among the American people.[226] More specifically, one study has found that the more the president mentions the issue of crime in his State of the Union Address, the more concerned people become.[227] In sum, the more the presidents talk about crime, regardless of whether it is in a substantive or a symbolic manner, the more important the issue of crime becomes for the American people.

The ability of the president to influence the American public on crime is important but only if it assists him in the passage of crime control policy in Congress. One of the most important means of obtaining a legislative victory is to ensure that the president's agenda is the congressional agenda. The agenda of Congress is generally marked by the number and type of committee hearings being held. Research into the ability of the president to influence congressional attention to the crime issue by the increase in congressional committees related to crime has found some support in that often what presidents talk about one year becomes a focus of attention for Congress the next year. As a result, the more presidents focus on the topic of crime, the more Congress holds congressional hearings related to crime.[228] Although gaining the attention of Congress is supportive of the president's ultimate goal—the passage of crime legislation—it is the presidents' ability to influence Congress to pass these laws that in the end has the most impact. In analyzing the presidents' ability to influence Congress in the passage of crime legislation, it has been found that presidents do have some qualified success in obtaining the passage of crime legislation.[229] While the president is not the sole participant in the policy process, his is a very powerful position, and it can generally be summed up that when the president speaks, the public and Congress listen.

STATE GOVERNMENT: GOVERNORS

The executive branch at the state level is the governor's office. (See Box 4.5.) The governor is the state's highest elected official and has many of the same powers and responsibilities as the U.S. president. Governors run for election on a party platform and serve for a four-year term in office. Many states have term limits on the number of times a governor can serve, and most tend to limit it to two consecutive four-year terms. Some states have other qualifications, such as Indiana, which allows governors to succeed themselves once, after which they must take a four-year respite before running again. In the Commonwealth of Virginia, governors can serve more than one term, but they may never succeed themselves; hence, effectively, they are limited to one term in office.

Role in the Policy Process

The governor's role in the public policy process is, in a sense, twofold. Governors serve as the chief executive of the state, much in the same vein as the president of the United States. They propose legislation to the state legislatures, make budget requests on an annual or biannual basis, and sign legislation into law. In addition, they have the power to veto legislation, give the annual

BOX 4.5
State Governors and their Political Affiliation as of June 2010

Alabama	Bob Riley, R	Montana	Brian Schweitzer, D
Alaska	Sean Parnell, R	Nebraska	Dave Heineman, R
Arizona	Jan Brewer, R	Nevada	Jim Gibbons, R
Arkansas	Mike Beebe, D	New Hampshire	John Lynch, D
California	Arnold Schwarzenegger, R	New Jersey	Chris Christie, R
Colorado	Bill Ritter, D	New Mexico	Bill Richardson, D
Connecticut	M. Jodi Rell, R	New York	David Paterson, D
Delaware	Jack Markell, D	North Carolina	Beverly Perdue, D
Florida	Charlie Crist, I	North Dakota	John Hoeven, R
Georgia	Sonny Perdue, R	Ohio	Ted Strickland, D
Hawaii	Linda Lingle, R	Oklahoma	Brad Henry, D
Idaho	Butch Otter, R	Oregon	Ted Kulongoski, D
Illinois	Pat Quinn, D	Pennsylvania	Edward Rendell, D
Indiana	Mitch Daniels, R	Rhode Island	Donald Carcieri, R
Iowa	Chet Culver, D	South Carolina	Mark Sanford, R
Kansas	Mark Parkinson, D	South Dakota	Mike Rounds, R
Kentucky	Steve Beshear, D	Tennessee	Phil Bredesen, D
Louisiana	Bobby Jindal, R	Texas	Rick Perry, R
Maine	John Baldacci, D	Utah	Gary Herbert, R
Maryland	Martin O'Malley, D	Vermont	James H. Douglas, R
Massachusetts	Deval Patrick, D	Virginia	Bob McDonnell, R
Michigan	Jennifer Granholm, D	Washington	Christine Gregoire, D
Minnesota	Tim Pawlenty, R	West Virginia	Joe Manchin, D
Mississippi	Haley Barbour, R	Wisconsin	Jim Doyle, D
Missouri	Jay Nixon, D	Wyoming	Dave Freudenthal, D

State of the State Address, and run the bureaucracy at the state level. As the president is one of the key players at the national level, this makes the governor one of the key policy players at the state level. On the other hand, the governor is also an important player, albeit less powerful, in national politics in that governors also lobby Congress for additional funding for pet projects and particular policies that will benefit their states. In addition to individual lobbying, governors will also lobby collectively. This is often done through the National Governors Association (NGA),[230] which is a forum for all fifty governors to come together to discuss policies that would benefit all their states. More important, however, the NGA is a lobbying group that can place pressure on Congress to pass specific policies proposed by the NGA.

In terms of criminal justice, governors oversee the bureaucracy that is responsible for public safety and emergency management. State-level police agencies were primarily a development in the early twentieth century, with the Pennsylvania State Police creating the first such agency in

1905. Prior to World War II, these agencies were formed as state-level detective bureaus generally involving themselves in cases that affected the state, such as state fraud cases. In the post–World War II era, with the construction of the interstate highway system, state police turned their attention to patrolling the highways and became more identifiable by today's standards regarding what most people think of when they think of state police agencies. There are, however, only 49 state police agencies, as Hawaii does not have the need for interstate patrol.

Many states also developed civil defense agencies during World War II as a means of protecting the home front during the war. Many of these were disbanded or rolled into the departments of public safety. In other states, they became the office of emergency management. In still other states, they were made a part of the state police function. More recently, with the September 11 terrorist attacks, many states, including Alaska, Texas, and New Jersey, have created state offices or departments of homeland security.

Although crime has generally had a history of being a local issue, states have always been looked to for providing additional resources to local governments or as the final level of government for dealing with the issue of crime. In the early twentieth century, the creation of the state police agencies brought the state more into a crime control role, albeit it was severely limited. In the 1920s, many of the states sanctioned surveys that addressed the rising levels of crime and what the states could do to address the various problems associated with crime. More specifically, these surveys often talked about changes in the organizational structure of the criminal justice process and how state oversight could improve justice. Although these surveys brought about some changes, it was not until after World War II that many would be actualized. It was the period of social change in the 1960s and 1970s that fundamentally changed the dynamics of the responsibility of the state in crime. As the federal government began creating various grant programs, in particular the LEAA, to funnel grants to local law enforcement, each state was required to create a state planning agency that would be responsible for moving these grants from the federal level to the local level. When the LEAA folded in 1981, many of these agencies became the state-level departments or divisions for criminal justice services, which are bureaucratic departments responsible for continuing to procure federal grants, conducting research, and disseminating crime information.

In the 1990s, when crime became such a major issue and was highlighted by President Clinton's "100,000 Cops" plan, the state governors also became heavily involved in the issue of crime. In fact, as much of the debate on Clinton's Crime Bill came in 1994, one member of the NGA observed that same year that the "top three issues in the gubernatorial campaigns this year are crime, crime, and crime."[231] The observation wasn't too far off the mark, as the issue of crime did play a major role in many of the gubernatorial campaigns, including the 1994 campaigns in Texas and Florida for President George W. Bush and his brother Jeb Bush, respectively. Many of the issues in these campaigns and others revolved around the death penalty and which candidate could appear the toughest. Other issues centered on creating tougher sanctions for certain crimes and creating mandatory minimums for certain offenses, especially those involving a firearm in the commission of a felony. In fact, taking the issue of firearms further, the issue of gun control became an important issue as more and more states moved toward loosening the restrictions of the past.[232] And still others during the 1990s were focused on building more prisons in order to house more offenders in an attempt to drive down crime. One author, Joseph Dillon Davey, has argued that the primary reason for the prison boom of the 1980s and 1990s was because of the advocacy by state governors in order to appear tough on crime.[233]

Since it seemed that most of the 1990s was about governors trying to appear tough on crime, that is probably why former Illinois Governor George Ryan's decision, as he was nearing the end of his term in office in 2000, to declare a moratorium on executions and to commute the death sentence of 167 death-row inmates was received with such controversy. Although his act was appealed to the Illinois Supreme Court, that court upheld the governor's power to commute sentences under the Illinois Constitution. The next governor, Rod Blagojevich (currently under indictment for bribery), continued the moratorium, but also upheld the state's right to sentence an individual to death. What is perhaps more interesting in this case is the fact Governor Ryan is a Republican and Governor Blagojevich a Democrat, thus blurring the lines between the positions of these two parties regarding the death penalty.

LOCAL GOVERNMENT: MAYORS

The executive branch at the local level is generally found within the local mayor's office. Municipal governments consist of local towns, townships, or cities. They do not constitute counties or parishes because these are not sovereign governments but rather are given power for administration by the state. Local municipalities, on the other hand, have their own sovereignty and are granted executive, legislative, and judicial powers. Mayors, like other executives, tend to serve in four-year terms through elective office by running on one of the two party platforms. Many of these municipalities have term limits similar to those at the state level. In addition, the mayor often has the power to veto any of the municipal ordinances passed by the city council, can appoint such people as the chief of police, and have the power to run the city administrative offices.

There is one distinct difference between the mayor as executive and the other levels of government, and that is the differing styles of municipal government. There are essentially three types of municipal governments: the strong mayor–weak council, the weak mayor–strong council, and the city mayor–city manager format.[234] In the strong mayor–weak council style of local government, the mayor is voted into office, serves as the chief executive officer, and presides over the city council. The mayor also has the power to vote on any bills, so along with all the other powers of the mayor's office, this gives the individual an enormous amount of power to control the bills that come before the council, the passage of the bills, and their implementation. In the weak mayor–strong council style of municipal government, the mayor is either elected or selected by the council but does not preside over the council and can vote only if there is a tie. In many cases, the mayor does not have any veto power over the city council, and all actions by the mayor must be approved by the council. Hence, control over the bureaucracy, such as the hiring of the police chief, rests more in the hands of the council. Finally, in the event that a municipal government has a city manager, duties between the mayor and city manager are split, with the mayor receiving more of the ceremonial duties and the city manager having more of the administrative duties. This can greatly weaken the office of the mayor (elected official) and strengthen the office of city manager (appointed official), but ultimately it is the relationship that these two have with the city council that will determine their power.

Role in the Policy Process

The mayor's role in the policy process is perhaps more complex because the type of municipal government employed will determine how active a role the mayor can actually play. In the strong-mayor system, the mayor plays an extremely important role in shaping crime policy in his or her city. In the weak-mayor system, he or she may advocate for a particular policy but may have no more say than other actors in the policy process. Mayors can also serve as lobbyists for state and federal funding, and they often do. Mayors can also join collectively to voice their advocacy for certain policies, often doing so under the U.S. Conference of Mayors, a federal lobbying interest group.[235]

In terms of crime policy, mayors play a significant role that usually centers on their selection, appointment, and working relationship with the police chief. This relationship is perhaps one of the most important ones in that if the citizens of a particular municipality believe that crime is a problem in their community and is not adequately being addressed, while they know the police chief is responsible for managing the department, it is the mayor that they generally hold accountable. Therefore, one source of vulnerability for a mayor as an elected official and one area of critical concern to them is the issue of crime.

Mayors in recent years have been instrumental in the implementation of community policing within cities and towns across the United States. In many cases, the ability to implement such a program begins with the hiring of a new chief and the mayor giving that chief a specific charge.[236] The implementation of such a program, however, can also be laden with political issues that surround the relationships between local government and citizens in specific neighborhoods that must be resolved for a program such as this to move forward.[237] The mayor is again only one actor in the process, but as the executive officer, he or she is a critical actor in the success of any program.

A leading example of the impact of a mayor as related to crime policy can be found in former New York City Mayor Rudolph Giuliani's administration. While New York City had attempted the implementation of community policing in the 1980s, specifically under Police Commissioner Lee Brown, when the administration changed hands in 1994 and Giuliani was ushered in as mayor, he hired William Bratton as his police chief to implement a tougher policy of crime control, often called zero-tolerance policing and one based loosely on the broken windows theory.[238] This method of targeting specific crimes and enforcing the law on smaller petty crimes did have a dramatic but controversial impact on New York City. While crime did rapidly fall during the 1990s, it was also falling nearly everywhere across the country.[239] And while many people cheered the police for finally cracking down on the criminals and derelicts, many cited the corruption and brutality of the police force as being a reflection of the Giuliani administration.[240] Although the police chief played an important role during the 1990s in policing New York City, its driving force was assuredly the mayor. More recently, the role distinction between police chief and Mayor has blurred as many former police chiefs have become the Mayor, such as Lee P. Brown in Houston, Jerry Sanders in San Diego, and Robert J. Duffy in Rochester, New York.

EXECUTIVE ROLE IN THE POLICY PROCESS

The executive role at the federal, state, or local level is extremely important to the police process. Whether president, governor, or mayor, these chief executives are instrumental in every step of the public policy process. As related to crime policy, each of these serves to address the problem of crime in a very similar manner, but there is one dichotomy here. While mayors have more direct influence on shaping crime policy, it is the president of the United States who usually garners more attention. And although presidents can assist in addressing the problem of crime, they are severely limited in what they can do, while mayors have far more powers to intervene in this particular policy area. Regardless, all three are instrumental in every step of the policy process.

Problem Identification

Presidents, governors, and mayors are often the individuals who are responsible for bringing many of the problems to the attention of governments. One venue where this most often happens is on the campaign trail. This is the one time that the individual who ultimately will find him or herself in office spends most of his or her time talking to citizens. As a result, they come to learn about many of the problems facing the United States as a whole, a particular state, or a city. Often they will acknowledge these problems and make promises about what they would do to address these problems if elected. Once in office, the executives try very hard to achieve the promises they make, and if they promised to address a particular crime problem, they usually try to at least place the problem on the government's agenda.[241] In other cases, while in office, executives are often given information through their administrative agencies that may make them aware of a problem, and hence they will attempt to place it on the government's agenda. A good regional problem, especially in the South and in rural areas, is the amount of abuse and pharmacy theft of the painkiller oxycontin. In still other cases, issues come to everyone's attention, and we often look to the executive to do something about the problem. No better example of this can be found than the events of September 11.

Agenda Setting

Once the problem has been identified, it is often the chief executive who will bring it to the attention of both the public and the appropriate legislative body. Presidents, governors, and mayors will often talk to the public about a specific problem in newscasts and conferences, and at these events they explain the types of policies they are proposing to address the problem. This serves two purposes: (1) to gain the attention of the public and demonstrate to them that the executive branch is attempting to address a particular problem and (2) to place pressure on the legislative body to take up the executive's policy proposal.

Formulation

Once a policy comes before the legislative body, be it Congress, a state legislature, or a city council, it is up to that body to determine exactly how the problem will be addressed and what the policy will ultimately look like. Although the legislative body is the one that will craft the final policy, the executive must stay involved in the process in order to see his or her vision and plans for addressing a specific policy come to reality. The executives do this by lobbying his or her party members in the legislative body, specific voting blocks within the legislature, and individual members as well. The purpose is to retain as much of the executive branch's original policy proposals so that when it comes to implementing the policy, the executive has the same powers and capabilities that he or she originally proposed. If changed too dramatically from what the executive originally wanted, then he or she must determine if the policy is still viable from his or her perspective or whether he or she should veto the bill.

Implementation

Once the legislative branch passes a specific policy, the responsibility for implementing that policy generally falls back to the executive branch. This is why the executive must remain active in the policy formulation process so that the policy that he or she proposes will be the policy that is implemented. Even if it is not, however, it is still the responsibility of the executive branch to implement the policy as the legislature requests because of the powers that the executive has in running the bureaucracy. How the executive responds to the legislative charge will greatly impact the policy's implementation.

Evaluation

Once the policy has been implemented, it is also the executive's responsibility to ensure that the policies are implemented as originally intended and that the policy has some impact. These two pieces of information are obtained through the process of policy evaluations, which is the responsibility of the bureaucracies and ultimately the executive. While the legislative bill may call for some type of evaluation, many do not. Regardless, the executive branch must ensure that process and impact evaluations are conducted to determine the type of policy change that is necessary. This information assists the executive in making future policy decisions.

Policy Decisions

Once the policy evaluations are released, it is the responsibility of the executive to determine how a particular policy will proceed. If the policy is successful, the executive may simply laud it or request for additional funding to enhance or expand the program. If the latter is done, then the executive must place the policy back on the agenda and again try to obtain the expansion of the program through a legislative bill. If the policy is not successful, the executive must make a policy decision on whether to kill the program or alter it. In either case, the executive must once again exercise the public policy process, and the cycle continues.

Conclusion

The executive branches of government, whether it is the president (national level), the governor (state level), or the city mayor (local level), are significant players in the policy process. Although all are constrained by the limitations of their office, it is their power to persuade the public and their respective legislative bodies that gives them an enormous amount of power to oversee crime policy in America. Whether it is placing an item on the agenda, advocating for the formulation of its proposed policy, or implementing a policy through its oversight of the bureaucracy, the executive branch clearly plays a very important role in the public policy process.

Notes

1. James Calder, *The Origins and Development of Federal Crime Control Policy: Herbert Hoover's Initiatives* (Westport, CT: Praeger Publishers, 1993); Nancy E. Marion, A History of Federal Crime Control Initiatives, 1960–1993 (Wesport, CT: Praeger Publishers, 1994).
2. Lance T. LeLoup and Steven A. Shull, *The President and Congress: Collaboration and Combat in National Policymaking* (Boston: Allyn & Bacon, 1999), p. 40. Still another means of understanding the division of these two presidential powers comes from Thomas and Pika in their delineation of "the formal powers vested in him by the Constitution and by statute and the informal resources inherent in the office." See Norman C. Thomas and Joseph A. Pika, *The Politics of the Presidency*, 4th ed. (Washington, D.C.: Congressional Quarterly Press, 1996), p. 211.

3. U.S. Constitution, art. II, sec. 2.

4. Jeffrey A. Segal and Robert M. Howard, "Justices and Presidents," in *Presidential Policymaking: An End-of-Century Assessment*, ed. Steven A. Shull (Armonk, N.Y.: M E Sharpe, 1999), pp. 168–82.

5. *Mapp v. Ohio*, 367 U.S. 643, 6 L.Ed. 2d 1081, 81 S. Ct. 1684 (1961).

6. *Miranda v. Arizona*, 384 U.S. 436, 16 L.Ed. 2d 694, 86 S. Ct. 1602 (1966).

7. *Gideon v. Wainwright*, 372 U.S. 335, 9 L.Ed. 2d 799, 83 S. Ct. 814 (1963).

8. Office of the Pardon Attorney, U.S. Department of Justice Web site, available online at www.usdoj.gov/opa/opa.html.

9. George C. Edwards III and Stephen J. Wayne, *Presidential Leadership: Politics and Policy Making*, 2nd ed. (New York: St. Martin's Press, 1990), p. 342; Office of the Pardon Attorney, U.S. Department of Justice Web site, available online at www.usdoj.gov/opa/opa.html.

10. Edwards and Wayne, *Presidential Leadership*, p. 342; Nancy E. Marion, *A History of Federal Crime Control Initiatives, 1960–1993* (Westport, Conn.: Praeger, 1994), pp. 103–4; David R. Simon and Stanley D. Eitzen, *Elite Deviance*, 4th ed. (Boston: Allyn & Bacon, 1993).

11. Gerald R. Ford, "Proclamation 4311, Granting Pardon to Richard Nixon. September 8, 1974," in *Public Papers of the Presidents of the United States* (Washington, D.C.: U.S. Government Printing Office, 1975), p. 104.

12. Edwards and Wayne, *Presidential Leadership*, p. 342.

13. Gerald R. Ford, 1975. "Remarks on Signing 18 Executive Warrants for Clemency. November 29, 1974," in *Public Papers of the Presidents of the United States* (Washington, D.C.: U.S. Government Printing Office, 1975), pp. 672–73.

14. Jimmy Carter, "Presidential Proclamation of Pardon. January 21, 1977," in *Public Papers of the Presidents of the United States* (Washington, D.C.: U.S. Government Printing Office, 1978), pp. 5–6; Edwards and Wayne, *Presidential Leadership*, p. 342.

15. Edwards and Wayne, *Presidential Leadership*, p. 342.

16. See U.S. Department of Justice, Presidential Pardons, available online at www.usdoj.gov/opa/pardonchartlst.htm.

17. Paul C. Light, *The President's Agenda: Domestic Policy Choice from Kennedy to Reagan*, rev. ed. (Baltimore: The Johns Hopkins University Press, 1991), pp. 158–60.

18. Ibid., p. 160.

19. Ibid.

20. Lyn Ragsdale, *Vital Statistics on the Presidency*, rev. ed. (Washington, D.C.: Congressional Quarterly Press, 1998), p. 366.

21. John H. Kessel, "The Parameters of Presidential Politics" (paper presented at the annual meeting of the American Political Science Association, New York, September 1972), p. 3, as cited in Light, *The President's Agenda*, p. 160.

22. Robert E. DiClerico, *The American President*, 4th ed. (Englewood Cliffs, N.J.: Prentice Hall, 1995), chap. 3; Thomas and Pika, *The Politics of the Presidency*, p. 211.

23. Kenneth J. Meier, *Politics and the Bureaucracy: Policymaking in the Fourth Branch of Government*, 3rd ed. (Belmont, Calif.: Wadsworth, 1993), pp. 167–68; William F. West, *Controlling the Bureaucracy: Institutional Constraints in Theory and Practice* (Armonk, N.Y.: M E Sharpe, 1995), Chapter 4.

24. West, *Controlling the Bureaucracy*, p. 94.

25. Kenneth J. Meier, *The Politics of Sin: Drugs, Alcohol, and Public Policy* (Armonk, N.Y.: M E Sharpe, 1994), p. 68.

26. Woodrow Wilson, *Congressional Government* (Cleveland: World, 1973), p. 53.

27. Roger H. Davidson and Walter J. Oleszek, *Congress and Its Members*, 6th ed. (Washington, D.C.: Congressional Quarterly Press, 1998), pp. 283–88; Edwards and Wayne, *Presidential Leadership*, pp. 312–16; Ragsdale, *Vital Statistics on the Presidency*, pp. 366–75; Thomas and Pika, *The Politics of the Presidency*, pp. 213–16.

28. Gerald R. Ford, "Veto of Legislation to Reclassify and Upgrade Deputy United States Marshals. August 13, 1974," in *Public Papers of the Presidents of the United States* (Washington, D.C.: U.S. Government Printing Office, 1975), pp. 13–14.

29. Ronald Reagan, "Memorandum Returning without Approval a Bill concerning Contract Services for Drug Dependent Federal Offenses. January 14, 1983," in *Public Papers of the Presidents of the United States* (Washington, D.C.: U.S. Government Printing Office, 1984), pp. 49–50.

30. William J. Clinton, "Message to the House of Representatives Returning without Approval the Departments of Commerce, Justice, and State, the Judiciary, and Related Agencies Appropriations Act, 1996. December 19, 1995," in *Public Papers of the Presidents of the United States* (Washington, D.C.: U.S. Government Printing Office, 1996), pp. 1910–11.

31. Franklin D. Roosevelt, "The President Directs the Detroit Race Rioters to Disperse. Proclamation

No. 2588. June 21, 1943" in *The Public Papers and Addresses of Franklin D. Roosevelt* (New York: Russell and Russell, 1943), pp. 258–59.

32. Lyndon B. Johnson, "Telegram in Reply to Governor Romney's Request for Federal Troop Assistance in Detroit. July 24, 1967," in *Public Papers of the Presidents of the United States* (Washington, D.C.: U.S. Government Printing Office, 1968), pp. 714–15.

33. Shirley Anne Warshaw, *The Domestic Presidency: Policy Making in the White House* (Boston: Allyn & Bacon, 1997), pp. 5–6.

34. It should be noted that many of the methods by which presidents can implement their crime control policies are also explanations for why they engage in crime control policy. For example, a president's response to a crisis, the inclusion of the crime issue in presidential campaigns, and the fact the national political party's platforms include a position on crime are explanations for why presidents engage in crime control policy (see Chapter 2), but they stand as an explanation for how they engage in crime control policies as well.

35. Daniel A. Smith, Kevin M. Leyden, and Stephen A. Borrelli, "Predicting the Outcomes of Presidential Commissions: Evidence from the Johnson and Nixon Years," *Presidential Studies Quarterly* 28 (2, 1998): 269–85, at 270.

36. Ibid.

37. James Doug Calder, "*Presidents and Crime Control: Some Limitations on Executive Policy Making*" (Ph.D. diss., Claremont University, 1978), pp. 138–45; Frank Popper, *President's Commissions* (New York: Twentieth Century Fund, 1970); Smith et al., "Predicting the Outcomes of Presidential Commissions," pp. 269–85; Thomas Wolanin, *Presidential Advisory Commissions* (Madison: University of Wisconsin Press, 1975).

38. Thomas and Pika, *The Politics of the Presidency*, p. 344.

39. James D. Calder, "Herbert Hoover's Contributions to the Administrative History of Crime Control Policy" (paper presented at the annual meeting of the Southwest Political Science Association, Dallas, March 25–28, 1981); Calder, "*Presidents and Crime Control,*" pp. 139–42; James D. Calder, *The Origins and Development of Federal Crime Control Policy: Herbert Hoover's Initiatives* (Westport, Conn.: Praeger, 1993), chap. 4.

40. See Randolph Boehm, ed., *Records of the Wickersham Commission on Law Observance and Enforcement*, Research Collections in American Legal History (New York: University Publications, 1997).

41. Calder, "*Presidents and Crime Control,*" pp. 138–45.

42. Gerald Caplan, "Reflections on the Nationalization of Crime, 1964–1968," *Law and the Social Order* 1973: 583–635.

43. President's Commission on Law Enforcement and Administration of Justice, *The Challenge of Crime in a Free Society* (New York: Avon, 1968).

44. John A. Conley, ed., *The 1967 President's Crime Commission Report: Its Impact 25 Years Later* (Cincinnati: Anderson/Academy of Criminal Justice Sciences, 1994); U.S. Department of Justice, Office of Justice Programs, *The Challenge of Crime in a Free Society: Looking Back, Looking Forward* (Washington, D.C.: U.S. Department of Justice, 1997); Samuel Walker, "Reexamining the President's Crime Commission: The Challenge of Crime in a Free Society after Ten Years," *Crime and Delinquency* 24 (1, 1978): 1–12.

45. National Advisory Commission on Civil Disorders, *National Advisory Commission on Civil Disorders Report* (Washington, D.C.: U.S. Government Printing Office, 1969), pp. 229–30; National Commission on the Cause and Prevention of Violence, *National Commission on the Causes and Prevention of Violence Final Report* (Washington, D.C.: U.S. Government Printing Office, 1969), p. 272; President's Commission on Law Enforcement and Administration of Justice, *The Challenge of Crime in a Free Society*, p. 284.

46. Thomas and Pika, *The Politics of the Presidency*, p. 264; Richard A. Watson and Norman C. Thomas, *The Politics of the Presidency* (New York: John Wiley & Sons, 1983), p. 305.

47. Executive Order 11111, Providing assistance for the removal of obstructions of justice and suppression of unlawful combinations within the State of Alabama, Signed: June 11, 1963, *Federal Register* page and date: 28 FR 5709; June 12, 1963; Executive Order 11118, Providing assistance for removal of unlawful obstructions of justice in the State of Alabama, Signed: September 10, 1963, *Federal Register* page and date: 28 FR 9863; September 11, 1963; Executive Order 11364, Providing for the restoration of law and order in the State of Michigan, Signed: July 24, 1967, *Federal Register* page and date: 32 FR 10907; July 26, 1967; Executive Order 11403; Providing for the restoration of law and order in the Washington Metropolitan Area, Signed: April 5, 1968, *Federal Register* page and date: 33 FR 5501; April 9, 1968; Executive Order 11404, Providing for the restoration of law and order in the

State of Illinois, Signed: April 7, 1968, *Federal Register* page and date: 33 FR 5503; April 9, 1968; Executive Order 11405, Providing for the restoration of law and order in the State of Maryland, Signed: April 7, 1968, *Federal Register* page and date: 33 FR 5505; April 9, 1968.

48. Executive Order 12564, Drug-Free Federal Workplace, Signed: September 15, 1986, *Federal Register* page and date: 51 FR 32889; September 17, 1986. See also Donald W. Crowley, "Drug Testing in the Rehnquist Era," in *The New War on Drugs: Symbolic Politics and Criminal Justice Policy*, ed. Eric L. Jensen and Jurg Gerber (Cincinnati: Anderson/Academy of Criminal Justice Sciences, 1998), pp. 123–39.

49. Executive Order 11236, Establishing the President's Commission on Law Enforcement and Administration of Justice, Signed: July 23, 1965, *Federal Register* page and date: 30 FR 9349; July 28, 1965.

50. Executive Order 11365, Establishing a National Advisory Commission on Civil Disorders, Signed: July 29, 1967, *Federal Register* page and date: 32 FR 11111; August 1, 1967.

51. Executive Order 11599, Establishing a special action office for drug abuse prevention, Signed: June 17, 1971, *Federal Register* page and date: 36 FR 11793; June 19, 1971.

52. Executive Order 11676, Providing for the establishment of an Office of National Narcotics Intelligence within the Department of Justice, Signed: July 27, 1972, *Federal Register* page and date: 37 FR 15125; July 28, 1972.

53. Executive Order 12590, National Drug Policy Board, Signed: March 26, 1987, *Federal Register* page and date: 52 FR 10021; March 30, 1987.

54. Executive Order 11669, J. Edgar Hoover, Signed: May 2, 1972, *Federal Register* page and date: 37 FR 9013; May 4, 1972.

55. Executive Order 12911, Seal for the Office of National Drug Control Policy, Signed: April 25, 1994, *Federal Register* page and date: 59 FR 21121; April 28, 1994.

56. Thomas and Pika, *The Politics of the Presidency*, p. 345.

57. Ibid.

58. Lance T. LeLoup, "Budget Policy Transformations," in Shull, *Presidential Policymaking*, pp. 204–23; Thomas and Pika, *The Politics of the Presidency*, pp. 268–71; Aaron Wildavsky, *The New Politics of the Budgetary Process*, 2nd ed. (New York: HarperCollins, 1992).

59. Wildavsky, *The New Politics of the Budgetary Process*, p. 21.

60. "Federal Crime Control Efforts," *Congressional Digest* 73 (6–7, 1994): 161–92.

61. Gregory A. Caldeira, "Elections and the Politics of Crime: Budgetary Choices and Priorities in America," in *The Political Science of Criminal Justice*, ed. Stuart Nagel, Erika Fairchild, and Anthony Champagne (Springfield, Ill.: Charles C Thomas, 1983), pp. 238–52; Greg A. Caldeira and Andrew T. Cowart, "Budgets, Institutions, and Change: Criminal Justice Policy in America," *American Journal of Political Science* 24 (3, 1980): 413–38.

62. Wendy L. Martinek, Kenneth J. Meier, and Lael R. Keiser, "Jackboots or Lace Panties? The Bureau of Alcohol, Tobacco and Firearms," in *The Changing Politics of Gun Control*, ed. John M. Bruce and Clyde Wilcox (Lanham, Md.: Rowman & Littlefield, 1998), pp. 17–44.

63. Ibid., p. 24.

64. Nancy Marion, "Presidential Agenda Setting in Crime Control," *Criminal Justice Policy Review* 6 (2, 1992): 159–84, at 162.

65. Steven A. Shull, *Domestic Policy Formation: Presidential-Congressional Partnership?* (Westport, Conn.: Praeger, 1983), p. 31.

66. Ibid.

67. Lyn Ragsdale, "The Politics of Presidential Speech-making, 1949–1980," *American Political Science Review* 78 (1984): 971–84, at 971.

68. Ibid.

69. Theodore J. Lowi, *The Personal President: Power Invested, Promises Unfulfilled* (Ithaca, N.Y.: Cornell University Press, 1985); Martin P. Wattenberg, *The Rise of Candidate-Centered Politics* (Cambridge, Mass.: Harvard University Press, 1991).

70. Samuel Kernell, *Going Public: New Strategies of Presidential Leadership*, 3rd ed. (Washington, D.C.: Congressional Quarterly Press, 1997).

71. See Lowi, *The Personal President*.

72. For a broader understanding of the politics of the presidency, see DiClerico, *The American President*.

73. A speech to the graduating class at Yale Law School, June 26, 1905, cited in Barry Mahoney, "The Politics of the Safe Streets Act, 1965–1973: A Case Study in Evolving Federalism and the National Legislative Process" (Ph.D. diss., Columbia University) (Ann Arbor, Mich.: University Microfilms International, 1976), p. 20.

74. Herbert Hoover, address before the annual luncheon of the Associated Press, April 22, 1929, cited in Mahoney, "The Politics of the Safe Streets Act, 1965–1973," p. 24.

75. National Commission on Law Observance and Enforcement, *Reports*, 14 vols. (1931) (reprint, New York: Arno Press, 1968).

76. J. M. Hepbron, "Local Crime Surveys: Their Origin, Purpose, and Accomplishments," *Social Forces* 24 (1927): 426–31.

77. Ibid.

78. Nancy E. Marion, *A Primer in the Politics of Crime and Criminal Justice* (New York: Harrow and Heston, 1995).

79. James D. Calder, "Presidents and Crime Control: Kennedy, Johnson, Nixon and the Influences of Ideology," *Presidential Studies Quarterly* 12 (1982): 574–89.

80. Ibid., p. 575.

81. See Caplan, "Reflection on the Nationalization of Crime, 1964–1968," pp. 583–638; Thomas E. Cronin, Tania Z. Cronin, and Michael E. Milakovich, *U.S. vs. Crime in the Streets* (Bloomington: Indiana University Press, 1981); Erika S. Fairchild and Vincent J. Webb, *The Politics of Crime and Criminal Justice* (Beverly Hills, Calif.: Sage, 1985); Kathlyn Taylor Gaubatz, *Crime in the Public Mind* (Ann Arbor: University of Michigan Press, 1995); Marion, *A History of Federal Crime Control Initiatives, 1960–1993*; Joachim J. Savelsburg, "Knowledge, Domination, and Criminal Punishment," *American Journal of Sociology* 99 (1994): 911–43; Stuart A. Scheingold, The Politics of Law and Order (New York: Longman, 1984); Scheingold, "Politics, Public Policy, and Street Crime," *Annals of the American Academy of Political and Social Science* 539 (1995): 155–68.

82. Mahoney, "The Politics of the Safe Streets Act, 1965–1973," pp. 72–73.

83. Barry Goldwater, transcript from the Republican National Convention, as cited in "Goldwater's Acceptance Speech to GOP Convention," *New York Times*, July 17, 1964.

84. Marion, *A Primer in the Politics of Crime and Criminal Justice*, pp. 34–37.

85. President's Commission on Law Enforcement and Administration of Justice, *The Challenge of Crime in a Free Society*.

86. See Conley, *The 1967 President's Crime Commission Report*.

87. Marion, *A History of Federal Crime Control Initiatives, 1960–1993*.

88. Advisory Commission on Intergovernmental Relations, *Safe Streets Reconsidered: The Block Grant Experience 1968–1975* (Washington, D.C.: U.S. Government Printing Office, 1977).

89. Ibid.; Conley, *The 1967 President's Crime Commission Report*; Marion, *A History of Federal Crime Control Initiatives, 1960–1993*.

90. Advisory Commission on Intergovernmental Relations, *Safe Streets Reconsidered*.

91. House of Representatives, *Hearings before a Subcommittee of the Committee on Government Operations, House of Representatives: The Block Grant Programs of the Law Enforcement Assistance Administration* (Washington, D.C.: U.S. Government Printing Office, 1971).

92. Ibid.

93. Marion, *A History of Federal Crime Control Initiatives, 1960–1993*.

94. Law Enforcement Assistance Administration, *LEAA Eleventh Annual Report, Fiscal Year 1979* (Washington, D.C.: U.S. Department of Justice, 1980).

95. Thomas J. Anton, *American Federalism and Public Policy* (New York: Random House, 1989); Robert F. Diegelman, "Federal Financial Assistance for Crime Control: Lessons of the LEAA Experience," *Journal of Criminal Law and Criminology* 73 (1982): 994–1011; John J. Dilulio, Steven K. Smith, and Aaron J. Saiger, "The Federal Role in Crime Control," in *Crime*, ed. James Q. Wilson and Joan Petersilia (San Francisco: ICS Press, 1995); Malcolm M. Feeley and Austin D. Sarat, *The Policy Dilemma: Federal Crime Policy and the Law Enforcement Assistance Administration* (Minneapolis: University of Minnesota Press, 1980); John K. Hudzik, *Federal Aid to Criminal Justice: Rhetoric, Results, Lessons* (Washington, D.C.: National Criminal Justice Association, 1984).

96. Calder, "Presidents and Crime Control"; Marion, *A History of Federal Crime Control Initiatives, 1960–1993*; Marion, *A Primer in the Politics of Crime and Criminal Justice*; Samuel Walker, *Sense and Nonsense about Crime and Drugs: A Policy Guide*, 3rd ed. (Belmont, Calif.: Wadsworth, 1994).

97. Marion, *A Primer in the Politics of Crime and Criminal Justice*, pp. 37–38.

98. Cronin et al., *U.S. vs. Crime in the Streets*, p. 122.

99. "The Federal Role in Crime Control," *Congressional Digest*, June-July 1994, pp. 161–92; Marion, *A History of Federal Crime Control Initiatives, 1960–1993*; Marion, *A Primer in the Politics of Crime and Criminal Justice*; President's Task Force on Victims of Crime, *Final Report* (Washington, D.C.: U.S. Government Printing Office, 1982).

100. Marion, *A History of Federal Crime Control Initiatives, 1960–1993*.

101. Ibid.

102. Robert J. Spitzer, *The Politics of Gun Control* (Chatham, N.J.: Chatham House, 1995), esp. chap. 5.

103. Elaine B. Sharp, *The Dilemma of Drug Policy in the United States* (New York: HarperCollins, 1994), esp. Chapter 4.

104. "Federal Crime Control Efforts."

105. David C. Anderson, *Crime and the Politics of Hysteria: How the Willie Horton Story Changed American Justice* (New York: Times Books/Random House, 1995); Sentencing Project, *The Lessons of Willie Horton: Thinking about Crime and Punishment for the 1990s* (Washington, D.C.: Sentencing Project, 1989).

106. George Bush, State of the Union Address, 1992, in *Public Papers of the President of the United States* (Washington, D.C.: U.S. Government Printing Office, 1993), pp. 156–63.

107. Ted Gest and Kenneth T. Walsh, "The New Crime (Talk) Wave," *U.S. News and World Report*, August 10, 1992, p. 23.

108. Mark Costanzo, *Just Revenge: Costs and Consequences of the Death Penalty* (New York: St. Martin's Press, 1997), p. 1.

109. U.S. Department of Justice, *The Violent Crime Control and Law Enforcement Act of 1994* (Washington, D.C.: U.S. Government Printing Office, 1994).

110. Midnight basketball was a much-politicized program that authorized funds to keep local basketball gymnasiums open into the early hours of the morning, providing local youth with a place to be after other businesses close.

111. N. E. Marion and R. Farmer, "Crime Control in the 2000 Presidential Election: A Symbolic Issue," *American Journal of Criminal Justice* 27 (2, 2003): 129–44.

112. Ibid.

113. W. M. Oliver, "The Homeland Security Juggernaut: The End of the Community Policing Era?" *Crime and Justice International* 20 (79, 2004): 4–10.

114. John W. Kingdon, *Agendas, Alternatives, and Public Policies*, 2nd ed. (New York: HarperCollins College Publishers 1994), p. 23.

115. Ibid.

116. Shull, *Domestic Policy Formation*, p. 17.

117. Bruce Miroff, "Monopolizing the Public Space: The President as a Problem for Democratic Politics," in *Rethinking the Presidency*, ed. Thomas Cronin (Boston: Little, Brown, 1982), pp. 218–32.

118. Christopher Bosso, *Pesticides and Politics: The Life Cycle of a Public Issue* (Pittsburgh: University of Pittsburgh Press, 1987), p. 261.

119. Ibid.

120. Light, *The President's Agenda*.

121. Ibid., p. 1.

122. Ibid., pp. 2–3.

123. Ibid., Chapter 1.

124. Ibid., p. 15.

125. Kingdon, *Agendas, Alternatives, and Public Policies*, pp. 24–27.

126. Light, *The President's Agenda*, p. 15.

127. Ibid., Chapter 2.

128. Ibid.

129. Ibid., Chapter 3.

130. Ibid., Chapter 4.

131. Ibid., Chapter 5.

132. Ibid.

133. Ibid., Chapter 6.

134. Ibid., Chater 7.

135. Kernell, *Going Public*.

136. Paul Brace and Barbara Hinckley, *Follow the Leader: Opinion Polls and the Modern Presidents* (New York: Basic Books, 1992), pp. 27–30.

137. Calder, *The Origins and Development of Federal Crime Control Policy*, pp. 198–203.

138. Michael William Flamm, "'Law and Order': Street Crime, Civil Disorder, and the Crisis of Liberalism" (Ph.D. diss., Columbia University, 1998); Donald Lee Scruggs, "*Lyndon Baines Johnson and the National Advisory Commission on Civil Disorders (The Kerner Commission): A Study of the Johnson Domestic Policy Making System*" (Ph.D. diss., University of Oklahoma, 1980).

139. Lyndon Baines Johnson, *The Vantage Point: Perspectives of the Presidency, 1963–1969* (New York: Holt, Rinehart and Winston, 1971), p. 549.

140. Light, *The President's Agenda*, p. 69.

141. Feeley and Sarat. *The Policy Dilemma*, p. 19.

142. Theodore J. Lowi, *The End of Liberalism: The Second Republic of the United States*, 2nd ed. (New York: Norton, 1979), pp. 292–94.

143. President's Commission on Law Enforcement and Administration of Justice, *The Challenge of Crime in a Free Society*.

144. As Freda Adler, past president of the Academy of Criminal Justice Sciences explains, "The LEEP fund program . . . for the first time, brought education and training into the various organs of government that are concerned with crime control," and the "LEAA spent $7 billion." She then goes on to say, "Let us never forget that without that massive expenditure of government funds, our profession would not exist, our schools and programs would

have remained pipe dreams." See Freda Adler, "Who Are We? A Self-Analysis of Criminal Justice Specialists," *ACJS Today* 14 (1, 1995): 1–21, at 1. Also, another past president of the Academy of Criminal Justice Sciences has stated, "Undoubtedly the Law Enforcement Assistance Administration, or LEAA, was the catalyst for the expansion of undergraduate programs. It was also instrumental in the creation of doctoral programs at John Jay College of Criminal Justice, the University of Albany, and Michigan State University." See Donna C. Hale, "Presidential Address: Delivered at the 34th Annual Meeting of the Academy of Criminal Justice Sciences, Louisville, Kentucky, March 1997. Criminal Justice Education: Traditions in Transition," *Justice Quarterly* 15 (3, 1998): 385–94, at 387.

145. Steven R. Donziger, *The Real War on Crime: The Report of the National Criminal Justice Commission* (New York: HarperPerennial, 1996), chaps. 2 and 3; Eric Schlosser, "The Prison-Industrial Complex," *Atlantic Monthly*, December 1998, pp. 51–77.

146. Marion, *A History of Federal Crime Control Initiatives, 1960–1993*; Marion, "Presidential Agenda Setting in Crime Control"; Nancy E. Marion, "Symbolic Policies in Clinton's Crime Control Agenda," *Buffalo Criminal Law Review* 1 (1, 1997): 67–108; Nancy Marion, "Symbolism and Federal Crime Control Legislation, 1960–1990," *Journal of Crime and Justice* 17 (2, 1994): 69–91.

147. Joseph Gusfield, *Symbolic Crusade: Status Politics and the American Temperance Movement* (Urbana: University of Illinois Press, 1963).

148. Murray Edelman, *Constructing the Political Spectacle* (Chicago: University of Chicago Press, 1988); *The Symbolic Uses of Politics* (Urbana: University of Illinois Press, 1964); *Politics as Symbolic Action: Mass Arousal and Quiescence* (Chicago: Markham, 1971).

149. Edelman, *The Symbolic Uses of Politics*, p. 6.

150. Edelman, *Constructing the Political Spectacle*, p. 8.

151. Barbara Hinckley, *The Symbolic Presidency: How Presidents Portray Themselves* (New York: Routledge, Chapman, and Hall, 1990), p. 7.

152. Cronin et al., *U.S. vs. Crime in the Streets*; John Hagan, "The Symbolic Politics of Criminal Sanctions," in Nagel et al., *The Political Science of Criminal Justice*, pp. 16–36; Marion, *A History of Federal Crime Control Initiatives, 1960–1993*; Marion, "Symbolic Policies in Clinton's Crime Control Agenda"; Marion, "Symbolism and Federal Crime Control Legislation, 1960–1990"; Joel Rosch, "Crime as an Issue in American Politics," in Fairchild and Webb, *The Politics of Crime and Criminal Justice*, pp. 19–36; Scheingold, *The Politics of Law and Order*; Stuart A. Scheingold, *The Politics of Street Crime: Criminal Process and Cultural Obsession* (Philadelphia: Temple University Press, 1991); Barbara A. Stolz, "Congress and the War on Drugs: An Exercise in Symbolic Politics," *Journal of Crime and Justice* 15 (1, 1992): 119–36.

153. Scheingold, *The Politics of Street Crime*, p. 177.

154. Cronin et al., *U.S. vs. Crime in the Streets*, p. 170.

155. Ibid.

156. Scheingold, *The Politics of Law and Order*, p. 87.

157. Bryan D. Jones, *Reconceiving Decision-Making in Democratic Politics: Attention, Choice, and Public Policy* (Chicago: University of Chicago Press, 1994), p. 106.

158. David Butler and Donald Stokes, *Political Change in Britain: The Evolution of Electoral Choice*, 2nd ed. (New York: Macmillan, 1974).

159. Ibid.

160. Victor E. Kappeler, Mark Blumberg, and Gary W. Potter, *The Mythology of Crime and Criminal Justice*, 2nd ed. (Prospect Heights, Ill.: Waveland Press, 1996), p. 49.

161. Jones, *Reconceiving Decision-Making in Democratic Politics*, p. 106.

162. Ibid.; Frank R. Baumgartner and Bryan D. Jones, *Agendas and Instability in American Politics* (Chicago: University of Chicago Press, 1993); Meier, *The Politics of Sin*; Barbara J. Nelson, *Making an Issue of Child Abuse: Political Agenda Setting for Social Problems* (Chicago: University of Chicago Press, 1984).

163. Scheingold, *The Politics of Street Crime*, p. 178.

164. Scheingold, Stuart A. 1995. "Politics, Public Policy, and Street Crime," *Annals of the American Academy of Political and Social Sciences* 539 (1995): 155–68, at 166.

165. Ibid., p. 166.

166. Jones, *Reconceiving Decision-Making in Democratic Politics*, chap. 5.

167. Paul Barrett, "Moving On: Though the Drug War Isn't Over, Spotlight Turns to Other Issues," *Wall Street Journal*, November 11, 1990; Jones, *Reconceiving Decision-Making in Democratic Politics*, p. 107.

168. The three previous Gallup Poll surveys asking respondents, "What is the most important problem facing the country?" received a 27 percent response of "drug abuse." These polls were conducted on May 7, 1989; July 21, 1989; and August 4, 1989. The president's speech was on September 5, 1989, and on September 10, 1989, when asked the same question, the response citing "drug abuse" rose to 63 percentage points. Drugs were, for the first time in the history of

the Gallup Poll, the "most important problem." See George Gallup, *The Gallup Poll: Public Opinion* (Wilmington, Del.: Scholarly Resources, 1945–1996); *The Gallup Organization home page*, "Gallup Social and Economic Indicators-Most Important Problem," available online at www.gallup.com/poll/indicators/indmip.asp; Kathleen Maguire and Ann L. Pastore, *Sourcebook of Criminal Justice Statistics 1997* (Washington, D.C.: Bureau of Justice Statistics, 1998).

169. Jones, *Reconceiving Decision-Making in Democratic Politics*, p. 107.

170. R. Michael Alvarez and John Brehm, "Are Americans Ambivalent towards Racial Policies?" *American Journal of Political Science* 41 (2, 1997): 345–74; Lawrence Bobo and James R. Kluegal, "Opposition to Race Targeting: Self-Interest, Stratification Ideology, or Racial Attitudes?" *American Sociological Review* 58 (1993): 443–64; Paul M. Sniderman and Thomas Piazza, *The Scar of Race* (Cambridge, Mass.: Harvard University Press, 1993); Paul M. Sniderman, Thomas Piazza, Philip E. Tetlock, and Ann Kendrick, "The New Racism," *American Journal of Political Science* 35 (1991): 423–47.

171. Thomas Bryne Edsall and Mary D. Edsall, *Chain Reaction: The Impact of Race, Rights, and Taxes on American Politics* (New York: Norton, 1991).

172. Martin Gilens, "Racial Attitudes and Opposition to Welfare," *Journal of Politics* 57 (4, 1995): 994–1014; James H. Kuklinksi, Paul M. Sniderman, Kathleen Knight, Thomas Piazza, Philip E. Tetlock, Gordon R. Lawrence, and Barbara Mellers, "Racial Prejudice and Attitudes toward Affirmative Action," *American Journal of Political Science* 41 (2, 1997): 402–19; Mark Peffley, Jon Hurwitz, and Paul M. Sniderman, "Racial Stereotypes and Whites' Political Views of Blacks in the Context of Welfare and Crime," *American Journal of Political Science* 41 (1, 1997): 30–60.

173. Steven E. Barkan and Steven F. Cohn, "Racial Prejudice and Support by Whites for Police Use of Force: A Research Note," *Justice Quarterly* 15 (4, 1998): 743–53; Kathlyn Taylor Gaubatz, *Crime in the Public Mind* (Ann Arbor: University of Michigan Press, 1995); Jon Hurwitz and Mark Peffley, "Public Perceptions of Race and Crime: The Role of Racial Stereotypes," *American Journal of Political Science* 41 (2, 1997): 375–401; Kevin M. Leyden, John C. Kilwein, and Willard M. Oliver, "Public Opinion and Crime: Who Fears Crime and Why?" (paper presented at the annual meeting of the Northeastern Political Science Association, Boston, November 1996); Kenneth J. Meier, "The Politics of Drug Abuse:

Laws, Implementation and Consequences," *Western Political Quarterly* 45 (1990): 41–69; Meier, *The Politics of Sin*; Willard M. Oliver, Kevin M. Leyden, and John C. Kilwein, "Drowning: The Subterfuge of Race by the Issue of Crime" (paper presented at the annual meeting of the Southern Criminal Justice Association, Richmond, Virginia, November 1997); Michael Omni and Howard Winant, *Racial Formation in the United States* (New York: Routledge, 1986); Peffley et al., "Racial Stereotypes and Whites' Political Views of Blacks in the Context of Welfare and Crime"; Mark Peffley, Todd Shields, and Bruce Williams, "The Intersection of Race and Crime in Television News Stories: An Experimental Study," *Political Communication* 13 (1996): 309–27.

174. Thomas Bryne Edsall and Mary D. Edsall, "Race," *Atlantic Monthly* 267 (5, 1997): 77.

175. Cited in Dan Baum, *Smoke and Mirrors: The War on Drugs and the Politics of Failure* (Boston: Little, Brown, 1996), p. 13.

176. John Ehrlichman, *Witness to Power: The Nixon Years* (New York: Simon & Schuster, 1982), p. 233.

177. Michael Tonry, *Malign Neglect: Race, Crime, and Punishment in America* (New York: Oxford University Press, 1995); Michael Tonry, "Racial Politics, Racial Disparities, and the War on Crime," *Crime and Delinquency* 40 (4, 1994), 475–94. See also Steven R. Donziger, *The Real War on Crime: The Report of the National Criminal Justice Commission* (New York: HarperPerennial, 1996), chap. 4; Samuel Walker, Cassia Spohn, and Miriam DeLone, *The Color of Justice: Race, Ethnicity, and Crime in America* (Belmont, Calif.: Wadsworth, 1996).

178. For an excellent discussion of the Willie Horton commercial and its political ramifications, see Kathleen Hall Jamieson, *Dirty Politics: Deception, Distraction, and Democracy* (New York: Oxford University Press, 1992).

179. Ibid., p. 41.

180. Thomas E. Patterson, *Out of Order* (New York: Vintage, 1994).

181. Scheingold, *The Politics of Law and Order*, p. 87.

182. Michael E. Milakovich and Kurt Weis, "Politics and Measures of Success in the War on Crime," *Crime and Delinquency* 21 (1, 1975): 1–10, at 3.

183. Marion, *A Primer in the Politics of Criminal Justice*, Chapter 7.

184. Task Force on the Federalization of Criminal Law, American Bar Association, Criminal Justice Section, *The Federalization of Criminal Law* (Washington, D.C.: American Bar Association, 1998).

185. Marion, *A History of Federal Crime Control Initiatives, 1960–1993.*

186. Jamieson, *Dirty Politics*; Darrell M. West, *Air Wars: Television Advertising in Election Campaigns 1952–1996*, 2nd ed. (Washington, D.C.: Congressional Quarterly Press, 1997).

187. See National Party Platform, Democratic Platform, and National Party Platform, Republican Platform (1960–1996). Platforms obtained from *World Book Encyclopedia, American Reference Library* (CD-ROM) (Orem, Utah: Western Standard, 1998).

188. See Ibid. This is clearly an area where more research is needed to comprehend not only how the issue of crime has expanded on the party platforms but also how the policy stances have converged over time and how closely presidents have adhered to this specific portion of the party platform.

189. Thomas and Pika, *The Politics of the Presidency*, p. 135.

190. Jeff Fishel, *Presidents and Promises: From Campaign Pledge to Presidential Performance* (Washington, D.C.: Congressional Quarterly Press, 1985); Gerald Pomper and Susan Lederman, *Elections in America: Control and Influence in Democratic Politics*, 2nd ed. (New York: Longman, 1980).

191. Joe Klein, "Crime Bill Garbage Barge," *Newsweek* 123 (February 28, 1994): 35.

192. Cronin et al., *U.S. vs. Crime in the Streets*, p. 172.

193. Kevin M. Leyden, Willard M. Oliver, and John C. Kilwein, "Is Crime Control Policy Another Form of Pork Barrel Politics?" (paper presented at the annual meeting of the Western Political Science Association, Seattle, November 1999).

194. Kenneth J. Meier, *Politics and the Bureaucracy: Policymaking in the Fourth Branch of Government*, 3rd ed. (Belmont, Calif.: Wadsworth, 1993), p. 83.

195. Robert J. Spitzer, "Promoting Policy Theory: Revising the Arenas of Power," *Policy Studies Journal* 15 (1987): 675–89, at 677.

196. Marc Allen Eisner, *Regulatory Politics in Transition* (Baltimore: The Johns Hopkins University Press, 1993), p. 202.

197. Task Force on the Federalization of Criminal Law, *The Federalization of Criminal Law*, p. 6.

198. Eisner, *Regulatory Politics in Transition*, p. 204.

199. Task Force on the Federalization of Criminal Law, *The Federalization of Criminal Law*, p. 7.

200. John J. Dilulio, Jr., "Federal Crime Policy: Time for a Moratorium," *Brookings Review* 17 (1, 1999): 17–21, at 17.

201. Task Force on the Federalization of Criminal Law, *The Federalization of Criminal Law*, p. 7.

202. Raymond Tatalovich and Bryon Daynes, *Moral Controversies in American Politics* (Armonk, N.Y.: M E Sharpe, 1998); Raymond Tatalovich and Bryon Daynes, *Social Regulatory Policy* (Boulder, Colo.: Westview Press, 1988).

203. Robert F. Meier and Gilbert Geis, *Victimless Crimes?* (Los Angeles: Roxbury, 1997); Edwin M. Schurr, *Crimes without Victims* (Englewood Cliffs, N.J.: Prentice Hall, 1965).

204. Tatalovich and Daynes, *Social Regulatory Policy*.

205. Robert M. Stein and Kenneth M. Bickers, *Perpetuating the Pork Barrel* (Cambridge: Cambridge University Press, 1995), p. 17.

206. Brace and Hinckley, *Follow the Leader*, p. 82.

207. Timothy J. Flanagan and Dennis R. Longmire, *Americans View Crime and Justice: A National Public Opinion Survey* (Thousand Oaks, Calif.: Sage, 1996); William G. Mayer, *The Changing American Mind: How and Why American Public Opinion Changed between 1960 and 1988* (Ann Arbor: University of Michigan Press, 1995); Benjamin I. Page and Robert Y. Shapiro, *The Rational Public: Fifty Years of Trends in Americans' Policy Preferences* (Chicago: University of Chicago Press, 1992); Mark Warr, "The Polls-Poll Trends: Public Opinion on Crime and Punishment," *Public Opinion Quarterly* 59 (1995): 296–310.

208. Michel Foucault, *Discipline and Punish: The Birth of the Prison* (New York: Vintage, 1977), p. 189. This citation was first discovered in William Lyons, *The Politics of Community Policing: Rearranging the Power to Punish* (Ann Arbor: University of Michigan Press, 1999), p. 11.

209. Brace and Hinckley, *Follow the Leader*; Elmer E. Cornwell, *Presidential Leadership of Public Opinion* (Bloomington: Indiana University Press, 1965); Michael B. Grossman and Martha Joynt, *The White House and the News Media* (Baltimore: The Johns Hopkins University Press, 1981); Stephen Hess, "I Am On TV Therefore I Am," in *Media Power in Politics*, ed. Doris A. Graber (Washington, D.C.: Congressional Quarterly Press, 2000), pp. 246–54; Richard Rubin, *Press, Party, and Presidency* (New York: Norton, 1981).

210. Doris Graber, *Crime News and the Public* (New York: Praeger, 1980); Doris Graber, *Mass Media and American Politics* (Washington, D.C.: Congressional Quarterly Press, 1989).

211. Graber, *Crime News and the Public*; Kaiser Family Foundation/Center for Media and Public Affairs Report, *Assessing Local Television News Coverage of Health Issues* (Menlo Park, Calif.: Henry J. Kaiser

Family Foundation, 1998); Ray Surette, *Media, Crime, and Criminal Justice: Images and Realities*, 2nd ed. (Belmont, Calif.: West/Wadsworth, 1997).

212. Albert P. Melone and Robert Slagter, "Interest Group Politics and the Reform of the Criminal Code," in Nagel et al., *The Political Science of Criminal Justice*, pp. 41–55; Ronald G. Shaiko, "Reverse Lobbying: Interest Group Mobilization from the White House and the Hill," in *Interest Group Politics*, 5th ed., eds. Allan J. Cigler and Burdett A. Loomis (Washington, D.C.: Congressional Quarterly Press, 1998), pp. 255–82.

213. See appendix in James Houston and William W. Parsons, *Criminal Justice and the Policy Process* (Chicago: Nelson Hall, 1998).

214. Shaiko, "Reverse Lobbying," pp. 255–82.

215. James David Barber, *The Presidential Character: Predicting Performance in the White House*, 4th ed. (Englewood Cliffs, N.J.: Prentice Hall, 1992), p. 5.

216. Ibid.

217. Ronald Reagan, *An American Life* (New York: Simon & Schuster, 1990), p. 40.

218. Calder, "Presidents and Crime Control: Kennedy, Johnson and Nixon and the Influences of Ideology"; Calder, "*Presidents and Crime Control: Some Limitations on Executive Policy Making.*"

219. Calder, "*Presidents and Crime Control: Some Limitations on Executive Policy Making,*" p. 161.

220. Ibid.

221. Calder, "Presidents and Crime Control: Kennedy, Johnson and Nixon and the Influences of Ideology"; Calder, "*Presidents and Crime Control: Some Limitations on Executive Policy Making.*"

222. Ibid.

223. DiClerico, *The American President.*

224. R. E. Neusdadt, *Presidential Power and the Modern Presidents* (New York: Free Press, 1990).

225. W. M. Oliver, *The Law and Order Presidency* (Upper Saddle River, N.J.: Prentice Hall, 2003).

226. W. M. Oliver, "Presidential Rhetoric on Crime and Public Opinion," *Criminal Justice Review* 23 (1998): 139–60.

227. W. M. Oliver, "The Pied Piper of Crime in America: An Analysis of Presidents' and Public's Agenda on Crime," *Criminal Justice Policy Review* 13 (2002): 139–55.

228. W. M. Oliver, "The Power to Persuade: Presidential Influence over Congress on Crime Control Policy," *Criminal Justice Review* 28 (1, 2003): 113–32.

229. W. M. Oliver and D. E. Barlow, "Following the Leader? Presidential Influence over Congress in the Passage of Federal Crime Control Policy" (paper presented at the annual meeting of the Academy of Criminal Justice, Boston, March 4–8, 2003).

230. See the National Governors Association Web site, available online at http://www.nga.org.

231. R. J. Gerber, *Cruel and Usual: Our Criminal Injustice System* (Westport, Conn.: Praeger, 1999).

232. J. M. Bruce and C. Wilcox, *The Changing Politics of Gun Control* (Lanham, Md.: Rowman & Littlefield, 1998); R. J. Spitzer, *The Politics of Gun Control* (Chatham, N.J.: Chatham House, 1995).

233. J. D. Davey, *The Politics of Prison Expansion: Winning Elections by Waging War on Crime* (Westport, Conn.: Praeger, 1998).

234. D. L. Martin, *Running City Hall* (Tuscaloosa: University of Alabama Press, 1982).

235. See the U.S. Conference of Mayors Web site, available online at www.usmayors.org.

236. W. G. Skogan and S. M. Hartnett, *Community Policing, Chicago Style* (New York: Oxford University Press, 1997).

237. W. Lyons, *The Politics of Community Policing: Rearranging the Power to Punish* (Ann Arbor: University of Michigan Press, 1999); W. E. Reed, *The Politics of Community Policing: The Case of Seattle* (New York: Garland, 1999).

238. G. L. Kelling and C. M. Coles, *Fixing Broken Windows* (New York: Free Press, 1996).

239. E. B. Silverman, *NYPD Battles Crime: Innovative Strategies in Policing* (Boston: Northeastern University Press, 1999).

240. A. McArdle and T. Erzen, *Zero Tolerance: Quality of Life and the New Police Brutality in New York City* (New York: New York University Press, 2001).

241. L. R. Jacobs and R. Y. Shapiro, *Politicians Don't Pander: Political Manipulation and the Loss of Democratic Responsiveness* (Chicago: University of Chicago Press, 2000).

5

Legislative Branches

INTRODUCTION

The federal, state, and local legislatures have the basic responsibility to provide a safe and secure environment where citizens can own property and seek happiness. They do this through considering and creating laws that attempt to prohibit people from committing acts that would be dangerous or potentially harmful to others. The resulting laws, called the criminal code, define what acts are prohibited and the punishment that may be applied if that act is carried out. The federal, state, and local legislatures are each involved in creating criminal laws or criminal codes that attempt to reduce crime. Each of these bodies also plays an important role in the policy process and has a major impact on the administration of criminal justice.

FEDERALIZATION OF CRIME

As the Founding Fathers were writing the U.S. Constitution and creating a new government for the nation, they viewed crime control as a function for the state and local government indicating their fear of a central police authority that was housed in the national government.[1] In Federalist 17, Hamilton wrote, "It will always be far more easy for the State governments to encroach upon the national authorities, than for the national government to encroach upon the State authorities." He also wrote, "There is one transcendent advantage belonging to the province of the State governments, which alone suffices to place the matter in a clear and satisfactory light,—I mean the ordinary administration of criminal and civil justice." This "would insure them so decided an empire over their respective citizens as to render them at all times a complete counterpoise, and, not infrequently, dangerous rivals to the power of the Union." Based on these ideas, the Founding Fathers defined only three acts as federal crimes in the Constitution, including treason against the United States, counterfeiting securities and currency, piracy and felonies committed on the high seas, and treason.[2] Instead, they created a system whereby states were able to define and prosecute nearly all criminal behavior in individual state courts.[3]

But over the past 200 years, crime became more of a national concern and the federal government has become more involved in crime control issues.[4] The trend toward more congressional action or intervention in crime-related issues is called the "federalization of crime." The federal government's role in the crime arena has increased dramatically since the 1960s and continues to be an important factor in many if not all areas of criminal justice. Many pieces of legislation concerning crime have passed, starting with the Interstate Commerce Clause, which is how crime came to be regulated by the U.S. Congress. The agency created by Congress in 1887 to enforce the Commerce Clause was the Interstate Commerce Commission, which would regulate railroad rates for goods carried in interstate commerce and was the first federal regulatory agency. Congress also passed the Comstock Law in 1873 and the Mann Act in 1910. The former law was intended to prevent any "obscene, lewd, or lascivious" material from being sent through the U.S. mail, while the latter law was intended to prevent the transportation of white women across state lines for purposes of prostitution.

The government's role in fighting crime was enhanced during Prohibition. The Eighteenth Amendment to the Constitution outlawed the manufacture and transportation of alcoholic beverages. To enforce the law, Congress created the position of federal Prohibition agents as part of the U.S. Treasury. Yet not only did the Eighteenth Amendment create a new class of criminals, those that manufactured, sold, or transported "intoxicating liquors," but it also spawned a new wave of street crimes because of the illegal black market, which in turn gave rise to the Mafia.

Congress also became involved in crime issues when it passed the 1934 Crime Bill, which regulated machine guns. Also called the National Firearms Act of 1934, it put regulations on machine guns, sawed-off shotguns and rifles, silencers, and concealable firearms other than pistols and revolvers and added a transfer tax of $200 on the purchase of machine guns. The new law also required existing firearm owners to register their arms within 60 days.[5] Congress modified the law in 1938 with another Federal Firearms Act. This time, the law required that any firearms dealer obtain a $1 license from the secretary of commerce before transporting, shipping, or receiving any firearm in interstate or foreign commerce. These dealers were, under the new law, forbidden to ship firearms in interstate commerce to any person who was under indictment for a crime, who had been convicted of a violent crime, or who did not have a state license to own firearms. The bill also required gun dealers to keep records of their sales and shipments. The federal license could be revoked if the dealer was convicted for a criminal offense or found to have violated the new law destination. Together, the 1934 and 1938 gun bills set the groundwork for all federal firearms law for the next three decades.[6]

There are many reasons for this recent trend beyond just gun control. One is the emergence and understanding of organized crime in America. Although organized crime had become a problem during the era of Prohibition, according to the FBI's very own J. Edgar Hoover, it was deemed to have been eradicated. However, realizations that this was not the case began to surface in 1950 and 1951, when the Senate Special Committee to Investigate Crime in Interstate Commerce, more simply known as the Kefauver Committee, traveled across the nation to hold hearings to probe into the existence of organized crime. Hundreds of top mobsters and law enforcement agents were called to testify in front of the committee. Because the hearings were televised, the American public was also able to hear the testimony and see the actual men and women who were involved in the organization. They were no longer mythical figures but real people who committed serious crime. Because of the media attention the hearings received and the popularity of the hearings by average Americans, it became one of the most important probes of organized crime in the United States. The hearings successfully publicized the facts about organized crime and proved the existence of an underground criminal organization that existed across the nation. When it was over, many citizens called on action from the federal government to get more involved and punish the members of the organized crime syndicates and to abolish the organization.

Another reason for the federalization of crime was the dramatic increase in drug abuse during the 1960s, especially by Caucasian, middle-class youth. Citizens saw that states were not able to stop the influx of drugs into the country or its use by so many people, so they called on Congress for action. Additionally, since there was a need to cooperate with other nations to deal with the importation of drugs, there needed to be an international approach to drug control, which states are not allowed to do. This emphasis would expand greatly during the Nixon administration and became hallmarks of both the Reagan and the Bush administrations.

Also during the 1960s, reported crime was increasing across America.[7] The FBI's Uniform Crime Report indicated that crime was increasing from 1.8 million in 1960 to almost 5 million in 1969.[8] Along with the increase in crime was an increase in public fear of becoming a victim of crime and more pressure on the government to make stricter penalties to deter potential offenders and at the same time lessen the chances of becoming a crime victim. Among the states around that time, there was a general perception that the federal government had more resources than the other levels of government to "solve" these problems, which tended to push the problem upward to the level of Congress.[9] Many citizens felt that the federal government had more money, more technology, and more personnel than states, thus making them more effective, potentially, to fight crime.

During this same time period, changes in the political scene also raised crime from the local and state levels to the federal level. Candidates for national public offices, including candidates for president and Congress, began to address crime-related issues (including drug use by youth, increased crime rates, and the natural ability of the federal government to fight crime), making crime control a viable campaign issue.[10] In 1964, conservative Republican Barry Goldwater and Democratic President Lyndon Johnson were the first to debate the crime issue at length and elevate it from a state concern to a national concern. Goldwater blamed the increase in crime on the liberal Democratic policies that were "soft on crime" and "coddled the criminals." He argued that conservative Republican policies toward crime would be more effective in reducing the crime rate and the resulting fear of crime across the nation.

Federal crime control policies became election fodder in many campaigns after that. As detailed in the previous chapter, in 1968, Nixon labeled himself the "law-and-order" president, arguing for stricter punishment and a more active federal role in crime control. In 1988, Democratic nominee Michael Dukakis was held responsible by a pro-Republican group for crimes committed by a convicted felon Willie Horton, who committed crimes while out on parole. George H. W. Bush and Bill Clinton debated the crime issue in 1992, and it was also an issue between George W. Bush and Al Gore in 2000.

In the most recent election in 2008, Barak Obama supported the death penalty for the most heinous crimes, but called for reforms to guard against wrongful convictions.[11] He argued for a national drug policy that included tougher enforcement measures as well as prevention and treatment. He believed in an individual's right to own a gun[12], but at the same time argued that there should be reasonable and commonsense gun-safety measures.[13] During the campaign, he promised to invest in innovative youth crime prevention programs to keep youth out of trouble and help them grow into law abiding citizens. He also supported prisoner reentry programs. Obama's opponent, John McCain, supported expanding the death penalty for federal crimes.[14] He believed in the second amendment and opposed gun control.[15] He supported the war on drugs, but at the same time believed that treatment was essential for eradicating illicit drug use.

Not only did the presidents and other politicians talk about crime, but they acted on it as well. Congress, in the 1968 Omnibus and Safe Streets Act, created the Law Enforcement Assistance Administration. This was a federal grant program that provided millions of dollars to states to help them become more effective at fighting crime. Under this program, Congress provided direct financial assistance to states and localities for research on crime and justice that allowed researchers to fund projects on the causes of criminal behavior, the decision-making processes with the criminal justice system, and the effectiveness of punishment programs. He promised, if elected president, that he would fight gang-related crimes, tougher punishments for violent offenders, and vocational training for prison inmates.

Additionally, Congress created many agencies or bureaucracies that are active in criminal justice. For example, the Office for Juvenile Justice and Delinquency Prevention was created by Congress in the Juvenile Justice and Delinquency Prevention Act of 1974. This office was created to coordinate federal, state, and local government programs related to juvenile delinquency and to develop a comprehensive plan for coordinating juvenile delinquency programs. The legislation also created the National Institute for Juvenile Justice and Delinquency Prevention, which is responsible for conducting research and evaluation projects related to juvenile delinquency. The DEA was created during the Nixon administration as a way to fight illicit drug use in our country, and the Department of Homeland Security was created after the terrorist attacks of September 11, 2001 during the Bush administration.

It has been argued that the federalization of crime is a positive trend for crime control. When the federal government takes the lead in fighting crime, it can raise issues and debate alternatives on the national level. In doing so, it can set the tone of the discussion about crime prevention and make communities and officials more aware of problems and solutions. Additionally, the federal government can establish a funding agenda for state and local governments to help them design programs without adding additional tax burdens on citizens. This allows the states to become more active in fighting crime and help them to respond to increased crime rates more effectively. States, counties and cities have received significant amounts of money from the federal government to run anticrime programs and now rely on federal money to fund a large portion of their criminal justice systems.[16] Another positive aspect of the federalization of crime is that the federal government is able to create national databases to find missing persons or solve crimes better than individual states. There are many crimes that can be most appropriately and effectively addressed by the federal government rather than states. Crimes such as drug trafficking or cybercrime are ones in which the offender can easily cross state (and international) borders, and thus would be more effectively fought at the federal level.

Of course, there are others who would argue that the push toward the federalization of crime is a negative trend. Some have argued that the federalization of crime is a shift in power from the state governments to the federal level so that it increases the power of Congress while decreasing the ability of states to respond to their own problems and make decisions for themselves. Instead, Congress now has power when it makes laws to tell people how to act or not to act and what the punishment will be for that behavior. Additionally, federalizing crime puts additional demands on the federal system, including demands for funding, more judges and other court personnel, police agencies, and correctional facilities.[17]

Critics of federalization have argued that the more active federal role in crime control is motivated by political concerns rather than a real concern for public safety and should therefore be limited. They point out that crime control is not an area noted in the Constitution as being under federal jurisdiction. Throughout the document, the Constitution is very specific as to what things the federal government will do and what things the state governments will do. Those powers or responsibilities that are under the jurisdiction of the federal government only are therefore denied to the states. Examples of these powers are printing money, declaring war, and conducting foreign policy. These are tasks that only the federal government can carry out, and states are denied this power.

Some authors have outlined specific times when the federal government should get involved in crime control. The federal government should get involved to protect the civil rights of citizens, and in emergency situations such as natural disasters, in order to protect the safety of the residents. Another time that federal action would be appropriate is when financial or technical assistance is needed by the states. This may happen if a state experiences a large-scale offense such as a terrorist act. In these cases, the offense may be "too big" for the states to handle, leaving the state overwhelmed. The federal government should also get involved in order to protect its own facilities, such as landmarks. Crimes where foreign nations are involved, or there are particularly dangerous subjects, may require federal action. Finally, if there are major local government officials or industries accused of criminal actions, federal involvement may be needed in order to ensure a fair and legitimate investigation of those charges.

Nevertheless, the federalization of crime has continued to expand, and Congress has become more involved in fighting crime than ever before. In recent years, Congress created more than 3,000 crimes that can be prosecuted by the federal courts, much of which had previously been left to the states.[18] Most of the legislation has been passed in the past forty years. In fact, "more than 40% of the federal criminal provisions enacted since the Civil War have been enacted since 1970."[19] In the 105th Congress alone, there were an estimated 1,000 bills relating to crime introduced for consideration, many of which would create new federal laws.[20] In addition, the federal government has created hundreds, if not thousands, of agencies aimed at different aspects of crime. Thus, over the years, crime control has become an issue over which Congress has become very active, and it has become a major responsibility for congressional action.

An example of an area in which Congress has become actively involved in a typically state offense is drunk driving. In 1996, the issue of drunk driving moved from the state to the national level when Congress passed the National Highway Safety Act. This legislative act established the National Highway Safety Bureau, which was responsible for funding research on drunk driving issues[21] and promoted the drunk driving issue before Congress and in other venues.[22] This action served to institutionalize alcohol abuse and drunk driving on the formal agenda of Congress and the federal government. The resulting congressional attention led to additional laws and the creation of new federal agencies to administer them.[23] Other offenses that are typically regarded as offenses against the state that are now also federal crimes include arson, carjacking, and failing to pay child support.[24]

Thus, crime control has become a policy venue for Congress, but it also remains one for the states. That means that the issues revolving around crime are simultaneously subject to the jurisdiction of several institutions rather than being within the domain of only one institution.[25] At this point, the federal, state, and local governments each pass laws and are involved in the policy process.

FEDERAL LEGISLATURE: CONGRESS

The legislative branch of the national government, defined in article I of the Constitution, is called Congress. This branch is made up of two houses: the House of Representatives and the Senate. Congress has a number of responsibilities, each of which is defined in the Constitution. These include fiscal powers (defining tax levels and the spending of money), foreign policy powers (ratifying treaties with other countries, confirming ambassadors and other public officials, and declaring war), commerce powers (the power to regulate commerce with foreign nations and among the several states), impeachment powers (the ability to remove a president or other high federal employee from office), confirmation powers (the authority to approve nominations made by the president for cabinet members, the U.S. Supreme Court, and lower-court justices, ambassadors, and other federal branch officials), amending powers (to amend the Constitution), and electing powers (to elect a president if the electoral college does not).

The primary purpose of Congress, however, is to create new laws and policies that, in the long run, will create and/or maintain a safe and secure society. The laws that they pass are considered federal offenses, and people convicted of these crimes are punished in the federal correctional system. Examples of federal crimes include treason, airplane hijacking, and counterfeiting currency.

Role in Policy Process

On the federal level, Congress plays an important role in the policy process. It plays a key role in problem identification, agenda setting, and policy formulation (or creating the law). Although Congress does not formally implement the law (that role belongs to the bureaucracies), it does assist in the funding aspects of implementation. Finally, Congress plays a role in the program evaluation and reassessment of the policy implemented by the bureaucracies.

PROBLEM IDENTIFICATION   The members of Congress are key players in identifying what problems throughout the nation are significant enough to demand attention. These elected officials determine what issues are discussed and even what issues are acted on. This may be the result of some event, called a "trigger event," that can often translate a social situation into a public issue. These are events that symbolize a situation, forcing it onto the public agenda.[26] Trigger events often put criminal justice problems onto the agendas of governments. An example would be the Virginia Tech massacre in 2007, which resulted in new federal legislation that improved the National Instant Criminal Background Check (NICS) system,[27] or the terrorist attacks of September 11, 2001, which resulted in action that created the USA PATRIOT Act.

Problem identification can also be triggered by media coverage. An increase in media coverage of an issue can eventually lead to the emergence of that issue on the congressional agenda. A good example of this is the extensive media coverage of drug abuse, which became a major topic on the congressional agenda for many years. As the increased media coverage of drug abuse occurred, various forces within Congress were activated, and they attempted to define the national response to the drug problem.[28]

Sometimes members of Congress get ideas from their constituency, or the people who elected them to represent them in Washington. They may have a particular concern and ask for their representative to propose legislation that will alleviate that concern. In this case, the constituencies identify the problem, and the representatives translate that into action.

Members of Congress can also be influenced in identifying a potential problem by members of interest groups or bureaucracies. These other unelected actors often attempt to convince the members of Congress that an issue is worthwhile for their attention. If they are successful in convincing the member of Congress about the importance of an issue, that topic may appear in front of Congress as a legislative proposal.

AGENDA SETTING   Topics for the political agenda come from a variety of sources. First, they can come from the members of Congress themselves. The members choose what issues will be given attention and brought to the forefront, and select what issues will be postponed until a later date or even ignored altogether. Some problems are given top priority, and others are dismissed for a later session. Every public official has his or her own preferred issues and ideas to support. Only a portion of these will succeed in securing a position on the congressional agenda.[29]

Individual members of Congress often serve as agenda setters. In a study of agenda setting in the Senate, Professor Jack Walker concludes that there are some "activist legislators, motivated by a desire to promote social change, and anxious to gain reputations as reformers [who] constantly search for issues that might be transformed into new items on the Senate's discretionary agenda."[30] Those members of Congress who push policy proposals are often referred to as "policy entrepreneurs." These members attempt to keep an issue alive, build support for it, get it on an agenda, and secure action on it.

In choosing to put an issue on the agenda, political leaders can be motivated by thoughts of political advantage, the public interest, or their political reputations.[31] Since crime issues often bring positive media attention to a member of Congress, they are often recognized as important problems and put on the congressional agenda. In many cases, however, this could be no more than an attempt to get positive media coverage and improve their public image.

In some cases, issues are put on the agenda as a result of a "moral panic." This is when there is a general hysteria about crime or a group of people that becomes defined as a threat to society's values and interests.[32] Generally, there is nothing out of the ordinary occurring, but the media present the issue in such a way that it becomes a threat. Chiricos argues that we have seen many moral panics in recent years that have either put issues on the political agenda or served to keep them on the agenda. He lists drugs (particularly crack cocaine) and juvenile violence as two moral panics that have resulted in legislation toward more punitive punishments for these offenses.[33]

Members of Congress often engage in agenda setting because they want to satisfy their constituents. Since many constituents are concerned with crime, it is easy to focus on crime issues to please the constituents. The resulting positive publicity is essential for elected officials.[34] Another reason a member of Congress would engage in agenda setting is to enhance his or her intra-Washington reputation. A member of Congress who successfully navigates a bill through the process of becoming a law may get a reputation of being a "heavyweight" who must be taken seriously. These members are successful at carving out a policy turf.[35] Of course, many members of Congress put anticrime legislation on the agenda simply because of a basic desire to set or create good public policy that will improve society as a whole.[36] Since crime is a major public policy issue and has remained so for many years, there are representatives who simply want to put forth a serious attempt to protect citizens and/or punish those who harm others.

The second source of agenda setting issues for Congress is the president. In some cases, the president may play a role in getting Congress to consider a policy proposal. The president may campaign on a particular issue and want Congress to follow through on the idea. In this case, the president must find enough support for the proposal not only to get the bill introduced in Congress but also to get enough votes to get it passed. The president may give speeches to Congress where he attempts to garnish support for his ideas, or he may go to numerous organizations and ask for their help in getting Congress to support a proposed bill.

The effectiveness of a president to work with Congress varies and depends on the president's personality or his relationship with the members of Congress. In some cases, the president's role as an agenda setter for Congress is diminished when Congress is controlled by the opposition party. In this case, the majority party leaders may be reluctant to accept the president's agenda as the starting point for policy dialogue. They take on more responsibility for agenda setting, drawing issues from the complex of matters under examination in committees and elsewhere in Congress. In selecting issues, they are influenced by public opinion, congressional support, triggering events, and other criteria.[37]

In some cases, an issue can even be put on the political agenda in the campaign for political office. Often, candidates running for office make campaign pledges or promises about how they will deal with a particular issue or problem if they are elected. In essence, the agenda can be influenced by those who are running for office, not just those who have been elected. Once in office, the candidate (now elected official) must follow through with that campaign promise, or risk a reputation of inaction. The first candidate to discuss the crime issue was Barry Goldwater in 1968, and since then it has been on the agenda of many candidates for office.[38]

The issues for the agenda may also come from interest groups. Each of these groups will frequently be competing with others for the attention of the legislator, each attempting to demonstrate or prove that its problem, as it has defined it, is the most needing of the attention of that public official.

In order to better understand the agenda-setting process in Congress, it is helpful to return to Cobb and Elder's distinction between a systemic agenda and an institutional agenda (see Chapter 3). The first consists of those issues that members of Congress agree merit their attention and are legitimate areas of concern for Congress. In this case, there is agreement that some type of action is needed. However, this agenda is vague and does not suggest specific policy options to solve the problem. The second type of agenda is the institutional agenda, in which there are explicit options or policy proposals suggested to solve a problem. This has been called an action agenda, which is more specific and concrete than a systemic agenda, where there are more fully developed plans.[39]

Some issues are always on the congressional agenda, whereas others come and go. For the most part, crime is always on the political agenda of most members of Congress, but the specific topics discussed and the extent to which they receive public attention vary. For example, illicit drugs were not a primary concern across the nation during the first part of the 1900s. Small blips of attention occurred in the 1930s, 1940s, and 1950s, but it was not until the mid-1960s that drug abuse emerged as a major issue. Even this attention was short lived, however, as the issue declined during the 1970s. It then began another increase in the mid-1980s. Overall, the topic of illicit drugs was on the systemic agenda of Congress during two periods: the late 1960s and the late 1980s.[40]

Finally, the agenda may be influenced by the bureaucracies that are responsible for carrying out policies created by Congress. These bureaucracies can provide information to the legislators about issues or concerns facing their communities and work aggressively to keep those issues in the forefront until they receive action. In the area of crime control, there are many bureaucracies that have developed a direct relationship with legislators and that are successful in influencing what topics are addressed by Congress. These can include the Justice Department, the FBI, or even the individual state attorneys general offices.

POLICY FORMULATION   The most significant role that the members of Congress play in the policy process surrounds the political tasks of policy formation and lawmaking.[41] This involves passing new laws that prohibit certain behaviors and at the same time setting punishments for those behaviors. Proposals are made to solve the problem that was identified in earlier stages. Once the different proposals are discussed, one of them is chosen as the best alternative to address the problem. The process for making new laws and/or punishments is complex and involves many different actors.

How a Bill Becomes a Law   The formal process of creating a new law may seem complicated because of its many steps; however, the process is logical and simple at the same time. The process was intentionally created to have many steps, allowing many people to potentially have access to lawmakers so that they have the chance to influence the final bill and/or law. This, in turn, helps prevent individuals from creating policies to benefit only themselves (rule by the elite).

The process begins when a proposal for a new law is written. Proposals can come from many sources, including but not limited to legislators, the president, interest groups, agencies, or even average citizens. Once that proposal is made, it must capture the attention of a member of either the House of Representatives or the Senate who will introduce the proposal by presenting it to a clerk of the House or Senate. That proposal is given a sequential identification number, such as SB 449 (for a proposal introduced into the Senate) or HB 226 (for a proposal introduced into the House). This simply means that the bill is the 449th bill introduced into the Senate or the 226th bill introduced into the House during that congressional session.

After the proposal is introduced into either the House or the Senate, it is referred to the most relevant committee, and the chairperson of the committee refers it to the most relevant subcommittee. Committees and subcommittees are simply small groups of House or Senate members that work on a proposal so that the entire House or Senate does not have to. This makes Congress more efficient. Once they get the proposal, the subcommittee members have many options. They can choose to do nothing, and the bill will die, or they can choose to hold hearings on the proposal where interested and knowledgeable people testify and provide subcommittee members with information about the problem. Based on this information, the subcommittee members can choose to mark up, or edit, the proposal. They then vote on the proposal. If the members vote no on the bill, it goes no further. If they vote yes, the bill heads back to the full committee. The committee also has the option of voting on the bill "as is," of holding hearings on the bill, or of doing research on the proposal. They can also choose to mark up the bill or to add amendments to it. A vote is taken in the committee, and if the vote is no, the bill dies. If the vote is yes, the bill goes on to the next step, which is consideration in the full House or Senate, depending on where the bill originated. Members then have the opportunity to debate the proposal. Debate could result in additional amendments or changes added to the bill, each of which must be voted on and either accepted or rejected by the entire membership. When debate is concluded, a vote is taken on the proposal. A simple majority is needed to approve it.

If the proposal has traveled through only one body, it must go through this process in the other body. For example, if a proposal was introduced only into the House, the proposal must go through the Senate. If the House acts on a bill and the Senate does not, the bill dies. A bill can be introduced into either the House or the Senate separately or into both at the same time. Some bills go through the entire process first in one body, then the other, while others go through both bodies of Congress simultaneously. In any event, once both bodies have passed a bill, they then send it to the president for his action. This can happen only if the bills that come out of the House and Senate processes are identical. If not, there is a conference committee, made up of members of the House and Senate. Here they try to iron out the differences between the two versions and come up with one version. If this is done, the compromise version must then be voted on by the members of the House and Senate for their approval. If both bodies do not accept the conference version, then either it has to go back to the conference committee or it will die. If the House and Senate vote positively on the bill, then it goes to the president.

The president then has a number of options. He can sign the bill, at which point the bill will go into effect on the date specified in the bill. The president can also choose to veto the bill, or reject the legislation. In this case, the president must send Congress a message outlining why he vetoed the bill. Congress can choose to override the president's veto by the vote of two-thirds of its members in both the House and the Senate. If this does not happen, the bill dies. Another option for the president is to not sign the bill within ten days of receiving it (excluding Sundays) and return it to Congress. If Congress adjourns during those ten days, then it is considered a "pocket veto," and it does not become law.

This entire process must be completed within a two-year span. This is because a congressional session is two years long and starts over every two years. At the end of each session, all the bills that were in the middle of this process are dropped. Each new Congress starts fresh every two years. Although the bills can be reintroduced into the next Congress, they are given new numbers and designations, and the process starts all over again.

House/Senate Judiciary Committees   Both the House and the Senate have, over the years, developed a system of committees and subcommittees that help the members get things done quickly and efficiently.[42] It is much easier for a committee or subcommittee with only a few members to look over a proposal and recommend changes or maybe debate issues than it is the entire membership of the House or Senate. Members who are not on the committees rely on the committees for their expertise and thus give them time to work on their own bills. On the whole, the committees play an important role in the policy process, but their efforts often remain unnoticed by the public.

To begin with, the makeup of the committee can have a lot of influence over the outcome of a proposal. A more liberal committee will more likely support a more liberal policy proposal, and a more conservative committee will more likely support a more conservative bill. The committee chairs are chosen by many factors. One of those depends on the majority party in the House or the Senate, and the second depends on the seniority of the individual member. Other members are added to the bottom of their party in that committee. They climb the seniority ranking by remaining on the committee and accruing years of seniority. New members of Congress want assignments to the most influential committees. When an opening occurs, it is filled by the next-highest-ranking majority party member. The assignments are handed out by the party leaders in the House and Senate when new members arrive.[43]

The chairmen are also responsible for appointing the committees' staff members and allocating the committees' budgets. The committees and subcommittees have staff and legal help to assist them. They help draft bills, develop political support, work with agency officials, and attempt to achieve compromises on disputed resolutions. Thus, committee and subcommittee staff possess substantial influence on the development of legislation.

Once it receives a proposal, the committee determines the content of the bill. These small bodies review suggestions for legislation. The committee can hold hearings on a proposed bill, and in this sense it is deciding the agenda of the full committees. It can amend the proposal, rewrite portions of it, or even write its own bills.[44] In the end, the membership makes recommendations to the whole Senate or House about the proposed bill. In most cases, a proposed bill is not submitted to the entire House or Senate for a vote without prior approval of a committee. Over time, the members develop expertise in a particular area and eventually can be regarded as more competent to make decisions concerning a policy than the whole committee or whole House.[45] The committee and subcommittee system actually encourages members to concentrate on particular policy areas. This creates policy specialists within Congress. Such specialization gives members more opportunity to influence policy in their areas of expertise.[46]

The individual committee and subcommittee members are often sought out by interest groups because of their expertise in an area.[47] The interest groups will provide information to the committee member and hope that the member will support that interest group during the hearings. Groups such as corporations, banks, law firms, unions, or lobbyists hand over billions of dollars to politicians in exchange for a return on their investments. It is hard to follow the money trail from contribution to legislation; however, members of Congress admit that people who contribute get to meet with members of Congress personally.[48]

The congressional subcommittees are not unbiased and in most cases show favoritism to the interests they are intended to oversee and control. This can be because members of Congress appointed to serve on a particular subcommittee tend to represent constituencies whose interests are affected by the policy in question.[49] Thus, the congressional members want to support their constituents and can do so by serving on committees which focus on topics of interest to those voters, thus potentially having an impact on the legislative proposals that come out of the subcommittee.

All the committees and subcommittees that have been set up by Congress over the years perform different functions. One type of committee is the conference committee. Any differences between the House and Senate versions of a proposed bill must be ironed out, as only one bill can be sent to the president for his approval. A conference committee is made up of members of both the House and the Senate, where they meet and attempt to come to a compromise between the two versions of the bill. If they are successful, the "compromise version" of the bill is returned to the entire House and Senate for a revote by the entire membership. If the differences cannot be worked out, then the bill dies or proceeds no further in the process. These committees are temporary and exist only for the process of coming up with a compromise bill. The members are appointed by the leadership of each house. They almost always include the chairs of both committees as well as the ranking minority party member. These conference committees are powerful actors in the policy process. They have a lot of power because they shape the final legislation. They are not obliged to accept either the House or the Senate wording of provisions. Instead, they may choose to write new wording themselves.[50]

Both the House and the Senate have committees and subcommittees that deal exclusively with criminal justice issues. These judiciary committees are among the most powerful committees in Congress. In the House, the relevant committee is the Committee on the Judiciary. This committee was established as a "standing" committee in 1813 and currently oversees legislation concerning civil and criminal judicial proceedings (including federal courts and judges), bankruptcy, espionage, terrorism, civil liberties, constitutional amendments, immigration and naturalization, interstate compacts, claims against the United States, national penitentiaries, presidential succession, antitrust law, revision and codification of U.S. statutes, state and territorial boundary lines, and patents, copyrights, and trademarks. They have oversight responsibility for the Departments of Justice and Homeland Security. As such, they must seek an appropriate balance between citizens' constitutional rights and national security. The Committee members also play a role in impeachment proceedings if that situation presents itself.[51]

The subcommittees of the House Judiciary Committee include the Subcommittee on the Constitution, Civil Rights, and Civil Liberties, the Subcommittee on Commercial and Administrative Law, the Subcommittee on Crime, Terrorism, and Homeland Security, and the Subcommittee on Immigration, Citizenship, Refugees, Border Security, and International Law. It can be seen that each subcommittee narrows in on a particular subject. When proposals are sent to the Judiciary Committee, they are further divided and sent to the most relevant subcommittee. Here, a small number of House members can work diligently on that proposal and help ensure its passage in the entire House of Representatives.

The Senate also has a committee that is devoted to issues surrounding crime and criminal justice: the Committee on the Judiciary. As one of the original "standing" committees, it was first authorized in 1816. The members consider legislation related to criminal justice, the expansion of the judicial system to new territories, and judicial salaries. They also consider legislation on terrorism, human rights, immigration, intellectual property rights, antitrust law, and internet privacy. When needed, the Senate Committee on the Judiciary plays a role in approving the president's nominees for federal judges. The subcommittees in the Senate include Administrative Oversight and the Courts; Antitrust, Competition Policy and Consumer Rights; the Constitution; Crime and Drugs; Human Rights and the Law; Immigration, Refugees and Border Security; and

Terrorism and Homeland Security.[52] As in the House, each of these subcommittees focuses on specific areas within crime and criminal justice. The members of each of the subcommittees are responsible for editing a proposed bill so that it can receive enough support from the members of the Senate to pass.

Congressional Bureaucracies   The ability of Congress to make effective policy has been enhanced by expanded assistance provided by staff and different research agencies. This is especially important because the issues that members are called on to resolve in recent years have become more complex. This means that they have a need for technical and expert assistance like never before.

Most if not all members of Congress have personal staff. This includes those people who work for the members of Congress either in Washington, D.C., or in their home districts. Congressional staff workers handle much of the actual writing of legislation. They must deal with the details of proposed legislation, such as the research and writing of bills, including the choice of words or phrases, the inclusion of particular provisions, and whether it will do what its supporters want done once enacted. They also have input as to the member's position on a bill. When the time comes, the staff members are involved with much of the bargaining over legislative details. In addition to helping with legislation, the staff assists the congressional member with administrative duties, such as answering phones and writing letters to constituents. They prepare the members of Congress for press interviews, give them guidance, handle constituents, screen lobbyists, and prepare the agenda for committee hearings. The staff can range from experienced attorneys who provide legal advice to college interns who may be responsible for making copies and disseminating them to interested people. On the whole, the staff for the individual members or the committees may be quite prominent because of their expertise in a specific area. In many instances, the staff are able to devote their full attention to one particular substantive policy area and become knowledgeable in that field. Of course, their immediate influence depends on the individual staff member and the congressional member.[53]

Another group of staff, the institutional staff, has also been developed to assist members of Congress in their legislative tasks. This refers to those agencies that provide informational services to members of Congress. Examples include the Congressional Research Service, the General Accounting Office, and the Congressional Budget Office. These offices provide members of Congress with research studies, policy evaluations, and budgetary data in a nonpartisan and objective manner. The Office of the Legislative Counsel, found within both the House and the Senate, was also created to help members make better policy. They employ several dozen lawyer-technicians who operate under strict rules of nonpartisanship and objectivity in order to perform the technical work in drafting legislation, which includes fitting it into the existing body of law.[54]

One agency designed to help members of Congress create informed laws is the Congressional Research Service (CRS). The CRS was created in 1914 as the research arm of the Congress. Currently housed within the Library of Congress, the CRS works for members of the Congress, committee members, and staff and provides nonpartisan analysis and research on issues related to proposed legislation. The CRS not only provides bill analysis but also identifies policy alternatives, assists in framing legislative proposals, develops quantitative databases, evaluates new research findings, and delivers expert testimony before congressional committees.[55]

Another congressional research agency is the General Accountability office (GAO). The GAO works as the investigative arm of Congress. Congress may ask the GAO to study the programs and expenditures of the federal agencies to determine if tax dollars are being spent effectively. The GAO also advises members of Congress and heads of agencies about ways to make programs more effective. Like the CRS, the GAO is independent and nonpartisan.[56]

A third research agency for Congress is the Congressional Budget Office. Since its creation in 1974, this agency provides congressional members with nonpartisan analyses of economic and budgetary information. The estimates it provides assist the members of Congress in preparing the federal budget each year. Their reports do not contain any policy recommendations to Congress, but instead focus on cost estimates, budget options, and long-term outlooks.[57]

Other Actors: Interest Groups, Media, Political Parties, and Public Opinion   Other actors, such as interest groups, media, political parties, and public opinion, also have an impact on the legislative process. Interest groups are actively involved in influencing the final content of the proposal as well as influencing legislators' voting on a proposal so that the final policy outcome reflects their interests. Political parties, most often the Republicans and Democrats, are also involved in attempting to influence legislation so that it reflects their political ideology. Public opinion, or the general feelings and ideas of the American public (the voters), additionally has an impact on the policies that are passed by Congress. The elected representatives are continually concerned with the views and opinions of their constituents, especially those who may be seeking reelection, and will keep those views in mind when voting on bills and creating policy.

Example of a Federal Crime Bill: The Brady Law   Many pieces of federal anticrime legislation have been created in Congress over the past thirty to forty years.[58] One example of federal anticrime legislation is the Brady Bill, more formally known as the Brady Handgun Violence Protection Act. This was first proposed after the attempted assassination of President Ronald Reagan on March 30, 1981. After the attack, a number of proposals were put forth that entailed a waiting period for the purchase of a handgun. The thought was that a mandatory waiting period before the purchase of a handgun would provide a "cooling-off" period for persons who were purchasing a gun during a moment of anger. It also gave the seller time to run a background check on the person purchasing a weapon to help identify those persons who were prohibited from owning a weapon.

Many versions of the bill were proposed in 1988, 1990, and 1991. For example, one early version proposed a seven-day waiting period and a background check for the purchase of a firearm. Another version required gun dealers to report the names of the people who buy more than one firearm within thirty days.[59] Yet another version prohibited anyone convicted of a violent crime or drug felony from ever purchasing a firearm.[60] None of these versions passed. The bill that eventually became law was introduced into the House of Representatives in the 103rd Congress in 1993. It was given the designation HB 1025 and referred to the House Judiciary Committee and subsequently to the House Crime Subcommittee. The subcommittee heard testimony from many interested parties, such as Jim and Sara Brady, who supported the bill, and the National Rifle Association, which opposed the proposal. The proposal was passed by the subcommittee on October 29, 1993, and sent back to the Judiciary Committee. The members of the committee approved the proposal on November 4, at which point the bill was referred to the House Rules Committee. Rule was granted on November 9, 1993. The members of the House held debate on the proposal and finally passed their version of the Brady Bill on November 10, 1993, by a vote of 238 to 189.

The Senate also introduced a version of the Brady Bill. Its version was introduced on February 24, 1993, and given the designation SB 414. The bill was placed on the calendar for debate on March 3, 1993, and after only limited debate, the members (on November 20, 1993) voted to indefinitely postpone their version of the bill and pass the House version instead. Because the Senate version included additional amendments, a conference was requested, and the House members agreed. The conference report was filed on November 22, and the House members immediately agreed with the conference version. The Senate agreed two days later with the stipulation that a proposal from Senator Done (R-Kans.) be considered at a later date. The final bill was sent to the president and was signed by President Clinton on November 30, 1993. The new law was given the designation PL 103-159. This indicated that the Brady Law was passed during the 103rd Congress and was the 159th bill signed during that session. The Brady Law became effective on February 28, 1994.

There are many other examples of federal legislation designed to reduce crime across the country. Box 5.1 gives a list of selected federal anticrime legislation since 1914, and Box 5.2 provides some of the details of particular federal anticrime laws.

BOX 5.1
Major Legislation Related to Crime

Year	Administration	Legislative Title
1914	Wilson	Harrison Act
1919	Wilson	National Motor Vehicle Theft Act
1922	Harding	Narcotic Drug Import and Export Act
1932	Roosevelt	Lindbergh Kidnapping Act of 1932
1934	Roosevelt	National Firearms Act of 1934
1934	Roosevelt	Fugitive Felon Act of 1934
1937	Roosevelt	Marijuana [sic] Tax Act
1938	Roosevelt	Federal Firearms Act of 1938
1956	Eisenhower	Narcotics Control Act of 1956
1961	Kennedy	Juvenile Delinquency and Youth Offenses Control Act
1964	Johnson	Criminal Justice Act of 1964
1965	Johnson	Drug Abuse Control Act of 1956
1965	Johnson	Prisoner Rehabilitation Act of 1965
1965	Johnson	Law Enforcement Assistance Act of 1965
1966	Johnson	Bail Reform Act of 1966
1966	Johnson	Narcotic Addict Rehabilitation Act of 1965
1966	Johnson	Federal Criminal Law Reform Act of 1966
1966	Johnson	Act to Extend the Law Enforcement Assistance Act of 1965
1967	Johnson	Act to Prohibit Obstruction of Criminal Investigations
1967	Johnson	Act to Create the Federal Judicial Center
1967	Johnson	District of Columbia Crime Act of 1967
1968	Johnson	Act to Provide Indemnity Payments for Police Officers
1968	Johnson	Omnibus Crime Control and Safe Streets Act of 1968
1968	Johnson	Juvenile Delinquency Prevention and Control Act of 1968
1968	Johnson	Gun Control Act of 1968
1968	Johnson	Traffic in or Possession of Drugs Act of 1968

BOX 5.1
Major Legislation Related to Crime (*continued*)

1970	Nixon	District of Columbia Reorganization and Criminal Procedure Act
1970	Nixon	Organized Crime Control Act of 1970
1970	Nixon	Comprehensive Drug Abuse Prevention and Control Act of 1970
1974	Ford	Juvenile Justice and Delinquency Prevention Act
1984	Reagan	Comprehensive Crime Control Act of 1984
1986	Reagan	Anti–Drug Abuse Act of 1986
1986	Reagan	The Firearms Owners' Protection Act of 1986
1988	Reagan	Anti–Drug Abuse Act of 1988
1990	Bush	Crime Control Act of 1990
1990	Bush	Gun-Free School Zones Act of 1990
1993	Clinton	Brady Handgun Violence Protection Act of 1993
1994	Clinton	Violent Crime Control and Law Enforcement Act of 1994
2003	Bush	Controlling the Assault of Non-Solicited Pornography and Marketing Act of 2003 (CAN-SPAM)
2006	Bush	Adam Walsh Child Protection and Safety Act of 2006
2008	Bush	Sex Offender Registration Law

BOX 5.2
Other Examples of Federal Crime-Related Bills

Juvenile Delinquency Prevention and Control Act of 1968

Provided financial assistance to state and local governments and provided training to juvenile justice personnel.

1968 Omnibus Crime Control and Safe Streets Act

Passed after the assassinations of Robert Kennedy and Martin Luther King, Jr.; provided money to state and local agencies to help them perform their duties; created the Law Enforcement Assistance Administration (LEAA) to improve the nation's criminal justice systems, provide for research into crime, and collect reliable statistics on crime and victims; and paid for higher education for criminal justice personnel and improved curricula in colleges and universities (LEAA 1980). In 1970, Congress amended the law to improve LEAA operations and its effectiveness.

Juvenile Justice and Delinquency Prevention Act of 1974

Consolidated federal juvenile justice policy under one department, the Office for Juvenile Justice and Delinquency Prevention, and set priorities for federal government involvement in juvenile delinquency prevention. The bill was revised in 1980 to require that all juveniles must be removed from adult jails and lockups within five years and again in 1984, which created the Missing Children's Assistance Act to locate and treat abducted youngsters. Extensive amendments in 1992

BOX 5.2
(continued)

addressed juvenile gangs, mentoring, and juvenile crime prevention.

Justice System Improvement Act of 1979

Made significant changes in the operations and organization of the LEAA. Signed on December 27, 1979, by Carter, it replaced LEAA with the Office of Justice Assistance, Research, and Statistics, the National Institute of Justice, and the Bureau of Justice Statistics.

The Anti–Drug Abuse Act of 1988 (ADAA-88)

Addressed the importance of coordination between federal and state authorities, between state and local criminal justice systems, and between state and local officials and substance abuse treatment and prevention; created the Public Housing Drug Elimination Program, which provided for grants to public housing authorities attempting to control drug-related problems; provided over $2 billion for antidrug activities, including increased drug education and treatment programs and broader federal drug interdiction efforts; also created the Office of National Drug Control Policy, headed by a "drug czar," to coordinate the national drug policy. Other provisions increased funding for school drug abuse and mental health programs, provided for more funding for drug abuse education throughout the country, increased efforts to deal with international narcotic problems, and provided for stricter criminal sanctions, including the use of the death penalty for major drug traffickers who intentionally kill someone as part of their drug-related transactions.

Crime Control Act of 1990

Provided for improvements in public defender services, implementation of "shock incarceration" programs in federal and state correctional systems, reforming the investigation process for child abuse cases, aiding crime victims through the Victims Rights and Restitution Act, authorizing a study of mandatory sentencing by the U.S. Sentencing Commission, and developing new offenses and penalties relating to the savings and loan scandals.

Brady Handgun Control Law of 1993

This law mandates a five-business-day waiting period before an individual can buy a handgun.

Violent Crime Control and Law Enforcement Act of 1994

Congress allocated over $22 billion to expand prisons, impose longer sentences, hire more police officers, and fund prevention programs; provided for a ten-year ban on the manufacture, trade, and possession of nineteen semiautomatic assault weapons; provided for mandatory life sentences on third conviction for a violent offense when the last is a federal offense; expands the number of federal crimes punishable by death; provides for "truth in sentencing" laws that require offenders to serve at least 85 percent of their prison sentences; and renders all prisoners ineligible for Pell grants.

Violence Against Women Act of 1994 (VAWA or Title IV of the Crime Act)

Part of the Crime Control and Law Enforcement Act of 1994; intended to reduce domestic violence and promote the arrest of batterers. It attempted to improve the police and prosecutors' response to these crimes and offers protections for victims, including the requirement that sex offenders pay restitution to their victims; strengthened protection orders against abusers and banned firearms possession by convicted domestic abusers; increased funding for battered women's shelters; and established federal penalties for sex crimes. Under VAWA, a national domestic violence hotline was created that promises to reach every community in the nation. Grants are available to the states and units of local government for programs in prosecution, education, outreach, and prevention.

USA PATRIOT Act of 2001

Gave federal officials greater authority to track and intercept communications for purposes of law enforcement and intelligence gathering. The bill created new crimes, new penalties, and new procedures that can be used against potential domestic and international terrorism. Despite its controversial components, it was reauthorized in 2010.

The Brady Bill, like all other proposals to Congress, had to pass through the formal process by which a bill becomes a law. However, there is also an informal process for policymaking, called the "iron triangle," or "cozy triangle," which some scholars argue is sometimes more important than the formal process itself. This refers to the informal relationships that have been developed between the bureaucracies or agencies that are involved in a particular issue, interest groups, and congressional committees and/or subcommittees. In the case of the Brady Bill, many interest groups influenced the final piece of legislation. For example, both anti-gun (or pro–gun control) groups such as Handguns Control Incorporated as well as pro-gun (or anti–gun control) groups such as the National Rifle Association have long-standing ties to members of Congress. Members of these two groups lobbied the members of the committees and Congress as a whole in an attempt to convince them to vote a particular way or to word the bill in a particular way. Although the exact influence of these groups is difficult to measure, the informal policymaking process cannot be ignored.

The relationships developed in the iron triangle are not the only influences that affect voting patterns by the members of Congress. When considering legislation, members of Congress will often vote on the basis of party loyalty. This can be an important decision-making criterion for many members of Congress. At the same time, party leadership pressures, ideological commitments, and constituency interests are also factors that members consider when deciding how to vote. Often, however, political party affiliation is the best single predictor as to how members of Congress will vote on legislative issues.[61]

OTHER ROLES   In addition to passing new policies, Congress plays other roles in the policy process. For example, members of Congress play an important role in the funding process. Congress allocates federal funds that allow agencies to implement laws or carry out congressional mandates. Without money, agencies would be hard pressed to hire the necessary personnel and equipment to follow through with the new law. Congress can choose to increase or decrease allocations to existing agencies as well, and by doing so, it is making an important political statement about the importance and effectiveness of that program.

Congress also has a role in the implementation of policies. Although it does not formally carry out the laws passed, Congress can influence administrative action and hold agencies accountable for what they do. Congress can hold committee hearings and investigations to gather information about the effectiveness of an agency or of a policy and can review the implementation of policies, publicize agency actions, put pressure on agency officials, and enhance the political reputations of its members.[62]

Another control device that Congress has is the specificity of legislation. The more detail that Congress puts in the legislation, the less discretion agencies usually will have. For example, Congress can include specific limitations on how the funds should be used in the statute or can specify deadlines for using the money. In some cases, strict rules or requirements may be incorporated into the body of a law, which become effective if an agency does not act in accordance with specific standards.[63] In other cases, committee reports that accompany bills include statements explaining how the legislation should be implemented by an agency. These reports do not have the force of law behind them, but agency administrators who choose to ignore them may pay a high political price.[64]

Yet another role that Congress plays in the policy process is an oversight function. Congressional oversight is the formal power granted to Congress to supervise and evaluate the administration and execution of federal laws and policies.[65] This can involve evaluation of existing programs to determine if they are effectively reaching their goals or being economically efficient. Or, it might involve evaluation of a proposed program to determine if it might work or which program should be chosen. Since members of Congress are not trained to carry out program evaluations or do not have the time to do so, they rely on the GAO to perform the technical analyses. Members of Congress or committees can call on the GAO to perform a statistical analysis of a program to determine if the program should be re-funded and, if so, on what level or whether it should be abolished entirely. In other words, members of Congress not only pass the initial legislation but also look over the shoulders of the implementors to try to ensure that their intentions are followed.[66]

In many cases, Congress plays a major role in oversight. The committees that initially adopted the legislation may choose to monitor how the agencies implement that legislation. If problems occur, the committee can then act legislatively to correct any deficiencies or things the agencies may be doing incorrectly. Sometimes, Congress may act indirectly by relying on its implicit authority over legislation and budgets to gain compliance from the agencies.[67]

Some might argue that congressional oversight might be the most important function a legislature performs, even though a member of Congress is more likely to be involved with the initiation and adoption of policy. By evaluating agency actions, the legislatures control the actions of agencies. The evaluations may be performed by casework, committee hearings and investigations, the appropriations process, the approval of presidential appointments; and committee staff studies. By doing so, members of Congress reach conclusions about the efficiency, effectiveness, and impact of policies and programs. Because of this, the evaluations can have profound consequences for the policy process.

Over the years, a different type of control over the agencies has been developed by Congress that allows the administrative agencies the flexibility they desire in the implementation of legislation while at the same time allowing Congress to maintain some control over how a policy is implemented. Called the legislative veto, it requires that either congressional approval be secured before an administrative action is taken or a specific action can be subsequently rejected by Congress or the committees. The legislative veto permits Congress to exercise control over what is done by the agency and gives Congress the ability to become involved in the details of the administration of the legislation. Even though the Supreme Court declared the legislative veto unconstitutional in 1983, it is still used on occasion. There may be provisions for legislative veto arrangements included in the law, or sometimes it is put in place by informal agreements between Congress and the executive.[68]

Congress also plays a public education role that revolves around informing the public about policy issues and solutions being debated and discussed. The members attempt to make the public more aware and educate their constituents about a given problem. They do this through traditional means, such as speeches and hearings, but have also begun to use the media, including the Internet, to reach out to the public.[69]

Theories of Law Formation

There are many theories that help one understand changes in laws over time or even the creation or formation of new laws. These theories also help demonstrate the public policy process. Some of these theoretical foundations originate in political science, whereas others come from the study of criminal justice.

The first theory is the theory of consensus, which finds its basis in criminal justice literature. According to this perspective, there is a general agreement, or consensus, about what the laws of a society ought to be and the punishment for breaking a law of society. In other words, most members of a community generally agree as to what is acceptable and unacceptable behavior, and the law is simply a way to make those values and ideas more formal. The creation of the law is a rational process whereby the law reflects a common conscience and interest of society. Most citizens, therefore, do not commit crime because they agree with the laws and the system rather than because of the threat of punishment.[70]

The second theory of law formation, called the theory of conflict, also finds its basis in criminal justice. Underlying this theory is the idea that there are many different interests in society that come into conflict with one another over the content of criminal law and punishments. One of these groups is able to dominate the others and influence the outcome of policy that emerges from Congress or another legislative body. The law, therefore, is not in the best interests of all of society but rather reflects the concerns or ideals of a particular group. This group uses the law and the policy process to express its interests and dominate over the others. According to this theory, people obey laws only because of the risk of punishment that is tied to the behavior.

A theory of law formation that has its roots in the study of political science is called elitism. This theory is much like the conflict theory and has to do with an elite group that has the power to influence policy to benefit its group or economic class. This theory was first described by C. Wright Mills in *The Power Elite* (1956) and then further described by Domhoff in *The Power Elite and the State* (1990). This theory underscores the fact that society is divided along class lines. An upper-class elite has emerged that is able to make policy to benefit their economic class. They often dominate policy decisions because they can afford to finance election campaigns and control key institutions, such as large corporations. Criminal justice policies reflect their positions at the expense of the lower classes.[71]

Another theory that focuses on the importance of groups in the policymaking process is called pluralism. This also finds its roots in the study of political science. The idea of groups playing a role in legislation was discussed by James Madison in Federalist 10. He notes that in a free society, people with similar interests will come together and create factions (or interests). The danger to this is that when these groups inevitably form, they could have a major impact on policy, especially if left unchecked. In response to this concern, the nation's founders created a government system whereby groups could have access to the policy process and, in the long run, compete with one another in their attempts to influence legislation. This is the essential nature of pluralism: Many groups form and vie for political power and control. Our system of government is set up with multiple access points, and groups compete with one another for control of policy. No one group or set of groups is ever completely successful at dominating the system; so the result is policy that is a rough approximation of the public interest.[72]

When pluralism is taken to an extreme, it is sometimes referred to as hyperpluralism. This is the next theory that helps us understand policymaking, and it finds its roots in political science as well. This is when too many groups become involved in the process and the government can get nothing done. Too many groups compete for power and hinder the government from being effective. Many groups are so strong that they divide the government and its authority. Government tries to satisfy every group, and the only outcome is confusing, contradictory, and muddled policy if anything is done at all.

Often, crime policies have been identified as "symbolic."[73] Symbolic policies are those that do not provide any tangible award, such as those that can be seen, felt, or used, to give a benefit to a particular group in society. Instead, symbolic policies provide intangible rewards that make us feel good or make us feel as though the politicians are acting on a particular problem. In the long run, however, symbolic policies do not result in real changes that solve a problem or provide additional benefits to those in need.[74] Many times, crime policies are identified as symbolic policies, as they produce no real changes in crime levels or treatment alternatives, but instead are emotionally satisfying and reassure constituents or interest groups that their concerns are being met and acted on.[75] Former Attorney General Edwin Meese III even admitted that sometimes Congress passes "misguided, unnecessary and harmful" anticrime laws because they are afraid of being considered "soft on crime" if they fail to act.[76]

An early example of how symbolic policies were used to help us understand criminal justice policy was by Gusfield when he examined Prohibition. He argued that Prohibition was a symbolic effort by white Anglo-Saxon Protestants to control the behavior (particularly with regard to drinking alcohol) of then-recent immigrant groups, including the Irish, Germans, and Italians. He shows that most people did not support the laws, and judges were left to support what were largely unenforceable laws.[77] A more recent example of symbolism is identified by Stolz (1992), who shows that antidrug legislation is a symbolic gesture to reassure the public that the government is addressing and solving the nation's drug problem when in fact there is very little impact on the problem.[78] Another example, also provided by Stolz, demonstrates the symbolic nature of the 1994 Violence Against Women Act. When Congress passed the act, it sent a message to the public that domestic violence is a serious criminal act that deserved severe criminal penalties.[79]

Yet another example of symbolic actions by the Congress is its action on the exclusionary rule that prohibits illegally seized evidence to be admitted into trial. McCoy writes that Congress proposed legislation that would allow a "good-faith" defense when evidence was seized illegally. Although the proposal did not pass through Congress, it probably would not have changed police accountability since the exclusionary rule only minimally deters police misconduct. Thus, the proposal sent a symbolic message to the public about the practice of good-faith searches by law enforcement but probably would not have made any changes.[80]

Symbolic offenses are also passed by state legislatures. Galliher and Cross (1982) provide an example of the use of symbolic policies, this time on the state level. They use Nevada's punishments for marijuana offenses as an example of how legislators passed laws that seem tough. However, it is recognized that the high penalties are seldom enforced, but the residents feel that the laws help give the state a more respectable image.[81]

Some might argue that the 1994 Crime Bill had strong symbolic elements included in it along with some major anticrime initiatives. The legislation provided a way in which federal legislators (i.e., members of Congress and even the president) could be seen as concerned about a rising crime rate. Because of this apparent show of concern, they agreed to support the proposed legislation.[82] This action demonstrates the symbolic nature of the bill.

STATE LEGISLATURES

The Constitution sets up a federal form of government where power is divided between the central government and state and local governments. These governments share power, meaning that each has responsibility in different areas. The Founding Fathers intentionally divided power between the federal and state and local governments so that no one branch could dominate the lawmaking process at the exclusion of the others. This means that no single level of government is independent and that each one can act as a "check" on the behavior of the others to ensure that one branch cannot make unfair policy. In other words, each branch oversees the actions of the others to ensure that they are acting constitutionally. While they are watching the behavior of the other branches, they are in turn being watched by the others. This ensures that the laws that are created are fair and in the best interest of all citizens. This is referred to as the process of checks and balances.

The Constitution defines the areas over which the federal and state governments have responsibility (as described previously). In essence, state governments are given jurisdiction in any area in which the Constitution has not prohibited action or in any area that has not been delegated to the national government. These are considered "reserved" powers, which are reserved for the states. Examples of reserved powers for the states are establishing taxes, spending fiscal resources, regulating intrastate commerce, maintaining a general police presence, and otherwise maintaining the health, safety, welfare, and morals of their citizens.

The presence of state governments allows for flexibility in meeting local problems. States may face different policy problems for which they have developed different solutions. Additionally, states may have differing amounts of money to spend on solving problems. Some may be forced to make tough choices about how to address some areas over others. The wide variety of problems and solutions found from state to state can also lead to confusion and inconsistency in policies across the nation. For example, there are variations in the definitions and punishments for victimless crimes, such as prostitution, gambling, homosexual behavior between consenting adults, and obscenity. These offenses and punishments have more variation from one state to the next. At the same time, these are the offenses that place a heavy burden on police and the courts. It should be noted, however, that the states generally have agreement on major, significant crimes, such as homicide, rape, assault, and robbery. Today, state and local governments retain control over many important public policy decisions in criminal justice. They have the predominant responsibility for policing and public security but are often influenced by federal initiatives, fiscal or otherwise.

Crime rates vary from one state to another, as do social environments, and states have found different programs to be variously successful in their particular jurisdictions as compared to others. The highest crime rates are in Texas and California, whereas the lowest are found in the least populous states, such as Vermont and North Dakota. Box 5.3 shows the crime index in each of the states as provided by the FBI's *Uniform Crime Report*. This shows the differences in crime between the different states.

Differences in State Legislatures

Each state has its own constitution that is subordinate to the Constitution. In each of these documents, each state has established the structure of its own government. Every state but Nebraska created a system with two legislative bodies. Nebraska has a unicameral legislature, meaning that there is only one legislative house. In the other states, the lawmaking bodies are bicameral (two houses). They have different names, such as legislature, general assembly, legislative assembly, or, in Massachusetts, general court. The upper state house is called the senate in every state, and the lower house is known either as the house of representatives, the assembly, or the house of delegates. Despite the differences in names, all have the same general responsibility: to make laws.

Each state's legislative system includes political parties, presiding officers, committees, and legislative staff, just like on the federal level. Each has some form of leadership, both formal and informal. This can include a president pro tempore in charge of the senate and a speaker in charge of the house. The officials in these positions are responsible for making sure the legislature runs smoothly and accomplishes its tasks. The leadership also assists in appointing committee members and chairs.

BOX 5.3
State Crime Index and Rate, 2008

State	Index/Rate	State	Index/Rate
Alabama	21,111/452.8	Montana	2,497/258.1
Alaska	4,474/651.9	Nebraska	5,416/303.7
Arizona	29,059/447.0	Nevada	18,837/724.5
Arkansas	14,374/503.4	New Hampshire	2,069/157.2
California	185,173/503.8	New Jersey	28,351/326.5
Colorado	16,946/343.1	New Mexico	12,896/649.9
Connecticut	10,427/297.8	New York	77,585/398.1
Delaware	6,141/703.4	North Carolina	43,099/467.3
Florida	126,265/688.9	North Dakota	1,068/166.5
Georgia	46,384/478.9	Ohio	39,997/348.2
Hawaii	3,512/272.6	Oklahoma	19,184/526.7
Idaho	3,483/228.6	Oregon	9,747/257.2
Illinois	67,780/525.4	Pennsylvania	51,036/410.0
Indiana	21,283/333.8	Rhode Island	2,621/249.4
Iowa	8,520/283.8	South Carolina	32,691/729.7
Kansas	11,505/410.6	South Dakota	1,620/201.4
Kentucky	12,646/296.2	Tennessee	44,897/722.4
Louisiana	28,944/656.2	Texas	123,564/507.9
Maine	1,547/117.5	Utah	6,070/221.8
Maryland	35,393/628.2	Vermont	844/135.9
Massachusetts	29,174/449.0	Virginia	19,882/255.9
Michigan	50,166/501.5	Washington	21,691/331.2
Minnesota	13,717/262.8	West Virginia	4,968/273.8
Mississippi	8,373/284.9	Wisconsin	15,421/274.0
Missouri	29,819/504.4	Wyoming	1,236/232.0

Source: FBI, Crime in the United States, 2008, available online at www.fbi.gov/ucr/cius2008/data/table_05.html.

Role in Policy Process

The state legislatures' roles in the policy process are very similar to those on the federal level. They are first and foremost responsible for creating policies that will make society safer by prohibiting actions that are dangerous and/or harmful. In the area of criminal justice, state legislatures are often more active than the federal legislature in making crime policy since this is primarily a state issue despite the recent increased role of the federal government. Through legislation, each state has evolved its own system of criminal justice, causing there to be differences between states. However, for the most part, state legislatures are very similar and play a consistent role in making policy.

PROBLEM IDENTIFICATION   State legislators, in similar fashion to those on the federal level, are key players in determining what issues will be given attention and ignored. They are influenced by members of the public, interest groups, bureaucracies, and even the media. In the case of states, they can also be influenced by the federal government. Often, the federal government will pass policies that act as models for the states to follow. Or, in some cases, the federal government will provide funding for programs, requiring that states follow certain stipulations to receive the money. In doing so, the federal government is influencing the actions and policy outcomes on the state level.

Over the past three decades, state and local governments have increased their involvement in organizations such as the National Governors Association and the U.S. Conference of Mayors and in many instances have established their own offices in Washington, D.C.[83] These agencies help states not only identify problems but also get these problems on the agendas.

AGENDA SETTING   The state legislatures influence the criminal justice agenda by proposing legislation that may be considered for law. They may be reacting to an event that occurred in their state or another state (a "trigger event"), or they may be "encouraged" to act by the federal government. In some cases, the federal government may have a policy that makes states act in a certain way. For example, the federal government declared that it would withhold federal highway funds to any state that did not lower the legal blood alcohol level to determine if a person is driving under the influence.[84] Although states were not formally required to change the blood alcohol level, most have come to depend on those funds and were in essence forced to change their drunk driving statutes.

The states' crime control agendas may be set by the governor who proposes a piece of legislation or by members of the legislature. The legislators are just as likely as the governor to try to set the state's policymaking agenda.[85] They want to get support from their constituents who become supporters and voters. They can also be influenced by interest groups, political parties, and private citizen groups, and they each want the agenda to reflect their concerns and provide benefits to their constituents.

One study of state legislator ideologies on crime control issues showed that legislators' attitudes toward crime police are complex and diverse. The members of the legislature had attitudes that differed dramatically about the causes and the solutions to crime problems. As a result of their findings, state legislators questioned how differences in opinions can affect policy. Obviously, there is a link between ideology and lawmaking that has significant implications for understanding criminal justice legislation.

Another study of state legislator attitudes toward one particular criminal justice policy (domestic violence) found that the legislators had different perspectives about the meaning of the policy and that the sources of their attitudes were very different. The results of this study showed that legislation did not vary in terms of the legislator's gender, education, political party, criminal justice contact, or criminal justice ideology but did vary in terms of the fundamental assumptions concerning the administration of criminal justice in America. As a whole, the legislators were supportive of legislation that increased the punishment for the offense, following the general trend across the nation at that time.[86]

POLICY FORMULATION   Probably the most obvious and important way state legislatures affect the policy process is by making legislation. This process of making a law on the state level is very similar to that at the national level. Generally, a proposal must be formulated, introduced into each house, referred to committees that may hold hearings, passed by a majority in both houses, sent to a conference committee to iron out any differences in the way the measure passed the two houses, and finally sent to the governor, who either signs or vetoes the measure. This process is true in every state but Nebraska, which lacks the need for laws to get approval from a second house. Specifically, the steps include the following:

1. *Drafting the bill:*   The proposal must be written in a technically appropriate form, and this often requires the legal skills of a lawyer. Some states have a staff of lawyers in a bill-drafting agency to assist in this part of the process. Often, legislators introduce bills for electoral purposes, claiming political credit for what they introduce and pass.[87] Ideas for a proposal can come from a variety of people, including the governor, legislators, interest groups, lobbyists, state agencies, constituents, and citizen groups.

2. *Committee review:*   The proposed bill is referred to the appropriate committee of the house in which it was introduced. Here, they receive a detailed review of the proposal. At this point, the proposal might receive consideration. Public hearings may be held where members of the public, interest group members, or other interested persons may testify either in support of or against a bill. A bill may be voted down at this point, or it may receive a positive vote and move on.

3. *Debate and vote by legislature:*   The entire membership of the legislature debates a proposal. Often, there may be political support or opposition in the entire body that was not present in the committee. When a proposal is scheduled for floor action, the bill often is given a second reading, meaning that it is put formally before the house for consideration. The third reading is the final passage of the bill.

4. *Governor's approval or veto:*   When a bill is presented to a state governor, he or she can sign it, in which case the proposal becomes a law. In all states but North Carolina, the governor can also choose to veto the proposal, in which case the proposal does not become law. However, a piece of legislation that has been vetoed can still become a law if the legislature overrides the veto. In some states, if the session has ended and the governor has not acted on the bill, it becomes law without the governor's signature. In other states, the governor's inaction is a pocket veto of the bill, and it is dead.

Like the national process for making a law, there are also many "outside" political influences on the legislatures during the lawmaking process. Since the early 1970s, citizen's participation in state policymaking has exploded.[88] People involved may include judges, commissions of lawyers, police, and prison officials. There is also action by interest groups, political parties, and governors. Business, labor, local governments, school boards, and other traditionally powerful groups still wield the most influence in state politics, but environmentalists, consumer advocates, and senior citizens have become more effective.

Additionally, most states have legislative reference services that provide pertinent information to legislators, make research reports on particular proposals, and maintain legislative records. Some states also have legislative councils comprised of professional staff members. These members carry out functions similar to those provided by legislative reference services and may prepare an annual legislative program. Some of these are listed in Box 5.4.

POLICY EVALUATION   Many state legislatures play an oversight function to guarantee that the programs being implemented by agencies are effective and cost efficient, similar to the oversight role played by Congress. Since legislators must decide whether to appropriate money to these programs, it is necessary to know if they are working or if they are a waste of

---

BOX 5.4

State Research Agencies

═══

Arkansas	Arkansas Crime Information Center: to provide information technology services to law enforcement and other criminal justice agencies in Arkansas
Hawaii	Crime Prevention and Justice Assistance Division of the Attorney General's Office
Minnesota	Criminal Justice Statistics Center: provides criminal and juvenile justice information, conducts research, and maintains databases for policy development
Maryland	Governor's Office of Crime Control and Prevention: administers millions of state and federal dollars in grant awards to other state agencies, local units of government, and nonprofit organizations responsible for adult and juvenile justice, public safety, victims' rights, and law enforcement in an attempt to prevent future victims of crime
Indiana	Indiana Criminal Justice Institute: serves as the state's planning agency for criminal justice, juvenile justice, traffic safety, and victims' services
Nevada	Office of Criminal Justice Assistance (Department of Public Safety): administers grant money to state and local units that perform law enforcement functions related to improving the criminal justice system with regards to the use and sale of controlled substances, faith-based and not-for-profit agencies providing drug treatment programs, prevention and education programs, and court programs.
Pennsylvania	Commission on Crime and Delinquency: established in 1978 to improve the criminal justice system in the state, they work to improve communication between agencies, and in turn increase effectiveness and efficiency.
Utah	Commission on Criminal and Juvenile Justice: serves as the state's Statistical Analysis Center. The Center is used by many agencies in order to create more effective criminal justice policy.

Sources: Indiana: www.state.in.us/cji/about.htm. Maryland: www.goccp.org//about. Arkansas: www.acic.org/about/index.htm. Hawaii: www.cpja.ag.state.hi.us/. Minnesota: www.mnplan.state.mn.us/cj/. Nevada: http://ocj.nv.gov/Welcome_Page.shtml.Pennsylvania: www.pccd.state.pa.us/portal/server.pt/community/pccd_home/5226. Utah: www.justice.utah.gov/Research/default.htm.

---

the taxpayer's money. States have different ways to evaluate programs. Many times, the evaluation is very simple and consists of legislators conferring with department heads, or the legislatures may complete their own evaluations. In some cases, the evaluation is much more complex and must be initiated by the state legislature. Most states have agencies that are responsible for reviewing and evaluating policies to determine if they are effective. This can be some kind of an auditor that evaluates programs and looks for efficiency or waste. Many states have sunset laws that provide that state agencies will be terminated unless they are periodically evaluated and reauthorized. This helps ensure that the programs are implemented in the way they were intended.

COMMITTEES To make the legislative process run smoothly and quickly, each of the state legislatures has created a committee system similar to that on the national level. This consists of standing (permanent) committees and temporary committees. Some states have created joint standing committees that are comprised of members of both houses. The primary function of the committees is to consider proposals and act on those proposals to increase the chance that it will be passed. In most cases, the committee members hear testimony, amend bills, and approve or reject them.

For the most part, the committees focus on different subject or topic areas. Each state has a committee that considers criminal justice issues, as described in Box 5.5. As this box shows, the agencies vary by state. The names are different from one state to the other, but the committees' jurisdictions are similar.

OTHER ROLES   The state legislatures often become involved in the appointment process for different personnel to head agencies or to act as members of committees for the state. The legislatures may hold hearings on nominees and may support or oppose them. By doing this, the legislatures play an oversight function over the state executive. The legislatures also have investigative functions that are intended to allow representatives to collect information relevant to proposed legislation but that can also be used to examine the activities of administrative agencies. Finally, state governments have intergovernmental functions, such as making decisions related to the proposal and ratifications of amendments to the Constitution, considering interstate compacts and agreements, passing legislation affecting local levels of government, and deciding whether to participate in federal programs.

Like federal legislatures, state lawmaking bodies play only a minor role in the implementation of policies created in the legislatures. Beyond defining the new policy through the legislation, the role of the state legislatures is minimal. Implementing the new policies is the primary responsibility of the bureaucracies and agencies affected by the new legislation. However, state legislatures can affect implementation through their role in funding the agencies. If the legislatures fund the new program adequately, the program has a better chance of succeeding than if it is minimally funded. The same is true of existing programs, which can see their budgets cut significantly by legislatures, thus reducing their ability to serve their clients. On the other hand, a legislature can also fund an existing program at a high level, thus providing more chance of successful program implementation.

Examples of State Legislation

Most criminal law has been enacted by state legislatures rather than by Congress. Because each state can define acts or behaviors as criminal as well as define an associated punishment for that act or behavior, there can be some variation from one state to another in either how a crime is defined or the punishment for conviction of that offense. Although there are too many state laws to list here, Box 5.6 has some examples of legislation passed by state legislatures to deter harmful behavior.

Relationship with Congress

The states have developed relationships with Congress in the area of crime control that allows the states to be even more effective in fighting crime. For example, state governments sometimes lobby the federal government to pass laws. In fact, the states have become important players in the shaping of many federally mandated policies. States can influence national policy through their elected congressional representatives. These state representatives fight for their state's interest when legislation is being considered.

BOX 5.5
State House and Senate Criminal Justice Committees/Subcommittees

State	House	Senate
Florida	Criminal & Civil Justice Policy Council	Criminal & Civil Justice Appropriations
	a. Civil Justice & Courts Policy Committee	Criminal Justice
	b. Public Safety & Domestic Security Policy Comm	
Mississippi	Corrections	Corrections
	Constitution	Constitution
	Judiciary A	Drug Policy
	Judiciary B	Judiciary, Division A
	Judiciary En Banc	Judiciary, Division B
	Juvenile Justice	
Louisiana	Administration of Criminal Justice	Judiciary A
	Civil Law and Procedure	Judiciary B
	Judiciary	Judiciary C
Pennsylvania	Judiciary	Judiciary
	Liquor Control	Law and Justice
North Carolina	Alcoholic Beverage Control	Appropriations on Justice and Public Safety
	Appropriations Subcommittee on Justice and Public Safety	Judiciary I
		Judiciary II
	Homeland Security, Military and Veterans Affairs	
	Judiciary I	
	Judiciary II	
	Judiciary III	
	Juvenile Justice	
Alabama	Judiciary	Constitution, Campaign Finance, Ethics and Elections
	Public Safety	
		Judiciary
Nebraska	Judiciary	

Sources: State Web sites. Florida House: www.myfloridahouse.gov/Sections/Committees/committees.asp, accessed 1/25/2010. Florida Senate: www.flsenate.gov/Committees/index.cfm?Tab=committees&CFID=183128211, accessed 1/25/2010. Mississippi House: http://billstatus.ls.state.ms.us/htms/h_cmtememb.xml, accessed 1/25/2010. Mississippi Senate: http://billstatus.ls.state.ms.us/htms/s_cmtememb.xml, accessed 1/25/2010. Louisiana House: http://house.louisiana.gov/H_Reps/H_Reps_StandCmtees.htm, accessed 1/25/2010. Louisiana Senate: http://senate.legis.state.la.us/committees/default.asp, accessed 1/25/2010. Pennsylvania House: www.legis.state.pa.us/cfdocs/legis/home/member_information/representatives_sc.cfm, accessed 1/25/2010. Pennsylvania Senate: www.legis.state.pa.us/cfdocs/legis/home/member_information/senators_sc.cfm, accessed 1/25/2010. North Carolina House: www.ncga.state.nc.us/gascripts/Committees/Committees.asp?sAction, accessed 1/25/2010. North Carolina Senate: www.ncga.state.nc.us/gascripts/Committees/Committees.asp? accessed 1/25/2010. Alabama Senate: www.legislature.state.al.us/senate/senatecommittees/, accessed 1/25/2010. Alabama House: www.legislature.state.al.us/house/housecommittees/,accessed 1/25/2010.

BOX 5.6
Examples of State Criminal Laws

Washington	Penal Code 9.35.010: "No person may obtain or attempt to obtain, or cause to be disclosed or attempt to cause to be disclosed to any person, financial information from a financial information repository, financial services provider, merchant, corporation, trust, partnership or unincorporated association. Violation of this section is a Class C felony."
Oregon	Chapter 163 section 149: "Criminal homicide constitutes aggravated vehicular homicide when it is committed with criminal negligence, recklessly or recklessly under circumstances manifesting extreme indifference to the value of human life by a person operating a motor vehicle while under the influence of intoxicants in violation of ORS 813.010 and (a) the person has a previous conviction for any of the crimes described in subsection (2) of this section; and (b) the victim's death in the previous conviction was caused by the person driving a motor vehicle."
	Chapter 163 Section 145: "A person commits the crime of criminally negligent homicide when, with criminal negligence, the person causes the death of another person. Criminally negligent homicide is a Class B felony."
Massachusetts	Chapter 151b, Section 3A: "All employers, employment agencies and labor organizations shall promote a workplace free of sexual harassment."
Florida	Chapter 561.1105: "In conducting inspections of establishments licensed under the Beverage Law, the division (the Division of Alcoholic Beverages and Tobacco of the Department of Business and Professional Regulation) shall determine if each coin-operated amusement machine that is operated on the licensed premises is properly registered with the Department of Revenue. Each month, the division shall report to the Department of Revenue the sales tax registration number of the operator of any licensed premises that has on location a coin-operated amusement machine and that does not have an identifying certificate conspicuously displayed as required by s. 212.05(1)(h)."
Alabama	Section 3-2-20: "The Director of Public Safety shall provide for taking up and impounding livestock or animals running at large upon state and federal aid highways which have been officially designated as such and regularly and customarily patrolled by the state highway patrol or upon the rights-of-way of such highways and, to that end, within the limit of the funds provided by this article, the Director of Public Safety is hereby authorized and empowered to contract with persons, firms or corporations within the several counties to take possession of and impound such livestock or animals."

Sources: Washington: http://law.onecle.com/washington/crimes-and-punishments/9.35.010.html. Oregon: http://law.onecle.com/oregon/163-offenses-against-persons/163.149.html. Massachusetts: http://law.onecle.com/massachusetts/151b.3A.html. Florida: http://law.onecle.com/florida/alcholic-beverages-and-tobacco/561.1105.html. Michigan: http://law.onecle.com/alabama/animals/3-2-10.html.

Many state and local government officials routinely seek to influence the content of national policies. Three factors seem to have been especially significant in generating this "intergovernmental lobby." One is the increasing professionalism in state and local governments. This gives these units the knowledge base and ability to meet with legislators and provide information that may influence legislation. The second is growth in federal grants-in-aid to state and local governments. These programs have the potential for the federal government to regulate the behavior of the state and local governments. Third are the many regulations and requirements that federal programs impose on the states and localities. Many times, these regulations are open to modification and give discretion and power to state and local officials.[89]

In fact, many states have hired lobbyists or even established offices in Washington, D.C., to keep track of proposed legislation that might impact their state. They might even lobby for their state's interests. For example, the National Governors Association (which used to be the Governors Conference) represents the interests of the nation's governors. The National Conference of State Legislatures pursues the interests of state legislatures. Additionally, the National League of Cities, the U.S. Conference of Mayors, and the Advisory Commission on Intergovernmental Relations are agencies that represent state interests in Washington.

The National Governors Association represents governors and their senior staff on Capitol Hill and the executive on issues that affect state governments. It is an agency through which state governors work to provide effective policies for their states. They have a "best practices" group that helps governors develop and implement innovative solutions to solving key problems in their states. They help governors learn about emerging issues and how to deal with them.[90] They press legislators and administrators to act favorably on requests for financial assistance and regulatory decisions.[91]

The National Conference of State Legislatures was founded in 1975 as a bipartisan organization to serve the legislators and their staff in the states, commonwealths, and territories and provides research, technical assistance, and other opportunities for legislators to exchange ideas. It also advocates for the interests of state governments in Congress and other federal agencies.[92]

States also lobby the federal government for financial assistance. When money passes from one level of government to another, it is referred to as fiscal federalism. There are many ways in which money can be provided to the states from the federal government. One of those is called "categorical grants." This money can be used only for the specific purposes declared by Congress or detailed in the federal administrative code. Categorical grants are provided to states for specific purposes and cannot be used for any other program or purpose. The state or local governments, when they accept the grant funds, then become obligated to comply with the requirements. There are generally two types of categorical grants. One of those is a formula grant, which is distributed to state and local governments based on a specific formula approved by Congress. The formula could include such factors as population, tax base, crime rates, and prison populations. The second type of categorical grant, project grants, are funds provided to state and local governments that cover the costs of a specific project or program. These are typically assigned after many competing proposals are reviewed.

Block grants are another type of federal funding. These grants can be used for many related purposes as long as they are consistent with the authorization as described by Congress. Block grants carry fewer restrictions and administrative regulations. With block grants, the recipients can decide how to use the funds among many possible purposes authorized in the legislation.

Another type of funding is general revenue sharing, under which the federal government provides funds to state and local governments based on a formula that takes into account many factors, as with formula grants described earlier. However, in this case, there are very few strings attached to the money. This type of grant increases the ability of state and local governments to make choices and spend money on programs of their choice. For the most part, this grant program no longer exists.

In 1994, when Congress passed the Crime Bill, state and local policymakers had the opportunity for federal financial support. In fact, a large share of the $30.2 billion provided by the bill went to state and local governments. The biggest portion ($8.8 billion) was to be used to hire approximately 100,000 state and local police officers in state and local police departments. Another $7.9 billion went to states in the form of construction grants to support prisons and correctional "boot camps." The third-largest share, $6.9 billion, was allocated to local communities by a formula grant in support of crime prevention programs. Smaller amounts ($1.8 billion) went to state and local governments to reimburse them for the costs of incarcerating illegal aliens convicted of felony offenses. Another $1.6 billion was provided by the federal government to finance the Local Partnership Act. As part of the legislation, there was a five-year limit on the funding, with a descending percentage of federal funds distributed over the period.[93]

Another way that states can impact policy is by their willingness to take on a federal law. The state or local government may decide to implement the law only minimally, whereas another state may decide to put more emphasis on the new law. Additionally, a national bill may set broad policy goals with few specific details or even only minimum details about a policy. This means that the state and local governments have a great deal of discretion or latitude in defining details and procedures for the implementation of that law. This, too, can greatly affect the success of the law.

On the other hand, a state can choose to oppose a federal law and pass legislation contrary to federal policy. To date, fourteen states have passed laws allowing for the cultivation and distribution of medical marijuana, laws that are in direct opposition to federal anti-drug policies that outlaw possession, selling or cultivating marijuana. During his campaign for the presidency, Obama claimed he did not support raiding legitimate dispensaries. In early March of 2009, Attorney General Eric Holder announced that the Justice Department would not arrest providers who were obeying the law. However, federal raids on marijuana dispensaries have continued. The DEA claims that federal law trumps state law, and that those who operate such businesses are violating federal law. Nonetheless, states have continued to support laws that allow the distribution of marijuana even though it clearly conflicts with federal laws.[94]

LOCAL GOVERNMENTS

Many citizens feel that federal institutions and agencies have grown too large to meet on a regular basis with concerned citizens. Additionally, for many people, federal agencies, which are typically based in Washington, D.C., are simply too remote to allow for a face-to-face meeting to discuss issues and seek common solutions. As a result, some Americans have become uninterested or even apathetic in national government. Instead, they are now turning to neighborhoods and communities to become involved in the political process and making decisions that directly affect their lives. They have found that the smaller the government unit, the greater the opportunity for participating in decisions.[95] In other words, the small units of government are more conducive to grassroots democracy, providing a sense of belonging. There can be close contact between political elites, leaders, and ordinary citizens, something that can't be done on the federal level.[96]

The focus of local governments is on neighborhoods or communities. These government agencies are responsible for the provision of a host of public services, including police and corrections. The ability of local governments to control their own area is called "local home rule." In most places, the state governments allow local governments to exist. This also means that they can dissolve them.

Types of Local Governments

There are many types or forms of local governments, each responsible for providing services to local communities. "To qualify as a local government under the U.S. Bureau of the Census definition, a jurisdiction must be an organized entity with governmental character and substantial autonomy."[97] There are over 82,000 local governments, including 19,000 municipalities, 3,000 counties, 17,000 townships, 15,000 school districts, and 29,000 special districts.[98] States create local governments, define their authority, determine possible forms of government they may adopt, and may even abolish local government. The amount of independent authority exercised by local governments varies from state to state and by type of government. There are five categories of local governments: counties, municipalities, towns and townships, special districts, and school districts (which is a particular kind of a special district).[99]

Counties are the basic administrative subdivision in a state and were created by states to manage activities of statewide concern at the local level. They generally have the broadest or far-reaching responsibilities, including the local administration of some state services, including law enforcement, justice, welfare, and roads. Often, states use counties as the basic administrative units for courts and law enforcement. All states except Connecticut and Rhode Island have counties, although in Louisiana they are called parishes and in Alaska boroughs. In some large cities, such as New York and San Francisco, the county government has merged with the city, but in most places, counties overlap and coexist with others. They are often concerned with jail expansion and law enforcement planning. The law enforcement agency in the county is the sheriff's department.

Townships are geographic entities rather than forms of government. In some states, a town is a medium-size city. In other states, a town is a form of local government where the community members meet once a year in the town hall to elect officers, pass ordinances, adopt budgets, and levy local taxes. The townships perform many of the functions that the county officials perform except at the local level. These types of government exist mostly in the midwestern states. In New England, the town rather than the county has been the predominant form of local government. In these areas, towns perform many of the same functions as counties, but they oversee a much smaller geographic area. In recent years, many townships have been replaced by elected councils and mayors. The law enforcement agency within the town is the constable.

Municipal governments, also called city governments, include towns, villages, and cities. These were created in response to the needs and demands of people living in close proximity. These governments come into existence only when they are incorporated by a charter that prescribes the basic structure of city government and outlines its powers.[100] Most cities are run by a city council. City council functions vary with the size of the population they serve. Overall, they concentrate on areas such as zoning or planning. There are differences in the council structure. There are usually five or nine members with council–manager forms. Some areas have a council–mayor form. In larger cities with this form of government, they play a more legislative role. In most places, council members are elected.

Elected municipal officials are represented by an organization called a state municipal league that assists officials in carrying out their jobs. Such leagues monitor state legislation, attempt to get favorable state action on financial issues, lobby for policies that affect them, act as a clearinghouse for information, sponsor training seminars, and provide networking opportunities. They are found in nearly every state and are usually located in or near the state capital.

Special districts are government bodies that surround a specific policy area or function. Examples include school districts and airports. They make policies that guide those specific geographic areas.

Most local government must, at least partially, rely on the states for money. However, in recent years, many local officials have also turned directly to the federal government for financial assistance. Most state representatives want to protect their communities they represent, so they actively fight to receive their share of funds.

Types of Offenses

Obviously, crime rates vary from one city to the next. For the most part, crime rates are highest in the largest cities with populations of over 250,000 residents. This fact may reflect not necessarily the actual violence in that city but rather the differences in police practices and the quality of police reporting. Box 5.7 indicates the number of criminal offenses reported in local areas.

Role in Policy Process

The local form of government plays a similar role to that of Congress and the state legislatures in the policy process except on a smaller scale. The local elected officials help establish a local system of criminal justice that, once again, has the goal of keeping the community safe from crime to the extent that it can.

BOX 5.7

Offenses Known to Law Enforcement, 2008

Alexander City, Alabama	204
Lincoln, California	55
Milford, Connecticut	68
New Smyrna Beach, Florida	120
Waterloo, Iowa	510
Shreveport, Louisiana	1,897
Peabody, Massachusetts	144
Golden Valley, Minnesota	0
Fremont, Nebraska	53
Newark, New Jersey	2,660
Oklahoma City, Oklahoma	5,400
State College, Pennsylvania	44
Watertown, South Dakota	35
Fort Worth, Texas	4,601

Source: FBI, Uniform Crime Reports, Crime in the United States, 2008, table 8; www.fbi.gov/ucr/cius2008/data.

PROBLEM IDENTIFICATION   Local officials and community members are key players in identifying problems in the local communities that need to be addressed. Problems can be identified by local law enforcement, community members, schools, and many other individuals. Once the problem is identified, it becomes a possible topic for the political agenda.

AGENDA SETTING   The members of the town councils, similar to members of the federal and state legislatures, are important in setting the agenda for the local government. They may be influenced by the public, schools, law enforcement, and store owners. Since the mayor acts as the chief executive of the city, he or she plays an important role in setting the public agenda. The agenda can also be set by city councils. However, conditions can be imposed on local governments by either state or local officials. In most cities, interest groups are not normally involved.

MAKE LOCAL LAWS   The process for making a law on the local level is not the same as the process for making a law on the national or state level. Instead, most local governments have regular city council sessions where the mayor presides. The mayor is traditionally viewed as the chief executive of the city. Most local governments have regular city council sessions. The sessions may result in a consensus. Council members are briefed on policy matters by administrators and have read the reports of zoning and other commissions before the session, and then a public meeting is held. Depending on the issue, the hearing may be intense. Often, city council decisions are made immediately following a public hearing. There are usually no committees. In most places, the public takes an active role in the process, depending on the issue.

OTHER ROLES   The local governments, like the federal and state governments, play little role in the implementation of the new policies they create. This responsibility is left to the bureaucracies and agencies that are relevant to the new program. Nor do they usually play a direct role in the evaluation of new policies, but there is some oversight by the service director and/or city council. Typically, all money that local departments receive and spend must be approved by these officials. Any grant money received from the state or federal government must also be approved by the city council, yet it still must be spent for the purpose it was intended. This is also monitored by the state auditor's office.

In some cases, a city council may ask an outside agency to come in and complete a program evaluation of some kind and then report that back to the requesting body. In this role, city government officials play an oversight function in attempting to guarantee that the agencies are carrying out the policy in the most cost-efficient and effective way possible.

EXAMPLES OF LOCAL LAWS AND ORDINANCES   Local laws and ordinances regulate behavior to protect the safety of the citizens in that local area. Typically, these are lesser offenses with less serious punishments. These laws are created by city councils, township supervisors, or similar groups. Examples of local laws and ordinances are found in Box 5.8.

Effect on State and National Policy Process

One might think that the local government plays little or no role in the federal or state legislative process. However, in recent years, specific organizations have been established to represent local interests in both of these political arenas. This is important because the local government can influence what the state and federal governments do. The state and government officials may not be aware of local issues, or they may differ with respect to how serious a specific problem is. The

BOX 5.8
Examples of Local Laws and Ordinances

Borough of Riverside; Northumberland County, PA	Ordinance No. 86-4: Junk Vehicle Ordinance: Section 1: It is declared to be a violation of this Ordinance to accumulate, store or have abandoned junk motor vehicles on any private or public property.
	Ordinance 1296: The Dog Law: If dogs are confined in outside quarters (including leashed), they shall be kept no closer than ten feet from the exterior limits of any neighboring dwelling. Any person who walks any dog within the Borough shall not permit such dog to be unattended. The dog shall be restrained by leash or other appropriate device of control so that it will not stray. Any person who walks such a dog shall immediately remove all feces deposited by such dog by any sanitary method and same shall be deposited in the owner's garbage or disposed of in some other sanitary method. The deposit shall be properly wrapped, packaged or protected so as to prevent unsightly disposal, smell or interference with the health and welfare of the community.
Town of Grand Chute, Wisconsin	Section 7.15: All swimming pools as defined above, whether in ground or aboveboard types, shall be enclosed with an adequate and secure fence at least 44 inches high above adjoining grate to prevent straying into pool area. For a violation of this ordinance he shall forfeit not more than $25.00 and the costs of prosecution and in default of such forfeiture and costs of prosecution shall be imprisoned in the County Jail until forfeiture and costs of prosecution are paid, but not exceeding five days.
Stillwater, Minnesota	Code 1980 & 38.02: No person may congregate or participate in any party or gathering of people from which noise emanates of a sufficient volume or of such nature to disturb the peace, quiet or repose of other persons.
	No person shall, between the hours of 10:00 p.m. and 8:00 a.m. drive or operate any minibike, snowmobile or other recreational vehicle not licensed for travel on public highways, in such a manner that it is plainly audible at a distance of 50 feet from its source.
	No person may engage in or permit construction activities involving the use of any kind of electric, diesel or gas-powered machine or other power equipment except between the hours of 7:00 a.m. and 10:00 p.m. on any weekday or between the hours of 9:00 a.m. and 9:00 p.m. on any weekend or holiday.
New Lenox, Illinois	Section 54-191: It shall be unlawful for any person to carry any concealed weapon in the village unless permitted to do so by state law.
	Section 54-211: It shall be unlawful for anyone to do any of the following acts within the corporate limits of the village: (a) Hunt, with or without the aid of a weapon or other device, any animal; (b) Trap, with or without the aid of a trap or other device, any animal; (c) possess or display any loaded weapon.

Sources: Pennsylvania: http://www.riversideborough.org/Ordinances.html. Ohio: http://www.fairfaxohio.org/index.php?view= article&catid=13%3Apolice-department&id=. Wisconsin: http://www.grandchute.net/gradchute/municipal+code/chapters/ chapter+7/chapter+7. Minnesota: http://www.stillwater.govoffice.com/index.asp?Type=B_BASIC&SEC=. Illinois: www.newlenox. net/code.html.

local governments can influence how the state and federal governments address problems and how much financial assistance they may receive.

Big cities are represented in the state and federal arena by the U.S. Conference of Mayors. This organization was created in 1932 as an agency to work to strengthen the relationships between the city and federal governments efforts and to help ensure that federal policy meets the needs of the cities. The Conference provides city mayors with leadership training and tools and provides a forum where mayors can meet and exchange information.[101]

Small and medium-size cities are represented by the National League of Cities. This national organization was created in 1924 to represent municipal governments and to strengthen cities across the nation. It conducts research, shares the information with city government officials, and represents city government interests in the national policy process.[102]

Small governments, such as towns and townships, are represented by the National Association of Towns and Townships. This organization works to strengthen the effectiveness of towns and township governments through educating lawmakers and other officials about how small governments operate. They also advocate for related policies in Congress and help local governments meet federal requirements for grants and other benefits.[103]

Finally, counties are represented in the state and federal arenas by the National Association of Counties, which was created in 1935 to give county officials a voice in the national legislative process. Today, they still represent county governments and their interests on Capitol Hill. They provide legislative, research, and technical help to county government and generally work as a liaison between county government and the national government.[104]

The National Association of Neighborhoods is a nonpartisan agency that was founded in 1975 by concerned individuals in neighborhoods as a way to improve the quality of life there. It works with community leaders, church leaders, and members of small businesses to support policies that will improve neighborhoods. It also works with national organizations to tackle neighborhood problems, such as crime prevention.[105]

Conclusion

The legislative branches of government, whether they be national, state, or local, have a dramatic impact on the policy process. Although the state is the primary branch in criminal justice policymaking, the federal government has become more active in recent years in the battle against crime. The legislatures are involved in the entire policy process, from problem identification to program oversight. While creating policy, the legislature is directly influenced by other political actors and in turn influences the legislatures.

Notes

1. James P. Lester and Joseph Stewart, Jr., *Public Policy: An Evolutionary Approach* (Belmont, Calif.: Wadsworth, 2000); Vivian E. Watts, "Federal Anti-Crime Efforts: The Fallout on State and Local Governments," *Intergovernmental Perspective* 18 (Winter 1992): 35–38.
2. Ibid; Barbara Stolz, *Criminal Justice Policy Making* (Westport, Conn.: Praeger, 2002).
3. Kathleen F. Brickey, "The Commerce Clause and Federalized Crime: A Tale of Two Thieves," *Annals of the American Academy of Political and Social Science* 543 (1995): 30–42; Kathleen F. Brickey, "Criminal Mischief: The Federalization of American Criminal Law," *Hastings Law Journal* 46 (1995): 1135; Sara Sun Beale, "Federalizing Crime: Assessing the Impact on the Federal Courts," *Annals of the American Academy of Political and Social Science* 543 (1996): 43–59.
4. Suzanne Cavanagh, "Crime Control: The Federal Response," in *Criminal Justice Policy Making*, ed. Barbara Stolz (Westport, Conn.: Praeger, 2002), pp. 21–26; James D. Calder, *The Origins and*

Development of Federal Crime Control Policy (Westport, Conn.: Praeger, 1993); Ted Gest, *Crime and Politics: Big Government's Erratic Campaign for Law and Order* (New York: Oxford University Press, 2001).

5. David T. Hardy, "The Firearms Owners' Protection Act: A Historical and Legal Perspective," *Cumberland Law Review* 17 (1986): 585–682. See also www.guncite.com/journals/hardfopa.html.

6. Hardy, "The Firearms Owners' Protection Act."

7. Stuart A. Scheingold, *The Politics of Law and Order* (New York: Longman, 1984), p. xi.

8. Nancy Marion, *A History of Federal Crime Control Initiatives, 1960–1993* (Westport, Conn.: Praeger, 1994), p. 9.

9. B. Guy Peters, *American Public Policy: Promise and Performance* (Chatham, N.J.: Chatham House, 1996), pp. 414–15.

10. T. E. Cronin, T. Z. Cronin, and M. E. Milakovich, *U.S. vs. Crime in the Streets* (Bloomington: Indiana University Press, 1981), p. x; Scheingold, *The Politics of Law and Order*, p. 77; James Q. Wilson, *Thinking about Crime* (New York: Vintage, 1975), pp. 71–86.

11. Bob Egelko, "Where Candidates Stand on Crime, Death Penalty," *San Francisco Chronicle*, February 10, 2008. Retrieved February 11, 2008, from www.dfgate.com/cgi-bin/article.cgi?file=/c/a/2008/02/10/INU.

12. N. Pickler (2008). Obama talks on gun violence in wake of shooting. Pantagraph Publishing, 18 Feb. Retrieved February 19, 2008, from www.pantagraph-com/articles/2008/02/16/news/doc47b5eb0ee; G. Johnson (2008). Gun control a gray area between McCain, Obama. Fox News Press, 15 October. Retrieved October 16, 2008, from www.foxnews.com/wires/2008Oct15/0,4670,CandidatesGuns,00.html.

13. D. Lightman (2008). Democrats Obama, Clinton tread softly on gun control. Houston Chronicle, 26 March. Retrieved March 27, 2008, from www.chron.comdisp/story.mpl/politics/565176.html.

14. Bob Egelko, "Where Candidates Stand on Crime, Death Penalty," *San Francisco Chronicle*, February 10, 2008; R. Garrity, "The Candidates and The Office of Sheriff" Sheriff Magazine (November 2008): 21–34.

15. Bob Egelko, "Where Candidates Stand on Crime, Death Penalty," *San Francisco Chronicle*, February 10, 2008; G. Johnson, (2008). "Gun Control a Gray Area Between McCain, Obama" Fox News Press October 15, available at http://www.foxnews.com/wires/2008Oct15/0,4670,CandidatesGuns,00.html.

16. Ted Gest, *Crime and Politics: Big Government's Erratic Campaign for Law and Order* (New York: Oxford University Press, 2001), p. 1.

17. Franklin E. Zimring and Gordon Hawkins, "Toward a Principled Basis for Federal Criminal Legislation," *Annals of the American Academy of Political and Social Science* 543 (1996): 5–26.

18. Lester and Stewart, *Public Policy*; Watts, "Federal Anti-Crime Efforts.

19. James A. Strazzella, *The Federalization of Criminal Law* (Washington, D.C.: American Bar Association, 1994), p. 7.

20. Ibid., p. 11.

21. James Jacobs, *Drunk Driving: An American Dilemma* (Chicago: University of Chicago Press, 1989).

22. Michael Laurence, "The Legal Context in the United States," in *Social Control of the Drinking Driver*, ed. Michael Laurence, John Snortum, and Frank Zimring (Chicago: University of Chicago Press, 1988), pp. 112–31, Frank R. Baumgartner and Bryan D. Jones, *Agendas and Instability in American Politics* (Chicago: University of Chicago Press, 1993), p. 163.

23. Baumgartner and Jones, *Agendas and Instability in American Politics*, pp. 163–64.

24. Laurie Asseo, "Rehnquist says 'Too Many Crimes Are Federalized'" *The Plain Dealer*, January 1, 1999, p. 18-A.

25. Baumgartner and Jones, *Agendas and Instability in American Politics*, p. 31.

26. Roger W. Cobb and Charles D. Elder, *Participation in American Politics: The Dynamics of Agenda-Building* (Baltimore: The Johns Hopkins University Press, 1983), pp. 84–85; Baumgartner and Jones, *Agendas and Instability in American Politics*, p. 129.

27. John Cochran, "New Gun Control Law is Killer's Legacy" January 12, 2008, ABC News retrieved on 2/11/2010 from http://abcnews.go.com/print?id=4126152; Jim Abrams, "House Tempers Background Checks for Guns" Washington Post, June 13, 2007; retrieved on 2/11/2010 from www.washingtonpost.com/wp-dyn/content/article/2007/06/13/AR2007061300970; Richard Simon, "Bush Signs Bill Geared to Toughen Screening of Gun Buyers" *Los Angeles Times*, January 8, 2008, retrieved on 2/11/2010 from www.latimes.com/la-na-guns9dec09,0,1232293,print.story.

28. Baumgartner and Jones, *Agendas and Instability in American Politics*, p. 158.

29. James E. Anderson, *Public Policymaking* (Boston: Houghton Mifflin, 2003).

30. Ibid.

31. Ibid.

32. Stan Cohen, *Folk Devils and Moral Panics: The Creation of the Mods and Rockers* (Oxford: Blackwell, 1992).

33. Ted Chiricos, "The Media, Moral Panics and Politics," in *The Criminal Justice System: Politics and Policies*, ed. George F. Cole, Marc G. Gertz, and Amy Bunger (Belmont, Calif.: Wadsworth, 2002), pp. 59–79.

34. John W. Kingdon, *Agendas, Alternatives, and Public Policies* (New York: HarperCollins, 1995), p. 39.

35. Ibid.

36. Ibid.

37. Anderson, *Public Policymaking.*

38. Elizabeth Hull, "Criminal Negligence: The Depoliticalization of Crime," *Public Perspective* (2001): 20–23.

39. Roger W. Cobb and Charles D. Elder, "Issue Creation and Agenda Building," in *Cases in Public Policy-Making*, ed. James E. Anderson (New York: Holt, Rinehart and Winston, 1982), pp. 126–38; Anderson, *Public Policymaking.*

40. Baumgartner and Jones, *Agendas and Instability in American Politics,* p. 153.

41. Ibid.; Stella Z. Theodoulou and Chris Kofinis, *The Art of the Game: Understanding American Public Policy Making* (Belmont, Calif.: Thomson, 2004).

42. Christopher J. Deering and Steven S. Smith, *Committees in Congress*, 3rd ed. (Washington, D.C.: Congressional Quarterly Press, 1997).

43. Thomas R. Dye, *Top Down Policymaking* (New York: Chatham House, 2001).

44. Ibid.

45. Peters, *American Public Policy.*

46. Anderson, *Public Policymaking.*

47. Dye, *Top Down Policymaking.*

48. Ibid.

49. Peters, *American Public Policy,* p. 29.

50. Dye, *Top Down Policymaking.*

51. U.S. House of Representatives, Committee on the Judiciary, Welcome page, retrieved 2/11/1020 from www.house.gov/about/subcommittee.html.

52. U.S. Senate, Committee on the Judiciary, retrieved 2/11/2010 at www.judiciary.senate.gov/about/sub-committees/index.cfm.

53. Kingdon, *Agendas, Alternatives, and Public Policies*, p. 39; Theodoulou and Kofinis, *The Art of the Game.*

54. R. H. Davidson and W. J. Oleszek, *Congress and Its Members*, 6th ed. (Washington, D.C.: Congressional Quarterly Press, 1998).

55. "About CRS," available online at www.loc.gov/crsinfo/whatcrs.html.

56. U.S. General Accountability Office home page, available online at www.gao.gov.

57. "Congressional Budget Office," available online at www.cbo.gov/AboutCBO.cfm.

58. Cavanagh, "Crime Control."

59. "Panel Addresses Hate Crimes, Gun Purchases and More," *Congressional Quarterly Weekly Report* 50 (August 8, 1992). 2368.

60. Ibid.

61. Anderson, *Public Policymaking.*

62. Ibid.

63. Ibid.

64. Ibid.

65. Theodoulou and Kofinis, *The Art of the Game.*

66. Peters, *American Public Policy,* p. 85.

67. Ibid.

68. Anderson, *Public Policymaking.*

69. Theodoulou and Kofinis, *The Art of the Game.*

70. Emile Durkheim, *The Division of Labor in Society* (New York: Free Press, 1964); Emile Durkheim, *The Division of Labor in Society,* trans. George Simpson (1893; reprint, London: Free Press of Glencoe, 1933).

71. Thomas R. Dye, "Elitism in a Democracy." In *Taking Sides*, ed. G. McKenna and S. Feingold (Guilford, Conn.: Dushkin, 1991), pp. 67–75; P. Bachrach, *The Theory of Democratic Elitism* (Boston: Little, Brown, 1967); T. Ferguson and J. Rogers, *Right Turn: The Decline of the Democrats and the Future of American Politics* (New York: Hill &Wang, 1986).

72. D. Truman, *The Governmental Process* (New York: Knopf, 1951); R. A. Dahl, *A Preface to Democratic Theory* (Chicago: University of Chicago Press, 1956); McKenna and Feingold; *Taking Sides;* A.M. Greely, "Building Coalitions," in McKenna and Feingold, *Taking Sides,* pp. 112–21.

73. Barbara Stolz, ed., *Criminal Justice Policy Making* (Westport, Conn.: Praeger, 2002), pp. 88–93.

74. Murray Edelman, *The Symbolic Crusade* (1967; reprint, Urbana: University of Illinois Press, 1985).

75. C. D. Elder and R. W. Cobb, *Political Use of Symbols* (New York: Longman, 1983).

76. Richard Carelli, "Push for Anticrime Laws Often Fruitless, Report Says," *Cleveland Plain Dealer,* February 16, 1999, p. 5–A.

77. Joseph R. Gusfield, *Symbolic Crusade* (Urbana: University of Illinois Press, 1963).

78. Barbara Stolz, "Congress and the War on Drugs," *Journal of Crime and Justice* 15 (1, 1992): 119–35.

79. Barbara Stolz, "Congress, Symbolic Politics and the Evolution of 1994 'Violence Against Women Act,'" *Criminal Justice Policy Review* 10 (3, 1999): 401–28.

80. Candace McCoy, "Congress Is (Not) Repealing the Exclusionary Rule! Symbolic Politics and Criminal Justice (Non)Reform," *Criminal Justice Review* 21 (1996).

81. John F. Galliher and John Ray Cross, "Symbolic Severity in the Land of Easy Virtue: Nevada's High Marihuana Penalty," *Social Problems* 29 (4, 1982): 380–86.

82. Peters, *American Public Policy*, pp. 414–15.

83. William T. Gormley, "Interest Group Interventions in the Administrative Process: Conspirators and Co-Conspirators," in *The Interest Group Connection*, ed. Paul S. Herrnson, Ronald G. Shaiko, and Clyde Wilcox (Chatham, N.J.: Chatham House, 1998), pp. 213–23.

84. Stolz, *Criminal Justice Policy Making*, p. 17.

85. John J. Harrigan and David C. Nice, *Politics and Policy in States and Communities* (New York: Pearson, 2004), p. 189.

86. Mark S. Hamm, "Domestic Violence: Legislative Attitudes toward a Coherent Public Policy," *Journal of Crime and Justice* 12 (2, 1980): 37–59.

87. Alan Rosenthal, *Legislative Life* (New York: Harper & Row, 1981).

88. Carl E. Van Horn, *The State of the States* (Washington, D.C.: Congressional Quarterly Press, 1996), p. 232.

89. Anderson, *Public Policymaking*.

90. National Governors Association, available online at http://www.nga.org.

91. Carl E. Van Horn, Donald C. Baumer, and William T. Gormley, Jr., *Politics and Public Policy* (Washington, D.C.: Congressional Quarterly Press, 1992).

92. "National Conference of State Legislatures," available online at www.ncsl.org.

93. Dennis L. Dresang and James J. Gosling, *Politics and Policy in American States and Communities* (New York: Pearson, 2004), pp. 76–77.

94. Steve Hymon, "DEA Raids 10 pot shops" LAtimes. com, July 26, 2007, available online at latims.com/news/local/la-me-medpot26jul26.1.1720060.story; Alex Johnson, "DEA to end medical marijuana raids" February 27, 2009, available at www.msnbc.com/id/29433708/print; "Fourteen Legal Medical Marijuana States" available at http://medicalmarijuana.procon.org/view.resources.php?resourceID=881; Coco Ballantyne, "Federal Raid on Callifornia marijuana dispensary has cannabis advocates clamoring for answers" Scientific American March 26, 2009, available at www.scientificamerican.com; Stephen Dinan and Ben Conery, "DEA pot raids go on; Obama opposes" The Washington Times, February 5, 2009, available at www.washingtontimes.com/news/2009/feb/05/dea-led-by-bush-continues-pot-raid.

95. Robert A. Dahl, "The City in the Future of Democracy," *American Political Science Review* 61 (1967): 953–70.

96. K. Newton, "Is Small Really So Beautiful? Is Big Really So Ugly? Size, Effectiveness, and Democracy in Local Government," in *Public Administration Debated*, ed. Herbert M. Levine (Englewood Cliffs, N.J.: Prentice Hall, 1988), pp. 101–13, at 101.

97. Ann O'M. Bowman and Richard C. Kearney, *The Resurgence of the States* (Englewood Cliffs, N.J.: Prentice Hall, 1986), p. 138; Ann O'M. Bowman and Richard C. Kearney, *State and Local Government* (Dallas: Houghton Mifflin, 1993), p. 138.

98. U.S. Bureau of the Census, *Census of Governments: Government Organization* (Washington, D.C.: U.S. Government Printing Office, 1987), p. vi.

99. Bowman and Kearney, *The Resurgence of the States*, p. 138; Bowman and Kearney, *State and Local Government*, p. 312.

100. Dresang and Gosling, *Politics and Policy in American States and Communities*, pp. 118–19; Harrigan and Nice, *Politics and Policy in States and Communities*, p. 130.

101. U.S. Conference of Mayors, available at www.usmayors.org.

102. National League of Cities, available at www.nlc.org.

103. National Association of Towns and Townships, available at www.natat.org.

104. National Association of Counties, available at www.naco.org.

105. National Association of Neighborhoods, available at www.nanworld.org.

6

Judiciary

Chapter Outline

INTRODUCTION

According to Alexander Hamilton, one of our Founding Fathers, the courts were intended to be an intermediate body between the people and the legislature and were responsible for, among other things, keeping the legislature within its boundaries.[1] He noted in Federalist 78 that the judiciary "will always be the least dangerous to the political rights of the Constitution; because it will be least in a capacity to annoy or injure them . . . (it) has no influence over either the sword or the purse; no direction either of the strength or of the wealth of the society, and can take no active resolution whatever. It may truly be said to have neither force nor will but merely judgment; and must ultimately depend upon the aid of the executive arm even for the efficacy of its judgments."

    Based on these ideas, the broad outline of the court system in the United States was initially established in article III of the U.S. Constitution. In part, article III states that "the judicial power of the United States, shall be vested in one supreme Court, and in such inferior Courts as the Congress may from time to time ordain and establish." In the Constitution, the U.S. Congress was given the power to set up whatever federal courts, other than the U.S. Supreme Court, became necessary. It also gave them the power to impeach, convict, and remove justices from the Supreme Court for crimes such as treason, bribery, or other high crimes and misdemeanors.[2] More details about the courts were filled in by Congress in the Judiciary Act of 1789. This congressional act set up a judicial system composed of a Supreme Court, which consisted of a chief justice and five associate justices; three circuit courts, each constituting two justices of the Supreme Court and a district judge; and thirteen district courts, each presided over by one district judge.[3] Despite these initial attempts to define the role of the court, it was left chiefly to the Supreme Court to define the exact jurisdiction and powers of the federal courts—itself included—with precision.[4]

    Since then, the courts have evolved into a complicated system of ensuring justice. To an outsider, the court can be a confusing place. It is often noisy and congested with what appears to be a focus on mass production. In some instances, the presiding judge accepts guilty pleas and plea bargains and imposes sentences ranging from fines to death. Despite this, the courts play many important roles, including a key role in the policy process and in criminal justice policymaking.

FUNCTION OF THE COURTS

The role of the courts stems from three sources. The first is article III of the Constitution, which defines the Supreme Court's original jurisdiction. The Supreme Court has original jurisdiction over specific kinds of cases or controversies, such as those affecting ambassadors or other public ministers and consuls and disputes to which the United States is a party between two or more states, between a state and a citizen of another state, and between a state (or its citizens) and foreign countries. It also has appellate jurisdiction, meaning that significant cases of constitutional issues can be appealed to it through lower courts. The jurisdiction of the Supreme Court is outlined in Box 6.1.

The second source of power from the courts is congressional legislation, which helps define the courts' jurisdiction. Congress can establish and/or change the jurisdiction of the federal judiciary, including the Supreme Court. As the Court's caseload increased, Congress expanded the Court's discretionary jurisdiction by replacing appeals with petitions for *certiorari*, which the Court may choose to grant or deny.

Third, the courts' power comes from their own interpretation of the previously mentioned powers together with their own rules for accepting cases.[5] The power of the federal courts to invalidate laws that are unconstitutional is widely accepted. This power is called judicial review, and it stems from *Marbury v. Madison* (1803). In this case, Chief Justice John Marshall interpreted the Judiciary Act of 1789 to have unconstitutionally expanded the Supreme Court's original jurisdiction as described in article III of the Constitution. At the same time, it also struck down an act of Congress. Over time, the Supreme Court also overturned a number of state laws that enforced its power of judicial review.[6]

Since *Marbury v. Madison*, it is widely accepted that the courts have the power to review the acts or laws made by Congress, the president, and state and local legislatures to ensure that the laws are constitutional. In other words, the courts review acts by others to determine if they are in conflict with the Constitution, federal laws, or federal treaties.[7] "With its rulings, the court engages the country in a dialogue over the meaning of the Constitution."[8] The courts can overturn laws that conflict with either a state or the federal Constitution.[9]

A second role of the courts is to resolve legal disputes between actors. In this role, the justices play the role of a third, neutral party who will apply the law to a dispute and resolve conflicts that may arise between two parties.[10] They are an outside, disinterested party that will look at the facts surrounding a situation in an unbiased way and attempt to bring the disagreement to an end.[11]

Additionally, the courts sometimes play administrative roles.[12] They get involved in the administration of policies.[13] For example, the courts sometimes must define laws more clearly when they are too vague or if there is disagreement about the exact meaning of a particular phrase or wording of a new law.

Some courts are also responsible for issuing search warrants, arrest warrants, or other related documents and thus play a role in arraignments, trials, and sentencing to ensure a defendant's due process rights. These are typically lower-level courts that ensure that the procedures for arresting a defendant, collecting evidence against that defendant, and the court process that decides if that defendant is guilty or not guilty is fair and that each defendant is afforded his or her rights as described and guaranteed under the Bill of Rights.

The different roles of the different courts can be easily understood when they are examined in light of Herbert Packer's two models of criminal justice described earlier.[14] The first, the crime control model, revolves around a presumption of guilt, followed by a high rate of apprehension and conviction, with a focus on speed and finality. The criminal process must not be cluttered up with ceremonious rituals (i.e., appeals or pretrial motions) that do not advance the progress of a

BOX 6.1
Summary of Supreme Court Jurisdiction

Original jurisdiction

1. Disputes between states
2. Some types of cases brought by a state
3. Disputes between a state and the federal government
4. Cases involving foreign diplomatic personnel

Appellate jurisdiction

1. All decisions of federal courts of appeals and specialized federal appellate courts
2. All decisions of the highest state court with jurisdiction over a case, concerning issues of federal law
3. Decisions of special three-judge federal district courts

Source: L. Baum, *The Supreme Court*, 6th ed. (Washington, D.C.: Congressional Quarterly Press, 1998), p. 12.

case. The second model, the due process model, relies on an assumption of human error and the need for fact-finding. Thus, it is imperative that there are legal protections in place to protect the innocent defendant. Taken together, these models show the dichotomy between the two roles of the court: to punish and to provide legal protections that guarantee a defendant's rights.

ORGANIZATION OF THE COURTS

The Constitution set up a dual system of courts, meaning that there are two court systems operating simultaneously. There are courts on the federal, state, and even local levels, all operating at the same time. Whether a court is federal, state, or local, it generally has the same responsibilities: to resolve disputes and maintain justice.

There are many kinds of courts with different responsibilities. Courts can be established either under a constitution or by legislation. The Supreme Court was established under the Constitution, but many state courts were created by legislation. Those established under the Constitution are called constitutional courts, and those established by legislation are considered legislative courts.

The courts differ as to their jurisdiction or their authority to hear a case. A court of general jurisdiction has the ability to hear a variety of cases. For example, county or district courts hear both criminal and civil cases involving such issues as murder, probate, divorce, and suits for monetary damage. A court of limited or specific jurisdiction hears only a narrow range of cases. For example, a juvenile court will hear only cases involving defendants of a specific age-group. Original jurisdiction means that a court is empowered to hear a case initially, as opposed to appellate jurisdiction, which means that a specific court can hear a defendant's appeal of conviction by the court of original jurisdiction.

The responsibilities of the different courts can be categorized by the type of court rather than level. There are two types of courts: trial and appellate. Trial courts are most well known for handling criminal cases where people or companies are charged with violating a law and causing harm to an individual or a group of individuals. They also handle civil cases, which are

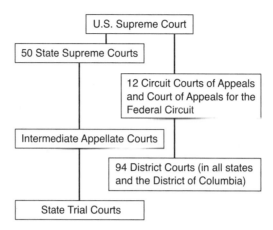

FIGURE 6.1   Relationship between State and Federal Court Systems.

disagreements between individual citizens, between individuals and private institutions (such as business firms), or between individuals and government agencies. In these cases, there is usually an adversarial process whereby the prosecution attempts to prove an offender's guilt and a defense attempts to prove an offender is not guilty. Presiding over the case is the judge, who will respond to questions of courtroom procedure. In some cases, a jury is present to help determine guilt or innocence.

Appellate courts have been granted the power of judicial review, meaning they review the acts of other courts/legislatures and determine if they are constitutional. Some appellate courts must hear all cases appealed to it, while others have discretion to choose what cases they will hear. These courts do not hear evidence as do the trial level courts but rather simply review court records and other legal documents to determine if errors or mistakes were made during trial. If a mistake is found, the court will not hear the case but rather remand it back to the lower court, where another trial may take place.

Figure 6.1 shows the organization of the court system in the United States and demonstrates the nature of the dual court system. The state courts are represented on one side and the federal on the other. The two systems overlap only when they reach the Supreme Court. In order for a case to be heard by the Supreme Court, it must go through either the state or the federal system, and this is determined by the type of offense committed. No case can go through both the federal and the state system concurrently (unless the crime included both federal and state offenses and the defendant is charged with such offenses).

Courtroom Personnel (Courtroom Work Group)

Regardless of the type of court, there are certain personnel who play a specific function in the court. These include the prosecution, defense, and judges. Each fulfills its own role but must also interact with others to process defendants through the system.

PROSECUTION   In a trial-level court, the prosecution is responsible for enforcing the law by filing criminal cases and bringing the state's case against the accused. The prosecutor is responsible for starting legal proceedings in a case, which begins when he or she files formal charges or grand jury indictment with the court. The prosecutor works with police to investigate possible violations of law, determines what the charge will be, interviews witnesses in criminal cases, reviews applications for arrest and search warrants, subpoenas witnesses, represents the government in pretrial hearings and in motion procedures, enters into plea-bargaining negotiations, prosecutes criminal cases, recommends sentences to courts on conviction, and represents the government in appeals.

There are prosecutors in the federal, state, and local court systems. At the federal level, they are called U.S. attorneys. These are the officials who are responsible for representing the people (the state) in the prosecution of federal crimes. They are appointed by the president and assigned to a U.S. district court jurisdiction. On the state or local level, the prosecution is referred to as a district attorney, state's attorney, county attorney, or prosecuting attorney.

The prosecution has a major impact on the court activities. His or her daily decisions can have a tremendous influence on the values in the community.[15] By determining which cases will be prosecuted, the charges to be made, and the bargains to be agreed on with defendants, the prosecution can make powerful statements about acceptable behavior.

The prosecution also affects others within the system since their actions could potentially influence the operations of the police, coroner, grand jury, and judge.[16] Prosecutors are the link between the police and the courts. When law enforcement arrests a suspect, the prosecution determines the specific charges to be brought against that suspect or if charges should be brought at all. In making that decision, the prosecution is determining the type of cases that go to the court and how many. Because of this, the prosecutor "has been called the most powerful single individual in local government. If the prosecutor does not act, the judge and the jury are helpless, and the police officer's word is meaningless."[17]

Prosecutors must also learn to work with (or in some cases manipulate) members of the media. Often, the prosecution deals with dramatic, sensational materials and information that the media wants to present in some fashion (i.e., print or broadcast). The media may call on the prosecutor for information about a case. Some prosecutors are able to use the media to create a favorable climate of opinion for the prosecution.[18]

In many jurisdictions (both state and local), prosecutors are elected. They are usually elected on a partisan basis for a four-year term. With the exception of the electoral process, there are few other public checks on their actions. The prosecutor's discretionary powers may be used so that the voters will be impressed with their abilities. Charges may be dropped to avoid difficult cases, investigations initiated at politically opportune times, and disclosures made of suspected wrongdoing by members of the opposition. Since they can use their staff for campaign work and hold offices where political contributions may be easily gathered, prosecutors may appear to be irresistible forces in local politics.[19] Prosecutors, like other political actors, have many ties to political parties. Prosecutors are recognized as having a lot of power within the system and as having many positions to fill. Thus, they have become key figures in local political organizations.[20]

DEFENSE Under the Sixth Amendment to the Constitution, an accused offender has the right to legal counsel who must serve the interests of the accused. The defense counsel is an attorney and an officer of the court but also a representative of the defendant. It is the defense attorney's role to see that his or her client is properly represented at all stages of the system (police station, initial appearance, preliminary hearing, arraignment, pretrial, trial, sentencing, and appeal), that the client's rights are not violated, and that the client's case is presented in the most favorable light possible within legal bounds. The defense attorney must make sure that the prosecution proves its case in court or has substantial evidence of guilt before a defendant pleads guilty or is convicted and punished.

The responsibilities of the defense include investigating the alleged offense; seeking pretrial release of the accused; interviewing the client, police, and other witnesses; discussing the matter with the prosecutor; filing motions to suppress evidence illegally obtained; representing the defendant at the various pretrial procedures, such as arrest, interrogation, lineup, and arraignment; entering into plea negotiations; preparing the case for trial, including developing tactics and strategy; filing and arguing legal motions with the court; representing the defendant at trial; providing assistance at sentencing; and determining the appropriate basis for appeal.

While they are defending indigent offenders, public defenders may also be impacting public policy and the policy process. When needed, public defenders may undertake activities to influence criminal justice policies that affect the status of indigent defendants. A public defender's office can initiate and sustain litigation that supports desired policy goals. Public defenders can force a court to halt a practice or order an action to assist defendants. In turn, then, they are establishing a long-term policy to protect all future defendants in some way.[21]

The Fifth Amendment to the Constitution guarantees the right to legal counsel in trial proceedings. If a defendant is unable to afford adequate legal counsel, the government must provide representation to that defendant. Over the years, state and local governments have devised different methods to ensure that indigent offenders have legal counsel. These methods include public defenders, assigned counsel, and contract counsel.

Public defenders are used in many of the most heavily populated urban areas as well as in the federal government.[22] A public defender is typically an attorney who is employed by the state or federal government and acts as legal counsel for indigent defendants. In some states, there is a statewide public defender's office that is headed by a chief public defender. In most states, the public defender's office is organized on the county level. In this situation, each office is autonomous. The attorneys working for the public defender's offices are salaried attorneys who represent all or most defendants deemed indigent.

These offices typically have high caseloads and are thus unable to spend significant time on any one case. As a result, they are often criticized for not being as legally qualified as private attorneys and thus provide a poor quality of legal counsel. They are also criticized for being overworked, not putting in as much time on cases, and lacking expertise in criminal law and plea bargaining. In many areas, the nonlegal community has a very negative perception of public defenders. However, most public defenders have years of experience and work diligently to provide a defendant with the best possible legal advice.

Another method to provide legal counsel to indigent offenders is by assigned counsel. This is the most common means of providing representation for the poor.[23] In this situation, the court assigns private attorneys to represent indigent defendants in court proceedings. In some areas, all qualified practicing attorneys are placed on a list that is used by a judge to select an attorney for a case. The attorney is usually reimbursed by the state or county for his or her services. This system is often used in rural areas that may not have a high caseload and do not have the need or the monetary support for a public defender's office. In some cities, the judges select attorneys, using a system of strict rotation from a list submitted by the bar association. In these cases, it is often the youngest attorneys who are called on to perform this service as a civic and professional duty. In other areas, the choice of attorneys for the indigent is limited to those who have indicated to the judge that they are willing to take such cases. This system distributes the burden of indigent representation among members of the bar.

The contract system is another method for providing legal counsel for indigents. Under this system, a county or township invites private law firms to submit proposals on the cost for providing a system of public defense. For example, the county may ask for a bid on the costs for providing legal representation for a certain number of cases. The government then selects the firm that provides the lowest bid. The chosen law firm is responsible for providing indigent defendants with legal representation in court. This is a newer system for providing public defense than the other systems, but its popularity has grown considerably, and now many states are using it to supplement an existing public defender's office system.[24]

In some states, a system of providing services to indigent offenders has evolved to become a mixed system, including elements of each of these methods. Some use a public defender's office alongside private attorneys. In this case, the public defender system operates simultaneously with the assigned counsel or contract system. Mixed systems allow states to draw on the strength of each to provide better advice to indigent offenders.

JUDGES   Judges in the courtroom have many responsibilities. They preside over the courtroom proceedings (even acting as an umpire during a trial), supervise jury selection, interpret and decide questions of law (questions about evidence), instruct (or "charge") the jury, sentence guilty offenders, ensure that a defendant's plea is voluntary, and preside over the plea-bargaining process. They also sign warrants, fix bail, arraign defendants, rule on legal motions drafted by the prosecution or defense, rule on motions to exclude evidence, and accept or negotiate guilty pleas through plea bargaining. Many judges also draft legal opinions setting forth reasons for their decisions. Their administrative duties include responsibility for support staff (getting help from bailiff and administrators), lending assistance in the preparation of the budget, keeping their dockets current (dates for hearing pretrial motions and for trial must be established), and management of the case flow within the court, such as scheduling cases and trials. Judges are supposed to ensure that all defendants are treated fairly.

Theoretically, judges are the most powerful figures in the courtroom. Their rulings and sentencing decisions influence the actions of police, defense attorneys, prosecutors, and other courtroom actors. They determine whether individuals will lose their liberty by being sentenced to a prison term and whether people will live or die by a sentence of death.

The behavior of trial judges and appellate judges differs. Trial judges rule on the appropriateness of the conduct of all others involved in the court process, including spectators. They decide if an attorney questions a witness inappropriately or if spectators are interrupting the legal proceedings. They determine what evidence is admissible and, during jury trials, which instructions of law the juries will receive. Only the judge can make a decision on any motions filed, questions of law, objections, and, in most states, the sentence imposed. They also have extensive control over probation officers and court clerks and, indirectly, over the police, for example, when they decide whether evidence was collected legally or whether a suspect was treated fairly.

Appellate judges have very different responsibilities and duties from the trial judge. They are responsible for examining the record of trial, trial brief, notice of appeal, and other matter submitted with the appeal to determine if the appeal is properly presented and the appropriate issues are presented properly before the court. They also preside over oral arguments and are involved in negotiating a decision among the justices considering the appeal. Finally, they must write an opinion that explains the logic and reasons for the decision.

Whether judges preside over a trial or an appellate court, there is a mystique surrounding the bench that sets them apart from the other courtroom personnel. They are referred to as "your honor" while they are seated far above the other actors in the courtroom. They are dressed in black robes, while others in the courtroom are dressed in business attire. Other courtroom personnel can be punished if they do not obey the orders of the judge. Most judges portray themselves as "above the fray" of politics and do not allow political considerations to affect their decisions.[25]

OTHER PERSONNEL   There are many other courtroom personnel who play a significant role in daily court procedures. These personnel often do not receive as much publicity as the major players (including the defense, prosecution, or judges) but are nonetheless just as important to the efficient functioning of the courtroom. They work regularly in the court and develop personal and professional relationships with the other actors over time. Without these personnel, the court could not function as it does.

One of those personnel is the court clerk, who assists the judge with many of the administrative duties that surround the trial process. The clerk performs such duties as docketing cases (scheduling cases), collecting court fees, arranging a jury pool, issuing jury summonses, and subpoenaing witnesses for both the prosecution and the defense. The clerk also maintains court records of criminal cases, including all pleas and motions made both before and after the actual trial. In addition, the clerk is responsible for administering the oath to jurors and witnesses before they testify (otherwise known as swearing them in), marking evidence as instructed by the judge, keeping a log of what exhibits have been admitted as evidence into trial, and maintaining the custody of any evidence admitted. Because the clerk is really the official record keeper of the court, he or she is responsible for all the legal documents filed with the court.

Another key position in the courtroom is the court administrator. This position was created in many courtrooms based on recommendations made by the National Advisory Commission on Criminal Justice Standards and Goals. The commission recommended that all courts with five or more judges have a court administrator to make the trial process more efficient. Connecticut was the first state to respond and created the first court administrator position in 1937. In some places, the court administrator has replaced the court clerk.

Court administrators handle the day-to-day routines of the court and assist judges in administrative and nonjudicial functions, such as record keeping, making courtroom arrangements, scheduling cases, case flow analysis, data gathering and analysis, personnel administration, research and planning, space utilization, facilities planning, and budget preparation and management. In some cases, the administrator helps manage the jury pool in an effort to reduce the time potential jurors waste waiting to be chosen for a jury or to help deal with requests to be excluded from jury duty. They may also collect court fees and fines and disburse judicial monies. The court administrators are typically appointed by individual judges.

Another courtroom personnel member who has become essential to the effective functioning of the court is the bailiff, sometimes called the "court officer." In most cases, the bailiff is an armed officer who helps keep order in the courtroom. The bailiff announces the judge's entry into the courtroom, calls witnesses, and helps prevent the accused from escaping. The bailiff will often assist the jury when it is not in the courtroom, especially if a jury is sequestered and is not allowed to have any contact with outside influences. In this case, the bailiff may bring jurors items they request, such as evidence presented at trial. In a federal trial, the bailiff is a deputy U.S. marshal.

The court reporter is another member of the courtroom personnel who is important in the trial proceedings. Sometimes known as the court recorder or court stenographer, the court reporter records all the events that occur in the courtroom. This includes the testimony of witnesses, oral arguments, instructions, and any words spoken during any court proceedings. The court reporter must keep track of all verbal comments made in the courtroom, including testimony, objections, rulings of the judge, the judge's instructions to the jury, arguments made by attorneys, and the results of conferences between the attorneys and the judge. These are often taken on a stenotype machine but are sometimes recorded with an audio recorder. The information is later transcribed in manuscript form. The transcripts become the official trial record and may be used if an appeal is made. In courts where there is no position of court clerk, the court reporter is also responsible for listing all exhibits offered into evidence.

Some other actors who are consistently involved in the courtroom but who are not employees of the court can include witnesses, parole officers, court psychiatrists, social workers, and defendants' families and friends. Each plays an important role in the disposition of each case that comes into the courtroom.

Together, these major courtroom personnel (judge, prosecution, defense, and other personnel) are often called the courthouse work group. These members of the court must work together and cooperate with each other on a daily basis to make decisions about and dispose of the defendants' cases. In most courtrooms, the same prosecutors, judges, and defense attorneys come into contact with each other as they represent or hear the same type of cases time after time, with the only difference being the defendant, the plaintiff, and the facts of the case. The court personnel are forced to interact with each other on a constant basis, and over time they come to know each other well and rely on each other to carry out a particular function to reach the ultimate goal of processing the defendant. As this happens, the courthouse work group develops a close network of mutual relationships. In addition to the formal interaction that must occur to keep cases moving through the system, the work group members often have informal discussions about the cases as well. These discussions, both formal and informal, help keep the court operating smoothly and efficiently.

Each member of the work group has a specialized position and is expected to carry out that role. All the members become proficient at their task and are responsible only for that task. New employees are socialized to be part of the work group. They learn the formal requirements of the job but also the informal rules of behavior. Eventually, the members may even come to share common goals and norms. Since the members often have similar educational backgrounds and career goals, they tend to share a social status with similar values that may be different from the predominantly lower-class defendants being processed. Actors within the work group who violate the norms are sanctioned, and those who cooperate are rewarded.[26]

THE PROCESS OF JUDICIAL SELECTION

There are many ways to place judges on the bench. Debate continues to rage over which method of judicial selection is "best" and results in the most qualified person serving as judge.[27] These methods include judicial election, appointment, or a combination of the two. No matter which method is used to seat a judge, his or her career is linked to the political arena.[28] The position of judge is a "political position to which . . . most bring a background of political activity and interest."[29] In seating a judge, there is controversy over judicial accountability versus judicial independence. Judicial accountability relies on elections of judges to make them responsive to the people. On the other hand, judicial independence (from merit appointments) allows a judge to make decisions objectively and without political pressure.[30]

Election

Some states have developed a system whereby the judges are elected. In most states, lower-court judges are elected, but in some, the appellate level justices are elected as well. The theory behind judicial elections is that the people can choose the type of judge they want serving the people. Throughout a campaign, a judicial candidate must impress the voters with his or her experience and qualifications. After a few years in office, if the judge does not live up to the voters' expectations, he or she is not reelected.[31] Additionally, it is argued that wealthy and powerful voters would not be able to control judicial appointments as they might be able to do if the judges are appointed. Most states decided to select judges through partisan ballots on the theory that this makes them accountable to the voters to the same degree as members of the legislative and executive branches.

The campaigns are partisan (where the candidate's political party affiliation is made known), nonpartisan (where the candidate's political party affiliation is not designated), or a combination of the two, sometimes referred to as a semipartisan system. This might happen when a primary election is partisan and candidates run on a party ticket, followed by a general election in which the candidates' political party affiliations are not identified. This is what occurs in Ohio, for example.

Until recently, most judicial campaigns were low key and did not receive much public attention or analysis. Since most justices are prohibited from discussing issues throughout a campaign (as most states have adopted a code of judicial conduct that prohibits a judge from announcing his or her views on disputed legal or political issues), they received little attention. As a result, voter turnout for these elections has been low—about 20 to 25 percent of eligible voters turn out to vote. This also meant that incumbent judges were often successfully reelected. In fact, incumbent justices won over 90 percent of the time.[32]

However, in more recent elections, the campaigns for state judicial positions have become multi-million-dollar political affairs with fund-raising and spending becoming major parts of the campaign. Judicial candidates now hire and rely on political consultants, lawyers, media advisers, political parties, and pollsters to help them win office. Some justices have even begun testing the limits of ethics rules that limit their speech, making vague promises about cases or policies during a campaign that were once prohibited.

Now, one of the major issues in judicial races revolves around campaign finance. Millions of dollars in campaign contributions are being raised for judicial races. There is obvious concern that some lawyers, interest groups, or corporations are exerting influence—or at least attempting to exert influence—on the outcome of these elections. In response, some states have tried to pass new ethics rules that limit what candidates can say and how much they can spend. But many court rulings said that the First Amendment prohibits these laws. Since they curtail political speech, they are in violation of the First Amendment and are thus unconstitutional.

The issues surrounding judicial campaigns have become so serious that two U.S. Supreme Court justices, Stephen Breyer and Anthony Kennedy, have spoken publicly about their concerns. Each has expressed concern that the money coming into judicial races is rising faster than money in other federal campaigns. At the same time, there has been an increase in the instances in which a judge may potentially rule on cases involving those big donors and cases in which judges are told that ruling against moneyed interests may cost them their seats.

There is a concern in states where judges are elected that they may make decisions that will increase or maintain their popularity rather than decisions based on law. Judges who are concerned about their next campaign may be tempted to ignore the Constitution and relevant statutes and make a popular decision. Or, they may avoid controversial, difficult, or unpopular decisions rather than risk opposition from voters in the next election. Or, they may follow the wishes of the campaign contributors and political party leaders who help them win elections and stay in office.

Furthermore, judicial elections do not permit judges to be chosen on the basis of their qualifications. Instead, judges are chosen in part because of their service to the party. "The selection of candidates for judicial office is not based on ideal criteria for selecting the 'most qualified' judge but focuses on such factors as who can raise the most campaign money, who has worked diligently for the party and who can win an election against the opposing party's candidate."[33]

Even if a campaign is nonpartisan, it does not mean the political parties are not involved. The party funds its chosen candidate regardless of whether the party affiliation is listed on the ballot and helps the candidate throughout the campaign by providing campaign volunteers, literature, and other campaign assistance. It is easy to discover which political party backs the candidates.

Appointment

In some states and the federal government, lower-court judges are appointed by an executive (governor or president) and confirmed by a judicial appointment committee that contains representatives from the state legislatures and the judiciary. The appointment is sometimes made by an executive and is then confirmed by the state senate, the governor's council, a special confirmation committee, an executive council elected by the state assembly, or an elected review board. In other states, the legislature appoints a judge. Eventually, the appointed judge must also be confirmed by voters in the next general election.

It is argued that since the electorate is uninformed about the courts and issues related to the courts, knowledgeable groups, such as bar associations, law professors, current members of the bench, and citizen groups, can advise the legislators and governors in appointing the state's judiciary. It is assumed that these individuals are able to choose qualified judges as opposed to the nonlegal community, which has little or no knowledge about the court system. It has also been argued that more and better-quality lawyers would be willing to seek judicial positions if they did not have to subject themselves to the rigors and frustrations of a public campaign.

The appointment process for seating judicial nominees is not without its fair share of politics. In fact, the nomination process is very political. In most cases, the executive does not personally know every candidate for a judicial position, and he or she must depend on others for advice. They might rely on a nominating commission, a bar association, or lay members within the legal community.[34] When selecting nominations, executives rely on certain factors. One is the candidate's merit. A candidate must have strong legal credential and unquestioned ethical behavior. Another factor is a nominee's personal and political friendship and support. Executives often "reward" political support for themselves or the party with a nomination.[35] The policy preferences of the nominee are crucial. President Reagan appointed four justices to the court, all with conservative views. President Clinton, on the other hand, nominated justices were more moderate.[36] President Obama nominated a liberal law professor, Goodwin Liu, to serve on the 9th Circuit Court of Appeals, which drew criticism from conservatives.[37] Executives also look to other symbolic factors when appointing a justice, such as a nominee's geographic background, religious preference, race, ethnicity, or gender.[38]

Most nominations sail through the approval process with no problems.[39] But on occasion, politics overshadows the process. There are many examples of the political influence surrounding judicial appointments. More recent examples are those of Robert Bork, Clarence Thomas, John Roberts, and Sonia Sotomayer. These nominations show some general themes surrounding judicial appointments: that judges have political backgrounds, they are members of the president's political party, have been active in party politics, and have held prior government positions either as a judge or prosecutor.[40] More information about judicial nominations to the Supreme Court is outlined in Box 6.2.

ROBERT BORK   Robert Bork was nominated in 1987 by President Reagan to be an associate justice on the Supreme Court to replace retiring Justice Powell. Bork was a graduate of the University of Chicago Law School and a professor of law at Yale University. He had served as

BOX 6.2
Nominations to the Supreme Court, 1969 to Present

Name	Nominated by	Replaced	Senate Vote	Years Served
Warren Burger	Nixon	Warren	74–3	1969–1986
Clement Haynsworth	Nixon	(Fortas)	45–55	Not confirmed
G. Harrold Carswell	Nixon	(Fortas)	45–51	Not confirmed
Harry Blackmun	Nixon	Fortas	94–0	1970–1994
Lewis Powell	Nixon	Black	89–1	1971–1987
William Rehnquist	Nixon	Harlan	68–26	1972 to present
John Paul Stevens	Ford	Douglas	98–0	1975 to present
Sandra Day O'Connor	Reagan	Stewart	99–0	1981 to 2006
William Rehnquist	Reagan	Burger	65–33	1986 to 2005
(Chief Justice) Antonin Scalia	Reagan	Rehnquist	98–0	1986 to present
Robert Bork	Reagan	Powell	42–58	Not confirmed
Douglas Ginsburg	Reagan	(Powell)	Withdrew	No action
Anthony Kennedy	Reagan	Powell	97–0	1988 to present
David Souter	G. H. W. Bush	Brennan	90–9	1990 to 2009
Clarence Thomas	G. H. W. Bush	Marshall	52–48	1991 to present
Ruth Bader Ginsburg	Clinton	White	96–3	1993 to present
Stephen Breyer	Clinton	Blackmun	87–9	1994 to present
John Roberts, Jr.	G.W. Bush	O'Connor	Withdrew	
John Roberts, Jr.	G.W. Bush	Rehnquist	78–22	2005–present
Harriet Miers	G.W. Bush	O'Connor	Withdrew	
Samuel Alito, Jr.	G.W. Bush	O'Connor	58–42	2006–present
Harriet Miers	G.W. Bush	(O'Connor)	Withdrew	
Sonia Sotomayor	Obama	Souter	68–31	2009–present

Source: L. Baum, *The Supreme Court*, 6th ed. (Washington, D.C.: Congressional Quarterly Press (1998), pp. 32–33, 51; United States Senate, Supreme Court Nominations, www.senate.gov/pagelayout/reference/nominations/Nominations.htm.

solicitor general in the Nixon administration and was well qualified to serve as a justice on the Court. Bork was an academic with nearly impeccable ethical credentials.

Despite that, there were many groups that got involved in the nomination process and voiced support or opposition to the nomination, including civil rights groups, women's groups, and abortion rights groups. These organizations found him to be insensitive to the needs of their members. They organized press conferences and sent mailings against the nomination.[41] On the other hand, conservative groups sponsored television ads and made telephone calls in favor of Bork.

During the confirmation hearings, Bork was questioned about how he would vote on specific cases. In answering the questions, he contradicted his past behavior.[42] Because of his contradictions, 1,925 law professors signed letters opposing Bork.[43] Eventually, the Judiciary

Committee voted 9 to 5 against the nomination, and he was defeated in the full Senate by a vote of 58 to 42.[44]

Even today, scholars debate if Bork received fair treatment. They point to the politicization of the nomination process and the range of players involved as well as the techniques they use to show support or opposition for a nominee.[38]

CLARENCE THOMAS   In 1991, President Bush nominated forty-three-year-old Clarence Thomas to be a Supreme Court justice to replace retiring Justice Thurgood Marshall. Thomas was the grandson of a sharecropper and as a child attended a Roman Catholic school run by white nuns for poor black children. He graduated from Yale Law School and had a successful political career. He served as chairman of the Equal Employment Opportunity Commission (EEOC), served on the U.S. Court of Appeals, was a federal appellate judge for sixteen months, and was an assistant secretary for civil rights in the Department of Education during the Reagan administration. Like Bork, Thomas was well qualified to serve on the Court.

Almost immediately, even before the confirmation hearings began, there were both supporters and opposition to Thomas's nomination. There were grassroots organizing, news conferences, rallies, public opinion polls, fund-raising, and negative advertising surrounding Thomas. Support for the Thomas nomination came from the Citizens Committee to Confirm Clarence Thomas, the U.S. Chamber of Commerce, the Coalition for Self-Reliance, the Coalitions for America, the American Conservative Union, Concerned Women for America, the Eagle Forum, the Family Research Council, the Council of 100, the Simon Wiesenthal Center, and Women for Judge Thomas. There was even a busload of friends, relatives, and neighbors from Georgia (Thomas's home state) that came to Washington, D.C., to support the nomination.

However, at the same time, an active grassroots movement against the nomination also began. This included Jesse Jackson, feminist groups such as the National Organization for Women, and labor organizations such as the American Federation of Labor–Congress of Industrial Unions (better known as the AFL-CIO). These groups claimed that Thomas was an unorthodox conservative whose legal theories could seriously damage the rights of all Americans, especially women and minorities. These organizations alleged that he failed to comply with antidiscrimination laws while he was chair of the EEOC and claimed that he criticized Supreme Court decisions that expanded the rights of privacy, endorsed affirmative action programs, and enforced school desegregation. Furthermore, they claimed that even though Thomas was admitted to Yale Law School under an affirmative action program that gave preference to black Americans; Thomas attacked affirmative action as more of a hindrance than a help. They claimed that Thomas cited welfare as a trap to prolong dependency and break up families. Other groups that came out against Thomas were the National Abortion Rights Action League; the United Church of Christ; the League of United Latin American Citizens; the Congressional Black Caucus; the National Education Association; Americans for Democratic Action; the Women's Legal Defense Fund; the Service Employees International Union; the Alliance for Justice; the American Association of University Women; the American Federation of State, County and Municipal Employees; the Coalition of Labor Union Women; the Nation Institute; the National Federation of Business and Professional Women; and People for the American Way. Even the American Bar Association (ABA) rated him as "qualified," which was a midlevel assessment of Thomas's legal ability. In fact, that is the lowest ABA rating of any Supreme Court nominee in the previous decade.

During the confirmation hearings, a former assistant of Clarence Thomas, Anita Hill, made startling charges of sexual harassment. Hill claimed that Thomas had sexually harassed her when they worked together at the Department of Education and the EEOC in the early 1980s. There were extensive hearings to determine the accuracy of the charges, but the Senate did not have strong enough evidence to confirm the charges. Eventually, the Democrat-controlled Senate voted to seat Thomas on the Court. The vote was 52 to 48, and Thomas became the first African American conservative Supreme Court justice in the Court's history.

JOHN ROBERTS President Bush originally nominated John Roberts to replace Justice O'Connor as an associate justice on July 19, 2005. When Chief Justice Rehnquist died on September 3, the Roberts' nomination was withdrawn and replaced with a second nomination to be chief justice. Roberts had clerked for Chief Justice William Rehnquist before practicing law at a private law firm. In that capacity, he argued 39 cases before the court. Prior to appearing before the Court, Roberts studied the personalities of the different justices so that he would know to whom he should direct his arguments. He also served as a Special Assistant to the Attorney General and as the principal deputy solicitor general in the Department of Justice. He served briefly on the D.C. Circuit Court before being nominated for the Supreme Court.

There was some controversy regarding Roberts' qualification for chief justice. Even thought the American Bar Association gave him a "well qualified" rating, some were opposed to the nomination. MoveOn.org was opposed to Roberts because as a lawyer for the Bush Sr. and Reagan administrations, he asked the Supreme Court to limit the ability of district courts to desegregate public schools. He also argued for a law banning doctors from even discussing reproductive options in many cases and argued to the Supreme Court that public schools could force religious speech on students.[45]

The National Council of Jewish Women was also opposed to Roberts. They argue that he did not support the right to privacy, civil rights, affirmative action, gender equality and the separation of religion and state. There were many other organizations opposing the nomination, such as the Alliance for Justice, the AFL-CIO (American Federation of Labor—Congress of Industrial Organizations), the Congressional Black Caucus, Equal Justice Society, Hispanics for a Fair Judiciary, NAACP Legal Defense and Education Fund, NARAL pro-Choice America, National Gay and Lesbian Task Force, National Organization for Women, National Urban League: Many others listed here.[46] He was opposed by the Lambda Legal Defense Fund.[47]

Conversely, the Roberts' nomination was supported by the Heritage Foundation, which issued a statement saying that Roberts had unquestionable integrity, that he had valuable experience, that he had a keen knowledge of the government and the federal justice system. They felt he understood how the law affects the lives of ordinary citizens.[48]

Confirmation hearings on the nomination began in the Senate Judiciary committee on September12. The Senate Judiciary Committee voted 13 to 5 to send the nomination to the Full Senate with favorable recommendations. On September 29, Roberts was confirmed by the entire Senate by a vote of 78 to 22.

SONIA SOTOMAYOR: Sotomayor was nominated to serve on the Supreme Court by President Barak Obama on May 26, 2009 to replace retiring Justice David Souter. She received a BA degree from Princeton University and a law degree from Yale University Law School. At the time of her nomination, Sotomayor was serving on the second circuit appeals court in New York, after being nominated to that position by President Clinton. Prior to that, she had nominated to be a district judge by George H.W. Bush. She was probably best known for issuing an injunction that ended a Major League Baseball strike in 1995.

The National Rifle Association and other pro-gun groups opposed her nomination because they argued that she did not support the Second Amendment right to own guns. Other groups supported the nomination. The American Bar Association, for example, gave her a "well quali-fied" rating.

Sotomayer's confirmation hearings in the Senate Judiciary committee began on July 13, 2009. On July 28, the Committee approved her nomination in a nearly party-line vote of 13 to 6. Her nomination was confirmed by the full Senate by a vote of 68 to 31. She became the first Hispanic and third female justice on the Supreme Court. It is expected that she would be a mod-erate or centrist judge,[49] or a "favorite of the left."[50]

LOWER FEDERAL COURTS   Appointment to lower federal courts is not as complex or public. Perhaps because there are many lower federal positions, the president and the Senate cannot spend as much time on each individual judge as with the nominees to the Supreme Court. Additionally, these judges have less of a potential impact on policy as opposed to Supreme Court justices. The justices appointed to federal appellate courts typically have served in political posi-tions in the past, have developed close ties to other members of the president's party, and share the general ideological positions as the president.[51]

But the appointment process is very political. One example of this is Daniel Manion. Daniel Manion was nominated to be a judge on the Seventh Circuit Court of Appeals by President Reagan in 1986. Manion had little experience in the federal court and no prior judicial experience. He also had no record of publications in law reviews, and some of his legal briefs given to the Senate had spelling and grammatical errors. There was even evidence that Manion at one time suggested posting the Ten Commandments in public schools and was associated with the John Burch Society. In the end, he was accused of being too conservative. The Senate vote was a 47 to 47 tie. In this case, the Senate rules allowed for a reconsideration of the vote. The vote was put off for several weeks, and a second vote was again a tie, 49 to 49. This time, the tie was broken by Republican Vice President Bush's vote in Manion's favor.

The politics surrounding court nominees was obvious during the Bush administration, when many of his nominations to fill open judicial seats both in federal district and appeals courts were blocked by Democrats in the Senate. Even though many appointments were ap-proved, there were many open positions. Bush then turned to using "recess appointment" to install nominees onto the bench, angering Senate Democrats who claimed that Bush was at-tempting to circumvent Constitutional procedures for seating federal justices.[52] Then, in December 2006, the Bush administration's Department of Justice fired seven US Attorneys, some say simply for political advantage. They claimed he did so because the fired attorneys did not investigate charges against Democratic politicians. The Bush administration pointed out that U.S. Attorneys serve at "the pleasure of the president" and that it was simply a personnel matter.[53]

Merit

The third method for seating a justice is the merit plan, also called the Missouri Plan. This was originally created in 1940 in Missouri to eliminate political patronage when judges were ap-pointed. Merit plans vary, but there are some general foundations. When a vacancy occurs in a judicial position, a judicial nominating commission made up of citizens and attorneys is estab-lished. The commission is usually made up of both lawyers and nonlawyers. It evaluates potential judicial appointees and sends the governor (or other decision-making body) the names of three potential judges. The governor then makes the appointment based on the list of names provided by the commission. The newly appointed judge serves a time in office, at which point he or she must be confirmed by the voters in a nonpartisan, unopposed election. In this race, the judge simply runs against his or her record. In this case, the ballot simply asks, "Shall Judge X remain in office?" If the judge is not approved by the voters, the process begins all over again with the committee nominating a successor. If the judge is approved, he or she remains on the bench but must go through the approval process at regular intervals.[54]

Although some might argue that the merit system is less political than other methods, it still has the potential of being influenced by political actors. When attempting to determine the "best" way to seat judges, one study concluded that "appointive methods are no more effective than the elective process in placing qualified judges on the bench, while neither method is successful in fulfilling philosophical expectations."[55] Thus, it appears as if each method has its benefits, but political influences cannot be removed from the judicial selection procedures completely.

FEDERAL COURT SYSTEM

The federal court system hears cases involving violations of federal laws. They hear both civil and criminal cases that are violations of acts of Congress, such as cases concerning counterfeiting, kidnapping, smuggling, and drug trafficking. There are different types of courts, each with its own jurisdiction.

Supreme Court

As noted earlier, the foundation for the Supreme Court is found in the Constitution, but the Supreme Court was actually created in the Judiciary Act of 1789. It is the nation's highest appellate court and is the court of last resort for all cases in the federal and state systems. It oversees both federal and state systems. The Supreme Court is made up of the chief justice and such number of associate justices as may be fixed by Congress. Currently, the number of associate justices is eight. The justices sit for life (or good behavior), but they may be removed by impeachment or voluntary retirement.

The jurisdiction of the Supreme Court is defined in the Constitution. According to article III, section 2,

> The judicial power shall extend to all cases, in law and equity, arising under this Constitution, the laws of the United States, and treaties made, or which shall be made, under their authority; to all cases affecting ambassadors, other public ministers and consuls; to all cases of admiralty and maritime jurisdiction; to controversies to which the United States shall be a party; to controversies between two or more states; between a state and citizens of another state; between citizens of different states; between citizens of the same state claiming lands under grants of different states, and between a state, or the citizens thereof, and foreign states, citizens, or subjects. In all cases affecting ambassadors, other public ministers and consuls, and those in which a state shall be party, the Supreme Court shall have original jurisdiction. In all other cases before mentioned, the Supreme Court shall have appellate jurisdiction, both as to law and fact, with such exceptions, and under such regulations as the Congress shall make.

The Supreme Court has both original and appellate jurisdiction. Original jurisdiction means that the cases will originate in the Court: these cases must be heard by the Court. Any cases that involve treaties made by the federal government, controversies in which the U.S. government is a party, and disputes between two states will go directly to the Supreme Court. The Court will hear those cases first. The Court also has original jurisdiction with discretionary cases, meaning that the Court may accept the case but is not required to hear it, as in cases brought by a state, disputes between a state and a foreign government, or cases involving a foreign diplomat.

The Supreme Court also has appellate jurisdiction. This means that the Court hears cases on appeal from a lower court. Despite the fact that the Court can basically decide what cases to hear, there are some appellate cases that it must hear (it has appellate jurisdiction with mandatory cases). If a federal court holds an act of Congress to be unconstitutional and the federal government is a party, if a U.S. court of appeals finds a state statute unconstitutional (a state law is in violation of the federal constitution), or if a state's highest court holds a federal law to be invalid or unconstitutional, the Supreme Court must hear the case.

The Supreme Court does not hear all cases that are appealed to it. It has discretion over the cases it will consider and can decide what cases to hear. The Court hears approximately 5 percent of the cases petitioned to it. Approximately 7,000 cases are passed on in the course of a term. In addition, some 1,200 applications of various kinds are filed each year that can be acted on by a single justice. The justices choose to hear only those cases that involve important issues or that are appropriate for the Court.

Some have argued that the court decisions have less influence today than in the past. The argument is made on two levels. First, the court is playing a smaller role in the lives of Americans. Most key issues, such as affirmative action or the death penalty, have been around so long that any cases coming to the court are highly specific cases that affect few people. Second, the court is hearing fewer cases than in the past. In 2006, the court heard fewer cases than at any other time in the past half-century.[56]

Over the years, the justices seated under different chief justices have listened to and made decisions in different ways. Some courts are more likely to follow a conservative perspective to criminal justice issues, while others follow the liberal approach. This has been evident in the most recent courts, including the Warren, Burger, and Rehnquist courts.

THE WARREN COURT (1953–1969)   The Supreme Court under Chief Justice Earl Warren became known as the most liberal Supreme Court in American history.[57] It addressed many significant social problems of the time, such as race relations. The members of this Court decided the landmark case of *Brown v. Board of Education of Topeka, Kansas*, which wiped out the legal basis for discrimination in education.[58] The Warren court also protected free speech[59] by broadening citizens' freedom to criticize public figures, by protecting freedom of the press,[60] and by an artists' ability to express him- or herself in unconventional and even shocking ways.[61] It also upheld equal representation through a series of reapportionment cases.

In terms of criminal justice, the Warren court weakened the "hands-off" policy that had been accepted by the Court until then. The Warren court became active in expanding the rights of persons accused of a crime. It wrote what amounted to a new constitutional code of criminal justice that put restraints on law enforcement, from investigation through arrest and trial, and applied the new code to state and local activities formerly outside federal standards.[62] As a result, "the police must obey the law while enforcing the law."[63]

The Warren court decided many landmark cases that still affect the criminal justice system today. It decided cases concerning stop and frisk, the right to counsel in a criminal proceeding, the accused's rights in a search and seizure, illegal confessions, interrogation, and confessions. These decisions have been called the "due process revolution"[64] because they expanded due process rights and applied them to the states for the first time.[65] The Warren court consistently upheld constitutional guarantees that were extended throughout the administration of criminal justice.[66]

THE BURGER COURT (1969–1986)   The Burger court was a court in political transition.[67] President Nixon replaced Chief Justice Warren with Warren Burger and also appointed three additional justices to the Court whom he expected to promote tough law-and-order policies. The Burger court was more conservative than the Warren court.[68] In fact, Burger had the second most conservative voting record on criminal justice issues by the time he retired from the bench.[69] The justices on the Burger court were seen as restrained by some because its decisions were generally less innovative and more conservative than those of the Warren court.[70] In the area of criminal procedure, the Court was less sympathetic to defendants than were previous Courts and less supportive of civil liberties. In *United States v. Ross* (1982), the Court expanded the power of police officers to search automobiles without warrants. In 1973, the Court gave the government more power to regulate obscene material in *Miller v. California*.[71]

THE REHNQUIST COURT (1986 TO 2005)   The Supreme Court under Chief Justice William Rehnquist has tended to decide cases on a more conservative basis, especially with the appointment of Justice Antonin Scalia. The Rehnquist court is much more conservative than either the Warren or the Burger courts.[72] It has been active in narrowing or overturning many Warren and Burger court precedents. On the whole, the Rehnquist court has been more restrained in its treatment of prisoners' religious freedom, due process protections, *habeas corpus*, and prison condition cases.[73] The Rehnquist court

> restricted habeas corpus review, allowed greater scope for police or other agencies to search or to administer drug tests, allowed states to secure prosecutions by using evidence that it had previously excluded, tolerated state regulations of abortions, disallowed affirmative action when quotas are used, refused to protect intimate relationships that are not conventional and refused to protect those who possess child pornography or women who seek to dance naked in adult-only clubs.[74]

ROBERTS COURT (2005–PRESENT)   Justice Roberts is the nation's seventeenth chief justice. He holds impeccable legal credentials and has a reputation for being a conservative. Today's court includes two women and an African-American. There are four conservative justices (Scalia, Thomas, Roberts, and Alito), two centrist justices (Breyer and Kennedy) and three who are considered to be liberal (Stevens, Sotomayer and Ginsburg). The justices currently serving on the Supreme Court are listed in Box 6.3.

It seems as if the Roberts court is continuing the recent traditions of limiting access to the nation's highest court. It also seems to be rolling back the concept of "standing" when attempting to sue so that members of a class must have suffered a specific harm rather than have an abstract "public interest."[75]

Roberts was only fifty two when he became Chief justice, so he may serve on the Court for many years. This means that he has the potential for influencing the court for many years.

POLITICS AND THE SUPREME COURT   Politics is supposed to remain outside the activities of the Supreme Court, but it often shows its face in its operations. The other branches of government often get involved in the Court's activities. Despite the image of being outside the political arena, judges are indeed a political organization.[76]

BOX 6.3

Members of the Roberts Court, 2010

Justice	Appointing President	Year Confirmed
Roberts	G. W. Bush	2005
Scalia	Reagan	1986
Kennedy	Reagan	1988
Alito	G. W. Bush	2006
Thomas	G. H. W. Bush	1991
Ginsburg	Clinton	1993
Breyer	Clinton	1994
Sotomayor	Obama	2009
Kagan	Obama	2010

Although justices must make decisions based on the law, the justices may interpret the laws differently, depending on their political views and political ideology. Studies show that Democratic and Republican judges do tend to vote differently on many important issues that come before the Court. Judges who come from the ranks of the Democratic Party have been more liberal than their colleagues from Republican ranks. Liberal justices tend to emphasize due process rights more than conservative justices, who tend to focus more on punishment. Democratic justices tend to favor the defense in criminal cases, whereas Republicans tend to favor the prosecution. Generally, Democratic judges tend to have more of an "underdog" orientation toward a variety of issues than do Republican judges.

Studies concerning judicial ideology and voting patterns show that the ideological stance of the justices does influence their voting behavior. In fact, "justice ideology is found to be a statistically significant determinant of justice voting in each of the policy areas examined."[77] These findings support Segal and Spaeth.[78] Thus, the political party affiliation of justices does alter the way in which they exercise their policymaking discretion when the circumstances of a case give them room to maneuver.

Although judges strive to be as neutral as possible,[79] they are often influenced by their political orientation, either liberal or conservative. Judges may be unable to ignore all their political beliefs and ideas when they assume the bench, and so, to some extent, their behavior can be differentiated on the basis of their party affiliation. This is important because their values and preferences can affect their decisions. This means that the law is based on the preferences of the justices involved in the case.[80] Most federal judges belong to the party of the president who appointed them, and they remain faithful to their party while in office. In fact, party identification is the single best predictor of judicial voting behavior.[81]

Politics and the Court: Congress   The relationship between Congress and the Supreme Court is not always friendly. Each branch acts as a check on the behavior of the other, which is another example of the separation of powers that was built into the government system.

First, Congress acts as a check on the behavior of the courts. When the Court makes a decision (thus making policy) that is opposed by the members of Congress, they may "go after" that decision and attempt to change it or alter it in some way. Congress can try to impact a decision in

TABLE 6.1 Reported Confidence in the U.S. Supreme Court, 2009 (%)

Question: I am going to read you a list of institutions in American Society. Please tell me how much confidence you, yourself, have in each one—a great deal, some, very little, or none: The U.S. Supreme Court?

	Great Deal	Some	Very Little	None
National	39	41	17	1
Sex				
Male	41	38	18	1
Female	35	44	16	1
Race				
White	39	43	15	1
Nonwhite	37	35	22	.5
Black	35	38	24	0
Age				
18 to 29 years	35	43	18	.5
30 to 49 years	41	41	16	.5
50 to 64 years	38	42	16	2
50 years and older	37	40	17	2
65 years and older	36	38	18	2
Education				
College postgraduate	53	37	8	1
College graduate	49	40	10	1
Some college	37	41	18	1
High school graduate or less	30	42	24	1
Income				
$75,000 and over	51	39	10	.5
$50,000 to $74,999	41	42	15	1
$30,000 to $49,999	37	40	17	2
$20,000 to $29,999	29	45	22	1
Under $20,000	27	43	27	1
Ideology				
Conservative	31	45	22	2
Moderate	48	37	12	.5
Liberal	38	45	14	1
Region				
East	40	38	19	1
Midwest	38	43	16	1
South	37	42	17	1
West	39	40	15	1
Politics				
Republican	35	44	18	1
Democrat	44	40	12	.5
Independent	36	40	20	2

Source: Sourcebook of Criminal Justice Statistics, available online at www.albany.edu/sourcebook/pdf/t215.pdf.

a number of ways. First, Congress may attempt to overturn a constitutional decision made by the Court by proposing and passing a constitutional amendment. A good example of this occurred in 1989, when the Supreme Court ruled 5 to 4 in *Texas v. Johnson* that flag burning was a form of political expression protected by the First Amendment. When it made that decision, the Court, in essence, made all existing state and federal laws banning the desecration of the flag invalid. President Bush immediately called on Congress to pass a constitutional amendment to prohibit flag burning, as did many other organizations and groups across the nation. But after congressional members and scholars recognized that such an amendment would entail amending the Bill of Rights, support for the amendment faded. The Senate voted on the proposed amendment, but the vote was not enough to pass the amendment. Another push to pass an amendment also failed in 1990.[82] It is generally not easy to get enough votes to pass an amendment and then to get ratification by states.

Alternatively, Congress can propose and pass new legislation that reverses, overrules, or modifies the Court's interpretation. This can be accomplished quicker than passing a constitutional amendment. Congress has, in the past, effectively passed legislation that reversed some of the Court's decisions that gave more rights to offenders charged with crimes. But since the legislation passed by Congress applied only to federal offenses and most crime is prosecuted on the state level, the congressional action had only limited effects and was seen as largely symbolic.[83]

According to Gallup's survey conducted in Sept 2007, 51 percent of Americans approve of the way the Supreme Court is doing the job; while 39 percent disapprove. It is related to their political party affiliation. 69 percent of Republicans approve of their job, while only 47 percent of independents and only 41 percent of Democrats approve.[84]

An example of this has to do with a Supreme Court decision made in 1943 in *McNabb v. United States*. In this case, the Court ruled that a confession obtained by police during an "unnecessary delay" in a suspect's arraignment could not be used as evidence in federal court even if the confession had been given voluntarily. A few years later, in 1957, the Supreme Court reaffirmed this decision in *Mallory v. United States*. In this case, the Court overturned the rape conviction of Andrew Mallory because police had not complied with the *McNabb* decision. In response, the House of Representatives in July 1958 passed what it termed "corrective" legislation that barred federal courts from disqualifying confessions that would otherwise be admissible as evidence in criminal cases simply because of a delay in arraigning a suspect. Although the Senate also passed a version of the bill, it died before final passage.[85]

The congressional oversight of the Supreme Court continued. In the late 1960s, the Court made two decisions that outraged many people. First, the Court decided the landmark case of *Miranda v. Arizona* (1966), in which the Court expanded and formalized new procedures revolving around criminal confessions. After *Miranda*, confessions were inadmissible as evidence in state or federal criminal trials if the accused had not been informed of his or her right to remain silent, if he or she had not been warned that any statement made might be used against him or her, and if he or she had not been informed of his or her right to have an attorney present during the police interrogation. In 1967, the Supreme Court decided in *United States v. Wade* that the identification of a defendant based only on a police lineup that took place when the defendant's attorney was not present was inadmissible evidence into court. These two decisions were very unpopular, and in 1968, Congress reacted, proposing a new law that made confessions admissible as evidence if given voluntarily, a clear attempt to overturn or modify the *Miranda* decision. The proposal also allowed that a confession made by a person in custody of law enforcement was admissible as evidence even if there was a delay in the defendant's arraignment. This legislation modified the Court's *Mallory* decision. Finally, the proposed law would modify the *Wade* decision by allowing the testimony of an eyewitness who could say that he or she saw the accused commit the crime for which he or she was being tried as admissible evidence in any federal criminal trial. Eventually, President Johnson signed the bill into law on June 19, 1968.[86]

This happened after the Supreme Court ruled in 2010 that the government cannot put bans on political spending by corporations during elections. The decision handed down in *Citizens United v. Federal Election Commission* overruled previous decisions that limited campaign spending by corporations. Immediately after the controversial decision was announced, questions emerged about what policy options were available to Congress to limit the impact of the decision. Two possible choices were noted. First, Congress could provide candidates or parties with additional access to funds to allow them to combat corporate influence in elections. Second, Congress could restrict spending under certain conditions or require those who spend money to provide additional information to voters. Many members of Congress spoke out against the decision, and multiple bills were proposed in Congress that would reverse the Supreme Court's decision.[87] But much of the response was symbolic, as any legislation banning political spending may, in the future, be deemed unconstitutional once again.

Of course, any action by Congress is reviewed by the Supreme Court to guarantee that it is legally fair and consistent with the rights guaranteed in the Constitution. This means that the judges act as a check on the behavior of Congress. This occurs when judges use their power of judicial review to reverse laws made by Congress. Of course, when the Court decides that a congressional act was unconstitutional, it is sometimes viewed as an illegitimate usurpation of congressional prerogatives.[88] In other words, it is taking away the power of Congress to make the laws and policies they deem necessary to better society in some way.

More and more, the policies enacted by elected representatives in Washington are challenged in the courts. Some people might argue that public policy is not fully legitimated until it has withstood judicial challenge. To become legitimate, policies often must await a decision by a federal court judge who decides that the action by Congress and the president does not conflict with the Constitution.[89]

By declaring congressional actions acceptable under the laws and the Constitution, the Supreme Court can legitimate the actions of Congress or other government decision makers.[90] If (or when) the Court upholds a law or policy created in Congress, for example, it is demonstrating that the law is legally valid and acceptable. Conversely, if the Court, on appeal, decides that a law is unconstitutional or unfair, it is declaring that the bill is not acceptable and that the actions of that legislative body were inappropriate. In other words, the members of the policymaking agency overstepped their boundary, making a law that was not consistent with the Constitution.

Another method used by Congress to reverse a Court decision is to use its appropriation powers to aid or hinder compliance with the Court's rulings. Congress can do this through its ability to authorize appropriations for salaries, law clerks, secretaries, and office technology. Although article III of the Constitution forbids reducing the salaries of justices, Congress can withhold salary increases.

Or the Senate may retaliate by trying to influence judicial appointments or may even impeach (or threaten to impeach) justices. If nothing else, this brings a lot of negative attention and media coverage to an individual judge or court. Congress can mount an attack on these judges with a series of verbal denouncements that allow congressional members to let off steam. If serious enough, federal judges can be removed from office by Congress.

Politics and the Court: Presidents   Like Congress, the executive branch also acts as a check on the behavior of the Supreme Court and vice versa. First and foremost, presidents will try to influence federal judicial policy by choosing nominees for the Court who share their party affili-ation and political philosophy and will make decisions and policies that reflect that particular po-litical ideology. Thus, the party affiliations of presidents influence their decisions about who to nominate for judicial seats. Republican presidents typically appoint conservative Republicans to judgeships, and Democratic presidents manifest a preference for moderate to liberal Democrats.[91] Once appointed, federal judges maintain their partisan views and make decisions that reflect those views.[92] Thus, the president's ability to affect Court policy is demonstrated in his opportunity to appoint like-minded justices to the bench, assuming that his appointments successfully pass the confirmation process.[93] In fact, most studies of judicial nominees find that presidents have been successful in shaping Court policy through their appointments.[94]

Once seated on the bench, most justices feel at least some degree of allegiance to the politi-cal actor (the president) who is responsible for their elevation to the Court.[95] Since justices tend to support their appointing presidents, the presidents can change the ideological composition of the Court through the power of appointment.[96]

Presidents also try to influence the decisions made by the Court. The president's ability to get his policy preferences implemented in certain policy areas is, to an extent, dependent on the degree to which the Supreme Court is willing to comply.[97] Presidents will sometimes reach out to other agencies and even to the public for support for his positions. One study by Yates shows that "presidents can use their tools of rhetoric, amicus activity, and popular prestige toward" influenc-ing court policy: "In short, presidents can contemporaneously affect the voting decisions of Supreme Court justices by sending public signals of their policy preferences."[98]

A president can also influence judicial policymaking through the activities of the Justice Department. The attorney general (a presidential appointee) and the staff of the Justice Department can emphasize specific issues according to the overall policy goals of the president. This is especially true because of the close relationship between the attorney general and the Supreme Court. The solicitor general, also a presidential nominee, can affect policy. The solicitor general is responsible for representing the U.S. government in federal cases. The policy positions of the U.S. government are represented by the solicitor general's office. The solicitor general may file amicus curiae briefs where the government has an interest in the outcome of a case. He or she can also determine which cases involving the federal government will be appealed to the Supreme Court. In this regard, the solicitor general can help the Supreme Court shape its docket. The views of the solicitor general are almost always consistent with the president's position.

Once a decision is made, the president may be able to influence the impact of that decision. A president may encourage the bureaucracies or agencies responsible for the implementation of that policy or resist a new judicial policy. Since many judicial decisions are implemented by the various departments, agencies, and commissions in the executive branch, the president can reach out to those people whom he appointed for their support or opposition to a new program. Or the president can propose legislation aimed at retaliating against the courts. Of course, the president cannot vote on that legislation, but he can propose it to Congress, making a strong public state-ment about the court's actions.

Politics and the Court: Other Actors   Other political influences affect the behavior of judges, including public opinion. Studies have shown that the Supreme Court does pay attention to pub-lic opinion and that this is reflected in the decisions they make. Mishler and Sheehan find that from 1956 to 1981, there was a reciprocal relationship between the public mood and the decisions made by the Court, with an approximate five-year lag. This means that it takes about five years for the public's opinion to register with the Court. This is also the amount of time it takes for the justices to perceive, interpret, and react to the changes. However, since 1981, the decisions were in the opposite direction from the public's opinion. At this time, the Court was more conservative despite a liberal resurgence in the public mood. This only served to widen a gap between public opinion and the Court's decisions.[99]

The public's opinion of the court changes over time. In June 2005, when Thomas became Chief Justice, 8 percent had a very favorable opinion of the Court. That poll showed that 49 percent said their opinion of the court was mostly favorable; 22 percent reported mostly unfavorable; 8 percent was very unfavorable, and 13 percent was unable to rate the Court. By 2007, those ratings had changed. The new poll reported that 18 percent had a very favorable opinion of the Supreme Court; 54 percent had a mostly favorable opinion of the Court. 14 percent had a mostly unfavorable opinion; 3 percent had a very unfavorable opinion, and 9 percent were unable to rate the Court.[100] More information about the public's confidence with the Court is found in Table 6.1.

The justices also rely on social science research when they are making their decisions. This can include books, government documents, and law reviews. Although justices vary as to how often they will do this, it appears that justices are more frequently relying on published information than before. It is more available than before, and it is used in the briefs of parties and amici.[101]

Lower Federal Courts

Article III, section 1, of the Constitution declares that the judicial power of the United States shall be invested in one Supreme Court and in "such inferior Courts as the Congress may from time to time ordain and establish." Congress has created many lower federal courts with differing jurisdiction, including Courts of Appeals, District Courts, and other courts with specific jurisdiction. These courts each deal with offenses against federal law rather than violations of state law.[102]

U.S. COURTS OF APPEAL   The U.S. courts of appeal are called intermediate appellate courts or the U.S. Circuit Court of Appeals. They were created in 1891 to reduce the number of appeals that had to be considered by the Supreme Court and to relieve the Court of considering all appeals in cases originally decided by the federal trial courts. They have the power to review all final decisions of district courts and to review and enforce orders of federal administrative bodies, such as the Food and Drug Administration, the National Labor Relations Board, and the Securities and Exchange Commission.

There are thirteen courts of appeal, each of which has jurisdiction over part of the country. Each circuit is identified by a number. (See Figure 6.2.) Eleven of the circuits are made up of three or more states, one is for the District of Columbia, and one is for the federal circuit. Circuit court offices are generally located in larger metropolitan areas, and the appellant must travel to that location to have his or her case heard. Each circuit has at least six permanent judges, but larger circuits have as many as twenty-eight. Each court of appeals normally hears cases in panels consisting of three judges, but in important cases, the judges may sit *en banc*. This means that the full membership of the court participates.

The U.S. courts of appeal have appellate jurisdiction and review records only from the federal district courts (not state courts) or from federal administrative agencies. They do not retry cases or make a ruling on the guilt or innocence of a defendant, nor will they determine issues of fact that might or might not support a conviction or dismissal (if a defendant was provided with legal counsel). The judges only analyze judicial interpretations of the law (both

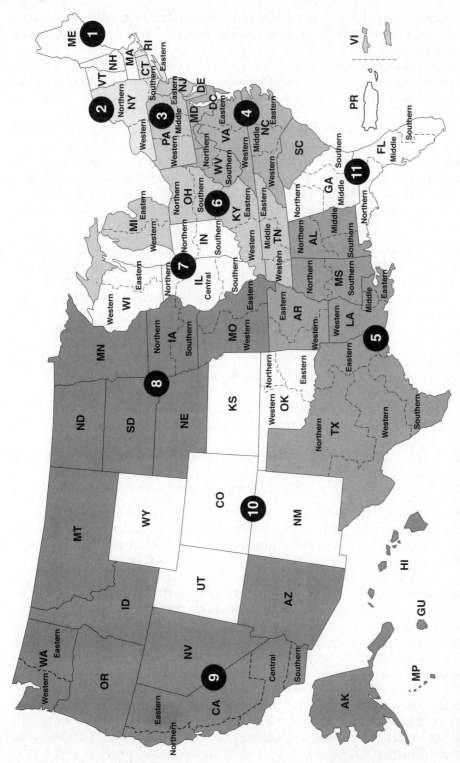

FIGURE 6.2 Geographic Boundaries of U.S. Courts of Appeals and U.S. District Courts.

statutory and constitutional), such as the charge (or instructions) to the jury, and consider constitutional issues involved in the cases they hear to determine if the decisions of the trial court are legally correct.

If the court of appeals determines that there are no errors of law in the district court, then the court upholds (or affirms) the decision of the lower court. However, if the court of appeals finds an error, it usually returns the case to the trial court. The trial court can either retry the case or dismiss the case.

The court of appeals generally receives far less media coverage than the Supreme Court, in part because its activities are not as dramatic and its decisions not as far-reaching. But this does not mean that the court of appeals is any less important. Its role in the legal system has increased significantly in recent years. In the 12-month period ending September 30, 2008, there were 61,104 appeals filed with the courts, representing a 3.8 percent increase from the previous year. About 22 percent of those appeals were made by criminals appealing their conviction, sentence, or both.[103]

U.S. COURT OF APPEALS FOR THE FEDERAL CIRCUIT   The Appeals Court for the Federal Circuit (or the Thirteenth Circuit Court) was created when President Reagan signed the Federal Courts Improvement Act of 1982. This created a thirteenth circuit court, which became the U.S. Court of Appeals for the Federal Circuit. The U.S. Court of Appeals for the Federal Circuit was developed to help sort out and develop cases that are significant enough to be heard by the Supreme Court. This court has national jurisdiction and is required to hear all cases appealed to it.[104] It also hears appeals from the district courts in patent cases, contract cases, and other civil actions in which the United States is a defendant. It also hears appeals from final decisions of other courts, including the U.S. Court of International Trade, the U.S. Court of Federal Claims, and the U.S. Court of Veterans Appeals. The jurisdiction of the court also includes the review of administrative rulings of different agencies, such as the Patent and Trademark Office, the U.S. International Trade Commission, the secretary of commerce, and the Merit Systems Protection Board.

The U.S. Court of Appeals for the Federal Circuit consists of twelve circuit judges. It sits in panels of three or more on each case and may also hear or rehear a case *en banc.* The court sits principally in Washington, D.C., but may hold court wherever any court of appeals sits.

U.S. DISTRICT COURTS   The U.S. district courts were created by Congress in the Judiciary Act of 1789 to lessen the demands on the Supreme Court. Presently, there are ninety-four district courts in the United States, divided into twelve geographic circuits. Each state has at least one district court, and some of the larger states (such as New York and California) have as many as four federal district courts, with the number of federal district judges ranging from two to twenty-eight, depending on the amount of work within its territory. These courts are the general trial courts for the federal system. They are courts of original jurisdiction, where federal cases are first heard. Usually, only one judge is required to hear and decide a case in a district court, but in some limited cases it is required that three judges be called together to make up the court. A defendant can request a jury trial in some cases. The justices are appointed by the president and approved by the Senate for a term of good behavior.

These courts are the basic point of entry for the federal judicial system. If a person is accused of a federal offense, this is the court that would determine guilt. These are the only federal courts in which attorneys examine and cross-examine witnesses. They are sometimes called the "workhorses" for the federal judiciary, as they have original jurisdiction over virtually all federal cases.

These are courts of general jurisdiction, so they have both civil and criminal jurisdiction. The courts preside over cases that involve civil actions arising under the Constitution, certain civil actions between citizens of different states, civil actions within the maritime jurisdiction of the United States, criminal prosecutions brought by the federal government, and civil actions in which the United States is a party. The civil jurisdiction of the district courts is limited to suits exceeding $10,000 in which a federal question is raised. The civil jurisdiction also includes questions involving citizenship rights suits between citizens who reside in different states, one state's suing another state or a citizen who lives in another state, or the federal government's being a party to the suit.

The criminal jurisdiction of the courts includes all cases where a federal criminal statute has been violated, such as civil rights abuse, kidnapping, assassination or attempted assassination of the president, postal violations, violations of federal fish and game laws, and cases involving interstate transportation of stolen vehicles or goods as well as interstate flight to avoid prosecution. Citizenship and rights of aliens are also included in the jurisdiction of the courts.

District courts may also serve as appellate courts for those matters tried before a U.S. magistrate. They also have appellate functions in dealing with certain writs of *habeas corpus.*

Many cases go through the federal district court each year. During the twelve months period ending in September 2008, criminal cases were commenced against 349,969 defendants in U.S. district court, a 4.3 percent increase over the previous year. Most of the defendants (81%) were charged with civil offenses, while the remainder were charged with criminal offenses.[105]

One case that appeared in a federal district court was *United States v. Microsoft,* based on a set of civil actions filed against Microsoft Corporation by the United States Department of Justice and twenty states. The plaintiffs alleged that Microsoft violated the Sherman Antirust Act by bundling its Internet Explorer web browser software with its Microsoft Windows operating system. In doing so, it was alleged that Microsoft unfairly restricted the market for competing web browsers. The case was heard in the D.C. District Court in 2000 (US v. Microsoft Corp. 87 F. Supp 2d 30 (D.D.C. 2000).[85] In 2001, the Department of Justice and Microsoft reached an agreement to settle the case.

FEDERAL MAGISTRATES/U.S. MAGISTRATE JUDGES Federal magistrates, formerly called U.S. commissioners, were created by Congress in the Federal Magistrates Act of 1968 to help federal district judges deal with increased workloads. They have trial jurisdiction over minor federal misdemeanor offenses; they also issue arrest warrants or search warrants to federal law enforcement officers (such as agents of the FBI and the Drug Enforcement Administration), conduct preliminary hearings, and set bail. In 1976, the magistrates were given the authority to review civil rights and *habeas corpus* petitions and make recommendations regarding them to the district court judges.

In December 1990, the title of "federal magistrate" was changed to "U.S. magistrate judge" as part of the Judicial Improvements Act. Now, full-time magistrate judges are appointed by district court judges for eight-year terms but can be removed for "good cause." There are currently 452 federal magistrates. There are also part-time magistrates who serve four-year terms. To be appointed, a judge must be a lawyer and a member of the state bar association. Since magistrate judges do not have the same qualifications as article III judges (i.e., presidential appointment, Senate confirmation, and protected tenure), magistrate judges are considered "adjuncts" of the federal courts who perform tasks delegated by the district judge.[106] Since magistrate judges were intended to be used according to the needs of each district court, the exact role they have differs from district to district. The judges in each district court establish the specific responsibilities of their magistrates. Generally, however, they serve three roles. First, they can be an additional judge who might oversee civil cases and share caseload responsibilities. For example, they can conduct a trial of a person accused of misdemeanor charges. Second, they can act as a "team player" who handles legal motion hearings, conferences, and other tasks to prepare cases for trial. They can hear and determine certain kinds of pretrial matters or conduct proceedings in a civil matter. Third, federal magistrates may act as a specialist who processes Social Security disability appeals or prisoner petitions for the district judges.[107]

OTHER FEDERAL COURTS   There are other federal courts that have jurisdiction over special areas. For example, the U.S. Claims Court hears cases in which the U.S. government has been sued for damages. They may also hear cases that concern disputes over federal contracts, unlawful "takings' of private property by the federal government, and other claims against the United States. The U.S. Court of International Trade handles cases involving cases of international trade and customs issues, appeals of U.S. Customs Office rulings. The U.S. Court of Military Appeals hears appeals of military courts-martial. There is also a Court of Appeals for the Armed Forces and the U.S. Tax Court.

STATE COURTS

Even though state courts may not receive as much attention as do federal ones, they remain an important power in the policy process. State courts do not receive as much attention as do governors and legislatures, but they make rulings and decisions on a wide range of important issues. Some of their decisions are reviewed by the Supreme Court.

Each individual state has established its own court system in their state constitutions. To that end, there is some variation in the court systems from one state to the next. Each state has its own unique court structure, but there are also many similarities between them. On the whole, these courts interpret state constitutions, statutes, and administrative regulations. Like federal courts, state courts hear both criminal and civil cases. Most states created a three-tiered system that includes courts of limited jurisdiction and general jurisdiction and appellate courts. But states call the courts different names. For example, the major trial courts in California are called superior courts but in Texas are called district courts.

Six states, Idaho, Illinois, Iowa, Massachusetts, Missouri, and South Dakota, have only one level of trial courts, so these courts hear all kinds of cases. Twelve states did not develop intermediate-level appellate courts. In these states, appeals are heard by the court of last resort. These states are Delaware, Maine, Mississippi, Montana, Nebraska, Nevada, New Hampshire, Rhode Island, South Dakota, Vermont, West Virginia, and Wyoming. Other states, Arkansas, Texas, and Oklahoma, have two courts of last resort: one for civil and one for criminal.

State courts hear cases concerning violations of state laws rather than federal statutes. Since most crimes are state offenses, the state-level courts (rather than federal courts) deal with most of the cases and offenders. These would include cases concerning murder, drug offenses, rape, assault, and theft, among other things. If federal and state laws conflict, the general rule is that the federal law prevails. In some cases, the decision surrounding who can try an offender becomes very political. Both federal and state agencies may feel entitled to convict an offender. This happened in the case of the D.C. sniper, where many states and the federal government wanted to prosecute him.

State courts are, like federal courts, political entities. Because they are responsible for arbitrating disputes about consequential matters, state courts have increasingly been drawn into

TABLE 6.2   Felony Convictions in State Courts, 2000 and 2006

Offense	Number	Percentage
Drug Trafficking 2000	203,400	22.0
2006	212,490	18.8
Violent Offenses 2000		
2006	165,360	18.2
Drug Possession 2000	116,300	12.6
2006	165,360	14.6
Larceny 2000	100,000	10.8
2006	125,390	11.1
Fraud/Forgery 2000	82,700	8.9
2006	96,260	8.5
Aggravated Assault 2000	79,400	8.6
2006	100,560	8.9
Burglary 2000	79,300	8.6
2006	99,910	8.8
Robbery 2000	36,800	4.0
2006	9,660	.9
Sexual Assault 2000	31,500	3.4
2006	32,200	2.9
Weapons Offenses 2000	28,200	3.1
2006	38,010	3.4
Other Violent Offense 2000	17,000	1.8
2006	21,980	1.9
Murder 2000	8,600	0.9
2006	8,670	0.8

Source: Bureau of Justice Statistics, "Felony Sentences in State Courts, 2000," *Bureau of Justice Statistics Bulletin* (Washington, D.C.: Bureau of Justice Statistics, 2003); "Felony Sentences in State Courts, 2006," *Bureau of Justice Statistics Bulletin* (Washington, D.C.: Bureau of Justice Statistics, 2009).

the political arena. State supreme courts must rule on key legal issues within a larger arena or environment of politics and policymaking. "Their interpretations of law are influenced by other institutions in government and politics. And their interpretations spur reactions by the same institutions: a supreme court decision is not necessarily the final word on a legal issue."[108]

For the most part, state courts can include the state supreme court, state appellate courts (which are organized by district), county or municipal courts (also called common pleas courts, which may include family courts, teen courts, juvenile courts, drug courts [for possession charges], or domestic courts), circuit courts, and trial courts for felony charges. State courts can include those at municipal and county levels and have jurisdiction over "traffic violations, divorces, wills, most contracts, crimes against persons and property, and the decisions and

TABLE 6.3	Mean Length of Felony Sentences Imposed in State Courts After Trial, 2006		
	Prison	**Jail**	**Probation**
Violent Offenses	149 months	6 months	40 months
Murder	275	9	42
Sexual Assault	172	6	42
Robbery	161	7	61
Aggravated Assault	98	6	39
Burglary	83	6	46
Fraud	59	6	36
Drug Possession	59	4	21
Drug Trafficking	85	7	40
All offenses	100	6	39

Source: "Felony Sentences in State Courts, 2006," Bureau of Justice Statistics Bulletin (Washington, D.C.: Bureau of Justice Statistics, 2009).

processes of state and local government institutions. Litigation in state courts includes, in other words, the areas that affect the daily lives of most people."[109]

Table 6.2 shows that, in 2000, state courts convicted about 924,700 adults of a felony offense.[110] Most were convicted for some type of drug offense. Table 6.3 indicates that the mean length of felony offenses ranges from 275 months for murder, and 59 months for fraud and drug possession charges.

State Supreme Courts

Usually called supreme courts, these courts are also called state judicial courts or supreme courts of appeal. In most cases, it is the court of last resort in the state because very few state cases ever reach the Supreme Court. Like the Supreme Court, state supreme courts also have discretion over the types of cases they choose to hear. In some states, death penalty cases are automatically reviewed by the state supreme court. If there is a question concerning the interpretation of state statute or the state constitution, the state supreme court can make a ruling.

State supreme courts have many functions. There are three general types of supreme court action. One is the interpretation of state statutes. By doing this, the court is shaping the meaning of the statute and at the same time its impact. Second, the state supreme courts are responsible for the development and interpretation of "common law" through which the basic legal rules are established almost entirely through state court decision rather than by legislatures. Third, the state supreme courts are responsible for interpreting federal and state constitutions. Their interpretations of the federal Constitution are subject to review by the Supreme Court.[111]

In most states, the supreme court is composed of between three and nine judges (most courts have either five or seven justices) who hear primarily civil cases and review cases on their record by reviewing the transcript. They typically hear cases as a group. The justices receive appellate briefs, hear oral arguments, discuss the cases, and issue written opinions to explain their decisions. They may have other powers, such as issuing judicial assignments, confirming the nomination of judges, and reviewing cases of alleged judicial misconduct.[112]

For the most part, state supreme courts hear primarily cases on appeals from the lower state courts. However, they can also have original jurisdiction in matters such as granting of certain writs, cases in which the state is a party, and disputes between counties within the state.

In some states, the supreme courts are called courts of last resort. In Oklahoma and Texas, there are two supreme courts—one having jurisdiction in civil cases and one having jurisdiction over criminal cases. State supreme courts usually have seven members, but some states have three and others nine.[113]

Regardless of their makeup, state supreme courts tend to operate in relative obscurity, and public knowledge about the courts is at best rudimentary. Despite this, the courts exert great influence. It is estimated that state supreme courts decide over 10,000 cases each year. In most of these cases, the litigants do not seek to appeal the decisions. This means that their decision is the final say. If the litigants do wish to appeal the decision, the Supreme Court either lacks the jurisdiction to hear it or declines to hear the appeal.[114] Again, this means that the decision of the state supreme court is the final one.

When deciding a case, members of a state supreme court typically turn first to the legal environment of the state, including the state's constitution, statutes, and/or legal precedents. A court may turn to decisions made by other state supreme courts in similar circumstances.[115]

The legal environment of the state can affect the decisions made by the state supreme court. The state laws affect the roles a state supreme court plays by defining the types of cases that can be adjudicated in state courts and thus brought to the state supreme court on appeal. The state laws also determine the authority of the state supreme court to regulate its workload and focus on important cases. Finally, the state laws provide most of the legal requirements the state high court is to apply and enforce.[116] Despite these legal constraints, the state supreme courts still maintain considerable discretion in defining the policy role they will play.[117]

Other State Appellate Courts

There are other, lower state appellate courts, most often called intermediate appellate courts. These courts are typically organized on a regional or even multicounty basis, and the structure of the appellate courts differs from state to state. Each state's appellate courts have little contact with those of the other states.[118] These are used in 36 states in the nation, especially in larger, more populated states, to relieve the caseloads of the state supreme court. They do not try cases but have appellate jurisdiction to review cases based on trial records. In other words, they do not conduct new trials or hear testimony to determine a defendant's guilt or innocence. Instead, they consider specific questions concerning alleged mistakes in the trial court. To do this, the justices consider detailed written arguments called appellate briefs that the lawyers for each side submit to argue the question at issue. In some cases, the lawyers involved in the case might be allowed to present oral arguments, and the justices will then discuss the case and vote to determine the outcome. One judge in the majority will write an opinion explaining the court's decision, and other judges may write opinions explaining why they applied different reasoning or arrived at different outcomes.

There are usually no juries in the lower appellate courts. Instead, judges, who usually sit on panels of three to nine judges, hear and decide appeals from trial courts. Thus, if a defendant believes that the procedures used in his or her case were in violation of his or her constitutional rights, he or she may appeal the outcome of his or her case. The courts will review cases to determine if a defendant's due process rights were granted and all procedures followed. They consider only the record of trial, the appellate briefs submitted by each side, and arguments made by counsel. In some jurisdictions, they are limited by law to hearing cases arising from specific lower courts or cases involving less than a specified dollar value. Most cases heard here are civil rather than criminal.[119]

Trial Courts of General Jurisdiction

Trial courts of general jurisdiction, which are sometimes called major trial courts or felony courts, have the power to process a wide variety of legal issues. They can hear all criminal cases, serious civil cases (in which the monetary amount in question is not limited), and some appeals cases, in some jurisdictions, from lower courts. They usually have exclusive jurisdiction over felony offenses, so they are the only court that has the authority to try felony cases. In these courts, the trials generally last a few days or even weeks or months. They sometimes oversee plea bargains made between the prosecution and the defense.

These courts are more formal in their proceedings than lower courts, and they employ full-time court personnel and record-keeping systems; they use juries, and they put more emphasis on formality and the protection of rights. In most states, a single judge presides over the trial court and is responsible for ruling on lawyers' motions concerning the admissibility of evidence and legal objections. The judge also instructs the jury on the law pertaining to a case before jury deliberation. If an offender is found guilty, a judge will also determine the most appropriate sentence for that person. Because trial courts keep a record of the proceedings, they are referred to as courts of record.

Trial Courts of Lower (or Limited) Jurisdiction

Limited jurisdiction courts are those courts where the judge can hear only certain, narrowly defined types of cases. These would be courts that deal with traffic offenses, juvenile crime, and minor criminal cases (misdemeanors). These courts are also called municipal and special courts (also called county or misdemeanor courts) and are at the bottom of the court hierarchy in the state court system. These courts usually hear cases of a minor nature, such as assault or shoplifting. They can be small-claims courts, which hear disputes involving less than $1,000 or $500 (depending on the state), traffic violations, parking tickets, or other minor offenses. These courts also hear civil cases, usually limited to cases where the damages in question are relatively small (usually under $10,000). There is usually a less severe punishment involved, either a fine of $1,000 or less and/or incarceration for a year or less in a local jail.[120]

There are judges present in the municipal courts, but in some cases they may try the cases in a more informal manner. Despite this, defendants appearing in these courts still have the same rights as they do in the major trial courts. There is often an emphasis on speed and routinization rather than constitutional procedures. Defendants can enter a plea and pay a fine in a matter of minutes. These are not courts of record, so there is no formal account kept of the proceedings.

Some states have created special courts with limited jurisdiction (thus called limited jurisdiction courts or sometimes specialty courts), that focus on a specific category of offense. These can include police courts, family court (child custody), juvenile court, probate court (divorce and estate issues), or drug court. They were developed to reduce the caseloads of the lower courts. They handle a large number of cases quickly and sometimes informally. Some examples of these specialty courts are shown in Box 6.4.

These courts are found in both rural and urban areas, but most exist in urban areas. They do not exist in every state or jurisdiction. Most common pleas courts have a single judge presiding, and no jury is present. Some areas may use a magistrate, referee, or justice of the peace in place of a judge. Decisions made by the judge can be appealed to a general jurisdiction court.[121]

BOX 6.4
Examples of Specialty Courts

Teen Courts

Teen courts, also known as youth courts, have become a popular intervention for young, usually first-time offenders who are charged with offenses such as theft, misdemeanor assault, disorderly conduct, and possession of alcohol. In many of the teen courts, there is an adult judge who serves as the judge and rules on legal terminology and courtroom procedure, but there is a youth judge who acts as the real judge. Other youth serve as attorneys, jurors, clerks, bailiffs, and other court personnel. The youth attorneys will present the case to the youth judge (or in some cases a panel of three youth judges), who decides the appropriate disposition for the defendant. In some cases, the teen courts do not use youth attorneys. Rather, the case is presented to a youth jury by a youth or adult. The youth jury then questions the defendant directly.

Most teen courts do not determine the guilt or innocence of a youth offender. Rather, they serve as a diversion alternative for young offenders. In many cases, the offenders must admit to the charges against them in order to qualify for teen court. Community service was the most common disposition used in teen court cases. Dispositions may also include victim apology letters, apology essays, teen court jury duty, drug/alcohol classes, and monetary restitution.

The number of teen courts nationwide grew from an estimated fifty programs in 1991 to between 400 and 500 programs in 1998, but most had been in existence for less than five years. Since they are so new and primarily experimental, most teen courts have relatively small caseloads.

Drug Courts

Since the mid-1980s, many state and local court dockets have become overloaded with drug cases, leaving fewer resources available to adjudicate serious, violent offenders. It became clear that incarceration did not help addicts break their addictions and that drug offenders sentenced to an institution were returning to the institution at high rates. It also became clear that drug treatment programs seemed to be effective in reducing both drug addiction and drug-related crime if participants remained in treatment for an adequate period of time.

Drug courts first began in 1980 as an experiment by the Dade County, Florida, Circuit Court. 48 states now have some type of drug court, as does the District of Columbia, Puerto Rico, Guam, a number of Native American Tribal Courts, and one federal district court. Defendants referred to drug courts are usually nonviolent offenders whose crimes were due to addiction, and those eligible for the drug court are identified soon after arrest. The program consists of weekly (or daily) counseling or therapy sessions, education programs, at least weekly urinalysis, frequent appearances before the drug court judge (biweekly or more often at first) for status updates, vocational programs, or medical services. After the participants become "clean," many programs require that they obtain a high school or GED certificate, maintain employment, be current in all financial obligations (including court fees and child support payments), and have a sponsor in the community. Many programs also require participants to perform community service hours in the community that is supporting them through the drug court program.

It is argued that drug courts provide more effective supervision of offenders in the community, more credibility to the law enforcement function (arrests of drug offenders are taken seriously), greater coordination of public services, and a more efficient court system.

The success of drug courts is becoming clear. Most participants tend to stay in the drug programs. The retention rates for drug courts show that more than 70 percent of participants are either still enrolled or have graduated. Traditional drug treatment programs have much lower retention rates. Drug courts have also been shown to have reduced recidivism rates. Recidivism among all drug court participants has ranged between 5 and 28 percent and less than 4 percent for graduates. Additionally, drug courts are generally less expensive than traditional punishments. The average cost for the treatment component of a drug court program ranges between $1,200 and $3,000 per participant, depending on the services provided. Savings in jail bed days alone have been estimated to be at least $5,000 per defendant. Drug courts can also reduce police overtime and other witness costs as well as grand jury expenses. In addition,

BOX 6.4

Examples of Specialty Courts (*continued*)

hundreds of families have been reunited as parents regain custody of their children. Many participants have received education and vocational training and have obtained employment.

Juvenile and Family Drug Courts

Family drug courts deal with cases that arise out of the substance abuse of a parent or child. These can include custody and visitation disputes; abuse, neglect, and dependency matters; petitions to terminate parental rights; guardianship proceedings; and other loss, restriction, or limitation of parental rights. Family drug courts provide immediate intervention in the lives of children and parents using drugs. Their goals

include helping the parent to become emotionally, financially, and personally self-sufficient and to develop parenting and "coping" skills adequate for serving as an effective parent on a day-to-day basis.

Juvenile and family drug courts are being started in many cities across the country. Since 1995, when the first juvenile and family drug courts were developed in Alabama, California, Florida, Nevada, and Utah, family drug court activity is under way in at least 35 states and the District of Columbia. The rapidly increasing popularity of these courts is reinforced by their success in reducing court backlogs and preventing substance abuse by juveniles and family members.

LOCAL COURTS

Some states have county courts or mayors' courts as the lowest level of general jurisdiction court. In some places, these are also called justice of the peace courts. Most have either a city or a county as their geographic area of jurisdiction. Local courts handle minor offenses, such as local ordinances (curfews). They may also perform marriage ceremonies. They have one judge presiding, but litigants can request a jury trial.[122] These courts are located primarily in small rural towns and villages. Some states have chosen to eliminate the justice of the peace officers.[123]

COURT BUREAUCRACIES

Over the years, many bureaucracies have evolved that exist to help the courts be more efficient and effective in performing their duties. Today, there are many bureaucracies that assist the courts in some fashion. They are located on all levels—federal, state, and local—and have different responsibilities.

One bureaucracy that assists court personnel is the Judicial Conference of the United States. This body is composed of the chief justice of the Supreme Court as the presiding member, the chief judges of each of the judicial circuits, one district judge from each of the twelve regional circuits, and the chief judge of the U.S. Court of International Trade. They meet twice a year to review and establish policy that revises the rules of procedure that may affect courts across the nation. They also make recommendations to Congress for approval of the changes.[124]

The Administrative Office of the U.S. Courts, created in 1939, helps oversee the administration of the federal judicial system. It gathers information and data on cases in the federal courts, such as case flow statistics. Once the information is gathered, the office acts as a clearinghouse for information as well as a liaison for the federal judicial system and the Judicial Conference in its dealings with Congress, the executive branch, individual judges, professional groups, and the general public. The Office also provides technology services to the federal courts.[125]

The Federal Judicial Center was created in 1967 as the research-and-development arm of the federal judiciary. It engages in research concerning the federal courts and makes recommendations that are intended to improve the administration and management of the federal courts. It is also responsible for developing educational and training programs for federal personnel who are employed with the federal judicial branch. Today, it is authorized to convene sentencing institutes that address major policy questions. It also partners with other organizations to develop research strategies that lead to new policies regarding sentencing.[126]

A final example of court-related bureaucracies is the Circuit Judicial Councils. These consist of all the judges of the circuit's court of appeals and other district judges. They come together and work to see that the district courts operate as effectively as possible. They monitor the caseloads of the district courts, oversee judicial assignments, and monitor the conduct of district judges. They also oversee the use of federal jurors, the assignment of magistrates, and the use of court reporters.

Conclusion

The courts on the federal, state, and local levels are a vital component in the criminal justice system and are responsible for interpreting the law and meting out justice. Many courtroom personnel work in these courts to help the judicial branch function smoothly. Politics plays an ever-present role despite the fact that the courts are, in theory, supposed to be insulated from political influence. Politics affects who serves on the bench (how they are chosen) and the decisions that come out of the courts. The makeup of the court is determined by politicians through a process of nomination and approval or through the political process of campaigns and elections. Their decision making, as often noted, is not always guided by neutral principles of law but rather by external political influences and the courts' political attributes.[127] In reality, there is little that the courts, including the Supreme Court, do that is entirely free of politics.[128] Despite this, the courts play an important role in the policy process. They affect each stage, from setting the agenda through review of the policy and the implementation of that policy.

Notes

1. Joan Biskupic and Elder Witt, *The Supreme Court and the Powers of the American Government* (Washington, D.C.: Congressional Quarterly Press, 1997), p. 49.
2. Ibid.
3. Robert A. Carp and Ronald Stidham, *The Federal Courts* (Washington, D.C.: Congressional Quarterly Press, 1991), p. 2.
4. Biskupic and Witt, *The Supreme Court and the Powers of the American Government*.
5. David M. O'Brien, *Storm Center: The Supreme Court in American Politics* (New York: Norton, 2003), p. 165.
6. Ibid., p. 29.
7. Biskupic and Witt, *The Supreme Court and the Powers of the American Government*, p. 13.
8. O'Brien, *Storm Center*, p. 28.
9. Herbert Jacob, "Courts and Politics in the United States," in *Courts, Law and Politics in a Comparative Perspective*, ed. Herbert Jacob, Erhard Blankenburg, Herbert M. Kritzer, Doris Marie Provide, and Joseph Sanders (New Haven, Conn.: Yale University Press, 1996), pp. 16–80.
10. John J. Harrigan and David C. Nice, *Politics and Policy in States and Communities* (New York: Pearson, 1994), p. 268.

11. Jacob, "Courts and Politics in the United States."

12. Dennis L. Dresang and James J. Gosling, *Politics and Policy in American States and Communities* (New York: Pearson, 2004), p. 352.

13. Harrigan and Nice, *Politics and Policy in States and Communities*, p. 268.

14. Herbert L. Packer, *The Limits of the Criminal Sanction* (Stanford, Calif.: Stanford University Press, 1968).

15. George F. Cole, *Criminal Justice: Law and Politics* (Monterey, Calif.: Brooks/Cole, 1984), p. 135.

16. Ibid.

17. Ibid., p. 136.

18. Ibid., p. 135.

19. Ibid.

20. Ibid., p. 3.

21. Brenda Hart Bohne, "The Public Defender as Policy-Maker," *Judicature* 62 (4, 1978): 176–84.

22. Alissa Pollitz Worden, "Privatizing Due Process," in *Courts and Justice: A Reader*, ed. G. Larry Mays and Peter R. Gregware (Prospect Heights, Ill.: Waveland Press, 1995), pp. 313–39, at 315.

23. Ibid.

24. Ibid.

25. Thomas R. Dye, *Top Down Policy Making* (New York: Chatham House, 2001).

26. Malcolm M. Feeley, "Two Models of the Criminal Justice System: An Organizational Perspective," *Law and Society Review* 7 (3, 1973): 407–25.

27. Elliot E. Slotnick, "Review Essay on Judicial Recruitment and Selection," in Mays and Gregware, *Courts and Justice*, pp. 200–215, at 201.

28. Jacob, "Courts and Politics in the United States."

29. Ibid., p. 19.

30. H. R. Glick, *Courts, Politics and Justice* (New York: McGraw-Hill, 1993).

31. Christopher E. Smith, *Courts, Politics and the Judicial Process* (Chicago: Nelson Hall, 1997), p. 152; Glick, *Courts, Politics and Justice.*

32. Nancy E. Marion, *Criminal Justice in America* (Durham, N.C.: Carolina Academic Press, 2002), p. 280.

33. Smith, *Courts, Politics and the Judicial Process*, p. 162.

34. Glick, *Courts, Politics and Justice.*

35. Robert Scigliano, *The Supreme Court and the Presidency* (New York: Free Press, 1971); Lawrence Baum, The Supreme Court, 7th Ed. (Washington, D.C.: C.Q. Press, 2001).

36. Sheldon Goldman, Elliot Slotnick, Gerard Gryski, Gary Zuk, and Sara W. Schiavoni, "Bush Remaking the Judiciary: Like Father Like Son?" *Judicature,* 86: 282–309, 2003.

37. Mark Sherman, "Obama Taps Liberal Scholar for Federal Appeals Court" *Akron Beacon Journal,* March 14, 2010, p. A2.

38. David W. Neubauer and Stephen S.Meinhold, Judicial Process: Law, Courts and Politics in the US (Boston: Wadsworth, 2010), p. 478.

39. Stephen Wasby, *The Supreme Court in the Federal Judicial System,* 4th Ed (Chicago: Nelson-Hall, 1993).

40. Neubauer and.Meinhold, *Judicial Process*, p. 180.

41. Ibid., p. 483.

42. O'Brien, *Storm Center*, p. 114.

43. Ibid., p. 115.

44. Glick, *Courts, Politics and Justice*, p. 138.

45. "Oppose John Roberts' Supreme Court Nomination" MoveOn.org Political Action: http:///pol.moveon.org/roberts/info.html; accessed 1/25/2101.

46. "John G, Roberts, Jr. Supreme Court Nominee Profile" National Council of Jewish Women: http://67,199.50.69/content_617,cfm; accessed 1/25/2010.

47. "John Roberts Confirmed" www.lambdalegal.ort/take-action/campaigns/courting-justice/nominations/john-roberts; accessed 1/25/2010.

48. "Heritage Foundation Legal Experts Laud Bush's Choice for High Court" July 19, 2005, accessed 1/25/2010.

49. Doug Bates, "Obama's Historic Pick for the U.S. Supreme Court" The Oregonian May 26, 20009; retrieved on 2/18/2010 and available from http://www.oregonlive.com/opinion/index.ssf/2009/05/obama_historic_pick_for_the_s.html.

50. "Favorites of Left Don't Make Obama's Court List: May 25, 2009, New York Times.

51. Jacob, "Courts and Politics in the United States."

52. Peter Brownfield, "Senate Dems to Block All Nominations" Fox News, Sunday, March 28, 2004; retrieved on 2/12/2010 from www.foxnews.com/printer_friendly_story/0,3566,115339,00.html.

53. "Gonzales Explanation of Firings Called 'Sorry Excuse'" CNN.Com; retrieved on 2/12/2010 from http://cnn.worldnews.printthis.clickability.com/pt/cpt?action=cpt&title=Gonzales.

54. Beth M. Henschen, Robert Moog, and Steven Davis, "Judicial Nominating Commissioners," in Mays and Gregware, *Courts and Justice*, pp. 340–56, at 340–41.

55. Michael B. Blankenship, Jerry B. Spargar, and W. Richard Janikowski, "Accountability v. Independence: Myths of Judicial Selection," *Criminal Justice Policy Review* 6 (1, 1992): 69–79.

56. David Von Drehle, "The Incredibly Shrinking Court," *Time* (October 11, 2007): www.time.com/time/printout/0,8816,1670489,00.html accessed 1/25/2010).

57. John A. Fliter, *Prisoners' Rights: The Supreme Court on Evolving Standards of Decency* (Westport, Conn.: Greenwood Press, 2001), p. 70.

58. Anthony Lewis, "Earl Warren," in *The Warren Court: A Critical Analysis*, ed. Richard H. Sayler, Barry B. Boyer, and Robert E. Gooding, Jr. (New York: Chelsea House, 1968); pp. 1–31, at 1.

59. Nadine Strossen, "Freedom of Speech in the Warren Court," in *The Warren Court: A Retrospective*, ed. Bernard Schwartz (New York: Oxford University Press, 1996), pp. 68–84; Harry Kalven, Jr., "Uninhibited, Robust and Wide-Open: A Note on Free Speech and the Warren Court," in Sayler et al., *The Warren Court*, pp. 98–111.

60. Ronald D. Rotunda, "The Warren Court and Freedom of the Press," in Schwartz, *The Warren Court*, pp. 85–103; John P. MacKenzie, "The Warren Court and the Press," in Sayler et al., *The Warren Court*, pp. 112–25.

61. Lewis, "Earl Warren," p. 1.

62. Ibid.

63. Ibid., p. 23.

64. Cole, *Criminal Justice*, p. 8.

65. A. Kenneth Pye, "The Warren Court and Criminal Procedure," in Sayler et al., *The Warren Court*, pp. 58–77, at 63.

66. Cole, *Criminal Justice*, p. 8.

67. Fliter, *Prisoners' Rights*, p. 94.

68. Lawrence Baum, *The Supreme Court* (Washington, D.C.: Congressional Quarterly Press, 1985).

69. Fliter, *Prisoners' Rights*, p. 94.

70. Glick, *Courts, Politics and Justice*.

71. Baum, *The Supreme Court*.

72. O'Brien, *Storm Center*, p. 167.

73. Fliter, *Prisoners' Rights*, p. 183.

74. D. F. B. Tucker, *The Rehnquist Court and Civil Rights* (Brookfield, Vt.: Dartmouth, 1995), pp. 6–7.

75. David W. Neubauer and Stephen S. Meinhold, *Judicial Process: Law, Courts and Politics in the US* (Boston: Wadsworth, 2010), p. 448.

76. O'Brien, *Storm Center*, p. xviii.

77. Jeff Yates, *Popular Justice: Presidential Prestige and Executive Success in the Supreme Court* (New York: State University of New York Press, 2002), p. 106.

78. Jeffrey A. Segal and Harold J. Spaeth, *The Supreme Court and the Attitudinal Model* (Cambridge: Cambridge University Press, 1993).

79. Christopher E. Smith, "The Capacity of Courts as Policy-Making Forums," in *Public Policy, Crime, and Criminal Justice*, ed. Barry W. Hancock and Paul M. Sharp (Upper Saddle River, N.J.: Prentice Hall, 2000), pp. 240–56, at 241.

80. Christopher E. Smith, *Politics in Constitutional Law: Cases and Questions* (Chicago: Nelson Hall, 1992).

81. C. E. Van Horn, D. C. Baumer, and W. T. Gormley, Jr., *Politics and Public Policy* (Washington, D.C.: Congressional Quarterly Press, 1992).

82. Biskupic and Witt, *The Supreme Court and the Powers of the American Government*, p. 346.

83. Ibid., p. 351.

84. Joseph Carroll, "Slim Majority of Americans Approve of the Supreme Court" September 26, 2007 www.gallup.com/poll/28798/Slim-Majority-Americans-Approve-Supreme-Court.asp; accessed 1/25/2010.

85. Ibid., p. 49.

86. Ibid., p. 351.

87. Adam Liptak, "Justices, 5–4, Reject corporate spending limit" New York Times, January 22,2010, available from www.nytimes.com/2010/01/22/us/politics/22scotus.html; "Supreme Court OKs Corporate Campaign Contributions" PBS Newshour, January 21,2010, available at www.pbs.org/newshour/bb/law/jan-june10/supremecourt_01–21.html; "Campaign Finance Policy After Citizens United v. Federal Election Commission: Issues and Options for Congress" OpenCRS; February 1, 2010, www.openers.com/document/R41054; see comments from Congressional members Charles E. Schumer, Chris Van Hollen, Hank Johnson, Jim Moran, Jerrold Nadler and Michael Capuano.

88. B. Guy Peters, *American Public Policy: Promise and Performance* (Chatham, N.J.: Chatham House, 1996), p. 91.

89. Dye, *Top Down Policy Making*.

90. Ibid.

91. James E. Anderson, *Public Policy Making* (Boston: Houghton Mifflin, 2003).

92. Ibid.

93. Yates, *Popular Justice*, p. 107.

94. Joan Biskupic and Elder Witt, *Congressional Quarterly's Guide to the U.S. Supreme Court*, 3rd ed. (Washington, D.C.: Congressional Quarterly Press, 1997); Norman C. Thomas and Joseph A. Pika, *The Politics of Presidency* (Washington, D.C.: Congressional Quarterly Press, 1996); Lawrence H. Tribe, *God Save This Honorable Court* (New York: Random House, 1985).

95. Yates, *Popular Justice*, p. 106.

96. Ibid., p. 108.

97. Ibid., p. 74.

98. Ibid., p. 102.

99. William Mishler and Reginald S. Sheehan, "The Supreme Court as a Countermajoritarian Institution?

The Impact of Public Opinion on Supreme Court Decisions," *American Political Science Review* 87(1, 1993): pp. 87–101; William Mishler and Reginald S. Sheehan, "Popular Influence on Supreme Court Decisions," *American Political Science Review* 88 (3, 1994): 711–24.

100. Sourcebook of CJ Statistics Online; accessed 1/25/2010.

101. James R. Acker, "Thirty Years of Social Science in Supreme Court Criminal Cases," *Law and Policy* 12 (1, 1990): 1–23.

102. Dresang and Gosling, *Politics and Policy in American States and Communities*, p. 354.

103. "U.S Court of Appeals-Judicial Caseload Profile" U.S. Courts; retrieved on 2/11/2010 from www.us-courts.gov/cgi-bin/cmsa2008.pl.

104. Carp and Stidham, *The Federal Courts*, p. 20.

105. U.S. Courts, "U.S. District Court-Judicial Case Profile" retrieved on 2/11/2010; available online at www.uscourts.gov/cgi-bin/cmsd2008.pl.

106. Christopher E. Smith, "From U.S. Magistrates to U.S. Magistrate Judges," in Mays and Gregware, *Courts and Justice*, pp. 37–50, at 37.

107. Ibid., p. 38; Carroll Seron, "Magistrates and the Work of the Federal Courts: A New Division of Labor," *Judicature* 69 (1986): 353.

108. Lawrence Baum, "Supreme Courts in the Policy Process," in *The State of the States*, ed. Carl E. Van Horn (Washington, D.C.: Congressional Quarterly Press, 1996), pp. 143–60, at 143.

109. Dresang and Gosling, *Politics and Policy in American States and Communities*, p. 354.

110. U.S. Department of Justice, Bureau of Justice Statistics, "Courts and Sentencing Statistics," available online at www.ojp.usdoj.gov/bjs/stssent.htm.

111. Baum, "Supreme Courts in the Policy Process," p. 143.

112. Smith, *Courts, Politics and the Judicial Process*, p. 32.

113. Dresang and Gosling, *Politics and Policy in American States and Communities*, pp. 359–61.

114. G. Alan Tarr and Mary Cornelia Aldis Porter, *State Supreme Courts in State and Nation* (New Haven, Conn.: Yale University Press, 1988), p. 1.

115. Ibid., p. 27.

116. Ibid., p. 41.

117. Ibid., p. 54.

118. Jacob, "Courts and Politics in the United States."

119. Dresang and Gosling, *Politics and Policy in American States and Communities*, p. 360; Smith, *Courts, Politics and the Judicial Process*, p. 32.

120. Glick, *Courts, Politics and Justice*.

121. Dresang and Gosling, *Politics and Policy in American States and Communities*, p. 360.

122. Ibid.

123. Ibid., p. 359.

124. Glick, *Courts, Politics and Justice*, p. 138.

125. Ibid.

126. Emily Z. Huebner, David R. Leathery, and Rya W. Zobel, "The Federal Judicial Center and the Probation and Pretrial Services System," *Federal Probation* 61 (1, 1997): 63–70.

127. Smith, *Courts, Politics and the Judicial Process*, p. 113.

128. Martin Garbus, *Courting Disaster* (New York: Times Books, 2002), p. 281.

7

Bureaucracies

INTRODUCTION

It has been shown that the U.S. Congress and other legislative bodies make many laws that are attempts to control criminal activity through either prevention (such as education programs like DARE or treatment programs) or punishment (to deter future crime). When Congress or other legislative bodies create a new law, their major responsibilities in the process are completed. The legislators now rely on others to carry out that new law, or implement it. This responsibility turns to the bureaucracies, which are the agencies that have been created to carry out or implement the laws and policies passed by federal, state, or local legislatures. Bureaucracies are the institutions of public administration in America.[1] They are the organizations at the national, state, or local level and provide services or benefits to particular clientele in accordance to the decisions made by legislators. They are responsible for the execution and delivery of public policies. Bureaucracies play an important role in providing services to those in need. They do things such as hire new personnel, make new regulations, create a new program, or a host of other activities to ensure that the new law is carried out as the legislative body intended.

Bureaucracies are found at all levels of government to provide a wide array of goods and services as well as regulate a wide range of activities. Bureaucracies exist in every country, without regard to race, creed, sex, or political system.[2] Hundreds of bureaucracies exist to help solve the crime problem or problems associated with criminal behavior. In terms of criminal justice, bureaucracies do things such as provide law enforcement to a community, oversee the functioning of the courts, provide programs within a correctional facility (including drug and alcohol treatment programs, anger management programs, and education programs), and even provide after-care programs for those inmates released from a custodial setting. Because of their vital importance in solving problems and in the policy process, bureaucracies are often called the fourth branch of government.

The bureaucratic agencies are typically the least visible political actor, as they are not elected officials, nor are they involved with political campaigns. However, these agencies have a major impact on all aspects of our lives, and every citizen has become dependent on the bureaucracy in one way or another, either directly or indirectly. Bureaucracies regulate behavior, redistribute our income, and distribute benefits to society. In fact, most of what we do is tied to government bureaucracy in some way. The Department of Agriculture and the Food and Drug Administration regulate what we eat. What we can listen to on the radio or watch on television is regulated by the Federal Communications Commission. When we drive to school or work, the car emissions are controlled by the Environmental Protection Agency, and the roads are overseen by the National Highway Traffic Safety Administration. The content and quality of our education is watched over by the Department of Education. While at work or school, employees are protected by the Occupational Safety and Health Administration. Our prisons, jails, and community corrections are overseen by the Department of Corrections on the federal level and by state departments of corrections on the state level. The overall safety and security of our nation is overseen by the new Department of Homeland Security.

Bureaucracies are not the simple, uniform phenomenon they are sometimes made out to be but instead are "a complex and varied phenomenon, not a simple social category or political epithet."[3] Bureaucracies differ by size, complexity, hierarchical organization, and degree of autonomy from the other branches of government.

Despite the differences, all bureaucracies have certain similarities. As defined by Anthony Downs, a renowned scholar of bureaucracies, an organization is a bureaucracy if it has certain characteristics. The first of these is that it is large and employs many people. The second is that it has full-time membership and the economic dependency of its members. In other words, a majority of its members are full-time workers who depend on their employment in the organization for most of their income. This implies that the employees have a serious commitment to the bureaucracy. Third is that its personnel are hired, promoted, and retained on a merit basis. This includes the initial hiring of personnel, their promotion within the bureau, and their retention therein, all of which are based at least partly on some type of assessment of the way in which they have performed or can be expected to perform their organizational roles. Fourth, the major portion of its output is not directly or indirectly evaluated in any markets external to the organization by means of voluntary quid pro quo transaction.[4]

All bureaucracies have some other defining characteristics in common as well. For example, all have some type of hierarchical structure of formal authority with a chain of command. Along with that is a division of labor among subunits, each of which specializes in a special task or function. There is also a hierarchical formal communications network that allows information to travel (or not travel) within the agency efficiently. Additionally, they have an extensive system of formal rules along with an informal structure of authority and an informal communications network. The operations within the bureaucracy are impersonal and formal, yet there is intensive personal loyalty and personal involvement among officials, particularly in the highest ranks of the hierarchy. The agency will adapt its structure, authority, and rules to suit the organization's goals.[5]

Every department, agency, and bureaucracy tends to develop its own organizational culture.[6] Every organization has a culture, which is a persistent and patterned way of thinking about the central tasks of and human relationships within an organization. Most bureaucratic cultures are supportive of the agency's function and client group and usually include beliefs about the value of the agency's functions and the importance of serving the clients. Culture is to an organization what personality is to an individual. Like human culture generally, it is passed on from one generation to the next. It changes slowly if at all. In fact, once entrenched, it becomes difficult to change the internal culture of the agency.[7] However, some agencies have, over time, developed multiple, competing cultures that can impede the effectiveness of the organization.[8] This can lead to disputes over what the bureaucracy should be doing. In the long run, the culture of the bureaucracy can have a significant impact on the behavior of bureaucrats, leading to inefficiency and an inability to provide the intended services.[9]

The term for the people or employees who work within these cultures at agencies throughout all levels of government is "bureaucrat." This is a public official who is hired, retained, and promoted through a merit system. On a very simple level, a bureaucrat can be considered a person who is employed by an agency. Most often, a bureaucrat is not elected to office but rather is appointed as a result of the political process. The public image of a bureaucrat is the person who is cold and impersonal and who carries out his or her job in an uncaring manner, typically seen as inefficient, legalistic, and unresponsive to any special needs a client may have.[10] There is a constant dilemma for agency officials because too much compliance on the rules is denounced as "bureaucratic" (in the dysfunctional sense), while using too much discretion and personal initiative is denounced as excess power or abuse of power.[11]

At the same time, however, people have high expectations of bureaucrats. They expect agency personnel to be neutral and not impose their own opinions over those of the elected representatives who were chosen by the voters to create laws. Second, people expect that bureaucrats will have an impersonal attitude toward those they serve to help ensure that all people will be treated the same without prejudice to one set of clients over another. Third, it is expected that bureaucrats will be detached from the objects or circumstances in each situation. For example, we expect that judges, prosecutors, and defense attorneys will be detached from their cases and focus on the administration of justice. Finally, we expect that bureaucrats will focus on justice, including fairness, equity, and due process.[12]

REPUTATION

Over the years, most bureaucracies have developed a negative image with the American public. This has happened for many reasons. One is that many people have become dissatisfied with government bureaucracy. They complain that bureaucracies have become too large and too powerful and that they regulate too many aspects of our lives. They regulate what we eat and drink, what we hear on the radio or see on television or in the movies, and what medicines we can use if we get sick. They regulate business practices, such as who can be hired, how many hours they can work, and how much they are paid. They regulate how we invest and borrow money from a bank. Of course, they regulate how a criminal defendant is arrested, tried, sentenced, and punished.

Because there is so much bureaucratic regulation, there are numerous cases of overlapping jurisdiction or responsibility, resulting in the wasteful use of resources that occurs when many bureaucracies exist in the same policy arena, carrying out the same or very similar functions. Critics often point to the inefficiency that sometimes occurs when bureaucracies become too large to function well. Over the years, bureaucracies have become known as being wasteful and incompetent.[13]

Critics of bureaucracies became more widely recognized in the mid-1990s. Citizens began to view bureaucrats as "lethargic, incompetent hacks who spend their days spinning out reels of red tape and reams of paperwork, all the while going to great lengths to avoid doing the job they were hired to do," and the agencies simply produced "waste, fraud, abuse, and mismanagement."[14] They blamed bureaucrats for many government failures and social problems. They argued that bureaucracies have even become dangerous in recent years[15] because there is a lack of control over the behavior and actions of the bureaucrats. They point to the general lack of congressional oversight of the bureaucracies and point out that no one has control over them because they are appointed rather than elected.[16]

Some presidents have attempted to reduce the size of bureaucracies and thus the bureaucracies' potential influence on regulating behavior. Presidents have criticized bureaucracies, claiming the agencies were out of touch with the needs of state and local communities and that the bureaucracies were tied up in red tape.[17] Presidents Jimmy Carter and Gerald Ford could agree on little else during their 1976 presidential contest other than that "'the bureaucracy' was a mess."[18] President Reagan also campaigned for reducing the size of the bureaucracy during both of his campaigns and even proposed getting rid of the Department of Education.[19] None of these presidents was able to successfully reduce the size of the federal bureaucracies. They found that once a bureaucracy has become established, it is hard to cut it back. Leaders of other countries have also found that the role of public bureaucracies has continued to grow and that the agencies have become more difficult to control.[20]

There are many weaknesses inherent in bureaucracies.[21] First, agency heads often become so consumed in their own bureaucracies and departments that they become immune to outsiders who may offer suggestions on how to adapt or improve the agency's service. Over time, they may also become so specialized and advanced that they feel too self-important and lose sight of the bureaucratic goals.[22] This can sometimes trickle down to lower-level employees, making it easy for the public to perceive this attitude.

Second, excessive reliance on rules, regulations, and red tape prohibits a bureaucrat from personalizing each case. Often there is little if any flexibility to deal with specific problems on an individual basis. People become numbers and are treated impersonally. Bureaucracies have even been accused of harming those people in need by being inflexible about rules that often contradict one another.[23]

Third, each bureaucratic agency must compete with the others for resources from Congress or the state legislature. Especially in recent years, when money has become more and more limited, bureaucracies must constantly prove the necessity, effectiveness, and efficiency of their programs. This may lead to inaccurate reporting of statistics to prove the effectiveness of a program to enhance its reputation in the legislature, ensuring its continued funding and longevity. They may spend more time making themselves "look good" in the eyes of the public and the legislatures than focusing on providing a necessary service.

Fourth, bureaucracies have been criticized for a lack of tangible goals. Since government agencies, particularly criminal justice agencies, do not have a profit motive, it is hard to determine what they are trying to do. In criminal justice, there is disagreement as to whether we should rehabilitate an inmate through education or training programs or simply punish them with long prison sentences. Further problems occur when there is a constant change of administrations, as there may be a lack of continuity or stability within the agency.[24] This is particularly true in criminal justice when one administration is supportive of a rehabilitative approach to treating inmates, whereas the next may be supportive of a conservative law-and-order approach that stresses strict and harsh punishments.

Finally, there is a concern about the accountability in bureaucratic agencies. This refers to the inability to hold bureaucrats responsible for the agency's actions. The president and Congress have some oversight over bureaucracies, but this is limited. There is often little oversight of agencies and their work.

Despite all this, we have come to rely on bureaucracies and the services they provide. Bureaucracies have been identified as being among the "most important institutions in every part of the world. Not only do they provide employment for a very significant portion of the world's population, but they also make critical decisions that shape the economic, educational, political, social, moral, and even religious lives of nearly everyone on earth."[25] Bureaucracies across the United States are more valuable today than in the past and are performing even more effectively than many people assume.[26] In fact, the public often underestimates the value of the functions and services provided by public agencies. Indeed, most agencies are not as wasteful and inept as is often assumed by the public. They may seem to perform badly because we have such high expectations of them, give them extremely complex functions, and expect them to perform multiple goals that are often difficult to measure and may even conflict with other goals and policies. They also have fragmented policies, which can lead to contradictory policies. We often hold them up to particularly high standards, and this makes their evaluation even more difficult.[27]

TYPES OF BUREAUCRACIES

There are different types of bureaucracies on the state and federal levels. There are bureaucracies surrounding both the president and Congress. The presidential bureaucracy begins with the White House office. This contains the president's press secretaries and special assistants who provide staff assistance to the president. The congressional bureaucracy includes the staff and various research agencies that help members of Congress function efficiently.

The first type of agency consists of the cabinet-level agencies, found within the executive branch. These agencies are probably the most familiar and well-known form of bureaucracy. There are currently fifteen executive-level departments, each headed by a cabinet secretary. Examples of these include the Department of Defense, the Department of Veterans Affairs, and the Justice Department. The departments have been established by Congress at different times over the past 200 years to address different needs as they evolved across the nation. The first three departments, those of state, treasury, and war, were created in the Constitution in 1789, and others have emerged slowly. The most recent department created was that of homeland security, created in 2003 after the attacks of September 11, 2001. These cabinet-level departments are highly organized. With the exception of the Department of Justice (which is headed by the attorney general), each department is headed by a secretary who is appointed by the president, to whom they are directly responsible. The departments are made up of several smaller bureaucracies and agencies that carry out different programs. The departments employ more

---

BOX 7.1
Cabinet-Level Agency—Department of Justice

The Department of Justice serves as counsel for its citizens. It represents them in enforcing the law in the public interest. Through its thousands of lawyers, investigators, and agents, the department plays the key role in protection against criminals and subversion, ensuring healthy business competition, safeguarding the consumer, and enforcing drug, immigration, and naturalization laws.

The Department of Justice was established by act of June 22, 1870 (28 U.S.C. 501, 503, 509 note),

with the attorney general as its head. The affairs and activities of the Department of Justice are generally directed by the attorney general. The attorney general represents the United States in legal matters generally and gives advice and opinions to the president and to the heads of the executive departments of the government when so requested. The attorney general appears in person to represent the government before the U.S. Supreme Court in cases of exceptional gravity or importance.

BOX 7.2

Independent Agency—Environmental Protection Agency

The mission of the Environmental Protection Agency (EPA) is to protect human health and to safeguard the natural environment—air, water, and land—on which life depends. The EPA was established in the executive branch as an independent agency pursuant to Reorganization Plan No. 3 of 1970 (5 U.S.C. app.), effective December 2, 1970. It was created to permit coordinated and effective government action on behalf of the environment. The agency is designed to serve as the public's advocate for a livable environment.

Office of Homeland Security: The EPA's homeland security responsibilities include federal leadership for some activities and significant involvement for others. The EPA serves as the lead federal agency charged with protection of the nation's water infrastructure from terrorist attack, cleanup of any biological or chemical attacks, and reduction of national chemical industry and hazardous materials sector critical infrastructure vulnerabilities. The EPA also has significant responsibilities in certain radiological attacks.

than 60 percent of all federal personnel. One example of a cabinet agency is the Department of Justice, described in Box 7.1.

The second type of agency consists of the independent agencies (or independent executive agencies). These are similar in size and influence to department agencies and perform executive functions, such as implementing public programs. They report directly to the president but are not part of the executive departments. Instead, they exist outside of executive departments. Some examples are the Veterans Administration, the General Services Administration, the Environmental Protection Agency, the Small Business Administration, the National Aeronautics and Space Administration, and the Office of Personnel Management. Box 7.2 shows more information about one Independent Agency, the Environmental Protection Agency.

There are also agencies referred to as independent regulatory commissions that are arms of Congress. Because of this, they are more independent from executive control than are federal departments. The president cannot dismiss commission members for political reasons. These commissions deal with making rules and establishing standards in various sectors of the economy, such as communications and finance. They seek to regulate certain segments of the economy. Examples are the Federal Reserve System, the Federal Trade Commission, the Federal Communications Commission, the Securities and Exchange Commission, and the National Labor Relations Board. One other independent regualtory Commission, the Occupational Safety and Health Review Commission, is described further in Box 7.3. For the most part, the people serving in the independent regulatory commissions do not have direct ties to the president or members of Congress.

A fourth type of agency is called a government corporation. These are agencies that were created to carry out a particular task and, in doing so, make a profit, similar to a business organization. The services provided by these bureaucrats are often used by the public. These are usually headed by either boards or commissions whose membership consists of representatives from both political parties. They are appointed to longer terms of office, helping guard against any possible partisan influence. Examples of government corporations are the U.S. Postal Service and Amtrak, which is described in Box 7.4.

Advisory committees also exist. These committees provide expertise to federal agencies and can be either temporary or permanent. Additionally, there are numerous minor boards, committees, and commissions that have been established by either Congress or the president for a specific purpose and are usually temporary.

BOX 7.3

Independent Regulatory Commission—Occupational Safety and Health Review Commission

The Occupational Safety and Health Review Commission works to ensure the timely and fair resolution of cases involving the alleged exposure of American workers to unsafe or unhealthy working conditions. The Occupational Safety and Health Review Commission is an independent, quasi-judicial agency established by the Occupational Safety and Health Act of 1970 (29 U.S.C. 651-678).

The commission is charged with ruling on cases forwarded to it by the Department of Labor when disagreements arise over the results of safety and health inspections performed by the department's Occupational Safety and Health Administration. Employers have the right to dispute any alleged job safety or health violation found during the inspection by the administration, the penalties it proposed, and the time given by the agency to correct any hazardous situation. Employees and representatives of employees may initiate a case by challenging the propriety of the time the administration has allowed for correction of any violative condition.

The Occupational Safety and Health Act covers virtually every employer in the country. Enforced by the secretary of labor, the act is an effort to reduce the incidence of personal injuries, illness, and deaths among working men and women in the United States that result from their employment. It requires employers to furnish to each of their employees a working environment free from recognized hazards that are causing or likely to cause death or serious physical harm to the employees and to comply with occupational safety and health standards promulgated under the act.

The commission was created to adjudicate enforcement actions initiated under the act when they are contested by employers, employees, or representatives of employees. A case arises when a citation is issued against an employer as the result of an Occupational Safety and Health Administration inspection and it is contested within 15 working days. The commission is more of a court system than a simple tribunal, for within the commission there are two levels of adjudication. All cases are assigned to an administrative law judge who decides the case. Ordinarily, the hearing is held in the community where the alleged violation occurred or as close as possible. At the hearing, the secretary of labor will generally have the burden of proving the case. After the hearing, the judge must issue a decision based on findings of fact and conclusions of law.

A substantial number of the decisions of the judges become final orders of the commission. However, each decision is subject to discretionary review by the three members of the commission on the direction of any one of the three, if done within thirty days of the filing of the decision. When that occurs, the commission issues its own decision. Once a case is decided, any party to the case adversely affected or aggrieved thereby may seek a review of the decision in the U.S. Courts of Appeals.

BOX 7.4

Government Corporation—U.S. Postal Service

The U.S. Postal Service provides mail processing and delivery services to individuals and businesses within the United States. The Postal Service is committed to serving customers through the development of efficient mail-handling systems and operates its own planning and engineering programs. It also protects the mails from loss or theft and apprehends those who violate postal laws.

The Postal Service was created as an independent establishment of the executive branch by the Postal Reorganization Act (39 U.S.C. 101 et seq.), approved August 12, 1970. The present Postal Service commenced operations on July 1, 1971.

The Postal Service has approximately 776,000 career employees and handles about 207 billion

BOX 7.4

(continued)

pieces of mail annually. The chief executive officer of the Postal Service, the postmaster general, is appointed by the nine governors of Postal Service, who are appointed by the president with the advice and consent of the Senate for overlapping nine-year terms. The governors and the postmaster general appoint the deputy postmaster general, and these 11 people constitute the board of governors. In addition to the national headquarters, there are area and district offices supervising approximately 38,000

post offices, branches, stations, and community post offices throughout the United States.

The U.S. Postal Inspection Service is the federal law enforcement agency that has jurisdiction in criminal matters affecting the integrity and security of the mail. Postal inspectors enforce more than 200 federal statutes involving mail fraud, mail bombs, child pornography, illegal drugs, mail theft, and other postal crimes as well as being responsible for the protection of all postal employees.

THEORIES OF BUREAUCRATIC BEHAVIOR

There are many theories to help us understand the behavior of bureaucracies: theories of political control, bureaucratic politics, public institutional theory, and public management as well as postmodern theory, decision theory, and rational-choice theory.[28] These theories help explain or help us understand bureaucratic behavior. There are probably too many to describe in any detail here, but there are some theories that have been recognized as fundamental to the field. One of those is called incrementalism. Under this theory, bureaucratic decisions tend to be made in gradual, limited steps rather than with bold dramatic changes.[29] In other words, most decisions made by bureaucrats only slightly modify previous decisions. Thus, change comes slowly in large organizations. Originally suggested by Charles E. Lindblom in 1959, incrementalism was also supported by Aaron Wildavsky, Richard Fenno, and Ira Sharkansky.

Another classic theory of organizational behavior was called "scientific management." Because it was originally presented by Frederick W. Taylor, this approach is sometimes referred to as Taylorism. The origins of scientific management can be found in business management, which sought to make the workplace more efficient and productive. Taylor analyzed the workplace and worker behavior within that environment in order to maximize productivity.[30] Taylor used a variety of experiments to determine how jobs should be structured. He then advocated a division of tasks. The management was to design the best division of the workload and the tasks required, and the workers would then respond. There would be incentives offered to the workers for optimal production,[31] including setting specific goals for employees, setting measures for work productivity, and providing feedback. It also used money as a motivator for the employees. Under this theory, it was the management's responsibility for training employees, selecting employees scientifically, providing a shortened workweek and rest pauses, and providing individualized work with individualized rewards.[32] Taylorism influenced public administrators into thinking that management in the public sector could be studied and applied scientifically.[33] It was a scientific approach to managerial decision making that was based on proven fact (e.g., research and experimentation) rather than on tradition, rule of thumb, guesswork, precedent, personal opinion, or hearsay.[34] Over the years, the principles of scientific management were used in bureaucracies to rationalize the structure and responsibilities of different levels of government and to organize day-to-day operations for some kinds of government agencies.[35]

In the 1970s and 1980s, the economic accomplishments of Japan led administrators and scholars to examine the ingredients of Japanese success. After studying the success of Japanese business, they found that their success was attributed in part to the Japanese management style and to techniques that tended to emphasize human relationships in a business setting. The results of many studies showed that employees who were provided with job security and provided with an opportunity to participate in decision making became more loyal to the company and also more productive. They also found that Japanese agencies have many characteristics that seem to produce creative organizations: missions and goals are clearly stated; the welfare of the employees is important; management committees and a board of directors exist; there is a sensitivity to opportunities and changes; long-range plans are put in place; communication is better, moving both horizontally and vertically through the organization; and there is a focus on lifetime employment, training, and the employee.[36] This new approach was called "Japanese management."[37] In particular, one of their techniques or tools that received some attention was the Quality Circle. This was made up of employees who shared similar work responsibilities and met on a regular basis with the goal of improving their work performance. It became a concept of worker cooperation through a team effort.[38]

A fourth approach to bureaucratic theory comes from Weber. He identified three types of leadership. The first is charismatic leadership, which adheres to an idea of traditional domination and legal rationalism. The leader's basis of legitimacy comes from the leader him- or herself, who generally holds some type of personal leadership that attracts people to the organization and to that leader. Traditional domination, the second type of leadership, bases decisions and action on the past. Something is done in a particular way simply because it is the way it has always been done. There is an emphasis on historic traditions rather than new and innovative styles. The third approach is called legal rationalism, where there are rational justifications for authority.

Together, these theories and ideas help us understand the behavior of bureaucrats and the bureaucracies in which they work. One concept they help explain is the power held by bureaucracies, including the source and the use of power by bureaucrats.

BUREAUCRATIC POWER

Since bureaucracies have a great deal of power, they are often referred to as the fourth branch of government. This power stems from three sources. First, bureaucrats have an excess of information and knowledge about the current issues that need attention. Many others, particularly lawmakers and executives, do not have that same information and knowledge base. This means that bureaucracies have power because there is an "asymmetry in information, understanding, and expertise."[39] Bureaucrats often simply know more than elected officials about what needs to be done and how to do it.[40] When it comes to criminal justice, one study found that

> most legislators have a limited interest in criminal justice affairs. The average lawmaker has never been employed in the criminal justice system, has never served on a legislative committee concerned with criminal justice policy, and has visited a prison only once in his life.[41]

Lawmakers must rely on bureaucrats for information and problems and solutions. This information gives bureaucracies the power to influence legislation and the voting patterns of legislators.

The second source of power is based on the discretion that is given to bureaucracies to decide key elements of new laws and policies that are created by Congress. Discretion, or the ability to decide how policies will be implemented, is given to the agencies by Congress. Discretion is needed by agencies because the problems being addressed by Congress are often too diverse or complicated for legislators to provide much guidance about how programs should be administered. The laws they create simply provide guidelines for bureaucrats about goals and must leave sufficient flexibility so that bureaucrats can adapt to the new policies, whether that be reorganizing current conditions or creating new ones.[42] Sometimes Congress will pass laws that require agencies to do things that they do not know how to do.[43] This gives agencies a great deal of discretion to decide policies[44] and thus a great deal of power. These decisions affect the lives of many people, including those providing the service and the clients.

Bureaucrats are often able to make these key decisions with little or no influence, input, or oversight from legislators, judges, or other political or public actors. Most often, bureaucratic policymaking is done secretly behind the scenes with few, if any, public hearings, and little debate or attention. They often do not gather facts and examine alternatives. Instead, the decisions that bureaucrats make are based on personal or cultural values. Since bureaucracies are not closely rule bound, the social and political values held by bureaucrats become even more important.[45] Often, the policy preferences of bureaucrats are not always representative of the policy preferences of their elected overseers.[46]

The third source of bureaucratic power stems from the ability of bureaucracies to make policy. Some agencies make regulatory policy, which is policy that regulates people's behavior or conduct. It can also regulate the behavior of companies. These regulations provide a way in which the government restricts "individual choice so as to keep conduct from transcending acceptable bounds."[47] This is made by independent regulatory commissions, such as the Food and Drug Administration and the Securities and Exchange Commission. In these policies, Congress sets general guidelines on regulatory policy, and agencies expand the guidelines into specific policy actions. Examples include highway safety regulations and criminal laws. These policies are often controversial, as they contain a sanction, such as a fine or imprisonment, or another method of coercion.

Bureaucracies also make redistributive policy, which entails taxing one group of people to provide benefits for a different group of people. These are designed to shape broad classes or groups of people, such as the poor, by providing them with some kind of benefit. Examples of this include health insurance, Social Security, and welfare programs. Similar to this is distributive policy, where agencies use tax revenue or other nonuser taxes to provide benefits directly to individuals. This includes national parks, health research, urban grants, and the progressive income tax.

The power of bureaucracies also stems from their size and importance. It seems that, in recent years, many bureaucracies continue to grow in size and gain in power with advances in technology, increases in the availability of information, and the growth in the size and complexity of society. Now bureaucracies play more of an active, essential role than ever before. Citizens rely on bureaucracies for services of all kinds, from protecting the safety of food and drugs to providing recreational facilities, such as national parks.

One of the primary goals of bureaucracies is to maintain their agency's survival. Most bureaucratic employees believe their work is important and resist efforts to reduce the activities, size, or budget of the agency for which they work. They press for increases in their own size and budgets and for additions to their own regulatory authority. They do not request a reduction in their authority, the elimination of a program, or a decrease in their budget or personnel. Instead, they seek higher pay, greater job security, and more power and authority. New policies are frightening because they may mean that an agency may be reorganized or even eliminated. They might not have the initiative or ability to develop new or innovative policy solutions. Their efforts may be further constrained by the political need to achieve accountability, efficiency, and effectiveness. Thus, there is a tendency for bureaucracies to formulate incremental proposals.[48]

Over time, this power held by bureaucracies has continued to increase as society has grown in size and complexity. But their behavior is continually monitored by interest groups, the media, and Congress in their oversight role.[49] The behavior of bureaucracies is limited by "laws, executive policies, and judicial decisions, not only in the policies it pursues but in the way it pursues them."[50] The behavior of bureaucracies is also impacted by other political actors, including the president, Congress, courts, interest groups, and other political actors.

POLITICS AND BUREAUCRACIES

Early political theorists realized the danger that politics could have on bureaucracies. As early as 1887, Woodrow Wilson argued that the dangers of political patronage could harm the effectiveness of bureaucratic administration, so every attempt should be made to keep politics out of bureaucracies.[51] Goodnow proposed a politics–administration dichotomy where politics and administration could be considered two different functions. However, he recognized that, in practice, politics was rarely separate from administration.[52]

Today, it is the case that bureaucratic agencies operate within the larger political system, and it is not possible to separate politics from bureaucratic behavior.[53] Bureaucrats interact on an almost daily basis with other government officials, including legislators, the executive branch, other administrators, and members of interest groups. Bureaucratic decisions are shaped by the political environment in which they must operate. In fact, politics is the driving force behind most bureaucratic behavior. The goals bureaucracies work for and the power they possess are largely dependent on how they cooperate with other actors in the political process, both within and outside government. Their behavior is also influenced by political developments, customs, laws, interest groups, the media, and political parties.[54]

At a basic level, there is a difference between liberals and conservatives concerning the role of politics in bureaucratic decisions. Many liberals today generally favor big government, especially if it is used to provide greater support for education, health care, programs for minorities, environmental protection, and worker safety. They tend to condemn government spending if it is used to support foreign aid to dictatorships, government assistance to parochial schools, or the purchase of computer equipment that might allow law enforcement to gather information about citizens' private lives. Conversely, most conservatives oppose government spending on welfare programs but favor it in national security, police protection, and some social concerns, such as antipornography campaigns.[55]

Presidents and Bureaucracies

Political parties and ideologies are not the only political influence on bureaucracies. In fact, the behavior of bureaucracies is overseen by other branches and cannot operate independently from them.[56] For example, the president or governor can set various broad policy goals that bureaucracies must work toward. Since the president can focus on only a few issues at a time, it leaves room for Congress to define others. At times, the goals set forth by the executive and legislative branches contradict each other.

The president can also reorganize bureaucracies. He can opt to put similar programs into the same department or separate different functions of the same bureaucracy. This may be done to reduce costs and/or the overlap of services. Sometimes this is done to improve the leadership or even the coordination of the agency.[57] President Nixon did this when he reorganized the agencies involved in the fight against drug use, resulting in the creation of the Drug Enforcement Agency (DEA).

Probably the most important relationship is the power of the president to appoint top personnel to many of the agencies and bureaucracies (often with the approval of the Senate). Some presidents have the opportunity to make almost 4,000 appointments outside the merit system, where employees are chosen solely on the basis of their qualifications.[58] It is expected that these appointees will make policy that is based on the president's ideology. If not, the president can remove them from office. It has been discovered that before presidential appointees take the oath of office, they are faithful to the president's principles, but after spending time in the agency, they sometimes "go native." In other words, they see the unmet needs of the clients and their unfulfilled agendas and start to support their loyal and hardworking employees rather than the policies of the president.[59]

As a result, presidents sometimes see the bureaucracy as their "natural enemy" and are always searching for ways to bring it under control. Most presidents would like to make even more appointments to bureaucracies or simply better ones. Some presidents encourage their "ideological allies" to be promoted into the top administrative ranks of senior civil servants.[60]

Congress and Bureaucracies

Congress retains enormous power over bureaucracies, and at this point in time, no agency can completely hide from Congress.[61] Congressional action has a major impact on the activities of bureaucrats. Obviously, Congress can write legislation that defines the actions of the bureaucracy, providing instructions that determine what agencies can and cannot do. They can write legislation to force agencies to do something or not to do it. They can also repeal, codify, or alter any rule made by an agency. Second, Congress can establish agencies and departments or can reorganize them. For example, Congress recently proposed a new agency, called the National Criminal Justice Commission that would be responsible for reviewing the criminal justice system. Additionally, Congress has fiscal controls through its budgetary power of appropriations. Through this power, Congress has been able to strengthen some bureaucracies while weakening others. Through the appropriations process, Congress can determine the number of employees an agency will have and how much money it will have (its budget). At times, bureaucratic leaders may even respond to changes in preferences held by the Congress (or even in the White House) in an effort to avoid budgetary sanctions.[62]

Third, Congress has personnel controls over the bureaucracy. Through the constitutional power to confirm presidential appointments, the Senate sometimes plays a role in selecting executive personnel and determining who will be employed by an agency. The Senate can either accept a presidential nominee or reject a nominee if it considers that person unqualified. This, in turn, can have an impact on policy as well. However, to some extent, this power is limited by civil service procedures that oversee the hiring and firing of some bureaucratic personnel. Congress cannot determine most of the agency employees, nor can it force employees it does not like to resign or determine the pay of individual agency members.[63]

Congress also has an oversight function through its power of investigation. For example, through committee investigations, members of Congress are able to investigate and examine the policies and operations of bureaucracies. They are given the power to examine police material, memoranda, and/or internal documents to determine if the agency was enforcing laws.[64]

Courts and Bureaucracies

The federal courts sometimes play a role in shaping bureaucratic behavior, even though they are often not as involved in the process as are other branches of government. Years ago, it was more difficult for the courts to alter the discretionary decisions of bureaucracies, but since the late 1960s, the federal courts became more involved in bureaucratic matters, making them much more intrusive in their oversight of bureaucracies.[65]

The courts help ensure that agency administrators do not exceed their statutory authority or that they do not ignore basic procedural requisites. The involvement of the courts also ensures that agency personnel conduct themselves in a manner that is not arbitrary, that they do not abuse their power of discretion, that they make important policy determinations logically and legally on the basis of facts, and that those policies do not violate the Constitution.[66] They can do this through making decisions that impact how procedures are carried out in bureaucratic agencies.

For example, throughout the 1960s and 1970s, decisions from the U.S. Supreme Court were influential in changing the procedures that police followed in the criminal justice system and in overseeing antidiscrimination practices.[67] Sometimes, federal judges have made decisions about detailed aspects of administrative decisions. For example, the courts determined the quality of living conditions for criminal offenders held in prison.[68]

The courts can also play an oversight function and review cases to determine whether government employees were improperly fired, whether a regulatory commission acted illegally in applying particular rules, whether correct and appropriate procedures were followed by a government agency in reaching its decisions, or whether specific agency rulings were in conflict with the law or the Constitution and were constitutional.[69]

Many times, bureaucratic agencies feel frustration, resentment, and anxiety when federal courts intervene into the daily administrative operations. At times, bureaucrats resent the judicial rulings that mandate certain procedures or policy changes in the operations of the agency. These court decisions serve to limit the discretion held by bureaucrats in running the operations.[70] However, now that bureaucrats know that there might be a legal challenge concerning their procedures, they are more careful to make and follow exact procedures. Some have argued that bureaucracies have even created rule-making procedures that are far more complex than what may be necessary just to protect themselves from legal action.[71]

Interest Groups and Bureaucracies

Like other branches of government, interest groups can influence bureaucratic behavior. Each bureaucracy or agency has a narrow policy interest that matches the concern or focus of the pressure group. This means that bureaucracies often have a great deal in common and often cooperate with each other to achieve their goals and to be successful in lobbying for and influencing the direction of public policy. Bureaucrats need the political support and influence of pressure groups in their exchanges with other political institutions. They also need the information that interest groups can provide so that they can make and defend their decisions. At the same time, the interest groups need access to the political process, and this in turn gives them influence in the policymaking process.[72]

Other Political Actors and Bureaucracies

The behavior of the bureaucracy is also influenced by other, nonelected officials. For example, the public influences government decisions. If the general public wants a particular service or even changes in how a service is provided, bureaucracies may respond and make appropriate changes to reflect that need. Keep in mind that the public's opinions are, at the same time, affected by the behavior of administrative agencies. For example, the behavior of law enforcement agencies can affect the public's perception of them. If police officers in a neighborhood are helpful, the public will have a positive reaction; if they are abusive and discriminatory, the public's opinion will probably be more negative.

The media can also help affect the behavior of the bureaucracy. The media can act as a "watchdog," looking for ineffective or wasteful (or even illegal) behavior on the part of bureaucrats. They can then make this public, affecting the reputation of the agency. Obviously, bureaucracies want to avoid that type of negative publicity.

Finally, political parties may play a role in the staffing of government agencies, particularly in the approval process of presidential nominees for office.[73]

ROLE IN THE POLICY PROCESS

Bureaucracies are often significantly involved in the policy process, both formally and informally. They help with the identification of problems, the formation of public policies, and the evaluation of policies. Most important, they are involved in the implementation of policies.

Agenda Setting

Bureaucracies play an important role in the agenda-setting stages of the policy process. Because bureaucrats work day in and day out with constituents who are identifying and dealing with new problems every day or work in the field themselves, they are more aware of the issues that need to be addressed by legislators. Or those same bureaucrats may be more aware of agency problems and departmental policies that are inefficient or ineffective. Because of their vast experience and specialized knowledge, agency officials are able to identify needed changes in existing policies as well as new problems that are appropriate targets for legislation. Thus, bureaucrats often have policy ideas that may eventually grow into law.[74]

However, bureaucrats cannot formally propose legislation to Congress. Instead, they must convince a member of Congress, either in the House of Representatives or the Senate, that a significant problem exists and that there is a need for action. That elected official will then be the person responsible for introducing the bill for action and sponsoring the bill throughout.

The suggestions for new laws or improvements in existing laws can sometimes come from the president, who in some cases appointed the bureaucrat to serve in the agency. The federal bureaucracy is often the most viable option for promoting administration policy directives that is available to the executive since it cannot, by itself, formally propose legislation to Congress.[75]

In identifying significant problems or issues, bureaucrats have power because they have knowledge about the real issues at hand. They have knowledge of both problems and possible solutions. This information becomes valuable to politicians who are often unaware of what is happening in the field and, at the same time, are concerned with making good public policy. Politicians must rely on bureaucrats to help them know when legislative action is needed.

Once the idea is proposed, there must be political and popular support for a new or changed policy. Getting this support is called consensus building. This is a competitive process whereby supporters attempt to persuade enough people that change is needed and in a particular direction. This decision is sometimes done with limited knowledge and is referred to as "muddling through." When a proposed policy satisfies the decision maker and suffices his or her need, it is called "satisficing." In this case, the "best" or "maximum" policy is not found. If policymakers do not know precisely what will work but understand what will not work or has not worked in the past, they can propose policies that eliminate poor practices. This is referred to as "remediality." In this case, policymakers do not ascertain what is "good." When plans change only at the margin, it is called "incrementalism."

Policy Formulation

The bureaucracy is not constitutionally empowered to make laws. However, bureaucracies are involved in the process of making policy in many ways, both formally and informally. Formally, bureaucracies and agencies often actively lobby and attempt to win acceptance of proposed legislation they favor or kill that which they oppose. They can do this by meeting individually with members of Congress or their staff or by testifying before congressional committees or subcommittees on proposed legislative issues. In some cases, the bureaucratic representative may assist a member of Congress in preparing speeches by giving him or her information or key phrases that may be helpful. To be more effective and to have the greatest chance of influencing congressional decisions, many agencies have opened congressional liaison offices to make their contacts with members of Congress more ongoing and effective.

Bureaucrats can help design or write legislation to address needed improvements or changes. It is often the case that many laws are drafted by bureaucrats or legislative aides with substantial assistance from bureaucrats.[76]

Often, bureaucrats testify in front of committees and subcommittees to give expert testimony about both problems and proposed solutions. In fact, it is routine for agency administrators to give advice and testimony to legislators and the executive branch when proposed legislation will affect their agency. "If an agency feels that proposed legislation will have some harmful or costly effect on it, the rationale against passage of such legislation will probably be considered legitimate, limiting the probability that such legislation will pass through the legislative process at least in recognizable form."[77]

The key role that bureaucracies play in the policymaking process cannot be overemphasized. Their role is so important that some have called it a "subgovernment," a term originally coined by Douglas Cater in 1965 to describe the interlocking networks of key actors that influenced public policy. He described a close interlocking network of congressional committees, executive branch bureaucracies, and powerful interest groups that worked with each other to influence and create public policy.

IRON TRIANGLES   In more recent years, the theory of the informal process by which a proposed bill becomes a law in Congress is called the iron triangle, or the cozy triangle. It describes the "behind-the-scenes" relationships or connections that exist between groups and legislative actors and that help determine the final policy that comes out of Congress. The other actors involved in the iron triangle (completing the three points of the triangle) are Congress (or congressional committees or subcommittees) and interest groups, each of which has a stake in particular programs. The theory implies that there is a relatively closed, autonomous policymaking system marked by more or less stable relations among a limited number of participants.[78] Each of these three actors gives something to the other, and each one gets something in return. The concept of the iron triangle helps demonstrate the importance of the bureaucracy in the policy process.[79]

Each of the actors or groups involved in the iron triangle provides a benefit to another actor and in turn receives a benefit. Each develops a "give-and-take" relationship with each other.

There are three linkages between the three actors. The first is between Congress (or the committees and subcommittees) and the bureaucracies. In this relationship, the bureaucracies give the legislators information about problems and the policy options. This is because the groups have the knowledge and expertise that the legislators do not. Instead, the legislators rely on the interest group members to help them understand the problem and the policy options for solving that problem. In return for providing that information to legislators, the interest groups hope to receive legislation that reflects the information they provided. "The final impact of interest groups on agency behavior depends on four factors: the extent to which the legislature wants and expects there to be an impact; the degree of discretionary authority possessed by agency members; the array of interests in the agency's environment; and the relationship between desired behavior and client incentives."[80] In return, the bureaucracies hope that the committee hearings and actions will be used to further the interests of the bureaucracies, especially if the committee is sympathetic and the bureaucracy has an opportunity to make an effective case for its programs.[81] In some cases, the committee members can have a significant impact on the proposed legislation. For example, the committee can choose to disapprove of any legislative proposal, proposed laws, or amendments that are disagreeable to the bureaucracy,[82] or an agency's budget can be reduced, padded, or even eliminated.

The second link is between bureaucracies and interest groups. The interest groups can provide the bureaucracies with the most recent information about the issues at hand or how constituents are feeling about those issues. In return for that, the bureaucracies can choose to define legislation in such a way as to benefit that interest group. In other words, bureaucracies can use their discretion to implement policies in such a way as to benefit the interest group members.

The third link in the iron triangle is between the interest groups and Congress (committees and subcommittees). In this relationship, the interest group can give Congress information (since it often has more detailed information about the problem at hand than the legislators), but it can also provide the legislators with campaign support and resources. This can include not only votes but also money, volunteers, and other campaign support. In return, the interest group hopes that the legislators will vote to support it when the time comes.

These relationships that have developed and become known as the iron triangle are not well publicized. Few bureaucrats or members of Congress would like to announce that they have been "captured" or that they were adherents to the cause of any special interest. But the relationships continue because they are out of the public eye.[83] Additionally, since everyone involved is benefiting in some fashion from the relationships that have been established, it remains a solid yet informal legislative structure.

If it is true, the iron triangle theory implies that a symbiotic interdependence exists between elite actors or groups who engage in the reciprocal behaviors with each other that, in the long run, control the decision-making process.[84] The same players deal with each other day after day and make the same policy decisions year after year. Because the relationships have become so established, there may be little debate or discussion about the merits of proposed programs.[85]

Some would argue that the iron triangle theory no longer applies to the policymaking process as it exists today. They claim that iron triangles were the dominant mode of policymaking from the 1940s to the 1970s[86] but that during the 1970s and 1980s the political world changed. There was a dramatic increase in the number of issues that arose, new interest groups were created, and government activities became more complex. For the first time, previously existing interest groups that had previously faced no or relatively little opposition found themselves facing competitive adversaries.[87] The concept of an iron triangle no longer seemed to be an accurate portrayal of the domestic policymaking process. It seemed oversimplified.[88]

Instead, the relationships referred to in the iron triangles were replaced by "issue networks." Such networks consist of bureaucrats, staffers, and interest group representatives connected in some fashion by their expertise in a particular policy area. The issue networks vary, depending on the issue area. There may be many networks in the same policy domain or area, each representing a different view of the issues and solutions. The concept of issue networks is much more complex than that of an iron triangle, but it still points to the informal, behind-the-scenes role that these actors play in the policymaking process.[89]

Policy Implementation

The policy process does not end with the passage of a law by Congress and its signing by the president. After this stage, the bill moves on to the implementation stage. The new bill goes to the departments and agencies of the executive branch of government charged with carrying out policy.[90] Most people do not consider bureaucracies to be major players in the policy process. However, the agencies play an important role because much of the policymaking process takes place within the agencies.[91]

The implementation stage of the policy process is the primary role in which bureaucracies are involved.[92] Implementation includes all the activities designed around carrying out the laws enacted by the legislative branch of government, meaning that they carry out the programs "thought up" by elected officials. In this regard, bureaucracies are responsible for the delivery of public services. This may include creating new organizations, agencies, departments, or bureaus to carry out new laws. It may also include the process of assigning new responsibilities and tasks to existing organizations and personnel. Bureaucratic agencies make many decisions and issue many rules that have far-reaching political and policy consequences. In the area of criminal justice, implementation may involve the development of treatment programs, rehabilitative programs, job training programs, or domestic violence programs. In criminal justice, bureaucrats responsible for implementing programs include police, court officials, and corrections personnel. All of them carry out the legislation or policies passed by Congress or a state legislature. In doing so, they have a great deal of discretion or decision-making power.[93]

Studies of policy implementation by bureaucrats are a relatively recent phenomenon. Before the 1970s, it was assumed that communities implemented policies in a similar fashion. But around that time, studies began to show that there were variations in how programs were implemented in different communities.[94]

This research indicated that there are many types or patterns of rule making that are carried out by bureaucracies that give them power.[95] The first revolves around their ability to make rules. Bureaucracies can make substantive rules whereby they fill in some of the details of the statutory provisions that may be lacking. These decisions have the same effect as a law. Their interpretations of the law and how it is enforced indicate how an agency views that law. Bureaucracies can also make procedural rules that describe an agency's organization and how it will conduct its various activities.

Bureaucracies make policy by informally interpreting the laws that are passed by Congress and making day-to-day decisions about how the laws will be carried out. This is because Congress, by attempting to phrase legislation in unoffensive language, may unintentionally make its intents about the law unclear to those who must implement the laws. Or it may pass symbolic laws that have the appearance of action and may not pay much attention to adding specifics and details in the legislation. The resulting legislation is often vague and ambiguous.[96] Phrases and terms are not spelled out or well defined, and goals are inconsistent or meaningless.[97] For example, Congress may pass a law to provide funding for indigent offenders, but who defines "indigent"?

Each law passed by the legislature varies in its specificity and clarity and the policy areas it attempts to influence. Vague terms are open to a number of different interpretations, and bureaucracies must choose between them. The bureaucracy is given the task of implementing difficult public policies with little or no guidance from the legislative body as to what standards to apply when considering options and solutions.[98] Bureaucrats must interpret the language of the legislation and decide on the specific details about policies before they can be put into effect. They are usually given a wide amount of discretion to interpret the laws, and they usually have a wide range of possible actions.

In essence, the Congress and the president are shifting policymaking from themselves to bureaucrats.[99] Thus, if the way in which the terms are defined and the final implementation of a policy turn out to be unpopular, Congress and the president can blame bureaucrats for the failed policy.[100] When bureaucrats are faced with making discretionary choices, they often exercise their discretionary authority in a manner that will increase their self-interested goals.[101] They will make decisions that will impact the department or themselves in the most positive way.

The decisions of bureaucrats may have a major impact on defining the client base as well as the distribution of goods. But it can become more complicated than this, as recognized by Gaus, who claimed that federal agencies not only carried out clearly understood directives from Congress but also were able to independently shape those directives and exercise discretionary policymaking authority while translating the vague intentions of statutes into specific government actions.[102]

Bureaucracies can also make policy through their adjudicative functions. Agencies can make policy when they apply preexisting laws or rules to particular situations on a case-by-case basis. In defining the rules and policies, bureaucracies are acting much like the courts. Bureaucrats are expected to be equitable, yet the day-to-day operations and rules must at times be selectively applied. Often, the public is not satisfied if implementation is the strict application of a detailed law. They expect and demand implementation that includes flexibility, creativity, and responsiveness to changes in needs. The bureaucracy must have the ability or the power to have discretion so that it can perform according to expectations.[103]

When implementation emanates primarily from clearly stated mandates or statutes, it is called top-down policymaking. This is optimal.[104] In this way, implementation will be more likely to capture the policy intentions of Congress more completely (which, of course, presumes that policy intentions precede implementation).[105] On the other hand, when policy intentions are not fully developed until they are negotiated, bureaucrats gain power because they decide to whom and how much they should communicate. This is called bottom-up policymaking.[106]

Since bureaucracies have so much discretion in making decisions and so much power to implement laws, the question then becomes whether public agencies represent the interests and values of the American public. Are these interests and values reflected in the policy actions of the bureaucracy? If the bureaucracy has the same values as the American people as a whole, then the decisions made by the bureaucracy will be similar to the decisions made if the entire American public passed on the issues.[107] This is called a representative bureaucracy. The bureaucracy is more reflective of the American public than Congress, which is heavily tilted toward the upper strata of society and does not reflect a variety of national interests.[108]

The rule-making procedures that bureaucracies have are not like those of the legislative process. Bureaucrats know the implementation procedures and what can and cannot be done.[109] They are the ones who deal with the problems on a daily basis; they know the specifics of the problems and the best way to solve the problems, probably even better than legislators.

Another source of rule-making power comes from the role of bureaucracies in law enforcement. Bureaucratic agencies may define policy through their various law enforcement actions. They may rigidly enforce a statute, choose to be more lax, or even ignore it. A policy may be applied in some situations or for some people but not in others. Law enforcement personnel often use their power to apply laws on a case-by-case basis, depending on the people involved and the facts. When implementing a program, a bureaucracy may be involved in using techniques of control that are designed primarily to make people do something, refrain from doing something, or continue to do something. There are many options, including noncoercive punishments, meaning that they do not involve imposing legal sanctions or penalties (these may involve inspections to determine whether it conforms to officially prescribed standards); licensing, which involves the government authorization to engage in a business or profession or to do something otherwise forbidden; loans, subsidies, and benefits that are means by which public purposes are advanced through financial aid; contracts with private companies; or general expenditures for purchasing goods and services that can be used by agency officials to attain their individual policy goals.[110]

How bureaucracies implement their programs (and the effect of those programs) is called program operations. The programs can impact many people both directly and indirectly. This would include such agency behavior as administering loans or grants, any possible benefits, and insurance. Bureaucracies often implement laws that help manage public properties, such as forests or parks. Often, these activities are not typically considered law enforcement, as they are not intended to regulate or shape people's behavior but nevertheless are sometimes very important to many people.[111]

Many bureaucracies make policy through their regulatory functions, meaning that they can levy fines and penalties for violations of regulations. In most cases, these are enforceable in federal court. The regulatory activity of bureaucracies expands each year. "Each year, federal regulatory bureaucracies issue thousands of rules and regulations, conduct thousands of inspections, investigate thousands of complaints, require businesses to submit hundreds of thousands of forms, hold thousands of hearings to determine compliance or noncompliance, issue thousands of corrective orders, and levy thousands of fines and penalties; federal regulatory bureaucracies are legislators, investigators, prosecutors, and judges—all wrapped into one."[112]

Bureaucrats also make administrative policy. Administrative rule making allows bureaucrats to make policy openly and directly. This refers to the ability or power of a bureaucracy to allocate scarce societal resources. In essence, the bureaucracy is determining who gets what, when, and how.[113] To have administrative power, the bureaucracy must have two characteristics: resources and autonomy.[114] It must have the resources to allocate a resource (money, a service, or a benefit), and it must have the autonomy, or the legal ability, to make the choices as to the allocation of that resource. If a bureaucracy holds these two characteristics and has the right to make those decisions, then it has a significant amount of power.

The discretion to decide policies is not held only by high-level administrators who can establish new programs and set priorities. "Street-level bureaucrats" also have power. People such as police officers and teachers have flexibility with respect to how they do their jobs. Police, as with many other personnel, have a lot of discretion in applying the law. In many cases, the law can be applied in some situations and not in others or to some persons or companies and not to others.

These street-level bureaucrats can be influenced by the attitudes and motives of officials and by external pressures and financial resources.

A classic argument that individual bureaucrats play an almost unavoidable role in policy-making is by Lipsky in *Street Level Bureaucracy* (1980). Lipsky's central argument is based on the idea that most street-level bureaucrats, such as policemen and teachers, typically must make decisions that are not governed by the guidelines or rules that were provided by the organization for which they work or that govern their work. These bureaucrats must make policy as a result of their day-to-day jobs. There is simply no way that the guidelines can foresee every situation the street-level bureaucrat may face, so they are forced to use their discretion and make their own decisions about what is the most appropriate course of action. For example, if an officer is called to a juvenile criminal case, there is no way a policy manual can describe what to do in each specific case. Thus, the officer must look at the facts of the case, things like the harm done and the prior record of the juvenile, and use his or her discretion to choose the best option to deal with that case. Because of that tremendous amount of discretion, street-level bureaucrats have significant policymaking power in the system.[115]

However, in most cases, those bureaucrats in upper management levels have more authority and discretion over final decisions than those bureaucrats who are employed in lower offices.[116] They make more formal decisions, such as budgetary ones. They get to decide how much money will be spent for services and programs and how the money will be divided among agencies and personnel. This also gives them a great amount of power in the policy process as well.

In sum, bureaucracies have a major role in implementing policy. They are given a great deal of decision making and discretion, which in turn gives them a lot of power in the political system.

Policy Evaluation

Bureaucracies are involved in the final stage of the policy process, which is policy evaluation. Here, bureaucracies are the evaluators, determining if programs work. But they are also the evaluatees, so to speak—the ones being evaluated.

All agencies are evaluated on occasion to look for inefficiency or waste. Many agencies want to get some idea of how their programs are working and what can be done to improve them. Many evaluations of policies and programs are produced within the administering agencies, either on their own initiative or at the discretion of Congress or the executive. The agencies can either evaluate themselves or have an outside agency complete the evaluation. When programs are evaluated, it is called evaluation research. This is done to give decision makers an idea about the effectiveness of programs.

A majority of evaluation is performed by nongovernmental actors, such as university scholars and research centers, and private research organizations, such as the Brookings Institution, the Urban Institute, and American Enterprise Institute. Often, pressure groups and public interest organizations, such as Common Cause or the Audubon Society, evaluate agencies to determine if they are meeting their goals. In many cases, the evaluation is funded by the National Institute of Justice or other federal agency.

There are many methods or techniques for the evaluation, including formative, summative, and process evaluations. Formative evaluations are designed to assist officials in making midcourse corrections or adjustments in existing programs. Summative evaluations are broader and more thorough in scope and are used to inform upper-level policymakers of the overall effects of important policies and programs. The evaluation process may discover a new problem or may uncover a new way to do something. An evaluation may show the need to downsize an agency or increase the agency. If problems are found, the whole process begins again. If the program is found to be effective or gets a positive review, it may be applied in other states or even on the federal level.

There are some agencies that have been created simply to evaluate programs. For example, evaluation activities may be undertaken by the General Accounting Office (GAO) on its own initiative because of directives in legislation, at the request of congressional committees, or sometimes at the behest of individual members of Congress. Copies of the GAO reports are sent to members of Congress and the affected agencies. The agencies are required by law to report to Congress and the Office of Management and Budget on actions taken in response to GAO's recommendation or on why they did not act.[117]

Typically, agencies are not strongly inclined to evaluate themselves. The conduct of their programs and day-to-day operations take precedence over more "distant" concerns, such as program evaluations. Moreover, evaluation would divert scarce funds from current operations. If an evaluation of program effectiveness was conducted and the results of the evaluation turned out unfavorable from the agency's perspective, it could be used as political ammunition by the agency's critics. In all, agencies do not have much incentive to evaluate themselves.[118]

In an effort to make agency evaluations more meaningful, Congress passed the Government Performance and Results Act of 1993. The intent of the law was to shift the focus of agencies from inputs and processes to outputs and outcomes—or results. Now, agencies are directed to work with Congress and its committees in formulating five-year strategic plans that are to include the following:

1. The annual performance goals for the agencies' major programs and activities
2. The measures that will be used to gauge performance
3. The strategies and resources required to achieve the performance goals
4. The procedures that will be used to verify and validate performance information

EXAMPLES OF FEDERAL CRIMINAL JUSTICE BUREAUCRACIES

There are many examples of federal bureaucracies that deal with criminal justice issues. These agencies vary in size, age, and policy area as well as power and ability to influence what goes on in Congress. Some examples are listed in Box 7.5. It can be seen that each of the agencies has a different focus, or jurisdiction, but all have the same goal of providing the best services to those people involved in the system as well as improving the system.

STATE AND LOCAL BUREAUCRACIES

The roles of state- and local-level bureaucracies are typically the same as those on the federal level, but they deal with state and local issues rather than federal ones. Each state and local government has developed its own organization of bureaucracies and defined the jurisdiction of those agencies. They each play a role in the policy process, including agenda setting and policy formulation, implementation, and evaluation. Each also has power, stemming from the same sources as noted for the federal agencies.

BOX 7.5
Examples of Federal Criminal Justice Bureaucracies

Office of National Drug Control Policy

Part of the Executive Office of the President; director is appointed by the president and is known as the "drug czar"; he or she is the administration's top official on drug policy and the director of national drug policy.

Department of Justice

Established in 1870 and headed by the attorney general, it is "the largest law firm in the nation." It is made up of lawyers and investigators who help protect citizens against criminal acts, ensure healthy competition of business, safeguard the consumer, and enforce drug, immigration, and naturalization laws. It also plays a significant role in protecting citizens through its efforts for effective law enforcement, crime prevention, crime detection, and prosecution and rehabilitation of offenders. It represents the government in legal matters generally, rendering legal advice and opinions, on request, to the president and to the heads of the executive departments.

Office of Pardon Attorney

Assists the president in making pardons. All requests for a pardon are forwarded to this office for investigation and review. The pardon attorney prepares a recommendation to the president for final disposition of each application.

Bureau of Prisons

Created to protect society by confining offenders in the controlled environments of prisons and community-based facilities that are safe, humane, and secure and that provide work and self-improvement opportunities to help offenders become law-abiding citizens.

DEA: Drug Enforcement Administration

The top federal agency in enforcing narcotics laws; created by Nixon in July 1973 through the Reorganization Plan No. 2 which merged four separate anti-drug agencies.

The Judicial Conference

Originally called the Conference of Senior Circuit Judges, was created by Congress in 1922; continually studies the actions of the courts and may make policy regarding the administration of the U.S. courts; suggests policies that encourage uniformity of procedures and court business; presided over by the chief justice of the Supreme Court; members include the chief judge of each judicial circuit, the chief judge of the Court of International Trade, and a district judge from each regional judicial circuit, who is elected by a majority vote of all circuit and district judges of the circuit represented.

Office of Justice Programs (OJP)

Established by the Justice Assistance Act of 1984 to provide federal leadership, coordination, and assistance needed to make the nation's justice system more efficient and effective in preventing and controlling crime; collects statistical data and conducts analyses; identifies emerging criminal justice issues; develops and tests promising approaches to address these issues; evaluates program results; and disseminates findings and other information to state and local governments.

U.S. Parole Commission

Has the sole authority to grant, modify, or revoke paroles of eligible prisoners serving sentences of more than one year, including military prisoners and D.C. Code prisoners housed in federal institutions; also responsible for the supervision of parolees and prisoners released on the expiration of their sentences with allowances for statutory good time and the determination of supervisory conditions and terms. The Sentencing Reform Act of 1984 abolished parole eligibility for federal offenders who commit offenses on or after November 1, 1987, and provided for the abolition of the commission on November 1, 1992. However, the Judicial Improvements Act of 1990 and the Parole Commission Phaseout Act of 1996 extended the commission in five-year increments through November 1, 2002.

National Institute of Justice

Established by Congress in 1968 as the major federal agency for criminal justice related research; conducts

(continued)

BOX 7.5

Examples of Federal Criminal Justice Bureaucracies (*continued*)

research in the causes and prevention of crime; evaluates federal anticrime initiatives; supports research to develop new approaches, techniques, systems, and equipment to improve law enforcement and administration of justice; makes recommendations to federal, state, and local governments on crime-related issues; and sponsors conferences and workshops.

U.S. Sentencing Commission

Plays a role in defining federal sentencing policies that balance punishment with rehabilitation. It has a research-and-development program, a help line to assist in sentencing issues, training sessions on the guidelines, and a clearinghouse for information queries, and it publishes numerous publications each year.

Source: Richard P. Conaboy, "The United States Sentencing Commission: A New Component in the Federal Criminal Justice System," *Federal Probation* 61 (1, 1997): 58–62.

Most state agencies work in combination with federal agencies to implement policies, especially those related to funding issues. In fact, most policy implementation takes place in an intergovernmental context. Often, the federal government gives the final authority for the implementation of policies to state officials.

This gives the states more opportunity to exert their influence over how a policy is enacted so that it will address the specific problems and goals of that particular state.[119] This intergovernmental structure of programs allows states to manipulate policy to increase benefits for their own state needs.[120] State governments manipulate federal programs either by having power to write legislation that carries out federal intent or by controlling the administration of federal programs.[121] As a result, most public services, including education, police services, and even welfare, are traditionally administered by cities and states. This means that most citizens are more familiar with local officials and services than those on the federal level.

EXAMPLES OF STATE AND LOCAL CRIMINAL JUSTICE BUREAUCRACIES

State bureaucracies that focus on criminal justice issues and problems have grown at a faster rate than federal ones to provide services to citizens, both victims and offenders. Some examples of state bureaucracies are listed in Box 7.6.

BOX 7.6

State Criminal Justice Research Agencies

New York State Division of Criminal Justice Services

The goal of the New York State Division of Criminal Justice Services is to make the state a safer place to live, raise families and run businesses. They do this through performing criminal history checks and finger-

prints, coordinating grants, providing law enforcement training, and providing information to other agencies and the public. They also have programs to manage sex offenders through public education and community outreach. The agency is working to reduce violent crime, crimes committed with firearms, human traffick-

BOX 7.6
(continued)

ing, and recidivism of inmates through reentry programs (http://criminaljustice.state.ny.us/ojis/index.htm).

New York State Division of Probation and Correctional Alternatives

The New York State Division of Probation and Correctional Alternatives was established in 1985 as an agency within the executive department. This agency is responsible for the operation of probation agencies and alternative correctional programs. The focus of their activity revolves around offender accountability, providing restitution to victims, providing courts with discretionary services, and assisting in funding and training of service providers (http://dpca.state.ny.us/nysdpca/mainpages/about1.htm).

New York State Office of Public Safety

The New York State Office of Public Safety oversees the police and peace officer certified training program that enhance the productivity and professional of law enforcement in the state. They are responsible for approving and certifying training instructors for police and security guards. Other tasks include highway safety, criminal investigation and youth crime.

New York State Department of Correctional Services

The mission of the New York State Department of Correctional Services is to protect the public by having incarcerated people able to return home less likely to revert to criminal behavior. This is done through providing treatment services that address the needs of all inmates within the institution. The agency offers opportunities for inmates to improve their skills and receive treatment to address their needs. This might include both medical and psychiatric serves. Opportunities for interaction between the inmate and their family members are provided as well. (www.docs.state.ny.us/mission.html)

New York State Crime Victims Board

The mission of the New York State Crime Victims Board is to provide compensation to innocent victims of crime in an efficient and compassionate manner, to fund direct services to crime victims via a network of community programs, and to advocate for the rights and benefits of all innocent victims of crime. In fiscal year 2007–08, the agency disbursed almost $27.5 million to victims across the state. (www.cvb.state.ny.us/about.htm)

Washington State Criminal Justice Training Commission

The mission of the Washington State Criminal Justice Training Commission is to train criminal law enforcement, corrections, and other public safety personnel in the state to enhance public safety. Training is provided for those interested in becoming bail bond recovery agents, corrections officers, K-9 team members, police, private security and tribal officers. (www.cjtc.state.wa.us/)

Illinois Criminal Justice Information Authority

Created in 1973, the Illinois Criminal Justice Information Authority has the mission to improve the administration of criminal justice in the state. The personnel collect and disseminate crime statistics, criminal justice–related research, and news about federal grant opportunities. Also housed within this agency are the Illinois Motor Vehicle Theft Prevention Council and the Capital Punishment Reform Study Committee. (www.icjia.org/public/index.cfm?metasection=about)

Colorado Department of Public Safety

The Colorado Department of Public Safety was created in 1984 when the state reorganized related agencies into one department. Today, the agency strives to provide a safe environment through law enforcement, criminal investigations, fire and crime prevention, reducing recidivism, and victim advocacy. Many departments are housed within this one agency, including the State patrol, the Bureau of Investigation, the Division on Criminal Justice, Fire Safety, Preparedness, and School Safety. Four commissions are part of the Department. These include the Cold Case Task Force, the Colorado Commission on

(continued)

BOX 7.6

State Criminal Justice Research Agencies (*continued*)

Criminal and Juvenile Justice, the DNA Working Group, and the Immigration Working Group. (http://cdpsweb.state.co.us/)

Texas Department of Criminal Justice

The mission of the Texas Department of Criminal Justice is to provide public safety, promote positive change in offender behavior, reintegrate offenders into society, and assist victims of crime. It also manages the offenders held in state prisons, jails, and private correctional facilities. The agency also provides funding and oversight of inmates assigned to community supervision (probation), and is responsible for the supervising any offenders who are on parole or mandatory supervision. (www.tdcj.state.tx.us/)

Conclusion

There are many horror stories about bureaucracies, but, as Goodsell argues, bureaucracies work.[122] They provide crucial services to the public and are, for the most part, efficient and fair. It has been proven that they have "staying power"[123] because they live forever, sometimes even outliving their usefulness. Nevertheless, the agencies play a key role in the policy process, from identifying issues (agenda setting) to policy implementation and evaluation. In these roles, bureaucracies have developed relationships with other political actors. They have also developed a significant amount of discretion and power to influence the behavior of others and also in designing policy. They can influence the design of the program, the level of service, and the client base. This truly makes bureaucracies the fourth branch of government.

Notes

1. Charles T. Goodsell, *The Case for Bureaucracy* (Chatham, N.J.: Chatham House, 1994), p. 5.
2. George Roche, "Bureaucracy: Enemy of the People," in *Public Administration Debated*, ed. Herbert M. Levine (Englewood Cliffs, N.J.: Prentice Hall, 1988), pp. 6–16, at 8.
3. James Q. Wilson, *Bureaucracy: What Government Agencies Do and Why They Do It* (New York: Basic Books, 1989), p. 10.
4. Anthony Downs, *Inside Bureaucracy* (Prospect Heights, Ill.: Waveland Press, 1967), pp. 24–5.
5. Ibid., p. 49; H. H. Gerth and C. Wright Mills, *From Max Weber* (New York: Oxford University Press, 1958).
6. B. Guy Peters, *The Politics of Bureaucracy* (New York: Longman, 1995).
7. Wilson, *Bureaucracy*, p. 91.
8. Ibid., p. 105.
9. Peters, *The Politics of Bureaucracy*.
10. Richard T. Green, "Impartiality and Administrative Statesmanship," in *Active Duty*, ed. Peter Augustine Lawler, Robert Martin Schaefer, and David Lewis Schaefer (Lanham, Md.: Rowman & Littlefield, 1998), pp. 91–111, at 91.
11. Brian C. Smith, *Bureaucracy and Political Power* (New York: St. Martin's Press, 1988), p. 7.
12. Green, "Impartiality and Administrative Statesmanship," p. 91.
13. Roche, "Bureaucracy," pp. 6–7.
14. Wilson, *Bureaucracy*, p. x.
15. Roche, "Bureaucracy," pp. 6–16.
16. Thoms R. Dye, *Top Down Policy Making* (New York: Chatham House, 2001).
17. Gary C. Bryner, "Limiting Bureaucratic Discretion: Competing Theories of Administrative Law," in Lawler et al., *Active Duty*, pp. 237–57.

18. Wilson, *Bureaucracy*, p. 235; Levine, *Public Administration Debated*, p. 1.

19. Levine, *Public Administration Debated*, p. 1.

20. Peters, *The Politics of Bureaucracy*.

21. L. Gulick, "Policy Roles of Public Administrators," in *Critical Cornerstones of Public Administration*, ed. P. Schorr (Boston: Oelgeschlager, Gunn and Hain, 1985), pp. 95–96.

22. L. C. Gawthrop, *Bureaucratic Behavior in the Executive Branch* (New York: Free Press, 1969), p. 25.

23. Roche, "Bureaucracy," pp. 6–7.

24. Gawthrop, *Bureaucratic Behavior in the Executive Branch*, p. 25.

25. Downs, *Inside Bureaucracy*, p. 1.

26. H. Brinton Milward and Hal G. Rainey, "Don't Blame the Bureaucracy!" in Levine, *Public Administration Debated*, pp. 16–28, at 25.

27. Ibid.

28. H. George Frederickson and Kevin B. Smith, *Public Administration Theory Primer* (Boulder, Colo.: Westview Press, 2003), p. 63.

29. Levine, *Public Administration Debated*, p. 162.

30. Ibid., p. 163.

31. George A. Krause and Kenneth J. Meier, eds., *Politics, Policy, and Organizations* (Ann Arbor: University of Michigan Press, 2003), p. 3.

32. Edwin A. Locke, "The Ideas of Frederick W. Taylor: An Evaluation," in Levine, *Public Administration Debated*, pp. 186–97, at 194.

33. Levine, *Public Administration Debated*, p. 163.

34. Locke, "The Ideas of Frederick W. Taylor," p. 186.

35. Levine, *Public Administration Debated*, p. 163.

36. Toyohiro Kono, "Japanese Management Philosophy: Can It Be Exported?" in Levine, *Public Administration Debated*, pp. 203–16.

37. Levine, *Public Administration Debated*, p. 164.

38. Ibid.

39. Thomas H. Hammond, "Veto Points, Policy Preferences, and Bureaucratic Autonomy in Democratic Systems," in Krause and Meier, *Politics, Policy, and Organizations*, pp. 73–103, at 74.

40. Ibid.

41. Mark S. Hamm, "Domestic Violence: Legislative Attitudes toward a Coherent Public Policy," *Journal of Crime and Justice* 12 (2, 1989): 37–59, at 50.

42. Phillip J. Cooper, "Conflict or Constructive Tension: The Changing Relationship of Judges and Administrators," in Levine, *Public Administration Debated*, pp. 83–95, at 83.

43. Milward and Rainey, "Don't Blame the Bureaucracy!" p. 23.

44. Francis E. Rourke, *Bureaucracy, Politics, and Public Policy*, 3rd ed. (Boston: Little, Brown, 1984).

45. Smith, *Bureaucracy and Political Power*, p. 7.

46. Hammond, "Veto Points, Policy Preferences, and Bureaucratic Autonomy in Democratic Systems," p. 74.

47. Kenneth J. Meier, *Politics and the Bureaucracy* (Monterey, Calif.: Brooks/Cole, 1987), p. 77.

48. Stella Z. Theodoulou and Chris Kofinis, *The Art of the Game: Understanding American Public Policy Making* (Belmont, Calif.: Thomson, 2004).

49. Dye, *Top Down Policy Making*.

50. Levine, *Public Administration Debated*, p. 114.

51. William E. Nelson, *The Roots of American Bureaucracy, 1830–1900* (Cambridge, Mass.: Harvard University Press, 1982).

52. Krause and Meier, *Politics, Policy, and Organizations*, p. 2.

53. Peters, *The Politics of Bureaucracy*.

54. Levine, *Public Administration Debated*, p. 41.

55. Ibid., p. 3.

56. Hammond, "Veto Points, Policy Preferences, and Bureaucratic Autonomy in Democratic Systems," p. 73.

57. John Rehfuss, *Public Administration as Political Process* (New York: Charles Scribner's Sons, 1973), p. 36.

58. Wilson, *Bureaucracy*, p. 257.

59. Ibid., p. 261.

60. Ibid., p. 257.

61. Ibid., p. 240.

62. Kevin Corder, "Structural Choice and Political Control of Bureaucracy: Updating Federal Credit Programs," in Krause and Meier, *Politics, Policy, and Organizations*, pp. 233–58, at 235.

63. Wilson, *Bureaucracy*, p. 238.

64. Levine, *Public Administration Debated*, pp. 41–42, 44; Bruce E. Fein, "Fighting Off Congress: A Bill of Rights for the Independent Agency," in Levine, *Public Administration Debated*, pp. 61–70; Stephen R. McSpadden, "Don't Cripple Congress," in Levine, *Public Administration Debated*, pp. 70–73; Rehfuss, *Public Administration as Political Process*.

65. Wilson, *Bureaucracy*, p. 279; Phillip J. Cooper, "Conflict or Constructive Tension: The Changing Relationship of Judges and Administrators," in Levine, *Public Administration Debated*, pp. 83–95, at 83.

66. Cooper, "Conflict or Constructive Tension," p. 83.

67. Levine, *Public Administration Debated*, p. 45.

68. Ibid.

69. Ibid.

70. Cooper, "Conflict or Constructive Tension," p. 83.

71. Wilson, *Bureaucracy*, p. 282.

72. Peters, *The Politics of Bureaucracy*, pp. 180–81.

73. Ibid., p. 201.

74. Rehfuss, *Public Administration as Political Process*, p. 158.

75. Francis Rourke, "Presidentializing the Bureaucracy: From Kennedy to Reagan," in *The Managerial Presidency*, ed. James P. Pfiffner (Pacific Grove, Calif.: Brooks/Cole, 1991), pp. 123–34; Terry M. Moe, "The Politicized Presidency," in Pfiffner, *The Managerial Presidency*, pp. 135–57.

76. Carl E. VanHorn, Donald C. Baumer, and William T. Gormley Jr., *Politics and Public Policy* (Washington, D.C.: Congressional Quarterly Press, 1992).

77. Robert Lorinskas, David Kalinich, and Dennis Banas, "Interest Groups and Criminal Behavior," *Journal of Research in Crime and Delinquency* 28 (2, 1994): 157–73.

78. Colton C. Campbell and Roger H. Davidson, "Coalition Building in Congress: The Consequences of Partisan Change," in *The Interest Group Connection*, ed. Paul S. Herrnson, Ronald G. Shaiko, and Clyde Wilcox (Chatham, N.J.: Chatham House, 1998), pp. 116–36.

79. Ibid.; James J. Gosling, *Understanding, Informing, and Appraising Public Policy* (New York: Pearson, 2004).

80. Wilson, *Bureaucracy*, p. 88.

81. Rehfuss, *Public Administration as Political Process*, p. 45.

82. Ibid., p. 45.

83. Eric M. Uslaner, "Lobbying the President and the Bureaucracy," in Herrnson et al., *The Interest Group Connection*, pp. 205–12.

84. Campbell et al., "Coalition Building in Congress."

85. Uslaner, "Lobbying the President and the Bureaucracy."

86. Ibid.

87. Ibid.

88. Ibid.; Campbell et al.

89. Uslaner, "Lobbying the President and the Bureaucracy."

90. Dye, *Top Down Policy Making*.

91. Ibid.

92. Theodoulou and Kofinis, *The Art of the Game*.

93. Barbara Stolz, *Criminal Justice Policy Making* (Westport, Conn.: Praeger, 2002), pp. 9–10.

94. Ibid.

95. James E. Anderson, *Public Policymaking* (Boston: Houghton Mifflin, 2003).

96. G. C. Edwards III and S. J. Wayne, *Presidential Leadership* (New York: St. Martin's Press, 1981); R. B. Reich, "Policy Making in a Democracy," in *Current Issues in Public Administration*, ed. F. S. Lane (New York: St. Martin's Press, 1994), pp. 430–31.

97. L. C. Gawthrop, *Bureaucratic Behavior in the Executive Branch* (New York: Free Press, 1969), p. 25.

98. Meier, *Politics and the Bureaucracy*, p. 46.

99. Dye, *Top Down Policy Making*, p. 140.

100. Ibid.

101. Frederickson and Smith, *Public Administration Theory Primer*, p. 63.

102. Ibid., p. 42.

103. Meier, *Politics and the Bureaucracy*, p. 53.

104. Dye, *Top Down Policymaking*.

105. Stuart S. Nagel, *Encyclopedia of Policy Studies*, 2nd ed. (New York: Marcel Dekker, 1994), p. 132.

106. Ibid., pp. 134–35.

107. Meier, *Politics and the Bureaucracy*, p. 528.

108. Norton Long, "Bureaucracy and Constitutionalism," *American Political Science Review* 46 (1952): 808–18.

109. Theodoulou and Kofinis, *The Art of the Game*.

110. Anderson, *Public Policymaking*.

111. Ibid.

112. Dye, *Top Down Policy Making*, p. 145.

113. Harold D. Lasswell, *Politics: Who Gets What, When How* (New York: Whittlesey House, McGraw-Hill, 1936).

114. Meier, *Politics and the Bureaucracy*, p. 14.

115. Frederickson and Smith, *Public Administration Theory Primer*, p. 63; Stolz, *Criminal Justice Policy Making*, p. 145.

116. Anderson, *Public Policymaking*.

117. Ibid.; Rehfuss, *Public Administration as Political Process*.

118. Anderson, *Public Policymaking*.

119. Lael R. Keiser, "Why It Matters whether State Bureaucrats as Opposed to Federal Bureaucrats Administer Federal Programs," in Krause and Meier, *Politics, Policy, and Organizations*, pp. 207–32; Edward Bardach, *The Implementation Game* (Cambridge, Mass.: MIT Press, 1980); Martha Derthick, *New Towns In-Town* (Washington, D.C.: Urban Institute Press, 1972); Robert P. Stoker, *Reluctant Partners: Implementing Federal Policy* (Pittsburgh: University of Pittsburgh Press, 1991).

120. Keiser, "Why It Matters whether State Bureaucrats as Opposed to Federal Bureaucrats Administer Federal Programs," p. 207; Glenn Beamer, *Creative Politics: Taxes and Public Goods in a Federal System* (Ann Arbor: University of Michigan Press, 1999).

121. Keiser, "Why It Matters whether State Bureaucrats as Opposed to Federal Bureaucrats Administer Federal Programs," p. 207; Lael Keiser, "Street-Level Bureaucrats, Administrative Power, and Manipulation of Federal Social Security Disability Programs," *State Politics and Policy Quarterly* 1 (2001): 144–64.

122. Goodsell, *The Case for Bureaucracy*.

123. Nicholas Henry, *Public Administration and Public Affairs* (Englewood Cliffs, N.J.: Prentice Hall, 1995), p. 11.

8

Public Opinion and the Media

Chapter Outline

INTRODUCTION

Both the media and public opinion are part of the political and legislative process in the United States. The media bring to the public's attention those issues that are most pressing and provide a forum for debate regarding both the political and the legislative process. Public opinion can either support a particular policy or legislative bill or voice its opposition to a particular policy or bill. In either case, public opinion helps shape the outcome of many policies. The media and public opinion often work in concert with one another by the media reporting on public opinion and public opinion shaping what the media report on, thus combining for a very powerful player in the policy process. While it is well recognized that both have a tremendous impact on government, few people realize that both have important influences on the criminal justice system. This chapter discusses the powers of both public opinion and the media in shaping the public policy process and demonstrate that the powers of each of these institutions can have an enormous impact on criminal justice policy.

PUBLIC OPINION

Public opinion is an important aspect of the American democratic system. It is also an important element in the public policy process in that it includes the formation of crime policy. The reason this is based on the traditional concepts of democracy that generally consist of rule by the people, a government that reflects the will of the people, and a government that makes decisions based on public interest.[1] But for American democracy to work today, there must be some means of gauging the will of the people. Although the ballot box, editorials, and town meetings are often used, these do not represent all the people, only those who are registered and vote, those who take the time to write, and those who attend the meetings, respectively. In order to engage the will of all the people, from the media to the politicians, society has come to generally accept public opinion, as gauged through public opinion polls, as a means to represent the will of the people. These polls are then used to help legislators shape policy in such areas as crime. As Roberts has explained,

> The beliefs of public officials about public preferences for criminal justice policies affect political campaigns, decisions in individual cases, and criminal justice policy. Politicians' beliefs about the nature of public opinion probably derive from three sources: shared conventional wisdom, the perception of an association between

electoral success and support for repressive criminal justice policies, and the publication of survey findings that seem to demonstrate public support for harsher sentencing. It is clear then that public officials' beliefs about public opinion influence criminal justice policy.[2]

Therefore, public opinion and the way we measure it has become a crucial and integral part of the public policy process.

Public Opinion Defined

Public opinion can be defined as the distribution of individual preferences or evaluations of a given issue, candidate, or institution within a population.[3] In this case, distribution means the proportion of the population that holds a particular opinion as compared to those holding opposing viewpoints or those with no opinion at all. For example, in a 2009 Gallup poll, a question related to support of the death penalty found that 65 percent of the people supported it, 31 percent opposed it, and 5 percent were unsure or had no opinion.[4] (See Table 8.1.) This type of public opinion poll informs public officials how many people favor the death penalty, how many are against it, and how many are not sure or have no opinion. Thus, when formulating policy in this area, they have at least some notion of the public's will.

The extent to which public opinion influences government policy has, however, been a subject of much debate since the early twentieth century. Initially, there was a strong belief that public opinion did in fact form public policy, and it was beginning to be formed by public opinion polls. Walter Lippmann, a social commentator in the early 1920s, became a strong opponent of this reality. Lippmann believed that the average American was unable to understand the issues or even the rudimentary facts of the issues placed before him and was therefore incapable of shaping and directing public policy.[5] As Lippmann so harshly stated, "If the voter cannot grasp the details of the problems of the day because he has not the time, the interest or the knowledge, he will not have a better public opinion because he is asked to express his opinion more often."[6] So distraught over the ignorance of the American people, he followed up his first book with a second titled *The Phantom Public*, which described the lack of a true public, one capable of making policy decisions, in what was deemed a democratic society.[7] It should be noted, however, that Lippmann based his books not on public opinion surveys but rather on his own personal insights.

This manner of thinking continued throughout the early twentieth century and with the advent of modern-day survey research commencing in the 1930s, it was reaffirmed through numerous evaluations of this research. From what is now considered classic literature discussing public opinion and its formation, there was a consensus that the American people lacked the knowledge to formulate policy through public opinion and that, in actuality, policy was formed by the "elite."[8] Rather than seeing public opinion shape policy preferences, supporting the ideas of a true democracy, these individuals argued that policy was in reality formulated by elites.[9] However, V. O. Key's book *Public Opinion and American Democracy*[10] provided the key summation to this way of thinking but also the turning point in the literature when he stated,

> Government, as we have seen, attempts to mold public opinion toward support of the programs and policies it espouses. Given that endeavor, perfect congruence between public policy and public opinion could be government *of* public opinion rather than government *by* public opinion.[11]

Key explored the possibility that public opinion did, in fact, shape government policy but perhaps not necessarily in a direct manner. He attempted to show that Americans did have an

TABLE 8.1   Attitudes Toward the Death Penalty, 2009

Question: Are you in favor of the death penalty for a person convicted of murder?

Demographics	Yes, In Favor (%)	No, Not In Favor (%)	Don't Know/Refused (%)
National	65	31	5
Sex			
Male	69	27	4
Female	61	34	5
Race			
White	69	27	5
Black	41	52	7
Non-white	55	40	5
Age			
18–29	56	40	4
30–49	66	29	5
50–64	69	28	3
50+	68	28	4
65+	67	27	6
Education			
College postgraduate	48	49	4
College graduate	71	24	5
Some college	63	34	3
High school or less	73	20	7
Income			
$75,000+	67	29	4
$50,000–74,999	62	35	3
$30,000–49,999	69	26	5
$20,000–29,999	60	36	4
<$20,000	58	40	2
Region			
East	55	38	7
Midwest	63	34	3
South	69	27	3
West	69	25	6
Politics			
Republican	81	16	3
Democrat	48	47	5
Independent	67	28	5
Ideology			
Conservative	75	21	3
Moderate	62	30	7
Liberal	47	52	1

Source: Adapted from Kathleen Maguire and Ann Pastore, eds., *Sourcebook of Criminal Justice Statistics—2010* (Washington, D.C.: U.S. Department of Justice, 2010), available online at www.albany.edu/sourcebook/.

impact on the policy process and that Americans were "rational" in their decisions; however, the effect was generated indirectly. As one author explains, "If a representative form of government is assumed, it is likely that the public, at least indirectly, influences the decisions of public officials who depend on their constituents for positions of power."[12] Key was able to demonstrate that people do make rational choices when they are presented the facts revolving around an issue. The problem, however, lies in the fact that most issues are fragmented and placed before the American people in an obscure manner, producing irrational decisions. As Key explains, "Voters are not fools . . . the electorate behaves about as rationally and responsibly as we would expect, given the clarity of the alternatives presented to it and the character of the information available to it."[13]

The use of public opinion surveys did not assist in the stand that the American people were capable of making rational decisions on policy, for it was after multiple studies in the 1950s and 1960s that a key publication basically supported Lippmann's previous statements.[14] The authors of *The American Voter* found that the American people knew very little about current issues in government, party platforms, or what they themselves felt government should do. One of the authors, Converse, would follow up this study with his seminal study on mass belief systems by looking at three key topics: attitude consistency, stability of opinions over time, and levels of conceptualization.[15] What Converse found was consistent across all three topics, namely, that the American people were minimally consistent and minimally stable and that most had minimal levels of conceptualization when it came to the formation of their opinions. Hence, the American people, by and large, were found to be ignorant and lacking in the necessary capacities to make policy decisions.

There were, however, some researchers during the 1960s who attempted to argue that the American people were not as ignorant as the majority of researchers were claiming. V. O. Key, Jr., became the most outspoken of the critics as he took the position that Americans were rational and "responsible" in their decisions.[16] However, it was not until the 1970s that a specific response to *The American Voter* was published that joined several authors together to refute the findings in their book titled *The Changing American Voter*. Nie, Verba, and Petrocik analyzed the American public from the 1950s to the 1970s on a variety of subjects and found that the American people were, in fact, consistent and stable as well as some cautionary evidence that the levels of conceptualization had risen during this time period.[17] The foundation of their argument was the fact that people change as a response to the changing environment and that, as the 1960s placed greater demands on the people, they responded with greater levels of political sophistication. This argument would later be challenged in another play on titles in *The Unchanging American Voter*, where Smith would argue that the changing environment thesis is inherently wrong and that there is a permanence to the levels of sophistication held by individuals that is exclusive of the environment.[18]

The entire argument would once again be captured by two key publications in the 1990s, both of which conducted extensive reviews of past public opinion surveys, analyzed a multitude of issues, and conducted a historical analysis to determine world and domestic events as they related to the time of each survey. One book, *The Rational Public,* by Page and Shapiro, found that the public as a collective is stable and consistent and has a high level of conceptualization despite limited information and can be relied on for guiding public policy.[19] The other book, *The Changing American Mind,* by Mayer, found that the American people were far less rational then Page and Shapiro articulated and that their collective opinion was not necessarily stable or consistent over time but changing.[20] In addition, Mayer also did not find the high levels of conceptualization that Page and Shapiro found and discovered the collective public to have minimal levels but having the potential for increasing them through education.

Public opinion research has continually demonstrated the convictions for both sides of the issue, leaving many to wonder which side is accurate. Is public opinion in the aggregate consistent and stable over time, or does it fluctuate and change with no clear direction? If it can be said that there is a relationship between the determinants of public opinion stability, consistency, and conceptualization with human rationality, then, perhaps like the need for a continuum between rational and irrational actors, there is a need for a continuum between minimum and maximum levels of these three topics. The degree to which public opinion would be considered at a minimum or maximum would be determined by various factors, such as external events, individual preferences, and levels of media attention to a particular subject.

This allows one to dig even deeper into the human psyche to determine how one derives opinions if they have very little knowledge on a particular subject. If the individual has a strong philosophy, a concrete belief system, and knowledge of the topic at hand, one could concede that this individual will make a sound decision—not one that is necessarily "right" or "wrong" but one that is consistent with their belief system. If, on the other hand, the individual does not have a strong belief system and lacks knowledge regarding the topic, how does this individual reach a conclusion? More specifically, how does that individual reach a conclusion that is not ignorant, irrational, or useless? One method of explanation has been that people utilize simplistic shortcuts to derive logical conclusions to the question posed, or "heuristics."[21] Although people may not have formal and highly cognitive belief systems or knowledge on a particular subject, they can take the information they already have, simplify the complexity of the issue, and make dependable choices.[22] One type of heuristic that the authors most often cite is the "likability heuristic," which is predicated on whether one likes or dislikes the topic in question. Although an individual may not understand a particular policy in question, he or she may understand that it is a Democrat-supported policy, and, being a lifelong Democrat, support it as well. Hence, a likability heuristic is one that allows people to shortcut larger policy questions of which they may have little or no information about.

The psychological process of reasoning and choice is then capable of being one explanation of how citizens reach their conclusions. If a citizen is consistent and stable and has a high level of conceptualization of an issue, then this strong belief system will carry one through the process of answering the question posed. However, no one can ever have every piece of information available at any given moment, and, therefore, even those who may fall into this category must still rely on some heuristics. Those who are not consistent in their opinions, who are unstable in their beliefs, and who have minimal levels of conceptualization stand in a position to utilize heuristics on a more frequent basis. In the end, heuristics, like rationalization and formation of opinion, seems to exist largely on a sliding scale. Perhaps in the end it is not the use of the heuristics at question but rather the length of the shortcut taken.

The Study of Public Opinion

The study of public opinion throughout the twentieth century has yielded a broad and vast multidisciplinary body of evidence.[23] It has also generated a number of methods used in an attempt to assess public opinion, and this has also generated a number of issues and controversies in the interpretation of this data. The specific methods used tend to fall in the category of surveys and focus groups. The former generally falls into two types of surveys—those that are representative surveys where national and statewide surveys use a probability sampling procedure to ensure that the final sample on which the public opinion research is based pulls from all characteristics of the population (e.g., race, gender, ethnicity, or class).[24] Examples of these types of surveys are found constantly in the daily newspapers when the media report on surveys conducted by the Gallup Poll organization and others as they relate to the public's opinion on crime, the death penalty, and other related topics. The other method is a nonrepresentative survey that simply mails out surveys to a population at random but does not try to ensure that all characteristics of the population are met.

The other common method, the focus group, is an intensive discussion that attempts to delve deeper into understanding people's opinion and perceptions about current issues. They tend to use small groups (no more than 15), are usually selected to be representative of the larger population, and will often meet multiple times or will be created in various locations with multiple groups. An excellent example of this method as it relates to crime is found in Kathlyn Gaubatz's in-depth focus group study that attempted to understand how her 24 participants perceived crime and what they felt should be done about the problem of crime.[25]

There are many problems with the use of public opinion surveys. The first is that the surveys make some assumptions that the public has a working knowledge about crime and criminal justice, and this is generally not the case. The public generally has an overinflated estimation of crime rates. In one study of criminal justice students who should have had a better grasp on the number of homicides in our country (currently around 15,000 a year), many estimated over 1 million homicides each year, which would mean that roughly one in every 280 Americans is murdered each year.[26] In addition to the problems of crime estimations, most Americans do not have a realistic understanding of the criminal justice system, legal rights, legislative changes, U.S. Supreme Court decisions, or media bias (see the discussion later in this chapter).[27] Finally, it should be noted that there can be problems with the surveys themselves in that the questions may be too simplistic, they may force answers because of the single-question format, and the survey or survey questions may not provide sufficient information for the public to make an informed decision.[28] In short, surveys can often impose limitations on understanding the public's will.

Keeping the various aspects of public opinion research methods in mind, it is also important to understand the many issues revolving around the topic of public opinion. As previously mentioned, it has long been recognized in the study of public opinion that people do not walk around with political information and political opinions in their minds, ready to draw on them at any moment when asked what opinion they have on a particular subject. In fact, it has largely been the case that people know very little about most of the subjects they are questioned on but can still provide the necessary answers about a particular subject.[29] Over the twentieth century, many authors have criticized the American public for their perceived ignorance, while others have extolled the virtues of their opinions in the aggregate, claiming that together they respond to situations far more realistically than politicians or so-called elites. This, then, is a critical juncture in much of the literature on public opinion. Although humans may be said to be more than irrational (and often to be a totally rational actor), how these rational or semirational actors reach their conclusions is of key concern.

Another area of public opinion study has looked at the effect of outside influence on the outcome of public opinion. As those preferences of the individual are translated into collective opinion, one must ponder whether such outside forces as external world and national events, elite and expert opinions, the media, and changes in the three key societal divisions of the social, economic, and the polity play a major role in the formation of opinion in the aggregate. Mayer demonstrated that external events in government, policy, and politics had the largest impact on public opinion, the greatest impact on foreign policy, and a significant impact on domestic policy.[30] One can find and understand many examples of this, ranging from the impact of wars, whether they involve Americans or not, to the impact of such domestic terrorist events as the

World Trade Center bombing, the Oklahoma City bombing, and September 11, 2001. These external factors can have a significant and lasting effect on collective opinion.

The views of the elite are other factors that can play a major role in the outcome of public opinion. Does the opinion of the elite influence public opinion, or does public opinion influence the opinions of the elite? This is a question that has been wrestled with by most researchers exploring public opinion, and most have found that there is a little of both at work.[31] Page and Shapiro find that in some situations, elite opinions influence public opinion, specifically through such things as news commentaries reflecting elite opinion and popular presidents. They also find that in some cases, elite control is so strong that they can manipulate or mislead the public into a policy preference. These authors are not alone in stating that elite opinion is a powerful method for guiding public opinion.[32] However, all these authors also recognize that public opinion in the United States is largely an independent force that more often influences elite opinion than vice versa.

A part of elite opinion shaping public opinion, however, is not a direct force but rather an indirect force that is filtered through the media. It is well recognized that the media have an impact on public opinion and that it is generally elite opinion that is filtered to the American people through the media. In addition to acting as a filter, the methods that the media utilize to present the information from elites or the method in which the news is "framed" can have a major impact on how the public perceives information and hence an impact on their collective opinion.[33] Although there seems to be little dispute today that the media have an impact on public opinion, a disagreement does arise in the determination as to what extent they play a role (see the discussion later in this chapter).

Finally, one additional influence found in much of the literature is the impact that the changing social, economic, and polity environments have on public opinion in the aggregate. Whether one is looking at a specific issue, such as race, or multiple policies across time, there is much to be said for these three key societal divisions influencing public opinion.

The key themes that arise in the majority of research are education and information. The amount of education bears on an individual's decision-making process, as does the amount of information one has access to. As the United States has grown and developed technologically, the system for sharing information has moved "from informationally void to informationally based."[34] This in turn has created a system whereby people are no longer lacking in information but rather are now bombarded with information, creating a new scenario for understanding the decision-making process. As Americans once made decisions based on little information, now they can make decisions based on too much information. And, as Converse articulates, "good decision making requires good information," the trend may be to look at how Americans process this overabundance of information.[35] Education, in the past often considered a key to learning new information, may now become the key for being able to sort through information to make the determination of what is beneficial and what is not.

PUBLIC OPINION OF CRIME

Similar debates exist in the area of public opinion of crime and its relationship with crime policy. The questions of public opinion of crime affecting crime policy and the debate over whether public opinion of crime is rational in the United States are hotly debated. Gaubatz has adequately expressed the problem when she explained that "while the body of available information about public opinion on crime and criminal justice is large, it is not sufficient."[36] Despite this insufficiency, two other authors, Hurwitz and Peffley, have perhaps stated the issue more succinctly when they explained that "we know two things about public opinion on crime—it is salient and it matters."[37] Research on public opinion of crime, like other areas of public opinion research, has demonstrated time and time again that there is a strong relationship between public opinion of crime and crime policy in the United States, but understanding how and what impact it has is still not very clear.[38] Crime has also been consistently found to be a highly salient issue,[39] but it has also been demonstrated to be a highly volatile issue in regard to both public and political agendas. As Scheingold has argued, "The movement of crime on and off the political agenda is not readily explicable in terms of the salience of the issue to the public."[40] The problem over salience, however, is often primarily a derivative of the difficulty in understanding what is meant by the concept of "public opinion of crime."

The Most Important Problem

It is generally the case that when the issue of the "public opinion of crime" is considered, the discussion centers around the concept of the public's "fear of crime." However, this concept, which has been explored across multiple disciplines, has generally demonstrated little agreement over what is meant by these terms.[41] While most people believe they understand what is meant by "fear" and "crime," these terms have the potential for multiple interpretations, and this becomes important for understanding the phenomenon of "public opinion of crime." The term "crime" is perhaps the easier of the two to define because most people tend to associate the term with what is often referred to as "street crimes."[42] Although the definition of crime can also include white-collar crimes, political crime, and computer-related crime, these are generally not the images that the American people conjure up when someone mentions the word "crime." What are generally envisioned are homicides, rapes, and robberies as well as the more "contemporary crimes," such as domestic violence, school shootings, and mass murders by disgruntled employees.

The more troublesome aspect is defining what is meant by the word "fear." Warr summarizes the problem when he explains that "the phrase 'fear of crime' has acquired so many divergent meanings in the literature that it is in danger of losing any specificity whatsoever."[43] In a scholarly sense, it has lost much of its meaning, but the term still invokes a certain understanding from the layperson. While scholars have attempted to adjust their understanding of the public's perception of the term, they have managed to generate additional explanations of the terms that provide a deeper and fuller understanding of this generic phrase.

Some scholars have suggested that "fear of crime" is in reality a "concern for crime" in that people understand crime to be a serious problem in their community and the level of "fear" is actually the level of "concern" they have from their understanding of the number, types, and seriousness of the crimes in their neighborhoods.[44] Citizens may become more concerned as they hear of more friends, relatives, neighbors, and associates being victimized from the local media or from seeing the "symbols" that they attach to crime occurring in their neighborhoods, such as graffiti, broken windows, and abandoned vehicles in the streets. Fear of crime is then a level of concern for crime rather than an emotional fear of crime or fearing personal bodily harm or loss.

In some cases, the term "fear of crime" is often not about crime per se but about the perceived risk of victimization.[45] This is not inherently about the emotional reaction that people have in fearing crime but rather a perception of the "risk" they face in becoming a victim of a crime. It is reasoned that those who perceive a high risk of crime, or that they or a friend may become a victim of a crime, will be more afraid. Hence, they do not have a "fear of crime," but they experience what is seen as a "fear of victimization."

Another approach to the "fear of crime" is by looking at the threat of crime that people believe they face.[46] In this definition, the focus is on the threat that people believe they would face if they were to place themselves in a specific situation. This "threat" perspective is usually generated from the survey questions, "Is there any area where you live—that is, within a mile—where you would be afraid to walk alone at night? How about at home at night—do you feel safe and secure or not?" These types of questions focus not necessarily on the behaviors one exhibits, such as walking around one's neighborhood at night, but rather on the level of threat an individual perceives one would have if one did take that midnight stroll.

Finally, the last perspective on "fear of crime" is oriented on the behavior that people exhibit.[47] It is one thing to say that one is concerned about crime, fears the victimization of crime, or perceives a threat by crime, but it is an entirely different matter to say that one does in fact change or alter one's behavior out of fear for one's safety. If people do lock their doors at night and refuse to go outside after dark, they are engaging in avoidance behavior, and hence the fear for their safety, or the "fear of crime," has altered their lifestyle. While a large majority of people may adjust their behavior in response to crime, either consciously or unconsciously, it is really a matter of degree as to the level of fear one has of crime in this instance. While one may lock the doors at night before going to bed and this may be a response to one's concern for their safety, this behavior may not translate into actual "fear of crime."

While the literature and studies on citizens' fear of crime are mixed and the definitions often muddled, one thing that can be drawn from the discussion is that Americans' fear of crime is a complex issue. The literature does not definitively state that all Americans fear crime and are paralyzed by this fear. However, it also does not provide us with a definitive answer that crime is not a concern of the American people and that the fear of crime is a complete social fabrication. That in turn leaves us somewhere in the middle, struggling to determine how much Americans fear crime and to what degree this is driving America's public policy on crime. As a result, it is important to utilize the indicators available to understand the level of fear that Americans have of crime.

To gauge the level of fear in the United States, the use of survey questions is the primary means available, and there are essentially two methods that can be employed, either the direct or the indirect. The direct method of assessing public opinion of crime, or "fear of crime," is to raise the issue of crime immediately, providing respondents' time to think only about the issue of crime, and then assess to what degree do they fear crime. As the issue of crime is raised for them, it is expected that the response that crime is a problem would consistently be high. The indirect method is to assess public opinion by couching the question not in terms of a specific issue, such as crime, but in terms of all the issues they are currently facing or believe are important. In this manner, the salience of crime may be high or low depending on how pressing the issue of crime is to respondents in terms of all the possible issues they feel are important. By looking at the responses to both direct and indirect questions over time, a better assessment of Americans' fear of crime, concern for crime, and the salience of crime can be made.

When people are asked directly how much they fear crime, the results are often mixed and tend to fluctuate. A study conducted in 1980 asked Americans if they were "highly fearful" of becoming the victim of a violent crime, and 40 percent of those surveyed answered in the affirmative.[48] However, a similar study conducted in 1989 asking a similar question found that only 12 percent of those surveyed reported being "very fearful," while 44 percent reported they were "somewhat fearful."[49] There is often a great deal of fluctuation in these types of questions, which are asked sporadically and in various formats, thus providing little understanding of Americans' fear of crime. Questions that have consistently been asked across time, otherwise known as trend data, are not abundant but do appear to provide a better estimate for the level of fear in the United States.

TABLE 8.2   Respondents Reporting Fear of Walking Alone and Feeling Unsafe at Home at Night, 1972–2009

Question: Is there any area near where you live—that is, within a mile—where you would be afraid to walk alone at night? How about when you're at home at night—do you feel safe and secure, or not

Year	Yes, Afraid (%)	Feel Unsafe at Home at Night (%)
1972	42	57
1975	45	55
1977	45	55
1981	45	55
1983	45	55
1989	43	57
1990	40	59
1992	44	56
1993	43	56
1996	39	60
1997	38	61
2000	34	66
2001	30	69
2002	35	64
2003	36	64
2004	32	67
2005	38	62
2006	37	63
2007	37	62
2008	37	63
2009	34	66

Source: Adapted from Kathleen Maguire and Ann Pastore, eds., *Sourcebook of Criminal Justice Statistics—2010* (Washington, D.C.: U.S. Department of Justice, 2010), available online at www.albany.edu/sourcebook/.

Poll Trends

The two well-known public opinion polls, the Gallup and Harris polls, have asked the American people for over three decades the key questions that have been utilized to gauge public opinion of crime.[50] The Gallup poll has asked the question, "Is there any area near where you live—that is, within a mile—where you would be afraid to walk alone at night?"[51] The response to this is very informative; for in 1975, the percentage of respondents who answered "yes" was 45 percent and in 1983, nearly a decade later, it remained at 45 percent. (See Table 8.2.) However, in 1996, it had dropped to 39 percent; in 2001, it was at a low of 30 percent; and has since stabilized in the mid-30s. Despite a modest gain from the mid-1960s to the mid-1970s, the answer to the question has remained very constant over time. In addition, the power of this survey question can be seen in

TABLE 8.3	Respondents Reporting Whether they Feel Afraid to Walk Alone at Night in their Own Neighborhood, 1973–2002

Question: Is there any area right around here—that is, within a mile—where you would be afraid to walk alone at night?

Year	Yes (%)	No (%)
1973	41	59
1974	45	55
1976	44	56
1977	45	54
1980	43	56
1982	47	53
1984	42	57
1985	40	59
1987	38	51
1988	40	59
1989	40	60
1990	41	58
1991	43	56
1993	43	57
1994	47	52
1996	42	57
1998	41	57
2000	39	60
2002	32	67

Source: Adapted from Kathleen Maguire and Ann Pastore, eds., *Sourcebook of Criminal Justice Statistics—2010* (Washington, D.C.: U.S. Department of Justice, 2010), available online at http://www.albany.edu/sourcebook/.

the fact that it was included in the General Social Survey (GSS) from 1973 to the early 2000s and it reported similar findings with the percentage-point levels of respondents stating "yes" in the low to mid-forties, with only the year 1987 deviating from this with a response rate of thirty-eight percentage points. (See Table 8.3.)

In turning to the Harris poll, which has asked the question, "In the past year, do you feel the crime rate in your area has been increasing, decreasing, or has it remained the same as it was before?" we find that the responses are very similar in that they are moderately high and remain relatively stable over time.[52] (See Table 8.4.) This would lead to the conclusion that the fear of crime has altered little over time despite the rising and declining crime rates during this same time period.[53] In addition, despite the fact that many argue that these two questions are poorly worded, the Gallup and GSS questions fail to mention the word "crime," and the Harris poll utilizes the term "crime rates" rather than simply "crime."[54] These two questions are the longest-running questions attempting to assess Americans' fear of crime that are available for understanding this phenomenon. As a result, they have become well used in a variety of disciplines for understanding Americans' fear of crime.

Because the two questions have often been criticized, two more recent questions have entered into the Gallup poll's repertoire of public opinion questions related to the issue of crime.

TABLE 8.4   Attitudes Toward Crime Rate in Own Area, 1967–1993

Question: In the past year, do you feel the crime rate in your area has been increasing, decreasing, or has it remained the same as it was before?

Year	Increasing (%)	Decreasing (%)	Remained Same (%)	Not Sure (%)
1967	46	4	43	7
1970	62	3	30	5
1973	48	7	40	5
1975	70	3	24	3
1978	46	7	42	5
1981	68	4	27	1
1982	59	6	34	1
1983	41	15	43	1
1984	33	21	44	2
1985	40	17	42	1
1991	55	5	39	1
1993	54	5	39	2

Source: Adapted from Kathleen Maguire and Ann Pastore, eds., *Sourcebook of Criminal Justice Statistics—2010* (Washington, D.C.: U.S. Department of Justice, 2010), available online at www.albany.edu/sourcebook/.

The first asks, "Is there more crime in your area than there was a year ago, or less?" (See Table 8.5.) This question presents the word "crime" in the question and remains focused on the respondents' "area," providing for a more specific answer to the issue of crime. Once again, the respondents' answers have remained fairly high and consistent over time in responding that there has been more crime in their area. In addition, a second question that has been utilized by the Gallup poll has shifted the focus from the respondents' "area" to asking about the level of crime throughout the United States. Surprisingly, the answers overwhelmingly state that there is more crime in the United States than the previous year, and although there was some decline in the late 1990s, the level stating that there is more crime in their area has returned to three-quarters of the respondents (74% in 2009), despite the realization that crime rates have remained low and stable. (See Table 8.6.) In sum, it is clear that when asked specifically about the issue of crime, citizens tend to respond in the affirmative that crime is a problem and that these responses have, for the most part, remained fairly consistent over time. Although this is assuredly not indicative of the actual rise and fall of the crime rates over time, it is an indicator that when Americans are asked specifically about the problem of crime, there is a tendency for them to respond that it is a problem, that they fear crime, and that there is more rather than less crime in their area and in the United States.

According to several researchers, because direct, or closed, questions can "sharply restrict frames of reference by focusing attention on the alternatives offered, no matter how impoverished those alternatives may be and no matter how much effort is made to offer respondents freedom to depart from them,"[55] the use of open and essentially indirect questions about crime are preferred. The most prominent of the indirect questions related to public opinion of crime, is derived from the Gallup poll's question, that has been asked consistently over time for the past fifty years and that is, "What do you think is the most important problem facing the country today?"[56] This question has been dubbed the "most important problem" time-series

TABLE 8.5   Attitudes Toward Level of Crime in Own Area, 1972–2009

Question: Is there more crime in your area than there was a year ago, or less?

Year	More (%)	Less (%)	Same (%)	No Opinion (%)
1972	51	10	27	12
1975	50	12	29	9
1977	43	17	32	8
1981	54	8	29	9
1983	37	17	36	10
1989	53	18	22	7
1990	51	18	24	8
1992	54	19	23	4
1996	46	24	25	5
1997	46	32	20	2
1998	31	48	16	5
2000	34	46	15	5
2001	26	52	18	4
2002	37	34	24	5
2003	40	39	19	2
2004	37	37	22	4
2005	47	33	18	2
2006	51	30	15	4
2007	51	29	17	4
2008	44	31	19	5
2009	51	29	16	4

Source: Adapted from Kathleen Maguire and Ann Pastore, eds., *Sourcebook of Criminal Justice Statistics—2010* (Washington, D.C.: U.S. Department of Justice, 2010), available online at www.albany.edu/sourcebook/.

question and is considered to be the best available gauge of the public's opinion as well as the public's agenda.[57] It can be considered a gauge of the public's agenda for the fact it provides an understanding of what the American people focus their attention on at any given time.[58] It is the citizens' policy preference and what they would like to see addressed by the government. In most cases, the public's agenda is operationalized through public opinion.[59] The public's opinion at any given moment on what they consider the most serious issue that the United States currently faces creates the "list" of policy issues that are deemed the public's "highest priorities."[60] This list, then, provides a legitimization process for government to begin addressing various issues through allocation of resources, implementation, and evaluation of various programs and policies.

The specific question asks the respondents to voice their opinion as to what they feel is the most important problem facing the nation, and the aggregated data are then utilized to detail where the public's concerns lie. This allows for the top problems facing the country to be examined and assessed against the entire world of problems facing the country. In regard to crime, it demonstrates that crime has been a highly salient issue that has had an on-again/off-again

TABLE 8.6   Attitudes Toward Level of Crime in the United States, 1989–2009

Question: Is there more crime in the United States than there was a year ago, or less?

Year	More (%)	Less (%)	Same (%)	No Opinion (%)
1989	84	5	5	6
1990	84	3	7	6
1992	89	3	4	4
1996	71	15	8	6
1997	64	25	6	5
1998	52	35	8	5
2000	47	41	7	5
2001	41	43	10	6
2002	62	21	11	6
2003	60	25	11	4
2004	53	28	14	5
2005	67	21	9	3
2006	68	16	8	9
2007	71	14	8	6
2008	67	15	9	9
2009	74	15	6	5

Source: Adapted from Kathleen Maguire and Ann Pastore, eds., *Sourcebook of Criminal Justice Statistics—2010* (Washington, D.C.: U.S. Department of Justice, 2010), available online at www.albany.edu/sourcebook/.

relationship over time. In the 1940s and 1950s, the aggregate response to the question was typically less than 1 percent. In the early 1960s, the responses jumped to levels averaging around 2 percent. It was not until 1968 that the response rate to crime being the "most important problem" would rise to such a level that it was considered the third most important problem. Crime would not become the number one problem facing the country until 1994 coinciding with President Clinton's support for the passage of the Violent Crime Control and Law Enforcement Act of 1994 and his "100,000 Cops" initiative. That year, 37 percent of those responding to the question felt that crime was serious enough to be the "most important problem," and several other national surveys supported these high response rates.[61] The following year, 1995, crime would once again be considered the "most important problem facing the country," and in 1996 it would move to the position of second "most important problem." By the turn of the twenty-first century, crime and drugs had fallen off the top problems facing the nation and after September 11, 2001, were replaced with the issue of war, terrorism, the economy, and high cost of living. (See Table 8.7.)

Who Fears Crime?

It is more or less clear that Americans fear crime. *Who* fears crime is another question that scholars have investigated. By investigating who fears crime, we gain insight into why people fear crime. Two of the most commonly analyzed attributes are gender and age. These two attributes reveal that women are more fearful of crime than men and that the elderly have a greater fear of crime than the young.[62] This is in spite of the fact that women and the elderly face a significantly

TABLE 8.7   "Most Important Problem" Over Time, 1968–2008

Question: What do you think is the most important problem facing the country today?

Year	Most Important	Second Most Important	Third Most Important
1968	Vietnam	Race relations	**Crime**
1969	Vietnam	**Crime**	Race relations
1970	Campus unrest	Vietnam	Foreign problems
1971	Vietnam	Economy	Foreign problems
1972	Vietnam	Inflation	**Drugs**
1973	Cost of living	**Drugs**	**Crime**
1974	Energy crisis	Cost of living	Government corruption
1975	Cost of living	Unemployment	Government corruption
1976	Cost of living	Unemployment	**Crime**
1977	Cost of living	Unemployment	Energy problems
1978	Cost of living	Energy problems	Unemployment
1979	Cost of living	Foreign problems	Energy problems
1980	Foreign problems	Cost of living	Energy problems
1981	Cost of living	Unemployment	**Crime**
1982	Cost of living	Unemployment	Budget cuts
1983	Unemployment	Inflation	Fear of wars
1984	Threat of war	Unemployment	Government spending
1985	Threat of war	Unemployment	Government spending
1986	Foreign tensions	Unemployment	Federal deficit
1987	Unemployment	Federal deficit	Economy
1988	Federal deficit	Economy	**Drugs**
1989	Economy	**Drugs**	Poverty
1990	**Drugs**	Federal deficit	Poverty
1991	Economy	**Drugs**	Poverty
1992	Economy	Unemployment	Poverty
1993	Economy	Unemployment	Poverty
1994	**Crime**	Economy	Unemployment
1995	**Crime**	Economy	Federal deficit
1996	Economy	**Crime**	Federal deficit
1997	**Crime**	Economy	**Drugs**
1998	**Crime**	Moral decline	Education
1999	Moral decline	**Crime**	Education
2000	Education	Moral decline	**Crime**/cost of living
2001	Moral decline	Education	**Crime**/government
2002	Terrorism	Economy	War
2003	War	Economy	Terrorism/ Unemployment
2004	War	Economy	Unemployment/Terrorism
2005	War	Economy	Terrorism
2006	War	Economy	Unemployment
2007	War	Immigration	Cost of Living
2008	Economy	Cost of Living	War

Source: Adapted by author from George Gallup, *The Gallup Poll: Public Opinion* (Wilmington, Del.: Scholarly Resources, Inc., 1964–1996), and *The Gallup Organization Homepage,* "Gallup Social and Economic Indicators—Most Important Problem," available online at www.gallup. com/poll/indicators/indmip.asp. Data obtained January 2002. Updated utilizing Kathleen Maguire and Ann Pastore, eds., *Sourcebook of Criminal Justice Statistics—2010* (Washington, D.C.: U.S. Department of Justice, 2010), available online at www.albany.edu/sourcebook/.

reduced chance of becoming the victims of crime. In regard to race, some studies suggest that Hispanics fear crime the most, followed by blacks and then whites.[63] Other attributes, such as those in the underclass, those that have been previously victimized, those with high exposure to the media, and those who live in urban settings, all showed higher rates of fear.[64]

Attributes such as these do not tell the whole story, of course; most important are the opinions that underlie these attributes and/or additional factors (such as experience) that might impact one's perception of crime. One factor that would seem to have the most impact on why someone would fear crime is prior victimization. While some researchers have found this to have a high impact on perceptions, others have found it to have a limited impact or no impact at all.[65] As Skogan and Maxfield's study explains, it is most likely the case that prior victimization "cannot account for much of the overall variation in levels of fear (of crime) in the general population, although it certainly may be linked to the fears of those who were directly victimized."[66] Another factor that may explain the high rates of fear is actually knowing friends and/or relatives who have been victimized.[67] Of course, many people fear crime even though they have not been victimized or do not know anyone who has been victimized. To understand this fear, we need to look at additional external factors.

The primary external factor found to play a role in affecting the public perception of crime is the media.[68] Graber reports in her research that 95 percent of the respondents stated that their primary source for information on crime was through the mass media, and Savelsburg demonstrates that the mass media reflect and form public opinion, leaving little doubt that the media are major players in the public opinion of crime in the United States.[69] However, where there exists much debate is specifically how the media impact the public perception of crime.[70] At the very least, the data demonstrate a strong correlation between the fear of crime and the rate of media exposure, especially high rates of television exposure (see the discussion later in this chapter).

One additional external factor that seems to impact an individual's fear of crime is living in an urban setting.[71] In general, research demonstrates that the larger the population size of a city, the greater the fear of crime.[72] There are many reasons for this higher rate of fear. They include an increased perception of risk, an increased awareness of the symbols of crime, and the higher rates of nonwhites living in the inner city.[73] In several survey studies, the relationship between higher rates of nonwhites living in an area and the fear of crime has been studied by focusing on the residential proximity of whites and blacks. Generally, these studies suggest that the closer whites live to blacks, the more whites fear crime.[74]

While there is some consensus on *who* fears crime, there is less consensus regarding *why* people fear crime. In a more recent survey of public opinion and crime issues, specifically the National Crime and Justice Survey conducted in 1995, the conclusions of who fears crime supported past research on the topic, but again the understanding of why people fear crime was mixed.[75] In a discussion of the articles based on this survey, Haghighi and Sorenson conclude that "future studies should include some contextual variables such as political, cultural, and community aspects in assessing fear of crime."[76] It is on the political contextual variables that we now focus.

IMPACT ON POLICY PROCESS

There is a large split in the understanding of whether elites impact on the public perception of crime or whether actual rises in crime and awareness to growing crime activity cause the public to become concerned, hence influencing the elites to "do something." A large body of research has focused on the fact that the elites play the major role in forming and shaping the public perception

TABLE 8.8	Reported Confidence in Selected Institutions

Question: I am going to read you a list of institutions in American society. Please tell me how much confidence you, yourself, have in each one—a great deal, quite a lot, some, or very little?[a]

Year	Criminal Justice	Police	U.S. Supreme Court	Newspapers	Television News
1996	19	60	45	32	36
1997	19	59	50	35	34
1998	24	58	50	33	34
1999	23	57	49	33	34
2000	24	54	47	37	36
2001	NA	57	50	36	34
2002	27	59	50	35	35
2003	29	61	47	33	35
2004	34	64	46	30	30
2005	26	63	41	28	28
2006	25	58	40	30	31
2007	19	54	34	22	23
2008	20	58	32	24	24
2009	28	59	39	25	23

[a]Data shown for responses "a great deal" or "quite a lot."

Source: Adapted from Kathleen Maguire and Ann Pastore, eds., *Sourcebook of Criminal Justice Statistics—2010* (Washington, D.C.: U.S. Department of Justice, 2003), available online at www.albany.edu/sourcebook/.

of crime[77] (Table 8.8). Others argue that people become concerned about crime and crime issues and that the actions taken by the state are actually reflections of the public's demands and frustrations with other societal events and demands on their sensibilities.[78] A more recent study, utilizing a regression analysis of crime rates, media initiatives, and state initiatives as correlated to crime as the most important problem facing the nation, concluded that both the elite and the media have been the key variables in shaping public concern on "street crime" and drug issues.[79] This then leads to the final question on whether public opinion shapes crime policy or whether crime policy, as formulated by the elites, forms public opinion of crime?

As one author concludes, "public opinion on crime and punishment is a complex mix of perception, reason, emotion, and social ideals of justice."[80] This statement once again gives credence to the multiple factors that make it difficult to determine the plausibility of which is the cause and which is the effect. Returning to Key's statement that public opinion most likely affects policy but most likely affects it indirectly is perhaps the best understanding for the public opinion–crime policy relationship as well. What one author concludes in a more recent study on public opinion provides some strong possibilities for explanation in that

> the rising tide of media attention captures the attention of political leaders, which promotes even more coverage and which may further increase public concern. Action is demanded from political leaders and the criminal justice system, and the salience of crime and justice issues is temporarily increased. Recurring cycles of this amplification process may lead to ill-considered, reactive, and dysfunctional legislation.[81]

Although certainly plausible, this relationship is distinctly a hypothesis that should be tested in the future to determine the cycle of public opinion, agenda setting, policymaking, and policy implementation as it relates to crime.

The final question that is brought to bear on the issue of public opinion lies in whether public opinion influences public policy or whether public policy influences public opinion. After all, as previously stated, in a democratic society the most highly desired goal is for the public to influence policy. What is found by the majority of research is that there is perhaps a synthesis of the two that depends on many of the previous factors discussed in order to determine the degree to which this is applicable. It becomes situationally based, focusing on the complexity of the issue, external events, how elites perceive the issue, how the media frame the issue, and key factors that involve the social, economic, and polity. Therefore, to state definitively that one affects the other is not plausible given the host of other factors, but it must be analyzed, as each individual component of public opinion has been, on a continuum. Based on the research, it may be safe to conclude that the end of the continuum closest to public opinion influencing public policy seems to bear the greater weight; however, there is the need for a caveat. It is perhaps V. O. Key, Jr., who recognized what is perhaps the key to understanding this relationship. He points out that public opinion does in fact shape public policy, but it does so indirectly, not directly, as a result of a multitude of factors, many of which have been previously described. One author, specifically focused on the topic of the public opinion of crime and criminal justice, has similarly concluded that "public opinion may well exercise an important, although indirect, influence on the criminal justice system."[82] The indirect effect, as related to crime, may lie in the public's fear of crime.

In order to understand the public's fear of crime in a political context, it is important to focus on how the public guides and controls public policy. There are multiple ways that the government can respond to public opinion, ranging from policymaking to policy funding. Public opinion can have either positive or negative effects; "public opinion may sometimes direct government to do something, but it more often constrains government from doing something."[83] One of the most serious constraints that any policy faces is the need for funding, and this can become even more acute if the public is not supportive.[84] One example is the recent health care debate; government appeared ready to respond to public opinion and provide national health care, but the public (and special interests) did not appear ready to bear the costs of this policy change. However, if the public is fully supportive of a particular policy, then public opinion may support the budget expenditures even if the budget is limited.

Crime appears to be such an issue. The public appears both willing to declare crime as a problem and willing to pay more money to combat crime. We feel that this concern coupled with commitment for spending is very important. In effect, it demonstrates that Americans have a very real concern or fear of crime. In other words, the fact that Americans are willing to ask government to spend more of their tax dollars to fight crime suggests the degree to which they fear crime is very real.

We have already noted that American's fear crime more despite the decline in the actual crime rate. A similar trend exists when one examines attitudes toward the level of spending to halt the rising crime rate. Survey data from the National Opinion Research Center has shown that in 1980, 69 percent of the people surveyed felt that "too little" was being spent on "halting the rising crime rate."[85] In 1994, the percentage of people who believed "too little" was being spent had risen to 75 percent.[86] The national average from 1980 to 1994 was 69 percent, and according to one study there is apparently little difference in this opinion across gender, race, age, education, income, occupation, region, religion, and politics.[87] The American people, by and large, feel that

TABLE 8.9	Respondents Indicating Too Little is Spent on Crime and Drugs	

Question: We are faced with many problems in this country, none of which can be solved easily or inexpensively. I'm going to name some of the problems, and for each one I'd like you to tell me whether you think we're spending too much money on it, too little money, or about the right amount. First (problem) are we spending too much, too little, or about the right amount on (problem)?[a]

Year	Halting the Rising Crime Rate %	Dealing with Drug Addiction %
1973	64	65
1974	66	60
1975	65	55
1976	65	58
1977	65	55
1978	64	55
1981	69	59
1982	71	57
1983	67	60
1984	68	63
1985	63	62
1986	64	58
1987	68	65
1988	72	71
1989	73	71
1990	70	64
1991	65	58
1993	71	60
1994	75	60
1996	67	58
1998	61	58
2000	59	59
2002	56	57

[a]Data shown for response "too little."

Source: Adapted from Kathleen Maguire and Ann Pastore, eds., *Sourcebook of Criminal Justice Statistics—2010* (Washington, D.C.: U.S. Department of Justice, 2010), available online at www.albany.edu/sourcebook/.

too little is being spent to address the problem of crime and are more or less willing to see the rate of spending increase. (See Table 8.9. Note: The survey question has not been asked since 2002.)

Generally, this call for more spending to deal with crime has become a reality. As we have seen, government expenditures on the "administration of justice" have risen significantly from 1965 to 1992.[88] From 1982 to 1992 alone, there was a 290 percent increase in expenditures at the federal level and a 154 percent increase in spending at the state and local levels.[89] In addition to these expenditures, additional funds were directed to specific crime programs, such as the Edward Byrne Memorial State and Local Law Enforcement Assistance Program and the portion of the Crime Control Act of 1994 directed at hiring 100,000 new police officers. All of these expenditures have been in response to factors other than "rising crime rates" since there has been a steady decline in crime rates during this period.

At this point, it must be understood that public opinion shapes and molds public policy by placing those issues of concern to the American people on the political agenda and that crime is a constant in American life. Despite the fact that crime rates have been falling for over ten years, concern for crime or the perception that crime is still rising continues unabated. Since objective crime rates do not correlate with the rise and fall of crime as a salient issue and since its placement on and off the agenda occurs for no explicable reason, the question that begs to be answered is, What forms the public opinion of crime? As one author has stated, "Salience is only partly a result of changes in objective phenomena," and "it is clearly influenced by media, political campaigns and all of the other diffuse sources."[90] We must then look to these other sources that create the public opinion of crime.

One study, centered on how people gather their information about crime, reported that it was derived from several sources, "by observation, from reports by those around them, from the media, and through direct personal experience."[91] Although gathering information and public opinion must be seen as two distinct events, the gathering of information does influence the individual opinion and hence the aggregate opinion. We should then consider all the information or stimuli revolving around crime, and this can be placed into two categories. The first category is personal, including not only personal experiences, such as being the victim of a crime, but also personal awareness of crime. This awareness is independent of the media and may be generated by a feeling about one's neighborhood, through information provided by friends and neighbors, or possibly from a sense of fear. The second category is the media, whether real news, documentaries, or fictitious entertainment. However, this must not be limited to thinking of the media as generating information on crime promoting crime, or reflecting "personal" incidents of crime but rather also as a conduit for information on crime. Almost everything else that we see and hear, whether it is presidential rhetoric on crime, the rise and fall of the crime rates, or the latest police incident, is communicated through some form of media: newspapers, radio, and especially television. The media are our primary sources for crime information, and this impacts, regardless of whether the media is the initiator or the conduit of crime information, the public opinion of crime.

The personal category is one source from which the public gathers their perception of crime.[92] Whether it is through actually experiencing crime as a victim, a witness, or having a close personal friend or relative who has been victimized, this can have an impact on the public's perception of crime. Equally, "when we hear friends and relatives talk about their experiences," we grow aware of the crime problem, and it may become a salient issue for an individual, but it will also affect opinion in the aggregate.[93] Although there is agreement to the fact that personal experiences and personal awareness do impact the public perception of crime, there is some debate as to the intensity. While some research has shown that personal experiences are so strong that they "override media images and evaluations,"[94] some consider it to be equal with the media,[95] while others have found no relationship between victimization and an increased or altered perception of crime.[96] There still exists much debate over the relationship of personal experience, personal awareness, and the perception of crime in the aggregate.[97] In any case, this personal influence stands alone from the influences of the media and works to some degree on the individual perception of crime and, in turn, whether directly or indirectly, on the public perception of crime.

The media, however, seem to play the larger role in forming public perception of crime. As Jacobs and Shapiro articulate, "There is substantial evidence now that public opinion is influenced by the messages and interpretations communicated through the mass media."[98] Essentially, "the news media reflect and form public opinion"[99] through various media but specifically through the newspapers, radio, and television. Adding the fact that Graber reports in her research that 95 percent of the respondents stated their primary source for information on crime was through the mass media, there is little doubt that the media play a major role in shaping public opinion.[100] In addressing the media, it is important to also look to those events at all stages of the policy process that influence the media or that the media report on, for despite the fact they are filtered to the public through the media, they have an impact on the public perception of crime in their own right. These events include both local and state politics regarding crime; congressional rhetoric; presidential rhetoric regarding the crime problem, federal, state, and local initiatives addressing the crime problem; and the criminal justice system, including the police, courts, and corrections.

Although Tip O'Neill explained that "all politics are local," one could easily articulate that "all crimes are local," especially street crimes. Violent, property, and drug abuse crimes are committed predominantly at the local level, and the politicization of crime also occurs mainly at the local level, with some response by the state level. When particularly heinous crimes or crime waves occur, it is the local and state politicians who must answer to the outrage of their constituents. In some cases, as members of the public, politicians may be just as outraged about the crime problem as their constituents and will utilize their position to either solve or at least alleviate the problem. Once local and state politicians begin politicizing the issue of crime, the media will then not only report on the speeches and programs implemented but will most likely explore crime as an issue and add their own commentary, thus providing information both directly and as a conduit for the American people.

Although crime is largely a local problem, the politicalization of crime creates, according to Scheingold, "something of a paradox: In local politics, where the burdens of crime are the most concrete and where the primary responsibilities for policymaking reside, crime is less a political issue than it is in national politics, where crime is an abstraction and policy responsibilities are minimal."[101] As Scheingold would describe in a later article, street crime is not only a salient issue but also a valence issue because very few people come out in support of crime. Therefore, although crime is a local political issue, it also makes its appearance, via the media, on the national level by way of both congressional and presidential rhetoric.

The congressional rhetoric in regard to crime has grown distinctly during the span of 30 years as "the national government of the United States assumed ever greater responsibility for making, administering, and funding the country's criminal justice policies."[102] As responsibility for crime has increased, so too has the rhetoric on crime. Because all the members of the House and Senate cannot ignore the fact that crime is a highly salient and valence issue and no politician wants to be seen as "soft on crime," the rhetoric of crime is attractive to the politician politically and is attractive to the media for ratings.

Although congressional rhetoric receives a great deal of attention by the news media and hence the public, nothing can compare to the ability of presidential rhetoric to shape the public opinion on crime. Numerous studies have been conducted to gauge the ability of the president of the United States to shape and form public attitudes, and it is generally accepted that presidents can influence the public's policy agenda.[103] However, once again, the majority of presidential rhetoric received, ranging from the State of the Union Address to the queries of the media themselves, is filtered through the media to the American people.

In the end, as local, state, and national rhetoric is heard on crime, the issue must move through the policy process as described earlier and must eventually be turned into some form of initiative that the governments can implement. Ranging from small modifications implemented on the local level, such as changing the way the police are deployed, to large federal bills attacking crime on multiple levels, such as the Omnibus Crime Bill of 1994, these types of initiatives receive a great deal of attention through the media as they are debated, voted on, and implemented. As Beckett found in her study on street crime and drug use and its effect on the public agenda, "State initiatives on crime and drugs is not consistently explicable in terms of public concern around those issues, but plays a consistent role in shaping public opinion."[104] As most state initiatives on crime are reported to the American people through the media, once again the shaping of public opinion on crime is processed through the media. However, Beckett also found, to some degree, that media initiatives on the issue of street crime and drug use also played a role in the public perception on these issues.

Finally, in the implementation stage of the policy process, it is the responsibility of the criminal justice system, consisting of the police, courts, and corrections, to carry out the initiatives. There is little doubt that the police are the most visible component of the criminal justice system and that the attention by the media to their actions are prominently displayed in all the various types of media. Whether it is coverage of an arrest by the police or a story on corrupt police officers, all the daily media coverage assists in forming the public's opinion of crime. Although not as visible as the police, the court system can have an impact on the public opinion of crime because of the media's review of certain cases, especially in highly visible cases or cases where individuals are released on a technicality. Although there is little research on the local and state courts' impact on public opinion, there is a large body of research pertaining to the relationship between the Supreme Court and public opinion. Finally, the often silent component of the criminal justice system, corrections, can also play a part in the public's perception of crime, especially during reports of prison riots, escapes, or prisoner lawsuits. Again, in the majority of situations, the public receives information of crime and the criminal justice system either processed through the media or directly from the media.

The final area to consider is the relationship between the information obtained through the media and the information obtained from personal experience and awareness. In conducting research to determine the effect of media on public perceptions of crime and personal experiences on the perceptions of crime, it becomes difficult to separate the two forms of information to determine which is the primary influence on public opinion.[105] It is then "more likely that there is a process of mutual reinforcement between the environmental cues ... and the individual's private information gained from personal experience" or personal awareness.[106] Additionally, the media report on the personal experience with crime when they cover incidents of crime for the evening news and on the personal awareness of crime when they "package" crime to present an overview or commentary on crime and drugs. Since the media are obviously such an integral part of public opinion, it is to a discussion of the media's role in the public policy process that we now turn.

THE MEDIA

The term "mass media" refers to "media that are easily, inexpensively, and simultaneously accessible to large segments of a population."[107] The media consist of print (all printed information, such as newspapers, magazines, and books) and broadcast media (television, radio, film, recordings, and the Internet). These make up the major source of information for most Americans. While some people tend to envision a very localized media because everyone has local newspapers and news stations, nothing could be further from the truth. For example, in regard to newspapers, while there are approximately 2,000 newspapers published daily in the United States, most tend to receive their news information from a handful of sources. Most of these newspapers subscribe to the Associated Press (AP) newswire, which is the largest news organization in the world. This service provides all the other newspapers stories that they can reproduce in their papers when they subscribe to the AP service. As a result, roughly one-half of all newspapers are providing the same story, usually with just a different headline. Taken further, the *New York Times* is often considered the newspaper of record, and so many newspapers in the country follow the

Times' lead. Read the *Times* one day and then a local paper over the next several days, and you will find many of the articles repeated. And while there are other major newspapers that smaller newspapers will pull from, such as the *Washington Post* and *USA Today,* these papers tend to get much of their news from the other sources as well. Therefore, despite the numerous choices available to the American consumer, the news tends to come from only a handful of sources.

It is also very clear that most Americans derive their news information from all the various media sources. According to a 1984 Roper poll, "20% of Americans received most of their news from both newspapers and television, 24% from newspapers without television, and 49% from television alone."[108] Another study, in 1992, found that 60 percent of Americans rely on television to provide them their news information.[109] A more recent study found that over 50 percent of Americans were now turning to the World Wide Web for their news. It is clear that most Americans gain their news from the media, but what about their crime news?

One study specifically related to the media's influence on crime, found that 95 percent of the respondents in the study reported their primary source for information on crime was the media.[110] A more recent study found that 96 percent of Americans rely on the media for their information about crime.[111] Simply stated, most people tend to gain their understandings and beliefs regarding crime from the media.

It has also been found through numerous studies of media content that crime reports are a consistent and durable news commodity.[112] As the saying goes, "if it bleeds, it leads." The media are quite taken with the topic of crime, so crime consists of a substantial portion of all the media. For example, research has demonstrated that between 22 and 28 percent of all newspaper stories are related to the issue of crime.[113] Crime on television has been found to consist of between 10 and 13 percent of all national televised news and over 20 percent of all locally televised news.[114] In sum, the proportion of crime news coverage tends to fall between 5 and 25 percent of the total news.[115] (See Table 8.10.)

The difference in the total percentage of total news coverage has to do with what the researchers were specifically analyzing in regard to media coverage, that is, the venue and the time period. Although crime is always a staple of the news media's reporting, it can also see rises in interest as well as declines. Or, there is also the possibility that the emphasis changes, such as moving from the crime of drugs to street crimes to school shootings to terrorism. All are crime related, but the specific subject matter may change. One example of how the reporting on crime can change is found in crime news reporting during the 1990s. It was found to have substantially increased during this time period. One study found that television and newspaper coverage of crime had increased by over 400 percent, and another study, looking at network coverage of murder, found that news coverage had increased by 336 percent between 1990 and 1995.[116] Succinctly stated, "Crime was the leading television news topic in the 1990s."[117]

Taken together, then, that the media have become the primary means of relaying information to the public about crime and that they have consistently made crime a staple of their daily reporting, it is easy to see why the media play a major role in the public policy process. Much of this centers on the fact that the media have the responsibility of reporting on crime because they can often simplify complex issues and explain them to the public in terms that can be readily understood. Because of this, people rely on the media for information about criminal behavior. Since most people have no personal, direct experience with crime, they must rely on the media to provide them with information about the crime problem.[118] As a result, the media can both reflect and form public opinion of crime.[119]

According to Marion, beyond the fact that the media are a primary news source, they can also be a source of entertainment.[120] This is especially true with crime. Crime themes appear on

TABLE 8.10   Most Common Local Television News Stories,[a] 1996

Topic	Number of Stories	Percentage
All topics		
Crime	3,397	20
Weather	1,838	11
Accidents/disasters	1,557	9
Human interest	1,271	7
Health	1,265	7
Crime topic breakdown		
Murders	—	29
Nonfatal shootings	—	7
Robbery	—	6
Assaults	—	5
Other violent crime	—	13
Other nonviolent crime	—	40

[a]Ranked by number of stories per topic.

Source: Adapted from Kaiser Family Foundation, "Crime Most Common Story on Local Television News," media release (Menlo Park, Calif.: Kaiser Family Foundation, March 12, 1998).

talk shows, in advertising, in pop/rock music, in comics, and in movies.[121] Stories about crime and criminals on infotainment shows such as *American Journal* or *A Current Affair* have also proliferated. In addition, there are true-crime shows, including *Cops* and *America's Most Wanted,* which receive high ratings. Documentaries such as *48 Hours* and *Prime Time Live* regularly have segments relating to criminal events or issues. The success of these shows points to the interest (or even obsession) that Americans have with crime.[122]

As a source of information and entertainment, Marion also explains that the media have a significant amount of power to influence criminal justice.[123] This can be seen in various ways. First, the media can alter the perceptions people have of the criminal justice system.[124] Since most people rely on the media to learn about crime, they believe what they see or read in the media and form an opinion about crime policy on the basis of that information. However, the way in which the media present the news can have an impact on public opinion of crime.

There are generally two ways that the media can present crime information. The first is the type of news that is generated by the media themselves, where the media are the initiators, such as news commentary. Here, the media have artificially created "crime waves" by linking various crimes together. The other way is the passage of news to the people in an informational style, where the media are merely considered conduits. The last point to be made with the media is that there exists some debate as to whether the media pass along information that is relatively accurate and unbiased or are misrepresenting the facts, distorting the event, and "packaging" it to their liking (Table 8.11).

When it comes to criminal justice, what the media show may not reflect reality. There are many examples of distortion by the media with regard to crime. For example, criminals on television are most often white, middle-class males with a high school social status and are older than actual criminals. The typical arrestee in real life is a young, poor, black male. The victims on television are portrayed as predominantly white, mostly young women, with whites overrepresented

TABLE 8.11 Sources Used in Specific Incident Stories

Sources	All Crimes %	Murder %	Rape %	Assault %	Robbery %	Burglary %	Larceny %
Police	27.7	29.1	35.6	54.8	44.3	50.0	33.8
Court	22.9	22.6	26.0	14.4	17.9	12.5	26.5
Defendant	9.5	12.5	11.0	4.8	2.1	5.6	1.5
Victim	8.3	6.5	11.7	8.7	11.5	12.5	16.2
Politician	3.8	1.9	.0	1.0	2.1	2.8	2.9
Witness	3.7	4.8	4.8	2.9	3.6	1.4	1.5
Citizen	3.4	3.5	1.4	1.9	2.9	1.4	4.4
Documents	3.4	3.1	2.7	1.0	2.1	1.4	2.9
Media	2.0	1.3	1.4	.0	1.4	.0	1.5
Experts	2.0	1.7	.0	.0	.7	.0	.0
Corrections	.8	.9	.7	1.9	1.4	.0	.0
	N 5,038	N 776	N 146	N 140	N 140	N 72	N 68

Source: Adapted from S. Chermak, "The Presentation of Drugs in the News Media: The News Sources Involved in the Construction of Social Problems," *Justice Quarterly* 14 (4, 1997): 699.

as murder victims. In actuality, the average victim is a young black male. Intrafamily violence is also underrepresented on television, but premeditated crimes are overrepresented.[125] In addition, the media tend to overemphasize violent crime, leading many to believe that this is the primary crime in the United States when in reality property crimes are far more common.[126]

The stages in the justice system portrayed in the media are also distorted.[127] The early steps of the process (law enforcement, investigation, and arrest) are emphasized, and the other steps are almost invisible, especially informal procedures, such as plea bargaining. Lawyers are often shown as actively investigating crimes, which rarely occurs. The media show weapons that are either completely inaccurate or completely accurate in their function—people either do not get shot or they get shot while moving far away—and also that these weapons can kill painlessly, which is another piece of misleading information. Most crimes are solved on television, but the clearance rate reported by the FBI is typically only one-quarter of all crimes. The offenses that are emphasized by the media are those that are least likely to occur in real life. For example, property crime is underrepresented and violent crime overrepresented.[128] Further, the media "exaggerate the most terrifying crimes and mislead people into thinking of the predatory stranger as the typical criminal."[129] The press tends to focus on street crime and to downplay corporate crimes, which may be more damaging and kill more people.[130]

Marion also explains that another way that the media can often distort reality is seen in the fact that the media, in all forms, are very selective of what they show and fail to show because of content, space, and a host of variables.[131] In doing this, "by attending to some problems and ignoring others, television [and the other media] news shapes the American public's political priorities."[132] A good example of this is the media's consistent reporting on street-level violence but very inconsistent reporting on white-collar crime. The only reason Enron was reported on was because numerous people discovered that their retirement savings had been wiped out (thus, the shock played well on the evening news), and the only reason that the media followed the Martha Stewart case was because she was Martha Stewart.

TABLE 8.12 Percentage of Crimes Presented in the Media and Crimes Committed

Crime	Newspaper Coverage %	Television Coverage %	Actual Crime %
Murder/manslaughter	30.6	28.8	.1
Rape	3.7	8.5	.7
Robbery	3.8	2.3	4.4
Burglary	2.6	1.5	21.2
Larceny	2.4	1.0	54.8
	N = 1,502	N = 388	N = 14,475,600

Source: Adapted from S. Chermak, "The Presentation of Drugs in the News Media: The News Sources Involved in the Construction of Social Problems," *Justice Quarterly* 14 (4, 1997): 696; Federal Bureau of Investigation, *Crime in the United States, 1990* (Washington, D.C.: U.S. Government Printing Office, 1991).

The media can also create an overinflated view of crime through repetition.[133] For example, in a local homicide, the media will report on the case as it "breaks" and will then follow up each night for a week regarding the investigation. When a suspect is arrested, arraigned, and brought to trial, the media can rehash the crime. If the individual is convicted and sentenced to prison, once again the media can retell the crime. Over and over again, the media keep repeating the story of the homicide, causing many to believe that each time (or at least each time a break in the reporting) a new homicide is occurring, thus inflating the public's reality (Table 8.12).

The media also tend to distort their news coverage of crime on the basis of the sources they uses for their stories. While one would think that in any crime the media would interview the victim, the victim's family, witnesses to the crime, suspects, and public officials, the reality is that most news reporting simply relies on the last set of people rather than any of the others. Public officials are generally more accessible; so the media form working relationships with them, and the bottom line is that they are easy to get in touch with, to interview, and to follow up with.[134] Most victims, witnesses, and suspects are difficult to get in touch with. They often do not interview well because they are not used to speaking to reporters or being in front of a camera, and they are hard to find after the interview for follow-up. The end result is that the media come to rely on public officials who often provide only one perspective regarding the crime.

The media also distort reality by reporting stories that are unique or very violent rather than typical crimes. When a criminal commits an unusual crime, such as the 1989 shooting of schoolchildren on a playground in Stockton, California, or the previously mentioned Martha Stewart case, the media will pick up the story and publicize it. However, the everyday crimes that occur most frequently, such as muggings or street crimes, are ignored. They occur too frequently to be of any interest to the average American. All this can contribute to the fear and cynicism exhibited in the previously discussed public opinion of crime. The unbalanced presentation of crime stories by the media results in concern about crime and drugs as well as in an unwarranted level of fear of crime by citizens.[135]

POWERS OF THE MEDIA

Marion, in her book *A Primer in the Politics of Criminal Justice,* states that "it is obvious that the media's impact on criminal justice and public opinion can be enormous."[136] Marion lists no less than seven powers that the media have that can impact the criminal justice policy process.

Influencing Public Opinion

The first power of the media, in whatever form it happens to take, is simply their ability to influence people's perceptions about crime and criminal justice. Unfortunately, that power can also be abused by altering the perceptions people have of the criminal justice system.[137] Since most people rely on the media to learn about crime, they believe what they see or read in the media and form an opinion about crime policy on the basis of that information. But beyond the power to influence public opinion, the media have many other effects on the system.

Influencing and Shaping Agendas

A second power of the media is their ability to influence the public agenda or shape public policy.[138] The media have the ability to draw attention to an issue and in essence inform the public about what issues are important and what issues are not. The public, then, demands action from legislators on those particular issues. In short, the media are defining problems that appear on the government's agenda by using (or even forming) the public's concerns, particularly about crime. The media can also keep an issue on the agenda once addressed by an executive or the legislature. If a problem has not been addressed fully, the media can also bring attention to this and demand further action.

In this capacity, the media act as a "linkage institution" that links government officials with public opinion.[139] This is important because, in theory, the ideas expressed by the public should be reflected in the policies created by government.[140] Therefore, "if a representative form of government is assumed, it is likely that the public, at least indirectly, influences the decisions of public officials who depend on the constituents for positions of power."[141] Further, when public opinion changes or shifts, the policies created by the government should reflect those changes.[142] The ideas expressed by the public in public opinion polls, such as the crime polls previously discussed, are reflected in the policies created by the government because politicians rely on the public for support of their policies.[143]

To guarantee that legislators are responsive to public opinion, legislators are elected every two, four, or six years. Elections, however, do not ensure that the public's opinions are incorporated into law. One reason is that individual officials can escape responsibility for policies.[144] They can blame inattention or inaction on other politicians. This is often done with criminal justice issues. Republicans will blame Democrats for inaction, and Democrats will blame Republicans for the same thing.

Whistle-Blowing

A third power of the media is whistle-blowing.[145] The media oversee the actions of many people, including politicians and actors in the criminal justice field. Reporters investigate these actors to determine if any wrongdoing has taken place, and, if so, they publicize it. In essence, this is supposed to keep people honest. A perfect example of the whistle-blowing function of the media is the investigations of the Watergate affair by Woodward and Bernstein in 1974. Many argue that the scandal would not have been discovered had it not been for the determination of these reporters in discovering the truth about the activities of the Nixon administration and his Committee to Reelect the President.

Causing Crime

Fourth, the media have the power to cause crime.[146] This can be seen on two levels. First, the media can influence the behavior of individuals when they show very violent acts that are then "copied" by someone who viewed those acts. These crimes are termed "copycat" crimes because they are crimes influenced by publicity about an original crime. These offenders incorporate major elements of the original crime into their own.

In addition, violence on television is often accused of causing violence in children. Some children are more likely to be violent or aggressive after watching violent television programs. Two federal government reports concerning research on television and crime were published on this problem. In 1972, a report to the surgeon general reported that there was a "tentative indication of a causal relationship" between violent television and violent behavior.[147] The second report, sponsored by the National Institute of Mental Health, concluded more strongly that television causes violence. Since these reports were published, an entire area of research has opened up in its exploration of this relationship, and the conclusions today remain very similar to those issued over thirty years ago.

Influencing Trials

A fifth power of the media is the ability to influence the trial process.[148] The media can cover a story so extensively before it comes to trial so that finding a jury without bias is difficult. Often, if there is too much publicity in a homicide case, prosecutors feel less able to plea-bargain the case and must pursue a trial and conviction.[149] Excessive media coverage has affected trials to such an extent that the convictions have been overturned. This is especially true when the case involves a terrible crime or when the defendants are celebrities. The coverage of these trials is rarely neutral, and this can make the jurors prejudge a case.[150] Examples of extensive media coverage include the cases of William Kennedy Smith, Jeffrey Dahmer, O. J. Simpson, Rodney King and the four Los Angeles police officers, and Scott Peterson, who was accused of killing his wife Laci Peterson and their unborn son, Connor. The media coverage of these cases affected the public's opinions about these individuals, and this may have prevented a fair and unbiased jury trial.

Deterring Future Criminal Behavior

Sixth, the media have the potential power to deter future or potential criminal behavior.[151] This is a theoretical argument based on deterrence theory, which provides that information about the plight of other criminals will deter potential criminals from committing crimes. In other words, if a person is considering committing a criminal act (or even similar act), he or she may choose to refrain from committing the offensive behavior. The media play a key role because they have the responsibility of publicizing the punishments for criminal behavior. This publicity may deter others from committing similar acts. This is called general deterrence and is the process of deterring members of the general public from committing crimes through publicizing criminal punishments.

Helping Fight Crime

Seventh, the media can also help fight crime.[152] Through the public service announcements about issues such as the dangers involved with drug abuse, the media may be helping someone choose not to abuse drugs. Other programs, such as McGruff the Crime Dog, may also help alleviate some crime. Crime-watchers and neighborhood crime watch programs also help increase awareness about criminal behavior.

IMPACT ON THE POLICY PROCESS

The vast literature exploring the relationship of mass media—and specifically television—to the public's opinion has been found to be varied in its results.[153] While some research has shown no direct relationship and others a limited relationship, a large body of research has found it to be a major influencing factor.[154] However, one cannot ignore the point that Iyengar and Kinder raise in stating that "in commanding attention and shaping opinion, television is now an authority virtually without peer."[155] This fact then raises the question as to whether the media have a direct impact, an indirect impact, or no impact at all on public opinion. Since the majority of Americans' understanding of the policy issues are formulated or, to borrow Iyengar's term, "framed" through the mass media, it only stands to reason that they must have some impact, however small.

While the predominant direction of the influence may not be clear, what is clear is that the media matter. The media influence the public, and the media influence the policymakers. While the media may also be influenced by the public and the policymakers, the impact of the media on everything else should not be lost in any attempt to figure out the "which-comes-first" controversy. The media not only influence the public and policymakers directly but also act as a medium for these other two actors in the policy process. The media report on the public's will through a variety of polls, those taken by independent firms (e.g., Gallup and Roper) as well as those in-house (e.g., ABC and CBS). By reporting on the polls regarding the public's position on something (e.g., gun control or the death penalty), the media give policymakers a list of things to focus their attention on or, if public approval is low, a list of things to ignore. But in either case, it is the media that inform the policymakers what the public wants.

Looking at the relationship from the opposite direction, we see the policymakers using the media to inform the public on their positions regarding certain policies. Since we tend to gain most of our knowledge about politicians through the media, the politicians are using the media as a means of influencing their constituents to support their policy positions. Although the media may be passive in relaying this information, more often than not they take a role through either questioning the policymaker, filtering the policymaker's message by editing what gets shown, or responding with the so-called experts to analyze what the policymaker said. Taken together, these demonstrate how the media can have a direct, indirect, or no impact on the policy process. If the media directly shape the news, they have a direct impact on public opinion and the policy process. If they relay public opinion poll information to the policymakers and policymakers' positions to the public, they are playing an indirect role. And if the media ignore a particular event or crime by accidentally or purposefully ignoring such a topic, in a sense they have no impact on the policy process.

The media's role in the public policy process—and particularly in the area of crime policy—is substantial. Because of the nature of the media's role, they also are not relegated to any one step in the public policy process but rather engage in all the steps in one form or another. As Surette has articulated, "In each local social, political and cultural environment, the media are seen as helping to shape criminal justice policy by establishing ongoing relationships with other local claims-makers including policy makers, lobbyists, and public officials."[156] Therefore, a review of the policy steps and the media's role in crime policy formation is helpful in understanding the media's role in the public policy process.

Based on the previous discussion about the media's powers, it should be evident that the media can be quite influential in the policy process, especially in the problem identification stage. Although much of the media's reporting on crime comes in a constant diet of crime stories, it also relays many of the major crime events and relays them to the American public. Because crime is always a staple of the news media reporting, it is always something the policymakers identify as a problem. This is the "constant stream of problems" in Kingdon's terms or the "equilibrium" according to Baumgartner and Jones. However, it is the sensational events, such as hate crimes and school shootings, which quickly move policymakers into action, thus identifying a problem and placing it on the public policy agenda. In many ways, it is the "punctuated equilibrium" that Baumgartner and Jones spoke of that makes crime problems into crime issues.

The other factor in much of this, as previously mentioned, is the fact that many of the problems that get identified as issues are really nothing more than problems. In other words, the media report on something as being a major social problem when in fact there is really no issue. Examples include the crack cocaine epidemic that the media reported on in the late 1980s. Research by Reinarman and Levine found that the use of cocaine had peaked around 1985 and was on the decline in the late 1980s, but that did not stop the media from identifying the crack cocaine epidemic as a major social issue.[157] Another example is the series of high school shootings in the mid-to-late 1990s. Despite the media heavily reporting on this problem and hyping the lack of safety in today's schools, the reality was that school violence had been on a decline throughout the entire decade, and these shootings were the exception and not the rule. In addition, it has been argued that by reporting on these shootings so heavily, the media generated copycat crimes, thus enhancing the artificial crime wave.

Another way of looking at the media's role in the problem formulation stage is conveyed by Sacco. He argues that often many personal problems are hyped by the media, thus becoming public issues. As he explains,

> If the news business is concerned with the production of crime problems, then the private troubles of criminal offenders and crime victims are the raw materials. These troubles are not simply reported on, however, since they are fundamentally transformed by the news-gathering process. Screened through a law enforcement filter, contextualized by advocacy claims and culturally resonant news themes, and shaped and molded by the conventions and requirements of commercial media, these private troubles become public issues.[158]

This in turn places the private problem on the public's agenda, placing it, as no politicians want to ignore the demands of their constituents, on the government's agenda. This is because politicians often interpret media coverage of an issue as a sign of heightened public concern.[159] Thus, the media contribute to and influence the next stage of the public policy process: agenda setting.

The media's role in the policy process, while part of every stage, is perhaps nowhere more evident than in the agenda-setting process. This relationship between public opinion, the media, and politicians is often what produces the agenda. In terms of crime policy, while politicians do often place many of the day-in-and-day-out types of crime issues on their agenda, the reality is that most crime policy is placed on the agenda when there is a crisis. Because there are so few true sources for the news, the news outlets can convey the importance of issues not only in one localized area but also across the states and the nation as a whole at the same time. This is one of the reasons that the federal government has become more involved in the issue of crime over the past 40 years. As all Americans receive largely the same news stories and the media frame these crime issues in the same way, people come to fear the same issue and demand that government do something about the problem. Whether it was riots in the late 1960s, drugs in the late 1980s, crime in the mid-1990s, or terrorism in the twenty-first century, the media present the same issue in all its outlets, raising the salience of the issue and creating the same demand for government action. And, since the salience often rises rapidly, these issues become a part of the agenda-setting process quite fast, and as a result there is an increased demand for the next two stages of the public policy process to be sped up as well.

It should also be noted, however, that the media can also assist in removing an issue from the agenda by no longer covering that issue. Drugs and the "war on drugs" were quite the staple of the media from 1985 to 1992. However, when President-elect Clinton chose to speak more about the problem of crime than about drugs, the media's attention shifted, and crime became the important issue beginning in 1994. Moreover, shifting the focus on a particular issue can change how the policy is dealt with. One example of this has been the changes in how crimes against the elderly have been perceived.[160] Mark Fishman conducted a study in 1978 that looked at the increase in media reporting in New York City, citing a crime wave against the elderly. He found that the media coverage had created the perception of an increased number of elderly victimizations when in fact the empirical data did not support this.[161] Another example could be highway safety. The solutions offered have changed over time, with building more highways being the solution of the 1950s, building better cars that of the 1960s, and putting drunk drivers behind bars that of the 1980s.

Once an issue is on the public policy agenda, policymakers must formulate policy that will address the problem, and once again the media can play a major role. The media are usually more adept at raising the issue than necessarily generating a particular solution. In the policy formulation stage, there are often numerous details and technicalities that the media—or, more specifically, the reporters—don't have time to delve into or the capacity to comprehend. Hence, the media either look for a simple angle that they can easily relay to the public or call on the "experts" to "float ideas" for how the problem could be dealt with. As a result, their role in the policy formulation stage becomes a process of analyzing and criticizing the policies that are put forth.

During the policy formulation stage, since many of the interest groups will often advocate a particular policy position, the media will often report heavily on these groups' positions. This can draw attention toward these particular policy proposals, draw attention away from them, or openly criticize the policy in order to reduce it as a viable option among policymakers. Using the example of highway safety, when the interest group Mothers Against Drunk Driving proposed the solution to traffic safety and a rise in instances of driving while intoxicated (DWI) in the late 1990s as being one of reducing the blood alcohol content (BAC) level across the country to .08, the media reported heavily on this proposal. As it reached the policy formulation stage, news reports continued to hype how this policy would reduce DWIs across the country. Congress entertained the policy, attached it to a transportation bill, and passed it prior to the end of the Clinton administration's second term (October 2000). Reporting on this policy has since shifted to the states coming into compliance with the transportation bill's demand that states pass legislation lowering their BACs to .08 or face losing their federal highway funding.

Once the policy is formulated and passed, the role of the media in the policy implementation stage is often very complicated. For example, "by giving widespread coverage to the president signing the Brady bill requiring gun registration, they added to its legitimacy. But by later reporting that many people were not registering their guns, the media may have encouraged widespread defiance of the law."[162] However, most policies at the implementation stage are not self-executing but rather require the work of the administration and its bureaucracy in order to move a policy forward. The media can be significant players in this particular stage, as they can report on how a policy is actually being implemented (or how it is not being implemented) and, if it is, how specifically the policy is being administered. The problem with media reports during this particular stage is that the journalists must have access to information, develop an understanding of the policy, and grasp the intricacies of the bureaucracies. The media can report on derelictions, ineptitude, and scandals during this stage, but they must uncover them first. Generally, most reporters do not have the time or the capacity for this type of reporting, so this form of investigative journalism is much rarer. In addition, just because a journalist investigates a particular policy does not mean that he or she will find any wrongdoing, thus potentially creating a very limited payoff in regard to a "story." As a result, media coverage of the implementation stage tends to be very sporadic and focuses on only a handful of policy issues at any given time.[163]

The final stage of the policy process, policy evaluation, is one in which the media are often engaged in their reporting. The reason the media so often become an integral part of this stage in the policy process is because government often has little will in this area. Once a policy is formulated and implemented, although there is usually some type of policy evaluation requirement attached to the policy, politicians generally do not care as much about the effectiveness or the efficiency of a policy. This is generally because of two factors: (1) they have satisfied their political obligation by *doing* something about a problem, and (2) they will usually have moved on to another policy issue by the time policy evaluations are conducted and released. Politicians will often treat any problems related to a policy evaluation as simply a new problem to pursue through the public policy process.

The media's role in the policy evaluation stage is most important when they force government to be held accountable for its actions. When the media inform the public about a particular problem with a policy, such as the D.A.R.E. program's failure to prevent kids from doing drugs, or, worse, when they expose corruption occurring because of a particular administrative or bureaucratic problem, such as the treatment of whistle-blowers in the FBI, they serve a very important role in allowing government to be held accountable for its actions. This is the true power of the press. This can then cause policies to be reevaluated, altered, or, in extreme cases, terminated. This is also why it is so crucial that media reporting not be biased, partial, or inaccurate, as the public may come to believe that government or a policy is wrong when in fact it is merely the distortions of the government or policy as portrayed by the media.[164] Yet, in either case, the media will have a tremendous impact on the public policy process.

In looking specifically at crime, studies have shown repeatedly that the media have a profound impact on obtaining public support for various crime policies. For example, media coverage on the drug crisis of the mid-1980s and the subsequent war on drugs led to a number of anti–drug abuse laws and increased penalties for drug crimes at the federal and state levels.[165] In 1994, news media coverage of the Clinton administration's "100,000 Cops" plan helped gain public support for the Violent Crime Control and Law Enforcement Act of 1994.[166] And, in the wake of September 11, the public demand for government to do something about terrorism nearly gave Congress a "blank check" to draft and pass the USA PATRIOT Act. Yet in the end, as Barlow, Barlow, and Chiricos have explained, "crime news may well be vital to securing popular consent for new criminal justice policies that are implemented in hopes of creating conditions conducive to a stable political economy, but [they] continually fail to have a significant impact on crime."[167] Or, as Surette has explained, "Media attention sometimes emerges as more important an influence on criminal justice activities than the legislation or policy initiative that its influence spurs."[168] In other words, the media are good at getting the public behind certain crime policies—but for all the wrong reasons. The media like to report what sounds good and sells well to the public, but this does not make for sound crime policy.

Conclusion

Both public opinion and the mass media play important roles in the American political process, and both have substantial impact on criminal justice. Both print and broadcast media serve as the principal means by which public opinion is expressed and altered. It is clear that "newspapers, television networks, and local stations shape the news and thus influence public officials and public opinion."[169] Unfortunately, the ability of the media to influence public concern with crime is based more on their coverage than on reported crime.[170] This means that the public's concern with crime is based not on reality but rather on the media's perception of reality,

which tends to be biased. Because of the biased presentation of crime issues and events, the public's opinion about crime and related policies may also be distorted.

The media can affect crime in other ways as well. For example, the media can influence the government's agenda, they can act as a whistle-blower against wrongdoing, they can cause or even prevent crime, and they can affect the jury's opinion about certain publicized cases. Through these powers, the media have become a very powerful political institution that has major impact on the criminal justice system both directly and indirectly.

Notes

1. B. Johnson and R. C. Huff, "Public Opinion and Criminal Justice Policy Formulation," *Criminal Justice Policy Review* 2 (1987): 118–32.

2. J. V. Roberts, "Public Opinion, Crime, and Criminal Justice" in *Crime and Justice: A Review of Research*, Vol. 16, ed. Michael Tonry (Chicago: University of Chicago Press, 1992), pp. 99–180.

3. J. M. Burns, J. W. Peltason, T. E. Cronin, and D. B. Magleby, *Government by the People* (Upper Saddle River, N.J.: Prentice Hall, 2000), p. 254.

4. Sourcebook of Criminal Justice Statistics-2002 (2003), "Attitudes toward the Death Penalty, 2001." Available online at www.albany.edu/sourcebook/pdf/t247.pdf.

5. Walter Lippmann, *The Phantom Public* (New York: Macmillan, 1925).

6. Ibid., pp. 26–27.

7. Walter Lippmann, *Public Opinion* (New York: Macmillan, 1992); Lippmann, *The Phantom Public*.

8. Angus Campell, Philip E. Converse, Warren E. Miller, and Donald E. Stokes, *The American Voter* (New York: John Wiley & Sons, 1960); Phillip E. Converse, "The Nature of Belief Systems in Mass Publics," in *Ideology and Discontent*, ed. David E. Apter (New York: Free Press, 1964), pp. 206–61.

9. Ibid.

10. V. O. Key, Jr., *Public Opinion and American Democracy* (New York: Knopf, 1967).

11. Ibid., p. 8.

12. P. J. Riley and V. M. Rose, "Public vs. Elite Opinion on Correctional Reform: Implications for Social Policy," *Journal of Criminal Justice* 8 (1980): 345–56.

13. Key, *Public Opinion and American Democracy*, p. 9.

14. Campbell et al., *The American Voter*.

15. Converse, "The Nature of Belief Systems in Mass Publics"; Philip E. Converse, "Popular Representation of Information," in *Information and Democratic Processes*, ed. John A. Ferejohn and James H. Kuklinski (Urbana: University of Illinois Press, 1990), pp. 234–38; Paul M. Sniderman, Richard A. Brody, and Philip E. Tetlock, *Reasoning and Choice: Explorations in Political Psychology* (New York: Cambridge University Press, 1991); Paul M. Sniderman, James M. Glaser, and Robert Griffin, "Information and Electoral Choice," in Ferejohn and Kuklinski, *Information and Democratic Processes*, pp. 117–35.

16. Key, *Public Opinion and American Democracy*; V. O. Key, Jr., *The Responsible Electorate: Rationality in Presidential Voting, 1936–1960* (Cambridge, Mass.: Harvard University Press, 1966).

17. Norman H. Nie, Sidney Verba, and John R. Petrocik, *The Changing American Voter* (Cambridge, Mass.: Harvard University Press, 1976).

18. Eric R. A. N. Smith, *The Unchanging American Voter* (Berkeley: University of California Press, 1989).

19. Benjamin I. Page and Robert Y. Shapiro, *The Rational Public: Fifty Years of Trends in Americans'*

Policy Preferences (Chicago: University of Chicago Press, 1992).

20. William G. Mayer, *The Changing American Mind: How and Why American Public Opinion Changed between 1960 and 1988* (Ann Arbor: University of Michigan Press, 1994).

21. Edward G. Carmines and James H. Kuklinski, "Incentives, Opportunities, and the Logic of Public Opinion in American Political Representation," in Ferejohn and Kuklinski, *Information and Democratic Processes*, pp. 117–35.

22. Sniderman et al., *Reasoning and Choice;* Sniderman et al., "Information and Electoral Choice."

23. Paul M. Sniderman, "The New Look in Public Opinion Research," in *Political Science: The State of the Discipline II,* ed. Ada W. Finifter (Washington, D.C.: American Political Science Association, 1993), pp. 219–45.

24. Roberts, "Public Opinion, Crime, and Criminal Justice."

25. K. T. Gaubatz, *Crime in the Public Mind* (Ann Arbor: University of Michigan Press, 1995).

26. M. Vandiver and D. Giacopassi, "One Million and Counting: Students' Estimates of the Annual Number of Homicides in the U.S.," *Journal of Criminal Justice Education* 8 (2, 1997): 135–44.

27. Roberts, "Public Opinion, Crime, and Criminal Justice."

28. Ibid.

29. Donald R. Kinder, "Diversity and Complexity in American Public Opinion," in *The State of the Discipline,* ed. Ada Finifter (Washington, D.C.: American Political Science Association, 1983), pp. 236–51; Sniderman et al., *Reasoning and Choice;* Sniderman et al., "Information and Electoral Choice."

30. Mayer, *The Changing American Mind.*

31. Page and Shapiro, *The Rational Public.*

32. Richard Brody, *Assessing the President: The Media, Elite Opinion, and Public Support* (Stanford, Calif.: Stanford University Press, 1991); Edward G. Carmines and James A. Stimson, *Issue Evolution: Race and the Transformation of American Politics* (Princeton, N.J.: Princeton University Press, 1989); James A. Stimson, *Public Opinion in America: Mood, Cycles, and Swings* (Boulder, Colo.: Westview Press, 1991).

33. Shanto Iyengar, *Is Anyone Responsible? How Television Frames Political Issues* (Chicago: University of Chicago Press, 1991); Shanto Iyengar, "Shortcuts to Political Knowledge: The Role of Selective Attention and Accessibility," in Ferejohn and Kuklinski, *Information and Democratic Processes*, pp. 160–85.

34. J. H. Kuklinski, "Information and the Study of Politics," in *Information and Democratic Processes,* pp. 391–95.

35. Converse, "Popular Representation of Information."

36. Gaubatz, *Crime in the Public Mind,* p. 10.

37. Jon Hurwitz and Mark Peffley, "Public Perceptions of Race and Crime: The Role of Racial Stereotypes," *American Journal of Political Science* 41 (2, 1997): 375–401, at 376.

38. For examples of public opinion and national criminal justice policy, see Timothy J. Flanagan, "Public Opinion and Public Policy in Criminal Justice," in *Americans View Crime and Justice: A National Public Opinion Survey,* ed. Timothy J. Flanagan and Dennis R. Longmire (Thousand Oaks, Calif.: Sage), pp. 151–58. For examples of public opinion and state criminal justice policy, see Bruce Johnson and C. Ronald Huff, "Public Opinion and Criminal Justice Policy Formulation," *Criminal Justice Policy Review* 2 (1987): 118–32.

39. Flanagan and Longmire, *Americans View Crime and Justice;* Julian V. Roberts and Loretta J. Stalans, *Public Opinion, Crime, and Criminal Justice* (Boulder, Colo.: Westview Press, 1997).

40. Stuart A. Scheingold, "Politics, Public Policy, and Street Crime," *Annals of the American Academy of Political and Social Science* 539 (1995): 155–68, at 163.

41. Bahram Haghighi and Jon Sorenson, "America's Fear of Crime," in Flanagan and Longmire, *Americans View Crime and Justice,* pp. 16–30; Stuart A. Scheingold, *The Politics of Law and Order* (New York: Longman, 1984); Scheingold, "Politics, Public Policy, and Street Crime"; Mark Warr, "Dangerous Situations: Social Context and Fear of Victimization," *Social Forces* 68 (1990): 891–907; Mark Warr, "The Polls-Poll Trends: Public Opinion on Crime and Punishment," *Public Opinion Quarterly* 59 (1995): 296–310; J. A. Will and J. H. McGrath, "Crime, Neighborhood Perception, and the Underclass: The Relationship between Fear of Crime and Class Position," *Journal of Criminal Justice* 23 (1995): 163–76.

42. Katherine Beckett, "Setting the Public Agenda: 'Street Crime' and Drug Use in American Politics," *Social Problems* 41 (1994): 425–47; Stuart A. Scheingold, *The Politics of Street Crime* (Philadelphia: Temple University Press, 1991); James Q. Wilson and Joan Petersilia, *Crime* (San Francisco: ICS Press, 1995); see introduction.

43. Mark Warr, "Fear of Victimization: Why Are Women and Elderly More Afraid?" *Social Science Quarterly* 65 (1984): 681–702.

44. Paul Lavrakas, "Fear of Crime and Behavioral Restrictions in Urban and Suburban Neighborhoods," *Population and Environments* 5 (1982): 242–64; Dan A. Lewis and Greta Salem, *Fear of Crime: Incivility and the Production of a Social Problem* (New Brunswick, N.J.: Transaction Books, 1986); Wesley Skogan, "Fear of Crime and Neighborhood Change," in *Communities and Crime*, ed. Albert J. Reiss Jr. and Michael Tonry (Chicago: University of Chicago Press, 1986), pp. 203–30; Wesley Skogan, "The Various Meanings of Fear," in *Fear of Crime and Criminal Victimization*, ed. W. Bilsky, C. Pfeiffer, and P. Wetzels (Stuttgart: Ferdinand Enke Verlag, 1993).

45. Kenneth F. Ferraro, *Fear of Crime: Interpreting Victimization Risk* (Albany: State University of New York Press, 1995); Randy L. LaGrange, Kenneth F. Ferraro, and Michael Supanic, "Perceived Risk and Fear of Crime: Role of Social and Physical Incivilities," *Journal of Research in Crime and Delinquency* 29 (1992): 311–35; Terance D. Meithe and Gary R. Lee, "Fear of Crime among Older People: A Reassessment of the Predictive Power of Crime-Related Factors," *Sociological Quarterly* 25 (1984): 397–416; Skogan, "The Various Meanings of Fear"; Mark Warr, "America's Perceptions of Crime and Punishment," in *Criminology: A Contemporary Handbook*, ed. J. F. Sheley (Belmont, Calif.: Wadsworth, 1991), pp. 145–81.

46. Skogan, "The Various Meanings of Fear"; Warr, "Dangerous Situations."

47. Skogan, "The Various Meanings of Fear."

48. Research and Forecasts, Inc., *America Afraid: How Fear of Crime Changes the Way We Live (The Figgie Report)*, ed. Andy Friedberg (New York: New American Library, 1983).

49. Frank A. Bennack, Jr. *The American Public's Hopes and Fears for the Decade of the 1990s* (New York: The Hearst Company, 1989).

50. Warr, "The Polls-Poll Trends."

51. Leslie McAney, "The Gallup Poll on Crime," *Gallup Poll Monthly*, December 1993, p. 18; Terance D. Miethe, "Fear and Withdrawal from Urban Life," *Annals of the American Academy of Political and Social Science* 539 (1995): 14–140; Scheingold, "Politics, Public Policy, and Street Crime."

52. Kenneth Ferraro and Randy LaGrange. "The Measurement of Fear of Crime," *Sociological Quarterly* 57 (1987): 71–101; Allen E. Liska and William Baccaglini, "Feeling Safe by Comparison: Crime in the Newspapers," *Social Problems* 37 (1990): 360–74.

53. Warr, "The Polls-Poll Trends."

54. Terry L. Baumer, "Testing a General Model of Fear of Crime," *Journal of Research in Crime and Delinquency* 22 (1985): 239–56; F. Clemente and M. B. Kleiman, "Fear of Crime in the United States: A Multivariate Analysis," *Social Forces* 56 (1977): 519–31; Ferraro, *Fear of Crime*; Carol B. Gardner, "Safe Conduct: Women, Crime, and Self in Public Places," *Social Problems* 37 (1990): 311–28; James Garofalo, "The Fear of Crime: Causes and Consequences," *Journal of Criminal Law and Criminology* 72 (1981): 839–57; Haghighi and Sorenson, "America's Fear of Crime"; Leslie W. Kennedy and Robert A. Silverman, "Significant Others and Fear of Crime among the Elderly," *Journal of Aging and Human Development* 20 (1985): 241–56; Randy L. LaGrange, Kenneth F. Ferraro, and M. Supancic, "Perceived Risk and Fear of Crime: Role of Social and Physical Incivilities," *Journal of Research in Crime and Delinquency* 29 (1992): 311–34; Miethe and Lee, "Fear of Crime among Older People"; Suzanne T. Ortega and Jessie L. Myles, "Race and Gender Effects on Fear of Crime: An Interactive Model with Age," *Criminology* 25 (1987): 133–52; Warr, "Fear of Victimization"; Peter Yin, "Fear of Crime as a Problem for the Elderly," *Social Problems* 30 (1982): 240–45.

55. H. Schuman and J. Scott, "Problems in the Use of Survey Questions to Measure Public Opinion," *Science* 236 (1987): 957–59.

56. George H. Gallup, *The Gallup Poll: Public Opinion* (Wilmington, Del.: Scholarly Resources, 1996).

57. Jeffrey E. Cohen, "Presidential Rhetoric and the Public Agenda," *American Journal of Political Science* 39 (1995): 87–107; Michael S. Lewis-Beck and Tom W. Rice, *Forecasting Elections* (Washington, D.C.: Congressional Quarterly Press, 1992); Nancy E. Marion, *A History of Federal Crime Control Initiatives, 1960–1993* (Westport, Conn.: Praeger, 1992); T. Smith, "America's Most Important Problems-A Trend Analysis, 1946–1976." *Public Opinion Quarterly* 44 (1980): 164–80.

58. Mayer, *The Changing American Mind*; Page and Shapiro. *The Rational Public.*

59. William J. Gozenbach, *The Media, the President, and Public Opinion: A Longitudinal Analysis of the Drug Issue, 1984–1991* (Mahwah, N.J.: Lawrence Erlbaum Associates, 1996), pp. 29–30; Mayer, *The Changing American Mind*; Page and Shapiro, *The Rational Public.*

60. Paul C. Light, *The President's Agenda: Domestic Policy Choice from Kennedy to Reagan*, rev. ed. (Baltimore: The Johns Hopkins University Press, 1991).

61. The specific polls consisted of a CBS News, CBS News/New York Times, the Wirthlin Group, and the Princeton Survey Research Associates surveys. See Warr, "The Polls-Poll Trends."

62. Baumer, "Testing a General Model of Fear of Crime"; Clemente and Kleiman, "Fear of Crime in the United States"; Ferraro, *Fear of Crime;* Gardner, "Safe Conduct;" Garofalo, "The Fear of Crime"; Haghighi and Sorenson, "America's Fear of Crime"; Kennedy and Silverman, "Significant Others and Fear of Crime among the Elderly"; LaGrange et al., "Perceived Risk and Fear of Crime"; Miethe and Lee, "Fear of Crime among Older People"; Ortega and Myles, "Race and Gender Effects on Fear of Crime"; Warr, "Fear of Victimization"; Yin, "Fear of Crime as a Problem for the Elderly."

63. Baumer, "Testing a General Model of Fear of Crime"; Haghighi and Sorenson, "America's Fear of Crime"; K. Parker, "Fear of Crime and the Likelihood of Victimization: A Bi-Ethnic Comparison," *Journal of Social Psychology* 133 (1993): 723–32; Wesley Skogan and Michael G. Maxfield, *Coping with Crime* (Beverly Hills, Calif.: Sage, 1981).

64. Baumer, "Testing a General Model of Fear of Crime"; Garofalo, "The Fear of Crime"; Haghighi and Sorenson, "America's Fear of Crime"; Skogan and Maxfield, *Coping with Crime*; Will and McGrath, "Crime, Neighborhood Perception, and the Underclass."

65. Doris A. Graber, *Crime News and the Public* (New York: Praeger, 1980); Jennie McIntyre, "Public Attitudes toward Crime and Law Enforcement," in *Perception in Criminology,* ed. Richard L. Henshel and Robert A. Silverman (New York: Columbia University Press, 1975); Skogan and Maxfield, *Coping with Crime.*

66. Skogan and Maxfield, *Coping with Crime,* p. 60.

67. Mayer, *The Changing American Mind.*

68. Garofalo, "The Fear of Crime"; Mayer, *The Changing American Mind*; Miethe, "Fear and Withdrawal from Urban Life."

69. Graber, *Crime News and the Public:* Joachim Savelsburg, "Knowledge, Domination, and Criminal Punishment," *American Journal of Sociology* 99 (1994): 911–43.

70. Vincent F. Sacco, *The Media, Crime and Criminal Justice* (Belmont, Calif.: Wadsworth, 1995).

71. Haghighi and Sorenson, "America's Fear of Crime."

72. Allen E. Liska, Joseph J. Lawrence, and Andrew Sanchirico, "Fear of Crime as a Social Fact," *Social Forces* 60 (1985): 760–71; Skogan and Maxfield, *Coping with Crime.*

73. Ferraro, *Fear of Crime;* Kenneth F. Ferraro and Randy LaGrange, "The Measurement of Fear of Crime," *Sociological Inquiry* 57 (1987): 70–101; Liska et al., "Fear of Crime as a Social Fact"; Skogan and Maxfield, *Coping with Crime,* Warr, "The Polls-Poll Trends"; Warr, "Dangerous Situations"; Mark Warr and Mark C. Stafford, "Fear of Victimization: A Look at the Proximate Causes," *Social Forces* 61 (1983): 1033–43.

74. Wesley G. Skogan, "Crime and the Racial Fears of White Americans," *Annals of the American Academy of Political and Social Science* 539 (1995): 59–71.

75. Haghighi and Sorenson, "America's Fear of Crime."

76. Ibid., p. 29.

77. W. Lance Bennett, *Public Opinion in American Politics* (New York: Harcourt Brace, 1980); Haghighi and Sorenson, "America's Fear of Crime"; Craig Reinarman and Harry Levine, "Crack in Context: Politics and Media in the Making of a Drug Scare," *Contemporary Drug Problems* 16 (1989): 535–77.

78. Gaubatz, *Crime in the Public Mind.*

79. Beckett, "Setting the Public Agenda."

80. Warr, "The Polls-Poll Trends," p. 302.

81. Flanagan and Longmire, *Americans View Crime and Justice.*

82. Roberts, "Public Opinion, Crime, and Criminal Justice," p. 162.

83. John W. Kingdon, *Agendas, Alternatives and Public Policies,* 2nd ed. (New York: HarperCollins College Publishers, 1994), p. 65.

84. Ibid.

85. Kathleen Maguire and Ann L. Pastore, *Bureau of Justice Statistics Sourcebook of Criminal Justice Statistics-1994* (Washington, D.C.: Bureau of Justice Statistics, 1995).

86. Ibid.

87. Ibid.

88. *Congressional Digest,* "The Federal Role in Crime Control," June/July 1994, pp. 161–92.

89. Ibid.

90. Shelly E. Taylor and Susan Fiske, "Salience, Attention, and Attribution: Top of the Head Phenomena," in *Advances in Social Psychology,* ed. L. Berkowitz (New York: Academic Press, 1978), p. 423.

91. Skogan and Maxfield, *Coping with Crime,* p. 123.

92. Ibid.

93. Mayer, *The Changing American Mind,* p. 285.

94. Graber, *Crime News and the Public.*

95. Mayer, *The Changing American Mind.*

96. McIntyre, "Public Attitudes toward Crime and Law Enforcement."

97. Vincent F. Sacco, "Media Construction of Crime," *Annals of the American Academy of Political and Social Science* 539 (1995): 141–54.

98. L. R. Jacobs and R.Y. Shapiro, *Politicians Don't Pander* (Chicago: University of Chicago Press, 2000), p. 223.

99. Joachim J. Savelsburg, "Knowledge, Domination and Criminal Punishment," *American Journal of Sociology* 99 (4, 1994): 911–43, at 923.

100. Graber, *Crime News and the Public.*

101. Scheingold, *The Politics of Law and Order,* p. 30.

102. J. J. Dilulio, S. K. Smith, and A. J. Saiger, "The Federal Role in Crime Control," in Wilson and Petersilia, *Crime,* p. 447.

103. W. M. Oliver, *The Law and Order Presidency* (Upper Saddle River, N.J.: Prentice Hall, 2000).

104. Beckett, "Setting the Public Agenda," p. 443.

105. Graber, *Crime News and the Public.*

106. Taylor and Fiske, "Salience, Attention, and Attribution," p. 421.

107. R. Surette, *Media, Crime and Criminal Justice* (Pacific Grove, Calif.: Brooks/Cole, 1992), p. 10.

108. C. Hellinger and D. R. Judd, *The Democratic Facade* (Belmont, Calif.: Wadsworth, 1994).

109. S. Anglobahere, R. Behr, and S. Iyengar, *The Media Game: American Politics in the Television Age* (New York: Macmillan, 1993).

110. Graber, *Crime News and the Public.*

111. K. Tunnell, "Film at Eleven: Recent Developments in the Commodification of Crime," *Sociological Spectrum* 12 (1992): 293–313.

112. Sacco, "Media Constructions of Crime."

113. K. Beckett and T. Sasson, *The Politics of Injustice* (Thousand Oaks, Calif.: Pine Forge Press, 2000).

114. R. Surette, *Media, Crime and Criminal Justice,* 2nd ed. (Belmont, Calif.: Wadsworth, 1998), p. 67.

115. Sacco, "Media Constructions of Crime."

116. Beckett and Sasson, *The Politics of Injustice,* p. 77.

117. Ibid.

118. D. Lewis, "Crime in the Media: Introduction," in *Reactions to Crime,* ed. D. A. Lewis (Beverly Hills, Calif.: Sage, 1981), p. 128.

119. Savelsburg, "Knowledge, Domination, and Capital Punishment."

120. N. E. Marion, *A Primer in the Politics of Criminal Justice* (New York: Harrow and Heston, 1995).

121. G. R. Newman, "Popular Culture and Criminal Justice: A Preliminary Analysis," *Journal of Crime and Justice* 18 (1990): 261–74.

122. M. Parenti, *Make-Believe Media: The Politics of Entertainment* (New York: St. Martin's Press, 1992), p. 113.

123. Marion, *A Primer in the Politics of Criminal Justice.*

124. C. E. Van Horn, D. C. Baumer, and W. T. Gormley, Jr., *Politics and Public Policy* (Washington, D.C.: Congressional Quarterly Press, 1992).

125. Lewis, "Crime in the Media," p. 132; Surette, *Media, Crime and Criminal Justice,* p. 35.

126. Sacco, "Media Constructions of Crime."

127. Marion, *A Primer in the Politics of Criminal Justice.*

128. Surette, *Media, Crime and Criminal Justice,* p. 34.

129. Scheingold, *The Politics of Law and Order,* p. 55.

130. M. Parenti, *Inventing Reality: The Politics of News Media* (New York: St. Martin's Press, 1993).

131. Marion, *A Primer in the Politics of Criminal Justice.*

132. Shanto Iyengar and Donald Kinder, *News That Matters* (Chicago: University of Chicago Press, 1987), p. 133.

133. Marion, *A Primer in the Politics of Criminal Justice.*

134. G. Potter and V. Kappeler, *Constructing Crime: Perspectives on Making News and Social Problems* (Prospect Heights, IL.: Waveland Press, 1998).

135. K. Beckett, "Setting the Public Agenda."

136. Marion, *A Primer in the Politics of Criminal Justice,* p. 111.

137. Van Horn et al., *Politics and Public Policy,* p. 234.

138. Marion, *A Primer in the Politics of Criminal Justice.*

139. Ibid.

140. Key, *Public Opinion and American Democracy.*

141. Riley and Rose, "Public vs. Elite Opinion on Correctional Reform."

142. Page and Shapiro, "Effects of Public Opinion on Policy."

143. P. C. Light, "The Presidential Policy Stream," in *The Presidency and the Political System,* ed. M. Nelson (Washington, D.C.: Congressional Quarterly Press, 1984).

144. Van Horn et al., p. 8.

145. R. Baker and F. A. Meyer, Jr., *The Criminal Justice Game* (North Scituate, Mass.: Duxbury Press, 1980); Marion, *A Primer in the Politics of Criminal Justice.*

146. Marion, *A Primer in the Politics of Criminal Justice.*

147. Parenti, *Make-Believe Media,* p. 118.

148. Marion, *A Primer in the Politics of Criminal Justice.*

149. Beckett and Sasson, *The Politics of Injustice.*

150. J. P. Levine, *Juries and Politics* (Pacific Grove, Calif.: Brooks/Cole, 1992).

151. Marion, *A Primer in the Politics of Criminal Justice.*

152. Ibid.

153. Sacco, "Media Construction of Crime"; Skogan and Maxfield, *Coping with Crime.*

154. Larry M. Bartels, "Messages Received: The Political Impact of Media Exposure," *American Political Science Review* 87 (1993): 267–85; Iyengar, *Is Anyone Responsible?*; Iyengar, "Shortcuts to Political Knowledge"; Sacco, "Media Construction of Crime"; Skogan and Maxfield, *Coping with Crime.*

155. Iyengar and Kinder, *News That Matters*, p. 133.
156. Surette, *Media, Crime, and Criminal Justice*, 2nd ed. p. 214.
157. C. Reinarman and H. G. Levine, "The Crack Attack," in *Images of Issues,* ed. J. Best (New York: Aldine de Gruyter, 1989).
158. Sacco, "Media Constructions of Crime," p. 153.
159. Beckett and Sasson, *The Politics of Injustice*, p. 85.
160. F. L. Cook and W. G. Skogan, "Convergent and Divergent Voice Models of the Rise and Fall of Policy Issues," in *Agenda Setting,* ed. D. L. Protess and M. McCombs (Hillsdale, N.J.: Lawrence Erlbaum Associates, 1991), pp. 189–206.
161. M. Fishman, "Crime Waves as Ideology," *Social Problems* 25 (1978): 531–43.
162. D. L. Paletz, "The Media and Public Policy," in *The Politics of News, the News of Politics,* ed. D. Graber, D. McQuail, and P. Norris (Washington, D.C.:

Congressional Quarterly Press, 1998), pp. 218–37, at 226.
163. Ibid.
164. T. E. Patterson, *Out of Order* (New York: Vintage, 1993).
165. K. Beckett and T. Sasson, "The Media and the Construction of the Drug Crisis in America," in *The New War on Drugs: Symbolic Politics and Criminal Justice Policy,* ed. E. L. Jensen and J. Gerber (Cincinnati: ACJS/Anderson, 1998), pp. 25–43.
166. Oliver, *The Law and Order Presidency.*
167. M. H. Barlow, D. E. Barlow, and T. G. Chiricos, "Economic Conditions and Ideologies of Crime in the Media: A Content Analysis of Crime News," *Crime and Delinquency* 41 (1, 1995): 3–19.
168. Surette, *Media, Crime, and Criminal Justice,* 2nd ed., p. 217.
169. Van Horn et al., *Politics and Public Policy*, p. 234.
170. Beckett, "Setting the Public Agenda."

9

Interest Groups

Chapter Outline

INTRODUCTION

An interest group, sometimes called a pressure group, special interest, organized interest, or faction, is a group of citizens who are organized and attempt to influence legislation so that it reflects their interests or policy goals. Simply put, interest groups are collections of individuals with similar goals who are dedicated to influencing public policy. They do this by putting pressure on government officials so that they adopt policies that favor their interests. They attempt to impact what laws or policies the government passes in order for the new law to "look like" what they want it to be.[1]

The term *interest group* encompasses all organizations whose activities revolve around influencing the creation or implementation of public policy. Interest groups attempt to give citizens an indirect role in the political process by acting as their representatives in the political process, voicing their opinions to elected officials.

The potential dangers of interest groups were recognized early on by the Founding Fathers. The ability of elite groups to become involved in the legislative process and succeed in dominating the laws that are enacted was a real fear of the Founding Fathers. They felt that interest group involvement in the legislative process could possibly lead to lawmaking by the few, or the elite. Madison warned about the dangers of factions in Federalist No. 10. However, Madison also knew that citizens must have a voice in the lawmaking process if a democratic government was to be successful. He envisioned a system whereby all interest groups could play an active role in the policy process. If this happened, it would promote competition among groups, thus reducing the potential power of any single group. In other words, the influence of each group could be counterbalanced by others so that no one group could extend too much power in the policy process. Today, the government has a system that allows for group participation in the lawmaking process, and many interest groups take advantage of those opportunities and get involved in the policy process in many ways.

INTEREST GROUPS AND PUBLIC POLICY

Interest groups attempt to influence decisions made within the public policymaking system on the federal, state, and local levels by convincing elected officials to vote in their favor or to enact or interpret policies in such a way that it benefits them. Many interest groups are supported by corporations, banks, insurance companies, investment houses, law firms, media conglomerates, professional and trade associations, and civic organizations. For example, the labor union is represented by the AFL-CIO, which has certain perspectives on issues and wants those perspectives reflected in the laws passed by the U.S. Congress and in the manner in which those laws are implemented by bureaucracies or agencies.

Over the years, interest groups and Congress have established a mutual exchange relationship where each actor gives and receives something beneficial. Interest groups desire to have favorable policy decisions. They have the technical information needed by members of Congress to write an effective bill as well as research staff and other support services. Interest groups provide that information in exchange for positive policy. Additionally, interest groups may be able to reward congresspeople for that vote and sometimes are able to influence, if not actually deliver, votes for them at election time.

Although it is difficult to tell how much direct influence interest groups have, most critics agree that they are very powerful. If a group has helped provide campaign assistance to a political candidate at some time, it is unlikely that the member of Congress will fail to meet with representatives of those groups that helped that member of Congress and even take their opinions into consideration when making policy. It has become clear that congressional members respond to groups that clearly communicate their interests and have the funding to convey their message effectively.[2]

There have been some notable trends in the behavior of interest groups in recent years. First, there has been a tremendous proliferation of interest groups since the 1960s.[3] The number of interest groups based in Washington, D.C., has become more numerous.[4] This growth in the number of interest groups provides an opportunity for more citizens to become involved in the policy process in some way, from a passive role to a more active participation.[5] They have also become more visible.[6] This attracts even more members, giving them more opportunities for involvement.

Not only has the number of interest groups grown, but they are now pursuing more diverse policy goals as well.[7] "Single-issue groups," which focus on one issue or set of related issues, make up one type of group that has seen a proliferation in recent years. Similarly, the number of citizen groups (also called public interest groups) has grown. Most of these groups were created since the 1960s and tend to view political action as the principal means of achieving their policy goals.

Another type of interest group that has seen a tremendous growth consists of political action committees (PACs). These groups, which emerged during the 1970s, are specialized forms of political fund-raising groups that are organized to collect and disburse contributions (meaning that they contribute) to campaign directly to federal political candidates. They are typically formed by corporations, labor unions, professional organizations, health organizations, trade associations, farm groups, ideological groups, environmental groups, and other types of organizations[8] as the election arm of an interest group. Once a union creates a PAC, the members donate money to support either an individual political candidate or many candidates.[9]

Interest group PACs are now a major source of campaign funding, especially for members of Congress. "Each PAC is a separate, segregated fund that collects money to contribute to political campaigns, to use in independent expenditures for or against a candidate, or to sponsor campaign ads supporting or opposing a policy."[10] PACs are regulated by the Federal Election Commission, which requires them to register their finances and political contributions periodically. The McCain-Feingold-Cochran Campaign Reform bill, passed by Congress in 2002, also placed new limits on campaign contributions made by PACs by banning soft money, or unregulated contributions.[11]

Independent PACs, also called nonconnected PACs, are issue, ideological and type-of-candidate PACs. This means they support a particular issue, ideology, or type of candidate. Some examples of conservative PACs are the National Federation of Independent Business or the PAC affiliated with the National Rifle Association. These PACs tend to support conservative political policies. An example of an independent PAC is the Realtors Association, which advocates specific policies that benefit their industry but does not really take sides with a political party. Another example is Emily's List, which supports female candidates for political office regardless of their political party identification.[12] Some PACs work to support labor issues, such as the Committee on Political Education, which is a nonpartisan political arm of the AFL-CIO Committee on Political Education.[13]

Another recent change that has affected the behavior of interest groups is the movement toward locating headquarters or offices closer to Washington, D.C., closer to the legislative action, rather than in other major cities, such as New York City or elsewhere.[14] The interest groups based in Washington have become more diverse and include private firms, public interest groups, state and local governments.

Technological advances and developments, such as the Internet, have led to significant changes in how interest groups operate. These changes have enabled interest groups to communicate not only with their members more often and in a more timely fashion but also with members of Congress.[15] Technology allows groups to reach out to their members (and potential members) at a low cost. The groups can use the quick and easy communication to educate the public and to help convince people of their ideas; they can also use it to help with fund-raising.[16]

These technological advances have allowed more interest groups to form or expand because it is easier for them to have contact with the public and convince them to join the organization. They are more able to participate in electoral politics since producing and mailing thousands of specially targeted materials two weeks before an election is no longer difficult.[17]

THEORIES OF INTEREST GROUP BEHAVIOR

The importance of groups in the democratic process has been described by many scholars. Truman, in his classic work titled *The Governmental Process* (1951), wrote that politics can be understood only by looking at the interaction of groups. He called this idea "group theory."[18] Robert Dahl, who in 1961 wrote *Who Governs*, described the pluralist theory. He completed a study of local politics to see just who influenced policy outcomes. Dahl found that in three areas, different groups were active and influential. He described a process by which loosely organized coalitions of groups and politicians became active on issues they cared about. Most people, according to Dahl, become interested in the issues that directly affect them, but most times, they are apathetic. He wrote that policymaking through group interaction is a positive virtue, not a threat to democracy. In group politics, the interest groups generally succeed in their goals of influencing the government. This happens so often that the government, in some way, provides a measure of protection to almost all interests in society. However, this does not mean that all interests get exactly what they want at all times from the government or that the policies always reflect what they want. Instead, all interests get at least some rewards.[19]

Theodore Lowi has termed this proliferation of groups and their growing access to government "interest group liberalism." Lowi recognizes the importance and the inevitability of government intervention in private activity but argues that organized groups have become the primary political actors that ensure that government is responsive to the needs of the various interests. The concern is not whether the government will intervene or to what extent but rather the manner in which the intervention will occur. Lowi recognizes that those closest to a problem or issue are probably the most competent to deal with it. Interest group liberalism encourages government to allow groups to cooperate in both the design and the implementation of policy. Lowi argues that policymaking operates with a delegation of authority from legislatures to administrative agencies who in turn delegate it to interest groups with whom they have developed relationships.

Thus, government passes public power into private hands and discourages public officials from making clear policy choices.[20]

Although elected officials respond to different groups on different issues, at times it may seem as if the political elites have a disproportionate amount of power. This idea was described by C. Wright Mills in *The Power Elite* (1956). In it, he claimed that American policies are ruled by a small group of wealthy and powerful individuals who are generally corporate executives, rich families, military leaders, and politicians. Because of their wealth, they have an unusual amount of pull with the legislatures, thereby becoming the true decision makers in society. Interests with more resources usually will obtain better results than interests that possess fewer assets and employ them less effectively.[21]

The unprecedented, unchecked, and even dangerous growth in the numbers of interest groups has led to yet another theory, that being hyperpluralism. As noted earlier, there has been a dramatic proliferation of interest groups. This increase in the number of groups and the resulting increase in the openness of the policy process do not necessarily mean better policies or ones that genuinely represent the national interest. Instead, government may be unable to process demands effectively, and openness may result in complexity, ineffective policy, and waste.[22]

CHARACTERISTICS OF INTEREST GROUPS

There are many types of pressure groups that are diverse in their interests, organization, size, and modes of operation. Despite their differences, each interest group has the same goal: to influence government. They actively seek to influence the outcome of the policy process through both positive activity (promoting new courses of government action) and negative activity (seeking to block changes in public policy).[23] Despite their differences, each interest group has similar characteristics. Some characteristics of interest groups are discussed in the following sections.

Lobbying   The term "lobbyists" comes from the practice of interest group representatives who would, many years ago, wait in lobbies to walk a legislator to his or her next meeting and have some face-to-face contact with that person. Today, that representative is called a "lobbyist" or simply a group representative. That person represents the group's perspective to the legislator or top staff official and regularly meets with the legislator to discuss matters of concern. By this action, the group attempts to alter the voting behavior of those legislators. But lobbyists can also direct their activity at any institution of government, including the legislative, judicial, or executive branches.[24] They often initiate lawsuits, start a letter-writing campaign, file a formal comment on a proposed regulation, or talk face to face with congresspeople or bureaucrats.[25]

Lobbying can be direct, which may include some time of direct contact between the legislator (or top staff member) and the lobbyists. This can be testifying at committee hearings, contacting government offices directly, presenting research results, or assisting in the writing of legislation. Lobbying can also be indirect, which includes letter or telephone campaigns or working through constituencies. In either event, those in government are reminded how strongly constituents feel about an issue. Usually, direct contact is most effective because it can make the member of Congress understand the group's position. However, letter-writing campaigns are easier now because of the popularity and acceptance of computers. The group can contact its membership, provide them with information, and urge them to sign a postcard or letter.[26] They may also use a system of coordinated calls that can tie up the phones on Capitol Hill for days.[27]

Influence   Each interest group has some kind of influence with legislators, but the ability to use that influence is unequal from group to group. The amount of influence an interest group wields depends on a number of factors, including the size of the membership, its monetary and other resources, its cohesiveness, the skill of its leadership, its social status, the presence or absence of competing organizations, the attitudes of public officials, and the site of the decision making in the political system. Obviously, groups with more influence are more effective in lobbying policymakers and more successful at having an impact on legislation.

Size/Membership   Every interest group has a membership who pays dues to the group on a yearly basis. For those dues, members usually receive a newsletter or magazine containing information about relevant issues. They also know that their interests are being represented in Washington.

Interest groups come in all types and sizes. Some groups have many members, while others have fewer. Some groups have geographic dispersion in congressional districts throughout the country, whereas others are located in a particular area.[28] Generally, larger interest groups have more members who pay dues or contribute financially to the groups. More members usually translate into more power and influence for the organization. Larger groups will usually have more money, resources, staff, and lobbyists to work on reaching their goals. In combination, these factors give larger groups more power and influence in lobbying legislators, judicial members, or even the executive branch. Some examples of larger interest groups include the Sierra Club, Friends of Earth, the U.S. Chamber of Commerce, the American Medical Association, and the American Bar Association.

Resources   Every interest group, large or small, has some resources they can use to influence legislators. This can include many things: money, people, or campaign support. The number of resources a group has can give it an advantage or disadvantage over the other groups in affecting legislation.

Of course, one of the most important resources is money, or financial support, for the candidate or politician. Some interest groups have large budgets, making them effective in providing financial assistance to candidates and already elected officials. Since each candidate must raise his or her own money for a campaign, the costs of which only continue to escalate, the financial contributions of interest groups are very attractive. Campaign contributions can even be made through PACs.

The Lobbying Disclosure Act of 1995 requires that groups disclose how much money they spend in their efforts to influence legislation. These reports indicate that each year, lobbyists spend more than $1.25 billion trying to influence policy. Obviously, groups with less money may have more difficulty influencing votes, especially if they are battling groups with more money available to them.

Resources can also be nonfinancial assistance. Some groups use their personal contacts to their advantage. This allows some groups to "schmooze" with legislators and convince them to vote a particular way. Other groups may provide people to be used as resources for a candidate; this may include helping with a campaign by handing out leaflets, going door to door, appearing at rallies, or preparing mailings. The larger the interest group, the more members it has to provide this resource.

Expertise   Each interest group has a different level of expertise in a different policy arena. With that expertise, a group is able to provide valuable information to assist a member of Congress to support or oppose proposed legislation. They may have expertise in one area (a single-issue group) or multiple areas. The members' expertise in an area will help determine the strength of an interest group. Those with considerable expertise may have more power, as more legislators may depend on them for that information.[29]

Focus or Goals   Interest groups vary as to their topic area. They can be narrow in scope and focus on one or two issues or issue areas, such as single-issue groups do. Or groups can be more general or broad, such as the American Civil Liberties Union, which takes on civil rights issues of all sorts. Examples of single-issue groups are Operation Rescue and the National Abortion Rights Action League, which focus on the abortion issue, or the National Rifle Association and Handgun Control, Inc., which revolve around the issue of the availability of guns.[30]

Longevity   Some interest groups are permanent, and others come and go quickly. Some were established over a hundred years ago, while others have emerged as the result of a recent social issue. Some stay around, while others may dissolve once the issue is addressed by legislators. Those groups with longevity typically have more power and influence simply because they have become more established in the policy arena.

Power   All interest groups have the power to influence legislators but to varying degrees. Power is the ability to get people to do what you want them to do. The distribution of power among interest groups has been described as not being a contest among equals.[31] The groups that can promise and deliver large numbers of votes to candidates and elected officials tend to be more influential and thus have more power. Of course, the ability to contribute campaign resources (either money or manpower) is also powerful. Groups that are well organized, large sized, and have a qualified leadership are more likely to have more influence than those that are poorly organized, poorly financed, and low in their social status.[32]

Organization   All interest groups have some type of organizational structure,[33] such as by-laws, a board of directors, and/or a governing board with formal authority over staff and operation of the group. The group's organization will usually include a division of labor that is based on function or issue.[34] Each position in the organization is assigned a specific task. Of course, the extent of organization will depend on the individual interest group. Some interest groups have a highly structured organization that mirrors that of a complex corporation, while others may be four or five people who simply work together on an informal basis. The organization will depend on many factors, including the number of members.

Build Coalitions   Most organizations will, in certain circumstances, build coalitions with other groups in an attempt to influence policies that they would never take on by themselves. Two or more groups may combine forces and pool their funds, resources, and/or staffs to work side by side to do this. If many interest groups share a point of view, they can divide the task, each group taking the members of Congress with whom it is most familiar. Coalitions usually last only until some resolution of an issue is reached.[35]

Catalyze Grassroots Support   Many interest groups reach out to group members or other interested individuals and get them involved in an effort to influence legislation. This is called grassroots support. Interest groups can organize and mobilize grassroots efforts to influence Congress and the White House by encouraging letters, phone calls, and visits by individual constituents and campaign contributors.[36] This way, the interest group can show the public's support or opposition to a proposal and attempt to sway the vote on a proposed bill. Some groups have the ability to easily mobilize their members and sympathizers, whereas others are less effective at this.[37]

Knowledge of Other Groups   Every interest group has information about the opposing groups so that they can counteract their initiatives. They understand their techniques and try to counter them with their own initiatives. They are also aware of other groups that may share similar goals. In this case, the groups may coordinate their efforts to be more successful in influencing legislation.

Educate the Public   Every interest group engages in research to uncover data on their own and then uses that to make people aware of the significance of the problem or issue at hand.[38] Groups will often work to disseminate their research findings about these political issues through a public relations campaign of some kind. They may purchase advertising space in newspapers and magazines, and they can publicize voting records of officeholders. Through educating the public, the interest group hopes that more people will join their organization, thus becoming a financial resource (when they pay dues) and a personal resource for the group.

ROLE IN POLICY PROCESS

For many years, political scientists have studied the role of interest groups in the policymaking process, yet the literature is sparse and diverse. The activities of an interest group are protected in the U.S. Constitution.[39] In a pluralist society, interest groups have many points of access to Congress and the process by which a bill becomes a law. The behavior, activity level, and role of these interest groups are varied. Some of the activity is focused on affecting the agenda, whereas other activity affects the alternatives considered by policymakers. Whatever it might be, the interest groups play a significant role in the policy process, including identifying the problem, setting the agenda, program evaluation, and some other roles.

Problem Identification

The role that interest groups play in initiating policy is key to the policymaking process. Public policy does not automatically occur and become a rational solution to an existing problem; rather, a problem must first be recognized. These problems are often brought to light by interest groups that are often more closely aware of the issues that must be faced by individuals working in the field every day. Since the workers are not usually able to travel to meet with legislators in Washington, interest groups will represent them and make their problems known to the elected officials serving there.

Lawmakers need to be made aware of one or more groups that are experiencing some type of dysfunction before they can act, and interest groups often do that. Take, for example, the issue of battered women. For many years, women were abused and battered by their spouses, but it was not recognized as a problem until women's organizations came forward to help identify the problem and shape people's perceptions of the victims and the offenders and demand some action by legislators to solve the problem. The issues surrounding battered women were eventually addressed by politicians, and action was taken. The women's groups were able to shape the social perceptions people had about the issue and identify it as a problem in need of congressional action.[40]

Interest groups, whether they are large or small, rich or poor, can help identify significant problems and turn those problems into political issues that become part of the political agenda that elected officials feel they must address. Interest groups can make elected officials and the general public aware of a particular issue that needs action.[41] This can be done in a variety of ways, either by meeting directly with members of Congress or their staff or through their constituencies in a letter-writing or telephone campaign as discussed previously. The interest group may also use the media to bring attention to the problem. In essence, the interest group is frequently responsible for bringing the issue to light in the first place. In fact, interest groups are a major source of demands for public policy action in the United States.

Agenda Setting

Once the problem has been identified, interest groups apply pressure on elected officials to have that issue placed on the agenda. Interest groups are major actors in supplying possible solutions to the problems identified earlier or advocating a certain proposal over another. Putting pressure on elected officials to deal with a problem can force them to give some attention to a serious issue of which they may not have been previously aware.[42]

Because interest groups cannot formally introduce legislation, they need to work with a "friendly legislator," a member of Congress who supports their ideas. This friendly legislator will introduce the legislation for the interest group, otherwise known as "dropping it in the hopper."[43]

Many interest groups focus on "negative blocking," through which interest groups attempt to block any new legislation that may reduce the existing benefits to interest group members. By blocking the legislation, the interest group is attempting to preserve any benefits that its members are currently receiving.[44] It attempts to discredit an alternative to the point that it is never seriously considered. Such a non-decision-making strategy is used to protect an existing policy.[45]

Many interest groups are effective in getting a criminal justice policy on the politicians' agenda. One of those is Mothers Against Drunk Driving (MADD). Created by a California mom whose daughter was killed by a drunk driver, this group was able to establish drunk driving as a major public problem during the 1980s. MADD effectively put the issue on the public's agenda even though there was no rise in the incidence or prevalence of drinking and driving accidents across the country. They claimed that the problems associated with drinking and driving had long existed and never been treated seriously by legislatures and the courts.[46] Other examples of criminal justice interest groups are listed in Boxes 9.1–9.4 below.

BOX 9.1

Criminal Justice Interest Groups Related to the Issue of Gun Control

Brady Campaign to Prevent Gun Violence

Supports sensible regulations to reduce gun violence, such as legislation to make it harder for convicted felons and mentally ill to get guns, and exposing corrupt gun dealers.

Coalition to Stop Gun Violence

Seeks to achieve freedom from gun violence. The group is comprised of 48 national organizations that work together to reduce gun violence. These organizations include religious groups, child welfare advocates, public health professionals and social justice organizations, each of which share a visions of non-violence.

Second Amendment Foundation

Promotes education and outreach regarding gun rights and responsibilities of gun owners.

Students for Concealed Carry on Campus

Supports allowing students, faculty and staff to carry concealed guns to campus for self defense.

BOX 9.1
(continued)

Citizens for the Right to Keep and Bear Arms
Promotes education and outreach regarding gun rights.

Law Enforcement Alliance of America
A gun rights group comprised of active duty and retired law enforcement officers, crime victims and other interested citizens. The organization attempts to explain police "use of force" policies, supports concealed carry laws especially for off-duty and retired law enforcement officers, and supports strengthening laws to punish violent criminals, including the death penalty.

Liberty Belles
An organization with a primary focus on women and gun rights, this organization seeks to dispel the myths about owning firearms. They often participate in outreach at community events at shooting ranges and rallies.

National Shooting Sports Foundation
Comprises gun manufacturers, distributors, retailers, sportsmen organizations and members of the media, the group supports the shooting, hunting and firearms industry.

Violence Policy Center
A national educational organization focused on reducing violence in America, especially relating to guns.

Gun Owners of America
Supports gun ownership and research. The group is known for being "the only no-compromise gun lobby in Washington." In 2004, they spent over $1.75 million to lobby Congress on gun legislation.

Jews for the Preservation of Firearms Ownership
A group of around 4,000 members, the organization works to preserve gun rights.

Mayors Against Illegal Guns
A coalition of mayors from different political parties that seeks to stop illegal trafficking in guns and make it easier to track guns used in crimes.

Pink Pistols
A gay gun rights group that supports firing range visits and political activism. They grade legislators based on their records of supporting issues relevant to the group.

American Hunters and Shooters
Committed to supporting the right to own guns, protect homes, and preserve liberties. The group is comprised of hunters who are committed to safe and responsible gun ownership.

BOX 9.2
Civil Liberties Interest Groups

American Civil Liberties Union (ACLU)
Renown interest group that focuses on protecting human rights and particularly constitutional rights of American citizens, especially First Amendment rights.

Anti-Defamation League (ADL)
Helps people counteract hate and helps victims of bias crimes; works with legislators, educators, and community and religious leaders to combat all forms of bigotry and prejudice; and has programs and materials that promote respect for all individuals.

Equal Justice USA
Wants to spark public scrutiny and concern about racial and class biases pervading the U.S. criminal justice system, capital punishment in particular; has a Moratorium Now! Campaign to bring about a national moratorium on executions, beginning state by state and gaining nationwide momentum; wants to deepen public understanding about how the death penalty is applied and how it violates human rights; and tries to recruit other groups to join the call for a moratorium on the death penalty.

BOX 9.3
Private Research Interest Groups

Criminal Justice Policy Foundation

Conducts surveys and research on solutions to criminal justice problems such as drug policy and policing practices.

Heritage Foundation

Nation's major conservative think tank dedicated to preserving America's traditional values.

Institute for Law and Justice (ILJ)

Private, nonprofit research and consulting firm that reviews legislation for impact analysis.

Police Executive Research Forum (PERF)

Partnership organization of academics and chiefs from the nation's largest cities dedicated to innovative policing, professionalism, research, and involvement in public debate.

Rand Corporation

Nonprofit institution and nation's major think tank on policy decision making, involved in a number of criminal justice-related issues, including crime control, drug laws, sentencing, and prison management.

Vera Institute of Justice

Nonprofit agency working to establish more humane alternatives to prison and the criminal justice system.

BOX 9.4
Criminal Justice Professional Organizations

Academy of Criminal Justice Sciences (ACJS)

Leading professional association devoted to scholarly study of criminal justice issues, composed primarily of college professors.

American Bar Association (ABA)

Lobby group composed primarily of lawyers working on solutions to the nation's crime problem.

American Correctional Association (ACA)

Leading correctional employee association for those interested in professionalism, runs a program that accredits prisons.

American Judicature Society (AJS)

Professional organization of nonpartisan judges, lawyers, and citizens working toward better judicial selection, ethics, and effectiveness in criminal justice.

American Society of Criminology (ASC)

Leading professional association devoted to the scholarly study of crime, composed primarily of college professors.

American Society for Industrial Security (ASIS)

Leading professional association for the private security industry.

International Association of Chiefs of Police (IACP)

Leading and oldest professional association for police professionalism.

National Organization of Black Law Enforcement Executives (NOBLE)

Policing organization of black police chiefs from across the nation.

Policy Formation

Interest groups play a major role in the policy formation stage of the policy process. Once an issue is placed on the agenda, there are many ways for interest groups to influence that proposal. They are key facilitators in the bargaining, negotiating, and compromising that take place during the lawmaking process.[47] Their involvement and effectiveness in the policy formulation stage reflect their resources and level of influence.[48]

Interest groups play a serious role in proposing potential legislation. Interest groups will often give the legislatures or even executive officials specific proposals for legislation that reflects their interest and will continue to work with that member of Congress to get a specific policy proposal turned into law. Those interest group representatives who push certain policy proposals are referred to as policy entrepreneurs. To do that, the policy entrepreneurs may provide information to members of Congress when they are drafting the proposal. They usually provide technical information about the likely impact of legislation or even the political ramifications of a bill. They can also provide relevant information to congressional committees and subcommittees when they are debating, or "marking up," the proposal. Because they are experts in the field and members of Congress generally do not have that information, interest groups are able to easily provide expertise, information, and status to members of Congress.

Since most of the work on a bill is done in committees, interest group lobbyists are more active here. At times, interest groups become most visible when they attempt to influence pending legislation. Interest groups may even persuade committees to hold hearings in the first place. Officials from interest groups are often called to testify in the hearings, and these activities bring a great deal of publicity to an issue. They may even get press coverage, which in turn may create public sympathy for the issues.[49]

The committee-based policymaking system that makes up the policy process actually helps interest groups succeed in influencing legislation. There are many opportunities to insert provisions that benefit a certain group.[50] Additionally, the committees are smaller than the entire body of the House or Senate and thus are easier to manage and influence. The small committees also facilitate the building of personal relationships. Over time, regular contacts allow lobbyists to prove that their information is reliable and that they can be trusted to assist the committee members in developing quality legislation.[51]

Sometimes, there is an implicit "threat" that the interest group will work to defeat a congressional member if he or she refuses to support the group's policies. Conversely, the interest group may promise electoral support if the member agrees to promote the group's proposals.[52] This potential threat or promise of support can influence actions by Congress.

However, even if an interest group successfully raises an issue and is able to have it placed on the agenda, the interest group does not always control the debate surrounding that issue.[53] It may be able to have the issue placed on the agenda but then is unsuccessful in influencing the alternatives considered.[54]

The role that interest groups play in the policy process and in policy formation in particular is understood in the concept of the iron triangle described earlier. In this relationship, interest groups give information to the legislators and to the bureaucracies. In exchange for that information, interest groups receive a "reward" from the other actors. Congress may pass legislation that is beneficial to the interest group and reflects its needs. Bureaucracies use their discretion to define and implement policies in their interests.

Citizens and groups of all stripes have a potential if not a lively interest in criminal justice issues. Many groups will place demands on the legislative system for action.[55] Each group may have different problems and approaches to solving those problems. Satisfying conflicting demands between groups is difficult for legislatures. There is always opposition to every proposal. Interest groups may reach out for support from the general public, but they also turn to professional groups. In fact, support from the public may be less vital and less powerful than even modest support from professionals who work within the ranks of the criminal justice system. Their proposals yield significant insights, and their support for a bill can influence others to support it as well.[56]

Many people complain about politicians' close relationships with interest groups, arguing that some groups are able to control the decisions of elected representatives, giving them too much power in the policy process. In essence, they argue that the groups are able to create policy proposals that reflect their interests rather than policy that is in the best interests of society.[57] Even some elected officials have attacked the undue influence of organized interests on the policy process, arguing that the lawyers and lobbyists who represent organized interests in Washington are narrow or selfish.[58] They claim that policy is consistent with the concerns of interest groups rather than what is "best." The public often attempts to limit the potential power or influence of groups through campaign finance laws, term limits, and restrictions on lobbying. But the influence of criminal justice interest groups remains strong in the policy process, as they argue that their actions are in the public interest. They are able to dominate and define the issues "on behalf of the public."[59]

Despite these concerns, Congress continues to rely on interest groups. "It is hard to imagine Congress functioning today without interest groups, given legislators' insatiable need for information relevant to policymaking."[60] Legislators need access to the information that is provided by the groups. They also need the campaign assistance provided by interest group members if the legislation successfully passes.

Program Evaluation

Interest groups are often involved in the final stages of the policy process, including program evaluation. They are often directly associated with program monitoring, as they closely follow programs that affect their constituents. If they discover a program that is not benefiting their members, they will often try to draw attention to shortcomings they observe. They may also decide to issue evaluative reports and contact people in the media. They may also lobby agency personnel to make changes in program implementation or go to court in an effort to exact compliance with the law.[61]

Other Roles

Interest groups have played a big role in campaigns and elections since the 1960s.[62] Interest groups attempt to influence who is elected into office, with the hopes of having their supporters who share their views elected into offices where they can be influential in passing legislation favorable to the group. By aiding incumbents in their reelection bids, the interest group can more easily approach policymakers to argue their cases.[63] In this way, the policies they support will be implemented.

To do this, interest groups will choose to endorse specific candidates.[64] These endorsements can often be very valuable. Interest groups can also contribute money to candidates and parties or organize fund-raising events; distribute voters' guides; provide volunteer labor to stamp envelopes or distribute campaign literature door to door; finance television, radio, and print advertising; and call citizens to encourage them to vote. In some cases, the groups recruit candidates or even attempt to influence the party platforms.[65] They can also choose to play an organizational role, helping the chosen candidate disseminate his or her message. This, in turn, will help deliver the votes to that candidate on election day.[66]

LOBBYING THE PRESIDENT   The influence of organized interest groups permeates not only the lawmaking process in Congress but also that of the federal executive agencies. Typically, interest groups do not lobby the president simply because they don't have that kind of access. But the groups' lobbyists will meet with other members of the executive branch, including department heads and other high-level bureaucrats. Obviously, the groups lobby for their own interests. They attempt to convince the bureaucrat of a particular need and that it is necessary to implement laws in a particular fashion to meet that need.

LOBBYING THE COURTS   Interest groups try to influence policy by exerting influence on the courts and judicial decision making. Interest groups lobby justices in an attempt to influence their decisions just as they lobby members of the legislature in an attempt to influence their behavior. Most of the time, judges are considered to be immune from the politics that are found in the other branches of government, and most justices have the image of being nonpolitical and above the political fray. The direct lobbying of justices at any level is considered a violation of judicial ethics. Few lobbyists would consider contacting a judge about a case, and few judges would react favorably to that type of contact.[67] This makes courts more difficult to lobby as compared to legislators or the executive branch. The interest groups' influence on the court's behavior is limited because of this. It is sometimes difficult for the group to achieve any significant influence over the justices' decisions.[68] However, going to court may be part of a broader group strategy used by interest groups to obtain government policies favorable to the group.

Most people would agree that today, members of the court are not immune from political pressures or the effects of organized pressure-group lobbying,[69] and interest groups actively attempt to advance their agendas in the courts. In fact, interest groups now view the judicial branch of government as a critical access point that they can attempt to influence.[70] They do this in many ways, including through litigation and in the process for selecting judges.

Litigation   The technique of bringing litigation to the courts became more popular in the late 1960s and early 1970s. At that time, political activists were looking for new methods for creating political change. To their benefit, the rules of standing were liberalized, giving them more opportunities to bring cases before the courts. Other interest groups saw how effective litigation was, so they began to do it themselves. As citizen groups began to win major victories in courts, litigation techniques became more popular with other groups.[71]

In recent years, there has been a significant increase in interest group litigation before the U.S. Supreme Court. Between 1986 and 1996, 76 percent of the full-opinion cases contained at least one amicus curiae ("friend of the court") brief.[72]

Since directly lobbying the courts is not well accepted, interest groups lobby the courts indirectly through litigation.[73] The most important basis for influence over the court is in written briefs and oral arguments. This way, group representatives try to shape policymakers' perceptions of the choices that they face. The groups commonly submit amicus curiae briefs in which they suggest legal strategies the court might follow to come to a particular conclusion. The briefs also try to draw the justices' attention to the political implications or ramifications of both the case and the decision. For example, these briefs often make note of the size of the group submitting the brief and the impact a particular decision would have on the group's membership, on the national economy, or on the social conditions and political activities in the nation.[74]

Often, interest groups will lobby the court to influence a decision or to delay the implementation of a policy if they have no other immediate way to change a policy quickly.[75] Some groups may attempt to lobby the courts if they do not have the access and resources to influence public policy in the legislative and executive branches.[76]

Interest groups use many litigation strategies to influence the court's decisions. It has become common for interest groups to use a test case, that is, to sponsor a case through the court system. They can locate a person who has been injured, who has suffered a loss, or who has a real grievance to serve as a plaintiff in a case. The group will then provide legal or financial assistance so that the case can go through the court system, even to the Supreme Court. Since interest groups have more resources than most individuals, they are able to provide the money to finance the case. They try to use the case to legally challenge the basic constitutionality of a law, government rule, or policy. The group may focus on a broad principle of law in order to obtain a general court ruling. "Typically, reform-seeking litigation involves a lawsuit against a governmental agency by an individual, often backed by an interest group, seeking judicial protection of an asserted constitutional right."[77] The groups know that a favorable court ruling must be applied to similar circumstances in the future, and this helps further their goals.

Interest groups often bring cases to trial concerning racial or gender-based discrimination. They have brought to court virtually all civil liberties cases and more than one-third of the cases involving business matters. In fact, the majority of important constitutional cases decided by the Supreme Court are brought by organized groups as test cases.[78]

Interest groups sometimes file amicus curiae briefs with the court. These are legal documents that provide legal and policy arguments in support of one of the parties to a case. When a group files these briefs, it does not directly participate in cases. The group is usually not a direct party but has an interest in the outcome of the case. If a group is not satisfied with the type or quality of legal argument being made by the parties in the case or if it is requested by the parties to submit an amicus curiae brief, it may provide an additional legal interpretation to those being used by the participants in the case. These briefs give the court another view on the possible implications of the decision and urge adoption of their favored resolution of legal disputes. They are also a way for groups to provide information to decision makers. By filing these briefs, the group is demonstrating to the court, the public, and their members that it is strongly committed to a certain position.[79]

Another way groups lobby the courts and persuade them to vote a particular way to influence policy is through class-action suits. These are cases in which a plaintiff claims to represent the interests of many people who have suffered harm. The dispute affects them in essentially the same way. There is not one specific individual plaintiff but many.

Finally, an interest group may use a Brandeis Brief to lobby the court. This type of brief stresses the social and economic conditions that are relevant to the case rather than formal law and precedent. These briefs can provide information on new ideas, information, or technology that can promote change instead of the traditional reliance on written law, which reflects the past thinking on an issue. Here, interest groups attempt to make the judges aware of the need to make new policies.[80]

There are other options that groups have to lobby the court. Some interest groups attempt to influence the court's decision as to whether to accept cases through participation in oral argument or the submission of legal briefs. Other groups attempt to lobby the court indirectly by holding demonstrations or starting a letter-writing campaign directed at the justices.

Both liberal and conservative groups have used litigation techniques to pursue their policy agendas for many years. Such techniques have led to many changes, including the improvement of living conditions in prisons and jails across the country.[81] Many groups use litigation to bring about change rather than try to lobby Congress. The American Civil Liberties Union, which concentrates on human rights issues; the National Association for the Advancement of Colored People, which focuses on racial equality disputes; the Sierra Club (an environmental group); and consumer and safety groups, such as Ralph Nader's organizations, have all done this.

In order for an interest group to effectively lobby a court, it needs to have certain characteristics. First, the group must have sufficient longevity to withstand the process of pursuing legal cases. Some cases may take years or even decades before benefits are seen. To be effective, an interest group must be stable over a long period of time. Second, a group must have adequate financial resources to afford the case. This may include a legal staff to maintain litigation. This becomes especially important when affluent interests or government entities that can afford to prolong the litigation process are involved. Third, interest groups must have the ability to generate well-timed publicity. This can create a positive public image, which in turn may enhance a group's ability to create financial support, favorable public opinion, and broader circulation of legal arguments and evidence.[82]

Since lawsuits can become quite expensive, litigation techniques are used more frequently by larger interest groups that have their own legal staffs.[83]

Selection   Interest groups try to affect policy by influencing who gets seated on the court. All judges must face some kind of political process to serve on the bench. They are either elected or appointed through a political process, and interest groups get involved in both of these processes. Interest groups know that the appointment of every justice to the Supreme Court can lead to major changes in policies that affect them. Thus, interest groups play a big role in the judicial appointment process.[84] For example, in 1987, when Robert Bork was nominated to the Supreme Court, there were 147 groups active in one or more phases of the process.[85]

Additionally, interest groups can be a valuable source of information about judicial nominees for both the senators involved in the process and members of the public. Interest groups can attempt to manipulate the press, the media, and public opinion in the judicial nominating process.[86] All these actions can potentially affect the nomination and/or approval of a candidate.

LOBBYING THE BUREAUCRACIES   Another tactic used by interest groups to affect the policy process is to lobby bureaucracies. This is because bureaucracies are so entrenched in the policy-making process and because of the close relationships that have developed between bureaucracies and interest groups (i.e., the iron triangle). This is especially important for those groups that are not as effective at lobbying the legislatures. And since most interest groups do not have direct access to the Oval Office,[87] they are unable to influence policy in that way. Instead, they can lobby the bureaucracies that do have access, such as cabinet departments and independent agencies. Congress and the president often delegate authority to these lower-level administrators who are then lobbied by special interests.[88]

Interest groups use a variety of techniques to influence decisions made by the federal bureaucracy. One of these is to use the "comment period," which the federal administrative agencies must provide as part of the rule-making process. Although this is not always an oral hearing, some statutes do require some kind of hearing where interested parties can relay their concerns.[89]

Another technique used by interest groups for influencing federal agency decision making is to influence particular members of Congress for a certain action. For example, the interest group can convince a member of Congress for the need to hold an oversight hearing that puts the offending agency in the spotlight, or the interest group can persuade a member of Congress to threaten an agency with an appropriations reduction if the agency does not rethink its position in a particular area.[90]

An interest group can also try to ensure that the top political executives, particularly those who run the agency, are supportive of the interest group's positions.

The interest group can mobilize a letter-writing campaign or schedule a series of personal visits to put pressure on the agency to act in a certain way.[91] The letters can come from constituents, supporters, other officials, or whoever may be influential in forcing the bureaucracy to perform in a way that would be acceptable to the interest group. The same is true of personal visits or personal contacts from either officials or supporters who may have some influence in encouraging a particular bureaucratic action.

There is some evidence that the influence that interest groups have has been declining over time because the contacts between interest group representatives and civil servants have declined. However, other research shows the opposite to be true and that the influence the interest groups have in affecting legislation is indeed strong.[92]

REVERSE INTEREST GROUP LOBBYING   Reverse interest group lobbying refers to officials attempting to lobby the lobbyists or interest group representatives. In other words, the government turns to the interest group. Government members and staff seek to mobilize interest group coalitions and their lobbyists so that the interest group leaders may then organize and mobilize their memberships to support or oppose proposed policies. Interest group members may become the targets for campaign solicitation by members of Congress who are seeking reelection. Reverse interest group lobbying typically does not involve letter-writing campaigns, but congressional members may turn to interest groups, such as law enforcement groups, defense attorneys, or other professional groups, for support for a bill.

These actions are, to some extent, limited by the Anti-Lobbying Act, which states that White House and executive branch officials may not coordinate efforts to mobilize support for administration policies with allied interest groups that are recipients of federal funds through contract and grants.

EXAMPLES OF FEDERAL CRIMINAL JUSTICE INTEREST GROUPS

For the most part, interest group activity in criminal justice is unique. While there are many groups that are influential at the national level that will, on occasion, be concerned with criminal justice, there are only a few groups that focus solely on criminal justice issues.[93] Box 9.1 shows some examples of effective interest groups that are involved in the criminal justice issue of gun control. Although they differ in their ideological perspective, they all seek to influence criminal justice legislation.

Interest groups in criminal justice have been divided into different types. There are legal and criminal justice professional associations, such as the American Bar Association, the National Black Police Association, the International Association of Chiefs of Police, and the National Legal Aid and Defender Association. These groups represent the interests of the particular group if legislation is proposed that will affect that group. In this case, such legislation might be procedures concerning arrests that may impact policing and court personnel. A second group of interests consists of reform groups, such as the National Council on Crime and Delinquency, which are concerned with reforming the criminal justice system to improve the way in which justice is meted out. A third type of group is made up of representatives from state agencies, such as the group representing state attorneys general. Civil liberties groups are another type of group, such as the American Civil Liberties Union, which helps ensure that the civil rights of all individuals are protected. Finally, there are issue-related groups, such as the National Coalition to Ban Handguns, which focus on specific issues.[94]

Probably the most well-known interest group that is active in criminal justice is the National Rifle Association (NRA), which was established in 1871. It is committed to promoting and protecting the rights of gun owners.[95] The group currently has around 4 million members and significant resources. In the 2008 presidential campaign, the NRA spent nearly 10 million to support or oppose candidates.[96] It has a large, geographically dispersed, and loyal membership. It also has the ability to quickly communicate with the members through state NRA chapters and gun clubs.[97] One division of the NRA is the Institute for Legislative Action. This is the "lobbying" group of the NRA. This group works to achieve laws that support pro-gun policies on the federal and state levels through lobbying techniques such as letter-writing, e-mails, faxes and telephone calls to officials. Another division of the NRA is the Political Victory Fund, a political action group (or PAC). They get involved in political campaigns by ranking the candidates based on voting records and public statements. The group claims that they have an 84 percent success rate in getting candidates elected to office who will support the NRA's policy position.

The NRA has many techniques for helping candidates. The organization gives political candidates for Congress a grade (from A to F) on their support for the group. Those who most actively support the NRA get an A. The grades are published in the *American Rifleman*. The NRA can also choose to endorse a particular candidate. Only those candidates who are allies of the NRA will receive its endorsement. The NRA often contributes money to the candidate's campaign. It uses both "in-kind" contributions, such as fund-raising and meet-and-greet events to help the candidates, and cash contributions. The NRA can also use independent expenditures to help its candidates, including radio or television ads to telephone banks.

STATE AND LOCAL INTEREST GROUPS

At the state level, criminal justice interest groups may play a major part in formulating legislation because state legislators frequently lack time and staff needed to cope with such matters.[98] Some would argue that private groups on the state and local levels have more power than on the federal level and can become the actual formulators of policy because the state political arena is smaller than the federal, giving the groups more opportunities to influence decisions made by policymakers.

The interest group environment is different from one state to another. There is some variation in the composition of the groups in different states. There are also differences in the amount of influence they have with the legislators. Generally, in states where political parties are strong, interest groups tend to be weak and vice versa.[99] Strong parties provide leadership in the policy-making process, and interest groups will function through them. In situations where there is a lack of political party leadership and organization, interest groups will fill the void.

Interest groups also get involved in local elections and community issues. At the local level, the focus of interest group activity is on the actions of government, including policy implementation and service delivery. Groups such as business groups (Chamber of Commerce), neighborhood groups, civic groups (League of Women Voters), labor unions, environmental groups, and ethnic groups become more involved. Some examples of interest groups in state and local systems are given in Box 9.5.

BOX 9.5

State and Local Interest Groups

Center for Court Innovation

A New York City interest group that conducts research on community courts and community-based initiatives.

Justice for All

An advocate for criminal justice reform out of Houston, Texas, aimed at making the criminal justice system better by protecting the lives and property of law-abiding citizens.

Maryland Network Against Domestic Violence

An advocate for victims of domestic violence that assists with referrals and providing medical and legal resources.

Research Triangle Institute

North Carolina-based think tank that conducts research on crime problems involving drugs, policing, and so on but mostly from an environmental perspective.

Texas State Rifle Association

State-level guns right group.

Conclusion

Interest groups play a significant role in the policy process from problem identification to policy formulation. There are many interest groups in criminal justice that are active in actions geared toward influencing legislation so that it reflects their perspective or their goals. Some interest groups are more effective at doing this than others. They must interact (or lobby) effectively with other political actors, including the president, courts, and bureaucracies, to help further their cause. One way this is done is through an attempt to influence who gets elected or appointed into office. But their ultimate goal is to influence the decision makers and policy implementers so that the decisions that are made support the interests of their group.

Notes

1. Jeffrey M. Berry, *The Interest Group Society* (Boston: Little, Brown, 1984); Michael A. Hallett and Dennis J. Palumbo, U.S. *Criminal Justice Interest Groups* (Westport, Conn.: Greenwood Press, 1993), p. xiii; Erika S. Fairchild, "Interest Groups in the Criminal Justice Process," *Journal of Criminal Justice* 9 (1981): 181–94, at 183.
2. Allan J. Cigler and Mark Joslyn, "Groups, Social Capital, and Democratic Orientations" in *Interest Group Politics*, ed. Allan J. Cigler and Burdett A. Loomis (Washington, D.C.: Congressional Quarterly Press, 2002), pp. 37–53.
3. Ibid., p. 3.
4. William T. Gormley, Jr., "Interest Group Interventions in the Administrative Process: Conspirators and Co-conspirators," in *The Interest Group Connection*, ed. Paul S. Hernson, Ronald G. Shaiko, and Clyde Wilcox (Chatham, N.J.: Chatham House, 1998), pp. 213–23.
5. Cigler and Joslyn, "Groups, Social Capital, and Democratic Orientations," p. 41.
6. Ibid., p. 3.
7. Mark J. Rozell and Clyde Wilcox, *Interest Groups in American Campaigns* (Washington, D.C.: Congressional Quarterly Press, 1999).
8. Paul S. Hernson, "Interest Groups, PACs, and Campaigns," in Hernson et al., *The Interest Group Connection*, pp. 37–51.
9. M. Margaret Conway, Joanne Conner Green, and Marian Currinder, "Interest Group Money in Elections," in *Interest Group Politics*, ed. A. Loomis (Washington, D.C.: Congressional Quarterly Press, 2002), pp. 118–40, at 119.
10. Ibid., p. 122.

11. "President Signs Campaign Finance Reform Act," available online at www.whitehouse.gov; Hoover Institution, "The McCain-Feingold-Cochran Campaign Reform Bill," available online at www.campaignfinancesite.org/legislation/mccain.html.

12. Conway et al., p. 122.

13. "What Is C.O.P.E.," available online at www.ibew332.org.

14. Cigler and Loomis, *Interest Group Politics*, p. 3; William T. Gormley, Jr., "Interest Group Interventions in the Administrative Process: Conspirators and Co-Conspirators," in Hernson et al., *The Interest Group Connection*, pp. 213–23.

15. Cigler and Loomis, *Interest Group Politics*, p. 3.

16. Christopher J. Boss and Michael Thomas, "Just Another Tool? How Environmental Groups Use the Internet," in Cigler and Loomis, *Interest Group Politics*, pp. 95–114.

17. Rozell and Wilcox, *Interest Groups in American Campaigns*.

18. David B. Truman, *The Governmental Process* (New York: Knopf, 1951).

19. Robert A. Dahl, *Who Governs?* (New Haven, Conn.: Yale University Press).

20. Theodore Lowi, *The End of Liberalism* (New York: Norton, 1979); Malcolm Feeley and Austin D. Sarat, *The Policy Dilemma: Federal Crime Policy and the Law Enforcement Assistance Administration* (Minneapolis: University of Minnesota Press, 1980).

21. C. Wright Mills, *The Power Elite* (New York: Oxford University Press, 1956).

22. Cigler and Loomis, *Interest Group Politics*, p. 29.

23. John W. Kingdon, *Agendas, Alternatives, and Public Policies* (New York: HarperCollins, 1995), p. 49.

24. Berry, *The Interest Group Society*.

25. Hallett and Palumbo, U.S. Criminal Justice Interest Groups, p. xiii.

26. Clyde Wilcox, "The Dynamics of Lobbying the Hill," in Hernson et al., *The Interest Group Connection*, pp. 89–99.

27. Ibid.

28. Kingdon, *Agendas, Alternatives, and Public Policies*, p. 51.

29. Robert Lorinskas, David Kalinich, and Dennis Banas, "Interest Groups and Criminal Behavior," *Journal of Research in Crime and Delinquency* 28 (2, 1994): 157–73.

30. Barbara Stolz, *Criminal Justice Policy Making* (Westport, Conn.: Praeger, 2002).

31. James E. Anderson, *Public Policymaking* (Boston: Houghton Mifflin, 2003); John P. Heinz, Edward O. Laumann, Robert L. Nelson, and Robert H. Salisbury, *The Hollow Core: Private Interests in National Policy Making* (Cambridge, Mass.: Harvard University Press, 1993).

32. Ibid.

33. Berry, *The Interest Group Society*.

34. Ibid.

35. Ibid.

36. Thomas R. Dye, *Top Down Policy Making* (New York: Chatham House, 2001).

37. Kingdon, *Agendas, Alternatives, and Public Policies*, p. 51.

38. Berry, *The Interest Group Society*.

39. Stolz, *Criminal Justice Policy Making*, p. 7.

40. Thomas M. Meenaghan, Keith M. Kilty, and John G. McNutt, *Social Policy Analysis and Practice* (Chicago: Lyceum Books, 2004), pp. 81–82.

41. Hallett and Palumbo, U.S. Criminal Justice Interest Groups, p. xvi.

42. Kingdon, *Agendas, Alternatives, and Public Policies*, p. 49.

43. Wilcox, "The Dynamics of Lobbying the Hill," pp. 89–99.

44. Kingdon, *Agendas, Alternatives, and Public Policies*, p. 49.

45. Peter Bachrach and Morton S. Baratz, *Power and Poverty: Theory and Practice* (New York: Oxford University Press, 1970); James Houston and William W. Parsons, *Criminal Justice and the Policy Process* (Chicago: Nelson Hall, 1998).

46. Craig Reinarman, "The Social Construction of an Alcohol Problem: The Case of Mothers Against Drunk Drivers and Social Control in the 1980s," *Theory and Society* 17 (1988): 91–120.

47. Stella Z. Theodoulou and Chris Kofinis, *The Art of the Game: Understanding American Public Policy Making* (Belmont, Calif: Thomson, 2004).

48. Ibid.

49. Berry, *The Interest Group Society*.

50. Wilcox, "The Dynamics of Lobbying the Hill."

51. Berry, *The Interest Group Society*.

52. Wilcox, "The Dynamics of Lobbying the Hill."

53. Kingdon, *Agendas, Alternatives, and Public Policies*, p. 50.

54. Ibid., p. 51.

55. Albert P. Melone and Robert Slagter, "Interest Group Politics and the Reform of the Federal Criminal Code," in *The Political Science of Criminal Justice*, ed. Stuart Nagel, Erika Fairchild, and Anthony Chapagne (Springfield, Ill.: Charles C Thomas, 1983), pp. 41–55.

56. Ibid.

57. Lowi, *The End of Liberalism*; E. E. Schattschneider, *The Semisovereign People* (New York: Holt, Rinehart and Winston, 1960).

58. Ronald G. Shaiko, "Lobbying in Washington: A Contemporary Perspective," in Hernson et al., *The Interest Group Connection*, pp. 3–18; Ronald G. Shaiko, "Reverse Lobbying: Interest Group Mobilization from the White House to the Hill," in Cigler and Loomis, *Interest Group Politics*, pp. 255–82.

59. Houston and Parsons, *Criminal Justice and the Policy Process*.

60. Burdett A. Loomis, "Interests, Lobbying, and the U.S. Congress: Past as Prologue," in Cigler and Loomis, *Interest Group Politics*, pp. 186–201, at 187.

61. Berry, *The Interest Group Society*.

62. Rozell and Wilcox, *Interest Groups in American Campaigns*.

63. Ibid.

64. Hernson, "Interest Groups, PACs, and Campaigns"; Rozell and Wilcox, *Interest Groups in American Campaigns*.

65. Rozell and Wilcox, *Interest Groups in American Campaigns*.

66. Hernson, "Interest Groups, PACs, and Campaigns."

67. H. R. Glick, *Courts, Politics and Justice* (New York: McGraw-Hill, 1993); Herbert Jacob, *Law and Politics in the United States* (Boston: Little, Brown, 1986).

68. Lawrence Baum, *The Supreme Court* (Washington, D.C.: Congressional Quarterly Press, 1985).

69. Karen O'Connor, "Lobbying the Justices or Lobbying for Justice?" in Hernson et al., *The Interest Group Connection*, pp. 267–88.

70. Ibid.

71. Berry, *The Interest Group Society*, p. 198.

72. John A. Fliter, *Prisoners' Rights: The Supreme Court and Evolving Standards of Decency* (Westport, Conn.: Greenwood Press, 2001), p. 39; Lee Epstein and Jack Knight, *The Choices Justices Make* (Washington, D.C.: Congressional Quarterly Press, 1998).

73. Glick, *Courts, Politics and Justice*; Jacob, *Law and Politics in the United States*.

74. Herbert Jacob, "Courts and Politics in the United States," in *Courts, Law and Politics in a Comparative Perspective*, ed. Herbert Jacob, Erhard Blankenburg, Herbert M. Kritzer, Doris Marie Provide, and Joseph Sanders (New Haven, Conn.: Yale University Press, 1996), p. 72.

75. Berry, *The Interest Group Society*, p. 198.

76. Christopher E. Smith, *Courts, Politics and the Judicial Process* (Chicago: Nelson Hall, 1997), p. 283.

77. Ibid., p. 282.

78. O'Connor, "Lobbying the Justices or Lobbying for Justice?"

79. Ibid.

80. Glick, *Courts, Politics and Justice*; Jacob, *Law and Politics in the United States*.

81. Smith, *Courts, Politics and the Judicial Process*, p. 282.

82. Ibid., p. 284.

83. Berry, *The Interest Group Society*.

84. O'Connor, "Lobbying the Justices or Lobbying for Justice?"

85. Christine DeGregorio and Jack E. Rossotti, "Resources, Attitudes and Strategies: Interest Group Participation in the Bork Confirmation Process," *American Review of Politics* 15 (1994): 1–19.

86. O'Connor, "Lobbying the Justices or Lobbying for Justice?"

87. Eric M. Uslaner, "Lobbying the President and the Bureaucracy," in Hernson et al., *The Interest Group Connection*, pp. 205–12.

88. Ibid.

89. Gormley, "Interest Group Interventions in the Administrative Process."

90. Ibid.

91. Ibid.

92. Ibid.

93. Hallett and Palumbo, *U.S. Criminal Justice Interest Groups*, p. xvii.

94. Stolz, *Criminal Justice Policy Making*, p. 84.

95. Kelly D. Patterson and Matthew M. Singer, "The National Rifle Association in the Face of the Clinton Challenge," in Cigler and Loomis, *Interest Group Politics*, pp. 55–77, at 56.

96. Eunice Moscoso, "NRA campaign against Obama carries $10 million price tag," Palm Beach Post, October 21, 2008.

97. John M. Bruce and Clyde Wilcox, *The Changing Politics of Gun Control* (Lanham, M.D.: Rowman & Littlefield, 1998), p. 15.

98. Anderson, *Public Policymaking*.

99. Sarah McCally Morehouse, *State Politics, Parties, and Policy* (New York: Holt, Rinehart and Winston, 1981).

PART THREE

The Criminal Justice System

10

The Police

Chapter Outline

INTRODUCTION

Police agencies are those government agencies that have some responsibility for enforcing the law and/or providing protection to our local communities. There are approximately 18,000 such agencies in the United States today, including over 50 federal law enforcement agencies, 49 state police agencies, over 12,000 municipal agencies, 3,067 sheriffs departments, and nearly 1,500 special police forces. These agencies are an important part of society, as they help ensure that society functions smoothly, thus allowing its citizens to lead stable and productive lives. These agencies are considered the first component in the criminal justice system, but they are also an integral part of the executive branch of government. As a result of their administrative (and bureaucratic) nature, they are a political entity that is affected by politics and that at the same time affects politics. This chapter looks at the role of policing in society, its history and contemporary status, its role in intergovernmental relationships, the various types of policing, and how policing fits into the policy process.

THE NATURE OF POLICING

The United States was founded on the principle of democracy. One aspect of creating a truly democratic society is to ensure that government does not usurp the powers of the people. To this end, Founding Fathers, after the creation of the U.S. Constitution, created the Bill of Rights—the first ten amendments to the Constitution—that established the rights and protections of American citizens against their government. And the most likely element of government that citizens will need to invoke these protections will often come at the hands of the police.

Policing in a Democratic Society

Citizens have rights and protections against police officers since they act as an agent of the government. Definitively, one of the most important of these protections is the Fourth Amendment, the right against unreasonable searches and seizures. Citizens cannot be arbitrarily stopped and searched, nor can they be arrested on simple suspicion. The Constitution provides these protections to prevent the police from taking power away from the people. However, the delicate balance here must be understood. In many instances, it is police who protect people's rights by ensuring that others' rights are not violated and, when violated, that order is restored. In other words, the same agency of government that stands in the greatest position to take away your rights is also the same agency that is established to protect your rights. This is the dilemma of policing in a democratic society.[1]

The true dilemma that is addressed here is the balancing of individual rights, those afforded to all citizens by the Constitution versus the maintenance of public order. On the one hand, we must ensure that individuals are afforded their rights, that they receive due process, and that they are not unfairly burdened by the system. On the other hand, it is the responsibility of the police to maintain order for all citizens, which may very well necessitate the violation, preferably legal violation, of individual rights. A simple example may suffice. If a group of juveniles hang out on a particular street corner, since it is a public street, they have that right. Yet, if the residents who live on the street corner feel threatened and passersby do not feel comfortable moving through the group on the sidewalk, this disrupts public order. A police officer comes along and is required to "do something" about the problem, as he or she is vested with the authority of government to resolve the situation. If the officer moves the juveniles along, he or she may very well be violating their right to peacefully assemble. If the officer arrests them for vagrancy, he or she may very well violate their rights against unreasonable seizures (arrests). If the officer does nothing, then the public order remains violated, and people living and walking in the area remain in fear. The officer must find a way to avoid violating the juveniles' individual rights while at the same time restoring public order to ensure that both individual rights and public order are maintained.

In order to ensure that police officers balance these rights, they are also given a number of tools that often seem to be as widely diverse. Police officers are given an enormous amount of discretion in the performance of their job in order to allow them the ability to achieve this balance. Police can choose to do nothing, give a verbal warning, issue a written warning, deliver an arrest summons, or physically make an arrest. There are some constraints, however, that are often dictated by the nature of the crime. If a police officer catches a murderer, it is unlikely he or she will let the murderer go or merely give a verbal warning, but as the types of crimes become more like the scenario described previously, an officer is given a wider latitude of discretion.

Police officer discretion is also restrained by a number of different sources. The law clearly places parameters on what police can and cannot do, as U.S. Supreme Court and circuit court decisions dictate police behavior. One only has to think of several landmark cases to recognize these limitations, such as *Miranda v. Arizona* (1966) regarding the famous Miranda warning or *Tennessee v. Garner* (1985) regarding police use of deadly force. In addition, police officers are also restricted in their behavior through various policies, procedures, rules, and regulations as delineated by either the agency they work for, the jurisdiction they work for, or the state. Finally, police officers are supervised to some degree, and management can place more restraints on an officer's use of discretion beyond the more formal policies found in departmental manuals.

Police as Street-Level Bureaucrats

One more aspect of discretion has to do with its location within the police hierarchy. Wilson has noted that in policing, "discretion increases as one moves down the organizational hierarchy."[2] Conversely, the higher one rises in the police department's chain of command, the less discretion one has. Because police officers on the street (and at the bottom of the hierarchy) have far more discretion than those at the top, police officers have been called "street-level bureaucrats."[3] Michael Lipsky, in his study of street-level bureaucracies—those public service agencies that interact directly with citizens in the performance of their duties—found that the nature of these agencies creates large conflicts between labor and management. This is because the police actually determine what the police departments do, whereas in most bureaucracies, decisions are made at the top and pushed down to the bottom. In other words, those at the bottom of the hierarchy tend to determine what those at the top do. This can create conflict within the agency primarily based on the officer's actions and his or her use of discretion.

Another aspect of policing that tends to make the role of the police a difficult one in a democratic society is based on the idea that government should reflect the will of the people. More specifically, government should reflect the values and norms of the society and community they serve. Extending this even further, it is argued that the police should reflect these same values and norms and that as these values and norms change over time, the police should change too. This expectation has been termed as the "impossible mandate" by Manning and Van Maanen[4] and serves to further describe the many roles that the police must serve in today's society.

Wilson, in his famous study, *The Varieties of Police Behavior*,[5] found that police do reflect the community's values and norms and that they tend to police in three different styles, depending on what the community desires. The first is the watchman style, which is more in line with maintaining public order with the most minimal amount of police intervention possible. The second style is the enforcer, which is the type of policing that strictly enforces any violation of the law. The third style is the service style, which attempts to perform its duties by providing a wide variety of services to better serve the public. That Wilson's study found different styles of policing raises questions as to whether these styles were really reflective of the community or the police organization; if they are truly reflective of the community, what happens when the community changes? Do the police change their style in accordance?

Taking this even further, the role of the police is so ill defined in society that the reality of the "impossible mandate" should be quite evident. The media (see chapter 1) convey a message of the police as being crime fighters, yet the reality of policing is that the crime-fighting role is only a fraction of this (usually cited as 20% of an officer's time). Police officers engage in civic programs and random patrols, and they appear in court, enforce traffic laws, respond to those in need of assistance, give directions to lost drivers, perform emergency medical services, answer legal questions, respond to civil disputes, serve papers, and write reports. The roles that typical police officers perform in one day are so diverse that they are truly the "jack-of-all-trades" and "master-of-none." Because of this, one author, Mark H. Moore, has called policing the "impossible job."[6]

Policing as an "Impossible Job"

Like the "impossible mandate," the "impossible job" focuses on the many roles that police play in society. The "impossible job" concept focuses heavily on the fact that the police, unlike other organizations, do not have one all-encompassing policy goal or objective. In private businesses, the primary goal is to make money. In organizations such as the Environmental Protection Agency, the overriding goal is to clean up the environment, and in fire departments across the country, it is to put out fires. In policing, as previously described, the goals and objectives are so numerous that the ability to perform the policing function is essentially impossible. There are tensions between the cost of policing and its outputs. Policing can become very expensive, and there is no real need to be highly efficient. The product that policing delivers is so varied that it is hard to really know what policing's "bottom line" is. In addition, the proper use of authority is often debated; whatever action a police officer in the previously mentioned street-corner scenario selected, the actions of the officer could be easily debated. Finally, the uncertain goals—fighting crime (which crimes?), law enforcement versus peacekeeping, crime control versus crime prevention, and reducing crime or reducing fear—all contribute to the complexities of policing.

Policing in a democratic society is a difficult task and one that appears to be getting more complex, not less. The implications for public policy should not be lost on the reader. What police officers do at the bottom can shape public policy. What police chiefs do at the top can shape public policy. And assuredly, how citizens perceive and react to the police can and will shape public policy. While the public policy that is being crafted at this level often applies primarily to the local process, these things have a way of rising much higher (e.g., police officer's actions resulting in a Supreme Court's decision affecting all police), and ideas at the top can often find their way down to the bottom (e.g., the passage of the Violent Crime Control and Law Enforcement Act of 1994 and its allocation of nearly $9 billion from the federal government to local police departments). Thus, police are not only an important actor within the criminal justice system but also an important player in the policy process. To understand this, it helps to look at how policing has become an important policy actor over time.

HISTORY OF POLICING

The history of policing is important to provide a more accurate picture of where we have been and where we should go in terms of ensuring a safe society. Police, police administrators, academics, and citizens should understand the strategies and police methods tried in the past to gain a better knowledge of what should be done in the future to help control criminal behavior.[7]

Policing today has its roots in the English system of policing. Dating back to the colonial era of America, when America was a part of England, as the new land became settled there was at least some need for a system of protection. As the majority of colonists during the 1600s tended to be English, they brought with them the system that they were familiar with from the old country. The system with which these English colonists were familiar consisted of the sheriffs, constables, and both the watch and the ward. Although all of these were common practices in England, with the colonists it really depended on where in America they settled that each of these was employed. Colonists settling in the southern colonies (e.g., Virginia and North Carolina) tended to favor the use of the sheriff. Those colonists settling in the northern colonies (e.g., New York and New Jersey) opted more for the constables. And where the larger urban areas began to grow, these cities and towns opted for either the watch or the ward, or both.

The sheriff was appointed by the colonial governor and served as the chief local government official.[8] His responsibilities included collecting taxes, conducting elections, maintaining bridges and roads, and various other duties. The constable also had some responsibility for enforcing the law and maintaining order but like the sheriff often had many duties that fell outside of what we today would consider policing. The watch consisted of men patrolling the city to guard against fire, crime, and disorder and occasionally checking taverns for drunks. At first, cities and towns employed only a night watch, but as these cities and towns grew larger, many were forced to create the day watch. As in England, these positions often started as volunteer positions. When that failed, it was made mandatory duty for all adult males. As even that tended to fail (for many purposefully failed to show and willingly paid the fine rather than serve), eventually the watch developed into paid positions, albeit poorly paid ones.

Colonial law enforcement was inefficient, often corrupt, and subject to political influence. The sheriff, constable, and the watch and the ward had little capacity to either prevent crime or apprehend offenders. The sheriff and constable were only reactive, responding to complaints brought to them. They did not engage in preventive patrol. There were too few watch members to deter crime. In addition, since the positions were paid so poorly, only the poorest members of society tended to serve on the watch. Victims had no convenient way to report crimes. If people wanted to engage in moral criminal offenses (e.g., gambling, drinking, or sexual behaviors), they simply had to bribe law enforcement officials to "look the other way." Thus, official law enforcement agencies played a relatively small role in maintaining law and order.[9]

During the Revolutionary War, peace was maintained by troops. After the war, peacekeeping reverted back to civilian control. Although the sheriffs, constables, and the watch and the ward continued in many jurisdictions, they were not highly favored because they were remnants of the King of England's rule. Citizens in the new United States began to reject many of England's former practices and advocated for individual rights as encapsulated in the passage of the Bill of Rights in 1791. The sheriffs and constables were thus minimized in importance because they posed a danger to individual rights and freedoms and the people wanted to limit police authority. As a result, the method of policing at the time was left in the hands of the local governments rather than by creating a national (or state-level) police force. This was done to ensure that local communities, rather than a national or state government distantly removed from them, could assert greater control over law enforcement and to promote the local police to reflect those communities. The resulting effect was a continuation of past English practices but with far less powers then they had previously held.

This method did not work well as America continued to grow from within and through mass immigration to this new and free country. In fact, as the cities grew, so too did the crime problem, and the old means of informal social control mechanisms, such as everyone knowing each other in the community, families asserting control over their children, and the church asserting its moral authority, began to fail. Crime and disorder were on the rise, and as crime, disorder, and riots broke out, there was no entity available to effectively respond to these problems. Perhaps the best example is in Boston, Massachusetts, for between 1834 and 1838, there were three major riots that ran rampant over the entire city, lasting for many days, killing and wounding numerous people, and causing enormous amounts of damage. As there was no one to stop the rioters, the riots ran their course. The people demanded something be done, and the answer lay across the Atlantic Ocean in London, England. There, Robert Peel had created the London Metropolitan Police Department, the first bona fide police department in the world. The solution to the problem in Boston was evident, and in 1838, Boston created the first police department in the United States. New York would follow in 1845 with the creation of its first police department.

Although these departments were modeled after the London Metropolitan Police Department, American police departments looked very different. While London started with a force of over 1,000 police officers, wearing uniforms and badges and under strict supervision, the American experiment with police departments tended to start with fewer than 100 officers, with no uniforms and under little supervision. The reason had much to do with the previously cited desires for a very limited government presence. Over 1,000 police officers wearing uniforms was thought to be too strong a government presence, and people feared that their rights would be lost. As a result, early American policing was highly ineffective, and because of a lack of supervision and the political climate of the time, they became highly corrupt and often brutal.

Political Era

Kelling and Moore have recognized three specific eras in the history of policing.[10] The first, known as the political era, began around 1840 and lasted until around 1900. During this time, many people from different backgrounds and cultures were coming into the country. In some communities, there was a breakdown in law and order that sometimes culminated in riots because of these social, economic, and political differences.[11] For example, as previously described, Boston, between 1834 and 1838, endured three major riots, and New York, in the lead-up to its creation of a police department, had similar experiences that destroyed large sections of the city, damaged numerous storefronts, injured hundreds of people, and killed dozens. People recognized the need for a police force but were unsure what it should be. The idea of an organized police force was a radical idea to many at the time, but the alternative was further widespread rioting.

What developed was a policing system that was closely linked to local politicians and inherently corrupt but at the same time extremely helpful to new immigrants. When many of these immigrants arrived in the United States, they were unfamiliar with the language, customs, and culture. Politicians helped them find jobs and homes or helped with troubled children. Sometimes they would provide money to buy medicine for a sick family member. The politicians, in return, expected (and received) support from these immigrants during elections.[12]

At the same time, the police also helped the immigrants. Police tasks included some crime prevention but also included a wide range of useful social services, such as assisting immigrants in establishing themselves in communities and finding jobs, housing the homeless during cold winter nights, and feeding the poor in soup kitchens. Because the police reflected some of the ethnic makeup of the area in which they lived and worked, they had positive relationships with those of the same ethnic groups. The police were familiar with their neighborhoods and maintained order in them. Policing was done mostly by foot patrol, which helped the officers come to know and understand the people they policed. Police were integrated into neighborhoods and enjoyed the support of many of its citizens.

However, politicians had influence over the police. At that time, politicians could hire police officers. Thus, local politicians could reward their friends with jobs, a major form of patronage. There were no personnel standards for serving as an officer, and there was no job security—the police who were appointed by politicians could also be fired on a whim by politicians. The police were obligated to politicians for their job and their job security. Thus, policing during the political era became closely linked to or even controlled by local politicians. The police and politicians worked together, but politics, through these political machines, influenced every aspect of American policing.

The closeness of police to political leaders and the lack of supervision of officers gave rise to widespread political corruption. Men with no education, bad health, and criminal records were hired as officers. They were vulnerable to being bribed in return for nonenforcement or lax enforcement of laws on drinking, gambling, or prostitution. There was very little in the way of formal training. In most places, new officers were handed a badge, a baton, and a copy of the department rules and sent out on patrol. There was a lack of communication, especially between police officers and a centralized headquarters, that made it impossible to respond to crimes. Supervision was also very weak. Officers could go weeks without seeing a supervisor, as they often went on and off duty from their homes. Even in those departments that required officers to serve their duty from the station house, much like firefighters do today, officers still would often not see their supervisors for days at a time. Thus, officers evaded duty and spent much of their time in saloons and barber shops. They had to pay bribes for promotion. Detectives were often used by politicians to obtain information for political purposes. On the whole, inefficiency, corruption, brutality, and a lack of professionalism were the chief results of this era of policing.

Reform Era

The period from 1900 to the 1970s is called the "reform era."[13] Change in policing came with an organized movement for police professionalism and attempts to free policing from the control of politicians. The reformers wanted to eliminate politics from policing and to hire qualified leaders and officers. Change also came from the civil rights movement's demands for equal justice as well as the development of advanced communications technology.

Most departments implemented civil service testing in an attempt to eliminate political patronage in the hiring and firing of officers. Officers were hired on the basis of their qualifications for the job and their ability to perform rather than their political connections. Departments emphasized their law enforcement roles over their social service role, which was now seen as the responsibility of social service agencies. Personnel standards were raised to include minimum recruitment requirements for intelligence, health, and moral character. Some departments created a formal training academy. There were calls for centralizing command and control within police departments. The departments became more military-like, with discipline and a chain of command.

New technology, such as two-way radios, telephones, and 911 emergency systems, helped police become more professional. Some communities decreased foot patrols and relied instead on patrol cars that allowed police to respond more quickly to calls for help. The police were concerned with reacting to crime and providing rapid response to all calls regardless of their urgency. Eventually, reliance on technology was viewed as a negative advancement. The police were spending less time on investigations and less time on the street, resulting in a loss of police relations with citizens. Citizens were not supportive of police and not providing them with information on crimes that police need.

Despite large increases in the size of police departments and in expenditures for new technology and new forms of equipment, police were not able to control crime or prevent its increase. Crime rose significantly during the 1960s, as did the public's fear of crime. Many minority citizens, especially African-Americans, did not perceive police treatment as fair or adequate. They protested not only police mistreatment but also lack of attention.

Both the civil rights movement and the antiwar movement brought new challenges to the police. The legitimacy of police and their role was brought into question. Students resisted police, minorities rioted against them, and the public, observing police behaviors and reactions on live television for the first time, questioned their tactics. Tensions between the police and the African-American community exploded in a series of riots across the nation from 1964 to 1968.

Community Era

Thus began the third era of policing, called the "community era."[14] The community era had its roots in a conference at Michigan State University in 1955 discussing the problems of police–community relations and how best to fix them. There was little political desire to fix any of the problems at the time, however, because life in America was rather tranquil. However, in the wake of the crime rate spiking upward, riots in the streets, demonstrations over civil rights and the Vietnam War, and campus unrest, police reactions brought to the forefront the political issues of the day and the weakness of police–community relations. Hence, with the problem being evident and a solution already existing, the movement toward improving police–community relations became political policy.

This policy was part of the Johnson administration's success in passing the Omnibus Crime Control and Safe Streets Act of 1968, which created the Law Enforcement Assistance Administration under the Department of Justice, part of the role of which was to funnel federal grants for police to state and local agencies. Many of these grants were focused on implementing the tenets of police–community relations. Police were often provided training regarding the various cultures they policed as well as special groups, such as juveniles, the elderly, and the handicapped. In addition, programs called "team policing" were begun in many cities during the early 1970s that consisted of special groups of officers working with the community to alleviate some of the problems particular to their neighborhoods. In concert with these programs, Neighborhood Watch programs were started all over America in an attempt to have citizens report more crimes and suspicious activities to the local police. Although many of these programs were aimed at improving police–community relations, the reality is that they had a negligible impact.

The reason for their lack of success had much to do with the way in which these programs were run. Team policing used special teams to work with the neighborhoods, while the rest of the police department continued their past practices. Hence, one small group of officers spoke of working with the community, while the rest seemingly worked against the community. In the Neighborhood Watch programs, police helped start these programs but abandoned them after the initial implementation. Without the guidance of the one entity these programs were supposed to help, they floundered until they were eventually abandoned and only the signs on the street corners remained. This was also combined with other problems; for example, the police tended to emphasize random patrols to prevent crime, rapid response to solve crimes faster, and more and better detectives to solve crimes. Research in the 1970s demonstrated that none of these long-held assumptions were valid. Finally, taking into consideration that with the implementation of the 911 system police were fast becoming tied to calls for service, policing was at a breaking point, and nothing seemed to work.

These factors caused many to consider what does work in policing, and the movement toward community policing in the early 1980s was seemingly the answer. Community policing is a shift from traditional, reactive policing to one that promotes working with the community to solve problems before crimes occur.[15] The police become partners with the community to create strategies to address the causes and reduce the fear of crime by increasing the interaction and cooperation between local police and the citizens. The goals are to reduce and prevent crime and to increase feelings of safety among residents and reduce fears of crime, to help develop closer ties to the community, and to engage residents in a joint effort to prevent crime.

Community policing refers to a number of different strategies, but they revolve primarily around getting the police on the street to interact more with the people.[16] Some departments have increased foot patrols to get officers out of their cars and onto the street. Some have created storefront police stations to make the police more accessible to the public. Others have distributed community surveys in an effort to define the public's perception of community problems so they can deal with those problems better. Some departments have sponsored youth activities to improve relations between youth and police and also to help deter juvenile crime. Finally, some departments have instituted more modern Neighborhood Watch programs where the police meet with citizens on a regular basis, usually monthly, to update the community on the information that the police have regarding crime and disorder in their neighborhoods and to give the community a chance to voice their perspectives on what problems exist. Then, working together to address these problems, the police and community develop a method for addressing these problems that shares the resources of the police with the resources of the community.

The ideas of community policing can be traced to Wilson and Kelling,[17] who acknowledged the importance of the community in crime control. They said that neighborhood disorder creates fear. In other words, neighborhood areas that are filled with street people, youth gangs, prostitutes, and the mentally disturbed are the ones most likely to maintain a high degree of crime. Some neighborhoods, particularly those in distress, give out crime-promoting signals. A neighborhood filled with deteriorating housing, unrepaired broken windows, and untended disorderly behavior gives out those crime-promoting signals. Honest citizens live in fear in these areas, and predatory criminals are attracted to them. To reduce crime and the fear of crime, according to Wilson and Kelling, police need citizens' cooperation, support, and assistance. To do this, police need to have more close contact with the people they serve and rely less on police cars that serve only to remove an officer from the community and alienate people. These citizens are potential sources of information to help police.

The move toward community policing quickly gained momentum, and it is now being used by large metropolitan police forces as well as small, rural departments. As more and more departments experienced success and saw public satisfaction with the police increase, community policing began to spread even further. However, the biggest impetus for the implementation of community policing in the 1990s came with the passage of the Violent Crime Control and Law Enforcement Act of 1994, which brought federal support for implementing community policing programs (see Chapter 1). The creation of the Office of Community Oriented Policing Services (COPS) under the Department of Justice began issuing grants to state and local agencies to hire additional police officers, purchase equipment, and provide training under the concepts of community policing and caused the number of agencies engaging in community policing to proliferate substantially. As a result, going into the twenty-first century, community policing has been the overriding police policy for most departments in the United States.

Homeland Security Era?

With the September 11, 2001, terrorist attacks on American soil, some have argued that we are now seeing the end of the era of community policing and the beginning of the homeland security era.[18] As America responded quickly to the attacks by educating themselves on terrorism and demanding action from government, the president and the U.S. Congress quickly began a process of restructuring government to focus on antiterrorism (prevention techniques) and counterterrorism (how to actively respond to terrorists) measures in order to meet these new demands. The creation of the Office of Homeland Security and its subsequent passage as a cabinet-level department as well as the passage of the USA PATRIOT Act are both inclinations that the national government is moving in this direction. In addition, many of the grants for local agencies have become centered on homeland security, and perhaps most telling was the fact that the Office of Community Oriented Policing Services (COPS) had its budget slashed by the Bush administration, but the Department of Homeland Security saw its budget allocations increase substantially. Funding for the COPS office was reinstated under President Obama (see Chapter 1), but only time will tell if American law enforcement has truly entered into a new era of policing.

Understanding the history of policing in America is important for grasping how police came to be an actor in the public policy process. However, also understanding the current status of policing in America helps us understand the complexities that this particular component of the criminal justice system brings to the table. It is easy to talk of the "police," but when we define what we mean, we begin to understand that police operate at many different levels and that across each level there are many different agencies. It is to understanding the contemporary status of policing that we now turn.

BOX 10.1

Agencies That Transferred into the Department of Homeland Security

- Department of Agriculture
  - Agricultural Quarantine Inspection Program
  - Plum Island Animal Disease Center
- Department of Commerce
  - Critical Infrastructure Assurance Office
- Department of Defense
  - Chemical and Biological Defense programs, including the National Bioweapons Defense Analysis Center (Biowatch)
  - National Communications System
- Department of Energy
  - Defense Nuclear Non-Proliferation
  - Energy Security and Assurance Center
- Department of Health and Human Services
  - Strategic National Stockpile
- Department of Justice
  - National Infrastructure Protection Center
  - Immigration and Customs Enforcement
  - Office of Domestic Preparedness
  - United States Citizenship and Immigration Services
- Department of Transportation
  - Transportation Security Administration
  - United States Coast Guard
- Department of the Treasury
  - Federal Law Enforcement Training Center
  - United States Customs Service
  - United States Secret Service
- Federal Emergency Management Agency
- General Services Administration
  - Federal Computer Incident Response

CONTEMPORARY POLICE

There are over 18,000 law enforcement agencies in the United States, all having different jurisdictions and therefore different responsibilities and powers. This means that no one agency has unlimited power. Most law enforcement agencies are found on the local level, with some at the state level and far less at the federal level. Although there are federal law enforcement agencies, there is no national police force in the United States, and federal law enforcement makes up less than 10 percent of all law enforcement agencies in the nation. Each agency, whether federal, state, or local, has a different jurisdiction and was created to enforce specific laws or help with particular situations. The role of each federal agency is specified by federal statute. The different agencies are described in the following sections.

Federal Law Enforcement

The federal law enforcement agencies are designed to protect the rights and privileges of U.S. citizens throughout the nation. Although there is no federal police force, there are over fifty federal law enforcement agencies that deal with federal offenses. The first federal law enforcement agency was the U.S. Marshals Service, created by Congress on September 24, 1789, through the passage of the Judiciary Act.[19] The U.S. Marshal Service is given the responsibility of judicial security, provides services for the federal courts (such as serving writs), and is in charge of fugitive investigations. The most recent change came in the wake of the terrorist attacks on September 11, 2001, when Congressional legislation created the Department of Homeland Security. This newly formed agency began operations on January 24, 2003. See Box 10.1.

As a result of the creation of the Department of Homeland Security (DHS), a number of federal law enforcement agencies fell under its organizational chart. The DHS has the following agencies that report to it: U.S. Customs and Border Protection (CBP), U.S. Immigration and Customs Enforcement (ICE), the United States Secret Service (USSS), the United States Coast Guard (USCG), and the Transportation Security Administration (TSA). The Department of Justice, however, still remains as the largest law enforcement umbrella organization, which has under its control the Federal Bureau of Investigation (FBI), Drug Enforcement Administration (DEA), the Bureau of Alcohol, Tobacco & Firearms (ATF), and the United States Marshal Service (USMS).

As of September 2004, federal agencies employed over 100,000 full-time personnel.[20] This was an increase of about 10 percent over 2002. Their duties include criminal investigation/enforcement (42%), police response/patrol (19%), corrections (18%), noncriminal investigations/enforcement (14%), court operations (3%), and security/protection (3%).[21] Three-fifths of federal officers were employed by the U.S. Customs and Border Protection (27,705), the Federal Bureau of Prisons (15,214), the Federal Bureau of Investigation (12,424), and the U.S. Immigration and Customs Enforcement (10,399).[22] In addition to the high number of employees in these agencies, there are also a number of very small and little-known federal law enforcement agencies, including those for Amtrak (317), the Tennessee Valley Authority (168), the National Marine Fisheries Service (141), and the Library of Congress (116).[23] Women accounted for approximately 15 percent of federal officers in 2004, about the same as in 2002.[24] Minority representation was approximately 30 percent in 2004, very similar to the years 1998 and 2002.[25]

Key Department of Justice Law Enforcement Agencies

FEDERAL BUREAU OF INVESTIGATION The Federal Bureau of Investigation (FBI) is housed within the Department of Justice and headquartered in Washington, D.C.[26] It is the principal investigative arm of the federal government. It is charged with gathering and reporting facts, locating witnesses, and compiling evidence in cases involving violations of federal law, including all federal statutes not specifically assigned to other agencies. This includes the investigation of espionage, sabotage, treason, subversive activities, and other actions related to national security; civil rights violations; murder and assault of federal officers; mail fraud; robbery and burglary of federally insured banks; kidnapping; interstate transportation of stolen vehicles; organized crime and drug trafficking; terrorism; and white-collar crime. The mission of the FBI is "to uphold the law through the investigation of violations of federal criminal statutes; to protect the United States from hostile intelligence efforts; to provide assistance to other federal, state, and local law enforcement agencies; and to perform these responsibilities in a manner that is faithful to the Constitution and the laws of the United States."[27] More recently, because of the terrorist attacks of September 11, FBI Director Robert Mueller has explained that "while we remain committed to our other important national security and law enforcement responsibilities, the prevention of terrorism takes precedence in our thinking and planning; in our hiring and staffing; in our

BOX 10.2
Directors of the Federal Bureau of Investigation[a]

Director	Assumed Office
Stanley W. Finch	July 26, 1908
A. Bruce Bielaski	April 30, 1912
William E. Allen, act.	February 10, 1919
William J. Flynn	July 1, 1919
William J. Burns	August 22, 1921
J. Edgar Hoover, act.	May 10, 1924
J. Edgar Hoover	December 10, 1924
L. Patrick Gray, act.	May 3, 1972
William D. Ruckelshaus, act.	April 27, 1973
Clarence M. Kelley	July 9, 1973
William H. Webster	February 23, 1978
John E. Otto, act.	May 26, 1987
William S. Sessions	November 2, 1987
Floyd I. Clarke, act.	July 19, 1993
Louis J. Freeh	September 1, 1993
Thomas J. Pickard, act.	June 25, 2001
Robert S. Mueller III	September 4, 2001

[a]The Federal Bureau of Investigation was created July 26, 1908, and was referred to as Office of Chief Examiner. It became the Bureau of Investigation (March 16, 1909), United States Bureau of Investigation (July 1, 1932), Division of Investigation (August 10, 1933), and Federal Bureau of Investigation (July 1, 1935).

Source: Federal Bureau of Investigation home page (2010), available online at www.fbi.gov/libref/directors/directmain.htm.

training and technologies; and, most importantly, in our investigations."[28] The FBI's jurisdiction includes a wide range of responsibilities that is ever changing in the criminal, civil, and security fields, but it has five areas that have been given priority. These are the areas that affect society the most: organized crime/drugs, terrorism, white-collar crime, foreign counterintelligence, and violent crime. See Box 10.2.

The FBI also offers important services to state and local law enforcement agencies. The FBI will help other agencies with things such as fingerprint identification, laboratory examination, and police training. The FBI Identification Division, established in 1924, collects and maintains a vast fingerprint file (over 181 million sets of fingerprints) that can be used by local police departments. It also acts as a national clearinghouse for criminal identification data and missing persons data. The FBI exchanges identification data with law enforcement agencies in more than 80 foreign countries. The FBI's crime laboratory, created in 1932, provides ballistic testing and handwriting analysis for local police and also helps them test and identify evidence such as hairs, fibers, blood, tire tracks, DNA, drugs, and other evidence. It has advanced forensic research capabilities as well. The FBI also allows states to use its National Crime Information Center, which is a database of information on stolen vehicles, stolen guns, stolen property, wanted persons with outstanding warrants, sexual predators, and so on. It also collects and disseminates crime statistics through its annual Uniform Crime Report.

The FBI has 56 field offices throughout the country to investigate federal offenses and assist state and local officials. Training for FBI agents is held at the FBI National Academy in Quantico, Virginia. Specially selected local law enforcement personnel may also receive training there.

The FBI, as part of the Department of Justice, is overseen by the attorney general of the United States. At this time, the FBI employs approximately 24,000 people, with 12,424 special agents across the nation and in foreign countries. In the wake of the terrorist attacks of September 11, the FBI ordered a major restructuring aimed at providing improved information sharing for the targeting of terrorists.

U.S. MARSHALS SERVICE   The U.S. Marshals Service is the nation's oldest federal law enforcement agency.[29] It was created by the First Congress in the Judiciary Act of 1789, eighty-one years before the creation of the Department of Justice. George Washington appointed the first thirteen U.S. marshals, who were given the authority to support and protect the federal courts within their judicial districts and to carry out all lawful orders issued by judges, Congress, or the president. This included serving subpoenas, summonses, writs, and warrants; making arrests; handling prisoners; and other orders issued by the courts. Marshals also performed administrative work for the courts: they handled all the money; paid fees for the attorneys, jurors, and witnesses; rented courtrooms and jail space; and hired bailiffs and janitors. They served as a link between the executive and judicial branches of government. Marshals were nominated by the president and approved by the Senate to four-year terms. At this time, the marshals were the major representatives of federal law enforcement. They performed most federal law enforcement functions until the formation of the Department of Justice. The marshals conducted the national census for 80 years (from 1790 to 1870), registered aliens, exchanged fugitives, and rented space from local authorities for federal courtrooms.

During this time, the marshals had considerable independence. They received no salary but were paid by various fees for services rendered. But much of that changed when the marshals received agency status in 1969. Today, the marshals are involved in a wide variety of federal law enforcement duties with approximately 3,233 deputy marshals to perform these duties. Marshals continue to perform judicial security. Protection of federal judicial officials, including judges, attorneys, and jurors, holds a high priority with the Marshals Service. Deputy marshals use the latest security techniques and devices at highly sensitive trials. The Marshals Service protects more than 2,000 sitting judges and countless other court officials at more than 400 court facilities throughout the nation. The Marshals Service also oversees each aspect of courthouse construction projects, from design through completion, to ensure the safety of federal judges, court personnel, and the public.

The Marshals Service is also involved in fugitive investigations, the one duty that has made it famous with the movie and television series *The Fugitive*. In 2003, the Marshals Service apprehended 55 percent of all federal fugitives. The agency executes more arrest warrants than all other federal law enforcement agencies combined regarding this duty. The marshals work with other law enforcement agencies at the federal, state, and local levels as well as with international agencies in the pursuit of fugitives.

In addition to these duties, the Marshals Service ensures the safety of witnesses who risk their lives testifying for the government in cases involving organized crime and other significant criminal activity. Since 1970, the Marshals Service has protected, relocated, and given new identities to over 7,500 witnesses. The marshals are also responsible for housing over 47,000 federal unsentenced prisoners each day in federal, state, and local jails. Approximately 75 percent of Marshals Service prisoners are housed in 1,300 state, local, and private jails. Thirty percent are housed in Federal Bureau of Prisons facilities. In areas where detention space is scarce, the Marshals Service uses Cooperative Agreement Program funds to improve local jail conditions and expand jail capacities in return for guaranteed space for federal prisoners. Finally, one other key duty of the Marshals Service remains the historical duties of serving the federal courts in the criminal process.

The director of the Marshals Service is appointed by the president and supervises the operations of the service throughout the United States and its territories, assisted by the deputy director, eight assistant directors, and a general counsel. The director answers to the attorney general. There are 94 marshals and approximately 3,233 deputy marshals and administrative personnel who operate from 427 office locations in all 94 federal judicial districts in the United States, from Guam, the Virgin Islands, the Northern Mariana Islands, and Puerto Rico and from Alaska to Florida. The Marshals Service is headquartered in McLean, Virginia.

DRUG ENFORCEMENT ADMINISTRATION   The Drug Enforcement Administration (DEA) was created in 1973 under the Nixon administration. Although it was a new agency, the DEA was actually derived from a number of other government agencies that had developed and changed over much of the twentieth century. It began with the passage of the Harrison Act in 1914, which established federal jurisdiction over the supply and use of narcotics. The act was primarily a tax law, but one section made it unlawful for any "unregistered" person to possess heroin, cocaine, opium, morphine, or any of their products. In 1919, the Volstead Act passed, ensuring the enforcement of Prohibition. The Prohibition Unit of the Revenue Bureau had a small unit called the Narcotics Division. When the Narcotics Drugs Import and Export Act of 1922 was passed, it strictly prohibited the importation of narcotic drugs for anything other than medicinal purposes.[30]

In 1930, the Narcotics Division became the Federal Bureau of Narcotics. It grew quickly under the leadership of Harry Anslinger, especially when he identified marijuana as a serious drug problem. As a result, Congress passed the Marijuana Tax Act in 1937. The Boggs Act of 1956 followed, which made any use of heroin illegal. In the 1960s, the quantity of drugs seized in the United States and overseas increased dramatically. So, in 1963, the President's Advisory Commission on Narcotic and Drug Abuse recommended numerous revisions to federal drug enforcement efforts. That resulted in the creation of the Bureau of Narcotics and Dangerous Drugs in 1968. Two years later, in 1970, Congress passed the Comprehensive Drug Abuse Prevention and Control Act. This established five schedules of drugs that classified controlled substances according to their abuse potential.[31]

In 1973, during the Nixon administration, all drug-related agencies were combined to form the DEA under federal Reorganization Plan Number 2.[32] The DEA became the primary federal agency responsible for the enforcement of federal laws concerning the use, sale, and distribution of narcotics and other controlled substances in the United States. It is also responsible for the investigation of drug seizures by U.S. Customs agents at border points and the regulation of the distribution of legal narcotics and drugs.

The DEA currently has approximately 10,000 staff members, about half of whom are special agents. It has headquarters in New York with agents throughout the country. There are 237 domestic offices and 80 foreign offices in 58 countries. The DEA helps local and state law enforcement in investigating illegal drug use and carrying out independent surveillance and enforcement activities to control the import of narcotics. It works with foreign governments in cooperative efforts aimed at destroying opium and marijuana crops and reducing the availability of narcotics. It tries to infiltrate drug rings and simulates buying narcotics in order to arrest drug dealers. It maintains regional laboratories to test seized drugs so that accurate records and measures can be presented at trials. The DEA's Office of Intelligence helps coordinate information and enforcement activities with local, state, and foreign governments. It also has a narcotics intelligence system that collects, analyzes, and disseminates data. It recently began sharing information with the FBI and the Department of Homeland Security in regard to the connection between terrorists using the illegal drug trade to fund its activities.

The DEA investigates major narcotic violators who operate at interstate and international levels. It is responsible for the seizure and forfeiture of assets derived from, traceable to, or intended to be used for illicit drug trafficking; enforcement of regulations governing the legal manufacture, distribution, or dispensing of controlled substances; management of a national narcotics intelligence system; coordination with federal, state, and local law enforcement; cooperation with counterpart agencies abroad; and training, scientific research, and information exchange in support of drug traffic prevention and control.

BUREAU OF ALCOHOL, TOBACCO, FIREARMS AND EXPLOSIVES   The Bureau of Alcohol, Tobacco, Firearms and Explosives (ATF) was originally part of the Internal Revenue Service but is now part of the Department of the Treasury.[33] It was originally created to enforce the ban on alcohol mandated under the Volstead Act and the Eighteenth Amendment to the Constitution, and it is most well known for battling bootleggers and gamblers during Prohibition. When Prohibition was repealed by the Twenty-First Amendment in 1933, the suppression of the illegal manufacture and sale of alcoholic beverages was less important. President Franklin D. Roosevelt folded many of these duties under the Alcohol Tax Unit within the Internal Revenue Service in 1933. The next year, with the passage of the first federal firearms laws, the Alcohol Tax Unit picked up the duty of enforcing these laws. This would remain the case until 1968, when duties would be shifted to the Alcohol, Tobacco, and Firearms Division, which would become an independent bureau under the Department of the Treasury in 1972.

Effective January 24, 2003, the ATF was transferred under the Homeland Security Act to the Department of Justice. The law enforcement functions of ATF under the Department of the Treasury were transferred to the Department of Justice. The tax and trade functions of ATF will remain in the Treasury Department with the new Alcohol and Tobacco Tax and Trade Bureau. In addition, the agency's name was changed to the Bureau of Alcohol, Tobacco, Firearms and Explosives to reflect its new mission in the Department of Justice.[34] The ATF currently has nearly 2,400 agents and helps control the sales of untaxed liquor and cigarettes. To the surprise of many, the agency still does seize illegal stills on occasion. The primary focus of the ATF, however, is on enforcing federal firearms laws. It has jurisdiction over the illegal sales, importation, and criminal misuse of firearms and explosives. It created the National Firearms Tracing Center, which processes hundreds of thousands of trace requests annually. The ATF issues federal firearm licenses and permits for the import and export of firearms.

Key Department of Homeland Security Law Enforcement Agencies

U.S. CITIZENSHIP AND IMMIGRATION SERVICES   The U.S. Citizenship and Immigration Service (USCIS) under the Department of Homeland Security was formerly known as the Immigration and Naturalization Service (INS).[35] With the creation of the Department of Homeland Security, the INS, which included the Border Patrol, was divided into two parts. The first part, under the USCIS, is responsible for overseeing the admission and naturalization process of aliens. The second part, the enforcement elements of the INS and specifically the Border Patrol, was merged with the responsibilities of the U.S. Customs Service and also placed under the Department of Homeland Security. As a result, one element handles the processing of aliens, whereas the other element (see the next section) handles the enforcement. The USCIS has approximately 18,000 employees.

U.S. CUSTOMS AND BORDER PROTECTION   The U.S. Customs and Border Protection is part of the Department of Homeland Security and is responsible for guarding points of entry into the United States and preventing the smuggling of contraband into (or out of) the country.[36] It ensures that taxes and tariffs are paid on imported goods and helps control the flow of narcotics into the country. It is also authorized to conduct investigations of aliens who are residing illegally in the United States or who have engaged in activities prohibited by law and to investigate people who attempt to illegally import aliens into the country. The U.S. Customs was originally part of the Department of the Treasury, but after the creation of the Department of Homeland Security, it was moved under this new agency and renamed U.S. Customs and Border Protection. The other agency with which it was combined was the Border Patrol, a uniformed enforcement division that was originally established in 1924 and served as part of the INS. It too was moved under the Department of Homeland Security and integrated with U.S. Customs. Border Patrol agents, now working together with members of Customs, are responsible for patrolling over 8,000 miles of international borders to prevent illegal entry of aliens into the United States. There are approximately 18,000 agents working this specific duty, and they make approximately 1.5 million arrests each year along the border with Mexico.

U.S. IMMIGRATION AND CUSTOMS ENFORCEMENT   The U.S. Immigration and Customs Enforcement (ICE) agency is the largest investigative agency in the U.S. Department of Homeland Security (DHS) with over 19,000 employees. Formed in 2003 as part of the federal government's response to the 9/11 attacks, ICE's mission is to enforce immigration and customs laws. The agencies that were either moved entirely or merged in part into ICE included the investigative and intelligence resources of the United States Customs Service, the criminal investigation resources of the Immigration and Naturalization Service, and the United States Federal Protective Service. The Federal Protective Service was transferred from ICE to the National Protection and Programs Directorate effective October 28, 2009.

U.S. SECRET SERVICE   The U.S. Secret Service was originally created by Congress in 1865 to investigate and enforce the laws against counterfeiting. However, after President McKinley was assassinated in 1901, protecting the safety of the president became its primary purpose. Because it was originally created to investigate counterfeiting, it was placed under the Department of the Treasury, where it had remained for over 125 years. Like many other agencies, it too was moved under the Department of Homeland Security with the reorganization of many government agencies.[37] Despite these changes, however, its duties and functions have remained the same. The Secret Service is mandated by statute and executive order to carry out two significant missions: protection and criminal investigations. The Secret Service protects the president and vice president, their families, heads of state, and other designated individuals; investigates threats against these individuals; protects the White House, the vice president's residence, foreign missions, and other buildings within Washington, D.C.; and plans and implements security designs for designated "national special security events." The Secret Service also investigates violations of laws relating to counterfeiting of obligations and securities of the United States; financial crimes that include but are not limited to access device fraud, financial institution fraud, identity theft, and computer fraud; and computer-based attacks on the nation's financial, banking, and telecommunications infrastructure.

State Police and State Highway Patrols

In addition to federal agencies, there are many kinds of state law enforcement agencies that have been established over time. Each has its own jurisdiction and own responsibilities. Since each state can establish its own law enforcement agencies, these vary from state to state. State law enforcement agencies can be state police, highway patrols, and state investigative agencies. State police are agencies that have statewide power over both traffic regulation and criminal investigation. Highway patrols have statewide authority to enforce traffic regulations and arrest nontraffic violators. They provide a variety of different law enforcement services. Some share responsibilities with local police agencies. They can enforce traffic laws on the main highways. Their responsibilities vary concerning investigative powers. Some provide crime lab services for local police departments.

State police or highway patrols were created by state legislatures to deal with crime in nonurban areas. Most states found that the invention of automobiles made it impossible for the local sheriffs departments to deal with highly mobile offenders, so state governors and legislatures created plans for police agencies that would be responsible to the state instead of being tied to local politics and the possible corruption found there. Although many states did develop state police agencies, others developed state highway patrols. Some states, such as California, actually developed both and still maintain these two distinct agencies.

One of the first state-level agencies formed was the Texas Rangers in 1835 (before Texas became a state). The Texas Rangers originally patrolled the Mexican border to protect it against bandits crossing over from Mexico as well as to protect settlers against Indian attacks. Other states followed suit with similar organizations; the Massachusetts State Constables was created in 1865 and the Arizona Rangers in 1901. These, however, were very narrowly defined state-level agencies and did not fully reflect the modern concept of state police. The first bona fide state police agency was the Pennsylvania State Constabulary, created in 1905 in response to the anthracite coal strikes and the often bloody conflicts between labor and management. This was a highly centralized organization with statewide police powers and broadly defined duties and a quasi-military style of leadership. It became the model for many state police forces, most of which were created over the next 20 years.[38]

Currently, every state but Hawaii has its own police force. There are approximately 80,000 state police employees across the nation.[39] They have jurisdiction over highways and enforce the traffic laws of their states. In some states, including New York and Pennsylvania, the state police are also fire, fish, and game wardens. In other states, such as Texas and West Virginia, there are special state police agencies that deal with these types of law violations. In Michigan, state police may be required to execute civil process in legal actions to which the state is a party. In Connecticut and Pennsylvania, state police conduct driver's licensing road tests. Some also carry out training academies for all law enforcement in the state, such as West Virginia, and others provide emergency medical services. Tables 10.1–10.3 give more information about local law enforcement agencies. Table 10.1 shows information on the number of state and local law enforcement agencies; Table 10.2 provides information on the educational requirements for those employed in local police departments; and Table 10.3 is an analysis of training requirements for new police recruits.

TABLE 10.1 State and local law enforcement agencies and employees (by type of agency, United States, 2004)

| Type of agency | Number of agencies | Number of employees | | | | | |
| | | Full time | | | Part time | | |
		Total	Sworn	Nonsworn	Total	Sworn	Nonsworn
Total	17,876	1,076,897	731,903	344,994	105,252	45,982	59,270
Local police	12,766	573,152	446,974	126,178	62,693	28,712	33,981
Sheriff	3,067	326,531	175,018	151,513	27,004	11,784	15,220
Primary state	49	89,265	58,190	31,075	708	31	677
Special jurisdiction	1,481	85,126	49,398	35,728	14,342	5,063	9,279
Texas constable	513	2,823	2,323	500	505	392	113

Source: U.S. Department of Justice, Bureau of Justice Statistics, *Census of State and Local Law Enforcement Agencies, 2004,* Bulletin NCJ 212749 (Washington, D.C.: U.S. Department of Justice, June 2007), p. 2.

Most state police crime laboratories aid local police departments in investigating crime scenes and analyzing evidence. Special services and technical expertise in such areas as bomb-site analysis and homicide investigations may be provided. They can provide accident investigations, conduct public information campaigns about traffic safety, and manage accident scenes involving hazardous material. Sometimes, state agencies will help local agencies conduct criminal investigations and make arrests or even investigate organized crime, fraud, narcotics violations, violent crime, arson, and motor vehicle theft.

TABLE 10.2 Minimum education requirements for new officer recruits in local police departments (by size of population served, United States, 2003)

| Population served | Total with requirements | Percentage of agencies requiring a minimum of | | | |
		High school diploma	Some college[a]	Two-year college degree	Four-year college degree
All sizes	98%	81	8	9	1
1,000,000 or more	98	72	18	7	1
500,000 to 999,999	99	72	13	9	5
250,000 to 499,999	99	84	8	4	3
100,000 to 249,999	98	81	13	3	2
50,000 to 99,999	100	76	17	6	1
25,000 to 49,999	99	77	10	11	1
10,000 to 24,999	99	82	7	9	1
2,500 to 9,999	99	83	7	9	<0.5
Less than 2,500	97	82	6	9	0

[a]Nondegree requirements.

Source: Adapted from *Sourcebook of Criminal Justice Statistics,* available online at www.albany.edu/sourcebook/.

TABLE 10.3 Training requirements for new officer recruits in local police departments (by size of population served, United States, 2003)

| | Average number of hours required[a] | | | | | |
| | Academy | | | Field | | |
Population served	Total	State mandated	Other required	Total	State mandated	Other Required
All sizes	628	588	40	326	147	179
1,000,000 or more	1,016	689	327	513	153	360
500,000 to 999,999	920	588	332	561	104	456
250,000 to 499,999	950	620	330	652	200	452
100,000 to 249,999	815	642	173	624	253	371
50,000 to 99,999	721	657	64	598	268	330
25,000 to 49,999	702	657	46	527	210	317
10,000 to 24,999	672	642	30	442	164	279
2,500 to 9,999	630	597	32	314	151	162
Less than 2,500	577	542	35	199	106	93

[a]Computations of average number of training hours required exclude departments not requiring training.

Source: Sourcebook of Criminal Justice Statistics, available online at www.albany.edu/sourcebook/.

Sheriffs Departments

Sheriffs departments are an interesting agency because of the government structure of counties. Counties exist by decree of the state and have no sovereignty. Therefore, county sheriffs offices exist through state authorization, but they work for the county commissions, which are an extension of state government. Some sheriffs departments are large, such as that of Los Angeles County, the largest in the nation, with over 8,000 sheriffs deputies, whereas some rural departments have no full-time officers, relying on either part-time officers or a mixture of part-time officers and the state police.[40] As of 2004, sheriffs departments had an estimated 175,018 sworn personnel serving in 3,067 departments (the same number of counties in the United States).[41]

The sheriff is usually an elected position. This system exists in every state except Rhode Island and Hawaii, where sheriffs are appointed. This means that they must be aware of the public's perceptions of them, the agency, and crime in their jurisdiction because of their concern regarding reelection. Because they are elected officials, they are directly involved in partisan politics in ways that municipal police chiefs are not.

Years ago, the sheriff was often the only legal authority in the territories. Today, the responsibilities of the sheriff depend largely on the size of the agency and the jurisdiction. Sheriffs can perform law enforcement duties, including serving civil process papers (summonses and court orders), patrol, traffic enforcement, and both accident and criminal investigations. The sheriff has extensive civil law authority and can make civil arrests (can detain people who have not committed any serious crime but may be a threat to public order or to themselves, such as the mentally ill) and can also provide court security, operate county jails, and investigate crimes. In some jurisdictions, the sheriff also acts as coroner, tax collector, overseer of highways and bridges, custodian of the county treasury, and provider of fire, animal control, and emergency medical services. Although the duties of the sheriffs departments vary depending on the jurisdiction they serve, there are essentially four models of sheriffs departments: (1) full-service models carry out law enforcement, judicial, and correctional duties; (2) law enforcement models carry out only the law enforcement duty; (3) civil–judicial models handle only court-related duties; and (4) correctional–judicial models handle all the responsibilities except law enforcement.[42]

Municipal Police Departments

Local or municipal law enforcement agencies operate at the city and town levels. Most departments (over half) are small departments with fewer than ten employees, but some departments have many officers, such as the New York City Police Department, which has nearly 38,000 sworn officers. As of 2004, local police departments across the nation had an estimated 573,152 full-time employees, including 446,974 sworn personnel.[43] This means that local police agencies represent nearly three-quarters of all law enforcement agencies in the United States, employing nearly two-thirds of sworn officers.

Most agencies are required to respond to calls for service, provide patrols, and enforce traffic laws. In fact, more than 99 percent of local police departments were responsible for responding to citizen calls for service, providing routine patrol services, and enforcing traffic laws. Ninety-one percent, including all but a few of those serving a population of 10,000 or more, were the primary investigating agency for crimes occurring in their jurisdiction. Many also are responsible for enforcing drug laws. About seven in eight local police departments had primary drug enforcement responsibilities. About a third had officers assigned full time to drug enforcement units, with over 13,000 officers so assigned nationwide. About a third of departments had officers assigned to multiagency drug task forces, with a total of more than 6,000 officers assigned full time nationwide.

Municipal police are the most important component of American law enforcement. There are far more local police officers than state police or federal agents. Most crime that occurs and most crime that is investigated is done so by local police. Hence, municipal police play a complex role in fighting crime. They have the heaviest responsibility for dealing with serious crime and are asked to provide a wide range of emergency services.

Special Police

There are other types of police departments that provide special-purpose services, serving particular government agencies. They include agencies such as transit police (such as the Washington, D.C., Metropolitan Transit Police), public housing police, airport police, public school police, university and college campus police, Indian tribal police, and park police. The coroner's, or medical examiner's, office is often considered a law enforcement agency because it has the responsibility to investigate crimes. The jurisdiction of these police is usually limited to specific boundaries that may fall within a larger overall jurisdiction. It must be remembered that most of these agencies are real police forces with training and recruitment procedures similar to others. The officers have general arrest powers, are certified by their respective states, and participate in the FBI's Uniform Crime Report program. For example, three-fourths of university and college campuses have a bona fide police department, while the others employ private security. In terms of school district police, many have their own police departments, but others utilize officers from local police departments or employ private security. Therefore, one cannot assume that just because the jurisdiction is not a municipal city or town, it does not employ a full-time police department. More information on U.S. Special Police Forces is given in Table 10.4

TABLE 10.4 U.S. special police—tribal police, 2000[a]

Agency name and location of administrative headquarters	Full-time sworn personnel			Bureau of Indian Affairs service population, 1999	Reservation land area (square miles)
	Total	Per 1,000 residents	Per 100 square miles		
Navajo Nation Department of Law Enforcement (AZ)	321	2	1	169,617	22,174
Tohono O'Odham Tribal Police Department (AZ)	76	4	2	16,981	4,453
Seminole Department of Law Enforcement (FL)	67	26	(b)	2,626	(b)
Gila River Indian Community Law Enforcement (AZ)	58	4	10	15,084	584
Oglala Sioux Tribal Police Department (SD)	58	1	2	40,873	3,159
Cheyenne River Tribal Police Department (SD)	53	5	1	10,589	4,260
Salt River Tribal Police Department (AZ)	51	8	63	6,655	81
Choctaw Law Enforcement Services (MS)	38	5	152	6,949	25
Saginaw Chippewa Tribal Police Department (MI)	37	36	17	1,026	218
White Mountain Apache Tribal Police Department (AZ)	36	3	1	13,161	2,628
Rosebud Sioux Tribal Law Enforcement (SD)	35	2	3	19,440	1,388
Oneida Indian Nation Police (NY)	33	17	(b)	1,893	(b)
Warm Springs Tribal Police Department (OR)	33	9	3	3,837	1,011
Colorado River Tribal Police Department (AZ)	32	16	9	1,942	361
Assiniboine and Sioux (Ft. Peck) Tribal Police (MT)	31	4	1	6,933	3,289
Yakima Tribal Police Department (WA)	31	2	1	15,968	2,153
Cherokee Police Department (NC)	30	4	36	7,456	83
Miccosukee Tribal Police Department (FL)	30	51	23	589	128
Turtle Mountain Band of Chippewa Indians Police Department (ND)	26	2	38	11,116	68
San Carlos Tribal Police Department (AZ)	25	2	1	10,834	2,911

[a]Number and rate (per 1,000 residents and per 100 square miles) of full-time sworn personnel, service population, and reservation land area in the twentieth-largest tribally operated law enforcement agencies.

[b]Reservation land consists of less than one square mile.

Source: Adapted from *Sourcebook of Criminal Justice Statistics*, available online at www.albany.edu/sourcebook/pdf/t157.pdf.

INTERGOVERNMENTAL RELATIONSHIPS

Traditionally in American policing, the only issue of intergovernmental relationships had to do with jurisdiction. As more and more police departments were added in the United States in the nineteenth and early twentieth centuries, the primary issue regarding how various agencies interacted tended to deal with determining the proper jurisdiction responsible for a crime. Early on, this tended to be among local jurisdictions, such as cities and towns or cities and counties. As the number of states creating state police agencies increased in the 1910s and 1920s, the problem over jurisdiction began to evolve to determine when a crime was in the jurisdiction and responsibility of a city or county and when it was within the jurisdiction of the state police. By the 1970s, the issue had become even more complex, as the number of federal agencies increased, as did the number of special police agencies throughout the United States. It was also at this time that the role of the federal government in fighting crime was heavily questioned. As crime rates rose in the 1960s and 1970s and local police were having a difficult time dealing with the problem, people began looking to the federal government to do something about the problem of crime. The question was, How could government respond, and how should they respond?

Federal Support

The President's Commission on Law Enforcement and the Administration of Justice, in its report *The Challenge of Crime in a Free Society*, argued that crime was largely the responsibility of the state and local governments.[44] However, it did envision a role for the federal government in addressing the problem of crime. It stated that the federal government has the direct responsibility for enforcing major criminal statutes, especially in the areas of kidnapping, bank robbery, counterfeiting, and tax evasion. The commission also stated that the federal government for years had provided information, advice, and training to state and local law enforcement and that it should continue to do so. Finally, it noted that it could bring the vast resources of the federal government to bear on the problems of crime in order to enhance state and local law enforcement. The commission essentially argued that the federal government should and does play a role in crime control.

Dilulio, Smith, and Saiger have articulated that the federal role in crime control really falls into three categories of anticrime strategies. The first is policymaking, where the "federal government can regulate a virtually unlimited range of activities believed to contribute to street crime (assault, rape, robbery, burglary, drug dealing, murder) and white-collar crime (fraud, deceptive business practices, illegal financial transactions)."[45] In fact, Congress has, since the 1970s, engaged more heavily in the passage of federal criminal laws. One report found that of "all federal crimes enacted since 1865, over forty percent have been created since 1970,"[46] demonstrating that the federal government has become more engaged in crime control policy over the past 40 years. Dilulio, Smith, and Saiger further explain that "only the federal government can regulate such things as immigration flows, interstate commerce, and global corporate activities,"[47] giving them exclusive rights to regulate crime in regard to certain types of criminal behavior. This is largely how the creation of so many federal law enforcement agencies in the twentieth century came about: Congress passing laws that then needed specific agencies to enforce. Still further, under the concept of policymaking, the federal government has the capability of establishing model policies and through its policymaking capabilities can encourage (through threat or attractive grants) state and local agencies to come into compliance with its policies. For example, when agencies adhere to the federal reporting mechanisms regarding the updates from the Uniform Crime Reports to the National Incident Based Reporting System (a "model policy" for reporting crime rates), they are given grants to assist them in the implementation process.

The second means is policy administration. In this case, "the federal government can declare an undesirable activity a federal crime, thereby bringing the full force of federal law enforcement (the Federal Bureau of Investigation, the Drug Enforcement Agency, even the U.S. military in overseas drug interdiction efforts), prosecution (U.S. Attorneys), and adjudication (literally 'making a federal case' before a federal court) to bear on the activity."[48] This is essentially an extension of the policymaking function of government. Once Congress passes a federal criminal law, it gives the administration the capability of enforcing that specific law and bringing the vast resources of the federal government to bear.

The third means of federal intervention in crime is through policy funding. As Dilulio, Smith, and Saiger explain, "The federal government can provide human, financial, and informational resources (technical experts or advisers, money, studies and statistics that compare crime trends across many jurisdictions) and is in a unique position to coordinate (or legally mandate) interjurisdictional anticrime plans."[49] This is the area where the federal government has the most power to influence the criminal justice system in the United States. When the federal government channels money to state and local governments, it has the most impact on the intergovernmental relations between these three levels of government. Examples of this abound, but the three major initiatives over the past 40 years have been the grants for police under the Omnibus Crime Control and Safe Streets Act of 1968 that were delivered by the Law Enforcement Assistance Administration, the Edward Bryne Memorial State and Local Law Enforcement Assistance Program block grants of the 1980s and 1990s, and the COPS grants of the 1990s that resulted from the passage of the Violent Crime Control and Law Enforcement Act of 1994, which created COPS to deliver these grants to state and local agencies (see Chapter 1). Each of these grants has had a profound impact not only on the departments receiving the grants but also on how policing is done overall. Table 10.5 shows grant allocations to states under the Byrne Grant Program.

State Support

The state's role in intergovernmental relations has become more complex as well. While the federal system dictates two levels of government, national and state, the state governments also can create or allow for the creation of independent (cities and towns) and dependent (counties) government police agencies. So, while state governments set the standards for all law enforcement agencies in their states, they do not have complete control over the functioning of these agencies. States can and do set standards for law enforcement certification, training standards, and recertification and can establish state-level policies and procedures that local law enforcement is required to follow. However, it is often the case that local law enforcement, through its actions and policies, can end up dictating state-level policy. In a sense, the state acts as a coordinator between the many local agencies within the state as well as acting as a channel for many of the federal initiatives. This can be grant money received from the federal government (e.g., the Bryne grants) or information being forwarded from local agencies to the national government (e.g., the Uniform Crime Reports).

Local Support

This then leaves the role of the local law enforcement agencies as questionable in regard to their specific role in the intergovernmental relationship. In other words, it would seem that they are merely the ones that receive benefits, dictates, or mandates and are simply the agencies that are responsible for executing the policies at the local level. While much of this is true, police agencies can also be the proving grounds for federal initiatives, intended or unintended, that will eventually

TABLE 10.5 Program funds allocation of Edward Bryne Memorial State and Local Law Enforcement Assistance (by jurisdiction, fiscal year 2003)

Jurisdiction	Funds allocated	Percentage to be passed through to local jurisdictions	Jurisdiction	Funds allocated	Percentage to be passed through to local jurisdictions
Alabama	$ 7,659,952	60.10	New Hampshire	$ 3,087,951	54.68
Alaska	2,189,951	24.14	New Jersey	13,500,953	59.23
Arizona	9,039,952	61.86	New Mexico	3,870,589	49.29
Arkansas	5,130,952	52.84	New York	28,542,953	65.16
California	51,258,953	67.34	North Carolina	13,116,953	42.41
Colorado	7,687,952	59.56	North Dakota	2,175,951	58.68
Connecticut	6,198,952	38.25	Ohio	17,487,589	64.06
Delaware	2,422,951	27.15	Oklahoma	6,245,952	45.79
District of Columbia	2,085,951	100.00	Oregon	6,285,952	49.95
Florida	25,063,953	64.85	Pennsylvania	18,831,953	56.04
Georgia	13,458,353	59.56	Rhode Island	2,795,951	41.05
Hawaii	3,044,951	49.53	South Carolina	7,119,952	47.05
Idaho	3,181,951	57.74	South Dakota	2,356,951	53.80
Illinois	19,209,953	65.51	Tennessee	9,524,952	60.11
Indiana	10,039,953	59.29	Texas	32,275,953	60.42
Iowa	5,453,952	48.19	Utah	4,569,952	52.34
Kansas	5,138,952	57.09	Vermont	2,150,951	29.32
Kentucky	7,098,952	38.50	Virginia	12,814,953	35.11
Louisiana	7,653,952	54.04	Washington	9,911,953	63.72
Maine	3,115,951	52.03	West Virginia	3,837,951	50.13
Maryland	9,042,952	43.52	Wisconsin	9,018,952	61.51
Massachusetts	10,400,364	36.52	Wyoming	1,982,951	61.59
Michigan	15,579,953	57.83			
Minnesota	8,418,952	65.72	Puerto Rico	6,765,952	0.00
Mississippi	5,360,952	56.93	Virgin Islands	1,427,951	0.00
Missouri	9,347,952	58.53	Guam	1,471,363	0.00
Montana	2,590,884	52.56	American Samoa	944,424	0.00
Nebraska	3,734,951	62.12	Northern Marianas	479,474	0.00
Nevada	4,366,952	72.11			

Source: Adapted from *Sourcebook of Criminal Justice Statistics,* available online at www.albany.edu/sourcebook/pdf/t114.pdf.

influence the federal model policies. In many cases, the federal government will make available grants for local agencies to attempt new programs aimed at improving police efficiency, lowering crime rates, or improving public satisfaction with the police. If these programs are found effective, they often become the model policies that the federal government advocates. In other cases, when an agency, without federal assistance, implements a program that is successful, the federal government may advocate this as the policy of the federal government and will support it through policy funding, as was seen under the COPS grants for local law enforcement to implement the tenets of community policing.

Many have equated intergovernmental relations with a white picket fence where the lateral slats are the various levels of government and the vertical posts are the different agencies that run through them. This is a depiction that may begin to help one understand intergovernmental relations, but it is perhaps far too simplistic in terms of understanding the public policy of crime and criminal justice in America. The issues of jurisdiction, policymaking, policy administration, and policy funding create an integral web of relations between the federal, state, and local law enforcement agencies, but there is no seamless agency that operates at all three levels. Rather, a better depiction may actually be a mosaic, for there are thousands of different agencies that somehow all come together, acting in concert, to create a picture that is our criminal justice system.

POLICE AND POLICY ISSUES

Police officers, police chiefs, and, more specifically, police organizations are engaged in the public policy process on a daily basis. The crime problems that police address on the streets in their cities, towns, and counties are the types of problems that public policymakers attempt to address in the passage of crime legislation. When police departments implement a particular program within their jurisdiction, they are implementing a program most likely devised as part of the implementation of a larger crime policy. And the outcomes of these programs and the new problems that arise often feed back into the public policy process, thus making the police a continual part of the policy cycle.

Police as Policymakers

Welsh and Harris provide a good overview of how police agencies become involved in the policy process.[50] They discuss the differences between policy, programs, and projects. They describe a policy as "a rule or set of rules or guidelines for how to make a decision"; a program as "a set of services aimed at achieving specific goals and objectives within specified individuals, groups, organizations, or communities"; and a project as "a time-limited set of services provided to particular individuals, groups, organizations or communities, usually focused on a single need, problem or issue."[51] So, for example, the policy could be the federal government's "war on drugs" and the various anti–drug abuse legislation it has passed. The program could be a series of crackdowns on the open-air drug markets found in their jurisdiction, while the project may simply be a police officer speaking at a school event about the dangers of drugs. The underlying problem in this case is drug abuse, but each of these—policies, programs, and projects—is working toward the same policy objective, namely, to reduce drug abuse in American society. When police officers engage in these programs or perform these projects, they are participating in the policy process.

In fact, Welsh and Harris go even further and describe the policy development of criminal justice agencies as consisting of its own policy cycle. The process includes analyzing the problem, setting goals and objectives, designing the program or policy, developing an action plan, developing a plan for monitoring the program, developing a plan for evaluating the outcomes, and finally initiating the policy or program.[52] This process is very similar to the public policy process, but this process operates at the micro (local) level, while the public policy process described in this text operates at the macro (national and state) level. However, the two are highly related, for, as discussed in terms of intergovernmental relations, it is often the case that a local program that achieves some degree of success may become the policy solution to a national problem and thus become part of the national public policy process. Or, conversely, a national public policy may see the implementation process as providing the police the necessary funds to implement a federal government program.

Police Issues

There are numerous examples of how either crime- or police-related issues can often become part of the larger public policy process. For example, police departments continually review their use-of-force policies and update these on the basis of changes in the law, court decisions, and new advances in technology. When they experience a series of use-of-force incidents in their agencies, the process that Welsh and Harris describe will often be invoked, with the goal of perhaps reducing the number of incidents or reducing the harm caused by these incidents. In Houston, Texas, for example, the police department had a number of use-of-force incidents between 2000 and 2004. In 2004, the newly appointed police chief requested a review of these incidents, and the solution to the problem was the implementation of Taser weapons to be issued to all officers. This is a case of the policy process playing out at the local level. One only has to look at the Rodney King situation in 1992 to understand how the issue of police use of force can surface onto the macro public policy process and to trace the impact that this incident had on policing throughout the 1990s.

Other examples of police issues that are part of the public policy process include police pursuits, police use of discretion, and police corruption. A more recent issue that was beginning to surface as perhaps one of the major public policy issues prior to the September 11 terrorist attacks was the issue of racial profiling by police. Here the issue was whether police motor vehicle stops were being conducted on the basis of reasonable suspicion or on the basis of racial profiling. The amount of attention paid to this issue by the media continued to increase in the late 1990s and early 2000, and many people suggested that the police were biased in who they stopped, searched, ticketed, and arrested. Research that has been conducted on this topic, however, has been extremely weak and wrought with methodological problems and has given mixed results.[53] This helped create the controversy over the issue, but it was largely supplanted with the terrorist attacks. This does not mean that racial profiling is still not an issue with which police departments must contend; it simply means that it is no longer one of the major issues on the agenda or one that is being actively considered by the public policy process.

In terms of understanding the issues of policing as being part of the larger public policy process, the debate over the proper method of police deployment speaks best to how police organizations are part of the public policy process. Over the past 30 years, the proper deployment of the police has become a topic of policy debate and has seen some of the most sweeping legislation and policy changes passed at the national, state, and local levels. It is to these particular methods of police deployment that we now turn.

Deployment of the Police

Policing in the twentieth century was largely taken for granted until the early 1970s. What has become known as traditional policing made a number of assumptions in regard to the way the police were deployed. It assumed that police officers riding around on patrol deterred crimes; that when crimes did occur, if the police could arrive on scene faster, the crimes would usually be solved; and that if no suspects were taken into custody, the detective units would be able to solve the crimes with their investigative skills and technology. No one really questioned these long-held assumptions until the early 1970s. Many of these assumptions were questioned and refuted, and since then policing has been searching for new, innovative ways to deploy its forces in order to provide safer communities and more effective law enforcement agencies. Determining the proper method for deploying police has become part of the public policy process over the past 40 years, as police policy has moved away from "traditional" policing and attempted such policies as community-oriented policing, problem-oriented policing, and zero-tolerance policing. More recently, with the September 11 terrorist attacks, part of the public policy process has been about determining the proper role for local police in terms of homeland security. All these philosophies and methods for deploying the police have worked their way through the policy process, but they came largely as a rejection of "traditional" policing in the 1970s. Understanding this is critical to understanding why police deployment has become a public policy issue.

TRADITIONAL POLICING   Traditional policing, as it is often referred to today, was really a part of the professionalization movement in policing as well as advancements in technology that built up throughout the early twentieth century. The goal among the early reformers was to disengage policing from politics and to develop a means to hold police more accountable. To do this, many of the social services offered by the police were minimized while the aspects of law enforcement were emphasized. In addition, police were seen as having the capability of deterring crime through their presence and restoring order through the power of arrest. Since it was the police that had the knowledge and training, the assistance of the public was minimized in importance, and all that was needed from them was, in the words of *Dragnet*'s Joe Friday, "just the facts."

As a result of the Omnibus Crime Control and Safe Streets Act of 1968, funding was allocated for improving policing in the wake of the rise in crime rates throughout the 1960s. The crime bill also allocated funding for research into policing, and such research institutes as the Police Foundation and the Rand Corporation received funding to conduct research in policing. The research findings that came out of this funding ended up challenging the assumptions that had long been held in policing, namely, that random patrols deter crime, that faster responses to crime solve more crimes, and that police detective training and technology solve more crimes.

The effectiveness of policing styles on crime was first tested in a research study in Kansas City, Missouri, by the Police Foundation. Published in 1974, the study looked at fifteen separate police beats that were divided into three groups.[54] The first group, a control group, retained normal police patrol (one car per beat); the second was a "proactive" response using two or three times the normal number of patrol officers; and the third was "reactive" in that its preventive patrol was eliminated and police responded only when summoned by citizens to the scene of a crime (police vehicles assigned to these beats entered them only in response to a call for service). The citizens living in the areas were not told of the experiment.

The preventive patrol experiment measured the impact of the different levels of patrol on criminal activity and community perceptions and attitudes. In addition, the study looked at police officer behavior and police department practices. Moreover, it looked at police response time, arrest practices, police officer use of time, and officer attitudes. The study found that variations in the level of patrol had no statistically significant effect on either criminal activity or citizen feelings of safety. In fact, the variations had little effect on residential or business burglaries, motor vehicle thefts, larcenies involving auto accessories, robberies, vandalism, or other criminal behavior. It found that citizens' fear of crime was not significantly affected by changes in the level of patrol and that citizen attitudes toward police were not significantly affected by the level of patrol. The variations had little effect on citizens' satisfaction with police or their fear of future criminal behavior. On the whole, the study suggested that the number of patrol cars on the street and their visibility to citizens has little effect on the crime rate. The different social interactions that police officers have with citizens, based on the type of policing, is found in Table 10.6.

TABLE 10.6 Comparisons of social interactions and structural components of various forms of policing

Social interaction or structural dimension	Traditional policing	Community policing	Problem-oriented policing	Zero-tolerance policing
Focus of policing	Law enforcement	Community building through crime prevention	Law, order, and fear problems	Order problems
Forms of intervention	Reactive, based on criminal law	Proactive, on criminal, civil, and administrative law	Mixed, on criminal, civil, and administrative law	Proactive, uses criminal, civil, and administrative law
Range of police activity	Narrow, crime focused	Broad, crime, order, fear, and quality-of-life focused	Narrow to broad—problem focused	Narrow, location and behavior focused
Level of discretion at line level	High and unaccountable	High and accountable to the community and local commanders	High and accountable primarily to the police administration	Low but primarily accountable to the police administration
Focus of police culture	Inward, rejecting community	Outward, building partnerships	Mixed, depending on problem, but analysis focused	Inward focused on the target problem
Locus of decision making	Police directed, minimized the involvement of others	Community-police coproduction, joint responsibility and assessment	Varied, police identify problems but with community involvement/action	Police directed, some linkages to other agencies where necessary
Communication flow	Downward from police to community	Horizontal between police and community	Horizontal between police and community	Downward from police to community
Range of community involvement	Low and passive	High and active	Mixed depending on problem set	Low and passive
Linkage with other agencies	Poor and intermittent	Participative and integrative in the overarching process	Participative and integrative depending on the problem set	Moderate and intermittent
Type of organization and command focus	Centralized command and control	Decentralized with community linkage	Decentralized with local command accountability to central administration	Centralized or decentralized but internal focus
Implications for organizational change/development	Few, static organization fending off the environment	Many, dynamic organization focused on the environment and environmental interactions	Varied, focused on problem resolution but with import for organization and intelligence support	Few, limited interventions focused on target problems, using many traditional methods
Measurement of success	Arrest and crime rates, particularly serious Part I crimes	Varied, crime, calls for service, fear reduction, use of public	Varied, problems solved, minimized, displaced	Arrests, field stops, activity location specific

Source: J. R. Greene, "Community Policing in America: Changing the Nature, Structure, and Function of Police," in *Policies, Processes, and Decisions in the Criminal Justice System*, vol. 3 (Washington, D.C.: U.S. Department of Justice, 2000). p. 311.

Although the study was criticized for its research design, it was a watershed event in American policing. It not only tested the effectiveness of patrol but at the same time challenged traditional assumptions about police preventive patrol. A similar Police Foundation study was conducted later in 1978 and 1979 on foot patrol in the Newark Foot Patrol Experiment.[55] In this study, some foot patrol beats received the same number of foot patrol officers, some received more, and others were the control beats with foot patrol officers responding only on the basis of calls for service. The experiment found that additional foot patrol did not reduce serious crime, but the different levels of police staffing did have a significant effect on citizen attitudes toward the police. Citizens were aware of the different levels of foot patrol, and residents in beats with added foot patrol officers consistently saw crime problems diminish in their neighborhoods. Like the Kansas City experiment, however, foot patrol staffing levels were not associated with the reduction of crime, an assumption dating back to the earliest days of policing.

Another study conducted by the Rand Corporation in the 1970s tested the long-held police assumption that rapid response to the report of a crime helped increase the clearance of crimes.[56] A good portion of police expenditures in the post–World War II era were to enhance the capabilities of the police to respond faster to reports of crime. Faster cars, more patrol cars, and the implementation of 911 were all aimed at speeding up response time. The Rand Corporation study, also in Kansas City, found that in the majority of cases (over 75 %), it would not matter how fast the police responded to a crime scene because of the long delay in citizens' reporting crimes to the police, on average 40 minutes. And although the researchers found that approximately 25 percent of all reported serious crimes could have increased the ability of the police to make an arrest, the reality was that they were able to do so in only less than 3 percent of all reported serious crimes. Therefore, another long-held assumption in policing was dispelled by research in the 1970s.

Finally, the Rand Corporation conducted another study in the mid-1970s that looked at the criminal investigation process to determine how effective it was in solving crimes.[57] The researchers looked at the investigation process and the technology being applied at the time in order to determine how effective, primarily through arrest and clearance rates, criminal investigations were. The researchers looked at what investigators do during the work hours, how they collected and processed evidence, how they prepared their cases for prosecution, and what type of proactive measures they used. Although there were many findings from this study, the primary finding was largely a refutation of another long-held assumption, namely, that police detectives' knowledge and skills, as well as the latest technology, solved cases. What the researchers found was that the detectives' skills and technology accounted for a small portion of cases solved and that what really solved most crimes were citizens, either witnesses, victims, or friends and relatives of either, coming forward to help the police.

Each of these studies in its own right challenged assumptions that had existed in policing for well over four decades. Random patrols do not deter crime, rapid response does not increase the number of suspects arrested or cases cleared, and highly skilled detectives and technology do not solve most crimes. The resulting effect of these three studies was that municipalities, facing fiscal constraints in the 1970s, began to reduce the number of police officers on staff. Police emphasis on rapid response continued, but it was tied largely to the 911 emergency response system. And the resources that detectives received were somewhat diminished also because of fiscal constraints. All this was counterintuitive because cutting police assumed that police focused only on crime control and did not provide other services. In addition, with the advent of 911, calls for service actually began to rise significantly during this same time period, necessitating more police, not fewer. Finally, detectives and technology are still an integral part of policing and are critical to putting victim and witness statements to use in a criminal investigation.

The larger impact that these studies had on the public policy process is that they left many questioning what works in policing. Since the methods of policing that had been employed for many decades were found ineffective, the solution was to try to determine how best to deploy the police to overcome these findings. The resulting impact was a movement away from "traditional policing" in the 1980s and 1990s to new methods of police deployment. The three main policies that were developed, largely from grassroots efforts, were community-oriented policing, problem-oriented policing, and zero-tolerance policing.

COMMUNITY-ORIENTED POLICING   One of the first innovative methods to come out of the negative criticism of traditional policing in the 1970s was community-oriented policing. Community policing is aimed at entirely altering the basic philosophy of twentieth-century policing by improving the relationship between the police and the public in order for the police and local neighborhoods to work together to address the problems of crime and disorder. The police become partners with the community to create strategies to address the causes of crime and reduce the fear of crime by increasing the interaction and cooperation between local police and the citizens. The goals are to reduce and prevent crime, to increase feelings of safety among residents and reduce fears of crime, to help develop closer ties to the community, and to engage residents in a joint effort to prevent crime.

The roots of community policing can be traced to Wilson and Kelling's "broken windows" theory, published in 1982 as a means of dealing with the question of what works in policing and how best to deploy the police.[58] The authors acknowledged the importance of community in local crime control. They said that neighborhood disorder creates fear. In other words, neighborhood areas that are filled with street people, youth gangs, prostitutes, and the mentally disturbed are the ones most likely to maintain a high degree of crime. Some neighborhoods, particularly those in distress, give out crime-promoting signals. A neighborhood filled with deteriorating housing, unrepaired broken windows, potholes, abandoned vehicles, and other untended disorderly behavior gives out those crime-promoting signals. It tells the criminals that no one cares about this particular neighborhood. Honest citizens then live in fear in those areas, and predatory criminals are attracted to the area, with honest citizens becoming victims.

To reduce crime and the fear of crime, according to Wilson and Kelling, police need citizens' cooperation, support, and assistance. To do this, police need to have closer contact with the people they serve and rely less on police cars, which serve only to remove an officer from the community and alienate people. These citizens are potential sources of information to help people. To elicit the help of communities, the police not only must work alongside them as coproducers in the fight against crime but also must be willing to share power with the citizens. Under community policing, power is shared between local groups and individuals and between citizens and law enforcement officials. To be effective, citizens must actively participate with the police to fight crime and disorder. Police departments must focus on the problems of the community rather than the needs of the police departments.

The move toward community policing began in the early 1980s with a few experiments and local attempts at programs, demonstration projects, and subtle changes in policing practices aimed at implementing the broken windows theory.[59] Eventually, by the late 1980s, more and more police departments began to move toward adopting the community policing methods within their agencies, and community policing rapidly spread throughout the United States. As agencies began to see much success with this grassroots method of policing, it caught the attention of national policymakers in the Clinton administration, and eventually community policing would become a national public policy (see Chapter 14).

PROBLEM-ORIENTED POLICING   Another method for more effective police deployment that came out of the late-1970s questioning of police practices is the concept of problem-oriented policing. Herman Goldstein, in an article published in 1979, advocated that police should focus on the ends rather than the means. He found that too often police became so obsessed with the procedures of policing that they forget the ultimate goal of reducing or eliminating crime and disorder. Goldstein argued that when it came to calls for service, police acted as if the call had no history and no future and that it was not related to any other problems the police department encountered. Police officers arrived on scene, dealt with the situation, and then left as if the problem was resolved. He argued that the symptoms of the problem were resolved for the moment but that the underlying problem remained. He also argued that often problems are related to one another, but because police are so fixated on the means, they fail to analyze the ends in policing. Thus, Goldstein advocated that police apply a simple problem-solving method to their work.

The article was more theoretical than practical, but it caught the attention of two researchers, Spelman and Eck, who attempted to take Goldstein's method and put it into practice. After consulting with Goldstein, they devised the SARA model for policing.[60] SARA (Scanning, Analysis, Response, Assessment) is a four-step problem-solving model. The first stage, scanning, tells officers to scan their environment for problems and try to see if various problems are related. For example, one city block may face the separate problems of burglaries, drug dealing, and prostitution. Responding to each of these crimes separately can be time-consuming and would require different police tactics. However, if the crimes were linked, one solution may resolve all three problems.

Once a problem is recognized and narrowly defined, the next step is to analyze the problem. In the analysis stage, the function is to gather as much information about the problem as possible. This may include police reports, talking with other officers, talking with the community, and analyzing the number of calls for service. Data collection helps the officer gain a fuller understanding of the problems, perhaps finding, as in the case mentioned previously, that all the burglaries are occurring in a specific apartment complex, all the drug dealers arrested are from a nearby neighborhood, and the prostitutes are nearly always the same ones and all drug addicted. As part of this step, police can gain a better understanding of the problems they face and how best to deal with them.

This leads to the third step in the SARA model: response. Officers use the data collected from the previous stage to help them develop possible responses to reduce or eliminate the problem. Once they have a list of options, they select the most viable option and implement it. For example, in the previously described scenario, if the drug addicts are committing burglaries to buy the drugs and prostitutes are present because of the dealers and users, then getting rid of the drug dealers may reduce the problems associated with all three crimes.

Finally, the fourth step of the SARA model calls for an assessment of the response. The key to this step is to determine if the response had any impact on the problem. If it did, then continuation of the response may be warranted. If it did not, then selecting and implementing another response may be necessary.

Problem-oriented policing, especially the SARA model, became a successful method of policing, whether implemented alone or as part of a larger community-oriented policing program. In its initial testing in Newport News, Virginia, in the early 1980s, it was found to successfully resolve a number of problems. The model then began to spread across the United States in the late 1980s and 1990s, and numerous police departments began requiring their officers to work on problem-oriented policing projects. Problem-oriented policing has been deemed by many to be a very successful method of policing.

ZERO-TOLERANCE POLICING   The other method of policing that was created in the mid-1980s came to be known as zero-tolerance policing. This method of policing became known widely in its implementation in New York City under Mayor Rudolph Giuliani beginning in the early 1990s. However, the concepts for zero-tolerance policing were also derived from the Wilson and Kelling article "Broken Windows."[61] While community-oriented policing focuses on the aspect of the article that stated that the police and community needed to work together to address crime and disorder, the zero-tolerance method focuses on the article's belief that minor crimes and disorder are what lead to more serious crime. Hence, police should enforce the minor crimes and disorder that are typically ignored, especially in large urban areas, in order to reduce serious crime. By removing the signs of disorder, those things that promote other crimes, police help send the signal that the neighborhood is not going to tolerate crime and disorder, thus restoring order and allowing law-abiding citizens to feel safe and to "take back their neighborhoods" from the criminals.

Zero-tolerance policing advocates an aggressive means of law enforcement in order to stop and deter future crime. One of the reasons for this, it is argued, is that in those neighborhoods that have already decayed and are experiencing distress, it will take the assistance of the police to address the problem of crime and disorder because citizens' level of fear is already high and they will be unwilling or unable to help. In addition, these types of neighborhoods tend to be highly transient and lack the communal ties and civic organizations that can assist in restoring order. Moreover, the goal of zero-tolerance policing is to focus on the "hot spots" of crime and disorder, those locations that tend to exhibit problems based on time, location, and individuals. By employing "crackdowns" on these certain types of crimes, locations, and violators, police can alleviate or eliminate these types of minor crimes and disorders, thus preventing the promotion of more serious crimes. Examples include the crackdowns on graffiti in the New York subways, the open-air drug markets in Washington, D.C., and even the targeting of the infamous "squeegeemen" on the street corners of New York City.

The success of zero-tolerance policing has been mixed, and it has been a highly controversial method of policing. Although New York City Mayor Giuliani favored the method and crime rates did fall dramatically throughout his tenure as mayor, crime rates were falling throughout the United States overall. There are many advocates for zero-tolerance policing,[62] and there have been many advocates against this method of policing.[63] While it is too soon to tell the true success of these police methods and more research is needed, zero-tolerance policing has assuredly been a controversial police policy over the past decade.

HOMELAND SECURITY   The concepts of community-oriented policing, problem-oriented policing, and zero-tolerance policing all came largely as a result of the challenges to traditional policing issued in the 1970s. More recently, however, a new concept of policing is beginning to unfold, and that is the role of policing in homeland security. In the wake of the September 11 terrorist attacks in 2001, the federal government has shifted to a policy of homeland security, and part of that has incorporated local firefighters and local police agencies. What is currently at issue is not so much determining *if* local police are going to play a role in this new public policy but rather *what* role they can play. Much confusion abounds in terms of what homeland security means: is it simply being more watchful for suspicious activities, is it intelligence gathering on the part of patrol officers, or is it standing guard at possible terrorist targets in their jurisdictions? And, beyond determining what role the police will play in homeland security, the natural extension of this is to ask who will pay. As the public policy of homeland security is clearly a national policy issue, it would seem that the policy will be an intergovernmental one driven by the presidential administration. This is becoming evident in the police incorporation of the National Management Framework's (NMF) centerpiece, the Incident Command System (ICS), into its policies and procedures. As police officers are commonly the first responders in an incident and for the fact that the incident command system allows for a management structure to respond to man-made and natural disasters, this is fast becoming the most common means of police officers engaging in Homeland Security. ICS allows for a multi-police agency response to major incidents, and when the response necessitates other areas of expertise (e.g., fire, hospital, schools, etc.), incident command allows for the incorporation of these agencies into what is known as a unified command—one command structure but one composed of multiple agencies and jurisdiction representatives.

Conclusion

The role of the police in our society is a complex mosaic of agencies (federal, state, and local) and roles (law enforcement, services, and order maintenance) that have built up over the course of America's history. The specific history of law enforcement in this country provides us with some understanding of where we are in terms of providing police protection today. While there are many types of policing, all provide several basic functions, such as crime prevention, criminal investigations, and various services. These functions are provided by law enforcement on the federal, state, and local levels. All these agencies are influenced by politics and, in turn, affect politics. In the same right, all these agencies are influenced by the public policy process and, in turn, affect the public policy process.

Notes

1. H. Goldstein, *Policing a Free Society* (Cambridge, Mass.: Ballinger, 1977).
2. J. Q. Wilson, *Varieties of Police Behavior* (New York: Atheneum, 1973), p. 21.
3. M. Lipsky, *Street-Level Bureaucracy* (New York: Russell Sage Foundation, 1980).
4. P. K. Manning and J. Van Maanen, *Policing: A View from the Street* (Santa Monica, Calif.: Goodyear, 1978).
5. Wilson, *Varieties of Police Behavior.*
6. M. H. Moore, "Police Leadership: The Impossible Dream?" in *Impossible Jobs in Public Management*, ed. E. C. Hargrove and J. C. Glidewell (Lawrence: University Press of Kansas, 1990), pp. 72–102.
7. N. M. Marion, *Criminal Justice in America: The Politics behind the System* (Durham, N.C.: Carolina Academic Press, 2002).
8. Ibid.; W. M. Oliver and J. F. Hilgenberg, Jr., *A History of Crime and Criminal Justice in America* (Boston: Allyn & Bacon, 2006).
9. Oliver and Hilgenberg, *A History of Crime and Criminal Justice in America.*
10. G. L. Kelling and M. H. Moore, "From Political to Reform to Community: The Evolving Strategy of Police," in *Community Policing: Rhetoric or Reality*, ed. J. R. Greene and S. D. Mastrofski (Westport, Conn.: Praeger, 1988).
11. Oliver and Hilgenberg, *A History of Crime and Criminal Justice in America.*
12. Marion, *Criminal Justice in America.*
13. Kelling and Moore, "From Political to Reform to Community."
14. Ibid.
15. W. M. Oliver, *Community-Oriented Policing: A Systemic Approach to Policing*, 3rd ed. (Upper Saddle River, N.J.: Prentice Hall, 2003).
16. Ibid.
17. J. Q. Wilson and G. L. Kelling, "Broken Windows: The Police and Neighborhood Safety," *Atlantic Monthly* 249 (March 1982): 29–38.
18. W. M. Oliver, "The Homeland Security Juggernaut: The End of the Community Policing Era?" *Crime and Justice International* 20 (79, 2004): 4–10.
19. Oliver and Hilgenberg, *A History of Crime and Criminal Justice in America*; U.S. Marshals Service home page (2004), available online at www.usdoj.gov/marshals/history/oldest.htm.

20. K. Maguire and A. L. Pastore, *Sourcebook of Criminal Justice Statistics*, available online at www.albany.edu/sourcebook/.

21. Ibid.

22. Ibid.

23. Ibid.

24. Ibid.

25. Ibid.

26. Federal Bureau of Investigation (2004), available online at www.fbi.gov/homepage.htm.

27. Ibid.

28. Federal Bureau of Investigation (2004), available online at www.fbi.gov/aboutus.htm.

29. U.S. Marshals Service (2004), available online at www.usdoj.gov/marshals/.

30. Marion, *Criminal Justice in America*.

31. Ibid.

32. Drug Enforcement Administration (2004), available online at www.usdoj.gov/dea/.

33. Bureau of Alcohol, Tobacco, Firearms and Explosives (2004), available online at www.atf.gov/.

34. Ibid.

35. United States Citizenship and Immigration Service (2004), available online at http://uscis.gov/graphics/aboutus/index.htm.

36. U.S. Customs and Border Protection (2004), available online at www.customs.gov/.

37. U.S. Secret Service (2004), available online at www.secretservice.gov/.

38. Oliver and Hilgenberg, *A History of Crime and Criminal Justice in America*.

39. Maguire and Pastore, *Sourcebook of Criminal Justice Statistics*.

40. Ibid.

41. Ibid.

42. L. P. Brown, "The Role of the Sheriff," in *The Future of Policing*, ed. A. W. Cohn (Beverly Hills, Calif.: Sage, 1978), pp. 227–28.

43. Maguire and Pastore, *Sourcebook of Criminal Justice Statistics*.

44. President's Commission on Law Enforcement and Administration of Justice, *The Challenge of Crime in a Free Society* (New York: Avon, 1968).

45. J. J. Dilulio, Jr., S. K. Smith, and A. J. Saiger, "The Federal Role in Crime Control," in *Crime*, ed. J. Q. Wilson and J. Petersilia (San Francisco: ICS Press, 1995), pp. 445–62.

46. J. A. Strazella, *The Federalization of Criminal Law* (Washington, D.C.: American Bar Association, 1998), p. 2.

47. Dilulio et al., "The Federal Role in Crime Control."

48. Ibid.

49. Ibid.

50. W. N. Welsh and P. W. Harris, *Criminal Justice Policy and Planning* (Cincinnati: Anderson, 1999).

51. Ibid., pp. 5–6.

52. Ibid.

53. W. J. Chambliss, *Power, Politics, and Crime* (Boulder, Colo.: Westview Press, 2001); H. M. MacDonald, *Are Cops Racist?* (Chicago: Ivan R. Dee, 2003).

54. G. L. Kelling et al., *The Kansas City Preventive Patrol Experiment: A Summary Report* (Washington, D.C.: Police Foundation, 1974).

55. Police Foundation, *The Newark Foot Patrol Experiment* (Washington, D.C.: Police Foundation, 1981).

56. W. G. Spelman and D. K. Brown, *Calling the Police: A Replication of the Citizen Reporting Component of the Kansas City Response Time Analysis* (Collingdale, P.A.: Diane Publishing), pp. iii–xx.

57. J. M. Chaiken, P. W. Greenwood, and J. Petersilia, "The Criminal Investigation Process: A Summary Report," *Policy Analysis* 3 (1977): 187–217.

58. Wilson and Kelling, "Broken Windows."

59. Oliver, *Community-Oriented Policing*.

60. J. E. Eck and W. Spelman, *Problem-Solving: Problem-Oriented Policing in Newport News* (Washington, D.C.: Police Executive Research Forum, 1987).

61. Wilson and Kelling "Broken Windows."

62. G. L. Kelling and C. M. Coles, *Fixing Broken Windows* (New York: Free Press, 1996); E. B. Silverman, *NYPD Battles Crime* (Boston: Northeastern University Press, 1999).

63. A. McArdle and T. Erzen, *Zero Tolerance: Quality of Life and the New Police Brutality in New York City* (New York: New York University Press, 2001).

11

Courts

Chapter Outline

INTRODUCTION

The courtroom actors, judges in particular, are viewed as being impartial and above the fray of politics. However, all the court actors are linked to the political system on the federal, state, and local levels, and they make decisions that are at times based on a partisan argument about public policy. Judges often use court opinions to express their views and preferences on policy alternatives and sometimes make decisions that have major, long-term impacts on procedures and policies. Each of the courtroom actors has a major role in the policy process.

POLITICS AND THE COURTS

Despite the image of being "nonpolitical" and outside the political arena, the justices serving on the courts and other courtroom personnel are political actors who are involved in the political system in many ways. They have developed relationships with other political actors that may affect how cases and ultimately public policy is decided.

Relationships with Other Political Actors

The courts check on the behavior of other branches of government, including the executive, legislative, and even the administrative agencies that are responsible for creating policies. The courts are responsible for overseeing the behavior of the other branches to ensure that they are acting in accordance with the U.S. Constitution, state constitutions, and even local laws. They are also influenced by interest groups and the opinions of voters. Over the years, the courts have created long-lasting relationships with these other groups of political actors.

 Over time, courts have developed a relationship with legislatures, whether it be the U.S. Congress or a state legislature, depending on the type of court involved. For example, state courts must sometimes interpret legislation that is passed by their state legislature to decide if a law is in agreement with both the state constitution and the federal Constitution. These same state courts have also developed a relationship in the same way with Congress. Sometimes, state supreme court justices must determine if the laws made by Congress are constitutional. Often state courts are forced to determine what is meant by vague terms in new legislation that were not defined fully in the legislation or to determine specifically how the new law should be applied in each case. Federal appellate courts, including the U.S. Supreme Court, have the same responsibilities and must review the acts of both Congress and state legislatures to determine if they are constitutional.

Courts must also learn to cooperate with other courts. For example, over time, state courts have developed a relationship with the Supreme Court, which must sometimes review the actions of state appellate courts to determine if the most appropriate action was taken. Since the Supreme Court is the supreme power of the land, state judges must follow the decisions of the Court. However, the individual state courts have some discretion as to how closely or to what extent they will follow the decisions.

The courts have also developed relationships with executives, meaning the president or the state governors. The courts on the state and federal levels can invalidate executive actions if they are not constitutional or are inappropriate. In some cases, the courts' decisions can initiate action by the legislature, especially if the decision is controversial.

Interest groups have also developed a relationship with the courts. Interest groups get involved with the courts through litigation. They also can choose to file amicus curiae ("friend of the court") briefs with the courts. These allow the interest group to support a litigant or present another point of view from that which might be argued. Interest groups use the briefs as a way to lobby the courts so that the decisions reflect the general concerns of the group.

The courts have developed a relationship with voters, who in some cases are responsible for electing the judges who serve on the courts. Unfortunately, most people do not know much about the courts. The media usually cover only the most sensational court cases or proceedings, and they are more likely to cover criminal than civil cases. This means that many people's perceptions are shaped by television shows or other media outlets and run a high risk of being faulty. This is only made worse during a judicial campaign, when judicial canons and laws in many states prohibit judicial candidates from discussing ongoing or hypothetical cases.

The courtroom personnel, including prosecution, defense, and others, also impact the policy decisions of the courts. No single actor in the courthouse work group can perform his or her tasks independently—they must work as a team to process cases. Because of this, the members of the group must consider the reactions of others in the work group when carrying out their task. Decision making becomes a shared process, and the work group can significantly affect what decisions are made and how they are made. As the work group becomes more established, there is greater certainty concerning how the individual actors will respond to certain cases. This means that there will be a high degree of stability in the courtroom, and the court will require less time and resources on each case. If this happens, the business of the court will proceed in a regularized manner. In short, if the relationships among the work groups are good, then things go well. If the relationships have not yet been established or if the work group has not established similar goals and individual tasks, then the flow of a case can be hindered.[1]

Influences on Judicial Decision Making

When justices are making their decisions, it is commonly assumed that they are making neutral decisions based only on the law and the Constitution. We like to think that when judges make a decision, they are no longer a Republican or a Democrat and that party affiliations are put aside. However, that is not always the case. Judges are not merely neutral arbiters of the law but also active political actors who come to the court with ideological baggage.[2] The majority of judges have been active in the political system for years and are associated with one political party. They were either appointed to serve as a justice through a political nomination and approval process or elected to serve as a justice through a typical political campaign. Political parties, interest groups (such as bar associations), political elites, and insiders each participate and influence the processes of judicial recruitment and selection at the state and national levels.[3]

Once on the bench, the justices' actions and decisions will reflect the philosophical and political preferences of the political party to which they belong.[4] Every judge does not think and act like every other judge. Instead, every judge is a product of his or her background, prior experience, party identification (ideology), religion, ethnicity, age, and sex. All these personal characteristics partly influence his or her decisions and predispose a judge to decide cases in certain ways. Since every legal decision made by the courts promotes one interest or value over another, it is important to understand these forces.

One of the political forces that impacts the courts' behavior is the political ideology of the justices. Evidence shows that a judge's political identification does indeed affect his or her behavior on the bench.[5] Judges can be labeled as either conservative or liberal. Generally, liberal justices, most often affiliated with the Democratic Party, support the rehabilitation and treatment of offenders rather than harsh punishment. They agree that societal factors are the basis of many criminal behaviors and that crime is often caused by disorganization in society. In accordance with this, liberal justices feel that efforts must be made to eliminate those social conditions that cause crime and that there must be policies that bring an end to social and racial injustice.[6] They tend to agree that law enforcement, courts, and corrections all lack the adequate resources to deal effectively with criminals.

Those justices supporting a conservative ideology tend to believe that government programs alone cannot create the conditions within society to solve crime. Instead, the federal government should provide states with the financial assistance needed to help them build more prisons. Conservative justices believe that state criminal justice officials should be allowed to legally hold dangerous or repeat offenders without bail. Additionally, they believe that the exclusionary rule should be changed so that evidence of a crime would be allowed in court proceedings if it were obtained by an officer acting in "good faith." Conservative justices also support mandatory sentences, increased use of capital punishment, and restrictions on the insanity defense.[7]

In addition to these ideas, it has been found that judges who affiliate themselves with the Democratic Party are more sympathetic than Republican judges to the consumer, the working person, and the defendant in criminal cases but less sympathetic to businesses such as utilities seeking to avoid regulation.[8]

Public opinion can also affect the decisions that come from the courts. Although most justices would deny being directly influenced by public opinion,[9] the decisions they make are in part affected by society and its culture. In fact, most scholars would agree that the Supreme Court's opinions generally track public preferences.[10] It is important to remember that the justices are social beings who are influenced by the actions and events around them and that they are not immune to shifts in public opinion.[11] Table 11.1 shows the public's thoughts regarding judicial sentencing of offenders based on demographics.

Public opinion may affect those judges who are elected more so than those who are appointed. Elected judges might be concerned with making decisions that reflect the wants and desires of the people. These justices may be more likely to be influenced by public opinion than those who are appointed. In this scenario, the justices are more apt to give the people what they want, within the confines of the law, so that their public approval ratings will increase.[12] In fact, Justice Felix Frankfurter supported this view when he wrote in *Baker v. Carr* (1962), "The Court's authority—possessed of neither the purse nor the sword—ultimately rests on sustained public confidence in its moral sanction."[13]

Of course, public opinion can also act as a check on the behavior of the courts. For example, if the Supreme Court has gone too far or too fast in its rulings, public opinion will curb the Court.[14] Especially for those justices who are elected, if their decisions do not match society's ideas about crime and justice, they face losing a reelection bid.

TABLE 11.1 Attitudes Toward Severity of Courts in Own Area, 2002

Question: In general, do you think the courts in this area deal too harshly or not harshly enough with criminals?

Demographics	Too Harshly (%)	Not Harshly Enough (%)	About Right (%)
National	9	67	18
Sex			
Male	12	64	19
Female	7	70	16
Race			
White	8	69	18
Black/other	16	60	16
Age			
18 to 20	14	48	34
21 to 29	12	68	15
30 to 49	9	70	16
50+	8	66	19
Education			
College	9	65	20
High school graduate	8	72	16
Less than high school	12	67	15
Income			
$50,000+	9	70	17
$30,000 to 49,999	8	70	18
$20,000 to 29,999	8	63	20
<$20,000	13	66	16
Politics			
Republican	2	77	18
Democrat	11	65	18
Independent	11	64	17

Source: Adapted from Kathleen Maguire and Ann Pastore, eds., *Sourcebook of Criminal Justice Statistics 2002* (Washington, D.C.: U.S. Government Printing Office, 2003), available online at www.albany.edu/sourcebook/.

Beyond political ideology and public opinion, other factors influence judicial behavior.[15] Research shows that judges who are elected versus those who are appointed have a different approach to policy. The research shows that judges who are elected are more liberal in cases that deal with consumers but less liberal in cases that revolve around the constitutional rights of criminal suspects.[16] Studies show that Democratic, non-Protestant, younger judges with little previous government or judicial experience take the liberal position more often than other judges.[17]

Whether a judge is a male or a female may also be an important factor in how cases are decided. Female judges, for example, appear to be stricter with female defendants than are male judges.[18] The race of the judge may also be an important factor in understanding judicial decisions.[19] Other research shows that black trial court judges are more equitable in their treatment of black and white defendants than are white judges concerning the decision to incarcerate. Additionally, white judges are more likely to be lenient to white defendants than they are to black defendants.[20] Finally, other characteristics that can affect a judge's decisions include his or her prejudicial career and the level of prestige of his or her law school education.

ROLE IN POLICY PROCESS

The courts' role in the policy process is a significant one, although at first glance it may not be as obvious as other actors, such as the state or federal legislatures. The role the courts play in the policy process is determined in part by the type of court they are.

Agenda Setting

The courts play a somewhat minor role in setting the agenda when compared to the legislatures, but it is significant nonetheless. The primary difference between the legislature and the courts in setting an agenda is that the courts are limited as to what problems they can address. One reason for this is that courts must wait for cases to come to them. Courts cannot actively seek out issues to address. Instead, they must wait for a case to come to them either through original or appellate jurisdiction or through litigation. Issues of public policy come to the courts in the form of legal disputes or disagreements that must be interpreted or resolved by the courts.[21] In addition, a court is able to hear only certain cases, depending on the jurisdiction of that court.

Trial courts respond largely to cases brought to them by the police, so they are limited in their ability to set their own agendas. However, the prosecutors can decide to accept or decline cases, giving them some discretion over their agenda. Appellate courts have a greater potential for determining their caseloads. They can choose what cases will appear in front of the court, thus setting their own agenda in that way. Of course, certain cases must be heard by the court (original jurisdiction). But often, courts decide what cases are significant enough to warrant their attention.

When they are deciding what cases to hear, the courts can assign some cases a higher priority than others. They can choose cases to reflect their perspective or their political ideology.[22] Even a refusal to hear a case and to become involved in the issue affects some of the interested parties. There are thousands of cases appealed to the courts each year. The cases that make it to the court depend in large part on the justices themselves. Their decisions to hear a case depend on their own individual understanding or interpretation of their jurisdiction and any rules that might govern access to the court.[23] Thus, the ability or power to decide what cases to hear enables the court to set its own agenda.[24] Table 11.2 shows the number and percent of felony convictions in state courts, and Table 11.3 gives the results of felony case sentencing in state courts.

TABLE 11.2 Felony Convictions in State Courts (by Offense and Method of Conviction, United States, 2000

Total Trials		Jury Trials		Bench Trials		Guilty Pleas	
n	%	*n*	%	*n*	%	*n*	%
45,700	5	29,300	3	16,400	2	879,200	95

Source: Adapted from Kathleen Maguire and Ann Pastore, eds., *Sourcebook of Criminal Justice Statistics 2002* (Washington, D.C.: U.S. Government Printing Office, 2003), available online at www.albany.edu/sourcebook/.

TABLE 11.3 Felony Sentences Information by State Courts

	Prison	Jail	Probation
Percent of felons	40%	28%	32%
Mean sentence length	55 months	6 months	38 months
Median sentence length	36 months	5 months	36 months

Source: Adapted from Kathleen Maguire and Ann Pastore, eds., *Sourcebook of Criminal Justice Statistics 2002* (Washington, D.C.: U.S. Government Printing Office, 2003), available online at www.albany.edu/sourcebook/.

The courts' decisions sometimes cause other institutions to respond to the issues raised and thus set the agenda of other institutions, such as Congress. This happened in the late 1980s after the Supreme Court issued a series of rulings that narrowed the scope of Title VII of the Civil Rights Act of 1964, which made it more difficult for plaintiffs to obtain relief from alleged racial or sexual discrimination in the workplace. Civil rights organizations and their supporters in Congress were angry at these decisions but did not have the support in Congress to pass legislation that would, in effect, overturn the rulings. Their opportunity came after the 1988 elections, when a majority of Democrats were elected to Congress. The newly elected Democratic majority realized that this was its chance to pass new legislation on civil rights and at the same time strengthen its support from minorities.[25] In the long run, the Supreme Court's decision eventually put the civil rights issue on the agenda of Congress.

State court judges may also become involved in setting the agenda by meeting formally or informally with legislators, governors, and other public officials about policy issues or proposals. They may also be involved in making formal advisory reports to state officials that may result in agenda setting. Additionally, court personnel may become involved in the policy process by appearing at legislative hearings to give information or expert advice. In fact, judges are often sought out by state officials on policy matters that may involve the organization and functioning of the courts or criminal law. Judges may also be asked to serve on various task forces that investigate a particular issue. Sometimes the recommendations made by the judicial personnel are supported by the bar association, which may be looked on favorably in the legislature.

Policy Formulation

Although courts don't have an obvious role in making policy like Congress or the state legislatures, it can be argued that courts are still intimately involved in making policy. With their power to interpret the law, courts can make policy. In criminal justice, the decisions of the Supreme Court have affected the rights of both criminal and juvenile defendants and set expectations for law enforcement and corrections.[26] Their decisions have long-term impacts on how the criminal justice system operates and how offenders are treated within the system.[27]

The courts' role in policymaking has been debated for many years, but their essential role in making rules and policy is now accepted by most scholars and nonscholars alike.[28] When the justices decide cases or make rulings clarifying a law (especially controversial ones), the courts are determining how things should be done in the future or what certain standards should be. The new procedures must be carried out or enforced by bureaucrats or others having responsibilities in that field, or risk legal penalties. In a very real sense, new law is being created.[29] In this manner, the courts are helping to set many public policies. A good example of this is when the courts make a decision concerning the procedures by which a person is arrested or homes are searched or even concerning the trial or sentencing proceedings. It is making a policy that must be followed by criminal justice personnel. Thus, the role of the courts is no longer reserved to reviewing acts of the legislature and ensuring the constitutionality of the laws. Instead, the court has been labeled a "superlegislature" that makes laws without the involvement of other political groups and with little oversight.[30]

When judges make policy decisions, it is sometimes referred to as "judge-made law" because it is made by judges rather than Congress. If their decisions seem to overturn the policies made by legislatures or governors, the judges are sometimes said to be practicing judicial activism. Conversely, when they do not challenge legislative or gubernatorial decisions and limit themselves to narrow interpretations of the law, they are said to be exercising judicial restraint.[31]

Both trial level courts and appellate courts are involved in making policy. Both are responsible for clarifying legislation and defining terms. Usually, if a trial judge makes a decision, the policy is not implemented until the issue has been examined by higher courts on appeal.[32] The Supreme Court and the state appellate courts have an especially important role in making policy. By using their powers of judicial review and statutory interpretation, their decisions affect the nature and content of public policy.[33] Over the years, the appellate courts have made some far-reaching policy pronouncements[34] that have directly affected people's lives in many ways.[35] For example, the Supreme Court has undertaken the lead in eliminating racial segregation and providing for civil rights, defining the limits of affirmative action, ensuring separation of church and state, deciding about prayer in schools, deciding about abortion, defining obscenity and pornography, ensuring equality of representation, defining the rights of criminal defendants, and even deciding the legitimacy of capital punishment.[36]

Sometimes, the decisions made by the courts mandate state and local government actions.[37] The courts have declared that seriously overcrowded prisons constituted cruel and unusual punishment, violating the Eighth Amendment to the Constitution. Judges then decided that they would take over the prison systems and run them directly in order to correct the situation or would make very specific policies that state administrators were obliged to follow.[38] Similar state court takeovers of prisons also occurred in Texas under *Ruiz v. Estelle* (1980) and in West Virginia in *Crain v. Bordenkircher* (1988).[39]

Although the concept of judicial policymaking is accepted, it is still controversial. Supporters argue that the courts are appropriate and positive forums for making policy because judges are insulated from interest groups, political parties, public opinion, and other political influences. Many judges do not have to worry about reelection (those who are appointed), so they can make a decision or take a course of action they see as most beneficial to society without any significant political backlash. Since judges are fairly well insulated from the political system, they can make decisions that are fair, being based on the law or the facts rather than on political factors.

This means that courts can make policy in areas that are politically unfeasible for politicians. Since many judges, particularly those on the federal level, are appointed for life or good behavior, they need not worry about the public's reaction to a particular decision or opinion and if that might affect a future reelection bid. A good example of this is the civil rights legislation in the 1950s and 1960s, which was extremely controversial at the time. Many politicians were hesitant to show support for either side of the legislation that would give minorities equal rights, particularly those representing southern states, because of a feared political backlash from angered constituents at home. However, the courts did not have to concern themselves with the public's opinions of their actions and were free to step in and make social policy that helped provide equal rights to minorities. This set of circumstances resulted in the *Brown v. Board of Education* (1954) decision, which mandated that public schools be desegregated. Over the years, hundreds of other decisions concerning controversial topics, including race, abortion, women's rights, voting rights, campaign finance, and even the 2000 presidential election, have been fought in the courts.[40]

Another argument in favor of judicial policymaking is that in a courtroom setting, both sides of an issue are represented by legal advisers, whereas in a legislature, you may have only one side represented by an interest group.[41]

On the other hand, those opposed to judicial policymaking argue that public policies or laws should be created or developed only by elected officials and that the courts are not effective arenas for policymaking. They argue that if a bad policy is made by elected officials, voters are able to hold those officials accountable and not reelect them. This cannot be done if a bad or an unpopular decision is made by the courts. Many judges are in office for good behavior and can be removed only for criminal offenses. Thus, they argue that judicial policymaking is undemocratic.

Another argument against judicial policymaking is that since judges must deal with many different cases and subject areas, they cannot become knowledgeable about any one specific area. They do not have the expertise required to make sound, effective policy and cannot give continued support to any one policy area. Additionally, because most judges attempt to stay out of politics, they do not meet regularly with people who could inform them about current problems and issues and even the effects of the proposed policies on client groups. Thus, when judges make a decision, it may be uninformed and incomplete and possibly even biased.[42]

Recently, the courts have become more involved in policy formation; they are also playing a more positive role, specifying not only what government cannot do but also what it must do to meet legal or constitutional requirements.[43]

Policy Implementation

Although the courts make policy, they have no way to implement that policy. By itself, the Supreme Court is almost powerless to influence the course of national policy.[44] Instead, it must rely on others (the relevant agencies) to implement and enforce its decisions.[45] It must persuade the agencies, as well as the American public, that its ruling and mandated change are needed and important.[46] To do this, the Court relies on its prestige and legitimacy to make people agree with and comply with its decisions.[47] To some extent, how effective the Court will be depends on how it is viewed by agencies and the public as a whole. Its power lies in the persuasiveness of its rulings and rests with other political institutions and public opinion.[48] If the Court's institutional prestige and positive public opinion are lacking, law enforcement may be called on to help implement its decision.[49]

The courts can maintain their prestige with other agencies by effectively communicating their rulings to the appropriate officials. One problem is that the decision may be so unclear that no meaning can be derived from the ruling.[50] Rulings that are not clear or that do not reach the most appropriate audience are not likely to be effective. Some rulings may be interpreted differently by different constituents.[51] If the decision is clear, there is little room for discretion.

How a decision is implemented by the agencies is continually reviewed by the courts, and if they see that a decision is not being implemented in a manner that remedies constitutional violations, then the court can step in and force further change. In *Brown v. Board of Education of Topeka, Kansas* (1954), the Supreme Court declared that schools must be desegregated. However, many states, particularly in the South, were opposed to the integration of schools and were hostile to the Court's decision. They refused to carry out the decision, so the Court members returned to the case in *Brown v. Board of Education of Topeka II* (1955), which forced the desegregation of the schools "with all deliberate speed." This is called the implementing decision of the *Brown* case. It is rare for the Court to decide cases twice, but in this situation Court members realized that the additional mandate was needed to force change.

Policy Evaluation

The courts play a significant role in the review of federal, state, and local policies through their power of judicial review. This is the power of the courts to determine the constitutionality of actions by the legislative and executive branches and to declare them null and void if they are found to be in conflict with the Constitution. The courts often review the constitutionality of legislative actions. "Judicial review motivates disgruntled litigants and frustrated interest groups to turn to the appellate courts for relief, and almost any political issue may reach the courts."[52] A good example of this occurred in 1989, when the Supreme Court declared the Flag Protection Act unconstitutional.

The courts also review the acts of presidents and governors, who are constantly attempting to influence public opinion by endorsing or opposing court rulings that deal with sensitive policies. They publicly express their own opinions and sometimes encourage others to either support or ignore the courts' decisions. Executives can decide whether to use their powers of the federal or state government to help implement the new judicial policy. In addition, executives and their appointees are occasionally involved in cases. They must respond to direct orders from the court to take a particular action.[53]

COURTS IN THE POLICY PROCESS: EXAMPLES

Most people now recognize that the decisions made by the courts, especially those by the Supreme Court, are in essence a way that public policy is created. Through this power, the courts can have a dramatic impact on the procedures that must be followed in the criminal justice system on the federal, state, and local levels. This pertains to police, courts, and corrections. Each of these parts of the criminal justice system must abide by the court's decisions if they are to remain relevant.

Incorporation

As written, the Bill of Rights (the first ten amendments to the Constitution) protects citizens only against action by the federal government. Early in the nation's history, the Supreme Court refused to extend the protections guaranteed in the Bill of Rights to state actions. But in the mid-1920s, the Court began using the Fourteenth Amendment's guarantee of due process to protect certain individual rights against infringement by the state.[54] The movement began when Associate Justice Hugo Black, in his dissenting opinion in *Adamson v. California* (322 U.S. 46, decided in 1947), argued that the Fourteenth Amendment made the entire Bill of Rights binding on the states.[55] The process by which the courts use the Fourteenth Amendment to apply the Bill of Rights to the states is called "incorporation."

Originally, the Supreme Court denied applying the Bill of Rights to the states, arguing that it applied only to federal agencies. The Court made this point clear in 1925 in the case of *Gitlow v. New York* (268 U.S. 652, decided in 1925). Gitlow had been indicted for publishing and distributing subversive documents that supported overthrowing the government. These publications had been outlawed in New York's criminal anarchy law. Gitlow argued that he should be able to publish such documents because of rights guaranteed under the First Amendment (specifically, freedom of expression) and his right to due process of law. He further argued that New York's anarchy laws violated these rights. The Supreme Court eventually upheld Gitlow's prosecution, deciding that New York's law did not conflict with constitutional guarantees. In other words, the Court held that the Bill of Rights did not apply to the states and that the New York law did not violate the Bill of Rights.[56]

Over the next few years, the Supreme Court slowly and selectively incorporated substantial portions of the federal Bill of Rights to the states.[57] In 1932, the Court extended the right to counsel, guaranteed in federal cases by the Sixth Amendment, to the states in the case of *Powell v. Alabama* (287 U.S. 45, decided in 1932). In this case, some young boys, known as the "Scottsboro boys," were charged with the rape of two white females on a freight train that was passing through Alabama. The accused were never asked if they wanted the aid of lawyers, and the first case came to trial without a defense attorney. Some lawyers eventually did act as defense counsel, but the defendants were convicted. The Supreme Court eventually reversed their convictions, stating that they were denied their right to counsel, which was a denial of due process under the Fourteenth Amendment.[58] The Court held that people accused of capital crimes were entitled to the assistance of legal counsel in their defense. In later years, the Court denied this right to defendants in noncapital cases (*Betts v. Brady*, 316 U.S. 455, decided in 1942).

The Supreme Court again used the Fourteenth Amendment to apply the Bill of Rights to the states in 1968. This time, the right to a jury trial was extended to state criminal defendants in *Escobedo v. Illinois* (378 U.S. 478, decided in 1964). In this case, Danny Escobedo was questioned at the police station about a murder for 14 hours without counsel even though he asked to see his attorney. Eventually, he made incriminating statements that the police claimed were a confession to the murder. The Court decided that the confession could not be used against the defendant because it was obtained after intensive police interrogation in which the accused asked for an attorney but was denied one. The justices claimed the confession was obtained in violation of his constitutional right to counsel and could not be used against him. Thus, his confession was rendered invalid because the accused was refused permission to see his lawyer prior to its execution.

Throughout the next few years, the Supreme Court continued to apply the Bill of Rights to the states in other decisions. The justices provided for legal counsel in all felony cases in *Gideon v. Wainwright* (372 U.S. 335, decided in 1963). In this case, they declared that indigent defendants are entitled to counsel in felony prosecutions.

Since then, the courts have continued to define how and when the rights protected in the first ten amendments to the Constitution should apply to the states. Early Supreme Courts interpreted the Constitution as limiting only federal behaviors but eventually changed that perspective. Thus, during the last half of the nineteenth century, the rights guaranteed to citizens in the federal Bill of Rights had applied only to federal prosecutions or other federal government actions. But because of incorporation, using the Fourteenth Amendment, the Court began to apply all the restrictions found in the Bill of Rights to states.

Miranda Rights

A second example of how Supreme Court decisions make policy and impact the criminal justice system surrounds the rights given to someone accused of a crime. The case of *Miranda v. Arizona* (377 U.S. 201, 1966) was decided under Chief Justice Earl Warren. This decision expanded the rights of those accused of committing a criminal offense. It required that police officers inform criminal suspects of their right to remain silent, that anything said can and will be used against them in a court of law, and of the right to be represented by legal counsel. Additionally, any evidence obtained in the case, if the accused has not clearly indicated that he or she clearly understands their rights, is not legally admissible in a future court proceeding.

Before the *Miranda* decision, it was not uncommon for law enforcement to obtain confessions from suspects by using physical or psychological abuse or even by misrepresenting or lying to them about their rights or lack thereof. As a result of the *Miranda* decision, police must inform a suspect of his or her rights before entering any confession or damaging statement as evidence. Accused persons have a right to remain silent, that whatever statement they make may be used in evidence against them, that they have a right to be represented by counsel during the interrogation, and that, if they are unable to afford assistance of counsel, a lawyer will be provided for them. Additionally, the *Miranda* ruling requires that, after the accused is arraigned or charged, he or she cannot be interrogated in the absence of legal counsel. Overall, the *Miranda* case had a significant impact on precharge, or custodial, interrogations of criminal defendants.

Some say that the decision made it more difficult to convict criminals who sometimes make statements about their guilt that cannot be admitted into trial because of a "technicality." Many guilty individuals may go free because they were not given the Miranda warnings or were given the warnings at the wrong time.

More recent Supreme Court decisions made by the justices in the Burger court have narrowed the scope of the *Miranda*-type decisions. The Burger court made some decisions that had the effect of narrowing the impact of *Miranda* without actually overruling it. One of those was *Harris v. New York* (1971), in which the Court held that statements made by a defendant without Miranda warnings could be used to impeach his or her credibility. Another was *Oregon v. Haas* (1975), which extended the Harris principle to a defendant whose request for an attorney had been ignored. Finally, in *Brown v. Illinois* (1975), the Court held that a confession is inadmissible, even though voluntarily made, if the arrest that preceded the confession was invalid (i.e., made without warrant or probable cause). Additional limitations or restrictions came from the Rehnquist court, which also decided cases in such a way as to narrow the scope of *Miranda*.

Even today, the Supreme Court is still defining Miranda rights. In February of 2010 the Court again addressed the issues revolving around Miranda when it decided *Florida v. Powell* the justices answered the question, "must a suspect be expressly advised to his right to counsel during questioning and if so, does the failure to provide this advice violate *Miranda v. Arizona*?" The care revolved around a convicted felon, Kevin Dwayne Powell, who was convicted of illegally possessing a firearm. Before he was questioned he was given a different version of the traditional Miranda rights that did not expressly state that he had the right to an attorney during questioning. He was convicted and sentenced to 10 years in prison.[59]

Powell's lawyers appealed, saying police did not tell the defendant he had a right to have a lawyer during questioning. The Florida Supreme Court overturned his conviction on grounds that Tampa police did not adequately convey to Powell that he was allowed to have an attorney. The U.S. Supreme Court supported the police department's version of the Miranda warnings, arguing that police do not have to explicitly warn suspects that their lawyer can be present during questioning.

In another decision concerning Miranda rights, the Supreme Court reviewed the facts behind *Berghuis v. Thompkins* (2010). In the case, the Supreme Court justices will consider the question of whether police may interrogate a suspect in custody when the suspect, after receiving Miranda warnings, has neither explicitly waived, nor explicitly invoked, his right to remain silent. The police arrested Van Chester Thompkins in Ohio for murder. He was read his Miranda rights and gave a verbal confirmation that he understood them, but refused to sign a form stating that. During questioning, he was mostly silent but occasionally responded with short verbal and nonverbal answers. Towards the end of the questioning, the defendant was asked if he prayed to God for forgiveness for shooting the victim, and he responded "Yes." Thompkins was later convicted of murder, attempted murder and firearm offenses. His defense appealed the conviction, arguing that he did not waive his right to remain silent. The U.S. Court of Appeals decided that the statement should have been suppressed because he had not waived his Miranda rights. Upon hearing the facts of the case, the Supreme Court decided in a 5-4 decision to reverse and remand the case to the Sixth Circuit court. They decided that

Thompkins failed to invoke his Miranda rights to remain silent when he voluntarily made a statement to the police about the case.

Three Strikes

About half of the states and the federal government have passed what has been called "three-strikes-and-you're-out" legislation, also referred to as the "habitual offender law."[60] This law requires offenders who have been convicted of criminal offenses on three occasions to be sentenced to life in prison. There is a wide range of legislation aimed at dealing with habitual offenders, and many different versions of this policy exist in different states.[61] Some states have implemented a "two-strikes provision," while others have enhanced their sentencing provisions for those people who are convicted of two strikeable offenses. For example, the law in California mandates 25 years to life in prison for any offender convicted of any felony following two prior convictions for serious crimes. It also doubles sentences on the second "strike," requires consecutive sentences for multiple counts, and limits "good-time" credits.[62] Other states have passed provisions that seek a mandatory life term without parole for three offenses. Some of the three-strikes provisions have eliminated discretion of judges,[63] while other states provide for some judicial discretion in sentencing three-strikes offenders. Still others have added eligibility criteria to existing habitual offender laws.[64] A few states have a "four strikes" law. In addition to all these variations in the law itself, there are also differences as to what is considered a strikeable offense. It could be the sale of drugs, escape from a correctional facility, treason, embezzlement, murder, a terrorist act, aggravated child abuse, carjacking, or any felony offense.

The three-strikes provisions are the result of many factors. First is the public's concern with the increase in the number and severity of violent crime. Many point to the inability of the criminal justice system to curb such violence as well as the widespread leniency toward repeat criminals. Politicians in many states have seized the issue and use it as a way to reach out to voters and further their campaigns.[65]

There has been concern that the three-strikes legislation will have profound effects on prison populations and overcrowding—that prison populations will increase.[66] One study done found that there indeed was a dramatic increase in prison populations in the first twelve months that the law was in effect, but the number of admissions has leveled off and even declined slightly.[67] In some states, there was a massive influx of new convicts, so thousands of nonfelons had to be released instead.

Many other effects of the legislation have been described, both short and long term. Some have been identified as follows:[68]

1. Thousand of cases will be prosecuted.
2. Many more trials will be required.
3. Many more jurors will be needed.
4. Many more hearings will be required to dispose of cases in municipal and superior court.
5. The arrest-to-sentencing case processing time will increase.
6. The number of preliminary hearings will increase.
7. The amount of time spent on preliminary hearings will increase.
8. The preliminary hearings will be longer.
9. Fewer felony cases are settling in municipal court.
10. Costs associated with defense representation by private attorneys on the conflicts panel will increase.
11. Other backlogs will develop.
12. System breakdowns will create delays in processing time.

13. Legal ambiguity will produce delays.
14. The pretrial jail population will increase.
15. The proportion of the jail population that is unsentenced will increase.
16. More high-security inmates will be held in jail.
17. Increased court security will be needed.
18. There will be sentenced-prisoner jail day savings (because they will be going to prison).
19. There will be county probation supervision day savings.
20. Civil matters may be forced out by the criminal court workload.
21. Developing backlogs are pushing less serious cases out.
22. Justice expenditures will increase substantially.

Some other unintended consequences of the three-strikes law have been suggested, showing that the law is not having the effect that was intended. Two studies show that the law is actually having the reverse effect: homicide rates are increasing. The first, by Marvell and Moody, presents the argument that criminals who face life in prison (from a third strike) are not deterred from committing a third offense. Rather, they may take steps to reduce their chances of being caught, prosecuted, and convicted but are not dissuaded from committing a homicide as part of their criminal offense.[69] Kovandzic, Sloan, and Vieraitis examined homicide rates of 188 cities across the United States from 1980 to 1999 and also discovered that homicide rates increased after passage of the three-strikes legislation. They point out that since these new laws may actually exacerbate homicides, policymakers should seriously consider repealing them.[70]

Studies show that the three-strikes legislation does not seem to be effective in deterring or reducing crime.[71] If anything, there is only a minimal impact on crime reduction.[72] It was even argued that the legislation might increase crime. If a third offense (or strike) will put offenders in prison for life, they have nothing to lose by killing police officers to evade arrest. Instead of decreasing violent crime, the law may even escalate it.[73]

Other research shows that three-strikes laws produce a 10–12 percent short-term increase in homicides, and that about .06 percent of violent crimes result in homicides that would not have occurred without the laws. The long-term impact, however, shows that there is a 23–29 percent increase in homicides. In other words, if there were no three-strikes law, the homicide rate would be 7 percent lower in the short term and 17 percent lower in the long term. These researchers also found no evidence that three-strikes laws have reduced crime, and that the laws resulted in little or no prison population growth.[74]

Those who support the legislation can cite many reasons to support it. The basic arguments advanced by proponents of the three-strikes concept are the following:

1. It will protect the public by incapacitating those chronic offenders who have demonstrated by their acts that they are both dangerous and willing to reform.
2. It will deter repeat offenders still on the street from committing further felonies.
3. It will save money by cutting down on the number of times that career criminals need to be processed by the system.
4. It is the "right thing to do." Aside from the savings and other effects, justice demands that those who repeatedly cause injury and loss to others have their freedom revoked.[75]
5. In most cases, the same offenders are the ones that offend over and over. Three strikes will put a repeat, serious offender in jail to save future victims and make the streets safer.

At the same time, there are many opponents of the legislation who would argue that the three-strikes policies are not a rational response to violent crime.[76] Some claim that it is cruel and unusual punishment since punishments under the legislation are not graduated and proportional to the offense that was committed. Critics of the legislation argue the following:

1. Substantial increases in the use of imprisonment over the past decade have had little if any effect on violent crime rates.
2. Life terms of three-time losers will require the allotment of expensive prison space to nonviolent offenders who are well past their peak ages of criminal activity.
3. The demand for jury trials, caused by the law's restrictions on plea bargaining, will actually raise the costs of the criminal justice system and cause further delays in resolving criminal cases.
4. The same amount of money applied to measures other than three strikes would reduce crime by a greater amount.
5. The third-strike penalty is an unduly harsh one for criminals convicted of certain felonies, such as drug possession.[77]
6. Since the third strike does not have to be violent, a petty offender, such as a person who steals something of little value, can be sent to prison for life.
7. The legislation is unfair because some jurisdictions have not passed it and in those that have, it is used more by some judges than others. Others argue that Three Strikes will be applied to minorities more often than the population as a whole. This means that people who commit similar offenses may be sentenced to widely varying sentences.

Greenwood and colleagues completed a cost-benefit analysis of habitual offender laws in California and found that these laws prevent 340,000 serious crimes per year but cost roughly $5.5 billion annually, or about $16,000 per serious crime prevented.[78] They went on to say that citizens will have to give up other things to pay for those costs. In other words, the money spent on the habitual offender laws could be spent elsewhere, either to increase police protection or attack the causes of crime or to help fund higher education.[79]

Other researchers have come to similar conclusions. A similar study that examined the costs of three-strikes policies in California found that the costs of the program are estimated to be approximately $5.7 billion a year. Additionally, the laws are estimated to add 276,000 inmates to the prison system in the state over the next three decades.[80] They go on to say that for what California will spend to incarcerate one third-strike burglar for forty years, it could provide two-year community college educations to 200 students.[81]

It has become apparent that the three-strikes provisions are being resisted.[82] Many three-strike cases are being downgraded,[83] and the law is not being applied uniformly.[84] Across California, for example, offenders in particular parts of the state are treated differently from offenders in other parts of the state. "In the more conservative southern part of the state (and in particular, Los Angeles and San Diego Counties), prosecutors continue to press for something close to full enforcement of the law. In the urban northern areas (San Francisco and Alameda County, Oakland), however, the courts have found ways to adapt."[85]

The Supreme Court has given split decisions on whether three strikes is cruel and unusual.[86] In *Ewing v. California* and *Lockyer v. Andrade*, the Court reviewed California's three-strikes law. The Court ruled that repeat offenders may be locked up for long periods of time and that a sentence of up to 50 years to life is not too extensive. However, in a dissenting opinion in the *Ewing* case written by Justice Breyer and supported by Justices Stevens, Souter, and Bader Ginsburg, the justices said that the sentence was out of proportion to the crime and thus unconstitutional.[87]

It seems to be that the three-strikes legislation was merely symbolic in that it has had little if any effect on either the public's safety or the criminal justice system.[88] The three-strikes law is only another legislative trick that attempts to make people feel safe by promising to take criminals off the street and putting repeat offenders in prison for life without regard for the seriousness of the offense committed. However, this law clogs state court systems with petty cases and condemns more nonviolent offenders to life sentences.[89]

The legislation is an example of how public opinion can have a profound effect on legislation and on the treatment of offenders.[90] These authors argue that there are dangers to allowing citizens to vote on major policy initiatives since it puts criminal justice policy too directly under popular control. The public voted for the law without a clear understanding of its effects and without considering the side effects. Sentencing decisions should be insulated from popular will. However, once these laws are passed, they are difficult to get rid of. In most states, once a law is passed, it can be changed only by a supermajority in both legislative houses.

Many years after the three strikes legislation was originally passed in California, it is still being debated. Supporters such as the interest group, Threestrikes.org, claims that there has not only been a significant decrease in crime, but the law has been responsible for a $54 billion in savings as a result of that reduced crime, three million fewer victims of crime, reduced growth in prison construction, and nearly 10,000 fewer murders (threestrikes.org). The group claims that there is a significant deterrence to the three strikes law. In 2004, the state of California put a proposition on the ballot (proposition 66) that would allow the citizens decide if the "Three Strikes" law should be amended. The proposition, if passed, would amend the law to require increased sentences only when the current conviction was for specified violent and/or serious felony. Additionally, a "violent" or "serious" felony was redefined so that only prior convictions for specified violent and/or serious felonies, brought and tried separately, would qualify as a second or third "strike" for a sentence increase. The proposition would allow for re-sentencing of offenders if the original sentencing offenses would no longer qualify as a violent or serious felony. Finally, the proposition would increase the punishment for specified sex crimes against children.[91] In the end, the proposal did not pass.

Exclusionary Rule

The Fourth Amendment to the Constitution provides for limits on police behavior, including the legality of searches and seizures and the collection of evidence against a person accused of a criminal offense. The police cannot stop, question, or search an individual without legal cause. Further, any evidence the police obtain illegally cannot be used in a court proceeding against a criminal defendant. This is called the exclusionary rule.

One of the first cases to go to the Supreme Court and define the Fourth Amendment's protections against illegal searches and seizures was *Weeks v. United States* (1914). Freemont Weeks was accused by federal law enforcement personnel of using the mail for illegal purposes. The agents searched his home without a valid search warrant and found letters and other materials that were subsequently admitted at trial, where Weeks was convicted. The Court held that the evidence was obtained by the agents through an unreasonable search and seizure and therefore should have been excluded from the trial. The Court held that the Fourth Amendment barred the use of evidence obtained through illegal search and seizure in a federal prosecution. However, the Court declined to apply the exclusionary rule to the states because it believed that states could develop their own remedies to handle improper searches by police.

In later years, the Warren court expanded the exclusionary rule, placing limits on the behavior of the police in collecting evidence and defining legal searches. In 1949, the Supreme Court gave initial forewarning to the states that it was considering making the *Weeks* doctrine binding on the states. The case was *Wolf v. Colorado* (1949). Here, Wolf was charged in a state court (Colorado) with conspiring to perform abortions. Evidence and patients' names were retrieved from his office without a valid search warrant. The patients were questioned, and the evidence was used at his trial. The Court decided that the evidence was admissible. In a broad sense, the Court did not impose federal standards of criminal procedure on the states but made statements about the behavior of state law enforcement in collecting evidence.

The Supreme Court first applied the Fourth Amendment to the states in the case of *Mapp v. Ohio* (367 U.S. 643, decided in 1961), specifically writing that any evidence seized illegally could not be presented as evidence in court. This case had to do with police officers who searched the house of Dolree Mapp looking for a suspect in a bombing case. Mapp refused to allow the officers into her home and demanded to see a search warrant. They waved a paper in front of her face, which she grabbed and put down her shirt. The officers retrieved the paper but later could not produce it. The officers proceeded to search through the house and find a trunk full of books and drawings the officers deemed as obscene material. Mapp was convicted and appealed the decision. Eventually, the case made its way to the Supreme Court, which decided that the due process clause of the Fourth Amendment requires the exclusion of illegally obtained evidence in state court proceedings. For the first time, the Supreme Court applied the federal standards to the behavior of the states.

States varied as to how strict they applied the *Mapp* decision and what evidence would be allowed into trial. Some people argued that the exclusionary rule served only to "handcuff" the police, giving criminal suspects too many rights and allowing the guilty to continue to commit crime. The Burger and Rehnquist courts have attacked the exclusionary rule and narrowed it. Their decisions have not eliminated the exclusionary rule but rather limited its applicability, giving police greater flexibility to conduct warrants without obtaining a search warrant.[92]

There are many examples of decisions where the Supreme Court has opened up the exclusionary rule to allow the police greater flexibility in gathering evidence. One of those cases was *Illinois v. Gates* (1983), in which the Court used an anonymous letter as evidence in support of a warrant. Here, the Court made it easier for police to search a suspect's home.

The Supreme Court has created two policies that have helped define when questionably obtained evidence can be admitted to trial. The first of those is "good faith." In the case of *U.S. v. Leon* (1984), the Court decided that when police rely on good faith in a warrant, the evidence seized is admissible even if the warrant is subsequently deemed defective. If police obtain evidence with a "less-than-adequate" search warrant, the evidence may nonetheless be admissible in court if the police in good faith obtained court approval for their search. The Court did add a caveat that if the police deliberately mislead a judge or use a warrant that they know is unreasonably deficient, it would be grounds to invoke the exclusionary rule.

The Supreme Court expanded the good-faith exception in *Illinois v. Krull* (1987). Here, a police officer from Chicago carried out a warrantless search of a junkyard instead using a state statute that allowed such inspections. The statute was later found to be unconstitutional. The Court held that the evidence the officer found after the search was admissible into trial because the officer could not be responsible for an illegal search when the legislature had passed the law and the officer had relied in good faith on that law.

The Supreme Court continued to define the good-faith policy in later decisions. In *Arizona v. Evans* (1995), police officers from Phoenix stopped a male suspect for a traffic violation. They ran a computer check on him that revealed an outstanding arrest warrant for him. As he was being arrested, he dropped a marijuana cigarette, and more marijuana was found in his car. However, a court had quashed the search warrant seventeen days earlier. Eventually, the trial judge refused to admit the evidence gathered during the traffic stop on the grounds that the computer error was caused by negligence on the part of the law enforcement authorities. It was unknown why the arrest warrant had not been removed from the police computer. The Court ruled that the evidence does not have to be suppressed under the exclusionary rule since it was designed as a means of deterring police misconduct, not mistakes by employees. Further, it does not apply where the police acted in objectively reasonable reliance on an apparently valid warrant.

The second policy created by the Supreme Court to help to define when questionably obtained evidence can be admitted to trial is inevitable discovery. This policy means that any evidence that is seized by police that is in violation of the exclusionary rule can be used at trial if it would have been found within a short time by independent means. This policy was defined by the Court in *Nix v. Williams* (1984).

Even today, the Court continues to define the nature of the exclusionary rule. In 2009, the Supreme Court ruled in *Herring v. United States* that evidence from an illegal search can be used in court if a police officer made an innocent mistake. By a 5-4 vote, the justices decided that good evidence, even if obtained in a bad search, can be used against a suspect, unless it was taken deliberately or recklessly. In the case, a police officer, Mark Anderson, was told by a clerk that a defendant had failed to appear in court on a felony charge. But after Anderson found methamphetamine and a pistol in Herring's car, the clerk called back to say the arrest warrant had been withdrawn. Chief Justice Robers said the mistake was a bookkeeping error and did not reflect on the officer's decision to violate the rights of the defendant.[93]

Capital Punishment

Over the years, the Supreme Court has reviewed the death penalty in light of the Eighth Amendment, which is intended to protect citizens against cruel and unusual punishment. In *Furman v. Georgia* (480 U.S. 238, decided in 1972), the Court outlawed the use of capital punishment as it was then practiced because it was being applied in an arbitrary manner. The Court agreed that there were too many difficulties in resolving guilt and innocence while also deciding on a punishment of life imprisonment or death. However, the majority of justices rejected the idea that capital punishment is inherently cruel and unusual. Five justices agreed that it was cruel and unusual as it was then practiced. At the same time, the justices suggested that new statutes could be created to conform to the standard of not being arbitrary. For example, they approved statutes that listed specific mitigating and aggravating circumstances that could be used as guidelines that should be considered by courts when deciding whether to apply the death penalty in a particular case. Thus, in the *Furman* decision, the Court effectively struck down all the nation's death penalty laws on the basis of the arbitrary and discriminatory manner in which capital punishment was administered.

In *Gregg v. Georgia* (428 U.S. 153, 1976), the Supreme Court decided that capital punishment was inherently cruel and unusual, and it limited the death penalty to certain types of premeditated murder, such as multiple killings, homicide committed in the course of another felony, or killing a police officer in the line of duty. The justices devised a bifurcated (two-step) system of trying capital cases whereby the first stage determines guilt or innocence and the second stage is for determining for or against capital punishment. This new procedure was given formal approval in the *Gregg* decision. Here the Court justices held that the proper procedure should include a separate penalty trial, followed by appellate review. In this way, inequity and unfairness in imposing death sentences could be prevented.[94] They decided on three elements that were sufficient to safeguard against arbitrary sentencing: (1) guided discretion, that is, sentencing guidelines that detail specific elements of crimes that make state-imposed death an appropriate sentence; (2) special consideration of mitigating circumstances; and (3) the requirement of automatic review by state appeals courts.

After the *Gregg* decision, states began to use capital punishment more often. The first person executed after the *Gregg* decision was Gary Gilmore, who was executed by firing squad in Utah 190 days after the *Gregg* decision. The death sentence has continued to be used in many states across the country with more frequency despite continuing and sometimes vocal opposition.

For many years, the Supreme Court continued to review state death penalty statutes. For example, in *Maynard v. Cartwright* (1980), the Court struck down an Oklahoma death penalty statute on the grounds that the state's phrasing of aggravating circumstances as crimes that are "especially heinous, atrocious or cruel" was unconstitutionally vague. The issue was again addressed in 1987 in *Sumner v. Shuman.* In this case, the Court struck down a Nevada statute that made the death sentence mandatory for murder perpetrated by a prisoner who was serving a life sentence without the possibility of parole at the time of the crime.

The issue of racial disparities and the death penalty has also been a question addressed by the Supreme Court. In the case of *McClesky v. Kemp* (1987), the Court rejected the argument that the Georgia death penalty statute should be invalidated because it was more likely to be used when the victims of capital murder were white than when the victims were African-American. Additionally, the death penalty was used more often when the offenders were African-American than when they were white.

Across the nation, the inmates on death row are more likely to be disproportionately African-Americans relative to their fraction of the total population.[95] One study of 249 executions and forty-nine commutations in New York State from 1935 to 1963 found that offenders with certain characteristics that made them seem more dangerous (i.e., blacks, felony murderers, and nonyouthful offenders) had higher execution rates than other groups.[96]

The question of racial disparities surrounding the application of the death penalty resulted in the 1994 Death Penalty Act, part of the 1994 Omnibus Crime Bill, which expanded the range of federal crimes that were subject to the death penalty. Under the new Crime Bill, sixty new offenses are punishable by death, including terrorist homicides, murder of a federal law enforcement official, large-scale drug trafficking, drive-by shootings, and carjackings that result in death. The bill also calls for the death penalty for large-scale, continuous drug enterprise offenses even if no death resulted.[97]

Those who are opposed to the bill claim that it removes constitutional due process and places strict limitations on *habeas corpus* appeals in federal court. The law limits prisoners on death row to one federal appeal, which must be filed within six months after the state appellate process has expired. Furthermore, it prohibits federal judges from granting appeals unless they find that the state court acted "unreasonably."[98]

USE OF DEATH PENALTY   The death penalty has been in almost continual use in this country since early in the colonial era[99] even though people have debated its merits continually. The debate over capital punishment became visible after the Revolutionary War.[100] This was about the same time that Cesare Beccaria published his *Essay on Crime and Punishments*, in which he argued that capital punishment was less helpful in preventing murder than life imprisonment at hard labor. By the early 1830s, many called for a complete abolition of the death penalty.[101] During the mid 1960s, Americans as a whole did not support using the death penalty.[102] Public opinion polls in 1966 showed that only 47 percent of the American public supported the use of capital punishment.[103] However, Americans' support of the death penalty has increased since 1966.[104]

Public support for the death penalty is now at a near record high.[105] A *Newsweek* poll from June 2000 shows that Americans are divided on which crimes merit the death penalty. As Box 11.1 shows, 38 percent of the country feel that the death penalty is appropriate for mass murders or brutal murders, whereas 23 percent feel that it should be used for offenders who commit violent crimes or major drug offenses. This also shows that 19 percent are opposed to capital punishment in all cases.

BOX 11.1
Public Opinion Concerning Death Penalty: What Offenses Deserve Death?

Only the most brutal murders, mass murders and serial killings	38%
Other types of murder, violent crimes and major drug dealing	23%
Oppose in all cases	19%
Don't know	8%
Only murder	12%

Source: Bureau of Justice Statistics, *Capital Punishment, 2003* (Washington, D.C.: Bureau of Justice Statistics, 2004).

Since 1983, the Supreme Court has removed many procedural blocks to using the death penalty, and as a result, there have been more people executed.[106] The number of people executed is shown in Box 11.2. It can be seen that the number of executions has risen dramatically in recent years. Across the United States, there have been 1,136 people executed since 1977, mostly in the southern states.[107] The method of execution is shown in Table 11.4.

BOX 11.2
Number of People Executed in the United States, 1977–2009

1976	0	1993	38
1977	1	1994	31
1978	0	1995	56
1979	2	1996	45
1980	0	1997	74
1981	1	1998	68
1982	2	1999	98
1983	5	2000	85
1984	21	2001	66
1985	18	2002	71
1986	18	2003	65
1987	25	2004	59
1988	11	2005	60
1989	16	2006	53
1990	23	2007	42
1991	14	2008	37
1992	31	2009	52

Source: Bureau of Justice Statistics, *Capital Punishment, 2003* (Washington, D.C.: Bureau of Justice Statistics, 2004); *Sourcebook of Criminal Justice Statistics Online,* 2009; Key Facts at a Glance (Washington, D.C.: Bureau of Justice Statistics); http://bjs.ojp.usdoj.gov/conetnt/glance/tablels/exetab.cfm.

TABLE 11.4 Method of Execution by State, 2008

Method	State
Lethal Injection	Alabama, Arizona, Arkansas, California, Colorado, Connecticut, Delaware, Florida, Georgia, Idaho, Illinois, Indiana, Kansas, Kentucky, Louisiana, Maryland, Mississippi, Missouri, Montana, Nevada, New Hampshire, New Mexico, New York, North Carolina, Ohio, Oklahoma, Oregon, Pennsylvania, South Carolina, South Dakota, Tennessee, Texas, Utah, Virginia, Washington, Wyoming
Electrocution	Alabama, Arkansas, Florida, Illinois, Kentucky, Oklahoma, South Carolina, Tennessee, Virginia
Lethal Gas	Arizona, California, Missouri, Wyoming
Hanging	Delaware, New Hampshire, Washington
Firing Squad	Oklahoma, Utah

Source: Bureau of Justice Statistics, *Capital Punishment, 2008* (Washington, D.C.: Bureau of Justice Statistics, 2009).

In 2008, thirty-seven inmates were executed in the United States. This was five less than were executed in 2007 (see Box 11.2). Those executions took place across nine states, including Texas (eighteen executed); Virginia (four executed); Georgia and South Carolina (each executed three); Ohio, Florida, Mississippi, and Oklahoma (each executed two); and Kentucky (one executed). Of the people executed in 2008, twenty were white and seventeen were black; all inmates executed were men.[108]

It costs more to execute a person than to keep him or her in prison for life. This is because a death penalty trial usually takes longer than others, there are more appeals (some of which are automatic), and there are more costs associated with housing a death-row inmate.[109] In addition, there are more intensive pretrial and presentence investigations, more extradition proceedings, more pretrial motions filed and heard, longer hearings, a greater likelihood of requests for psychiatric and/or medical evaluations of defendants, more complex jury selection procedures, more frequent use of sequestered juries, more witnesses, longer sentencing proceedings, a higher proportion of appeals, longer appellate proceedings, more requests for clemency, and higher prosecution and defense attorney costs.[110]

Numerous studies have shown that the death penalty does not deter crime any more effectively than other punishments. One reason is that it is not carried out consistently and promptly.[111] "In fact, the evidence from nearly forty years of research runs overwhelmingly against the proposition that the death penalty deters any more effectively than other severe punishments."[112]

The Supreme Court continually makes decisions regarding the appropriateness and legality of the death penalty. In 2008, the Court decided the case of *Kennedy v. Louisiana* in which it struck down a Louisiana statute that allowed the death penalty for the rape, but not murder, of a child. The court held that since the law did not keep with the national consensus that the death penalty should be used only for the worst offenses, it was unconstitutional. They pointed out that there are no inmates on death row for any offense that did not involve murder. In other words, the decision prohibited states from executing those offenders who rape children but do not kill them because the "death penalty is not a proportional punishment for the crime."[113]

Another important decision was handed down by the Supreme Court in 2008 concerning the three-drugs that are commonly used to execute inmates by lethal injection. Two inmates,

Ralph Baze and Thomas Bowling, were sentenced to death in Kentucky. They argued that executing them by lethal injection would amount to cruel and unusual punishment because the drugs
used caused an unnecessary risk of inflicting pain. The Court rejected their argument by a vote of
7-3 and upheld Kentucky's method of execution.

A short time later, Ohio executions were postponed after the execution team attempting to
carry out the lethal injection of death row inmate Rommell Broom was unable, after two hours,
to find a suitable vein to insert an IV. State officials immediately granted stays of execution for
other inmates scheduled to be put to death, but then announced they would switch to another
protocol for lethal injection that involved only one drug instead of the typical three drug method.

The next inmate scheduled to be executed, Kenneth Biros, appealed his sentence to the
U.S. Court of Appeals for the Sixth Circuit. He argued that it would be unconstitutional to execute him with a one-drug injection, because it would amount to "human experimentation." The
court denied his appeal and he was executed on December 8, 2009. It took about ten minutes for
him to die.

There have been other cases in which the courts, both on the federal and state levels, have
continued to define issues surrounding the death penalty. The cases define with more clarity the
method of execution, timing, and type of inmate who can be sentenced to death and the situation
surrounding the execution. There is no doubt the courts will continue to hear similar cases in the
future as the country defines the issue more clearly.

Prison and Jail Conditions

In recent years, the federal courts have become one of the principal agents of change in the nation's prisons and jails. The courts have ordered new and different policies to be put into effect by
mandating improvements in institutional services, ordering the early release of thousands of inmates, and appointing special personnel to design and implement administrative plans to create
changes in correctional facilities to improve many aspects of institutional life.[114] These court orders have significant and far-reaching effects.

For many years, inmate rights were not recognized by the court system. Inmates had few
legal rights. At that time, prisoners were basically slaves of the state and could be worked merci-
lessly. They could be beaten for minor rule infractions, starved, and forced to live in filthy conditions. The courts rarely if ever stepped in to provide help.[115] Prisoner lawsuits were unheard of.
The courts took a "hands-off" policy toward inmates, preventing judges from becoming involved
and attempting to change conditions. Combined with the lack of concern by the public, little was
done to help inmates. Slowly, things began to change. Efforts to secure rights for prisoners began
in the middle of the twentieth century.[116] Because of the idea of incorporation and other events,
such as the 1971 riots in Attica prison in New York and the civil rights movement, people started
to change the way they viewed inmates' rights.

During the Warren court (1953–1969), inmates' access to the courts for rights violations
expanded. The Supreme Court formally incorporated the Eighth Amendment's ban on cruel and
unusual punishment to the states, guaranteed legal assistance for inmates, and generally weakened the hands-off policy. The Court did little to expand the substance of prisoners' rights in
areas such as religious freedom, medical care, prison overcrowding, and prison conditions. It was
not until the Burger court (1969–1986) that the courts began to intervene actively in the administration of prisons. During this time, district court judges ordered changes in the physical conditions of prison facilities, the treatment of inmates, staffing, food and medical care, and prison
overcrowding. The decisions of the Burger court supported the expansion of prisoners' rights.

Many jurisdictions had judicial orders to change and improve their systems for health care services, staff training practices, sanitation standards, food services, inmate grievance procedures, and the constitutionality of prison conditions "in their totality."[117] The decisions made by the justices protected the religious freedom of prisoners (*Cruz v. Beto*, 1972), mail privileges (*Procunier v. Martinez*, 1974), and due process guarantees in disciplinary actions (*Wolff v. McDonnell*, 1974) and held state death penalty statutes unconstitutional (*Furman v. Georgia*, 1972).

In 1972, the National Prison Project of the American Civil Liberties was formed. This group was a legal advocate for inmates that took the policies of capital punishment and other prison conditions to court.[118] The courts responded by declaring that prisoners did not forfeit all constitutional protections when they entered a prison, and they made decisions to help force changes within the prisons and improve the treatment of inmates. The federal judiciary played a major role in the reform of the nation's prisons and jails. Over time, they have expanded legal protections given to inmates. In many decisions, they have created changes in prison staffing and procedures and have been successful in reducing inmate populations.[119]

Despite the argument that prisoners should not be given many rights because they committed criminal acts and have harmed society, there is general agreement today that inmates should be provided basic human rights. It is sometimes pointed out that harsh conditions within prisons may actually cause more violence within the institution and will serve only to increase the inmates' anger and resentment, increasing the chances of reoffending when released from the institution.[120]

One legal option open to inmates is to file a writ of *habeas corpus*. This allows inmates to challenge the fact of their confinement in reference to decisions made during their trial and sentencing. If granted, a writ of *habeas corpus* orders the person responsible for the detention (prison warden or local jailer) to produce the petitioner in court so that a judge can determine the constitutionality of the detention. The Supreme Court used to be reluctant to review the actions of prison wardens and jailers unless there was clear evidence of constitutional violations. The *habeas corpus* law was originally passed by Congress in 1867. The law authorized federal courts and judges to grant writs when any person is restrained or deprived of liberty in violation of the Constitution or law.

Many *habeas corpus* petitions are typically filed by death-row inmates, allowing them to raise different constitutional claims in each one. They can use the petitions to overturn their convictions and sentences or simply to delay their sentence.

Now the most popular method of challenging prison conditions is to use civil rights cases based on post–Civil War litigation. In these cases, prisoners allege that state officials have violated their constitutional protections found in the First, Fourth, Fifth, Eighth, and Fourteenth Amendments to the Constitution and Bill of Rights. These suits are also called Section 1983 suits because they are filed under Section 1983 of the Civil Rights Act of 1871.

The third way inmates use to challenge conditions within prisons is to use the Eighth Amendment to the Constitution, which forbids cruel and unusual punishment. Although the amendment was originally intended to restrict forms of barbaric punishment and torture, this has been applied to both capital punishment and prison conditions.

The Supreme Court under William Rehnquist made decisions that were generally more conservative. It has redefined constitutional provisions concerning criminal procedure, cruel and unusual punishment, the death penalty, and *habeas corpus*,[121] making them stricter. The Rehnquist court has reversed some of the rights guaranteed to inmates and has made decisions that have, in effect, limited *habeas corpus* petitions. In *Teague v. Lane* (1989), the Court decided that *habeas corpus* petitions could not be available in the federal courts to state prisoners who are seeking to establish new constitutional rules announced since their conviction became final. In *McClesky v. Zant* (1991), the Court ruled that death-row prisoners, following exhaustion of state court appeals, should be allowed only one round of federal court review through petitions for *habeas corpus* unless there are extraordinary circumstances.

The majority of justices on the Supreme Court today support a more limited role for federal courts in judging inmate claims and defer to prison administrators in those cases. Chief Justice Rehnquist almost always votes for the government in cases involving the rights of criminal defendants and prisoners. In *Turner v. Safley* (1987), the Court significantly limited the religious and expressive freedoms for inmates by adopting a new standard for review of prisoners' constitutional rights cases. It held that the proper standard of review in determining the validity of prison regulations that restrict inmates' constitutional rights is whether the regulation is "reasonably related to legitimate penological concerns." In effect, the decision lowered the standard of scrutiny for determining the constitutionality of prison rules.[122]

The Supreme Court weakened due process guarantees set in *Wolff v. McDonnell* (1974) in the case of *Sandin v. Conner* (1995). In this case, the Court established a new standard for determining when due process protections apply to inmates' disciplinary hearings. It ruled that the Fourteenth Amendment's due process protections come into play only when inmates face the loss of good-time credits or other extraordinary results that impose an "atypical and significant hardship."

When Congress passed the Anti-Terrorism and Effective Death Penalty Act in 1996, it also affected *habeas corpus* petitions. The new law raises the standards for federal court *habeas* review of state criminal proceedings. Under the statute, federal judges cannot grant a writ of *habeas corpus* unless a state court decision upholding a prisoner's conviction is "unreasonably wrong" or flatly contradicts clearly established Supreme Court rulings. The new law also imposes a statute of limitations on the filing of *habeas corpus* petitions. Now inmates have one year from the time their conviction becomes final to file, but if the state provides counsel in a postconviction proceeding, the state prisoner has only six months to file a *habeas corpus* petition.

***RUIZ V. ESTELLE*: TEXAS** One of the first cases to recognize the issue of inmate rights was *Ruiz v. Estelle* (1980).[123] The case was brought against W. J. Estelle, Jr., who was the director of the Texas Department of Corrections, by David Ruiz, a prisoner who claimed that the conditions in the corrections facilities, and particularly in "the hole," were inhumane. Ruiz claimed that the prison administrators exposed prisoners to physically deteriorating, dangerous, and overcrowded conditions.[124] They often allowed select inmates to carry weapons, gave them privileges for keeping things quiet, and allowed inmates (called tenders) to make counts, search cells, frisk other inmates, and administer discipline.

The Supreme Court's decision required numerous changes in the way that Texas ran its prisons. For example, the Texas Department of Corrections was asked to do the following:

- Bring an end to the use of tenders
- Double the number of corrections officers
- Retrain the veteran officers
- Revise the procedures for handling inmate grievances
- Change the methods used to classify inmates to reduce the number of maximum-security inmates
- Improve the health delivery system to give inmates easy access to state-of-the-art medical treatment
- Provide a single cell for each inmate[125]

The *Ruiz* decision became the most comprehensive civil action in correctional law history.[126] The Supreme Court forced sweeping changes in the philosophy of the Texas Department of Corrections as well as its leadership and management practices. The decision altered almost every aspect of the operation of the prison.[127]

***GUTHRIE V. EVANS:* GEORGIA**   On September 29, 1972, Arthur S. Guthrie, Joseph Coggins II, and fifty other black inmates of the Georgia State Prison at Reidsville signed a four-page complaint with the federal courts in Georgia concerning the conditions within the prison. Although the case did not go to the Supreme Court, the decision nonetheless led to one of the most detailed and comprehensive remedial decrees ever imposed on prison facilities.[128] The case became known as *Guthrie v. Evans* (Civil Action No. 73-3068, S.D. Ga. 1973). In the end, the judge overseeing the case stated that the segregation, overcrowding, poor medical care, miserable conditions, and unfair treatment of black and white inmates constituted cruel and unusual punishment. This decision resulted in extensive changes in nearly every aspect of prison operations.[129] In the end, there were sixty-one orders handed down by the courts that were intended to improve existing problems within the Georgia State Prison. There were three major areas of concern:

1. Physical health and safety of inmates
2. Due process of law and the equal protection of the laws in both the treatment of inmates and the employment practices of Georgia State Prison employees
3. Improvements in medical services, vocational and educational programs, and a rehabilitative incentive plan for Georgia State Prison inmates[130]

On the whole, the case resulted in sweeping changes and a general rebuilding of the prison facility. There was also a rational restructuring of correctional authority and operations. Today, many authorities refer to this prison as a "constitutional prison." There are now single-cell living arrangements; up-to-date medical, sanitary, and custodial conditions; and procedures for disciplining inmates that are nondiscriminatory.[131]

***RHEM V. MCGRATH* AND *RHEM V. MALCOLM:* NEW YORK CITY**   Yet another prison where court decisions improved the rights of the inmates was in New York City's most decrepit jail, known as the "Tombs." In 1970, the inmates filed a class-action suit against city officials, alleging that they were being held in inhumane and unconstitutional conditions.[132] As proof, they gave evidence that most inmates were held three in a cell and most of the time that the third inmate slept on the concrete floor without a mattress or blanket. The case was called *Rhem v. McGrath.*

Early in the morning on August 10, 1970, the inmates being held in the Tombs overpowered the guards who were supervising breakfast and took control of the ninth floor. Five of the guards were held for eight hours. The inmates presented their grievances to the incoming mayor of New York, John Lindsay, and the head of the Department of Corrections (called the commissioner of corrections), George F. McGrath.[133] When McGrath was replaced as commissioner by Benjamin Malcolm in January 1972, the case became known as *Rhem v. Malcolm.*

The inmates argued that incarceration at the Tombs did the following:

1. Violated protections against due process. They argued that because they were not yet convicted of a crime, they were to be held under the least restrictive conditions necessary to ensure their appearance at trial.
2. Violated the equal protection clause because they were being held in harsher conditions than those inmates who had been convicted of a crime.
3. Violated the Eighth Amendment against cruel and unusual punishment.[134]

CRAIN V. BORDENKIRCHER: WEST VIRGINIA   In the West Virginia Penitentiary, inmates lived in cells that were poorly ventilated or heated, that had sewage leaking into them, and that were infested with rats and lice. In 1982, thirty-six inmate petitions were consolidated and brought to trial in *Crain v. Bordenkircher*.[135] In a state court, a state circuit judge ruled that the conditions within the prison violated the inmates' constitutional rights against cruel and unusual punishment and other rights established in the laws in the state.[136] Judge Recht concluded that the conditions within the penitentiary violated the Constitution's prohibition against cruel and unusual punishment as well as the West Virginia constitution and statutes.[137] He noted in particular the small cells and the lack of adequate medical care. Nonetheless, the prison administrators failed to act, and on New Year's Day 1986, riots broke out, and three inmates were killed. After the riot, attacks and counterattacks between inmates and guards continued. Inmates were known to throw urine, feces, and boiling water on guards. Guards were also assaulted with broom handles and other makeshift weapons. Those inmates who chose not to participate in the attacks were themselves victims, being attacked by other inmates. The guards retaliated by turning off the electricity for long periods of time, allowing the unit to become and remain cold, and refusing to enter the tiers unless absolutely necessary.[138]

Recently, California experienced severe overcrowded prisons resulting in a legal action against the state. The original case, *Coleman v. Schwarzenegger*, was originally filed in April 1990 and tried in front of a U.S. magistrate judge. He found that the state was unable to provide timely health care for inmates because of overcrowded conditions in prisons. A similar case, *Plata v. Schwarzenegger*, found that prison medical care was substandard. In response, Governor Schwarzenegger declared a state of emergency surrounding the state's prison system. In August, 2009, a panel of three federal judges ordered California to reduce its prison population by 40,000.[139] The state was given 45 days to submit a plan to reduce the population. The plan included building more prison facilities, arranging with other states to house more of California's inmates, and changing sentences for some criminals. Schwarzenegger also called for deporting illegal immigrants serving time in California prisons for nonviolent crimes.

The three-judge panel rejected the Governor's plan, ruling that it failed to meet certain requirements, and ordered the state to submit a revised plan. The state appealed the decision to the U.S. Supreme Court in an emergency appeal and asked for more time to devise a plan. The Supreme Court rejected the appeal, explaining the case would be "premature" because the order only required a plan rather than any action.[140] State officials submitted a revised plan in November 2009, and in January 2010, the three-judge panel ordered the state to carry it out. At the same time, they stayed the population reduction order until a pending appeal is decided, so that it will not take effect immediately.

Although the prison conditions in California remain a concern, the courts are, and will continue, to oversee the care provided to inmates in the future. As poor conditions are discovered, whether it is in California or another state, the courts will act to protect the rights of inmates as it relates to overcrowding.

Conclusion

Despite much controversy surrounding the policy-making role of the courts, they have become important actors in the policymaking process. They have made many key policies with regard to criminal justice that have helped provide rights to individuals, whether involved in the criminal justice system or not, and protect constitutional safeguards. The courts are able to do this when other branches of government cannot.

Several factors would seem to guarantee continued judicial involvement in policy formation. One is the growing influence of the government, especially the courts, on people's lives. Part of this is due to the increasing litigiousness in at least some segments of the population. In recent years, Americans have become adept at converting political issues into legal issues that the courts are then called on to decide. The second reason is the failure or refusal of the legislative branches to act on some problems, opening the doors for the courts to step in to decide issues surrounding social problems. Third is the dissatisfaction that often arises when the courts demonstrate a willingness to get involved and make rulings on issues that are unsatisfactory to some people. At this point, judicial activism, more than judicial restraint, currently characterizes the actions of the courts, and their willingness to get involved in social issues that come to the forefront is clearly evident.[141] Fourth, the courts are able to develop specific policies, whereas legislatures' policy decisions tend to sweep with a broad stroke across all relevant situations without regard for the subtle but potentially important differences between specific circumstances.[142] Based on these trends, it is doubtful that the courts will back away from their policymaking role.

Notes

1. George F. Cole, *Criminal Justice: Law and Politics* (Monterey, Calif.: Brooks/Cole, 1984), p. 239.
2. John A. Fliter, *Prisoners' Rights: The Supreme Court and Evolving Standards of Decency* (Westport, Conn.: Greenwood Press, 2001), p. 37.
3. Cole, *Criminal Justice*, p. 3.
4. Fliter, *Prisoners' Rights*, p. 37.
5. Robert A. Carp and Ronald Stidham, *The Federal Courts* (Washington, D.C.: Congressional Quarterly Press, 1991), p. 142.
6. Cole, *Criminal Justice*, p. 1.
7. Ibid., p. 2.
8. Stuart Nagel, "Political Party Affiliation and Judges' Decisions," *American Political Science Review* 50 (1961): 843–50; Sidney Ulmer, "The Political Party Variable in the Michigan Supreme Court," *Journal of Public Law* 11 (1962): 352–62; Philip L. Dubois, *From Ballot to Bench: Judicial Elections and the Quest for Accountability* (Austin: University of Texas Press, 1980).
9. David M. O'Brien, *Storm Center: The Supreme Court in American Politics* (New York: Norton, 2003), p. 338.
10. Jeff Yates, *Popular Justice: Presidential Prestige and Executive Success in the Supreme Court* (New York: State University of New York Press, 2002), p. 8.
11. O'Brien, *Storm Center*, p. 338.
12. Helmut Norpoth, Jeffrey A. Segal, William Mishler, and Reginald S. Sheehan, "Popular Influence on Supreme Court Decisions," *American Political Science Review* 88 (3, 1994): 711–24.
13. Ibid.
14. O'Brien, *Storm Center*, p. 337.
15. H. R. Glick, *Courts, Politics and Justice* (New York: McGraw Hill, 1993).
16. Stuart S. Nagel, *Comparing Elected and Appointed Judicial Systems* (Beverly Hills, Calif.: Sage, 1973).
17. Glick, *Courts, Politics and Justice*.
18. John Gruhl, Cassia Spohn, and Susan Welch, "Women as Policymakers: The Case of Trial Judges," *American Journal of Political Science* 25 (1981): 308–22; Carp and Stidham, *The Federal Courts*, p. 142.
19. Carp and Stidham, *The Federal Courts*, p. 142.
20. Susan Welch, Michael Combs, and John Gruhl, "Do Black Judges Make a Difference," *American Journal of Political Science* (1988): 126–36; Carp and Stidham, *The Federal Courts*, p. 142.
21. Carp and Stidham, *The Federal Courts*, p. 9; Christopher E. Smith, *Courts, Politics and the Judicial Process* (Chicago: Nelson-Hall, 1997), p. 289.
22. John Hagan, "The Symbolic Politics of Criminal Sanctions," in *The Political Science of Criminal Justice*, ed. Stuart Nagel, Erika Fairchild, and Anthony Champagne (Springfield, Ill.: Charles C Thomas, 1983) pp. 27–40.
23. O'Brien, *Storm Center*, p. 190.
24. Ibid., p. 165.
25. Herbert Jacob, "Courts and Politics in the United States," in *Courts, Law and Politics in a Comparative Perspective*, ed. Herbert Jacob, Erhard Blankenburg, Herbert M. Kritzer, Doris Marie Provide, and Joseph Sanders (New Haven, Conn.: Yale University Press, 1996).
26. Barbara Stolz, *Criminal Justice Policy Making* (Westport, Conn.: Praeger, 2002), p. 177.

27. Jacob, "Courts and Politics in the United States."

28. B. Guy Peters, *American Public Policy: Promise and Performance* (Chatham, N.J.: Chatham House, 1996), p. 91; Thomas R. Dye, *Top Down Policy Making* (Chatham, N.J.: Chatham House, 2001); John J. Harrigan and David C. Nice, *Politics and Policy in States and Communities* (New York: Pearson, 2004), p. 268; Dennis L. Dresang and James J. Gosling, *Politics and Policy in American States and Communities* (New York: Pearson, 2004), p. 352.

29. Dresang and Gosling, *Politics and Policy*, p. 353; W. Murphy, *Elements of Judicial Strategy* (Chicago: University of Chicago Press, 1964); C. A. Johnson and B. C. Cannon, *Judicial Policies: Implementation and Impact* (Washington, D.C.: Congressional Quarterly Press, 1984); James E. Anderson, *Public Policy Making* (Boston: Houghton Mifflin, 2003).

30. O'Brien, *Storm Center*, p. 28.

31. Harrigan and Nice, *Politics and Policy*, p. 269.

32. Christopher Smith, "The Capacity of Courts as Policy Making Forums," in *Public Policy, Crime and Criminal Justice*, ed. Barry Hancock and Paul M. Sharp (Upper Saddle River, N.J.: Prentice Hall, 2000); pp. 240–56, at 250.

33. Anderson, *Public Policy Making*.

34. Smith, "The Capacity of Courts as Policy Making Forums," p. 250.

35. Smith, *Courts*, p. 287.

36. Dye, *Top Down Policy Making*.

37. Peters, *American Public Policy*, p. 92.

38. Peters, *American Public Policy*, p. 92; citing Federal Judge Frank Johnson in Alabama literally took over the prisons and mental hospitals of that state. See *Wyatt v. Stickney*, 344 F. Supp. 373 (M.D. Ala 1972), and *Pugh v. Locke*, 406 F. Supp. 318 (M.D. Ala. 1976).

39. John J. Dilulio, Jr., *Courts, Corrections and the Constitution* (New York: Oxford University Press, 1990).

40. Smith, "The Capacity of Courts as Policy Making Forums"; Martin Garbus, *Courting Disaster* (New York: Times Books, 2002).

41. Smith, "The Capacity of Courts as Policy Making Forums," p. 242.

42. Ibid.

43. Anderson, *Public Policy Making*.

44. R. A. Dahl, "Decision-Making in a Democracy: The Supreme Court as a National Policy-Maker," *Journal of Public Law* 6 (1957): 279, 293.

45. Jeff Yates, *Popular Justice: Presidential Prestige and Executive Success in the Supreme Court* (New York: State University of New York Press, 2002).

46. O'Brien, *Storm Center*, p. 336.

47. Yates, *Popular Justice*, p. 1.

48. O'Brien, *Storm Center*, p. 314.

49. Carp and Stidham, *The Federal Courts*, p. 9; Smith, *Courts*, p. 197.

50. Glick, *Courts, Politics and Justice*.

51. G. Alan Tarr, "The Effectiveness of Supreme Court Mandates," in Nagel et al., *The Political Science of Criminal Justice*, pp. 73–86.

52. Jacob, "Courts and Politics in the United States."

53. Glick, *Courts, Politics and Justice*, p. 412.

54. Joan Biskupic and Elder Witt, *The Supreme Court and the Powers of the American Government* (Washington, D.C.: Congressional Quarterly Press, 1997), p. 244.

55. Herbert A. Johnson, *History of Criminal Justice* (Cincinnati: Anderson, 1988), pp. 272–73.

56. Biskupic and Witt, *The Supreme Court and the Powers of the American Government*, p. 287.

57. Johnson, *History of Criminal Justice*; Biskupic and Witt, *The Supreme Court and the Powers of the American Government*, p. 288.

58. Biskupic and Witt, *The Supreme Court and the Powers of the American Government*, p. 289.

59. John Frank, "Nation Follows Tampa Case" Tampa Bay Times December 6, 2009l, retrieved 2/18/2010 and available at www.tampabay.com/news/courts/us-supreme-court-to-decide-were-tampa-police-cle.

60. Ted Gest, *Crime and Politics: Big Government's Erratic Campaign for Law and Order* (New York: Oxford University Press, 2001).

61. David Schichor and Dale K. Sechrest, eds., *Three Strikes and You're Out* (Thousand Oaks, Calif.: Sage, 1996), p. vi.

62. Peter C. Greenwood, Peter Rydell, Allan F. Abrahamse, Jonathan P. Caulkins, James Chiesa, Karyn E. Model, and Stephen P. Klein, "Estimated Benefits and Costs of California's New Mandatory-Sentencing Law," in Schichor and Sechrest, *Three Strikes and You're Out*, p. 54.

63. Schichor and Sechrest, *Three Strikes and You're Out*, p. vi.

64. James Austin, "The Effect of 'Three Strikes and You're Out' on Corrections," in Schichor and Sechrest, *Three Strikes and You're Out*, pp. 166–67.

65. Schichor and Sechrest, *Three Strikes and You're Out*, p. vi.

66. Austin, "The Effect of 'Three Strikes and You're Out' on Corrections," p. 169.

67. James Austin and John Irwin, *It's About Time: America's Imprisonment Binge* (Belmont, Calif.: Wadsworth, 2001), p. 204.

68. Robert C. Cushman, "Effect on a Local Criminal Justice System," in Schichor and Sechrest, *Three Strikes and You're Out*.

69. Thomas B. Marvell and Carlisle E. Moody, "The Lethal Effects of Three Strikes Laws," *Journal of Legal Studies* 30 (2001): 89–106.

70. Tomislav Kovandzic, John J. Sloan, and Lynne Vicraitis, "The Unintended Consequences of Politically Popular Sentencing Policy," in *The Criminal Justice System: Politics and Policies*, ed. George F. Cole, Marc G. Gertz, and Amy Bunger (Belmont, Calif.: Wadsworth, 2004).

71. Jerome H. Skolnick, "What Not to Do about Crime," *Criminology* 33 (1, 1995): 1–13.

72. Austin and Irwin, *It's About Time*, p. 214.

73. C. Stone Brown, "Legislative Repression," in *Criminal Injustice: Confronting the Prison Crisis*, ed. Elihu Rosenblatt (Boston: South End Press, 1996), pp. 100–107, at 102.

74. Thomas B. Marvell and Carlisle E. Moody, "The Lethal Effects of Three-Strikes Laws," The Journal of Legal Studies (January 2001), pp. 89–106.

75. Greenwood et al., "Estimated Benefits and Costs of California's New Mandatory-Sentencing Law," p. 54.

76. Cushman, "Effect on a Local Criminal Justice System," p. 101.

77. Greenwood et al., "Estimated Benefits and Costs of California's New Mandatory-Sentencing Law," p. 54.

78. Ibid., p. 81.

79. Ibid., p. 82.

80. Vincent Schiraldi, "The Undue Influence of California's Prison Guard Union: California's Correctional-Industrial Complex," *In Brief* (October 1994): 1; Skolnick, "What Not to Do about Crime," p. 4.

81. Noah Baum and Brooke Bedrick, "Trading Books for Bars: The Lopsided Funding Battle between Prisons and Universities," *In Brief* (May 1994): 5.

82. Cushman, "Effect on a Local Criminal Justice System," p. 106.

83. Ibid., p. 104.

84. Ibid., p. 106.

85. Malcolm Feeley and Sam Kamin, "The Effect of 'Three Strikes and You're Out' on the Courts," in Schichor and Sechrest, *Three Strikes and You're Out*, pp. 135–54, at 148.

86. Frank A. Zeigler and Rolando V. Del Carmen, "Constitutional Issues Arising from 'Three Strikes and You're Out' Legislation," in Schichor and Sechrest, *Three Strikes and You're Out*, pp. 3–23, at 4.

87. Stephen Henderson, "Supreme Court Upholds Three-Strikes Law," *Miami Herald* (March 5, 2003), available online at www.miami.com/mld/miamiherald/news/nation/5323838.htm?template.

88. Austin and Irwin, *It's About Time*, p. 213.

89. Brown, "Legislative Repression," p. 102.

90. Franklin E. Zimring, Gordon Hawkins, and Sam Kamin, *Punishment and Democracy: Three Strikes and You're Out in California* (New York: Oxford University Press, 2001).

91. "Proposition 66: Limitations on 'Three Strikes' Law, Sex Crimes, Punishment, Initiative Statute" Legislative Analyst's Office, 2004; accessed on 2/18/2010 and available at www.lao.ca.gov/ballot/2004/66_11_2004.htm.

92. M. S. Vaughn and R. del Carmen, "The Fourth Amendment as a Tool of Actuarial Justice: The 'Special Needs' Exception to the Warrant and Probable Cause Requirements," *Crime and Delinquency* 43 (1997): 78–103.

93. David G. Savage, "Supreme Court Limits 'Exclusionary Rule,'" Los Angeles Times, retrieved on 2/18/2010 and available at www.articles.latimes.com/2009/jan/15/nation/na-supreme-court-police15.

94. Johnson, *History of Criminal Justice*, pp. 272–73; Biskupic and Witt, *The Supreme Court and the Powers of the American Government*, p. 283.

95. Hugo Adam Bedau, "The Case against the Death Penalty," in Rosenblatt, *Criminal Injustice*, pp. 209–29, at 215.

96. Joshua D. Freilich and Craig J. Rivera, "Mercy Death and Politics: An Analysis of Executions and Commutations in New York State, 1925–1963," *American Journal of Criminal Justice* 24 (1, 1999): 15–29.

97. Brown, "Legislative Repression," p. 105.

98. Ibid., p. 106.

99. Herbert H. Haines, *Against Capital Punishment* (New York: Oxford University Press, 1996), p. 7.

100. Ibid.

101. Ibid., p. 8.

102. Franklin E. Zimring and Gordon Hawkins, *Capital Punishment and the American Agenda* (New York: Cambridge University Press, 1986), p. 39.

103. Haines, *Against Capital Punishment*, p. 45.

104. Phoebe C. Ellsworth and Samuel R. Gross, "Hardening of the Attitudes: Americans' Views on the Death Penalty," *Journal of Social Issues* 50 (2, 1994): 19–52.

105. Ibid.

106. Haines, *Against Capital Punishment*, p. 3.

107. Tracy Snell, "Capital Punishment, 2008-Statistical Tables" (Washington, D.C.: Bureau of Justice Statistics, Office of Justice Programs, U.S.

Department of Justice), available at www.bjs.ojp.usdoj.gov/content/pub/pdf/cp08st.pdf.

108. Tracy Snell, "Capital Punishment, 2008–Statistical Tables" (Washington, D.C.: Bureau of Justice Statistics, Office of Justice Programs, U.S. Department of Justice), available at www.bjs.ojp.usdoj.gov/content/pub/pdf/cp08st.pdf.

109. Bedau, "The Case against the Death Penalty," p. 225.

110. Haines, *Against Capital Punishment*, pp. 169–70.

111. Bedau, "The Case against the Death Penalty," p. 212.

112. Haines, *Against Capital Punishment*, p. 173; Thorsten Sellin, *The Death Penalty* (Philadelphia: American Law Institute, 1959); Ruth D. Peterson and William C. Bailey, "Murder and Capital Punishment in the Evolving Context of the Post-Furman Era," *Social Forces* 66 (1988): 774–807; Gary Kleck, "Capital Punishment, Gun Ownership and Homicide," *American Journal of Sociology* 84 (1979): 882–910.

113. Michael Doyle, "Supreme Court rejects Death Penalty for Child Rape" June 25, 2008; retrieved on 2/18/1020 from www.mcclatchydc.com/homepage/v-print/story/42117.html.

114. Malcolm M. Feeley and Roger A. Hanson, "The Impact of Judicial Intervention on Prisons and Jails: A Framework for Analysis and a Review of the Literature" in *Courts, Corrections and the Constitution*, ed. John J. Dilulio, Jr. (New York: Oxford University Press, 1990), pp. 12–49.

115. Dilulio, *Courts, Corrections and the Constitution*, p. 3.

116. Fliter, *Prisoners' Rights*, p. 45.

117. Dilulio, *Courts, Corrections and the Constitution*, p. 4.

118. Fliter, *Prisoners' Rights*, p. xvi.

119. Ibid., p. xvii.

120. Ibid.

121. Ibid., p. 145.

122. Ibid., p. 155.

123. The state case was decided in 1980, and the Fifth Circuit case was decided in 1983.

124. Ben M. Crouch and James W. Marquart, "Ruiz: Intervention and Emergent Order in Texas Prisons," in Dilulio, *Courts, Corrections and the Constitution*, pp. 94–114, at 94.

125. Dilulio, *Courts, Corrections and the Constitution*, p. 60.

126. Crouch and Marquart, "Ruiz," p. 94.

127. Ibid.

128. Bradley S. Chilton and Susette Talarico, "Politics and Constitutional Interpretation in Prison Reform Litigation: The Case of Guthrie v. Evans," in Dilulio, *Courts, Corrections and the Constitution*, pp. 115–37, at 117.

129. Ibid.

130. Ibid., p. 119.

131. Ibid., p. 122.

132. Ted S. Storey, "When Intervention Works: Judge Morris E. Lasker and New York City Jails," in Dilulio, *Courts, Corrections and the Constitution*, 138–72, at 138.

133. Ibid., p. 139.

134. Ibid., p. 146.

135. Bert Useem, "Crain: Nonreformist Prison Reform," in Dilulio, *Courts, Corrections and the Constitution*, pp. 223–48, at 229.

136. Ibid., p. 224.

137. Ibid., p. 229.

138. Ibid., p. 237.

139. Cheryl Miller, "Federal Judges Order California to Cut Prison Population" Law.com, 8/5/2009, retrieved 2/18/2010 from www.law.com/jus/law/LawArticleFriendly.jsp?id=1202442793708.

140. Caleb Groos, "California Prison Reform: Too Little Too Late?" Findlaw Blotter, September 14, 2009, retrieved on 2/18/2010 from http://blogs.findlaw.com/blotter/20009/09/california-prison-reform-too-little-too-late.html.

141. Anderson, *Public Policy Making*.

142. Smith, "The Capacity of Courts as Policy Making Forums," p. 241.

12

Corrections

Chapter Outline

INTRODUCTION

The corrections system includes any correctional policy, program, or agency that has the aim or goal of "correcting" any behavior that society finds unacceptable or that has been made illegal by a legislature, typically through punishment or rehabilitation. There are federal, state, and local correctional systems and facilities, each of which is set up to hold or rehabilitate criminal offenders who violate laws of their jurisdiction. Each of the corrections agencies and the personnel who work there, along with any groups that support agencies, personnel, or inmates, have a significant impact on the policymaking process.

The federal corrections agencies deal with offenders convicted of federal offenses, such as terrorism or drug smuggling. The federal government funds these programs and oversees the treatment of the inmates held there. They are overseen by the Department of Corrections, which has control over the federal prisons located throughout the nation. There are also a small number of federal detention facilities that function as jails. Usually, the federal government relies on contracts with local jail facilities for the vast majority of its short-term needs. State and local facilities hold inmates convicted of state and local statutes, but they are still overseen by the federal government.

Across the United States, each individual state has also developed its own unique system of corrections, so variations exist from state to state. In most states, an agency has been created to oversee the administration of correctional programs. One way to know the goals of a state correctional agency is to look at the mission statement of its department of corrections. For example, the mission statement for the Texas Department of Criminal Justice states that the purpose of the organization is to "provide public safety, promote positive change in behavior, and reintegrate offenders into society."[1] Similarly, the Department of Corrections for Illinois states that its mission is to "protect the public from criminal offenders through a system of incarceration and supervision which securely segregates offenders from society, assures offenders of their constitutional rights and maintains programs to enhance the success of the offender's reentry into society."[2]

Corrections agencies are distinguished from other, typical agencies in that people do not come willingly to prisons. They are forcibly brought through the gates and prevented from leaving by guards, walls, and fences. While inside the prison, the inmates are required to live according to the dictates of the administration that also restrict their movements. Because almost every minute of the inmates' lives are controlled by the rules of the institution, as enforced by the staff, the prison is considered a closed institution.[3]

Prisons carry out a number of functions. First, they must keep the inmates within their custody. Second, many institutions use inmates to produce a product, typically through a prison industries program. Finally, institutions are sometimes responsible for the treatment of inmates. This can be through education, drug or alcohol treatment, or vocational training programs.[4]

The primary goals of the corrections agencies throughout the United States revolve around punishment (deterrence) and rehabilitation. These goals focus on either protecting the public or rehabilitating the prisoner, but most correctional programs are a mixture of goals.[5] The majority of correctional programs include some element of retribution or punishment whereby wrongdoers are punished because they committed an illegal act and should be given their just deserts. This often includes incapacitating the offender, who is then prevented from reoffending by the punishment imposed, either temporarily or permanently. Of course, executed offenders never reoffend. There are also fines and other sentences that serve, at least partially, to punish an offender. These punishments are also set up to function as a deterrent to potential criminals, preventing future criminal behavior. There are two types of deterrence. One is general deterrence, in which offenders are punished to deter others from committing criminal acts. The other is specific deterrence, where an individual commits a crime, is punished for it, and finds the punishment so unpleasant that the offense is never repeated. If society can deter crime from occurring, it can also at the same time protect its citizens from violence and harm.

Most programs also include elements of rehabilitation, which incorporates an underlying premise that punishment can reform or change an offender's character and make him or her less likely to reoffend in the future. Sometimes referred to as the "medical model," it assumes that something is wrong with the offender that causes him or her to commit crime. Whatever is wrong can be fixed so that the person will not offend again. Education and job training are two examples of rehabilitative programs offered to inmates that offer them a chance to improve themselves so that they can function as productive citizens. While in prison, offenders can receive an education and marketable skill so that when they return to the outside world, they can find profitable employment and no longer be forced to steal or commit additional crimes. In other words, when inmates are released from a rehabilitative program, they will be able to gain employment that provides an income instead of relying on crime to obtain what they want or need.

The corrections system can be categorized by the government body that oversees it (i.e., federal, state, and local systems) and also by the level of punishment provided (maximum, medium, and minimum security). There are also separate facilities for men, women, and juveniles who have been charged with or convicted of criminal offenses. Within these categories, there are many varieties of programs and punishments designed to deal with different offenders. Each plays a role in the policy process and must deal with many controversial policies.

Politics and Corrections

Generally, there are two approaches to corrections policies that are supported by politicians on all levels of government. The first is the liberal approach to punishment, which involves less strict punishments, focusing instead on rehabilitation programs, such as furlough programs. The emphasis here is on providing due process, equal protection of the law, and protection against cruel and unusual punishment as well as the reform of the inmate.[6] This approach acknowledges the role of social inequality in causing crime; for example, the lack of educational opportunities, a lack of employment, and racism cause a person to commit crime. It is based on the medical model, where deficiencies within an inmate can be identified and the appropriate treatment provided so that the inmate can change his or her behavior and become a productive member of society. Under this assumption, crime is the product of moral default of society.[7] There is an underlying assumption that the individualized treatment of offenders would be most effective in preventing future involvement in crime.[8] This approach was the basis for indeterminate sentencing, whereby an inmate's release date depends on a desired behavioral change. In other words, inmates are released when they are deemed to be "rehabilitated."

Rehabilitation saw its heyday during the 1960s. At this time, community corrections became very popular because it had the intention of reintegrating offenders into society so that they could become productive members of the community rather than returning to a life of crime. It was thought that community corrections could restore family links, help offenders obtain employment and education, and secure a sense of place and pride in their daily lives. As a result, administrators started using probation and parole more often. Additionally, smaller institutions located near urban areas rather than large institutions located in rural settings were designed to hold offenders. Sometimes community corrections programs included special programs within the structure of the community that were designed to create links between the offender and the community.[9]

The second approach to corrections policy is the conservative approach, which involves stricter punishment, few inmate rights, and strict and certain punishments for criminal behavior. Under this philosophy, criminal behavior is made through free choice and is the result of inadequate control by the offender. Thus, there is a need for speedy punishment when criminal activity occurs. The corrections system would be more effective if there were swift and certain punishment with a greater use of imprisonment, including more and longer prison terms. In this way, crime would be reduced.[10]

The sentencing policy that resulted from the conservative approach revolved around determinate sentences. These required judges to impose punishments that were commensurate with the crime committed rather than the character or background of the criminal. An inmate's release date is firm, not dependent on an inmate's behavioral changes. When politicians who supported this philosophy were elected into office, they changed the focus of the justice system to reflect this approach, but they also put more emphasis on the rights of crime victims than on the offender.

In recent years, the federal government has been more conservative and thus supports policies that reflect the conservative point of view concerning corrections. It is currently politically popular to support a "get-tough-on-crime" stance toward offenders and punishment. As a result, the system has become more punitive, with the rehabilitation of offenders taking second place to punishment of offenders. New laws mandate longer prison sentences, abolish parole, and make prison life harsher.

There may be some serious consequences as a result of these conservative policies that have been implemented, such as an increased number of people in prisons (overcrowding and poor conditions within the prison) or at least more people under correctional supervision. There may also be increased costs for providing more incarceration services. Additional consequences involve increased stress on correctional officers and other personnel.

Restorative Justice

The concepts surrounding restorative justice constitute a new paradigm or approach to criminal justice. This entails a more proactive system that puts an emphasis on preventing crime at early stages so that society is protected from harm. The underlying belief is that offenders can change if they accept responsibility for their actions. The concept rejects the traditional punishment mechanisms, using incarceration only as a last resort, and shifts the focus of punishment to actively involve both the victim and the offender. It is based on a belief that the extensive use of punishment as a deterrent has failed because it does not involve the victims and offenders in making decisions about criminal sentences. Restorative justice works to repair the injury caused by the crime by shifting the role of the offender from being a passive recipient of punishment to an active participant in repairing the harm done. The use of mediation, restitution, community service, and police–community partnerships to resolve conflict is common.[11]

HISTORY

Over time, the corrections system has evolved in the United States to become what it is today. The opposing political ideologies (i.e., conservative and liberal) are reflected in the dominant criminal justice policies of the time that are made to help deal with offenders. As the prominent ideology changes, the approach to correctional programs shifts as well.

The initial experiment in confining offenders convicted of criminal offenses took place in 1790 and involved converting sixteen cells at the Walnut Street Jail in Philadelphia, Pennsylvania, into housing for convicted felons. This became America's first penitentiary and was referred to as the Philadelphia, or Pennsylvania, system. The prison revolved around a system of solitary confinement, manual labor, and Bible study in their cells. The prisoners were kept separate from each other as well as from the outside world. The aim of this system was one of penance.[12]

The Walnut Street Penitentiary evolved into the Eastern State Penitentiary in 1829, which remained in use until 1970. At Eastern, they used the basic format of confining offenders to solitary cells but used a congregate work environment. Another approach at that time was the "Auburn model" in New York State, which required inmates to work during the day, but they were prohibited from talking or even exchanging glances.[13] The purpose of these early institutions was to punish the offender and at the same time prevent further harm to the inmates, which results from contact with other inmates. This was done by disallowing communication between inmates. This form of punishment was popular from about 1870.[14]

The "Big House," referring to maximum-security prisons, was popular across the United States throughout the first half of the twentieth century. Here, prisoners worked in jobs that kept them occupied, such as working in rock piles. The tasks were not meant to be productive or make a profit. The inmates simply "did their time."

As this discussion illustrates, until the 1930s, the dominant view of corrections was primarily punishment and deterrence. Most felt that criminals could not be rehabilitated or changed into law-abiding citizens, so they ought to be punished.[15] However, there was a shift in the dominant approach to correctional policy across the United States at about that time. Most states supported removing harsh discipline from prisons and replacing it with educational, vocational, and treatment programs for inmates. This approach to treating an inmate rather than on strict punishment was called "rehabilitation" and was popular from the 1930s until the 1970s among correctional personnel. At this time, the term "penitentiary" was replaced with "correctional institution" and "prison guard" with "correctional officer" to demonstrate the focus on rehabilitation rather than punishment.

The use of rehabilitation as the primary theory of criminal justice policy was initiated largely by President Johnson's Commission on Law Enforcement and Administration of Justice, which was established in 1965 to investigate the causes and nature of crime. The 1967 final report from the commission reflected the liberal perspective that crime could be prevented if social inequalities were corrected. It was a strong endorsement of treating inmates instead of punishing them.[16] Crime was conceptualized as a social problem that resulted from basic inequalities in society, such as employment and educational differences. The offender was viewed as a victim of society's ills. It was hoped that prisoners could be rehabilitated to rejoin society in a productive capacity by using psychology or counseling or teaching marketable skills.[17] On the whole, the primary purpose of prisons was to produce changes in the characters, attitudes, and behavior of convicted offenders.[18]

The rehabilitative approach dominated in the United States for most of the twentieth century.[19] During this time, there was a tremendous expansion of community-based programs.[20] There were also shifts to indefinite prison sentences. But as time went on, the concept of rehabilitation began to weaken among correctional administrators, politicians, and scholars.[21] Administrators found that many of the assumptions on which the ideas were based were vague and ambiguous.[22] It became clear that correctional institutions were not as effective in rehabilitating offenders as previously thought, as many released inmates ended up back in prison.[23] The nation also witnessed increased violent crime rates, an increase in the use of illegal drugs, and worsening race relations.

Scholars soon discovered empirical data that seemed to show that correctional treatment programs were not effective in preventing repeat criminal activity. In a relatively short time, new research seemed to show that real rehabilitation was not possible and that rehabilitative programs were misdirected.[24] One of those landmark research projects was conducted by Robert Martinson in 1974, titled "What Works." In this study, Martinson surveyed 231 experimental studies of juvenile and adult offenders of both sexes.[25] He concluded that "nothing works."[26]

Combined, all these factors fostered a conservative "lock-'em-up" attitude. These events signaled the end of rehabilitation as a primary focus for correctional policy. The rehabilitation era was replaced by the "conservative era" of punishment, which was popular from 1975 to 1995.[27] From then on, criminal justice policy was dominated by a very different approach to dealing with criminal offenders.[28] Conservatives argued that the liberal rehabilitation programs failed to reduce crime.[29] The "conservative revolution" redefined crime as a criminal justice problem and rejected both social explanations of and social solutions to crime.[30] They blamed increasing crime rates and recidivism rates on the ineffectiveness of rehabilitation programs.

This period was dominated by harsh punishment rather than treatment of offenders. One popular idea of that era was determinate or mandatory sentences, whereby offenders must serve a sentence for a fixed number of years regardless of their participation in any type of rehabilitation or educational program. This included a well-defined prescription of punishments: The punishment for the more serious offenses would be greater than that for the less serious ones. Many states turned to determinate sentencing and sentencing guidelines in which the state legislature rather than the judiciary decides what the sentence should be for each offense.

Conservative reforms throughout the 1990s also attempted to limit the discretion of parole boards by requiring a higher percentage of inmates' sentences be served before they are eligible for parole. In some states and in the federal government, "truth-in-sentencing" laws have eliminated parole. Inmates do not get time off for good behavior within the institution. A more recent idea to the conservative approach is the "three-strikes-and-you're out" approach to sentencing.

Some would argue that we are now in a period of "overt politicization." They argue that policymakers ignore research findings, instead supporting any policy that shows short-term promise. For example, the policy of using mandatory minimum sentences has become popular even though many studies have shown that the people receiving the mandatory sentences are among the most benign in terms of their prior record. Most politicians do not want to take the political risk of failing to address crime and being labeled soft on crime, so they support programs that provide immediate results.[31]

For the most part, the overall mission and goals of correctional agencies will depend to a large extent on which political ideology is dominant at the time. The emphasis on rehabilitation by liberal party members creates certain procedures that are significantly different than those created by conservative party members.[32] Over time, there is an ebb and flow of correctional ideologies, with one approach dominating the other, then vice versa. Nonetheless, while the philosophical ideology and stated goals of the prison and the criminal justice system have fluctuated over time, the basic concept of imprisoning people in cages remains the central feature of our correctional system.[33]

PRISON POPULATIONS

As of February 2010, there were 208,799 inmates in federal prisons. Of those, 16.7 percent were held in minimum-security, 38.4 percent in low-security, 29.6 percent in medium-security, and 11.1 percent in high-security prisons (4 % have not been assigned to a security level). The majority of the federal inmates were male (93.4 % versus 6.6 % female), white (57.6 %), and U.S. citizens (73.3 %). The average inmate age was 38. Most of the inmates were charged with drug offenses (51.6 %), followed by weapons offenses (15.1 %), immigration (11.3 %), robbery (4.5 %), burglary (3.5 %), extortion (5.0 %), and homicide (2.8 %).[34]

Box 12.1 shows the number of inmates in state or federal prisons from 1995 to 2002. It shows that the number of inmates has continued to increase over time, peaking at 2 million in 2002. The states with the highest prison populations are California, Texas, Florida and New York and those with the lowest are North Dakota, Wyoming, Vermont, Maine, and New Hampshire. However, when the population of the state is taken into consideration and the states are compared by the rate of incarceration (as opposed to number of inmates), the states with the highest rates of incarceration become Louisiana, Mississippi, Texas, Oklahoma, and Alabama. The states with the lowest rates of incarceration are Maine, Minnesota, North Dakota, Rhode Island, and New Hampshire. Maine had the highest percent change in its number of inmates (an 11.5% change), and Alaska had the lowest (they had a 3.8% change).[35]

BOX 12.1
Number of Inmates in State or Federal Prisons and Jails, 1995–2002

1995	1,585,586
1996	1,646,020
1997	1,743,643
1998	1,816,931
1999	1,869,115
2000	1,937,482
2001	1,961,247
2002	2,003,331

Source: Bureau of Justice Statistics, "Prisoners in 2002" (December 2002).

TABLE 12.1 Incarceration Rate in State or Federal Prison of Inmates Sentenced to One Year or More, 2007

Type of Prison	Rate per 100,000 U.S. Residents
Federal	59
State	447
Total	506

Source: Public Agenda, available online at www.publicagenda.org/citizen/issueguides.crime/getfacts.

Table 12.1 shows the incarceration rate for those inmates who are serving a sentence of over one year in either a state or a federal prison. There is a higher incarceration rate for state prisons, as might be expected.

Additionally, at the end of 2002, over 4.7 million adult men and women were under federal, state, or local probation or parole jurisdiction.[36] Some of this increase in the prison population has been attributed to the truth-in-sentencing policies that were adopted in many states and to other mandatory sentencing policies.

Table 12.2 shows the percentage of inmates in state and federal prison by their offense. This shows that most inmates in state facilities committed violent offenses, followed by property and drug offenses, with public order offenses being the least often committed offense. Most of the inmates in federal prison were convicted of drug offenses, followed by public order offenses and violent offenses, with property offenses being the offense for which offenders are least often arrested. This also shows that on the federal level, from 2007 to 2008, the number of inmates convicted for drug offenses and violent offenses decreased slightly, whereas convictions for public order and property offenses increased.

Table 12.3 shows the average time served by violent offenders in 2003–04. On average, the longest sentences were given to offenders who were convicted of sexual offenders, followed by murder and robbery. Long terms of probation were given for sexual abuse, murder, drug offenses and embezzlement.

TABLE 12.2 Percentage of Inmates in State and Federal Prisons by Type of Offense

State (2006)		Federal (2008)	
Violent	50.2%	Violent	8.5%
Property	20.9%	Property	6.1%
Public order	8.4%	Public order	32.5%
Drug	20.0%	Drug	52.15%
Other	0.5%	Other	2%

Source: William J. Sabol, Heather C. West, and Matthew Cooper, "Prisoners in 2008" (Washington, D.C.: U.S. Department of Justice, Office of Justice Programs, Bureau of Justice Statistics), December 2009; available at http://bjs.ojp.usdoj.gov/content/pub/pdf/p08.pdf.

TABLE 12.3 Average Sentence Length for Inmates Sentenced October 1, 2003–Sept 30, 2004

	Incarceration (Months)	Probation (Months)
All violent offenses	59.7	32.2
All Property Offenses	27.4	39.2
All Drug Offenses	83.6	41.0
Murder	111.20	42.0
Assault	44.8	32.7
Robbery	105.3	42.8
Sexual abuse	112.2	44.3
Embezzlement	16.0	40.1
Counterfeiting	24.1	38.4

Source: Mark Motivans, Steven K. Smith, "Compendium of Federal Justice Statistics, 2004" (www.ojp.usdoj.gov/bjs).

There is a great deal of evidence to support the idea that the people who are under the control of a correctional authority (federal, state, or local) are not an accurate representation of the nation's population. Most inmates in state correctional institutions tend to be young African-American and Hispanic males who are uneducated and unemployed or marginally employed in low-paying jobs.[37] African-American males make up 6 percent of the U.S. population, yet they represent nearly 50 percent of prison inmates.[38] Additionally, African-Americans tend to serve far longer sentences than whites for similar offenses. In the federal correctional system, sentences for African-Americans are 20 percent longer than those given to white defendants for similar crimes.[39] In the mid-1990s, about half of the prison inmates across the country were African-American, but they made up only 13 percent of the nation's population. One in fourteen adult black males was locked up in a prison or jail on any given day.[40]

There are other discrepancies between races. African-American males have an 18 percent chance of serving time in a juvenile or adult prison at some time in their lives, while white males have only a 3 percent chance.[41]

It has been argued that these racial disparities in arrests, jailing, and imprisonment have become only worse after 1980 and that they had little to do with changes in crime patterns.[42] It was argued that the increase in the number of African-American men and women who are under correctional control is due to arrests and convictions for possession and sale of drugs. It has been reported that African-Americans made up almost 40 percent of those arrested for drug-related violations. Based on these and other figures, it was estimated that, if the current rate of incarceration of African-Americans continues, 63 percent of all African-American men between the ages of 18 and 34 will be incarcerated, mainly for minor offenses, by 2020.[43]

CONGRESS AND CORRECTIONS

For many years, crime control was considered a state issue and dealt with primarily by the states. However, this has changed, and in recent years crime control and corrections has become an important part of the federal government's agenda. A quick review of some recent examples of congressional legislation dealing with corrections provides an insight into the types of bills the U.S. Congress passes.

In the 108th Congress (2003-04), a new law related to prison conditions (S 1435; PL 108-79) was proposed signed into law by President Bush. The new law, called the Prison Rape Elimination Act of 2003, required the Bureau of Justice to carry out an analysis of the incidence and effects of prison rape in federal, state, and local institutions. The bill would also provide for information, resources, recommendations and funding to protect inmates in the future from becoming victims of rape within a correctional facility. To do this, a new panel, called the Review Panel on Prison Rape, was created and given the mandate to collect information on the victims and perpetrators of prison rape. The panel members would then determine effective methods to deter prison rapes.

The members of the 110th Congressional session (2007-08) continued to debate bills related to inmates. One new law passed in this session (HR 7082: PL 110-428), the Inmate Tax Fraud Prevention Act, amended the Internal Revenue Code so that the Secretary of the Treasury would be permitted to disclose the tax return information of certain prisoners who have been identified as having filed false tax returns. Another new law this session (HR 3992; PL 100-416) was termed the Mentally Ill Offender Treatment and Crime Reduction Reauthorization and Improvement Act of 2008. This law approved funding for adult and juvenile mental health programs that revolved around the identification and treat mentally ill offenders. Provisions of the law provide for training officers and campus security so they are better able to respond to incidents involving mentally ill individuals, and provide for computerized systems to improve responses to people with special needs. The bill also establishes money for the use and expansion of mental health courts.

The 111th Congress (2009-10) acted on a proposal (HR 4218/ PL 111-115) that would prevent inmates, fugitive felons, and probation or parole violators to receive social security. The bill, called the No Social Security Benefits for Prisoners Act of 2009, was passed extremely quickly by the House and Senate. The bill was originally introduced into the House of Representatives on December 8, 2009, and signed by the president on December 15, 2009.

Other proposals have been introduced into the Congress during the 111th Congress but have yet to be passed. In January 2009, the Judiciary Committee in the Senate received a bill (S 41) that, if passed, would require inmates in federal institutions to work a fifty hours a week. The "Prisoner Opportunity, Work, and Education Requirement Act" (also called the POWER Act) would require federal inmates to not only work, but to engage in job training in addition to educational and like skills study. In the House of Representatives, the Crime, Terrorism and Homeland Security Subcommittee is considering a bill (HR 2450) that would require nonfederal prisons who are holding federal prisoners (under a contract with the federal government) to make the same information available to the public that federal prisons are required to make available. The members of the same subcommittee are considering another bill (HR 4328) that would give credit to an inmate who participated in educational, vocational, treatment, assigned work, or other developmental programs. The credit could be used toward lessening their sentence.[44]

CORRECTIONAL BUREAUCRACIES

Over the years, many federal bureaucracies or agencies have been established to oversee the corrections system across the nation. The primary federal agency that oversees the corrections system is the Bureau of Prisons, established in 1929. When this was done, the federal government, for the first time, ended its reliance on state prison facilities to maintain those who violated federal criminal laws.[45] Currently, the Bureau of Prisons is divided into six regions: mid-Atlantic, north-central, northeast, south-central, southeast, and western. The central office is located in Washington, D.C.

The Bureau of Prisons oversees many institutions that house a wide variety of offenders. These facilities are of different security levels so that inmates can be housed in the most appropriate manner. Security levels are based on such features as the presence of external patrols, gun towers, security barriers, or detection devices. They are also based on the type of housing found within the institution, internal security features, and the staff-to-inmate ratio. Each facility is placed in one of five groups: minimum, low, medium, high, and administrative.[46]

Part of the Bureau of Prisons is the National Institute of Corrections. Located within the U.S. Department of Justice (Federal Bureau of Prisons), it is headed by a director who is appointed by the U.S. attorney general. There is also a 16-member advisory board whose members are also appointed by the attorney general. The National Institute of Corrections was established to provide training, technical assistance, information services, and policy/program development assistance to federal, state, and local corrections agencies. It also provides leadership to influence correctional policies practices and operations nationwide in areas of emerging interest and concern to correctional executives and practitioners as well as public policymakers.[47]

A relatively new federal agency that deals with correctional issues is the White House Office of Faith-Based and Community Initiatives. This office, headed by Jim Towey, was established by President George W. Bush to strengthen and expand the role of faith-based and community organizations in providing solutions to various social problems. Some of its priority areas include at-risk youth and ex-offenders. It provides grant money, resources, and legal guidance.[48]

One more example is the U.S. Parole Commission, headed by Chairman Edward F. Reilly, Jr. The mission of the Parole Commission is to promote public safety and "strive for justice and fairness in the exercise of its authority to release and supervise offenders under its jurisdiction." The commission is responsible for granting or denying parole to federal offenders and making determinations regarding the conditions of parole supervision for these offenders.[49]

COURT DECISIONS AND CORRECTIONS

From 1787, when the courts were created, until the 1960s, the federal courts followed a "hands-off" doctrine regarding offenders and prison conditions related to inmate litigation.[50] They did not regulate how states treated their inmates. But eventually, using the doctrine of incorporation, the federal courts began to apply the Eighth Amendment to the U.S. Constitution to the behavior of state officials and began to provide for due process and equal protection to inmates. After World War II, federal courts also began to express a concern for the rights of minorities.[51] At this time, African-Americans made up the majority of the inmate population in many state prisons. As the civil rights movement grew, Black Muslim inmates, often assisted by lawyers with civil rights experience, began to successfully challenge correctional policies and procedures.[52] The "prisoners' rights movement," as it was called, thus grew out of the civil rights movement.

The traditional hands-off policy stopped in the Warren court, when the U.S. Supreme Court became more involved in prison reform. Since then, federal judges have in some cases ordered state officials to dramatically change the way they operate their prisons and jails and how they treat their inmates.[53] There have been many legal cases in recent years that have challenged both the treatment of inmates and the conditions within the prison facility, such as overcrowded conditions, double bunking of inmates in cells meant for one person, inadequate health care, and unsanitary conditions. There have been numerous court orders to change procedures within correctional facilities.

There were many key cases that helped provide humane treatment for inmates. For example, in *Jones v. Cunningham* (1963), the Supreme Court ruled that state prison inmates could employ a writ of habeas corpus not only to challenge the legality of their imprisonment but also to contest the conditions of their incarceration. Another early decision was *Cooper v. Pate* (1964), in which the Court established the general principle that prison inmates had constitutional rights. In this case, the justices held that prisoners possessed standing to sue in federal court under the Civil Rights Acts of 1871.[54]

The entire prison system in Arkansas was found to be unconstitutional and in violation of the prohibition on cruel and unusual punishment found in the Eighth Amendment to the Constitution. This was decided in *Holt v. Sarver* (1969). In this case, a U.S. district court found deficiencies in the facilities, safety, medical services, staff practices, and security of the institutions. Additionally, the court ruled that conditions within the prison, including violence at night in the prison dormitories, the robbery of new inmates of all their possessions, and forcing prisoners to pay bribes to get medicine, also constituted cruel and unusual punishment.[55]

In 1978, conditions within the Arkansas prison system once again came under federal court orders. This time the case was *Hutto v. Finney* (437 U.S. 678, decided in 1978), which involved the practice of punitive isolation whereby four to eleven inmates, some with hepatitis and venereal disease, were housed in a windowless cell measuring eight feet by ten feet. There was no furniture, and the inmates were forced to sleep on mattresses placed on the floor. There was only one toilet in the room, and this could be flushed only from outside the cell. There was only one source of water. Order was maintained by guards using nightsticks and mace. Inmates were given only one four-inch square of "grue," a pastry that provided around 1,000 calories per day. The Supreme Court justices once again found the conditions to be in violation of the Eighth Amendment guarantee against cruel and unusual punishment.[56]

The Texas prison system also came under court order. In 1980, the case of *Ruiz v. Estelle* went to the U.S. district court. This was a class-action lawsuit that alleged that the policies of the Texas Department of Corrections were unconstitutional and even a threat to the safety of the inmates. The district court judge presiding over the case ordered the Texas Department of Corrections to make dramatic changes in its prison system. The district court declared that state prison officials had to halt overcrowding of inmates (sometimes two or three in a cell meant for one), reduce the use of force by prison employees, double the number of correctional officers, retrain veteran officers, eliminate internal inmate control of prison activities, upgrade inmate health care, improve inmate disciplinary practices, liberalize good-time policies, revise the handling of inmate grievances, establish more elaborate hearing processes, revise the classification system, close or upgrade the prison hospital, and correct problems concerning fire and safety standards.

Texas responded by spending millions of dollars to improve the state's correctional facilities. But in 1987, U.S. District Court Judge William Wayne Justice ruled that these requirements had not been met by the Texas Department of Corrections and therefore that the state was in contempt of court. The judge ruled that if the problems were not remedied by April 1987, he would fine the state approximately $800,000 per day.[57]

The justices slowly began to define some concepts, such as due process. In *Wolff v. McDonald* (418 U.S. 539, 94 S. Ct. 2963, decided in 1974), the Supreme Court justices declared that inmates were entitled to a notice of the charges against them, a written statement of the evidence, the right to call witnesses and present evidence, and a hearing before an impartial disciplinary board. Litigants retained some noninmate rights. However, in *Meacham v. Fano* (427 U.S. 215, 96 S. Ct. 2532, decided in 1976), neither assignment to a particular prison nor transfer between prisons is subject to any sort of constitutional requirement of due process. Then, in 1983, the Court decided *Hewitt v. Helms* (459 U.S. 460, 103 S. Ct. 864), in which the justices decided that prison administrators were not required to give an inmate a full-blown adversarial review of the facts before placing him or her in administrative segregation. Mississippi and Oklahoma were also found to be similarly deficient and under court orders.[58]

During the 1970s, activists concerned about the treatment of inmates banded together and formed the National Prison Project. Through this organization, they began to fight inhumane prison conditions across the nation. By the end of 1983, eight states had their prison systems declared unconstitutional; twenty-two had facilities operating either under a court order or consent decree, and nine others were engaged in litigation.[59] By 1995, thirty-nine states were under court order to improve prison conditions. Since then, prisoners have used the courts to win rights to practice religion, to correspond with people outside the prison, and to receive books and magazines.[60]

There are many other cases that demonstrate the expansion of inmate rights. The federal government, even today, continues to oversee conditions within state correctional facilities. In fact, filings by state prisoners increased in the federal courts over 120 percent between 1970 and 1983. In fact, as of July 21, 1995, all state prisons in Louisiana were under federal court supervision. Attorneys for inmates successfully argued that "the Department of Public Safety and Corrections did not properly manage four critical areas: prison overcrowding, violence, inmate programming, and medical services."[61] Because of the involvement of the courts, the nature of correctional policy has changed. The courts now provide an oversight function to guarantee that inmates are provided basic human rights.

The intrusion of federal courts into state correctional policy is controversial, particularly when they have taken over full operating responsibility or ordered increased state and local expenditures for prisons. Important questions concerning the proper division of power between the national government and the state governments have been raised, as have questions about the competence of federal court officials to run state prison systems. But some states have operated prisons under less-than-humane conditions.[62]

Over the past few years, hundreds if not thousands of cases involving prison conditions and the treatment of inmates have been litigated.[63] However, recent court decisions are reversing that trend, as are congressional actions. Proposals to restrict prisoner lawsuits were part of the "Contract with America" that many Republicans supported in 1994. At that time, the Republicans, who had gained the majority in Congress, wanted to reform prisoner lawsuits on the argument that many of them were frivolous and cost millions of dollars for the states to litigate. Two senators in particular, Orrin Hatch (R-Utah) and Spencer Abraham (R-Mich.), were also concerned about excessive prisoner lawsuits.[64]

In response, the Prison Litigation Reform Act was proposed in Congress as a means to curtail prisoner lawsuits and in turn return power for prisoner management to the states. It was an attempt by the Republican Congress to reduce the number of lawsuits filed by both federal and state inmates. President Clinton signed the bill on April 26, 1996.

The new legislation requires that inmates use all administrative remedies before filing suit under federal civil rights laws. Additionally, no prisoner may file suit if on three or more prior occasions the action or appeal was dismissed on the grounds that it was frivolous or malicious or failed to state a claim on which relief may be granted unless the prisoner is in immediate physical danger. The new law also imposes restrictions on the ability of inmates to proceed in the manner of a pauper (which means that they do not have to pay a filing fee). The law also makes it easier for state and local governments to terminate or modify consent decrees and court orders that govern conditions in federal and state prisons and local jails.[65]

CORRECTIONS AND THE POLICY PROCESS

The corrections agencies have an influential role in all aspects of the policy process, from start to finish. They operate within the federal, state, and local political environment and are concerned about improving the policy toward correctional programs and the treatment of inmates involved in those programs. The legislation may also affect their work environment and their safety.

Problem Identification

Since inmates rarely have the opportunity to meet with politicians and discuss their concerns, they must rely on others who are sympathetic to their causes. This can be corrections agencies or interest groups that are aware of problems and play a role in helping to identify problems within corrections systems that need attention. All these groups become involved in the problem identification stage of the policy process and help convey problems to legislators. Such problems include those regarding inmates as well as work environments to support the employees of correctional programs. Thus, they are concerned with prisoner rights issues as well as the safety of the employees who are part of the corrections systems.

Problems are sometimes identified by the many corrections bureaucracies and agencies that have been established to deal with these issues at all levels of government. Officials within the Bureau of Prisons often help identify problems such as conditions within the prisons or the treatment of the inmates. They may provide guidelines to states concerning conditions within an institution.

Problems can also be identified by interest groups that have formed around the concerns of inmates. An example of this is the American Civil Liberties Union (ACLU), which often gets involved in correctional issues. The ACLU has a division called the National Prison Project (NPP), which originated in 1972 after the Attica prison riot. The NPP's purpose is to protect the adult and juvenile offenders' Eighth Amendment rights against cruel and unusual punishment. The NPP has frequently become involved in prison reform litigation, and it often takes a public position on different correctional issues in order to influence policymaking. The attorneys for the NPP often draft model legislation to help advise state legislatures about alternatives to incarceration. Finally, the NPP also serves as a resource center for the law governing the policies of corrections. In recent years, the NPP has become involved in such issues as reducing incarceration, improving the conditions of confinement, placing an emphasis on rehabilitation and treatment programs, halting the transfer of child offenders to adult facilities, giving some attention to the concerns of female prisoners, decriminalizing mental illness, and eliminating private prisons.[66]

Another interest group that is sometimes at odds with the ACLU is the American Jail Association. It is an organization designed to support the employees who operate and are employed in local jails across the country.[67]

Often a problem will be identified as the result of a triggering event, such as a riot or other prison disturbance. For example, the Attica uprising in New York resulted in major changes in the administration of prisons there and elsewhere and the rights given to the inmates. This trigger event helps bring issues to light, such as overcrowding, religious rights, and other inmate rights issues. These types of events sometimes force legislators to recognize a problem.

Agenda Setting

Correctional agencies, interest groups, and the general public all help set the political agenda by convincing legislators and staff of relevant issues or problems that need attention. Again, since the majority of people involved in the corrections systems as inmates are not able to convey their issues to elected officials in Washington, other groups must do that on their behalf. Each of these actors can provide information to legislators indicating the extent of the problem and convince them that some action is needed. The key is to convince a legislator or staff member that the problem is significant enough to warrant the attention of the legislative body.

One group that consistently helps set the political agenda in criminal justice is the ACLU. In recent years, the ACLU gave its support to the Prison Rape Reduction Act (S 2619) but noted that more needed to be done to solve the problem. The bill would establish a commission to study the extent of prison rape and its long-term effects.[68] The organization also urged opposition to the Federal Prison Industries Competition Contracting Act of 2001 (HR 1577), a bill that would end prison employment programs. The ACLU claimed that prison industries are key in reducing recidivism, easing inmates' reentry into society after release, and providing some measure of future prospects to unskilled and undereducated inmates.[69]

Sometimes, the agenda reflects the public's opinions about crime and punishment rather than reality. Polls continue to show that the public is concerned about crime and tends to favor conservative policies, such as the death penalty and periods of long incarceration. Politicians pick up on this and, as representatives of their constituents, place more conservative, "get-tough" policies on the agenda.

Policy Formulation

Interest groups and bureaucracies concerned about criminal justice issues get involved in the policy formulation aspect of the policy process. Obviously, each group has a certain perspective on the issues and their own ideas about the best way to solve the problem. Thus, they get involved to convince legislators to act in a certain way.

Interest groups and bureaucracies use the same techniques in attempting to have an effect on the final policy. They do this by meeting with legislators and staff often to discuss the problem and lobby them for a potential solution. They try to convince them to vote a particular way. The groups also try to influence policy by helping legislators and their staff write proposals for legislation that reflects their perspective about the problem and the best solution. Furthermore, the interest groups may provide information to the legislators through hearings in committees and subcommittees.

One interest group that is involved in attempting to influence legislators on corrections issues is the AFSCME Corrections United, an organization of the American Federation of State, County, and Municipal Employees (AFSCME). This is because many prison guards and corrections officers are unionized and represented by AFSCME. The organization fights for better pay and benefits as well as safer working conditions for corrections officers and other employees in the field of corrections.[70]

Program Implementation

Correctional agencies at the federal, state, and local levels are the ones responsible for implementing policies passed by Congress. On the federal level, the Bureau of Prisons oversees the implementation of correctional services, whereas each state has created an agency to do this. Such agencies implement programs within prisons as well as those outside prisons (e.g., community corrections) for men, women, and juveniles. To this extent, they have a lot of power to define terms, services, and clients that may be left undefined by Congress. The bureaucracies must respond to congressional mandates but do so to varying degrees. Some bureaucrats will follow the mandates more closely than others. They must also meet standards set by the courts.

Program Evaluation and Reassessment

Correctional agencies must evaluate their programs to determine if they work and if they are cost efficient (how much the program costs). This can be done by the agency itself or by an outside agency that is hired to evaluate a program.

It is often difficult to determine if a program worked, especially in a social science such as criminal justice. There are a host of other factors that can influence a person's behavior, so determining if a program caused a behavioral change is difficult. To say with certainty that "program X caused behavioral change Y" (referred to as causality) is tenuous. Sometimes the methodological designs used by researchers to determine if a program worked can be complicated and at other times much simpler. Sometimes two studies on the same program or policy can show opposite results. A classic example concerns studies done on capital punishment. Some studies show that the death penalty deters crime, while others show that it does not.[71]

Determining the cost effectiveness of a program is just as difficult. What exactly is "cost effective"? This definition will differ from person to person. Although researchers can complete a cost-benefit analysis on each program implemented in criminal justice and determine exactly what the costs and benefits of a program were, it sometimes requires that a monetary cost be applied to elements that cannot be sold in the market. For example, how does one put a monetary value on a human life? Or on the value of justice? There are essential elements to criminal justice programs that cannot be addressed simply through monetary means. Additionally, even if a program is determined to be cheaper, it does not necessarily mean it is better at achieving the goals of the system.

One area where issues surrounding the implementation costs of a program helped guide policy choices is private prisons. Some legislatures decided that one way to deal with a dwindling budget for corrections (at the same time the public demands for more incarceration) was to use private prisons. It was anticipated that they would have lower construction costs as well as lower administrative costs. However, there is little evidence of a reduction in costs and even some evidence of increased administrative problems.[72]

These evaluations are sometimes initiated by Congress or a state legislature. They are looking for effectiveness as well as waste and inefficiency. If a program is found to be effective, the legislators may continue to fund it with high appropriations. Additionally, the program might be put into effect in other jurisdictions or expanded to other prisons or inmate populations.

However, if the analysis shows waste and inefficiency, then legislators are faced with choosing the fate of that program. They may not choose to re-fund the program, or they may put the funding into other programs. They may simply choose to reorganize or restructure the program in an attempt to improve it.

ISSUES FACING CORRECTIONAL ADMINISTRATORS

There are many issues that correctional administrators must face on a day-to-day basis. These are areas in which a policy has been made by a legislative body and then implemented by a bureaucracy. Some of these are described in the following sections.

Overcrowding

Many state correctional facilities are dealing with overcrowded institutions, meaning that a correctional facility is holding more inmates than it has capacity. The effects of overcrowding can lead to violence within the institution (both inmate to inmate and inmate to staff), health problems (for both inmates and staff), stress-related injuries (for both inmates and staff), prison disciplinary problems, and even recidivism. Box 12.2 shows the extent of prison overcrowding across the nation. The figures indicate the percentage overcapacity of state prisons in 2002. The federal prisons are at 133 percent of capacity, and states range from 201 percent overcapacity in

---

BOX 12.2
Overcapacity Percentages of State Prisons, 2008 (Highest/Lowest)

Alabama	98/188%	Montana	93/93%
Alaska	111/116%	Nebraska	113/141%
Arizona	79/88%	Nevada	86/118%
Arkansas	95/100%	New Hampshire	98/133%
California	106/204%	New Jersey	96/132%
Colorado	120/137%	New Mexico	48/52%
Connecticut	N/A	New York	99/105%
Delaware	123/167%	North Carolina	100/116%
Florida	88/88%	North Dakota	132/139%
Georgia	103/103%	Ohio	127/127%
Hawaii	96/137%	Oklahoma	94/94%
Idaho	108/113%	Oregon	94/94%
Illinois	133/150%	Pennsylvania	101/101%
Indiana	88/88%	Rhode Island	88/93%
Iowa	64/64%	South Carolina	98/98%
Kansas	92/92%	South Dakota	97/97%
Kentucky	93/95%	Tennessee	70/71%
Louisiana	114/115%	Texas	85/87%
Maine	109/109%	Utah	75/77%
Maryland	97/97%	Vermont	80/101%
Massachusetts	140/140%	Virginia	93/93%
Michigan	97/97%	Washington	111/125%
Minnesota	101/101%	West Virginia	98/118%
Mississippi	75/75%	Wisconsin	125/125%
Missouri	96/96%	Wyoming	75/80%

Source: William J. Sabol, Heather C. West, Matthew Cooper, "Prisoners in 2008" (December 20009) Washington, D.C.: U.S. Department of Justice, Office of Justice Programs, Bureau of Justice Statistics, http://bjs.ojp.usdoj.gov/content/pub/pdf/p08.

Alabama to 71 percent overcapacity in Idaho. As a response to the problem, states have implemented different methods to divert convicted offenders from prison. Some states have built new prisons or have increased the size of the current prisons by changing existing facilities, such as converting a gymnasium into a dormitory. Still other states have turned to diversion programs (that divert offenders from prison), probation, intensive probation, house arrest, electronic monitoring, boot camps, house arrest, and shock probation or split sentences to reduce prison populations. Community corrections, or the use of early release of inmates (sometimes called "emergency release"), have also been used to reduce populations. Despite these changes, mandatory sentencing laws, truth-in-sentencing laws, and three-strikes policies have resulted in the continued increase of prison populations.

A special three-judge panel ruled that reducing California's prison population by about 40,000 inmates over two years was necessary to improve medical and health care of the inmates. Schwarzenegger proposed sending inmates to private prisons, building additional prisons and sending criminals convicted of drug possession, receiving stolen property, theft, and check fraud to county jails.[73] In 2009, the Supreme Court rejected California's challenge to a preliminary court order forcing the state to reduce its prison population. The justices turned down California's request to delay a federal court order requiring the state to present a plan to reduce the population of its prisons by 40,000. The Court refused to extend a deadline for telling a special three-judge panel how the state will reduce its prison population by about 25 percent over two years.

Private Prisons

Because of issues of overcrowding and financial issues, many state policymakers are turning to private prisons to help house inmates and provide correctional needs for inmates. This involves turning to the private sector to provide care and treatment for inmates.[74] Private prisons can be defined as "a contract process that shifts public functions, responsibilities, and capital assets, in whole or in part, from the public to the private sector."[75] Or, it can be the "government's use of the private sector (both for-profit and not-for-profit) to deliver public policies and improve the content and implementation of public programs."[76] In 2001, it was estimated that 5.3 percent of sentenced, adult population were incarcerated in private prisons.[77] By the end of 2008, this number had increased to 8 percent.[78]

Based in Nashville, Tennessee, the Corrections Corporation of America (CCA) is the nation's largest provider of private prisons.[79] Other companies that provide private prison services are Wackenhut Corrections Corporation; Management and Training Corporation; Cornell Corrections, Inc.; Correctional Services Corporation; McLoud Correctional Services, LLC; Marantha Production Company, LLC; Alternative Programs, Inc.; Dominion Management; and CiviGenics, Inc.[80]

The privatization of prisons can take many forms. One of the most common of those is when specific services are contracted out.[81] For example, a state may enter into a contract with a private company (or hire a private firm) to provide government services, such as mental health and substance abuse counseling to inmates or educational services and job training/placement services.[82] Or, a state may contract out for community residential services, such as halfway houses, drug treatment facilities, and alcohol treatment programs. In these cases, private contractors may provide for the management of inmates on a per diem basis. In other cases, a private contractor might provide direct food or laundry services or medical and dental care.[83] A more radical approach is when the government transfers ownership of assets and management responsibilities to the private sector, leaving the government with a limited or nonexistent role in the financial support, management, and oversight of the sold asset.[84] In this case, the states have chosen to allow private companies to oversee the complete operation of a facility. These companies assume total control over the inmate population.[85]

In some states, prison privatization may be a response to recent court orders demanding an improvement of living conditions and a reduction of overcrowding.[86] Private prisons may be able to respond more quickly to court orders because private prisons can be constructed more quickly than state prisons since they do not have all the state requirements for bidding and contractors and do not need a bond issue or voter approval.

There are other benefits to private prisons. Private corporations can provide correctional services in a more cost-effective manner than the public sector, and some short-term savings can be realized.[87] The state relies on private sector competition to ensure that the good or service is delivered at the lowest possible cost and at a high quality.[88] In some cases, private contractors can be more cost efficient than the public sector because they have an incentive to seek new and innovative approaches to reducing the cost of the service. If they do not keep costs low while at the same time maintaining the quality of the service, they could lose any contracts. There is no similar incentive in the public sector.[89] There may also be an opportunity for experimenting with new policy ideas and possibly untapped expertise in providing care and treatment of inmates.[90] The government can hire specialists and people with other talents without necessarily adhering to the affirmative action requirements.[91] Yet others argue that private industry cannot do a worse job than is presently being done by state and local agencies.[92] Additionally, political debts can be paid off with private prisons.[93]

Another benefit to private prisons is that union employees (with generous salaries and benefits) are replaced by nonunion employees who do not require as much training and salary.[94] Critics also argue that the need to lower the costs of the services will require that the contractor cut corners by hiring inexperienced and unqualified personnel. The administrators in private prisons find ways to keep people inside the institution because they profit from keeping people there, rather than finding ways to return them to their communities. In essence, overcrowding and reduced services mean higher profits. There are allegations of higher violence because of the overcrowding and untrained staff. One study of private prisons actually found a greater number of inmate-on-inmate assaults at private than at public prisons and that the rates of staff assaults, riots, fires and other disturbances were comparable.[95] Unfortunately, since there is not as much oversight by the state, there is a serious potential for abuse directed against an imprisoned labor force.

Others would argue that the privatization of prisons leads to more problems within the correctional facility and therefore that the state should not give up this responsibility. They argue that holding, punishing, and/or treating offenders is—and should remain—a state responsibility and that state officials should not turn over that responsibility to private corporations. Corrections should not be a "for-profit" industry. They point out that there seem to be many problems associated with private prisons. One study found that privately operated prisons seem to have more systemic problems in maintaining their facilities. They found more escapes and drug use and higher staff turnover. Overall, the study concludes that there were serious problems with privately operated prisons.[96]

Despite these issues, private prisons are being used by the majority of states in an effort to reduce overcrowding and cost issues. Whether these prisons remain a popular option to reach these goals remains to be seen.

Inmate Labor

The use of inmates in prison industries has long been a controversial policy used by some prison administrators for a variety of reasons. Allowing inmates to participate in the program can teach them a trade to help them become less prone to committing additional crimes once released. The programs also help reduce "idle time" of inmates, thus reducing violence within the prison. Finally, prison industries can help make money for the institution as it sells its products.

The Federal Prison Industries was created by President Franklin D. Roosevelt in December 1934 in Executive Order 6917. This established a corporation to oversee the manner and extent of prison industries to be implemented in correctional facilities across the nation.[97] Congress also passed legislation that same year to help fund UNICOR, a wholly owned government corporation responsible for the operation of the industries within the federal prisons. UNICOR became heavily involved in the production of military equipment during World War II. In fact, several prison industries operated more than one shift per day and seven days a week during the war.[98]

Early prison industries focused on several labor-intensive types of industries. However, because of public outcry about the program, prison industries remained stagnant from the 1940s through the early 1970s. Members of the general public argued that prison industries displaced civilian jobs. They were also accused of mistreating offenders with low wages and low compensation. There were other issues surrounding inmate safety and security. The public still does not always support prison industries programs. Because of this, in 1985, Chief Justice Warren Burger made many speeches and wrote an article called "Prison Industries: Turning Warehouses into Factories with Fences." It helped promote public acceptance of the prison industries program, demonstrating the potential effectiveness of programs for inmates.

In 1979, Congress removed some of the barriers to interstate shipment of prison-made goods. Called the Private Sector Prison Industry Enhancement Certification Program, it permitted certified states to sell goods made by prisoners on the open market. The program was revised in 1984 to increase the number of certified states that could take part.

Today, UNICOR provides products to federal agencies at fair market prices. It develops products that minimize competition with private-sector industry and labor. In 1995, UNICOR earned a profit of more than $46 million on $459 million in sales. This profit was possible because of the low wages given to the inmates, which ranged from 23 cents to $1.15 an hour.[99] It seems as if many prisoners are anxious to work, whatever the job or pay, because it is better than doing nothing. In addition, the small amount of cash or savings is better than none at all. The prison industries also save the state money. Prisoners in Delaware helped save the state $25 million by working for 15 cents an hour constructing a new prison.[100]

Today, states have a variety of prison industry programs. Some states have agricultural programs, carpentry, plumbing, electrical, bricklaying, cement work, welding, painting, surveying programs, and manufacturing programs. They also do prison maintenance, food service, and laundry within the prison. They make office furniture, dormitory furniture, metal storage cabinets, and general office supplies. Some areas have used prison labor to build new prisons and to work on other construction projects. In other states, inmates do public works projects.

In 2009, New York voters were asked to consider allowing inmates to voluntarily perform work for nonprofit organizations in Proposal 2. Before the proposal, the state Constitution said that "no person in any prison . . . shall be required or allowed to work." In 2007, the state of Washington had a measure on the ballot to authorize prison labor programs and it passed by 60.71 percent of the vote.

Prison labor became an issue once again when the Department of Corrections in Kansas closed a minimum security unit, which meant that the state lost thousands of hours of inmate labor they used for park maintenance, construction and landfill maintenance.[101]

Public opinion for prison labor was changed in Florida, when the Sheriff presented new inmate labor programs that were being used to save taxpayers' dollars. State officials argued that the work programs were designed to raise the work ethic of selected inmates and give them a productive way to spend their sentences. In that state, inmates poured concrete slabs, put in plumbing and electrical systems, and erected structures needed for all programs. The state has also developed a Swine program that processes pork products; a cattle program; and an ornamental plant program for landscaping and horticulture training for inmates.[102] Many inmates who participate in this program receive a sense of achievement and have lower recidivism.

In another county in Florida, the sheriff announced that inmate labor saved over $6,000 in one month. The inmates removed seats from lecture halls, pulled trees, leveled mulch and pressure washed public buildings; they removed weeds and cut overgrowth, trimmed bushes and trees, and set up tents, tables and chairs, and hung banners for special events.[103]

Inmate labor has been under consideration in other places as well. Charlottesville, Virginia considered using inmate labor to save money on labor costs for the city. It was proposed that nonviolent offenders on work release programs be used for street cleaning.[104] Officials in Huston, Texas, were considering a similar program.[105]

STATE CORRECTIONS

On the state level, the corrections agencies house convicted offenders who violate state laws, including murder, rape, robbery, drunk driving, and domestic violence. Over the years, states have developed their own prison systems, so they vary from one state to another. The states provide for any treatment and/or education programs for inmates within the facilities. All states have developed not only the traditional prison systems to hold serious offenders but also alternatives to prisons for less serious offenders. These can include community alternatives, such as furloughs. State correctional programs are funded and administered by the individual states with additional funding provided by the federal government.

The correctional facilities administered by federal and state agencies can be further divided by the security level of the institution. These are maximum-, medium-, and minimum-security facilities. Minimum-security facilities assume that the inmates housed there are not likely to try to escape and would probably not commit major felonies even if they did escape. Maximum-security institutions usually hold individuals who have been convicted of the most serious crimes against persons and property. In those states that have it, the death penalty may be carried out within this institution. Medium-security institutions fall somewhere in between these two. A prisoner would find it difficult to escape, but at the same time, rehabilitation programs are provided to inmates with the hope that these inmates will be provided skills to live a productive, crime-free life after release from the institution.

In recent years, a new category of prison has emerged. These have been called "supermax" prisons, such as California's Pelican Bay, which opened in 1979. Supermax prisons are permanent lockdown facilities where inmates are housed in windowless cells twenty-three hours a day and are not allowed to communicate with other prisoners. The inmates eat, sleep, and live their entire lives alone in a cell. Each cell has a concrete slab for a bed, an immobile concrete stool, and a small concrete writing platform. There is no congregate exercise, job program, or religious service. All reading materials are strictly censored, and educational programs are severely restricted if

BOX 12.3

Incarceration Rate by State: Inmates in State or Federal Prison with a Sentence of More Than 1 Year, 2008 (per 100,000 Residents)

Alabama	634	Montana	368
Alaska	430	Nebraska	247
Arizona	567	Nevada	486
Arkansas	511	New Hampshire	220
California	467	New Jersey	298
Colorado	467	New Mexico	316
Connecticut	407	New York	307
Delaware	463	North Carolina	368
Florida	557	North Dakota	225
Georgia	540	Ohio	449
Hawaii	332	Oklahoma	661
Idaho	474	Oregon	371
Illinois	351	Pennsylvania	393
Indiana	442	Rhode Island	240
Iowa	291	South Carolina	519
Kansas	303	South Dakota	412
Kentucky	492	Tennessee	436
Louisiana	853	Texas	639
Maine	151	Utah	232
Maryland	403	Vermont	260
Massachusetts	218	Virginia	489
Michigan	488	Washington	272
Minnesota	179	West Virginia	331
Mississippi	735	Wisconsin	374
Missouri	509	Wyoming	387

Source: William J. Sabol, Heather C. West, Matthew Cooper, "Prisoners in 2008" (December 2009) Washington, D.C.: U.S. Department of Justice, Office of Justice Programs, Bureau of Justice Statistics, http://bjs.ojp.usdoj.gov/content/pub/pdf/p08.

allowed at all. Visits by family members are restricted. The prisoners have little face-to-face contact with other people, even guards. The guards monitor the inmates from control booths that have video cameras. The prison administration attempts to minimize any human contact and maximize sensory deprivation.[106]

The number of inmates in state prisons varies dramatically from one state to the next. As Box 12.3 shows, the state with the highest incarceration rate (inmates per 100,000 people) is Louisiana, with a rate of 853. The state with the lowest rate is Maine, with an imprisonment rate of 151.

The federal government can impact the state systems through grant programs. For example, the U.S. Department of Justice's Violent Offender Incarceration/Truth in Sentencing Incentive Grant Program gives grants to states interested in building or expanding correctional facilities if they can guarantee that they will implement truth-in-sentencing laws requiring violent offenders to serve a substantial portion of their sentences. Approximately $10 billion has been authorized by this program through fiscal year 2000.[107]

LOCAL CORRECTIONS

Correctional facilities are also administered by local government agencies, typically by a county-level agency. These facilities usually hold the least serious offenders convicted of misdemeanor offenses (for which the sentence is a short term of one year or less) or those charged with an offense and awaiting arraignment, trial, or sentencing. In these cases, the jail serves as a pretrial detention center. Jails may also hold probation, parole, and bail-bond violators and absconders or may temporarily hold juveniles pending their transfer to juvenile authorities. At times, jails are responsible

---

BOX 12.4
Community-Based Correctional Options

Probation

This option allows those convicted of crimes to live in the community as long as they abide by certain restrictions and conditions in lieu of incarceration. If they violate the conditions of their probation, then the offender may be required to return to prison.

Parole

This option releases inmates from prison so they are allowed to live and work in the community but under certain restrictions, such as reporting to a parole officer on a regular basis, either face to face or by telephone. Parolees may not be allowed to drink, drive a car, change jobs, move, or marry without permission. A violation of parole may mean a return to prison.

Work Release

If a judge determines that a convicted criminal is not likely to be a future danger to society, the judge may allow the individual to work regular hours at a job and then to spend the rest of the time, including evenings and weekends, in jail.

Electronic House Detention

This technology allows for using the home or apartment of a convict as a type of prison. A judge may order an individual to wear an electronic bracelet or anklet that emits signals to a receiver in the home. Should the receiver fail to get the signals, it automatically dials a central computer and notifies law enforcement officials. The receiver can be programmed to allow the individual to keep a work schedule, go to classes, or participate in a treatment program.

Boot Camps

These programs are often used for juvenile offenders. They are based on military boot camps for new members of the military and are designed to teach discipline. The daily schedule is intense and rigorous and includes demanding physical activity as well as psychological, drug, and alcohol counseling.

Intensive Sanctions (Intensive Supervision Programs)

Here, probation officers see offenders almost daily and assign a heavier set of requirements to the offender than is usually associated with probation or parole. Most offenders are required to work full time, pay restitution to victims, be in treatment or vocational training programs, and provide community service.

for holding mentally ill persons pending their movement to appropriate health facilities (or even individuals for the military) for protective custody, for contempt, and for the courts as witnesses.

Jails are administered by elected county sheriffs who may have a background in law enforcement but not necessarily in prison administration or corrections. Most jails are administered locally with funding coming from local budgets that are partially funded by state allocations. Federal funding also exists for local facilities. However, in some states (including Alaska, Connecticut, Delaware, Hawaii, Rhode Island, and Vermont), the jails are administered by state officials rather than by county sheriffs.[108] In a few places, the jails are administered by a specific local department devoted to corrections.

Most jurisdictions have also developed a system of community-based correctional programs that are most often administered on the local level (typically by the county) but partially funded by states. There are numerous community-based programs. The major ones are listed in Box 12.4.

Conclusion

The corrections systems attempt to keep society safe from harm by incarcerating dangerous offenders and/or rehabilitating offenders who have that potential. Like other elements in the criminal justice system, the actors in the correctional field are not immune to the political forces around them. The correctional actors have become active in the policy process, having a potentially dramatic impact on the policies that are proposed and passed and how they are implemented.

Notes

1. Robert M. Freeman, *Correctional Organization and Management* (Boston: Butterworth-Heinemann, 1999), p. 32.
2. Ibid.
3. George F. Cole, *Criminal Justice: Law and Politics* (Monterey, Calif.: Brooks/Cole, 1984), pp. 314–15.
4. Ibid.
5. Alexander C. Lichtenstein and Michael A. Kroll, "The Fortress Economy: The Economic Role of the U.S. Prison System," in *Criminal Injustice: Confronting the Prison Crisis*, ed. Elihu Rosenblatt (Boston: South End Press, 1996), pp. 16–39, at 17.
6. Samuel Walker, "Putting Justice Back into Criminal Justice," in *The Criminal Justice System: Politics and Policies*, ed. George F. Cole and Marc G. Gertz (Belmont, Calif.: West/Wadsworth, 1998b), p. 493.
7. Francis A. Allen, *The Decline of the Rehabilitative Ideal* (New Haven, Conn.: Yale University Press, 1981), p. 3.
8. L. Goodstein and J. Hepburn, *Determinate Sentencing and Imprisonment: A Failure of Reform* (Cincinnati: Anderson, 1985).
9. Cole, *Criminal Justice*, pp. 316–17.
10. James Austin and John Irwin, *It's about Time: America's Imprisonment Binge* (Belmont, Calif.: Wadsworth, 2001), p. xiii.
11. Curtis R. Blakely and Vic W. Bumphus, "American Criminal Justice Philosophy: What's Old-What's New?" *Federal Probation* 63 (1, 1999): 62–66, at 64; P. Hahn, *Emerging Criminal Justice: Three Pillars for Proactive Justice System* (Thousand Oaks, Calif.: Sage, 1998); G. Bazemore and M. Umbreit, *Balanced and Restorative Justice for Juveniles: A Framework for Juvenile Justice in the 21st Century* (Washington, D.C.: U.S. Department of Justice, Office of Juvenile Justice and Delinquency Prevention, 1997).
12. Marc Mauer, *Race to Incarcerate* (New York: New Press, 1999), p. 3; M. P. Roth, *Crime and Punishment: A History of the Criminal Justice System* (Belmont, Calif.: Wadsworth, 2005).
13. Mauer, *Race to Incarcerate*, p. 4.
14. Roth, *Crime and Punishment*.
15. John J. Harrigan and David C. Nice, *Politics and Policy in States and Communities* (New York: Pearson, 2004), p. 288.

16. Freeman, *Correctional Organization and Management*.

17. Harrigan and Nice, *Politics and Policy in States and Communities*, p. 288.

18. Allen, *The Decline of the Rehabilitative Ideal*, p. 2; Roth, *Crime and Punishment*.

19. Allen, *The Decline of the Rehabilitative Ideal*, p. 5.

20. Walker, *Popular Justice*, p. 205.

21. Elliott Currie, *Confronting Crime: An American Challenge* (New York: Pantheon, 1985); Allen, *The Decline of the Rehabilitative Ideal*.

22. Allen, *The Decline of the Rehabilitative Ideal*, p. 51.

23. Harrigan and Nice, *Politics and Policy in States and Communities*, p. 288.

24. Allen, *The Decline of the Rehabilitative Ideal*, p. 57.

25. Harrigan and Nice, *Politics and Policy in States and Communities*, p. 288.

26. Robert Martinson, "What Works? Questions and Answers about Prison Reform," *The Public Interest* 35 (1975): 22–54.

27. Walker, *Popular Justice*, p. 211.

28. Ibid., p. 210.

29. Walker, "Putting Justice Back into Criminal Justice," p. 494.

30. Freeman, *Correctional Organization and Management*, p. 83.

31. Alfred Blumstein, "Interaction of Criminological Research and Public Policy," *Journal of Quantitative Criminology* 12 (4, 1997): 349–61.

32. Freeman, *Correctional Organization and Management*, pp. 82–83.

33. Mauer, *Race to Incarcerate*, p. 4.

34. Federal Bureau of Prisons, "Quick Facts" (2010), available online at http://www.bop.gov/about/facts.jsp.

35. Paige M. Harrison and Allen J. Beck, "Prisoners In 2002" (revised 8/27/2003), Washington, D.C.: U.S. Department of Justice, Office of Justice Programs.

36. www.ojp.usdoj.gov/bjs/pandp.htm.

37. Austin and Irwin, *It's about Time*, p. 3.

38. Lichtenstein and Kroll, "The Fortress Economy," p. 20.

39. Ibid., p. 21.

40. Mauer, *Race to Incarcerate*, p. 124.

41. Lichtenstein and Kroll, "The Fortress Economy," p. 21.

42. Michael Tonry, "Racial Politics, Racial Disparities, and the War on Crime," *Crime and Delinquency* 40 (4, 1994): 475–94.

43. Chambliss, *Power, Politics and Crime*, p. 79.

44. More information on these bills is available at http://thomas.loc.gov.

45. Herbert Johnson, *History of Criminal Justice* (Cincinnati: Anderson, 1988), p. 231.

46. www.bop.gov.

47. www.nicic.org.

48. www.whitehouse.gov/government/fbci/mission.html.

49. www.usdoj.gov/uspc/mission.htm.

50. Freeman, *Correctional Organization and Management*, p. 165; A. J. Bronstein, "Prisoners and Their Endangered Rights," *Prison Journal* 65 (1, 1985): 3–17.

51. Freeman, *Correctional Organization and Management*, p. 165.

52. Ibid.

53. Bradley Chilton, *Prisons under the Gavel: The Federal Takeover of Georgia Prisons* (Columbus: Ohio State University Press, 1991).

54. W. A. Taggart, "Redefining the Power of the Federal Judiciary: The Impact of Court-Ordered Prison Reform on State Expenditures for Corrections," *Law and Society Review* 23 (2, 1989): 501–31.

55. Walker, *Popular Justice*, p. 185.

56. Johnson, *History of Criminal Justice*, p. 282.

57. Ann O'M. Bowman and Richard C. Kearney, *State and Local Government* (Boston: Houghton Mifflin, 1993).

58. Taggart, "Redefining the Power of the Federal Judiciary."

59. Ibid.

60. Walker, *Popular Justice*, p. 187.

61. Freeman, *Correctional Organization and Management*, p. 242.

62. For two instructive state histories, see C. B. Hopper, "The Impact of Litigation on Mississippi's Prison System," *Prison Journal* 65 (1, 1985): 54–63, and G. Larry Mays and W. A. Taggart, "The Impact of Litigation on Changing New Mexico Prison Conditions," *Prison Journal* 65 (1, 1985): 38–53. For a focused discussion of Eighth Amendment litigation, see B. L. Ingraham and C. F. Wellford, "The Totality of Conditions Test in Eighth-Amendment Litigation," in *America's Correctional Crisis*, ed. S. D. Gottfredson and S. McConville (New York: Greenwood Press, 1987), pp. 13–36.

63. John A. Fliter, *Prisoners' Rights: The Supreme Court and Evolving Standards of Decency* (Westport, Conn.: Greenwood Press, 2001), p. xix.

64. Ibid., p. 2.

65. Ibid.

66. Freeman, *Correctional Organization and Management*, p. 167; "ACLU National Prison Project" (2001), http://archive.aclu.org/issues/prisons/npp_mission.html.

67. www.corrections.com/aja/about/index.html.

68. "ACLU Calls Prison Rape Reduction Bill Positive Step, but Says More Needed to Protect Current

Victims" (2002), http://archive.aclu.org/news/2002/n073102a.html.

69. "ACLU Opposes End to Prison Work Programs: Calls Inmate Employment Important for Rehabilitation" (2002), http://archive.aclu.org/news/2002/n042402b.html.

70. See www.afscme.org/workers/67.cfm.

71. Don C. Gibbons, "The Limits of Punishment as Social Policy," in *Public Policy, Crime, and Criminal Justice*, ed. Barry W. Hancock and Paul M. Sharp (Upper Saddle River, N.J.: Prentice Hall, 2000), pp. 280–94.

72. Alida V. Merlo and Peter J. Benekos, "Adapting Conservative Correctional Policies to the Economic Realities of the 1990s," in Hancock and Sharp, *Public Policy, Crime, and Criminal Justice*, pp. 295–307.

73. Don Thompson, "High Court rejects challenge to California prison plan" Yahoo News; retrieved 2/18/2010 and available at http://fe43.news.spl.yahoo.com/s/ap/20100119/ap_on_re_us/us_supreme_court_california.

74. Lawrence F. Travis, Edward J. Latessa, Jr., and Gennaro F. Vito, "Private Enterprise and Institutional Corrections: A Call for Caution," *Federal Probation* 49 (December 1985): 11–16, at 11.

75. Austin and Irwin, *It's about Time*, p. 65.

76. Nicholas Henry, *Public Administration and Public Affairs* (Upper Saddle River, N.J.: Prentice Hall, 2004), p. 318.

77. Scott D. Camp and Gerald G. Gaes, *Growth and Quality of U.S. Private Prisons: Evidence from a National Survey* (Washington, D.C.: U.S. Department of Justice, Federal Bureau of Prisons, 2001).

78. William J. Sabol, Heather C. West, Matthew Cooper, "Prisoners in 2008" (December 20009) Washington, D.C.: U.S. Department of Justice, Office of Justice Programs, Bureau of Justice Statistics, http://bjs.ojp.usdoj.gov/content/pub/pdf/p08.

79. Lichtenstein and Kroll, "The Fortress Economy," p. 32.

80. Camp and Gaes, *Growth and Quality of U.S. Private Prisons*.

81. Austin and Irwin, *It's about Time*, p. 65.

82. Freeman, *Correctional Organization and Management*, p. 122; Stephen Moore, "How to Privatize Federal Services by 'Contracting Out,'" in *Public Administration Debated*, ed. Herbert M. Levine (Englewood Cliffs, N.J.: Prentice Hall, 1988), pp. 223–30, at 223.

83. Freeman, *Correctional Organization and Management*, p. 123.

84. Austin and Irwin, *It's about Time*, p. 65.

85. Freeman, *Correctional Organization and Management*, p. 123.

86. Ira P. Robbins, "Privatization of Corrections," *Federal Probation* 48 (March 1986): 24–30, at 26.

87. Freeman, *Correctional Organization and Management*, p. 122; Henry, *Public Administration*, p. 321.

88. Moore, "How to Privatize Federal Services by 'Contracting Out,'" p. 224.

89. Ibid.

90. Travis et al., "Private Enterprise and Institutional Corrections," p. 11; Moore, "How to Privatize Federal Services by 'Contracting Out,'" p. 224.

91. Henry, *Public Administration*, p. 321.

92. Robbins, "Privatization of Corrections," p. 26.

93. Henry, *Public Administration*, p. 318.

94. Freeman, *Correctional Organization and Management*, p. 122; Henry, *Public Administration*, p. 123.

95. Austin and Irwin, *It's about Time*, p. 81.

96. Camp and Gaes, *Growth and Quality of U.S. Private Prisons*.

97. www.presidency.ucsb.edu/site/docs/ppus.php?admin=032&year=1934&id=199.

98. Harry E. Allen and Clifford Simonsen, *Corrections in America: An Introduction*, 4th ed. (New York: Macmillan, 1986).

99. Lichtenstein and Kroll, "The Fortress Economy," p. 30.

100. Ibid.

101. "Inmate Labor Loss Bemoaned" The Topeka Capital-Journal May 15, 2009; retrieved on 2/18/2010 from http://cjonlline.com/news/state/2009-05-15/inmate_labor_loss_bemoaned; Associated Press, Parks Losing Inmate labor" February 16, 2009, Topeka Capital Journal; retrieved on 2/18/2010 from http://cjonline.com/stories/021609/kan_388330211.shtml.

102. "Pasco Sheriff's Office Expands Inmate Labor Programs" Pasco Sheriff's Office; accessed 2/18/2010 from www.pascosheriff.com/websmart/Pasco/static/InmatePrograms2009.htm.

103. Eugene Morris, "Inmate Labor Saves More than $6,000 in October" News Release #2009-108, Alachua County Sheriff's Office, November 19, 2009, retrieved 2/18/2010 from www.alachuasheriff.org.

104. Henry Graff, "Charlottesville Turning to Inmate Labor" NBC29, Feb. 26, 2009, retrieved on 2/28/2010 from www.nbc29.com/Global/story.asp?s=9910673&clienttype=printable; see also Tasha Kates, "More Jailbirds to pick up after Local Litterbugs" Daily Progress, March 6, 2009, retrieved on 2/26/2010 from www2.dailyprogress.com.

105. Chris Moran, "Inmate Labor Plan on Table" Houston Chronicle, Dec 7, 2009, retrieved on

2/18.2010 from www.chron.com/disp/story.mpl/sports/bk/bkn/675832.html.

106. Corey Weinstein and Eric Cummins, "The Crime of Punishment: Pelican Bay Maximum Security Prison," in Rosenblatt, *Criminal Injustice*, pp. 308–21, at 310; Erica Thompson and Jan Susler, "Supermax Prisons: High Tech Dungeons and Modern Day Torture," in Rosenblatt, *Criminal Injustice*, pp. 303–7.

107. Mary Dallao, "Prison Construction Trends," *Corrections Today* 59 (2, 1997): 70–72.

108. G. Larry Mays and Joel A. Thompson, "The Political and Organizational Context of American Jails," in *American Jails: Public Policy Issues*, ed. Joel A. Thompson and G. Larry Mays (Chicago: Nelson Hall, 1991), pp. 3–21, at 12; L. L. Zupan, *Jails: Reform and the New Generation Philosophy* (Cincinnati: Anderson, 1991).

13

Juvenile Justice

Chapter Outline

INTRODUCTION

Over the past 50 years, a juvenile justice system has evolved to help deal with juveniles who have been either accused of committing criminal acts or declared delinquent by the court system. Nationally, the juvenile justice system consists of thousands of public and private agencies that deal with thousands of youth, with a total budget amounting to hundreds of millions of dollars. This gives the juvenile justice system an important role in the policy process.

There are juvenile justice systems on both the federal and the state level. At the federal level, there are limited cases where a juvenile is adjudicated delinquent. An act of juvenile delinquency is a violation of federal law committed by a person younger than eighteen. However, federal law requires that prosecutors go forward with a case only if they can certify that there is a substantial federal interest and that the state does not have jurisdiction (or refuses jurisdiction), that the state does not have adequate programs or services for that juvenile, or that the offense is a violent felony, a drug-trafficking or importation offense, or a firearms offense. The federal government does not have a formal, separate system for juveniles per se; rather, a juvenile who is arrested is adjudicated by a U.S. district court judge or magistrate in a closed hearing without a jury. If the juvenile is adjudicated, a hearing concerning the disposition of the juvenile is then held. The judge or magistrate can order restitution, probation, or commitment to a correctional facility. A juvenile may also be tried as an adult if the offense charged is a violent crime, involves drug trafficking or importation or the use of a firearm, or is a repeat offense.[1]

In 1995, there were charges filed against 240 juveniles for alleged acts of juvenile delinquency in the federal system. About a third of the cases involved a violent offense (32%), and a lesser proportion involved a drug offense (15%). The average length of commitment was 34 months. The majority of juveniles charged with federal offenses were placed on probation.[2]

Each state has also developed its own system for dealing with youthful offenders, including a juvenile code and a special court structure to deal with children who are in trouble. Since the system in each state has evolved separately, there is some variation between states but at the same time many similarities between them.

Whether it is the federal, state, or local level, the juvenile justice system is concerned with juveniles who violate the law. A juvenile delinquent is a minor child who violates the penal code. The age that defines a minor child varies from state to state and ranges from 15 to 17. A youth can be found guilty of violating the criminal code similar to an adult but can also be convicted of a status offense, which is an action for which only juveniles can be held accountable. In other words, there are acts that are illegal only for juveniles. These include behaviors such as truancy; smoking; drinking; swearing; running away; disobeying the orders of parents, teachers, or other adults; and violating curfew.

The juvenile justice system was created to protect and guide juveniles who might be in trouble with the law. The system is geared to protecting the juvenile rather than punishing him or her. Because of this purpose, there are some differences between the adult and juvenile courts. For one, there are some different terms and procedures in the two courts. A youth is not referred to as a "criminal" but rather as a "delinquent child." A youth is not "arrested" per se but rather is "taken into custody." A youth is not taken to jail or placed into a prison but instead is placed in a "detention facility," "treatment center," or "training school." There is no trial in the juvenile court but rather an "adjudicatory hearing." Finally, a juvenile is not "convicted" of an offense but rather "adjudicated."

In addition to a separate court structure for juvenile offenders, most police agencies also have a juvenile component, and there are about 3,000 juvenile correctional facilities across the country. But other institutions are also involved in helping juvenile offenders, including mental health systems, schools, and networks of private social service programs.

AMOUNT OF JUVENILE CRIME

There is a perception that juvenile crime continues to increase across the country, although the pattern of juvenile crime is difficult to determine. Not all juveniles who commit crimes are actually arrested and formally brought into the criminal justice system as either juveniles or adults. Many juveniles who commit offenses are never caught, and some who are caught are given a warning and released or diverted from the system in some other fashion.

One way to measure the number of juvenile offenses is through the number of arrests. The Office of Juvenile Justice and Delinquency Prevention, the federal agency that tracks juvenile crime, reported that 2,111,200 juveniles were arrested for criminal acts in 2008. Of these, 96,000 were for violent crimes.[3] The statistics show that the number of juveniles arrested for criminal offenses has decreased steadily between 1997 and 2008, as shown in Table 13.1. Males commit more

TABLE 13.1   Estimated Juvenile Arrests, 1997–2008

	1997	1999	2000	2001	2008
Violent crime	123,45010	103, 880	98,860	96,520	96,0000
Property crimes	701,500	541,500	518,800	491,400	439,600
Nonindex offenses	2,013,350	1,823,420	1,751,740	1,685,580	1,575,500
Total	2,838,300	2,468,800	2,369,400	2,273,500	2,111,200

Source: H. Snyder, C. Puzzanchera, and W. Kang, "Easy Access to FBI Arrest Statistics 1994–2001" (2003), available online at http://ojjdp.ncjrs.org/ojstatbb/ezaucr/ucr_display.asp?Select_State=0&Select; OJJDP "Juvenile Arrests 2008" (December 2009) Office of Justice Programs, Department of Justice; available online at www.ojp.usdoj.gov.

TABLE 13.2 Juvenile court cases			
Year		**Year**	
1960	405,000	1998	1,798,000
1965	554,000	1999	1,179,000
1970	836,000	2000	1,701,800
1975	1,051,000	2001	1,687,200
1980	1,092,000	2002	1,675,500
1985	1,161,500	2003	1,673,700
1990	1,345,800	2004	1,688,300
1995	1,345,800	2005	1,697,900

Source: Statistical Briefing Book, Office of Juvenile Justice and Delinquency Prevention, available online at www.ojjdp.ncjrs.gov/ojstatbb/court/qa06204.

homicides than females. In 2006, males committed 1165 homicides and females committed 88. Most homicides are committed with a firearm. In 2006, 902 homicides involved a gun, whereas 353 did not.[4]

There is concern that there is a disproportionately high number of minority juveniles in the system. In 2007, 47 percent of the youth arrested for violent crimes were white, 51 percent involved black youth, and 1 percent was Asian. The racial composition of the general population in the country is 78 percent white, 17 percent black, and 5 percent Asian. This trend has been labeled "disproportionate minority contact" or DMC. Further, from 1985 to 2005, the number of delinquency cases for black youth increased 97 percent, but only 24 percent for white youth.[5]

Another way to examine the amount of juvenile crime is to look at how many juveniles appear in court. Table 13.2 shows that from 1960 to 2005, the number of juveniles committing offenses serious enough to appear in front of a court has increased steadily. Table 13.3 indicates that most offenses are public order offenses, followed by property offenses, personal offenses and then drug law violations. Females comprise between 20 and 30 percent of the cases. The majority of defendants were white.

There have been fewer juveniles placed in residential facilities in recent years. In 1997, there were 105,055 juveniles held in youth facilities, which increased to 107,856 in 1999. After that, the

TABLE 13.3 Juvenile Court Cases, by Offense, 2005			
	Number of Cases	**Female (%)**	**White (%)**
Total Delinquency	1,697,900	27	64
Person Offenses	429,500	30	57
Property Offenses	598,600	27	67
Drug Law Violations	195,300	20	74
Public Order Offenses	474,400	28	63

Source: Statistical Briefing Book, Office of Juvenile Justice and Delinquency Prevention, available online at www.ojjdp. ncjrs.gov/ojstatbb/court/qa06204.

TABLE 13.4 Population of Juvenile Residential Placement

	1997	1999
Delinquency	98,913	104,237
Status	6,877	4,694

Source: Melissa Sickmund, "Juveniles in Corrections" (Washington, D.C.: U.S. Department of Justice, Office of Justice Programs, 2004); p. 3.

juvenile residential population dropped to 104,413 in 2001, 96,655 in 2003 and then to 92,854 in 2006.[6] That year, 15 percent of the juveniles in residential facilities were females. Forty percent of the juveniles were black, 35 percent were white, 20 percent Hispanic, 2 percent American Indian and 1 percent Asian. Most of the juveniles were sentenced for personal crimes (34%), followed by property crimes (25%), technical violations (16%), public order offenses (11%), drug offenses (9%), and status offenses (5%).[7]

Juvenile residential placement facilities vary in their degree of security. It is more common for facilities to have fences, walls, and surveillance equipment. In 1999, it was reported that seven out of ten juveniles were confined by at least one locked door or gate. Seventy-two percent were held in a locked facility, whereas 28 percent were held in a staff-secure facility.[8] Those juveniles held for status offenses were more likely to be confined in staff-secure facilities than in locked ones.[9] See Table 13.14.

THEORIES OF JUVENILE DELINQUENCY

There are many theories to explain why juveniles commit crime and how the system can prevent further harm by juveniles. Some of these are in Box 13.1. The theories range from personal choice to physical characteristics of offenders, such as an extra Y chromosome that makes some juveniles more prone to violence. Another theory is based on the premise that those juveniles with a particular body type are more likely to commit criminal offenses. Other theories center more around the structure of society and its focus on criminal behavior. For example, class conflict sometimes is acknowledged as the source of crime, as are differences in opportunities available to members of different classes. Although the focuses of the theories are different, each one attempts to determine the underlying reason for the criminal behavior. If we understand why criminal acts are committed by juveniles, our criminal justice system will be better equipped to deal with that offender and prevent further crime.

EVOLUTION OF THE JUVENILE JUSTICE SYSTEM

The juvenile justice system has not always been an integral part of the criminal justice system in America but rather has evolved over time. In colonial America, there was no separate criminal justice system for juveniles who committed criminal offenses. At that time, it was illegal for children to show rebelliousness or disobedience, play ball in public streets, or sled on the Sabbath. Children between seven and fourteen who committed one of these crimes were considered to be responsible for the act, and they were punished appropriately. Children over the age of 14 were believed capable of both the act and the intent to carry it out, which made them eligible for more

BOX 13.1
Theories of Juvenile Delinquency

School	Description	Theorist
Classical	Individuals have free will and reasoning and make rational choices based on pleasure and pain; crime can be prevented through increased punishment.	Beccaria: *On Crimes and Punishment* (1764) Bentham: *An Introduction to the Principles and Morals of Legislation* (1789)
Biological and biosocial	Behavior is caused by an internal mechanism or physical property that predisposes one to criminality; criminal behavior based on biological makeup of individual; crime can be prevented through treatment of offender.	Sheldon (1944): Body types (somatype) can determine criminal behavior; mesomorphs (muscular and large) are more likely to commit crimes than endomorphs (short, fat, and round) or ectomorphs (bony, thin, and skinny).
		Lombroso; Ferrero (1867; 1911): Criminals are atavistic or less developed than noncriminals; likely to have protruding jaws, long arms, high foreheads, unusual number of fingers, bad teeth, abnormal nasal features, and deep, close-set eyes.
		Murray (1976): Learning disabilities cause criminal behavior; a disorder or deficiency of speech, hearing, reading, writing, or arithmetic may affect behavior.
		Jacobs, Brunton, and Melville (1965): Males with an extra Y chromosome (XYY males) are more likely to commit crimes.
Psychological	Differences in intelligence, personality, or other factors cause delinquency; these might include early life experiences, incomplete socialization, or poor development of personality.	Freud: A person's personality is made up of the id, the ego (the social identity that is exhibited through behavior, and the superego (a result of the early moral training, providing the rationale for refraining from various types of behavior); crime is caused where there is a conflict between the id and the superego.
		Fink (1938): Delinquents are deficient in basic moral sentiments that are inherited from parents.
		Goddard (1912): Criminal behavior is the result of weak intelligence by studying the Lakkikak family, where one line came from a "respectable girl" and resulted in governors, senators, doctors, and other good people; the other line came from a barmaid and produced prostitutes, alcoholics, and criminals.
Social disorganization and anomie	Social and economic inequalities cause people to commit crimes.	Durkheim (1933), Anomie theory: This describes the inability of individuals to recognize the necessity of different jobs and payoffs and the inability to control the egoistic urges within themselves.
		Burgess (1967) and Shaw, and McCay (1942, 1969): These theorists debated if delinquency is more a product of economic conditions and local-based traditions and values than ethnic culture.
		Merton (1957), Strain theory: This describes a lack of agreement between goals and means to achieve those goals.

BOX 13.1
(continued)

School	Description	Theorist
Class based	Delinquency is concentrated in lower class, and a high number of lower-class youth do poorly in school; poor school performance is related to delinquency and attributed to a conflict between the dominant middle-class values of the school system and values of the lower class; lower-class male delinquency is committed largely in a gang context as a means of developing more positive self-concepts.	Cohen (1955): Lower-class boys feel ill equipped to compete in middle-class society; middle-class orientation is set up so that lower-class youths cannot succeed, yet these youths are expected to follow the goals of the middle class; often, boys of lower classes may join together in groups that provide alternative means of gaining status.
		Cloward and Ohlin (1960): Differential opportunity; Illegitimate opportunities are available when legitimate opportunities are blocked; when youth find that educational opportunities and good-paying jobs are not available to them, they will pursue delinquent activities instead.
		Shaw and McKay (1942): Delinquency rates are highest in and around the central business district and highest in the lowest economic areas and in areas of foreign-born and African-American heads of households.
		Miller (1958): The lower class operates under a distinct set of cultural values or focal concerns; these are trouble, toughness, smartness, excitement, fate, and autonomy; adherence to these provides status and acceptance in lower classes but conflict with middle-class values; deviant behavior is the by-product of following the subcultural focus concerns.
Interpersonal and situational theories	Personal interactions cause people to learn about and accept criminal behavior as normal.	Sutherland (1939), Differential association: Criminal behavior is learned and more easily learned in some areas; it is learned in the same fashion as conforming behavior from the people with whom an individual comes into contact; a person becomes delinquent because of an excess of definitions favorable to violation of law.
		Matza (1964), Drift: People drift between different modes of behavior; a person who is deviant at one point in time may be a model citizen at another time.
Control	People must be controlled if criminal tendencies are to be repressed.	Empey (1982) and Hirschi (1969): People need to create a bond to society that is set in childhood; a weak bond allows for deviance; the bonds include attachment, commitment, involvement, and belief.
		Reckless (1967), Containment: An individual controls his or her own behavior; outer containment deals with the influences of the family, peers, and environment in molding behavior; inner containment deals with individual strengths such as a good self-concept and internalized moral codes.
Labeling	People are labeled as criminal	Lemert (1951), Becker (1973), and theory and learn to fulfill the label. Wolfgang (1972): An individual uses his or her deviant behavior as a means of defense, attack, or adjustment to the problems created by the societal reaction to him or her; actions of an individual correspond to a label.

BOX 13.1
(continued)

School	Description	Theorist
Radical	Criminal behavior is the result of repressive efforts of ruling class to control the subject class.	Turk (1969), Quinney (1970), and Chambliss (1974): The competition for wealth is the key to conflict; the economically powerful use the law to maintain their dominance; the law is made by the powerful, and it is in their interests to keep the powerful in power.

Sources: G. S. Becker, "Crime and Punishment: An Economic Approach," *Journal of Political Economy* 76 (1968): 169–217; D. J. Shoemaker, *Theories of Delinquency* (New York: Oxford University Press, 1996).

severe punishment. When misconduct occurred, the juvenile's family was primarily responsible for punishing the child.[10] But when more severe punishment was needed, the colonists used whipping or some other form of corporal punishment. If the crime was serious enough, the colonists punished children by imprisonment.

Throughout the colonial period to the nineteenth century, it was thought that misbehavior by juveniles was caused by poverty and lower-class environments.[11] Public officials used the same methods to deal with criminal youth as they used to handle poor people, who were also viewed as a threat to society. One way to deal with the poor was to provide training that would help them become productive members of society. To accomplish this, the juveniles should be removed from the bad influences and substandard training of the parents.[12]

This era was termed the "era of institutionalization," during which many juveniles were removed from their families and homes and sent to institutions where they could be "trained." Many juveniles faced broad definitions of criminal behavior, and many were sent away for acts for which they would not have been punished had they been adults (status offenses). For example, in Massachusetts, officials could commit to prison "rogues, vagabonds, common beggars, and other idle, disorderly and lewd persons."[13] Juveniles were housed with adults in often inhumane settings without heat and adequate food and clothing.

The Philadelphia Society for Assisting Distressed Prisoners, organized in 1776 by several prominent Quakers, investigated these jail conditions. They criticized the failure of jails to segregate men from women, juveniles from adults, and felons from misdemeanants.[14] Eventually, a new approach to punishing juveniles was created. The houses of refuge, created by the Reformers, were intended to remove the juvenile from the environment that was causing crime (i.e., the city) and replace it with institutional, rehabilitative care where the child could be reformed and saved rather than punished. They tried to make the houses of refuge warm, supportive places resembling a home or school rather than a prison.[15] The institutions were seen as less cruel than earlier systems of control and more capable of turning the deviant into a productive member of society.[16] The first House of Refuge was established in New York City in 1825. Boston and Philadelphia created their own houses of refuge that were racially segregated.

The houses of refuge enforced silence among the inmates. The juveniles wore uniforms and marched to and from different activities. There was also the use of swift punishment that included corporal punishment.[17] Since the rationale and setup of the houses of refuge reflected concern for the poor and the need for training, work programs became the centerpiece of the program of rehabilitation. Often the juveniles were contracted out to employers as apprentices. Unfortunately, the children were often bribed, beaten, and subjected to incarceration if the monetary interests of the administrators were at stake.[18] Those boys who failed to make their quota were whipped. They were paid very little, denied adequate clothing, and physically abused.[19]

Over time, the houses of refuge were replaced with reform schools, which were state institutions intended for the long-term incarceration of their more serious offenders. Massachusetts established the first State Reform School for Boys in 1847. For the most part, the reform schools resembled the houses of refuge. There was a strict regimen of work, education, and religious instruction that was intended to rehabilitate the juvenile offenders.[20] By 1880, almost every state, excluding those in the South, had a government-supported boys' reformatory and a separate girls' institution. Many states had created "cottage" reformatories that were intended to mirror a family and home setting. Here, surrogate parents would oversee the training and education of a small number of kids. Discipline was mixed with care. Often these reformatories were located in the country to separate the youth from the city.[21]

In the late nineteenth century, people saw a need to reform the system for juvenile offenders. The separate juvenile justice system expanded gradually, culminating in the first separate court for juveniles, established on July 1, 1899, in Cook County, Illinois, in the Juvenile Court Act (1899 Ill. Laws 132 et seq.). This statute created a "children's court" with jurisdiction not only over delinquent children under sixteen who committed criminal offenses but also over a variety of other situations, such as homeless or abandoned children, children dependent on the public for support, or neglected children who were without proper parental care. The act was unique because it was based on a rehabilitative approach rather than punishment. It was hoped that keeping kids out of adult court and jails where they were corrupted by hardened criminals could prevent troubled youths from becoming more involved with crime.

The juvenile court was based on a system of informal procedures that were intended to make it less intimidating for the juvenile. Formal courtroom procedures found in the adult court, such as lawyers, strict rules of evidence, and testimony under oath, were discouraged. Courtroom procedures were informal and had no adversary procedures that might prevent the court's ability to determine the best treatment for the child. The judge assumed more of a paternal attitude toward the juvenile and attempted to determine what the child needed to keep him or her away from crime.

Between 1920 and 1960, the juvenile court became an accepted and inherent part of the criminal justice system. In the 1950s, an increase in juvenile crime and more youth entering the juvenile system caused concern among public officials and citizens.[22] They responded with developing more training and counseling programs and psychotherapeutic interventions.[23]

The rights of juvenile offenders were expanded during the 1960s to include due process considerations, such as the right to counsel and protection against self-incrimination.[24] But changes in the nature of crimes committed by youth, including increases in violent crime, involvement in crack cocaine and other drugs, and gang activity (combined with a conservative political climate during the mid-1980s), saw a return to policies of punishment and criminalization for juveniles. This resulted in a gradual reduction in treatment-oriented policies and services between 1985 and 1990.[25]

Since 1990, many states have passed legislation that has changed the way in which delinquent youths are processed in the system. Recent policies toward juvenile justice stress the punishment and control of young offenders. Some states have passed laws to lower the age at which juveniles can be tried as adults, enacted stricter punishments for drug- and gang-related offenses, and introduced stringent treatments, such as boot camps, for all juvenile offenders.

Community-based programs have been eliminated in many jurisdictions, and institutions combining different types of juvenile offenders have been reintroduced.[26]

As with correctional policy for adults, there have been cycles of treatment/rehabilitation versus punishment in the juvenile system. As seen with adult offenders, there is no consensus as to the best way to deter, treat, or punish juvenile criminal offenders. For years, scholars and practitioners have debated if crime could be reduced by either punishing or treating offenders.[27] Allen points out that the rehabilitative ideal, particularly for juveniles, actually led to an increased severity of penal measures. He explains that judges were authorized to intervene punitively in juvenile cases that would be ignored if committed by an adult. Further, the use of indeterminate sentences allowed for lengthened periods of imprisonment. In the long run, the rehabilitative ideal led to more incapacitation than treatment.[28]

Bernard shows that these cycles, one consisting of largely punitive policies, followed by a predominantly rehabilitative phase, have been repeated three times since 1820. He calls this the "Cycle of Juvenile Punishment."[29] He presents the argument that many juveniles who were first brought through the juvenile system and then go on to commit additional crimes may not have committed additional crimes if they had been punished severely for the earlier offenses. He argues that the leniency of the juvenile court simply encourages juveniles to laugh at the system and to believe that they will not be punished no matter what additional crime they commit. Thus, they feel free to commit serious crimes more frequently and with greater impunity.[30] In response, officials begin to "toughen up" the punishments for juvenile offenders, and the lenient responses become less accepted. Despite the tough policies, juvenile crime rates remain high. This, then, generates efforts to provide even harsher punishments. However, when the punishments become more severe, they are not applied to the juvenile. Some minor offenders may even be released without any punishment. The juvenile crime continues to be high, so officials conclude that harsh punishment may be increasing crime, causing the offender to be angry and bitter toward society. Taking this into account, officials again make changes to the juvenile system.[31]

JUVENILE JUSTICE SYSTEM TODAY

Today, our legal system still recognizes that many young people are incapable of making mature adult judgments and that responsibility for their acts should be limited. Some children may know that an act is illegal, but they may be incapable of fully understanding the consequences of their behavior and the harm it may cause. There are elements of both conservative and liberal approaches to juvenile crime in today's system. There has recently been a "toughening up" of juvenile correctional policy in many states. For example, many states have passed laws that allow the transfer of a juvenile to an adult court where juveniles are removed from the jurisdiction of the juvenile court so they can be tried and punished as adult offenders. Nonetheless, there are also many aspects of rehabilitation in the juvenile system, especially involving status offenders, where they are placed in educational or treatment programs instead of in a residential facility.

There has also been a focus on preventing juvenile crime before the juvenile becomes a serious offender. Many experts are questioning the effect of early childhood experiences on juvenile behavior. Research in this area seems to show that early events in children's lives may be the precursors of criminal behavior, including the relationship between a child and his or her parents. Some risk factors of delinquent behavior include early use of alcohol and drugs, ties to antisocial friends, early expressions of aggression, poor parent–child relations, and even low intelligence.[32]

Although the jurisdiction of juvenile courts now varies from state to state, judges are generally given broad jurisdiction over problems involving children and their families. These problems include establishment of paternity, child abuse and neglect, foster care, termination of parental rights, adoption, truancy, runaway youth, children in need of services, youth with mental illness and other disabilities, crimes committed by family members and partners against one another, civil orders of protection for family members and youth, and crimes committed by and against youth.

When a juvenile comes into the system, there are many decisions that are made by many different actors that affect the outcome of the case. These actors include probation officers, defense attorneys, prosecutors, and judges. The following discussion provides a quick overview of the juvenile system and the actors' roles.

Most children initially come into contact with a police officer. At that time, the police can simply warn the child, call the parents, or make a referral to a social service agency. If the offense is serious enough, the police can arrest the juvenile. If a youth is taken into custody, he or she is referred to the juvenile court.

If the police decide to file a petition (similar to bringing charges in an adult case) and take the child into custody, the child may be brought to the station house lockup and then to a county detention program or intake program prior to a court appearance. The primary issue is whether the child should remain in the community or be placed in detention or in a shelter home. This decision is made by the relevant court personnel in a detention hearing.

The Model Juvenile Delinquency Act, which serves as a guideline for state codes, stipulates that the detention hearing be held within 36 hours. The officials can release a child to his or her parents, or they can choose to put the child in secure detention, which is often the equivalent of jail. This involves putting the juvenile in a locked facility with other youths who are awaiting further court action or transfer to a state correctional facility. Normally, the detention hearing results in a decision either to remand the child to a shelter or to release the child. At this point, the child has a right to counsel and other procedural safeguards.

In some cases, a youth may be detained pending a trial if there is a danger to him- or herself or others. Authorities can also choose to put the youth in a nonsecure detention facility, which is usually for those youth who are involved in less serious crimes and do not pose much of a threat to society. These usually entail small group homes where they can go to regular school during the day.

There must also be an intake decision. This is when a court official, either a probation officer or a prosecutor (or both), decides whether to file a court petition of delinquency, status offense, neglect, abuse, or dependency in a case. The officer can choose not to file a petition but instead try to resolve the matter without resorting to a formal petition against the child. This might be called an informal adjustment and occurs frequently.

If the crime is serious, the juvenile court prosecutor may initiate a petition against the child. This begins the trial process, called adjudication, which is the trial state of the juvenile court process. The adjudication hearing is held to determine the facts of the case. If the child denies the allegation of delinquency, an adjudicatory hearing is scheduled. Here a judge determines whether there is enough evidence to establish the petition and decides what to do if there is enough evidence. The court hears evidence on the allegations in the delinquency petition. This is a trial on the merits of the case, and the rules of evidence are similar to the criminal proceedings in adult cases. Every child is given procedural rights similar to criminal proceedings for adults: right to representation by counsel, right to confront witnesses, and so on.

The adjudication process typically begins with some sort of initial hearing. At this hearing, juvenile court rules of procedure normally require that the child be informed of his or her right to a trial and that the plea or admission be voluntary. This step is similar to the plea, trial, and sentencing decisions in adult court.

The decision to transfer the juvenile (a waiver) to the adult court may be necessary in cases where the offense was serious. This decision creates an adult criminal record rather than a confidential juvenile record.

The disposition decision is next. If the adjudication or trial finds the child to be delinquent or in need of supervision, the court initiates a social study of the child's background. This is called a predisposition report. On completion of the report, an appropriate disposition leading to a correctional and rehabilitation program is provided. The judge decides what should be done to treat the child. Judges are given much leeway in such decisions, and some of the options are listed in Box 13.2.

BOX 13.2
Punishment Options for Juvenile Delinquents

Aftercare or Parole

Similar to that for adults; provides transitional supervision between a stay of incarceration and freedom in the community; offender must abide by certain conditions or face reincarceration.

Juvenile Probation

The primary form of community treatment for juveniles; a juvenile is placed within the community under the supervision of an officer of the court (a juvenile probation officer). For the probationary period, the juvenile is subject to rules and conditions that must be followed; if those are violated, probation can be revoked and the juvenile sent to prison or other custodial option.

Intensive Probation Supervision

The probation officer has smaller caseloads than with typical probation; allows the officer to provide almost daily contact with the offenders and monitor their actions.

Wilderness Probation

Offenders take part in an outdoor camp and must perform tasks to increase their discipline and self-esteem.

Diversion

The offender is diverted from the prison; represents the view that the juvenile system is too punitive and ineffective.

Community Corrections

The offender is given treatment in the community, which often permits him or her to stay in the home and maintain family relationships.

Restitution

Reimbursing the victims of an offense or donating to a charity; may either be an independent option or a condition of probation.

Community Service Restitution

The juvenile must assist a community organization.

Residential Programs

Provide a juvenile with a "home away from home"; the juveniles move into and live in this setting, either a group home or foster home that is staffed by counselors who provide counseling, education, or job training; the juveniles can attend school or participate in school and community activities; these homes hold twelve to fifteen youth.

Nonresidential Community Treatment

In these programs, the youth remain at home with their families yet receive necessary counseling, education, employment, diagnostic, and casework services for the youth and other family members.

Institutionalization

Usually reserved for more serious or repeat juvenile offenders; typical institutional settings involve treatment programs, counseling, vocational, and/or education training; usually followed by an aftercare program such as parole.

Intermediate Custodial Facilities

A residential facility that allows the offender to have more freedom in the community.

BOX 13.2
(continued)

Juvenile Jails

House only juveniles and are completely separate from those for adults.

Reformatories or Training Schools

Long-term custodial institutions; the offenders are deprived of some or all of their liberty; have an emphasis on punishment but also elements of rehabilitation, such as education and counseling; the goal is to effect a significant change in the values, attitudes, and behavior of the offender.

Probation Camp

An alternative to an institution for some juveniles where they follow a strict physical regimen for usually six months to a year; the offenders receive some re-socialization treatment (psychological counseling) or educational and vocational training; the juvenile must show progress, or a judge may resentence the offender to a reformatory institution for long-term treatment.

Boot Camp

An army-like setting that was popular in the 1990s; a tough method for treating juvenile offenders that emphasized physical conditioning and military-style discipline; after an evaluation by the OJJDP that showed no reduction in recidivism, the popularity of boot camps declined.

Source: Lewis Yablonsky, *Juvenile Delinquency into the 21st Century* (Belmont, Calif.: Wadsworth, 2000), pp. 426–30.

Although confidentiality has been the standard for the juvenile court, many states have passed statutes to permit for more openness. In 2004, fourteen states have opened delinquency hearings to the public except on special order of the court. In other words, the statutes state that all hearings must be open to the public except in certain cases when it is in the best interest of the child. In 21 other states, statutes have opened delinquency hearings for some types of cases, depending on the age of the juvenile or type of case. In most states, court records are being made available to a wider variety of individuals and agencies. Further, most states have school notification laws under which schools are notified when students are involved with police or courts for committing delinquent acts.[33]

POLITICS AND JUVENILE JUSTICE

Although most people would like to think that the juvenile justice system operates only in the best interests of the children who come into it, it is the case that political factors have a great influence on the daily operations of the system. As with the adult system, politics affects what goes on in the juvenile justice system and in turn affects how the juveniles are treated and/or punished. The political actors include the U.S. Supreme Court, the U.S. Congress, interest groups, and bureaucracies.

Liberal and Conservative Approaches to Juvenile Justice Policy

As noted in previous chapters, there are different views concerning the approaches that should be taken to prevent or punish juvenile crime. The conservative approach tends to support longer, harsher punishments for those juveniles who commit criminal acts, whereas the liberal approach supports more treatment, rehabilitation, and education of criminal violators to prevent any future criminal acts.

The prominent underlying ideology toward juvenile justice policy has changed intermittently over the past 30 years, the emphasis shifting from rehabilitation to punishment. During the 1970s and 1980s, the focus leaned toward an individual treatment model that encouraged placing juvenile offenders in nonsecure, community-based programs. However, since the early 1990s, this approach has been replaced by policies that support strict sanctions and incarceration.[34]

Since the 1970s, the main focus of the juvenile justice system has been toward "getting tough." During this time, there has been a national concern about serious, violent crimes committed by juvenile offenders. Many states have passed legislation that has made the punishments for juveniles more tough.[35] This includes longer sentences (mandatory minimums) and easier (and more frequent) transfer of juveniles to adult criminal court.

The Supreme Court and the Rights of Juveniles

Early in the nineteenth century, juveniles were tried along with adults in criminal courts. Under common law, children under age seven were presumed immune, that is, lacking the moral responsibility to be criminally responsible (the infancy defense). Children between ages seven and fourteen were presumed not to be criminally responsible, and prosecutors had to prove that an individual juvenile was culpable. Youth ages fourteen and older were deemed responsible for their criminal acts as adults.

Since the 1960s, the Supreme Court has made many decisions to define the rights of juveniles accused of crimes. Initial changes came in the case of *Kent v. United States* (1966). Kent, who was sixteen, was arrested and charged with housebreaking, robbery, and rape. Because he was a juvenile, he was sent first to a juvenile court. After an investigation, the juvenile court waived jurisdiction, and Kent was sent to an adult court. He had no hearing and no assistance of counsel, and there was no statement of the reasons for the judge's decision to transfer the matter to the adult court. Additionally, the judge did not allow Kent's attorney to review any of the files, nor did he conduct a hearing on the matter. The waiver decision was made by the judge acting alone. Kent's counsel filed a motion for a hearing on the question of a waiver, but the juvenile court entered an order waiving jurisdiction without a hearing. Kent was indicted, tried, and convicted on six counts of housebreaking and robbery but acquitted on two rape counts by reason of insanity.

In its decision of *Kent v. United States* (1966), the Supreme Court said that the defendant has certain minimum safeguards, including the right to a hearing, the right to the assistance of an attorney, and a statement of the reasons for transfer if the judge decides to transfer the case to adult court. They decided that there must be a meaningful right to representation by counsel and a hearing on the issue of transfers to criminal court. In other words, the juvenile court must conduct a hearing before a juvenile is transferred to an adult criminal court. By making that decision, the Court established that procedures concerning waiver must measure up to the essential of due process of law, including a formal hearing, the right to legal counsel, and access to social records.

In re Gault (1967) was also a landmark case that established the constitutional right of children to have appointed counsel in juvenile delinquency proceedings. In this case, 15-year-old Gerald Gault was charged with and convicted of making an obscene phone call to a female neighbor and was sentenced to the Arizona State Industrial School (a juvenile correctional facility) for an indeterminate period though not to exceed his twenty-first birthday. During his trial, Gault never had access to a lawyer, was not allowed to confront or cross-examine his accusers, and was not allowed to appeal the decision. There was no written record of his confession or his court hearing, and his sentence was longer than that an adult would have received for the same offense. The Supreme Court overturned Gault's conviction, ruling that he had been denied several basic rights. Supreme Court Justice Abe Fortas announced, "Under our Constitution, the condition of being a boy does not justify a kangaroo court." Fortas said that Gault was entitled to the following:

- Adequate notice of the precise nature of the charges brought against him
- Notice of the right to counsel and, if indigent, the right to have counsel appointed
- The right to confront witnesses and have them cross-examined
- The privilege against self-incrimination, which applies to juvenile and adult proceedings

The Supreme Court held that juveniles at trial, faced with incarceration, were entitled to many of the rights granted to adult offenders, including counsel, notice of the charges, cross-examination of witnesses, and protection against self-incrimination. Overall, the *Gault* decision mandated a more formalized juvenile court system.

In both the *Kent* (1966) and the *Gault* (1967) case, the Supreme Court made clear its intention that the legal protection of due process be expanded for juveniles. Over time, there were other cases that helped expand the rights of juveniles brought into the criminal justice system. One of those was *In re Winship* (1970). In this case, a 12-year-old boy was accused of stealing $112 from a woman's purse in a locker. The Court addressed the question of standard of proof in juvenile cases, which has to do with how strong a case must be to prove delinquency. In its decision, the Court extended the reasonable-doubt standard of proof to juvenile delinquency proceedings where there was the possibility of commitment to a locked facility. The Court ruled that the standard of proof in a delinquency proceeding that could result in a child's commitment must be "proof beyond a reasonable doubt" rather than a "preponderance of the evidence."

Yet another case that expanded the rights of juveniles was *McKeiver v. Pennsylvania* (1971). This case helped define the rights of a juvenile in a jury trial. The Supreme Court ruled that juveniles were not to be afforded the constitutional right to a jury trial in a delinquency proceeding. This aspect of the adversarial process was not appropriate for the juvenile justice system.

In *Breed v. Jones* (1975), the Supreme Court made the waiver process more explicit by ruling that states cannot first adjudicate a juvenile as delinquent and then waive or transfer the youth to adult court, as this is a violation of double jeopardy. In this case, the Court established that the double-jeopardy clause of the Fifth Amendment to the Constitution extends to juvenile offenders through the Fourteenth Amendment's due process clause. After this case, juveniles could not be tried in a juvenile court and transferred to an adult court for a similar action.

Some questions surrounding the interrogation of juveniles accused of crimes were addressed in *Fare v. Michael* (1979). Here, a juvenile murder suspect consented to an interrogation after he was denied the opportunity to consult with his probation officer. The Supreme Court ruled that there is no constitutional mandate to allow a suspect to speak with his or her probation officer. In other words, a child's request to see his or her probation officer at the time of interrogation did not operate to invoke his or her Fifth Amendment right to remain silent. According to the Court, the probation officer cannot be expected to offer the type of advice that an accused would expect from an attorney.

The Supreme Court ruled that a juvenile who is awaiting court action can be held in preventive detention if there is adequate concern that the juvenile would commit additional crimes while the primary case is pending further court action. In *Schall v. Maring* (1984), the Court ruled that the juvenile does have the right to a hearing on the preventive detention decision and a statement of the reasons for which he or she is being detained. In this case, the Court upheld a state statute allowing the placement of children in preventive detention before their trial. The Court concluded that it was not unreasonable to detain juveniles for their own protection.

The legality of searches in a school was addressed in *New Jersey v. T.L.O.* (1985). In this decision, the Supreme Court determined that the Fourth Amendment applied to school searches. The Court adopted a "reasonable suspicion" standard as opposed to "probable cause" to evaluate the legality of searches and seizures in a school setting.

Two final cases in which the Supreme Court addressed the rights of juveniles were *Stanford v. Kentucky* (1989) and *Wilkens v. Missouri* (1989). In these cases, the Court concluded that the imposition of the death penalty on a juvenile who committed a crime between the ages of sixteen and eighteen was not unconstitutional and that the Eighth Amendment's clause concerning cruel and unusual punishment did not prohibit capital punishment in these cases.

In 2009, the Supreme Court considered if it was cruel and unusual punishment to sentence teenagers to life in prison for their criminal behavior. The cases, *Graham v. Florida* and *Sullivan v. Florida*, revolved around two Florida men who were serving life in prison with no chance of parole for nonhomicidal crimes they committed as teenagers. Terrance Graham committed an armed burglary when he was 16, and Joe Sullivan committed sexual battery when he was 13. The inmates argued that sentencing a juvenile to life in prison violates the Eighth Amendment. Although Florida argued that such sentences are not extreme, the Supreme Court ruled that those in prison for non-murderous crimes committed as juveniles should be given a chance to demonstrate that they have matured enough that they are fit to rejoin society. The court did not rule that those in prison should automatically be released or resentenced. The Court also ruled that, in the future, no juvenile who committed a crime that did not involve murder should be given a life term in prison. Thus, over the years, the Supreme Court has clarified many issues regarding the rights of juveniles who have entered the justice system. Only a small number of the cases that helped define the rights afforded to juveniles are listed here. This is only one example of a political organization affecting the treatment of juveniles. Another is Congress.

Congress and Juvenile Justice

The Supreme Court is not the only federal branch of government to have an impact on the juvenile justice system and to provide rights to juvenile offenders. Congress has also passed many pieces of legislation to help states create effective juvenile justice systems. Congress not only passed new legislation but also provided financial assistance to states. As the costs of juvenile justice grew, the federal government gave the states more money.[36]

Congressional involvement in preventing juvenile crime first started in 1909, when the White House sponsored the Conference on Children and Youth. During this conference, President Theodore Roosevelt expressed the need for national involvement in all youth issues and urged the formation of the Children's Bureau, which eventually became the primary federal instrument of change. It launched the first federally sponsored juvenile delinquency–related research endeavors, such as the study of the District of Columbia's juvenile court law (1914) and the study of children before Connecticut courts (1914). They also sponsored a questionnaire measuring the extent of the American juvenile court movement (1918) and a survey of organizations and methods of ten juvenile courts (1912).

In 1929, President Hoover appointed the Wickersham Commission to investigate the national crime problem. In 1933, the Civilian Conservation Corps was created. As part of this, a program was developed for jobless males ages 18 to 25. They established the National Youth Administration (1935) to employ college and high school students in part-time jobs. These attempted to get juveniles employed and away from crime.

During the Great Depression, the Children's Bureau expanded its interest in preventing juvenile delinquency. It began to study court and probation reports, investigated institutional care and treatment of delinquent children, and provided technical guides for community and court services for children on probation.

Most federal juvenile justice- and family-related policymaking efforts were eliminated during World War II. During this time, the government sponsored only three major forums related to juvenile crime because of the war: the Fourth White House Conference on Children and Youth (1940), the National Commission on Children and Youth (1942), and the National Conference on Prevention and Control of Juvenile Delinquency (1946). The Interdepartmental Committee on Children and Youth was created in 1948 to coordinate youth-serving activities sponsored, organized, and funded by several federal departments.

Throughout the 1950s, the federal government developed new ways to combat juvenile delinquency. The Federal Youth Corrections Act of 1951 provided training and rehabilitation programs for youths who violated federal laws. The next year, the Children's Bureau gathered a group of experts and asked them to recommend ways to decrease rising delinquency rates. In 1954, the Children's Bureau created the Juvenile Delinquency Service to provide technical assistance to states, localities, and public and private agencies; prepare and publish standards and guides for these agencies and the courts; and recommend necessary federal and state legislation.

The Senate Subcommittee to Investigate Juvenile Delinquency was created and was kept busy through the 1950s. The subcommittee conducted hearings between 1953 and 1958 and eventually recommended a comprehensive federal program to assist states and local governments in strengthening and improving delinquency programs.[37]

The FBI's *Uniform Crime Report* indicated at that time that crime by juveniles had more than doubled since 1950 and that arrest statistics for juveniles were increasing. In response, Congress passed the Juvenile Delinquency and Youth Offenses Act of 1961 to help control and prevent juvenile delinquency. It gave the Department of Health, Education and Welfare the ability to provide categorical grants to state and local governments to allow them to plan and create projects aimed at reducing juvenile crime. Large sums of money were channeled to state and local governments through this program. It also served to set the framework for future federal juvenile justice policy.[38]

The president at the time, Lyndon Johnson, was also active in helping to prevent juvenile crime. He created the President's Commission on Law Enforcement and Administration of Justice in 1965 and included a provision to examine the juvenile justice system and make recommendations for future federal efforts. The commission's 1967 report provided several recommendations, including the need for active support of diversion programs for juveniles, support for projects to reduce unemployment, improved standards of living, new community-based residential facilities and youth service bureaus, increased educational opportunities, increased quality of public education, and a complete overhaul of the juvenile justice system.[39]

The President's Commission on Law Enforcement and the Administration of Justice issued its report in 1967. The commission suggested that the juvenile justice system needed to provide underprivileged youth with jobs and education that would lead to success. The commission also recognized the need to develop effective law enforcement procedures that would control hard-core youthful offenders and provide them due process of law when they came before the courts.[40]

The Juvenile Delinquency Prevention and Control Act of 1968 was then passed by Congress. It was enacted to carry out some of the commission's recommendations. The bill initially authorized a three-year $150 million grants-in-aid program to strengthen state and local juvenile justice and delinquency prevention efforts as well as to coordinate all federal youth development activities.

However, the act lacked specific focus. Its objectives were prevention and control, but neither substantive distinctions between the two approaches nor differentiations between treatment needs of certain types of youth were made. Additionally, most funds assisted the state organization of juvenile planning bureaucracies rather than the creation of new youth programs.[41]

The Juvenile Justice and Delinquency Prevention Act of 1968 created the Youth Development and Delinquency Prevention Administration, which was to help states develop new juvenile justice programs, particularly focused on diversion programs for youth, decriminalization, and decarceration. In 1968, Congress also passed the Omnibus Safe Streets and Crime Control Act. Title 1 of this law established the Law Enforcement Assistance Administration (LEAA) to provide federal funds to improve the adult and juvenile justice systems.[42]

By the end of the 1960s, the federal government had adopted new responsibilities for juvenile crime. The President's Commission on Law Enforcement and Administration of Justice had suggested a massive public program for juvenile justice reform, and Congress was attempting to comply with the recommendations.

The Juvenile Delinquency and Youth Offenses Act of 1961 and the Juvenile Delinquency Prevention and Control Act of 1968 assumed new federal obligations for delinquency prevention and control. The Juvenile Delinquency Prevention and Control Act of 1968 was a national effort to help states and cities develop and maintain programs that had the goal of deterring delinquency and assisting those juveniles who had committed crimes. Together, these programs gave millions of dollars to the states.

Regulating the federal money that was being provided to the states became a concern. In response, Congress passed the Crime Control Act of 1970, which created the Interdepartmental Council to coordinate all federal juvenile delinquency programs that were being administered by the Department of Health, Education and Welfare. In 1972, Congress amended the Juvenile Delinquency and Prevention Act of 1968 to force state and local governments to develop and adopt comprehensive plans to obtain federal assistance.[43]

Because juvenile crime continued to receive much publicity during this time, the Nixon administration established the National Advisory Commission on Criminal Justice Standards and Goals in 1973. Its final report on juvenile justice and delinquency prevention identified 12 major concepts that were central to the development of standards and goals for juvenile justice:

1. Increase family stability
2. Develop programs for families needing service, including families with children who are truant or who run away, families with children who disregard parental authority, and families with children who use intoxicating beverages or who are under 20 years old and commit delinquent acts
3. Develop programs for children who are neglected or physically abused
4. Develop programs for young people to prevent delinquent behavior before it occurs
5. Develop diversion activities whereby youths are processed out of the juvenile justice system
6. Develop dispositional alternatives so that institutionalization can be used only as a last resort
7. Extend due process to all juveniles
8. Control the violent and the chronic delinquent
9. Reduce the proportion of minorities who are victims of delinquent acts and who are clients in the juvenile justice system and increase the proportion of minority policymakers and operators in the juvenile system
10. Increase the coordination among agencies to improve the operation of the juvenile justice system and to increase resources and knowledge about how to deal with juvenile offenders

11. Improve research
12. Allocate resources, especially to the many states that do not have their own resources to deal with juvenile programs[44]

The recommendations of the National Advisory Commission formed the basis for the 1974 legislation called the Juvenile Justice and Delinquency Prevention (JJDP) Act of 1974. In this legislation, Congress expressed its concern for the need to safeguard children's rights. The act promoted placing offenders in the least restrictive appropriate treatment setting; establishing community-based programs in place of large, custodial institutions; and diverting youth from formal juvenile justice system processing.[45] Additionally, this act eliminated the old Youth Development and Delinquency Prevention Administration and replaced it with the Office of Juvenile Justice and Delinquency Prevention (OJJDP) within the LEAA.

In addition to creating the OJJDP, the 1974 JJDP Act established the Coordinating Council on Juvenile Justice and Delinquency Prevention as an independent cabinet-level body. It was established to coordinate all federal juvenile delinquency programs and to determine the most appropriate federal roles and policies, improve the effectiveness of federal programs in reducing delinquency, increase the organizational and managerial efficiency of federal activities, and facilitate implementation of effective programs at the state and local levels.[46]

Between 1973 and 1975, there was a plethora of federal financial assistance for juvenile delinquency projects available to states through at least ten separate entities. Each grant opportunity had its own requirements and goals. The programs were combined when the JJDP Act was passed.

The JJDP Act was a landmark federal commitment to juvenile justice. It reflected organizational and philosophical shifts in the government's approach to juvenile justice. The responsibility for youth issues was transferred to the Department of Justice. In addition, the federal juvenile delinquency programs were reorganized so that they would have a more coordinated approach. To do this, the Coordinating Council on Juvenile Justice and Delinquency Prevention was also created.[47] The OJJDP began overseeing federal grant programs in 1975.

Amendments were made to the JJDP Act in 1977 that required all state juvenile detention and correctional facilities to be monitored to determine if they were suitable for juvenile offenders. The amendments also expanded funding of special programs that dealt with school violence, youth advocacy, and youth employment.[48]

Throughout the 1970s, the most important goals of federal legislation were removing juveniles from detention in adult jails and eliminating the coincarceration of juvenile and status offenders. During this period, the OJJDP stressed the creation of formal diversion and restitution programs around the United States.[49]

The JJDP Act was reauthorized by Congress and President Carter in December 1980. This extended the act another four years and made some major changes. This time, OJJDP became a separate organization that now operated under the authority of the U.S. attorney general within the Department of Justice. The administrator of OJJDP, a presidential appointee, was given the ability to implement JJDP Act provisions. The new role of the OJJDP was to develop and implement programs to reduce or even prevent juvenile criminal behavior.[50] Additionally, the LEAA was phased out.

The Reagan administration proposed in March 1981 that the OJJDP be terminated while at the same time substantially cutting back other federal criminal justice agencies.[51] But in December 1981, OJJDP was reinstated into the federal budget for two more years.

Throughout the 1980s, the OJJDP shifted its priorities from reducing the stigma attached to juvenile offenders to the identification and control of chronic, violent juvenile offenders. This goal was in line with the Reagan administration's more conservative views of justice. The federal government poured millions of dollars into research projects designed to study chronic offenders, predict their behavior, and evaluate programs designed to control their activities.[52]

When Congress reauthorized the JJDP Act in 1992, it reemphasized the importance of lawyers in juvenile delinquency proceedings. Congress charged the OJJDP with developing a program to enhance the quality of due process available to children in juvenile court by improving the level of legal representation in delinquency proceedings.

Recent sessions of Congress have passed bills related to juvenile crime. In the 109th Session of Congress (2005–06), members debated a bill (HR 864) that would provide programs and activities to prevent underage drinking. The Sober Truth on Preventing Underage Drinking Act (the STOP Act) required the Secretary of Health and Human Services to establish the Interagency Coordinating Committee on the Prevention of Underage Drinking, which is to produce a yearly report on each state's performance in preventing or reducing underage drinking. The bill was signed into law (L 109-422).

During that same Congress, the members passed a bill (HR 4472; PL 109-248) called the Adam Walsh Child Protection and Safety Act of 2006. The new law created the national Sex Offender Registration and Notification Act and created a three-tier classification system under which offenders must register after being convicted of a sexual offense.

In the next Congress, the members passed a proposed bill (S 1738) that would require the Department of Justice to improve the Internet Crimes Against Children Task Force, to increase resources for regional computer forensic labs, and to make other improvements to increase the ability of law enforcement agencies to investigate and prosecute child predators. The bill was named the Providing Resources, Officers and Technology to Eradicate Cyber Threats to our Children (PROTECT) Act. The bill was signed into law (PL 110-401). Congress also passed a law (S 1829; PL 110-240), called the Protecting our Children Comes First Act of 2007, to revise and expand the grants for the National Center for Missing and Exploited Children.

It is clear that even today, Congress continues to debate and make legislation that impacts the juvenile justice system and how juveniles are treated in the system. Congressional action also has a dramatic impact on the funding that is provided to states that allows them to implement programs for juveniles.

Interest Groups and Juvenile Justice

There are many interest groups that lobby legislators on the federal and state levels and try to influence legislation so that it will reflect their interests. One example of these is the Coalition for Juvenile Justice (CJJ). Based in Washington, D.C., the CJJ serves as a resource on juvenile delinquency prevention and other juvenile justice issues. Each state created an advisory group, as required in the JJDP Act, whose members are appointed by governors. Called state advisory groups, they provide assistance and guidance to elected officials so that they can meet federal requirements to receive funds, administer federal funds, and generate local citizen involvement in reducing youth crime and violence. In 1980, the National Coalition of State Juvenile Justice Advisory Groups was founded. In early 1993, the organization's name was changed to the Coalition for Juvenile Justice.

The CJJ has taken many positions on issues related to juvenile justice. For one, it opposes new laws that try and sentence youthful offenders in adult criminal courts, except in the rare cases of chronic and violent offenders, and then only at the discretion of a juvenile court judge. Under no circumstance does the CJJ support sending a child younger than age 15 into the adult system. The CJJ also opposes the death penalty for any individual whose offenses were committed before age 18. It is opposed to the unequal treatment of minority youth in the juvenile justice system, believing that all children deserve to be treated the same regardless of race, ethnicity, or other factors.

The Juvenile Justice and Delinquency Prevention Coalition is another group that works to promote policies that keep children out of trouble but also to protect those youth who have entered the system. It organizes congressional briefings, provides congressional and administration staff with the latest information and research, and provides grassroots support for legislation, among other things.[53]

Bureaucracies and Juvenile Justice

Probably one of the most well-known and largest bureaucracies that deals with criminal justice issues is the Office of Juvenile Justice and Delinquency Prevention (OJJDP). This federal agency was created by Congress in 1974 to improve juvenile justice policies and practices on both the federal and the state level. It sponsors many research studies on juvenile crime, establishes training programs, helps set policies to guide federal juvenile justice issues, disseminates information about its research and other pertinent information, and provides funding awards to states to provide state and local programs that assist juvenile offenders.[54]

All states have state-level bureaucracies that are responsible for implementing programs to assist juveniles. For example, Texas has the Texas Juvenile Probation Commission to help provide a quality level of probation services to juveniles. It helps provide probation services to juveniles as an alternative to the commitment of juveniles, and it provides financial aid to help local communities establish and improve their probation services. The agency also helps set uniform standards among agencies and develop a communications system among state and local agencies to improve the quality of their contacts. Texas also has the Texas Youth Commission, which operates the institutional component of the juvenile justice system. It provides for the care, custody, rehabilitation, and reestablishment of juveniles in the community. Like such commissions in most states, this one oversees both institutional and community-based residential programs.[55]

Florida also has a Department of Juvenile Justice with four core functions: prevention and victim services, detention, probation and community corrections, and residential and correctional facilities. Its overall mission is to protect the public and reduce juvenile crime in the state.[56] Kansas has the Kansas Juvenile Justice Authority, the goals of which are to deal effectively with violent, serious, and chronic juvenile offenders; provide individualized care; work to strengthen families; provide education and work experience to juvenile offenders to develop skills; cooperate with other agencies; and provide leadership.[57]

Some other state juvenile justice agencies are the Department of Youth Services (Alabama), the California Youth Authority, the Division of Youth Corrections (Colorado), the Louisiana Office of Youth Services, the Juvenile Justice Advisory Committee (Massachusetts), the New Jersey Juvenile Justice Commission, the Oregon Youth Authority, the Virginia Department of Juvenile Justice, and the West Virginia Division of Juvenile Services.[58]

ROLE IN POLICY PROCESS

Usually, juveniles who are "at risk" of committing criminal offenses or those who already have committed an offense do not have access to the political system and are unable to have much influence on the policy process. Instead, the interest groups and bureaucracies that revolve around juvenile justice become their surrogates and represent the interests of the youth in the political process. These groups often play a major role in defining policy that concerns how juveniles are treated and what programs and services are available to those youth. They help ensure that juveniles are provided the rights guaranteed to them under the U.S. Constitution.

Problem Identification

Most often, juveniles who face problems that result in criminal behavior cannot help identify major problems that need to be solved to prevent further juvenile offenses. Additionally, in most cases, legislators may be completely unaware of any new issues and problems in the juvenile system, as they have limited contact (if any) with the system. The major way in which issues pertaining to the juvenile justice system are identified is through interest groups or bureaucracies, such as those noted previously, who deal with juvenile offenders bringing the problems to light. They can attempt to persuade legislators that issues need more attention or more money. In some cases, a trigger event, such as a school shooting, may help identify a problem that can be addressed by legislators.

At the federal level, the Juvenile Justice Advisory Committee of the OJJDP advises the president and Congress on matters related to juvenile justice.[59] At the state level, there are many agencies that help identify problems. One of these is the Texas Juvenile Probation Commission, which was described earlier. This organization helps educate lawmakers, juvenile justice professionals, and the public regarding the issues and needs of the juvenile justice system.[60] Occasionally, executives at either the federal or the state level may appoint a task force made up of practitioners, academics, and/or other experts in the field (such as psychologists or doctors) who will develop a set of recommendations to deal with a problem or issue. Often these task forces have more legitimacy behind them, as they are composed of people with a certain expertise who have the impression of wanting to make effective policy without regard for politics.

Agenda Setting

The same bureaucracies or interest groups that identify new problems must also be effective in persuading legislators to put new issues that concern juvenile justice on the political agenda. Since agencies and interest groups are formally unable to put the issue on the agenda themselves, they must be able to persuade a legislator about the extent of the problem and the need for attention. As noted earlier, a trigger may help show legislators that a problem exists. For example, after the Columbine High School shooting, some of the surviving students met with legislators in Washington, D.C., who then proposed legislation to Congress so that another school shooting could be prevented.

For the most part, it is relatively simple to get juvenile justice on the agenda. Most politicians will be supportive of programs to help juveniles and prevent juvenile crimes as long as the proposed program shows some signs of being effective. It is easy for politicians to be supportive of these programs, as it brings them positive media coverage.

Occasionally, presidents may even be able to put the issue of juvenile delinquency on the political agenda. In fact, President Kennedy focused on issues surrounding juvenile justice, arguing that stopping adult crime begins with helping at-risk youth and presenting the need for congressional action on the issue.

Policy Formulation

Criminal justice bureaucracies or interest groups help influence legislation by testifying in front of committees and subcommittees and providing information to legislators. These three actors (bureaucracies, interest groups, and congressional committees) work together both formally and informally (through the iron triangle) to make policy. They provide each other with the information needed to make a policy that will deal with a problem effectively.

Any task forces and research groups that were put together by the executive branch may also propose policy solutions for problems and work for those proposals. They can testify in front of Congress or may work to influence public opinion concerning a particular issue. Since these task forces sometimes have more legitimacy, their actions may seem more powerful and have more impact on the final legislation that is passed.

Program Implementation

Programs to deter or prevent juvenile offenses or those that help juvenile offenders who are in the system are implemented by the bureaucracies, such as state juvenile justice departments and agencies that oversee the juvenile justice system in that state. They have been given broad discretion to define terms and phrases that were left undefined in legislation passed by the legislative body. Bureaucracies on the state and local levels sometimes have discretion over how to spend federal grant monies made available to them. This ability to define the specifics of a bill or how to spend money gives them significant power in the implementation stage of the policy process.

Almost every state has some services for juveniles that are provided through the local government, while others are implemented at the state level. Residential programs (commitment) for delinquents and any aftercare programs tend to be implemented by states, whereas probation and readjudication detention of juveniles are most often local responsibilities. In some states, such as Florida and Maine, there is a state executive agency that has control of all delinquency services. In other states, such as Ohio and California, the organization of juvenile services is characterized by local control of probation and sometimes detention services. Other states have a combination of implementation, such as Georgia, which has a mix of state-controlled and locally controlled delinquency services. They have largely state-run agencies but with significant local control in the more populous cities in the state.[61]

Program Evaluation and Reassessment

Programs to assist juveniles are constantly under review from federal research agencies, such as the OJJDP or the General Accountability Office. These studies attempt to determine if the programs are successful in helping juveniles out of a life of crime. After a study is completed, the results are usually published and made available to the public and other practitioners in the field. If the program has been successful, other communities may decide to implement a similar program in their jurisdiction. If not, the program will, more than likely, not be re-funded and may be disbanded. The Juvenile Justice Advisory Committee of the OJJDP is one organization that is responsible for evaluating the progress and accomplishments of juvenile justice activities and projects. Another agency within the OJJDP that is involved in the evaluation stage is the Disproportionate Minority Contact Office (DMC). The DMC coordinator organizes the planning, implementation, and evaluation of efforts to reduce the disproportionate number of contacts between minority youth and law enforcement.[62]

The Justice Research and Statistics Association works with the OJJDP to "develop and enhance juvenile justice evaluation capacity in the states. The goal of this project is to provide useful resources and practical technical assistance to local and state policymakers, program administrators and staff, and evaluators to strengthen their ability to implement and utilize evaluation studies and their findings."[63] After completion of the project, a "national Advisory Group ... will review the findings."[64] This is an example of a metaevaluation.

Many places have a research and planning division of their agencies that collects data and publishes that information in annual publications to distribute the data to key decision makers. They then use this to determine if programs are cost effective and if they should be re-funded.

JUVENILE JUSTICE ISSUES

There are many examples of key issues that personnel working in the juvenile justice system must face on a daily basis. Some of these issues have serious implications for how juveniles are treated (or the level of punishment they receive) and what their chances are of successfully becoming a productive and crime-free member of society.

Preventive Detention

The physical detention of juveniles to prevent or deter additional future juvenile crime is a controversial policy that many jurisdictions use. Detention refers to the temporary care of children in physically restricted facilities pending court disposition or transfer to another agency. The detention of a juvenile can be either before adjudication, where some juveniles are placed in a detention facility overnight until parents can be notified, or while they are awaiting trial. Or, they may be detained if the court presupposes that a juvenile might commit another offense dangerous to him- or herself or the community. In some cases, juveniles may be detained if they are violators from other jurisdictions.

Until recently, the placement of juveniles in adult facilities was a common policy. In some areas, juvenile offenders are still held alongside adult offenders. This is usually done only in rural areas where there is no opportunity for separate facilities. It has been shown that juveniles who are housed alongside adults can become the victims of adults, of the staff, and of their own hands. According to federal guidelines, all juveniles within state custody must be separated from adult offenders, or the state could lose federal funds for juvenile justice programs. Separation requires that juveniles have either totally independent facilities or separate areas within shared facilities so that juveniles and adults do not have either planned or accidental contact.

The decision about what to do with youth after their arrest and before the trial has been debated for years. Some youth are released under community supervision whereas others are placed in secure detention facilities. Sometimes, the parents do not want the children at home, or in other situations there may be a lack of alternatives for the youth. It has been argued that pretrial detention removes children from their homes and schools, but also increases the chances that they will be moved further into the justice system. It has also been said that these children are more likely to meet gang members within the institution, and delays the access they may have for appropriate mental health services.[65]

Those opposed to detention not only point to the dangers of harm or violence directed at the juvenile prisoners but also argue that many juveniles are not given the same or equal rights as an adult who may be facing a loss of freedom through detention. Although juveniles do have the right to a detention hearing where evidence is provided and a determination is made as to the need for detention, many accusations of unfair treatment remain. Some argue that the poor and minorities are placed in detention more often than wealthy, majority juveniles. They argue that every year, thousands of juveniles are held in detention and corrections facilities. Most juvenile facilities are overcrowded, leading to dangerous and unhealthy conditions.

Most professionals agree that juvenile detention centers should be reserved for those youth who present a clear and substantial threat to the community or to themselves. Many jurisdictions have created more approaches to detention, such as day resource centers, detention alternative programs, or family shelters. Other options can include those listed in Box 13.2.

Despite the fact that the JJDPA of 1974 requires that states separate adults and juveniles at all stages, more than 8,000 youth are held in adult jails, where they face serious risk of abuse and assault. It has been estimated that children held in adult facilities are five times as likely to be sexually assaulted, twice as likely to be beaten by staff, 50 percent more likely to be attacked with a weapon, and eight times as likely to commit suicide than children confined to facilities that hold only juvenile offenders.[66]

Currently, about 70 percent of youth in secure detention centers are being held for nonviolent offenses such as status offenses or other minor offenses. This could be emotionally harmful to youth, and may increase the likelihood of future delinquent behavior.[67]

Juveniles and the Death Penalty

Some states allowed for the death penalty in cases where the offender was a juvenile when the crime was committed, but in early 2005, this practice was deemed unconstitutional by a Supreme Court decision. In their decision, the justices raised significant questions concerning the development of the human brain and whether juveniles are mature enough to be subject to capital punishment. Most people recognize that adolescents are more susceptible to peer pressure than adults and that bigger issues within society are often at least partially responsible for juvenile crime.[68] Further, many would argue that current American standards of decency reject the death penalty for juveniles.[69] The increase in juvenile homicide and in brutal, senseless offenses committed by juveniles in the past decade makes this debate more critical than ever.

Those who oppose the death penalty for juvenile offenders find that it has little deterrent effect on youngsters who are impulsive and do not have a realistic view of the destructiveness of their misdeeds or their consequences; therefore, the capacity of the young for change, growth, and rehabilitation makes the death penalty particularly harsh and inappropriate.

Supporters of the death penalty for youth often argue that juveniles, particularly "older" juveniles (i.e., sixteen or seventeen years old) have the capabilities to understand the consequences of their crimes. Additionally, the prevention of further crime by the specific juvenile offender, as well as others, requires the swift and certain punishment for that offense.

For many years, the Supreme Court allowed for capital sentences for juvenile offenders. For example, the Court addressed the question of teenagers on death row in the 1982 case of *Eddings v. Oklahoma*. After hearing the facts of the case, the members of the Court reversed the death sentence of a 16-year-old male who had been tried as an adult in criminal court. The Court argued that young people tend to be less mature, less responsible, and less self-disciplined than adults and are therefore also less able to consider the long-range implications of their actions. Thus, a court, when deciding whether to apply the death penalty in a juvenile case, must consider a defendant's young age and his or her young mental and emotional development. The Court, however, did not address the larger question of whether imposing the death sentence on the offender was prohibited because he was only 16 years old at the time the offense was committed.[70]

In 1988, the Supreme Court again addressed whether the death penalty applied to juveniles in the case of *Thompson v. Oklahoma* (487 U.S. 815). The specific question in this case was whether imposing the death penalty on an offender who was 15 years old at the time of the murder violated protections against cruel and unusual punishment. The defendant, William

Thompson, was a 15-year-old with a record of three convictions for violent assaults with deadly weapons. He was convicted of the first-degree murder of his brother-in-law after he savagely beat him, shot him, and then cut up his carcass with a knife. Thompson received the death penalty for his offense. The Court overturned Thompson's death sentence by a vote of five to four on the fact that Oklahoma did not specify any minimum age of eligibility for the death sentence. Only four justices held that the death sentence for crimes committed by people under 16 years old is necessarily cruel and unusual. In short, the Court concluded that the Eighth Amendment prohibited application of the death penalty to a person who was younger than 16 at the time of the crime. The Court did not address the issue of whether the Constitution prohibited the use of the death penalty for juveniles who were 16 or 17 years old when they committed their crime, leaving the possibility of executing older teenagers open. At the same time, the case indicated that a growing portion of the population was very uncomfortable with the idea of putting minors to death.[71]

The following year, the Supreme Court again faced the issue, this time upholding the death penalty for juveniles. This time the case was *Stanford v. Kentucky* (429 U.S. 361, 1989). In this case, Stanford was seventeen when he committed murder. The Court ruled that it is not cruel and unusual punishment for a state to execute an offender who was 16 or 17 at the time of their crime. The Court stated,

> We discern neither a historical nor a modern societal consensus forbidding the imposition of capital punishment on any person who murders at 16 or 17 years of age. Accordingly, we conclude that such punishment does not offend the Eighth Amendment's prohibition against cruel and unusual punishment.[72]

In March 2005, the Supreme Court ruled that juveniles who were younger than 18 at the time of their offense could not be executed, stating in their five-to-four decision that the practice of executing juveniles was a violation of the cruel and unusual clause of the Eighth Amendment to the U.S. Constitution. The case, *Roper v. Simmons* (S.Ct., 205 WL 464890), revolved around Christopher Simmons, who was 17 when he broke into the house of Shirley Crook. He abducted her, hog-tied her, then threw her, bound and gagged, into a river to drown. He then bragged to his friends that he could get away with the crime because of his age. Simmons' death sentence was reversed by Missouri's Supreme Court, and the U.S. Supreme Court justices backed that ruling.

In reaching their decision, the justices argued that medical and social-science evidence consistently demonstrates that teenagers are too immature to be held accountable for their crimes. In essence, the justices argued, juveniles lack maturity and are particularly susceptible to peer pressure. Juveniles are also more agreeable to reform than are adults.

The *Simmons* decision means that more than 70 juveniles on death row in approximately 20 states across the nation will not be executed. Instead, their death sentences will be vacated and life sentences imposed.

The decision that states could not impose the death penalty on juveniles who commit serious, brutal criminal offenses was praised by some, but others maintain that at least some juvenile offenders are capable of understanding the seriousness of their offenses and should pay the ultimate penalty for that offense. In years to come, the Supreme Court may continue to ban the execution of juveniles or may choose to allow it under certain circumstances.

Racism in the System

As with the adult criminal justice system, there are allegations of racism in the juvenile justice system as well. These allegations, however, are controversial. There are many statistics to show that

TABLE 13.5 Custody Rates by Race, 2006

Race	Rate per 100,000
White	170
Black	767
Hispanic	326
American Indian	540
Asian	85

Source: Statistical Briefing Book, Office of Juvenile Justice and Delinquency
Prevention, available online at www.ojjdp.ncjrs.gov/ojstatbb/court/qa06204.

minority juveniles are overrepresented in the system. For example, the ratio of the custody rate for minorities to that for whites was 2.9 to 1.[73] Other statistics show that in 2008, black youth were involved in 52 percent of juvenile violence crime arrests and 33 percent of juvenile property crime arrests, even though they make up only 16 percent of the youth population.[74] Since 2004, the arrest rate for aggravated assault increased 4 percent for black juveniles while the white rate declined 9 percent. The robbery rate increased 56 percent for black youth whereas only 30 percent for white youth.[75] These numbers demonstrate an overrepresentation of minorities in the juvenile justice system. It has also been argued that "an Afro-American male born today will, if present imprisonment and crime rates continue, have more than a one in four chance of being in state or federal prison before he dies."[76] Table 13.5 shows the custody rates of juveniles in the system broken down by race. This shows that there are far more minorities in the system than whites per 100,000 people.

There are also statistics to show that minority juvenile offenders are treated differently in the punishment phases. Of the juveniles held in custody for criminal acts. Thirty-nine percent where white, 38 percent were black, 19 percent Hispanic, 2 percent were American Indian, and 2 percent were Asian.[77] Again, these statistics show the different treatment given to whites and minorities.

The disproportionate number of juveniles who come into contact with the juvenile justice system has been terms "disproportionate minority contact or DMC." Through the Office of Juvenile Justice and Delinquency Prevention, grant money has been made available to those states who design programs to reduce DMC within their states. The ultimate goal of the program is to ensure equal and fair treatment for every youth in the system.[78] In 1992, the Juvenile Detention Alternatives Institute was developed to help states reduce the number of children who are detained, to minimize the number of youth who reoffend, and to improve the conditions of confinement.[79]

However, there is another side to this argument, and there is evidence to show that there is not as much racism in the system as one might think. A study done by Pope and Snyder focused on data collected from the National Incident Based Reporting System. After analyzing the information and controlling for other characteristics, they concluded that, for violent offenses, there was no difference in the overall likelihood of arrest for white juveniles and nonwhite juveniles. They did find that the likelihood of juvenile arrest was affected by several other characteristics. They found that a juvenile was more likely to be arrested when there was a single offender, there were multiple victims, or there was victim injury or when the victim and offender were family members (rather than strangers). The odds of arrest also increased when the offender was male and when the victim was an adult or white. In fact, because of the association of these other incident characteristics with offender race, a greater proportion of white juvenile offenders were arrested than were nonwhite juvenile offenders for most person offenses (e.g., robbery, aggravated assault, and simple assault).[80]

Another study of juvenile arrests that looked at data from the National Crime Victimization Survey between 1980 and 1998 showed that the serious violent offending rate for black juveniles was higher than the rate for white juveniles. For 1980–1998, the offending rate for black juveniles was, on average, 4.1 times higher than the offending rate for white juveniles. On average, the arrest rate for black juveniles was 5.7 times higher than for white juveniles.[81]

According to the studies, the argument can be made that minority youth commit more crimes than white youth, are involved in more serious incidents, or have more extensive criminal histories. This is why they tend to be overrepresented in secure facilities even if no discrimination by system decision makers occurs. Thus, minority youth may be overrepresented within the juvenile justice system because of behavioral and legal factors.[82]

Thus, there is evidence to support both sides of this argument. More research in future years may give the edge to one side or the other.

Serious, Violent Juvenile Offenders

In most states, a juvenile is defined as a boy or girl under the age of 18. In some states, the age is sixteen, and in very few it is 15. Many juveniles commit petty offenses that really are not very serious. However, there are more and more juveniles committing brutal, violent criminal acts, such as homicide, aggravated assault (including weapons offenses and attempted murder), robbery (including armed robbery), kidnapping, voluntary manslaughter, rape or attempted rape, and arson of an occupied building. There are also juveniles committing felony larceny/theft, auto theft, fraud, dealing in stolen property, burglary, breaking and entering, carjacking, extortion, forgery and counterfeiting, embezzlement, drug trafficking, arson (other than of an occupied dwelling), and violations of weapons and firearms regulations/statutes. These juveniles have been labeled serious, violent juveniles (SVJs). An SVJ does not include those youth who commit status offenses, minor forms of aggression (simple assault, juvenile fist fights), violations of ordinances, vandalism, drunkenness, malicious mischief, disorderly conduct, and traffic and motor vehicle law violations. Rather, they are typically involved in serious forms of delinquency.[83]

SVJ offenders are a distinct group of juveniles who tend to start criminal behavior early in their lives and continue to offend into their later years.[84] Even in early childhood and adolescence, SVJ offenders tend to have behavior problems, such as aggression, dishonesty, property offenses, and conflict with authority. They tend to have multiple problems at home and at school with things such as truancy, substance abuse, and mental health problems. They often have a lack of strong social ties, antisocial peers, and a poor attitude toward school.[85]

Since SVJ offenders often begin to show behavior problems and delinquency early in their lives, the need for early intervention has been identified. The prevention of SVJ involves family- and parent-focused components, child-focused components, and peer-based components, such as conflict resolution.[86] Some professionals argue that programs that target children before they begin school can identify potential SVJ offenders and work to prevent such behavior. These programs include early (preschool) home visits to teach parent–child interaction techniques, other programs for preschoolers to help parents support their children's development, programs for school-age children to reduce involvement with antisocial peers and reduce aggressive behavior, and programs for adolescents, such as anti–drug use classes.[87]

Gangs

A juvenile gang is understood to be a group of juveniles who come together to commit serious criminal behavior. The typical definition of a gang is three or more individuals who engage in criminal activity and who identify themselves with a particular sign or name. However, it is much more complicated that this. Klein offers one widely accepted definition of a gang:

> Any denotable adolescent group of youngsters who (a) are generally perceived as a distinct aggregation by others in their neighborhood, (b) recognize themselves as a denotable group (almost invariably with a group name) and (c) have been involved in a sufficient number of delinquent incidents to call forth consistent negative responses from neighborhood residents and/or enforcement agencies.[88]

Generally, gangs are groups that exhibit characteristics that set them apart from other groups of juveniles.[89] A gang is a specific form of a group that becomes involved in activities and behaviors that include conflict. There are social gangs, in which membership is based not on "self-protection" but on feelings of mutual attraction and friendship. But there can also be delinquent gangs that are organized primarily to carry out delinquent acts. Other gangs have been identified as violent gangs, which become a vehicle to act out hostility and aggression.[90]

All gangs have a name and territorial neighborhood base. Joining a gang involves some type of an initiation rite that often includes the commission of a delinquent act. Senseless violence is an important gang activity, as is drug use.[91]

The OJJDP's 2007 National Youth Gang Survey found that there were more than 27,000 active gangs across the United States and more than 788,000 gang members, a 7.7 increase from 2002.[92] Most police departments have gang units that attempt to identify these gang members and their crimes. They also have programs that attempt to convince gang members to leave the gangs and to prevent others from ever joining. Social intervention programs that provide counseling or other attempts to change the values of gang members are also attempts to get juveniles out of gangs. There are also programs to make meaningful opportunities available to at-risk youth.

Despite all the attention given to gangs, there is some evidence that gang violence and crime is not as serious a problem as we are led to believe. McCorkle and Miethe conclude that during the late 1980s and early 1990s, the reaction to gang violence in Las Vegas was nothing but a "moral panic." As a result of the increased media attention gang violence received, there was new legislation that was overstated when compared to the actual threat posed by gangs. Although criminal gang activity did increase at the time, the political reaction to it was exaggerated, say McCorkle and Miethe. They argue that the nature, frequency, and severity of a social condition such as gang violence are often grossly exaggerated in order to justify further political action. In this case, gang violence simply was not as serious as it was made out to be.[93]

Transfer to Adult Court

Some juveniles are transferred from juvenile court to adult criminal court in a process known as a waiver, bind-over, or removal. All state statutes allow for this kind of transfer to allow for the adult criminal prosecution of juveniles.[94] It typically occurs through a judicial waiver, a prosecutorial decision, or a specific statute that excludes certain youth from the juvenile court.[95] Forty-six states currently have judicial waiver provisions whereby the juvenile court judge can waive jurisdiction for those juveniles who have committed serious violent offenses. Sometimes the prosecution has the discretion to choose, in certain cases, whether to initiate cases in juvenile or adult court. This is called direct file law, and it occurs in 15 states.[96] Twenty-nine states have statutory exclusion provisions that grant adult courts original jurisdiction in certain juvenile cases. In these states, the legislatures have decided what kinds of cases should be heard in the adult courts, taking the decision making out of the prosecutors' hands.[97]

Some states allow for transfer between the ages of 14 and 17. However, others restrict waiver proceedings to mature juveniles and specify particular offenses. Other jurisdictions have defined the bind-over process on the basis of a juvenile's past record and current offense.

Recently, many states have amended their waiver policies to automatically exclude certain offenses from juvenile court jurisdiction. These statutes that remove certain juveniles from the jurisdiction of the juvenile court because of offense, age, or previous record have become increasingly popular.[98] In many states, 16- and 17-year-old offenders who have been charged with rape, murder, or armed robbery are automatically bound over to adult court.

Opponents say that the process is done unfairly and that children tried in adult criminal court may be incarcerated under conditions so extreme that the children will be permanently damaged. They also argue that these juveniles may be given a stigma that may be attached to a conviction in criminal court. In their eyes, labeling children as adult offenders early in life may seriously impair their further educational, employment, and other opportunities. The juveniles transferred to adult court are disproportionately minority, and this demographic trend is increasing.[99]

Often, the bind-over laws are political responses to juvenile crime.[100] The bind-over process provides the illusion of doing something about juvenile crime—a "quick fix."[101] The new laws come from today's political concerns and interests in maintaining the legitimacy of juvenile justice. When juveniles continue to commit serious violent offenses and brutal acts of juvenile violence, they are threatening the system. Diverting the most violent offenders from the juvenile justice system satisfies public and official demands to see these serious delinquents punished in a public, criminal court.[102]

Nonetheless, the number of cases waived to criminal court via judicial waiver is increasing.[103] The new law is simply shifting the legal decision from juvenile justice officials to criminal justice officials.[104]

In most cases, states have a "once an adult, always an adult" clause, meaning that if a juvenile who has been prosecuted as an adult once and subsequently accused of a new offense, he or she will from then on be tried as an adult. Others require the juvenile to be of a certain age or to have committed a serious offense to be tried in adult court for subsequent offenses.[105]

The OJJDP has concluded that youth transferred to adult court had higher rates of recidivism and reoffended more often than youth offenders who remained in the juvenile courts.[106]

Conclusion

Despite early attempts to prevent juvenile crime with a distinct juvenile justice system geared toward rehabilitating juvenile offenders rather than punishing them, juveniles continue to commit sometimes serious offenses. In recent years, the public has become more concerned with the seriousness of the offenses and have called on politicians to react, which they have done by passing more severe and harsh punishments for juvenile offenders. The system today has become more punishment oriented than in earlier years, but it retains many elements of the treatment programs the Founding Fathers supported. Despite this, the juvenile justice system must face many serious issues, such as preventive detention, racism, serious violent youth, and transfers to adult court. To solve the problems that arise in the juvenile justice system, many organizations and personnel have become involved in the policy process in an attempt to make the system more effective in reducing juvenile crime.

Notes

1. John Scalia, *Juvenile Delinquents in the Federal Criminal Justice System* (Washington, D.C.: U.S. Department of Justice, Bureau of Justice Statistics, 1997).
2. Ibid.
3. "Juvenile Arrests 2008" Office of Juvenile Justice and Delinquency Prevention, Office of Justice Programs, U.S. Department of Justice; available online at www.ojp.usdoj.gov.
4. Federal Bureau of Investigation, Supplementary Homicide Reports for the years 1980–2006. Washington, D.C.: FBI.
5. Federal Advisory Committee on Juvenile Justice, Annual Report 2009, Washington, D.C.: Office of Juvenile Justice and Delinquency Prevention, Office of Justice Programs, U.S. Department of Justice; accessed 2/18/2010 from www.facjj.org, page 7; Mark Soler and Lisa M. Garry "Reducing Disproportionate Minority Contact: Preparation at the Local Level" September 2009; Washington, D.C.: U.S. Department of Justice, Office of Justice Programs, Office of Juvenile Justice and Delinquency Prevention, available at www.ojp.usdoj.gov/ojjdp.
6. Statistical Briefing Book: Juveniles in Corrections (Washington, D.C.: Office of Juvenile Justice and Delinquency Prevention, Office of Justice Programs, U.S. Department of Justice), available online at www.ojjdp.ncjrs.gov/ojstatbb/corrections/qu08201.asp?
7. Statistical Briefing Book: Juveniles in Corrections (Washington, D.C.: Office of Juvenile Justice and Delinquency Prevention, Office of Justice Programs, U.S. Department of Justice), available online at www.ojjdp.ncjrs.gov/ojstatbb/corrections/qu08201.asp?
8. Ibid., p. 16.
9. Ibid., p. 17.
10. Gayle Olson-Raymer, "National Juvenile Justice Policy: Myth or Reality?" in *Juvenile Justice Policy*, ed. Scott H. Decker (Beverly Hills, Calif.: Sage, 1984), p. 21.
11. Ibid.
12. John T. Whitehead and Steven P. Lab, *Juvenile Justice* (Cincinnati: Anderson, 1996), pp. 41–42.
13. Samuel Walker, *Popular Justice: A History of American Criminal Justice* (New York: Oxford University Press, 1998), p. 105.
14. Ibid., p. 43.
15. Ibid., p. 105; Whitehead and Lab, *Juvenile Justice*, p. 43.
16. Simon I. Singer, *Recriminalizing Delinquency: Violent Juvenile Crime and Juvenile Justice Reform* (New York: Cambridge University Press, 1996), p. 27.
17. Whitehead and Lab, *Juvenile Justice*, p. 43.
18. Ibid., pp. 42–43.
19. Walker, *Popular Justice*, p. 106.
20. Ibid., p. 107.
21. Whitehead and Lab, *Juvenile Justice*, p. 44.
22. Walker, *Popular Justice*, p. 168.
23. Whitehead and Lab, *Juvenile Justice*, p. 53.
24. Jeffrey M. Jenson and Matthew O. Howard, "Youth Crime, Public Policy and Practice in the Juvenile Justice System: Recent Trends and Needed Reforms," *Social Work* 43 (4, 1998): 324–34, at 327.
25. Ibid., p. 328.
26. Ibid.
27. James Q. Wilson, "Never Too Early," in *Serious and Violent Juvenile Offenders*, ed. Rolf Loeber and David P. Farrington (Thousand Oaks, Calif.: Sage, 1998), pp. ix–xi, at ix.
28. Francis A. Allen, *The Borderland of Criminal Justice* (Chicago: University of Chicago Press, 1964).
29. T. J. Bernard, "What Stays the Same in History?" in *Exploring Delinquency*, ed. Dean G. Rojek and Gary F. Jensen (Los Angeles: Roxbury, 1996), pp. 3–8, at 7.
30. Ibid.
31. Ibid.
32. Wilson, "Never Too Early," p. x; Kevin N. Wright and Karen E. Wright, "A Policy Maker's Guide to Controlling Delinquency and Crime through Family Interventions," in Hancock and Sharp, *Public Policy, Crime and Criminal Justice*, pp. 349–64.
33. Juvenile Offenders and Victims: 2006 National Report, p. 109.
34. Jenson and Howard, "Youth Crime, Public Policy and Practice in the Juvenile Justice System," p. 324.
35. Charles Smith, Pul Alexander, Garry Kemp, and Edwin Lemert, *A National Assessment of Serious Juvenile Crime and the Juvenile Justice System: The Need for a National Response Vol. III: Legislation, Jurisdiction, Program Interventions, and Confidentiality of Juvenile Records* (Washington, D.C.: U.S. Department of Justice, 1980); Marc Miller, "Changing Legal Paradigms in Juvenile Justice," in *Intervention Strategies for Chronic Juvenile Offenders*, ed. Peter W. Greenwood (New York: Greenwood Press, 1986); Michael F. Aloisi, "Emerging Trends and Issues in Juvenile Justice," in Hancock and Sharp, *Public Policy, Crime and Criminal Justice*, pp. 365–80.
36. Olson-Raymer, "National Juvenile Justice Policy," p. 27.

37. Ibid., p. 30.
38. Ibid., p. 31.
39. Ibid., p. 32.
40. Larry J. Siegal and Joseph J. Senna, *Juvenile Delinquency* (St. Paul, Minn.: West, 1991), p. 408.
41. Olson-Raymer, "National Juvenile Justice Policy," p. 37.
42. Siegal and Senna, *Juvenile Delinquency*, pp. 408–9.
43. Ibid.
44. Ibid., p. 409.
45. Jenson and Howard, "Youth Crime, Public Policy and Practice in the Juvenile Justice System," p. 328.
46. Olson-Raymer, "National Juvenile Justice Policy," p. 40.
47. Ibid., p. 34.
48. Ibid., p. 38.
49. Siegal and Senna, *Juvenile Delinquency*, p. 409.
50. Ibid.
51. Olson-Raymer, "National Juvenile Justice Policy," p. 39.
52. Siegal and Senna, *Juvenile Delinquency*, p. 410.
53. "Juvenile Justice and Delinquency Prevention Coalition" (2004), available online at www.building-blocksforyouth.org/issues/federaladvocacy/jjdpwho.html.
54. "About OJJDP" (2004), available online at http://ojjdp.ncjrs.org/about/about.html.
55. "The Texas Juvenile Justice System" (2004), available online at www.tjpc.state.tx.us/about_us/juv_justice_overview.htm.
56. "Learn More about the Department of Juvenile Justice" (2004), available online at www.djj.state.fl.us/AboutDJJ/agency/about_us_index.html.
57. "About the Juvenile Justice Authority" (2004), available online at http://jja.state.ks.us/about.htm.
58. "State Juvenile Justice Grants Information Links" (2004), available online at www.jrsa.org/jjec/state_info/header.html.
59. http://ojjdp.ncjrs.org/statecontacts/categorydefinitions.html.
60. "The Texas Juvenile Justice System" (2004), available online at www.tjpc.state.tx.us/about_us/juv_justice_overview.htm.
61. Patrick Griffin and Melanie Bozynski, "National Overviews," State Juvenile Justice Profiles (Pittsburgh: National Center for Juvenile Justice, 2004), available online at www.ncjj.org/stateprofiles/.
62. http://ojjdp.ncjrs.org/statecontacts/categorydefinitions.html.
63. Justice Research and Statistics Association, "Juvenile Justice Evaluation Needs in the States: Findings of the Formula Grants Program Evaluation Needs Assessment" (2004), available online at www.jrsa.org/pubs/reports/jj_needs_assessment.htm.
64. Ibid.
65. Federal Advisory Committee on Juvenile Justice, Annual Report 2009, Office of Juvenile Justice and Delinquency Prevention, Office of Justice Programs, U.S. Department of Justice; accessed 2/18/2010 from www.facjj.org, page 12.
66. Building Blocks for Youth, "Children in Adult Jails" (2004), available online at www.buildingblocksforyouth.org/issues/adultjails/factsheet.html.
67. Federal Advisory Committee on Juvenile Justice, Annual Report 2009, Office of Juvenile Justice and Delinquency Prevention, Office of Justice Programs, U.S. Department of Justice; accessed 2/18/2010 from www.facjj.org, page 11.
68. B. C. Feld, "The Juvenile Court Meets the Principle of the Offense: Legislative Changes in Juvenile Waiver Statutes," *Journal of Criminal Law and Criminology* 78 (1987): 471–533.
69. V. L. Streib, *Death Penalty for Juveniles* (Bloomington, Ind.: Indiana University Press, 1987), p. 34.
70. Sickmund, *Juveniles in Corrections*, p. 22.
71. Feld, "The Juvenile Court"; Sickmund, *Juveniles in Corrections*.
72. Sickmund, *Juveniles in Corrections*.
73. Statistical Briefing Book, Office of Juvenile Justice and Delinquency Prevention, available online at www.ojjdp.ncjrs.gov/ojstatbb/court/qa06204.
74. Charles Puzzanchera, "Juvenile Arrests 2008" (December 2009), Office of Juvenile Justice and Delinquency Prevention, Office of Justice Programs, U.S. Department of Justice, available at www.ncjrs.gov/pdffiles1/ojjdp/228479.pdf.
75. Ibid.
76. Wilson, "Never Too Early," p. ix.
77. Howard N. Snyder and Melissa Sickmund, *Juveniles Offenders and Victims: 2006 National Report* (Washington, D.C.: U.S. Department of Justice, Office of Justice Programs, Office of Juvenile Justice and Delinquency Prevention), available online at http://ojjdp.ncjrs.gov/ojstabb/nr2006/downloads/chapter7.pdf.
78. Jeff Slowikowski, "Disproportionate Minority Contact" October 2009, Office of Juvenile Justice and Delinquency Prevention, Office of Justice Programs, U.S. Department of Justice, available at www.ncjrs.gov/pdffiles1/ojjdp/228306.pdf.
79. Mark Soler and Lisa M. Garry, "Reducing Disproportionate Minority Contact: Preparation at the Local Level" (September 2009) Office of Juvenile Justice and Delinquency Prevention, Office of Justice Programs, U.S. Department of Justice, available at www.ncjrs.gov/pdffiles1/ojjdp/218861.pdf.

80. Ibid., p. 14.
81. Ibid., p. 13.
82. Ibid., p. 12.
83. Rolf Loeber, David P. Farrington, and Daniel A. Waschbusch, "Serious and Violent Juvenile Offenders," in Loeber and Farrington, *Serious and Violent Juvenile Offenders*, pp. 13–29, at 15.
84. Ibid.
85. Ibid.
86. Gail A. Wasserman and Laurie S. Miller, "The Prevention of Serious and Violent Juvenile Offendings," in Loeber and Farrington, *Serious and Violent Juvenile Offenders*, pp. 197–247, at 199–207.
87. Ibid. For other prevention strategies, see Richard F. Catalano, Michael W. Arthur, J. David Hawkins, Lisa Berglund, and Jeffrey J. Olson, "Comprehensive Community and School Based Interventions to Prevent Anti-Social Behavior," in Loeber and Farrington, pp. 248–83; James C. Howell, "Promising Programs for Youth Gang Violence Prevention and Intervention," in Loeber and Farrington, pp. 284–312; David M. Altschuler, "Intermediate Sanctions and Community Treatment for Serious and Violent Juvenile Offenders," in Loeber and Farrington, pp. 367–85.
88. M. W. Klein, *Street Gangs and Street Workers* (Englewood Cliffs, N.J.: Prentice Hall, 1971), p. 13.
89. Whitehead and Lab, *Juvenile Justice*, p. 127.
90. Lewis Yablonsky, *Juvenile Delinquency into the 21st Century* (Belmont, Calif.: Wadsworth, 2000), pp. 178–80.
91. Ibid., p. 181.
92. Arlen Egley, Jr. and Christina E. O'Donnell, "Highlights of the 2007 National Youth Gang Survey" (Washington, D.C.: U.S. Department of Justice, Office of Juvenile Justice and Delinquency Prevention, 2009).
93. Richard C. McCorkle and Terance D. Miethe, "The Political and Organizational Response to Gangs: An Examination of a "Moral Panic" in Nevada," *Justice Quarterly* 15 (1, 1998): 41–64.
94. Patrick Griffin, "National Overviews," *State Juvenile Justice Profiles* (Pittsburgh: National Center for Juvenile Justice, 2004), available online at www.ncjj.org/stateprofiles/.
95. Alida V. Merlo, Peter J. Benekos, and William J. Cook, "Waiver and Juvenile Justice Reform: Widening the Punitive Net," *Criminal Justice Policy Review* 8 (2–3, 1997): 145–68.
96. Griffin, "National Overviews."
97. Ibid.
98. Merlo et al., "Waiver and Juvenile Justice," p. 151.
99. Ibid., p. 152.
100. Simon I. Singer, "The Automatic Waiver of Juveniles and Substantive Justice," *Crime and Delinquency* 39 (2, 1993): 253–61.
101. Merlo et al., "Waiver and Juvenile Justice," p. 153.
102. Singer, "The Automatic Waiver."
103. Merlo et al., "Waiver and Juvenile Justice," p. 151.
104. Singer, "The Automatic Waiver."
105. Griffin, "National Overviews."
106. Federal Advisory Committee on Juvenile Justice, Annual Report 2009, Office of Juvenile Justice and Delinquency Prevention, Office of Justice Programs, U.S. Department of Justice; accessed 2/18/2010 from www.facjj.org, page 13; R.E. Redding, Juvenile Transfer Laws: An Effective Deterrent to Delinquency? Washington, D.C.: U.S. Department of Justice, Office of Justice Programs, Office of Juvenile Justice and Delinquency Prevention; available at www.ncjrs.gov/pdffiles1/ojjdp/220595.pdf.

PART FOUR

Criminal Justice Policy

14

Criminal Justice Policy: A Case Study

Chapter Outline

INTRODUCTION

To fully understand the public policy of crime and criminal justice, it is helpful to look at the process through a specific example. Case studies provide this deeper understanding and give us a broader understanding of how the public policy process works. A case study focuses primarily on the process of how a specific crime issue becomes a public policy. By paying close attention to how an issue moves through the public policy process, one can gain greater insight into the nuances of this process. Issues in criminal justice clearly abound, and case studies could easily be conducted on such enduring issues as drug abuse, gun control, and the death penalty. In addition, more recent issues, such as the three-strikes legislation in California, the USA PATRIOT Act, or the Unborn Victims of Violence Act passed in light of the Scott Peterson case, would serve as good case studies for the criminal justice public policy process. However, for the purposes of this book, one specific case is used to highlight a number of varying aspects of the public policy process.

The case study selected here centers on the grassroots community policing movement, how it became a national public policy with the passage of the Violent Crime Control and Law Enforcement Act of 1994, and how this particular policy was implemented and what evaluations have been done to date. Although this act was a comprehensive bill, the primary emphasis here is placed on the centerpiece of the legislation, namely, the "100,000 Cops" initiative that was aimed at implementing or supporting community policing programs in local police and sheriff's departments across the United States. And while a bill from 1994 may seem somewhat "dated," the issue of this particular bill, the "100,000 Cops," and the Office of Community Oriented Policing Services (COPS), became an issue once again in the 2008 election, demonstrating it is still an example of modern criminal justice politics.

The method for reviewing this case study is to move the reader through the specific steps of the public policy process: problem identification, agenda setting, policy formulation, policy implementation, and policy evaluation. Reviewing each step in the process allows the reader to understand the material previously covered as it relates to each step in the process. And by applying the public policy process to this specific example in criminal justice, the goal is to demonstrate the importance of the public policy process in shaping our criminal justice system today.

COMMUNITY POLICING AND THE VIOLENT CRIME CONTROL AND LAW ENFORCEMENT ACT OF 1994

Problem Identification

Crime rates, especially violent crimes such as murder, rape, and robbery, peaked around 1991 and 1992, according to the Federal Bureau of Investigation's *Uniform Crime Reports*. The crime topics of the day tended to include drug abuse and the "war on drugs," remnants of the crack

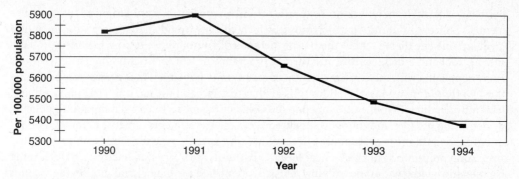

FIGURE 14.1 Crime Index by Year, 1990–1994. *Source:* Federal Bureau of Investigation, *Uniform Crime Reports—1996* (Washington, D.C.: Federal Bureau of Investigation, U.S. Government Printing Office, 1997).

cocaine epidemic from the late 1980s, and an increase in juvenile violence in the late 1980s. In addition, legislation such as the Brady Bill continued to surface as a public policy that drew attention to the issue of gun violence, and other topics tended to be emphasized by the Bush administration, such as the exclusionary rule, the death penalty, *habeas corpus,* and the insanity defense.[1] And, although President George H. W. Bush had successfully made crime a part of his campaign in 1988 in the presidential election of 1992, he was deftly undercut on this issue by the Democratic nominee, Bill Clinton. Whereas Bush had made drugs his issue, Clinton made crime his issue.

While drugs and crime were seen as problems throughout the United States, at the local level, police departments across the nation found a solution in the umbrella rubric known as community policing. Community policing developed at the grassroots level in the early 1980s, coming out of local police demonstration projects that were often funded by the National Institute of Justice and the Bureau of Justice Assistance. Community policing came about out of the rejection of traditional policing practices in the 1970s, largely as a result of various studies that found that long-held assumptions in policing were found not to hold up under close scrutiny. If such methods as random patrols, rapid response, and the application of technology to criminal investigations were not found to have any impact on crime, police agencies, administrators, and academics continually returned to the question, "What does work?"

An article published in a 1982 edition of the *Atlantic Monthly* by James Q. Wilson and George L. Kelling posited the broken windows theory and provided an answer to the question. In their theory, they articulated that when people no longer care about their community, the conditions of that neighborhood often send signals to people that no one cares. This allows for disorder and minor crimes to pass unnoticed, which, as Wilson and Kelling argued, lead to more serious crime. As run-down neighborhoods are rife with potholes, abandoned vehicles, and broken windows that remain unfixed, these environmental cues send crime-promoting signals to derelicts and criminals. Once disorder begins to take hold and minor crimes become common, eventually the neighborhood will decay and become crime ridden. The key to fixing the broken windows is for police to target these minor crimes and disorders in order to prevent more serious crimes, and by working with the community on a more personal basis, police officers can come to know who belongs to a neighborhood and who does not.

This concept of police–community partnerships became the primary basis of a shift in policing practices. Police began to articulate changes in policing under this new model of policing. Although there was no set pattern to how community policing was to be implemented, police–community partnerships in which citizens would share power with the police made up one key theme. Other themes or methods of community policing included problem solving, foot and bicycle patrols, and various programs. As Cordner has pointed out, what was really happening with the implementation of community policing is that change was occurring through three dimensions: the philosophical, the strategic, and the tactical.[2] The philosophical level moved policing from eschewing public assistance to embracing citizen input into policing by delivering broader and more personalized services. The strategic dimension focused on re-orienting operations to work more effectively, within specific neighborhoods, and to emphasize crime prevention. At the tactical level, community policing was focused on developing partnerships with the public, solving mutually identified problems, and employing various programs aimed at these ends.

The various types of programs under community policing tended to fall into three categories: strategic, neighborhood, and problem-oriented policing.[3] The methods of strategic policing adopted the concept of cracking down on minor crimes and disorder to bring the community out from behind closed doors. The federal government implemented its own method of strategic policing known as "weed and seed," which aimed to remove the criminal and disorderly elements of the community to allow new "seeds" to be planted by the citizens living in the neighborhood. The neighborhood policing methods focused on bringing police and citizens into contact with one another on a daily basis and included foot/bike patrols, neighborhood substations, and police–community meetings that would occur on a routine basis. Problem-oriented policing tended to generally adopt the SARA model for addressing specific problems in a neighborhood. Under community policing, however, SARA would be conducted by both police and citizens rather than police alone as was originally intended.

Although the 1980s was seen as the beginning of the community policing era, community policing moved through three generations of the way in which it was implemented.[4] During the early 1980s, it consisted of various experiments, test sites, and demonstration projects. As previously stated, these tended to be grassroots attempts at innovation within police deployment. As there was much success with these innovations, community policing moved to a second generation, marked by the diffusion of these early projects and programs. Community policing essentially diffused rapidly across the United States in the late 1980s, mostly among large and medium-size departments. While many departments continued to receive federal and state grants to assist in the implementation of community policing, most agencies adopted the tenets of community policing without the strings attached. While many of these agencies jumped on the bandwagon because community policing was the latest fad in policing, many signed on because the alternative was continuing past practices that were not deemed effective. Community policing offered hope for effective change.

The public responded well to the concepts of community policing, and the media reported quite heavily on it by the early 1990s.[5] Not only was it becoming a buzzword among police chiefs and sheriffs, it was becoming something of a household term. While this was clearly more prevalent in policing circles, the term "community policing" tended to resonate with both the media and the public. The implications here for the problem identification step in the public policy process began to take shape. The problem, as always, was crime. A solution for many local jurisdictions was the movement to community policing. The early police chiefs and sheriffs who were testing these programs and adopting the precepts of community policing were serving to shape future policy. In addition, because the term "community policing" tended to receive a favorable reaction from the public and the media, it established itself as a viable policy for many departments.[6] Eventually, with some changes, community policing would become a viable public policy on the national level.

It should be noted, however, that ideology did play a role in the perceptions of community policing. As previously detailed, people have differing ideologies, but politically they tend to fall into two camps: conservative or liberal. Community policing would appear at first blush to represent a more liberal perspective on crime control because of its emphasis on community partnerships and power sharing as well as its focus on due process. Conservatives would not necessarily care for community policing because it does not represent a conservative viewpoint on how best to deal with crime. As Craig Uchida, a senior-level official in the Justice Department, stated, "I don't think [the Republicans] cared. They viewed community policing as part of a liberal, soft-on-crime agenda. It didn't resonate well for them."[7] In fact, Ted Gest, in his book *Crime and Politics*, offers a good example of the negative response of conservatives (Republicans) to the concepts of community policing when he described the attorney general striking community policing from a draft of recommendations to combat violent crime because "it sounds too much like social work."[8] Recognizing the ideological basis and perceptions of policymakers is important for understanding the success of a public policy. Community policing by itself was not going to win the heart and minds—and, more important, the votes—of the Republicans.

Agenda Setting

In 1992, Governor Clinton (D-Ark.) sought the Democratic Party's nomination to run against President Bush, the Republican incumbent. As part of his endeavor for winning the Democratic nomination, he positioned himself as a "law-and-order" president from the commencement of his campaign and offered himself as a more moderate Democrat. This was intended to highlight the differences between his stance on crime and the views of his likely Democratic primary contender, New York Governor Mario Cuomo.[9] Governor Cuomo had a strong record of opposing the death penalty, making him vulnerable to attacks and being portrayed as "soft on crime." Clinton had learned from the mistakes made by the Democratic candidate, Governor Michael Dukakis (D-Mass.), when he ran against then Vice President Bush in the 1988 presidential campaign. Bush was able to portray Governor Dukakis as soft on crime because of his strong views against the death penalty and through the successful use of the Willie Horton television ad, which depicted a convicted felon who was released on a weekend furlough and raped a young woman.[10] Clinton did not want to repeat these mistakes and created for himself a strong stance on crime while still retaining many of the traditional liberal policies aimed at rehabilitation, drug treatment, and various programs focused on improving the quality of life in inner cities. The tactic worked, and although Clinton did not start off as the Democratic front-runner, he was able to secure the Democratic nomination for president through a shrewd campaign and various political circumstances.

Governor Clinton had campaigned heavily on crime while seeking the Democratic nomination and began targeting his rhetoric at President Bush in order to position himself as the candidate who would be toughest on crime. Clinton utilized the 1992 Democratic Party platform as the basis for his crime control strategy, which took the stance that "crime is a relentless danger to our communities. Over the last decade, crime has swept through our country at an alarming rate."[11] The platform stated that "Democrats pledge to restore government as the upholder of basic law and order for crime-ravaged communities. The simplest and most direct way to restore order in our cities is to put more police on the streets."[12] In addition to more police, the party platform called for the creation of a Police Corp, modeled after the military's Reserve Officer Training Corps (ROTC), to implement the concepts of community policing, target white-collar criminals, favor innovative sentencing and punishment options, and expand drug counseling and treatment programs.[13] Clinton promised not only to support the party platform, which, with the exception of the call for drug counseling and treatment, had become more moderate, but also to support a much more conservative approach in his policies on crime control. In other words, by linking the more liberal method of crime control, community policing, with a more conservative approach to policing, adding more police officers on the streets, Clinton was positioning himself for an ideological compromise that might allow for the passage of a bill in the U.S. Congress.

Thus, the centerpiece of Clinton's campaign on crime was promising to add an additional 100,000 police officers to America's streets under the auspices of community policing and to create a police corps through the use of a "national service trust fund."[14] The initiative was meant to send a clear message to the American electorate that the Democrats could be just as tough on the crime issue as the Republicans, all of which could be delivered through the sound bite "100,000 Cops." As one author explained, "By encapsulating the crime initiative within the call for 100,000 Cops, the Clinton campaign had accomplished the dual goals of shifting the debate on crime and providing the media and the public a clear message that cut through the complexities of federal crime policy."[15] While this was clearly his most successful initiative regarding crime, it was not his only initiative. It became clear by the end of the summer and early fall of 1992 that Clinton had an extensive crime control plan that would be underwritten by a host of new and old initiatives.

Clinton supported an expanded use of the federal death penalty, and to successfully highlight this fact, during the campaign he returned to Arkansas four times to oversee the execution of death-row inmates.[16] He favored the expanded use of juvenile "boot camp" programs for nonviolent, first-time offenders.[17] He advocated an increased use of law enforcement and judicial resources to fight the war on drugs.[18] He also supported background checks on all handgun purchases (as well as a waiting period) and the ban of some automatic weapons.[19] Complementary to the issue of firearms, he heavily favored the passage of the Brady Bill, but rather than portraying his reasons in terms of the traditional liberal viewpoint, he articulated that he was a supporter of the Second Amendment and wanted only to protect Americans and the police.[20] In one campaign speech in Houston, Texas, Clinton, surrounded by police officers, stated, "It is crazy to believe that we shouldn't at least try to give our police officers a fair fight in the fight to keep our streets safe. That's why I believe you ought to be for the Brady Bill."[21] In addition, he also supported increased cooperation between the federal, state, and local governments; programs oriented on reducing child and spousal abuse; and making public schools safer environments.[22] Finally, Clinton did support some of the liberal ideas in his campaign's anticrime agenda, such as a health and education approach to illegal drugs, but again Clinton was able to frame the issue and convey a tough stance on a traditionally liberal policy position. In one attack against President Bush on the issue of drug treatment, Clinton argued,

> Bush confuses being tough with being smart, especially on drugs. Bush thinks locking up addicts instead of treating them before they commit crimes . . . is clever politics. That may be, but it certainly isn't sound policy, and the consequences of his cravenness could ruin us.[23]

In sum, as one author concluded,

> Clinton's agenda for crime control in 1992 was varied. It was both conservative and liberal, and included illicit drug abuse, law enforcement issues, victims, domestic violence, firearms, white collar crime, prisons, and safe schools. On the whole, Clinton's agenda was much more conservative than one would ordinarily expect

from a liberal candidate for president. It encompassed many areas that were traditionally Republican strongholds but also included liberal approaches as well. This was a surprise to both the Republicans and the public, and helped to get Clinton elected into office that year.[24]

Clinton's crime control policies were most assuredly part of his success with the crime issue. However, it was also in part due to how he handled the crime issue throughout the campaign. For Clinton, crime was an offensive issue rather than the defensive issue it had been for other Democratic candidates, especially in 1988.[25] He succeeded in making the issue a positive one— one that did not divide the American electorate but rather united it under a cause that everyone could support. This was illustrated in his campaign speech in Houston when he stated,

> We cannot take our country back until we take our neighborhoods back. Four years ago this crime issue was used to divide America. I want to use it to unite America. I want to be tough on crime and good for civil rights. You can't have civil justice without order and safety.[26]

In addition, he worked hard at winning the endorsement of the police associations and police unions[27]; he convincingly utilized several television advertisements demonstrating his pro–death penalty stance[28]; he incorporated crime, drugs, and gun control into his political agenda publication *Putting People First*, filling up six of 172 pages[29]; and he took advantage of any opportunity to surround himself with police officers in staged photo opportunities.[30] This strong stance by Clinton on crime, coupled with the fact that President Bush downplayed the crime issue in the 1992 campaign, did not mention it during the Republican Convention, and was unable to replicate his 1988 crime symbol (namely, Willie Horton), gave Clinton the upper hand in regard to the crime issue. As one author so caustically remarked, "There was little about Clinton's crime control record in Arkansas that Bush could taunt him about the way he mocked Dukakis as a patsy for every dark-skinned murderer in Massachusetts."[31] All told, Clinton had succeeded in matching the Republicans on the crime issue and by the end of the election had managed to steal it from them.[32] In November 1992, Clinton won the election over the incumbent, George Bush, and on January 20, 1993, he was sworn-in as the forty-second president of the United States, "well-positioned to make crime a key substantive and political success of his administration."[33]

It has been demonstrated that the shift from a campaign for president to actually becoming president is a crucial time period for any president in regard to policy formulation.[34] This would especially be true for President-Elect Clinton, who was a Democrat taking over the White House after 12 years of Republican rule. During the transition period, he selected two moderates, Al From and Bruce Reed, to handle his domestic policy agenda.[35] They would write a memo in late December 1992 recommending that Clinton capitalize on the momentum he had managed to gain on the crime issue against President Bush by making crime a central issue on his agenda.[36] Their advice was to draft and transmit to Congress, in the first 100 days in office, a crime bill that would utilize all his campaign promises regarding crime, to include adding 100,000 new police officers; creating more boot camps for first-time, nonviolent offenders; expanding the death penalty; and adhering to his stance on gun control.[37] In addition, they recommended that he ban the importation of certain assault rifles through the use of an executive order.[38] Between his campaign promises and his ability to beat President Bush on the crime issue, coupled with his policy advisers recommending that he focus on crime, the president was left in a strong position to capitalize on the issue of crime. It quickly became apparent, however, that Clinton would lose the initiative by ignoring both the advice and his campaign promises.

All presidents come into office with a certain amount of political capital based on their electoral victory.[39] As DiClerico has pointed out, "Clinton's win provided him with very little capital" because of his low winning percentage.[40] In addition to the political capital on entering office, presidents can add to this capital through their reputation for competent leadership and the ability to enhance their public support.[41] In this matter, DiClerico explained that "Clinton has not been particularly successful on either count."[42] In regard to the crime issue, although he had the political capital coming into office, he did not display competent leadership, nor did he do anything to enhance public support for the various initiatives he proposed. In regard to all substantive policy considerations, he completely ignored the issue of crime on taking office.[43]

This total disregard for the issue of crime is evident in the fact that the White House declined to draft any crime legislation or to pressure Congress to draft and pass a crime bill during the first 100 days of the Clinton presidency. The majority of his first six months in office were spent dealing with such issues as gays in the military, a deficit-reduction package, motor-voter registration, the family and medical leave act, the North American Free Trade Agreement (NAFTA), and his health care initiative.[44] In addition, while the president called for $100 billion in increased spending for sixty-one separate programs, the centerpiece of his campaign on the crime issue, the "100,000 Cops" initiative, was nowhere to be seen.[45] In fact, in regard to the budget and crime, Clinton actually called for funding cuts, including a $206 million cut from aid to local police agencies, a $40 million cut from the FBI budget, and $331 million in cuts for prison construction.[46] Moreover, although he drafted a number of executive orders in his first 100 days on abortion counseling, abortions in military hospitals, fetal tissue research, and the RU-486 birth control pill, the order banning the importation of assault rifles was shelved.[47] Finally, in regard to speeches, Clinton did include crime in his address before a joint session of Congress on his administration's goals, but its emphasis was on signing the Brady Bill,[48] and he would make two speeches before law enforcement officials, one in the Rose Garden at the White House[49] and one at the National Law Enforcement Officers Memorial.[50] The former simply mentioned a "100,000 police officers" initiative, while the latter was strictly ceremonial. All told, the president did very little during the first six months in office, leaving one journalist to remark, "President Clinton has not determined to make crime-fighting one of the cornerstones of his administration. And that's a big mistake."[51]

Several authors cite three factors that contributed to Clinton's decision to drop the crime issue: politics, personnel, and priorities.[52] Politically, it was said that President Clinton "concluded that crime had been irrelevant to his victory in the 1992 campaign, and thus was not an essential element of his mandate or important to his political future."[53] As a result, Clinton's capital was spent on other items on his agenda as previously detailed. In terms of personnel, the key to the lack of a focus on crime was a result of the fact that some members of the Clinton transition team (Al From, Will Marshall, and Robert Shapiro) did not become members of his administration.[54] In addition to his White House staff, Clinton found himself mired in difficulties in getting crucial members of his cabinet appointed who could have assisted in the area of crime, namely, the attorney general and the "drug czar." In regard to the attorney general, Clinton had to endure public challenges of his first two choices, both of whom ended up withdrawing from the process,[55] and was not able to appoint Janet Reno to the position until March 12, 1993, three months into the administration.[56] In regard to the drug czar, Clinton was slow in announcing the appointment, which came on April 28, 1993, and Lee P. Brown was not sworn into office until July 1, 1993, six months into the administration.[57] Finally, it has been said that Clinton's priorities were simply overshadowed by issues that were not a part of the "New Democrat" ideas but were relegated to many "old issues," such as the economy, health care reform, and children's welfare.[58] As one Senior White House official stated in an interview,

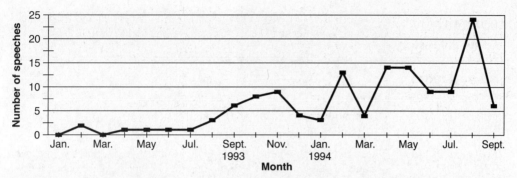

FIGURE 14.2 Clinton's Speeches on Crime, January 1993–September 1994. *Source:* Data collected by author from successive volumes of the paper version of *Public Papers of the Presidents* (Washington, D.C.: U.S. Government Printing Office) and the electronic version obtained in *World Book Encyclopedia: American Reference Library* (Orem, Utah: Western Standard). Data include speeches on the topic of "crime" under the headings of "remarks," "addresses," "interviews," "tele-conferences," and "radio addresses."

> If we had done a crime bill at the beginning of the term, it would have passed with bi-partisan support, been a great credit to the administration, and set an entirely different tone for the administration. If we had done any of the New Democrat ideas, it would have helped us build a working coalition, so we could do more unpopular stuff later. [59]

In the end, Clinton's first 100 days in office were marked by a number of political setbacks and an emphasis on several very controversial issues, and although Clinton had a high success rate for legislation being passed that he had supported, most of these bills consisted of narrow margin victories.[60] All this would contribute to the movement of his public approval rating from a high of 58 percent on taking office to a low of 38 percent by June 1993, the lowest level for any post–World War II president at that point in his term.[61] Whether because of his inexperience, his poor transition from candidate to president, or his poor handling of the office of the presidency, Clinton's first six months in office were difficult, and he was in need of an issue on which he could win. Crime was potentially that issue.

Clinton's reentry into the crime rhetoric did not come until August 11, 1993, one week after the Republican leadership in Congress had announced it would be proceeding with an omnibus anticrime bill that it hoped to pass by Thanksgiving. Their plan called for many of the same provisions that had failed to pass Congress two years earlier[62] as well as many of the bills that had been reformulated the previous year[63] and were believed to have bipartisan support.[64] The proposals consisted of federal aid to local law enforcement, building more prisons, mandatory minimum sentences, a greater use of the death penalty, and the three-strikes provision that would give life imprisonment to a third-time convicted felon. As a result of this announcement and in dire need of a legislative victory, Clinton seized the anticrime rhetoric and unveiled his plan. The path the bill took toward becoming law is described in Box 14.1.

In order to respond to the Republican proposal and once again seize the crime issue for the Democrats, the White House began drafting a proposal and a speech for Clinton to deliver before the bills could be introduced in either the House or the Senate. The proposal was based largely on the "compromises reached in the conference report on the Bush administration's crime bill, which had been blocked in the Senate in its final stages."[65] In addition, it was composed of a

BOX 14.1
Crime Bill History

House Actions

October 26, 1993	Referred to the House Committee on Judiciary.
October 28, 1993	Committee consideration and markup session held.
October 28, 1993	Orderd to be reported (amended).
November 3, 1993	Reported to House (amended) by House Committee on Judiciary. To allow grants to develop more effective programs to reduce juvenile gang participation and juvenile drug trafficking. To allow grants for residential drug treatment in correctional facilities, to allow grants to increase police presence and expand cooperation between law enforcement and public. House reported 103-324. November 3, 1993: Placed on the Union Calendar, No. 175, which is the calendar for all appropriation and revenue bills.
November 3, 1993	Called up by House under suspension of the rules.
November 3, 1993	Passed House (amended) by voice vote.
April 26, 1994	A similar measure, HR 4092, was laid on the table without objection.
August 10, 1994	Rules Committee H. Resolution 517 reported to House.
August 11, 1994	Rule H. Resolution 517 failed passage of House (waiving points of order in regard to grants for substance abuse treatment, juvenile gang participation, and police presence).
August 16, 1994	Rules Committee Resolution H. Resolution 522 reported to House (procedural maneuvering).
August 21, 1994	Rules Committee Resolution H. Resolution 526 reported to House. Waiving points of order against further conference report to accompany H.R. 3355, to amend crime bill.
August 21, 1994	Rule H. Resolution 526 passed House. Agreed to by yea-nay vote, clearing the measure for Senate action. On this date, there were many one-minute speeches urging passage of the crime bill, but most were symbolic rhetoric based on erroneous assumptions and poor information.

Senate Actions

November 4, 1993	Received in the Senate, read twice. Placed on Senate Legislative Calendar under General Orders. Calendar no. 272.
November 19, 1993	Measure laid before Senate by unanimous consent.
November 19, 1993	Senate struck all after the Enacting Clause and substituted the language of S 1607.
November 19, 1993	Passed Senate in lieu of S 1607 with an amendment by yea-nay vote, 95–4. Record vote no. 384.
November 19, 1993	Senate ordered measure printed as passed with amendments of the Senate numbered. On this day, Senate also began consideration of Brady Bill, which was ultimately passed and signed into law.
March 23, 1994	Message on Senate action sent to the House.

BOX 14.1
(continued)

May 11, 1994	Message on House action received in Senate and at desk; House requests a conference and House amendments to Senate amendment.
May 19, 1994	Considered by Senate.
May 20, 1994	Message on Senate action sent to the House.
August 22, 1994	Conference papers; Senate report on managers' statement and message on House action held at the desk in Senate.
August 25, 1994	Point of order that the Conference Report violates Section 306 of the Congressional Budget Act raised in Senate.
August 25, 1994	Motion to waive the budget act with respect to the measure agreed to in Senate by yea-nay vote. Record vote no. 293.
August 25, 1994	Point of order fell when the motion to waive the budget act was agreed to in Senate.
August 25, 1994	Cloture motion on the conference report presented in Senate.
August 25, 1994	Cloture on the conference report invoked in Senate by yea-nay vote, 61–38. Record vote no. 294.

Conference Actions

November 19, 1993	Senate insisted on its amendment, requested a conference. April 21, 1994: On motion that the House agree with amendments to the Senate amendment agreed to without objection. This motion was in regard to the crediting of "good time" for federal inmates not be awarded unless he or she has earned a high school diploma or a GED certificate.
April 21, 1994	On motion that the House insist upon its amendments to the Senate amendment and request a conference agreed to without objection. The debate centered on the truth in sentencing provision in that, if inserted as written, it would require states that had an indeterminate sentencing provision to incarcerate people for longer periods of time, and no money is provided to the states to do so.
April 21, 1994	On motion that the House instruct conferees filed by recorded vote, 191–222 (role no. 145).
April 21, 1994	The Speaker appointed conferees: Brooks, Edwards (CA), Hughes, Schumer, Conyers, Synar, Moorhead, Hyde, Sensenbrenner, and McCollum.
May 17, 1994	The Speaker appointed additional conferees from the Committee on Agriculture; the Committee on Banking, Finance and Urban Affairs; the Committee on Education and Labor; the Committee on Energy and Commerce; the Committee on Government Operations; the Committee on Merchant Marine and Fisheries; the Committee on Natural Resources; the Committee on Post Office and Civil Service; the Committee on Public Works and Transportation; the Committee on Rules; and the Committee on Ways and Means to look at various sections in the proposed legislation and amendments as committed to the conference.

BOX 14.1
Crime Bill History (*continued*)

May 19, 1994	Senate disagreed to the House amendments to the Senate amendment and agreed to request for a conference by voice vote. This disagreement mostly involved provisions to increase police presence, cooperation with public, etc.
May 19, 1994	Senate conferees instructed on motion by Senator Domenici agreed to in Senate by voice vote. Senator Domenici proposed an amendment requiring the death penalty for gun murders in commission of a federal crime.
May 19, 1994	Senate conferees instructed on motion by Senator Hatch agreed to in Senate by voice vote.
May 19, 1994	Senate conferees instructed on motion by Senators Conrad and Mack agreed to in Senate by yea-nay vote, 74–22. Record vote no. 123. This proposed amendment required states to have a truth in sentencing provision requiring inmates to serve 85 percent of time if the state is to receive federal money for prison construction.
May 19, 1994	Senate conferees instructed on motion by Senator Gramm agreed to in Senate by yea-nay vote, 66–32. Record vote no. 124. To establish a Violent Crime Reduction Trust Fund.
May 19, 1994	Senate conferees instructed on motion by Senator Biden agreed to in Senate by yea-nay vote, 94–4. Record vote no. 125. A rather lengthy motion to establish a Violent Crime Reduction Trust Fund; funding for state and local crime prevention programs; and construction/operation of secure prison facilities, boot camps, jails, and other local facilities. To establish tough penalties for violent criminals, to propose the Violence Against Women Act, provide funding for federal law enforcement, to establish the Senior Citizens Against Marketing Scams Act, to introduce rural crime provisions, and to provide funding for training law enforcement.
May 19, 1994	Senate conferees instructed on motion by Senator D' Amato agreed to in Senate by yea-nay vote, 51–47. Record vote no. 126. Senator D'Amato proposed mandatory prison terms for use of firearms in the commission of a crime.
May 19, 1994	Senate appointed conferees Biden, Kennedy, Metzenbaum, DeConcini, Leahy, Hatch, Thurmond, Simpson, and Grassley.
June 16, 1994	Conference held.
June 16, 1994	On motion that the House instruct conferees agreed to by the yeas and nays, 264–149 (roll no. 253).
June 22, 1994	On motion that the House instruct conferees agreed to by the yeas and nays, 338–81 (roll no. 264).
June 22, 1994	The Speaker appointed a conferee.
June 23, 1994	On motion that the House instruct conferees failed by recorded vote, 143–247 (roll no. 274).
June 30, 1994	On motion to instruct conferees agreed to by recorded vote, 348–62 (roll no. 314).
July 20, 1994	On motion that the House instruct conferees agreed to by the yeas and nays, 291–128 (roll no. 340).

BOX 14.1

(continued)

July 26, 1994	Conference held (July 27, 1994).
July 28, 1994	Conferees agreed to file conference report.
August 10, 1994	Conference report H. Report 103-694 filed in House. By a vote of 6–4, the committee voted to waive all points of order against the conference report and allow it to be filed as read.
August 19, 1994	On motion to recommit the conference report agreed without objection.
August 19, 1994	The Speaker appointed conferees as additional conferees: Schroeder, Frank (MA), and Castle.
August 21, 1994	Further conference report H. Report 103-711 filed in House.
August 21, 1994	Conferees agreed to file conference report (additional conference report).
August 21, 1994	House agreed to conference report by recorded vote, 235–195 (roll no. 416).
August 22, 1994	Conference report considered in Senate (August 23, 24, 25, 1994).
August 25, 1994	Senate agreed to conference report by yea-nay vote, 61–38.
September 13, 1994	President Bill Clinton signed into law the Violent Crime Control and Law Enforcement Act of 1994.

number of the proposals put forth by Clinton during his campaign. What it did not consist of was any input from the attorney general or the Department of Justice.[66] In the end, the proposal was mainly a 102nd Congress bill with some Clinton campaign initiatives tacked on to make it appear that the entire proposal was being put forth by the White House.[67]

On August 11, 1993, President Clinton would present his plan in a Rose Garden ceremony, surrounded by the vice president, the attorney general, Senator Biden (D-Del.) (Today the vice president of the United States), Representative Brooks (D-Tex.), and various members of the law enforcement community. Clinton would argue that "the first duty of any government is to try to keep its citizens safe" and proposed that his plan would add 100,000 police officers to the streets, pass a waiting period on the purchase of handguns, and limit the number of *habeas corpus* appeals by death-row inmates. As if tearing a page from his campaign rhetoric, Clinton would conclude that "for too long, crime has been used as a way to divide Americans with rhetoric . . . it is time to use crime as a way to unite Americans through action."[68] In addition, Clinton would draft two memorandums to the secretary of the treasury directing him to cease the importation of specific assault pistols and to limit the number of gun dealer licenses by conducting more intensive background checks and closer oversight.[69] President Clinton would reiterate this initiative to the American people on August 14, 1993, in his weekly radio address.[70] The crime issue was clearly back on the government's agenda.

To understand how community policing and the "100,000 Cops" ideas found their way onto the agenda, it is important to review the different policy models. Although one could find some support for the garbage can model or iron triangles, it would appear that these are too simplistic to apply to the "100,000 Cops" initiative. The garbage can model may be an accurate depiction because it took a number of different actors to bring this bill onto the government's agenda, but it does not provide any great depth of understanding that can be carried to other similar bills.

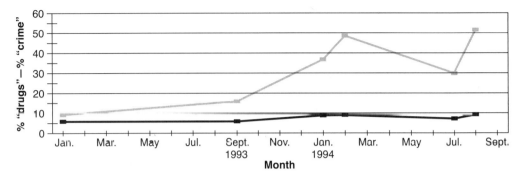

FIGURE 14.3 Crime as "Most Important Problem," January 1993–September 1994. *Source:* George Gallup, *The Gallup Poll: Public Opinion* (Wilmington, Dela.: Scholarly Resources, Inc., 1945–1996); *The Gallup Organization Homepage*, "Gallup Social and Economic Indicators—Most Important Problem," available online at http://www.gallup.com/poll/indicators/indmip.asp (data obtained January 2000); Kathleen Maguire and Ann L. Pastore, *Sourcebook of Criminal Justice Statistics 1997* (Washington, D.C.: Bureau of Justice Statistics, 1998).

The iron triangles concept does work to some degree, as the executive bureaus, congressional committees, and interest groups would all play a part in passing the initiative, but their part was largely minimized in the agenda-setting process and would be more fully realized only as the policy was being drafted.

The issues networks of Hugh Heclo do serve to explain the vast number of connections being made among conservatives and liberals for various aspects of the movement of the bill onto the agenda. Yet these networks didn't fully form until the next stage of the public policy process: policy formulation.

Anthony Down's issue-attention cycle actually works well here for describing the movement of community policing onto the agenda. Crime could be said to have existed in the preproblem stage in the early 1990s as crime rates were rising; criminal justice scholars and practitioners were paying close attention to the problem of crime and the rising crime rates, but it had not yet resonated with the American people. Perhaps a better explanation is that America's attention was focused on the problem of drug abuse in the late 1980s and that by the early 1990s it was becoming clear that the war on drugs would never be won; thus the issue was actually in Down's fourth stage of "gradual decline of intense public interest." Therefore, the question is, what brought crime into Down's second stage of "alarmed discovery and euphoric enthusiasm"? The answer may well be President Clinton himself.

According to Oliver, after Clinton entered into office, despite the fact that the crime rhetoric at least in part helped him achieve the oval office, he dismissed the policy for other issues, such as gays in the military and health care.[71] It wasn't until late in 1993 that, with the controversy over the former policy and the approaching defeat of the latter, he returned his attention to crime. Crime during the early part of 1993 was not a major part of either the newspapers or television news coverage, nor was it listed very high as one of the "most important problems" facing the nation. This is perhaps rightly so because according to the monthly crime index, crime did not increase until the summer months; crime rates were actually on a two-year decline going into 1993. Then in late 1993, when Clinton began talking about the issue of crime and his proposals for a crime bill, newspaper and television coverage of crime began to rise, as did the public's concern over the issue. Clinton, through his ramped-up rhetoric on crime, moved the issue of crime

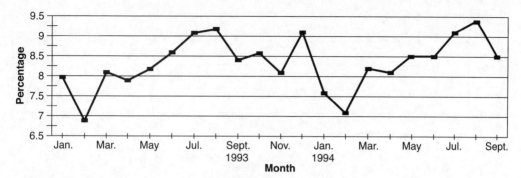

FIGURE 14.4 Crime Index Total by Month, January 1993–September 1994. *Source:* Federal Bureau of Investigation, *Uniform Crime Reports—1996* (Washington, D.C.: Federal Bureau of Investigation, U.S. Government Printing Office, 1997).

into Down's second stage of "alarmed discovery and euphoric enthusiasm." This can be seen especially in light of the August and September coverage of crime by the newspapers and television media and the fact that crime became the number one problem facing the nation in September 1994.

Perhaps the other policy model that fits the Crime Bill the best and explains how it reached the government's agenda is Kingdon's policy streams. The three streams—the problem, the political, and the policy streams—all came together in the summer of 1994 and created the window of opportunity for the passage of the Crime Bill. The problem was obviously crime, whether a true problem or one artificially constructed by the Clinton administration. The political stream was both the Republicans and the Democrats desiring to craft a bill on crime but not necessarily with the same policy ideas. This brought the policy stream to bear on the problem and brought the political stream together as the Republicans favored the Police Corps and the addition of "100,000 cops" and the Democrats favored the concepts of community policing. As the three streams converged, community policing and the "100,000 Cops" initiative was on the government's agenda. Now the question was, could a compromise be agreed on in the crafting of the Violent Crime Control and Law Enforcement Act?

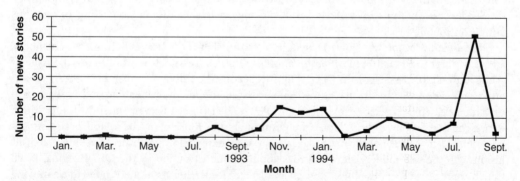

FIGURE 14.5 Television Coverage of Crime, January 1993–September 1994. *Source:* Data collected by author from Vanderbilt University, *Television News Archive* (Nashville: Vanderbilt University, 1998), data obtained from *Television News Archive* home page at http://tvnews. vanderbilt.edu/index.html and was downloaded in January 2000. The keyword search used "Clinton and Crime."

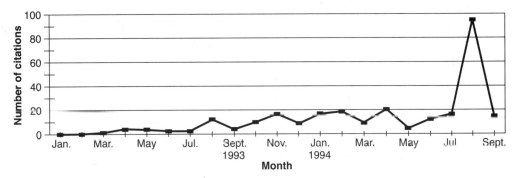

FIGURE 14.6   Newspaper Coverage of Crime, January 1993–September 1994.   *Source:* The original chart, which provided the data from January 1993 to April 1994, appeared in Tony G. Poveda, "Clinton, Crime, and the Justice Department," Social Justice 21 (3, 1996): 73–84, at 81. Data were collected from The National Newspaper Index (1992–1994), which is a database that indexes the following newspapers: New York Times, Wall Street Journal, Washington Post, Christian Science Monitor, and Los Angeles Times. This chart was created by reevaluating the original data through each of the cited newspaper's individual index from January 1993 to September 1994. In both the original and this chart, the keyword search used was "Clinton and Crime."

Policy Formulation

Despite Clinton's foray back into the area of crime control policy, the White House did little to draft the legislation, which some cited as evidence that Clinton was merely using the crime event to boost his public rating.[72] In any event, the drafting of the anticrime legislation was left to Senator Biden and Representative Brooks, both of whom introduced the legislation in their respective houses on September 23, 1993.[73] Both proposals authorized federal aid to hire 50,000 new police officers, expanded the use of the federal death penalty, revised the rules for death-row appeals, and allocated funds for drug treatment.[74] The differences between the two bills consisted of the House proposal, which allowed for a waiting period on handgun purchases while the Senate version did not, and the House bill extended the death penalty to sixty-four crimes, while the Senate version limited it to forty-seven.[75] Congress was on the way to passing an omnibus crime control bill.

President Clinton was slow to respond to the initial introduction of bills in both chambers, and it was not until October 9, 1993, in another radio address that he would raise the issue of crime and call for passage of the Crime Bill,[76] repeating the call on October 23, 1993, in yet another radio address.[77] In the meantime, Senator Biden, despite overwhelming odds, managed to get a bipartisan bill passed on November 19, 1993.[78] The House, however, under the leadership of Representative Brooks, did not fare as well. Although the House managed to approve 11 single-subject bills, the passage of the main legislation was extremely slow partly because of liberal disillusion with the way the legislation was developing and obstruction by the Congressional Black Caucus over portions of the bills[79] as well as a lack of leadership from the White House moving the House toward conference committee.[80] As a result, Congress was able to pass only a watered-down version of the Brady Bill,[81] a parental kidnapping bill,[82] and a child protection bill.[83] The 103rd Congress would have to wait until the second session to pass the main legislation, and President Clinton would have to wait to get his Crime Bill.

Although during the recess Clinton would call for Congress to return in the second session and pass the anticrime legislation[84] and invoke a call for the legislation in his State of the Union Address,[85] it became clear that Clinton was not taking an active role and was leaving the leadership to both Biden and Brooks.[86] As a result, the bill would languish in the House, subject to additional markups, rather than going directly to conference, until well into the summer of 1994.[87] Despite a continued call for passage of the legislation in a number of radio addresses,[88] Clinton and the Democrats lost the initiative, and by summer the Republicans were able to walk away from what had been mainly a Democratic bill with bipartisan support without any political damage. They were in a position to take control of the bill, and both the congressional Democrats and the White House were forced into a position of having to compromise.

The bill that was being formulated during this time was largely a compromise bill that incorporated policies that reflected the ideology of the Democrats with policies that reflected the ideology of the Republicans. The differences were often highlighted by the bill's incorporation of a variety of prevention programs, including what would become a controversial program: midnight basketball. This program provided funding to local communities to keep their recreation centers open longer in order to provide youth with a place to go at night where they could be more closely monitored and thus less likely to commit crimes. In addition, other programs included in the bill were drug treatment programs for prisoners, and the Senate version of the bill also included a ban on various assault weapons.[89]

On the Republican side of the bill, there was additional money for prison expansion not only for the federal government but for the state prison systems as well. In addition, portions of the bill included an expansion of the various crimes that could net one the death penalty as well as more severe punishments for other crimes. And, despite the concept of adding "100,000 cops" to the streets of America for community policing, the concept of adding police is often seen as more a conservative approach to crime control, not a liberal one. In other words, some of the bill's proposed legislation truly had bipartisan support but often for different reasons. In other cases, it was simply a matter of allowing for a quid pro quo. If the Democrats can have midnight basketball, the Republicans can have prison expansion. And if the Republicans can have tougher sanctions, the Democrats can have drug treatment for prisoners.

As the bill continued to be formulated, most of the various proposals by both sides remained. The assault weapon ban was removed, and it is believed that this was in response to public opinion polls that found that the public highly favored this type of ban. Had the assault weapon ban been incorporated into the omnibus bill, it would not have received the attention it deserved or, rather, the attention a bill by itself could generate, so it was removed from the bill.[90] However, the ability to get the final bill passed was starting to come into question.

Although the final bill was touted as being a bipartisan bill, this was not because the two parties worked together; rather, they really worked against each other. In addition, various factions of both parties were beginning to place the bill in jeopardy during the summer of 1994. In fact, divisions over the bill were so contested that there was a realization in early May that in order for the bill to pass, Clinton would need to secure the support of 36 Republicans to make up the deficit caused by Democrats who were arguing against the bill.[91] At one point during the summer, the House version of the ban included a provision that would allow for the use of statistical evidence regarding racial discrimination in death penalty cases. As a compromise, the discrimination portion of the bill was dropped, and the assault weapon ban was reinserted into the bill. The dropping of the discrimination challenge pleased the conservatives, while the inclusion of the ban on certain assault weapons pleased the liberals. The bill was not gaining ground toward passage but was merely languishing in bipartisan debate.

The presidential rhetoric increased dramatically during August in the hopes that passage could be achieved, and Clinton utilized every means of communication available to him, including radio addresses, remarks to specific groups such as police organizations,[92] and a number of exchanges with reporters. It was at this point that Clinton began drawing on the earlier creation of a "war room" to deal with domestic policy issues, such as crime, and by employing a strategy of direct lobbying, national outreach, and constituency group mobilization that developed into a form of "reverse lobbying."[93] His appeals managed to win him the support of a number of U.S. city mayors (including New York's Rudolph Giuliani, a staunch Republican),[94] the support of the public,[95] and the support of a number of interest groups oriented on crime control.[96] While this did take away some of the moderate Republicans from the partisan strategy of the Republican leadership, many of the Democrats walked away from the final bill as well.[97] For the first time, President Clinton became actively involved in the passage of the Crime Bill beyond the pressure he was trying to keep on public opinion and interest groups. The White House began actively seeking votes from Democrats who had walked away or were undecided and to solicit the help of many of the moderate Republicans.[98]

At the Capitol, the bargaining over the crime bill began on the afternoon of August 19, 1994, and did not end until August 21, 1994. During these negotiations, the Republicans were able to achieve a victory by driving down the amounts spent on various social programs, such as drug treatment, and by the afternoon of August 21, a procedural motion was made to bring the bill to the floor.[99] The motion was carried by a vote of 239 to 189, with 42 Republicans, 196 Democrats, and 1 Independent voting yea. A second vote followed, which was defeated, on "a motion to recommit the conference report to accompany the bill to the committee of conference."[100] Finally, the bill was voted on with 235 voting in favor, 195 voting against, and 5 abstaining. In the end, 188 Democrats, 46 Republicans, and 1 Independent voted in favor of the bill. As DiClerico summed up the crime bill: "The circumstances surrounding its passage tarnished much of the luster that might have come the president's way. After a humiliating procedural vote in which fifty-eight House Democrats—including twenty committee and subcommittee chairs and a deputy whip—abandoned the president, a concession forced by Republicans reduced the bill's funding by some $3 billion."[101] In the end, Clinton and the Democrats claimed victory, but so did the Republicans—the Democrats for stealing the crime issue from the Republicans and the Republicans for watering down the "liberal" components of the Crime Bill. On September 13, 1994, on the South Lawn of the White House and with much political fanfare, President Clinton signed the Violent Crime Control and Law Enforcement Act of 1994 into law, with several of his campaign promises intact.[102] The comments Clinton made upon signing the bill are shown in Box 14.2. Table 14.1 gives a description of the final bill as signed by Clinton.

As there is no specific format for how a policy is formulated, the creation and passage of the Violent Crime Control and Law Enforcement Act of 1994 demonstrates many of the difficulties in creating legislative policy. Factors such as ideology, political partisanship, and the influence of interest groups all came to bear on the creation of this policy. Although later touted as a successful bipartisan bill, it should be clear that this bill was really a demonstration in political compromise between the two parties, not in the sense that they came together to craft a mutually agreed-on bill but rather in the sense that they engaged in a form of a quid pro quo where members of Congress were able to retain their crime control policy in the bill by allowing others (generally of the opposition party) to keep their crime control policies in the final bill.

In addition, it is interesting to note the type of policy that was encapsulated in the Crime Bill. The community policing and "100,000 Cops" initiative was clearly meant to be nothing more

BOX 14.2

Remarks by President Clinton at the Signing of the Crime Bill, September 13, 1994

The American people have been waiting a long time for this day. In the last 25 years, half a million Americans have been killed by other Americans. For 25 years, crime has been a hot political issue, used too often to divide us while the system makes excuses for not punishing criminals and doing the job, instead of being used to unite us to prevent crime, punish criminals, and restore a sense of safety and security to the American people.

One of the reasons that I sought this office is to get this bill because if the American people do not feel safe on their streets, in their schools, in their homes, in their places of work and worship, then it is difficult to say that the American people are free.

When I sign this crime bill, we together are taking a big step toward bringing the laws of our land back into line with the values of our people, and beginning to restore the line between right and wrong. There must be no doubt about whose side we're on. People who commit crimes should be caught, convicted and punished. This bill puts government on the side of those who abide by the law, not those who break it; on the side of the victims, not their attackers; on the side of the brave men and women who put their lives on the line for us every day, not the criminals or those who would turn away from law enforcement. That's why police and

prosecutors and preachers fought so hard for this bill, and why I am so proud to sign it into law today.

In a few weeks I will name the head of our program to put 100,000 new police on the street. And early next month, the Justice Department will award grants to put new police on the street in 150 more cities and towns that applied last year.

Today we remember the thousands of officers who gave their lives to make our nation safer, whose names are inscribed in a stone memorial just a mile away from here. We remember the innocent victims whose lives were lost and whose families were shattered by the scourge of violent crime.

My fellow Americans, this is about freedom. Without responsibility, without order, without lawfulness, there is no freedom. Today, the will of the American people has triumphed over a generation of division and paralysis. We've won a chance to work together. So in that spirit, let us rededicate ourselves today to making this law become the life of our country, to restoring the sense of right and wrong that built our country, and to make it safe not in words, but in fact, in the lifeblood of every child and every citizen of this country who believes in the promise of America. Let us make it real.

Thank you and God bless you all.

Source: White House Web page, available online at www.whitehouse.gov.

than a distributive or "pork-barrel" policy. The grants were intended to go not where crime was highest in the United States but rather to any and every jurisdiction in the United States that simply applied. According to Herman Goldstein, it was "a symbolic gesture with relatively little practical use."[103] Making the grants a distributive policy allowed every member of the House and Senate to claim credit that they were doing something to deal with the problem of crime in their district or state. The program was not about getting money to where the problem was but about getting money to where the constituents were.

In addition, many of the policies in the Crime Bill were also regulatory in that they increased the severity of sentences for some crimes or created new criminal violations. One could also argue that many of the policies were focused on morality policy, as there were a number of titles in the Crime Bill that received funding to deal with such crime problems as violence against women, child pornography, and drunk driving. The Crime Bill was truly an amalgam of policies all thrown together under the one bill. But it was the centerpiece—the allocation of $8.8 billion over six years to add more police officers to the street under a community policing initiative—that would prove the most cumbersome to implement.

TABLE 14.1   Violent Crime Control and Law Enforcement Act of 1994

Congressional appropriations for 1996 in the Violent Crime Control and Law Enforcement Act of 1994[a]

Title 1	Public safety and policing	$1.85 billion
Title 2	Prisons	$1.07 billion
Title 3	Crime prevention	$678 million
Title 4	Violence against women	$274 million
Title 5	Drug courts	$150 million
Title 6	Death penalty	None
Title 7	Three strikes legislation	None
Title 8	Mandatory minimum penalties	None
Title 9	Drug control	None
Title 10	Drunk driving provisions	None
Title 11	Firearms	None
Title 12	Terrorism	None
Title 13	Criminal aliens and immigration	$332 million
Title 14	Youth violence	None
Title 15	Criminal street gangs	$1 million
Title 16	Child pornography	None
Title 17	Crimes against children	None
Title 18	Rural crime	$37 million
Title 19	Federal law enforcement	$145 million
Title 20	Police Corps and law enforcement officers' training and education	$20 million
Title 21	State and local law enforcement	$211 million
Title 22	Motor vehicle theft protection	$1.5 million
Title 23	Victims of crime	None
Title 24	Protection for the elderly	$900,000
Title 25	Senior citizens against marketing scams	$2 million
Title 26	Commission membership and appointment	None
Title 27	Presidential summit on violence and national commission on crime prevention and control	$1 million
Title 28	Sentence provisions	None
Title 29	Computer crime	None
Title 30	Protection of privacy of information in state motor vehicle records	None
Title 31	Violent crime reduction trust fund	$4.3 billion
Title 32	Miscellaneous	None
Title 33	Technical corrections	None
Total appropriations for 1996		$9.07 billion

[a]In the event of no expenditures, it is generally the case that either a new law was created or an old law was modified.

Source: W. M. Oliver, *Community-Oriented Policing: A Systemic Approach to Policing* (Upper Saddle River, N.J.: Prentice Hall, 2004).

Policy Implementation

The Violent Crime Control and Law Enforcement Act of 1994 is the largest crime bill in the history of the United States and dedicated over $36 billion to be spent between 1994 and the end of 2000. The largest of this funding, $8.8 billion, was to be allocated for the "100,000 Cops" program. This crime legislation was sweeping in the fact that it not only provided for new police officers to be hired under the concepts of community-oriented policing but also added new laws, altered old ones, allocated funds to build new prisons, and dedicated additional funding for the FBI, the Drug Enforcement Administration, the Immigration and Naturalization Service, U.S. attorneys, the federal courts, and the Treasury Department. In addition, it banned the manufacture of 19 military-style assault weapons, expanded the death penalty in nearly 60 federal offenses, created the registration requirements of sexually violent offenders, and initiated the federal three-strikes provision. Moreover, it targeted illegal immigration into the United States along the borders, generated additional research funding for DNA analysis, and allocated grant funding for the establishment of boot camps for violent offenders.[104] It was clearly the most sweeping crime legislation passed to date and would not only have a profound impact on federal law enforcement and federal laws but also pose sweeping changes at the state and local levels.

As a result of the "100,000 Cops" initiative and for the fact that a number of the provisions within the Crime Bill were related to the concepts of community-oriented policing, Attorney General Janet Reno created a new office within the Department of Justice to oversee the community-oriented policing grants and those related to them. This would include the $8.8 billion in community policing grants authorized for 1994 through 2000, the establishment of a Police Corps, and a number of crime prevention grants. On October 9, 1994, Reno formally established the Office of Community Oriented Policing Services (COPS), and three days later it would deliver its first series of grants to state and local law enforcement agencies. In the meantime, the search for a director was conducted, and the chosen candidate was Hayward (California) Police Chief Joseph E. Brann. On December 19, 1994, President Clinton named Brann to be the director on the basis of his experience with implementing community-oriented policing. Brann's background is described in Boxes 14.3 and 14.4.

BOX 14.3

Meet the First Director of the Office of Community Oriented Policing Services (COPS): Joseph E. Brann

Joseph E. Brann was appointed by President Clinton to head the U.S. Department of Justice's Office of Community Oriented Policing Services (COPS) on December 19, 1994. This new component of the Justice Department was tasked with the responsibility of advancing community policing nationally and funding 100,000 additional police by the year 2000.

Director Brann began his law enforcement career in Santa Ana, California. He served with that police department from 1969 to 1990. In 1990, the City of Hayward, California, a community of 125,000 people, located in the San Francisco Bay area appointed Brann as their police chief. While in Santa Ana, he designed, developed, and managed a wide array of community policing and crime prevention programs which led to the appointment by President Clinton for the role of "Top Cop," the name the media has given the director.

Director Brann received his bachelor's degree in criminal justice from California State University at Fullerton in 1975 and a master's degree in public administration from the University of Southern California in 1979. During the Vietnam conflict, Brann served as a member of the U.S. Army. He is also a graduate of the Federal Bureau of Investigation National Academy.

Source: COPS Web page, available online at http://www.usdoj.gov/cops.

BOX 14.4

COPS Director Says Training Is Integral to Organizational Change

Joseph E. Brann was sworn in as director of the Office of Community Oriented Policing Services (COPS) on Dec. 19, 1994. Brann formerly served as police chief in Hayward, Calif., a community of 125,000 people, located in the San Francisco Bay area. During his tenure in Hayward, Brann implemented a nationally respected community policing program that has been used as a model by police departments across the country. He has also lectured and written on community policing.

Before becoming chief of the Hayward Police Department, Brann served in the Santa Ana, Calif., Police Department from 1969 to 1990. While in Santa Ana, a community of 300,000, Brann designed, developed and managed a wide array of community policing and crime prevention programs that have been recognized as national models.

Brann received a bachelor's degree in criminal justice from California State University at Fullerton in 1975, followed by a master's degree in public administration from the University of Southern California in 1979. During the Vietnam Conflict, Brann served in Korea as a member of the U.S. Army. Brann is also a graduate of the Federal Bureau of Investigation National Academy.

Q: How should community policing training affect a department's organizational structure?

A: A police agency must go through an organizational and cultural transition if it is to move successfully into community policing. It requires chief executives, top administrators, middle managers and others to challenge and set aside some of their prior beliefs and management techniques. It is not an easy process. But I have seen this happen successfully numerous times, and training assistance helps.

Training and education are also helpful in encouraging traditional, rule-driven organizations to adopt new models of organizational management, and have proven to be more effective in both the corporate and public sectors.

Q: How is this transition process achieved through training?

A: You start with the basics. Community policing is value-oriented, not rule-driven, and establishing that foundation steers the process. Historically, police training focused on teaching technical skills and adherence to the "right" procedures. Those aspects are still important. But the transition to community policing requires an emphasis on outcomes and expectations, which is why a mission statement or "a sense of purpose" is essential. Once that's established, the process is underway.

The next step in training is to work with strategies and methods that move a department's personnel into activities through their awareness of established values, goals and the department's mission. Every aspect of the organization should be evaluated, and if necessary, strategies and methods should be refined or improved through the training. Remember, a key element of this philosophy is its adaptability. As long as values and objectives are kept in sight, the right kind of activities will occur.

Q: Do you feel that organizational change can effectively occur without community policing training, or is the training integral to change taking place?

A: I think training is essential. A very simple example relates to the delegation skills and discretion exercised by chief executives, middle managers and supervisory personnel. If they have been engaged in the same type of command activities for many years, it's often very hard for them to give up some of their authority. But decentralization in a department, where and when it's possible, is a positive goal. Decentralizing decision-making to ensure that appropriate decision-making and discretion are exercised at the lowest possible level leads to enhanced effectiveness of officers on the street, and their success benefits the entire organization and the community.

Training is helpful and often necessary in luring police executives away from traditional methods that are comfortable, even though they might not always be effective. It is important for executives to build upon the training and information that has been established. But I don't think it is advisable for a department to try to establish a community policing operation without the training tools that are now available.

Q: What are your plans for COPS-sponsored training and technical assistance?

A: In our first year the COPS office focused on awarding hiring grants, and with more than 25,000 additional

BOX 14.4
(continued)

officers now funded, it paid off. During that time, we began to use the Community Policing Consortium to assist with our training and technical assistance efforts.

In the near future, additional COPS-funded community policing training will be provided to complement the Consortium. We're still busy evaluating the best techniques, methods and subject areas, and we're eager to hear what people want from us in training and how they want it delivered.

We will be funding regional community policing training centers in different areas of the United States.

We're also looking at going beyond traditional classroom lectures that seem to predominate in police training. Perhaps problem-solving exercises in the field that include interaction with key community agencies and community groups are more effective. In remote areas where trainee-trainer interactions are difficult, we'll be looking at things like interactive computers, CD-ROMS, teleconferencing, and satellite networks to bring people together. It's important to remember that there is no one way to do this.

Source: Reprinted with permission from "COPS Director Says Training Is Integral to Organizational Change," Community Policing Exchange, March/April 1996.

A Washington, D.C., office was established in the fall of 1994, and the agency began to focus primarily on delivering the grants to state and local agencies that centered on the hiring of the "100,000 cops." Quickly, however, it would begin a series of grants that would center on providing technology and assistance grants to local agencies as well as funding specific community-oriented policing programs. Finally, the COPS office would turn its attention more fully toward providing training to agencies that were undergoing the process of implementing community-oriented policing. However, in this area, they would have assistance from a preestablished agency that would eventually find it organizationally under the COPS office, namely, the Community Policing Consortium.

The Community Policing Consortium was created and funded in 1993 by the Department of Justice under the Bureau of Justice Assistance. The Consortium initially was a combined effort by the International Association of Chiefs of Police, the National Sheriff's Association, the Police Executive Research Forum, and the Police Foundation. These four agencies would pool their resources to provide training and technical assistance to five community-oriented policing demonstration sites, including St. Petersburg (Florida), Knoxville (Tennessee), Denver (Colorado), Austin (Texas), and Hillsborough County (Florida). The Consortium also conducted meetings with community-oriented policing leaders in the field and created a monograph titled *Understanding Community Policing: A Framework for Action*, which has had widespread dissemination among police agencies in the United States. In 1994, the Community Policing Consortium would add the National Organization of Black Law Enforcement Executives to its list of partner organizations and would begin offering an array of training curriculums on community-oriented policing. A vast majority of police agencies would receive their first training from the Community Policing Consortium from 1993 through 1994, largely because it was the most progressive and accessible training on community-oriented policing available. By the end of 1994 and the beginning of 1995, however, with the establishment of the COPS office, the Community Policing Consortium would move out from under the Bureau of Justice Assistance and fall under the responsibility of the COPS office. The appropriations allocated to the office are outlined in Table 14.2, and the mission statement of the organization is found in Box 14.5.

TABLE 14.2 Authorization and appropriations for COPS grant program, fiscal years 1995–1999

Fiscal year	Amount authorized (in billions)	Amount appropriated (in billions)
1995	$1.3	$1.3
1996	$1.9	$1.4
1997	$2.0	$1.4
1998	$1.6	$1.4
1999	$1.4	—
Total	$8.2	$5.5

Source: U.S. General Accounting Office (1997) and COPS office data.

The Community Policing Consortium's primary mission is to deliver community-oriented policing training and technical assistance to police and sheriffs departments that are COPS grantees. The training sessions are generally held at the state and regional levels and use curricula designed by the Community Policing Consortium that reflect the knowledge it obtained from early work with a number of agencies and police leaders. The Community Policing Consortium presents general community-oriented policing training as well as more specific types of training focusing on sheriffs departments, problem solving, and community partnerships. In addition, it has also created training workshops on cultural diversity training, personnel deployment strategies, and "train-the-trainer" courses. Moreover, the Consortium has, in the name of information sharing, created several publications, including the *Community Policing Exchange*, the *Sheriff Times*, and *Community Links*. These and other publications and resources have contributed greatly to the education and training of police and sheriffs departments across the country.

The most visible aspect of the COPS office has been hiring grants that allow state and local agencies to hire additional police officers to assist in their transition to community-oriented policing. However, the grants have essentially fallen into four categories: (1) hiring grants, (2) technology/assistance grants, (3) special programs, and (4) training grants. Because of the impact that these grants have had on community-oriented policing, it is important to understand the types of grants that have been made available, how they are delivered, and how they have been subsequently

---

BOX 14.5

Office of Community Oriented Policing Services (COPS) Mission Statement

We, the staff of the Office of Community Oriented Policing Services, dedicate ourselves, through partnerships with communities, policing agencies, and other public and private organizations, to significantly improve the quality of life in neighborhoods and communities throughout the country.

We will accomplish this by putting into practice the concepts of community policing in order to reduce levels of disorder, violence, and crime through the application of proven, effective programs and strategies. We will meet the needs of our customers through innovation and responsiveness. We will create a workplace that encourages creativity, open communication, full participation, and problem-solving.

We will carry out these responsibilities through a set of core values that reflect our commitment to the highest standard of excellence and integrity in public service.

Source: COPS Web page, available online at www.usdoj.gov/cops.

BOX 14.6

Office of Community Oriented Policing Services (COPS) Grants

"100,000 COPS"

Phase I

- The initial officer hiring grants in the Fall of 1994.

COPS AHEAD (Accelerated Hiring Education and Deployment)

- Officer hiring grants for jurisdictions of 50,000 population or more.

COPS FAST (Funding Accelerated for Small Towns)

- Officer hiring grants for jurisdictions with less than 50,000 population.

Troops to COPS

- Grants for local law enforcement agencies to hire military veterans under Community Policing.

Universal Hiring Program (UHP)

- All officer hiring grants fell under this title in 1996.

Technology

COPS MORE (Making Officer Redeployment Effective)

- Grants to police agencies to purchase equipment, technology, hire civilians, or pay for officer overtime with the goal of placing more officers on the street.

Training

Community Policing Consortium

- A partnership of five leading policing organizations dedicated to training and technical assistance on Community Policing.

Regional Community Policing Institutes (RCPIs)

- Regional training institutes founded on local/state partnerships to deliver Community Policing training.

Programs

3-1-1

- A grant to establish a non-emergency phone number (311) to alleviate calls to 911.

Advanced Community Policing

- Grants to allow police departments to further develop an infrastructure to institutionalize and sustain Community Policing practices.

Anti-Gang Initiative

- Grants to allow local police and community to address the problem of youth violence as it relates to gang activity.

Community Policing to Combat Domestic Violence

- Grants for local law enforcement agencies to address the problems of Domestic Violence from a Community- and Problem-Oriented approach.

Police Corp

- Grants modeled after the military's R.O.T.C. (Reserve Officer Training Corps) that allow tuition waivers for college students who are willing to commit to a service obligation with a local police department upon graduation.

Problem Solving Partnerships

- Grants for local police and community to address a specific problem such as burglaries, drug dealing, or street-level prostitution.

Source: COPS Web page, available online at www.usdoj.gov/cops.

utilized by agencies across the country. The process for grant allocation to local police agencies is found in Box 14.6, and the amounts provided to those agencies are shown in Box 14.7.

When Director Brann took over the COPS office, one of his concerns was that the original intent of the Crime Bill was to assist in the establishment of community-oriented policing in state and local agencies, not to just hire "100,000 cops." As he has said on a number of occasions,

BOX 14.7

Office of Community Oriented Policing Services (COPS) Total Grant Awards by State or Jurisdiction and Estimated Number of Officers "Hired"[a], September 1994–January 1999

State	Number of Cops "Hired"	Total Award ($)
Alabama	1,350.9	77,389,652
Alaska	239.0	15,209,890
Arizona	1,754.5	119,150,937
Arkansas	1,006.3	54,532,181
California	12,420.4	786,610,627
Colorado	1,004.8	58,631,732
Connecticut	993.2	63,684,222
Delaware	416.8	21,077,232
Florida	5,549.6	327,848,873
Georgia	1,959.6	109,887,637
Hawaii	467.9	16,825,662
Idaho	262.1	16,011,129
Illinois	4,624.8	280,614,060
Indiana	1,207.3	67,945,232
Iowa	551.3	35,322,281
Kansas	655.2	40,263,205
Kentucky	1,027.8	54,555,594
Louisiana	1,737.4	81,654,437
Maine	232.1	15,326,199
Maryland	2,176.0	120,899,007
Massachusetts	2,699.3	169,032,784
Michigan	2,965.0	164,389,018
Minnesota	1,169.4	69,467,763
Mississippi	1,030.7	51,763,453
Missouri	1,936.0	105,978,248
Montana	232.4	13,967,961
Nebraska	424.6	24,017,548
New Hampshire	365.6	20,647,938
New Jersey	3,557.2	212,939,141
New Mexico	611.5	33,649,953
New York	10,230.4	623,851,524
North Carolina	2,168.5	107,682,410
North Dakota	197.0	11,846,831
Ohio	3,137.4	189,667,949

BOX 14.7
(continued)

State	Number of Cops "Hired"	Total Award ($)
Oklahoma	823.4	46,762,896
Oregon	1,084.5	74,447,597
Pennsylvania	3,105.0	170,219,796
Rhode Island	322.3	15,133,544
South Carolina	843.3	51,489,109
South Dakota	268.8	17,663,021
Tennessee	1,754.3	102,853,533
Texas	4,139.6	252,212,739
Utah	726.5	50,262,101
Virginia	1,877.3	134,585,881
Vermont	174.8	11,395,996
Washington	1,595.7	106,712,869
West Virginia	546.7	28,811,806
Wisconsin	1,018.4	62,951,529
Wyoming	65.4	3,952,639

Jurisdiction	Number of Cops "Hired"	Total Award ($)
American Samoa	30.0	1,126,006
Guam	40.0	2,959,343
North Mariana Islands	45.0	2,429,679
Puerto Rico	2,856.6	98,364,050
Virgin Islands	114.6	8,403,229
Washington, D.C.	809.0	19,542,751

[a]The estimated number of officers "hired" is based on actual grants to hire new police officers and other grants, such as technology or secretarial support, that free an officer from administrative duties to work the street, thus counting as an "officer hired."

Source: Office of Community Oriented Policing Services home page, Freedom of Information Act, Grantee Report, March 1999, available online at www.usdoj.gov/cops/.

"This is the Office of Community Oriented Policing, not the office of 100,000 Cops." He therefore set out to ensure that agencies understood that the grants were to complement and assist in the implementation of community-oriented policing. However, he was also well aware that when it came to the delivery of the grants, he did not want to make the same mistakes made under the old Law Enforcement Assistance Administration in providing block grants. Brann has stated, "In the past money was fueled through the states via block grants. This created too many layers of bureaucracy. Police wanted this removed to make the implementation more efficient and more effective."[105] In the structuring of the new hiring grants, Brann explained that "this office looks to customer orientation. Community-Oriented Policing is focused on the customer, the citizens. In our case focusing on the customer means focusing on local law enforcement."[106] The simplicity of the paperwork required to apply for one of the hiring grants and the fact that all grant applications go directly to the COPS office have earned high levels of satisfaction from the law enforcement community.

The first hiring grants to be delivered to state and local law enforcement agencies were announced on October 12, 1994, only three days after the formal establishment of the COPS office and prior to the hiring of the director. They were dubbed "COPS: Phase I grants" and consisted of the first $200 million in grants that were allocated to 392 state, municipal, county, and tribal law enforcement agencies. The grants allowed for the hiring of more than 2,700 additional officers in these agencies, and the COPS office was on its way toward reaching the "100,000 Cops-on-the-Beat" goal. The reason the COPS office was able to so quickly fund these agencies was because the Bureau of Justice Assistance (BJA), in anticipation of the president signing the bill and the funds being available for hiring the officers, was the agency that solicited applications and granted the Phase I awards.

These grants were awarded by the BJA through a very detailed grant process, similar to other BJA grant procedures. As a result, agencies had to complete a detailed application and mail it to the BJA, which then conducted an extensive review of the applications. The agencies then had to wait until the BJA approved the final grant award before beginning the recruitment, hiring, and training of the officers. As a result, the Phase I grant process was slow, and departments became disappointed in the grant process.[107] Most of the problems were indicative of the fact that an older bureaucracy was dealing with the grant awards and hence were utilizing award procedures that had developed over a period of ten years. At that rate, it would take well over ten years to fund all 100,000 officers, something the COPS office did not technically have. Therefore, a new grant delivery mechanism needed to be employed by a new agency: the office of Community Oriented Policing Service (COPS).

In response to a suggestion from the U.S. Conference of Mayors to expedite the grant application process for the COPS FAST and COPS AHEAD programs (described in the following), the COPS office designed a two-step application process to try to get new officers on the street months earlier than they would be under traditional grant award processes.[108] First, for COPS AHEAD, the COPS office used a one-page initial application to determine the number of officers whom jurisdictions could recruit and train. Approved jurisdictions were notified of proposed funding levels, cautioned that the funding was tentative, and warned that if the subsequent application was not approved, the COPS office would not be held liable for officers hired.[109] In COPS FAST, grant decisions were made on the basis of one-page applications for which agencies were then required to later submit additional information and a brief budget.

Once the applications were received for the COPS AHEAD and COPS FAST grants, they were reviewed by a panel of consultants, and unless the applying agency was negligent in completing the application, they were awarded the grant. The grant itself would fund 75 percent of an officer's pay and benefits for three years, up to a maximum of $75,000 per officer. The local agency would have to fund the other 25 percent of the grant's match, and they would have to agree that the officer would be an additional hire and not one previously working for the agency. In other words, supplanting of grants was considered illegal under the grant process. In addition, the agency would have to provide a guarantee that at the end of the three-year period, the additional officer hired would not be fired despite the fact the agency would now have to fund that officer at 100 percent.

On November 1, 1994, Attorney General Reno announced the next two series of grants that would be funded by the COPS office for hiring grants replacing the COPS: Phase I grants would be handled by the COPS office rather than the BJA. They were COPS AHEAD (Accelerated

Hiring Education and Deployment) and COPS FAST (Funding Accelerated for Smaller Towns). The grants were identical to the Phase I grants, except the COPS AHEAD grants were for agencies serving populations of 50,000 and over, while COPS FAST were grants for agencies serving populations under 50,000. This essentially did nothing more than divide up the grants into large-city police agencies and small-town and rural agencies. However, because some of the provisions within the Crime Bill of 1994 did specify that at least half the funding should go to small-town and rural agencies, the division of the grants allowed for this provision to be better monitored.

In June 1995, the COPS AHEAD and COPS FAST grants were superseded by the Universal Hiring Program (UHP), under which any agency could apply for the same three-year, 75 percent funded grant to hire an additional officer. The only difference under the funding provision with the UHP program seemed to be the clause that waivers for the nonfederal match requirement could be requested if "extraordinary fiscal hardship" could be demonstrated. This was most likely a result of a number of agencies applying for hiring grants, receiving their award notification from the COPS office, and later having to withdraw from the grant process because the local jurisdiction could not afford the 25 percent match or would be unable to continue funding the officer at 100 percent after the third year. In one study, it was found that approximately 10 percent of all COPS hiring grant applicants had to withdraw from the grant process for these reasons.[110]

On December 14, 1994, Attorney General Reno, just prior to the hiring of Director Brann, would announce the fourth COPS grant program known as COPS MORE (Making Officer Redeployment Effective). These grants were again directed toward agencies that were attempting to implement community-oriented policing, but rather than hiring new officers, they were attempting to expand the time that current officers had available to work the beat. The MORE grants were once again based on a simple application that could be completed with relative ease by any law enforcement agency and either mailed, faxed, or sent electronically to the COPS office. These grants were specifically to purchase new equipment and/or technology, to procure support resources (such as civilian personnel), or to pay overtime for officers. The concept was that if any of these would allow the officers' administrative tasks to be completed more efficiently, this would allow officers more time to work the beat, hence interacting with citizens and solving problems. For example, if the use of laptop computers would allow the typical officer to complete a report in one hour rather than the standard two hours, this would save one hour of an officer's time. If the standard number of reports an officer completed was two per day, then this would save two hours a day, five days a week, for a full year, thus yielding what would hypothetically be equivalent to hiring a part-time officer. What was most interesting was the fact this figure would then be utilized by the COPS office to reach the goal of adding "100,000 cops."

The other requirements to the COPS MORE grants were very similar to the hiring grants in that the COPS office would fund 75 percent, while the local agency had to match the other 25 percent, and the grant could not be used to supplant funding already dedicated by the local agency for equipment, civilian personnel, or overtime. These grants have been well received by police agencies across the United States, mainly for their ease of application and flexibility in their use. In many cases, agencies simply preferred to apply for the COPS MORE grants primarily because the matching requirements would not be as high for the local jurisdiction. However, most of the agencies that had applied for some form of hiring grants had also applied for one of the COPS MORE grants. After the first series of COPS MORE grants came out in 1995, the grants have been renamed each year with the fiscal year attached to the grant series, such as COPS MORE '98 grants.

The third series of grants that the COPS office began to offer beyond the hiring grants and equipment/technology grants were in the area of special programs. Although some resembled both of these former type of grants, many of the programmatic grants were oriented toward addressing a specific problem or exploring an innovative solution under the community-oriented policing philosophy. All these grants were published as grant proposal applications, requesting agencies to submit their specific plan under the guidelines the COPS office would provide, and after a review would be awarded to specific agencies for specific dollar amounts. Again, those agencies implementing community-oriented policing—and especially those agencies having received a hiring grant—were the most likely to also receive one of the special programmatic grants.

One of the first of these grants was very similar to the hiring grants and was called Troops to COPS. It was announced on May 2, 1995, that the Troops to COPS program would provide an agency up to $50,000 if it were to hire a qualified military veteran as a law enforcement officer under community-oriented policing. The benefits to the agency were that the grant money could be used to help defray the costs of the new officers' equipment, uniforms, or vehicles in the first three years of service and that the grant money did not require a matching amount. The benefit to the federal government was primarily that the U.S. military was undergoing some drastic cuts in manpower, and this provided the incentive for an agency to hire the separating veteran. A number of military soldiers were hired under this program.

The next program, announced on September 13, 1995, was the first true programmatic community-oriented policing initiative sponsored by the COPS office and was called the Youth Firearms Violence Initiative. These were grant applications for cities to develop innovative community-oriented policing and enforcement efforts to curb the rise in violence associated with young people and firearms. Agencies could apply for a one-time grant of up to $1 million under this initiative. The awards were made to ten cities, including Baltimore (Maryland), Bridgeport (Connecticut), Richmond (Virginia), and Seattle (Washington). Most of the initiatives centered on strategic-oriented policing tactics with such things as curfew enforcement, civil sanctions against local gangs, and firearms confiscation programs.

On April 3, 1996, the COPS office would announce a similar program that was geared toward antigang initiatives. Once again, agencies were encouraged to apply for up to $1 million in funding in order to address the problems gangs posed to communities through drive-by shootings, graffiti, and threats and intimidation. Fifteen agencies would receive these grants, including Austin (Texas), Indianapolis (Indiana), Miami (Florida), and Salt Lake City (Utah). The majority of initiatives centered on a combination of strategic-oriented and neighborhood-oriented policing methods, as most were designed to utilize the "hot spots" and targeting methods as well as mobilizing the community to strengthen local community efforts to keep children from joining local gangs.

Another series of programmatic grants was titled Community Policing to Combat Domestic Violence. These grants were open to agencies to apply for up to $1 million to address domestic violence training under the community-oriented policing philosophy, to create problem-solving and community-based partnerships at the local level, or to assist in changing police organization so that it would be more responsive to domestic violence situations in that community. The eligibility was restricted to agencies practicing community-oriented policing for at least two years, but the benefit, like the Youth Firearm Violence and antigang initiatives, was that no local match to the grant was required. On June 20, 1996, 336 communities across the country received more than $46 million under this grant program.

Perhaps one of the more interesting grants coming from the COPS office was utilized to address the growing problem of officers being tied to having to respond to 911 calls or, more specifically, calls to 911 that were not emergencies. An innovative concept to create a nonemergency alternative to 911 was created, and the pilot project of "311" was born. Through a COPS grant in cooperation with AT&T, the Baltimore Police Department was granted $350,000 to implement the 311 nonemergency phone number along with an aggressive public education campaign in order to reduce the number of 911 calls, leaving 911 for its original intent: emergency calls only. The pilot project was apparently highly successful in that it reduced the number of nonemergency calls to 911 while giving the public a phone number they could easily remember for making routine calls to the police department for assistance.

One key provision under the Violent Crime Control and Law Enforcement Act of 1994 had called for the creation of a Police Corps, modeled after the military's ROTC. The concept was to utilize grant money to defray the cost of a college education by having enrolling college students apply for the scholarships that could be applied toward the cost of tuition, fees, books, supplies, transportation, room, board, and other miscellaneous expenses. In turn, the student, on graduation, would agree to serve at least four years with a state or local police agency. The first grant was awarded in the fall of 1996 to Brian Shane Maynor, who was the son of an officer killed in the line of duty and was enrolled at the University of North Carolina at Chapel Hill. He was granted $7,500 for each year of college. In the first two years of the Police Corps Scholarship program, Congress had appropriated over $30 million toward this program.

A number of additional COPS grant programs have included a series of grants known as Problem-Solving Partnerships. These partnerships were to be innovative community-oriented policing programs that would combine police and community members to focus on a specific crime or disorder problem in the neighborhood, such as auto theft, street-level drug dealing, or prostitution, and to develop innovative solutions for addressing these types of problems. Another series of grants focused on advanced community policing, for which 117 agencies received grant awards to further develop their organizational infrastructure to complement the implementation of community-oriented policing. Another programmatic grant series was announced in 1998 as School-Based Partnership Grants, which were focused on utilizing the methods of community-oriented policing within local schools, essentially treating the school as a specific neighborhood. Finally, another grant initiative was titled the COPS Methamphetamine Initiative, which was awarded to six cities to develop community-oriented policing strategies to deal with the production and use of methamphetamines, especially among youth.

The fourth and final area of grants created by the COPS office was in the area of training and technical assistance. Although the COPS office would take control of the Community Policing Consortium, which would continue to provide a variety of training curricula to police agencies across the country, the COPS office turned to another mechanism for delivering community-oriented policing training. The newest grant series was solicited in the fall of 1996 for collaborative efforts among police, community, government, and academic institutes to come together to form regional community policing institutes (RCPIs). These RCPIs would be created to establish a more lasting legacy of the COPS office, which, based on its original mandate, was to sunset at the end of 2000. Technically, that would also mean that the Community Policing Consortium would be required to sunset, leaving no means for agencies to receive training and technical assistance. The RCPIs were to be created to fulfill this need and, in the words of Director Brann, "create a legacy of the COPS office." The RCPIs were to accomplish this through a one-year grant of up to $1 million, followed by up to two more years of funding, at which point they would be required to seek other sources of funding in order to stay in existence.

The RCPIs were to form as a partnership created to provide comprehensive and innovative education, training, and technical assistance to COPS grantees and other policing agencies throughout a designated region. Some of the regions would include cities and their surrounding areas (e.g., Los Angeles), others would consist of entire states (e.g., West Virginia), while still others would encompass multiple states (e.g., the Minnesota Community Policing Institute). The RCPIs would draw on their collaborative partnerships to bring to a collective table all the resources and support of the partner organizations. The RCPIs would have the latitude to experiment with new ideas, to expand the traditional training curricula, and to develop curriculum that supported community-oriented policing within their specific region. The RCPIs were also created with the intent that each would conduct research on community-oriented policing in their region as well as evaluate internally the success of their training curriculums. Finally, the RCPIs were required to create specialty training areas on which they could become the "experts," on developing curriculum for and sharing the training with their regional agencies as well as the other RCPIs. On May 30, 1997, the COPS office announced that 35 RCPIs would be established across the country, funded at nearly $1 million each. The regional institutes developed are illustrated in Box 14.8.

The Violent Crime Control and Law Enforcement Act of 1994 allocated funding for the addition of the 100,000 cops to support the concept of community policing to be added to state and local agencies across the United States. The policy allowed for the employment of these officers at 75 percent for three years of an officer's pay and benefits, and it allowed for the funding of technology, staff support, and training. The bill also allowed for the use of technology and staff support that would free an officer to be able to work the street, which officially counted as the addition of a police officer under the redeployment aspects of the bill. However, it did not delve deeply into how specifically the grants would be distributed and what specific criteria would be used to determine where the funds went. The entire process was left to the discretion of the Justice Department. As one can see through the policy implementation of the "100,000 Cops" initiative, the bureaucracies have an enormous amount of power when it comes to the implementation of a congressional bill such as the Violent Crime Control and Law Enforcement Act of 1994. While Congress provided the outline for how the grant system would work, the COPS office was given the power of filling in the details, thus contributing greatly to the formation of this policy. This would come to bear on how the policy was later evaluated by a number of internal and external studies.

Policy Evaluation

There is a great need for multiple assessments to be conducted on the COPS office because this office will have what is most likely the single-greatest impact on policing in the United States to date. More important, it will have the definitive impact on the concepts and philosophy of community-oriented policing because all the grant money, programs, equipment, technology, and resources have been focused on community-oriented policing. While the early innovations and the fast diffusion of community-oriented policing across the country throughout the 1980s and early 1990s has promulgated community-oriented policing, the COPS office has provided the infrastructure to institutionalize community-oriented policing within state and local agencies across the country. However, the criteria that one uses to assess the COPS office will most likely yield how the office is perceived to be doing. Hence, truly understanding the impact this office has had on community-oriented policing will most likely take years to fully and accurately assess.

To understand this problem with assessment, one could evaluate the COPS office in much the same manner as their U.S. Department of Justice counterpart, the BJA, as a grant-making institution. In this assessment, one would look at the efficiency of the COPS office to deliver the grants to state and local law enforcement agencies. In most assessments, it would be fairly accurate to say that they have done an outstanding job. They responded to the needs and requests of local law

BOX 14.8
Regional Community Policing Institutes (RCPIs)

State	RCPI Grant Recipient	RCPI Specialty
Arizona	Arizona Peace Office Standards and Training	Building partnerships
	Navajo Department of Law Enforcement	Problem solving
California	Los Angeles County Sheriff's Department	Violence prevention
	Sacramento Police Department	Neighborhood revitalization
	San Diego Police Department	Problem solving
Colorado	Department of Public Safety	Building partnerships
Connecticut	New Haven Police Department	Building partnerships
Florida	Gainesville Police Department	Problem solving
	St. Petersburg Junior College	Executive training
Georgia	Kennesaw State University	Technology
Illinois	Illinois State Police	Organizational change
	University of Illinois at Chicago	Building partnerships
Indiana	Fort Wayne Police Department	Strategic implementation
Kansas	Wichita State University	Rural community policing
Kentucky	Eastern Kentucky University	Rural community policing
Louisiana	Louisiana State University	Building partnerships
Maine	University of Maine	Rural community policing
Maryland	Johns Hopkins University	Ethics and integrity
Massachusetts	Boston Police Department	Ethics and integrity
Michigan	Michigan State University	Organizational change
Minnesota	League of Minnesota Cities	Organizational change
Missouri	Missouri Western State College	Training
New Jersey	John Jay College of Criminal Justice	Problem solving
North Carolina	Charlotte-Mecklenberg Police Department	Crime mapping
Ohio	Great Oaks Institute	Building partnerships
Oklahoma	Association of Chiefs of Police	Management and leadership
Oregon	Board of Public Safety Standards/Training	Community team training
Pennsylvania	Pennsylvania State University	Building partnerships
Tennessee	Knoxville Police Department	Organizational change
Texas	Sam Houston State University	Building partnerships
	University of Texas at Austin	Problem solving
Virginia	Department of Criminal Justice Services	CPTED
Washington	Washington State University	Organizational change
West Virginia	Department of Criminal Justice Services	Statewide implementation

Source: Office of Community Oriented Policing Services home page, Regional Community Policing Institutes, available online at www.usdoj.gov/cops/.

enforcement agencies to expedite the grants and make the application forms easy to complete. By allowing for a two-part grant process, where the first part was a one-page application that would allow for preliminary grant acceptance, agencies could begin the process of hiring the officer, later followed up by a slightly more detailed form including the date by which money was to be transferred. Thus, the COPS office was able to truly expedite the grant process in an age when most bureaucracies do not have the capability of responding that fast. They also responded to the local agencies' desire to bypass state review and control over the grants, hence ensuring that the grant process would remain streamlined. In addition, if one were to look at the level of grant authorization, local agencies had to be pleased in the process, for 92 percent of jurisdictions that applied for a grant received initial approval in the first series of COPS AHEAD and COPS FAST grants.[111] Finally, if one looks at the goal of adding 100,000 cops to America's police and sheriffs departments by the end of 2000, the fact that as of early 1999 the COPS office had funded over 92,000 officers demonstrates that the COPS office would in fact meet its goal. Therefore, as a grant-making institution, the office could be considered to have been highly successful.

However, delivering the grants and monitoring the grants are two different things. Assessing the ability of the COPS office to monitor the grants that were awarded so fast in the fall of 1994 and all of 1995, a General Accounting Office report found that the ability of the COPS office to administer the grant was exceptional but that the ability to monitor and evaluate the financial and programmatic impact of the grants was less than adequate.[112] Although the grantees are required to submit progress and accounting reports on a periodic basis, these are simple budgetary forms that do not reveal much in the way of the true use of the grant awards. In fact, it was found that the COPS office would occasionally make periodic contacts by telephone but few on-site visits. Further, those agencies receiving grants under the COPS FAST program were most likely to receive only phone contacts because the number of agencies under this grant program was high but the number of officers hired was less. Whereas the COPS AHEAD grant recipients stood a higher chance of an on-site visit because the number of agencies under the grant award was less and the number of officers they hired was high.

The primary reason cited by the COPS office for failure to monitor the agencies receiving the awards was the fact that the agency was limited in manpower and was concentrating more fully on the process of making grant awards rather than following up on grant awards made.[113] The COPS office began with less than 100 personnel to support its large operation, but by 1997 it was up to approximately 180 personnel and by 1999 had exceeded 200. Although there was clearly always an intent to monitor the grants (part of the original mandate for the COPS office), clearly the hiring of the 100,000 cops took precedence. The reasons given by police departments for not applying for the grants are described in Table 14.3.

This limited amount of monitoring is important for a number of reasons, but two are perhaps most significant: agencies maintaining the grant after receiving the award and supplanting of the grant. In the first, because the grants are only an award for up to three years at 75 percent of an officer's pay, at the end of the three-year period there is a question as to the disposition of the officers. Will they be retained by the police agency, or will they be fired or laid off? This question has surfaced with the COPS office, which has noted that the agencies are required to maintain the officer after the end of the three-year grant because it is part of the agreement to receiving the grant. However, Director Brann has also noted that the statute needed to be further defined and that communities could not be expected to maintain hiring levels indefinitely but that a reasonable period for retaining the officers funded by the COPS office had not been determined.[114] It also appeared that in the fall of 1998, the question would be raised once again because it would be the first time many of the grants would begin to expire. In anticipation of this

TABLE 14.3 Reasons law enforcement agencies did *not* apply for a COPS grant

Reason	Number of agencies	Percentage
Cost-related factors	4,215	62.5
Could not ensure continued funding	2,745	40.5
Could not meet 25 percent match	1,198	17.7
Other cost reason	272	4.0
Regulations for use of funds too restrictive	576	8.5
Lack of information/deadline	572	8.4
Did not need additional officers	501	7.4
Other reasons	265	3.9
Political/city decisions	206	3.0
Paperwork requirements too burdensome	153	2.3
All reasons equally important	25	0.4
Do not know	267	4.0

Source: General Accounting Office (1995) telephone survey results.

event, a number of grants were extended or new grants were given to agencies that had officers whose grants were about to expire, thus delaying the inevitable. In one report, there was at least some anecdotal evidence that several agencies had essentially laid off the officer, while in others, the simple accounting figures demonstrated that sometime in the future, a police department having hired multiple officers would not be able to maintain those officers.[115] For example, the Los Angeles Police Department announced that it would hire an additional 710 officers through COPS grants at a staggered rate of hiring for 1998, 1999, and 2000. However, at the end of the three-year period for all the grants, it was estimated to cost the City of Los Angeles over $70 million a year to maintain these officers—a figure that even in the best of times could greatly offset any budget.[116] The total number of officers funded is outlined in Table 14.4.

The other major problem with failing to monitor the grants falls under the issue of agencies supplanting their grant money. When agencies agree to the COPS grants, they also acknowledge that they will not supplant the funds they receive. In other words, the grant awards are to be used

TABLE 14.4 Officers funded and COP grant totals, through February 1999

Grant type	Officers funded	Grant totals
PHS	2,003	$148,421,993
Phase I	2,570	$189,027,136
AHEAD	3,976	$282,944,668
FAST	6,049.5	$394,422,013
MORE	35,851.7	$966,924,476
UHP	41,874	$3,027,412,482
Total	92,324.2	$5,009,152,768

Source: U.S. Department of Justice, Office of the Inspector General, *Special Report: Police Hiring and Redeployment Grants*, Report No. 99-14 (April 1999), available online at www.usdoj.gov/oig/au9914/9914toc.htm.

above and beyond the normal operating budget of the police or sheriffs department and cannot be used to pay for an already hired or employed police officer or sheriff's deputy. However, especially with a limited amount of monitoring, agencies could simply utilize the grant money to pay for a previously hired officer by adjusting the budget or reducing the number of officers the city is required to employ and then hiring the difference through a COPS grant. Although the U.S. General Accounting Office acknowledged that supplanting was probably occurring, it states that "it is difficult to establish with certainty that supplanting has not occurred because of the lack of evidence to determine what would have occurred in the absence of a grant."[117] Having spoken with several agency/city accountants in regard to supplanting, one city accountant explained, under condition of anonymity, that the city had a mandate to employ five full-time officers. To obtain one of the grants and help defray city costs, they simply reduced the number of required full-time officers to four when they had an officer quit and then utilized a grant to hire a fifth "additional" officer. Although this is only one case, one must question how often this occurs.

Another problem that has been often cited is the means by which the COPS office calculates the "number of officers hired" to meet the 100,000 officers goal. During the 1992 presidential campaign, President Clinton continually called for adding 100,000 police officers to the streets of America. Again in the 1996 presidential campaign, both President Clinton and Vice President Gore continued this call and touted the advantages of hiring these "100,000 police officers." In the vice-presidential debate, Al Gore stated, "Clinton promised to pass a plan that would put 100,000 new police officers on the streets. It is law." No one would think at the time that this meant anything other than adding 100,000 bodies, but the Violent Crime Control and Law Enforcement Act of 1994 was actually very clear, albeit not often discussed, in that the use of equipment could account for the "hiring" of a new officer. Hence, the use of a COPS MORE grant to add laptop computers to the department's equipment could actually count as having hired three new officers. Despite having been written into the original law, authorizing the COPS office to utilize this type of budget "trickery" leaves one with a less-than-positive assessment of the "hiring of 100,000 police officers." See Box 14.9.

Finally, a problem that has been noted by several researchers as well as from several studies that have been conducted is based on the method in which grants have been delivered. The primary reason for adding additional police officers to state and local agencies through the grant process was to help reduce the problem of crime in cities and towns across the United States. However, although agencies with higher crime rates were in fact more likely to apply for COPS grants, there is little in the way of a relationship between crime rates and whether an applicant jurisdiction was awarded the grant.[118] In addition, several reports have found that cities, such as Oklahoma City, with a 1994 violent crime rate nearly twice the national average, had not applied for any of the COPS grants because they were not able to afford the local match.[119] Moreover, several authors have made the argument that because the grants are not based on a rational effort to disburse the grants based on official crime rates and because they are not a zero-sum game (one recipient's allocation is not dependent on what another recipient receives), these grants are more a distributive form of policy than a regulatory type of policy, as most crime policy tends to be categorized. In other words, they are grants that allow politicians to claim how many officers have been hired in their jurisdiction and how they are responsible for helping the local police and sheriffs departments, thus helping them win votes on the crime issue.

One very important and significant study in the field of criminal justice that was a result of a mandate by Congress to assess what works in the area of crime control policy was published in 1997 under the title *Preventing Crime: What Works, What Doesn't, What's Promising*. This study was led by Lawrence Sherman at the University of Maryland, and it found that "in general, the

BOX 14.9

U.S. Department of Justice Office of the Inspector General Special Report—Police Hiring and Redeployment Grants (COPS)

The following is a summary of the results of the U.S. Department of Justice's Office of Inspector General grant audits of 149 grants to various agencies throughout the country.

For the 149 grant audits, we identified about $52 million in questionable costs and about $71 million in funds that could be better used. Our dollar-related findings amount to 24 percent of the total funds awarded to the 149 grantees. The following are examples of when we would question costs or recommend funds to better use.

- Costs incurred are unallowable according to statutory or regulatory provisions.
- Costs incurred are not supported by documentation.
- Funds were improperly or incorrectly accounted for.
- Funds remain unspent after a reasonable amount of time.
- Essential grant requirements were not met.

The following weaknesses appear to cut across all types of grantees that we audited regardless of size or location.

- 20 of 145 grantees (14%) overestimated salaries and/or benefits in their grant application.

- 74 of 146 grantees (51%) included unallowable costs in their claims for reimbursement.
- 52 of 67 grantees receiving MORE grants (78%) either could not demonstrate that they redeployed officers or could not demonstrate that they had a system in place to track the redeployment of officers into community policing.
- 60 of 147 grantees (41%) showed indicators of using federal funds to supplant local funding instead of using grant funds to supplement local funding.
- 83 of 144 grantees (58%) either did not develop a good faith plan to retain officer positions or said they would not retain the officer positions at the conclusion of the grant.
- 106 of 140 grantees (76%) either failed to submit COPS initial reports, annual reports, or officer progress reports, or submitted these reports late.
- 137 of 146 grantees (94%) did not submit all required Financial Status Reports to OJP or submitted them late.
- 33 of 146 grantees (23%) had weaknesses in their community policing program or were unable to adequately distinguish COPS activities from their pre-grant mode of operations.

Source: U.S. Department of Justice, Office of the Inspector General, *Special Report: Police Hiring and Redeployment Grants*, Report No. 99-14 (April 1999), available online at http://www.usdoj.gov/oig/au9914/9914toc.htm.

evidence suggest that federal appropriations to prevent crime through additional policing is most effective when allocated on the basis of serious crime rather than on the basis of population size."[120] The researchers state that the grants relate primarily to population size because those jurisdictions with higher population rates tended to be the agencies that applied for more grants. In addition, they explain the implications that can be drawn from this scientific conclusion:

> One is the "promising" finding that across all large cities, more police produced less serious crime. A second is the finding that each additional police officer assigned to a big city prevents six times as many serious crimes each year as an officer assigned by population. A third conclusion is the finding that directed patrol in crime hot spots "works" to prevent crime in those hot spots, the greatest micro-level concentrations of crime. A fourth conclusion is the "promising" finding that police can reduce gun crime by intensified enforcement of the laws against carrying concealed weapons.[121]

As a result of this national assessment of "what works" in the area of policing, this report to Congress made the recommendation that Congress should "consider revising the statutory allocation formula based not only on city-level violent crime, but beat-level and block level crime as well. Such a revision would be more effective in directing federal funds as precisely as possible for maximum crime prevention."[122] Finally, the authors of the report also focus their conclusions on the fact that the COPS grants are intended to be applied toward the implementation of community-oriented policing. They state, "While COPS language has stressed a community policing approach, there is no evidence that community policing *per se* reduces crime without a clear focus on a crime risk factor objective."[123] Thus, they conclude that while the "scientific evidence indicates the COPS program is effective, it also suggests it could be more effective if its funding was more focused upon police programs of proven effectiveness," such as directed patrols toward "hot spots" and problem-oriented policing on a beat-level and targeted basis.

In 1999, an individual researcher, Arthur Sharp, conducted a survey of police departments receiving COPS grants to determine police chiefs' perceptions of the effectiveness of the program.[124] The feedback he received was very positive in terms of the grants, the grant process, and the ability to hire additional officers. One of the more serious issues raised was the ability of the police departments to pick up the entire budget of the newly hired officers at the end of the three-year grant period. For those agencies that hired a dozen or more police officers through the UHP grants, that would potentially increase the cities' expenditures by over $1 million a year, something not feasible for many municipalities. Another issue that often arose from this survey of police chiefs was that the grants were intended to support the implementation of community policing. Many chiefs argued that they surely needed additional officers, but they did not necessarily need to hire community policing officers, thus putting them somewhat at odds with the intent of the grant. Other issues that the report raised included the uncertain connection between adding police officers to the streets and the drop in crime rates and that the number of police officers hired versus the number claimed by the COPS office may not have been realistic. These questions would continue to be raised by many in regard to the COPS program.

In 1998, the COPS office undertook a major evaluation of its own by conducting what is known as a process evaluation, which looks to see how successfully the COPS program was implemented, not the impact the program had. The report was published by the National Institute of Justice in August 2000 and was titled *National Evaluation of the COPS Program—Title 1 of the 1994 Crime Act.*[125] The report explained that the COPS program had four specific goals: (1) to increase the number of officers deployed in American communities, (2) to foster problem solving and interaction with communities by police officers, (3) to encourage innovation in policing, and (4) to develop new technologies for assisting officers in reducing crime and its consequences.[126] It then detailed the various initiatives under the COPS program (e.g., hiring grants) in order to provide some background on the program. The evaluation, the report explained, was funded by the National Institute of Justice and was conducted by the Urban Institute as an independent review of the COPS program. In order to conduct the evaluation, the Urban Institute researchers attempted to address seven specific questions: (1) How did local agencies respond to the exchange offered by the COPS program? (2) What distribution of COPS funds resulted form localities' application decisions through the end of 1997? (3) How did COPS hiring grantees accomplish their hiring and deployment objectives through mid-1998, and how did they expect to retain the COPS-funded officers? (4) How did COPS MORE grantees succeed in acquiring and implementing technology, hiring civilians, and achieving the projected redeployment targets through mid-1998? (5) What increases in policing levels were projected and achieved by local agencies using COPS resources? (6) To what

extent had the COPS program succeeded by mid-1998 in encouraging grantees to build partnerships with communities, adopt problem-solving strategies, and participate in prevention
programs? and (7) To what extent did grantee's organizations change through 1998 to support
and sustain community policing?[127]

The findings of the process evaluation were mostly positive but held a number of qualifications. In terms of how local agencies responded, the COPS office found that while 19,175 agencies were eligible for grants, only 10,537 (55 percent) applied, and 761 (7 percent) had withdrawn
from the application process. The problem, as previously cited, was the financial constraints of
many localities for the matching grants. In terms of the distribution, the researchers found that,
for the most part, the funds went to jurisdictions with no particular bias, and it highlighted that
agencies with the highest murder rates received the majority of funds in an attempt to link murder with crime in order to show that, like the Sherman report cited earlier, COPS programs encouraged funds to go where the most crime occurs. In terms of hiring, the evaluation found that
agencies were mostly successful and that police were deployed in community policing activities
but that it was too soon to tell whether there was retention after the grants expired. The report
also highlighted that the MORE grants were successful and popular with local police agencies and
that every $100,000 spent on technology equated to 6.12 full-time equivalent officers. In other
words, for every $100,000 spent on technology, the COPS grants essentially gained six "officers"
who counted toward the 100,000 total. As for the fifth question, the evaluation found that,
through 1997, 41,000 grants had been awarded and 39,000 officers hired. It projected that by
2001, there would be 57,200 officers hired but that the number would stabilize at 55,400 by 2003.
The rest of the "100,000 Cops" would be derived from the MORE technology grants. Finally, in
terms of the last two questions, the researchers reported that the COPS program did help advance
community policing in the United States, but they were also quick to point out that community
policing has many different meanings for different agencies. See Table 14.5.

The *National Evaluation of the COPS Program* gives the impression that the program was
very successful, but it should be noted that this conclusion is derived primarily from a process
evaluation, not an outcome evaluation. In other words, if one asked if the COPS office gave out
grants to local agencies like it said it would, the answer is a resounding yes. There is little doubt
that the COPS office achieved the goal of funneling money from the federal government to state
and local police agencies. However, it is the methods employed in the grant process that often
come into question. Although the Crime Bill of 1994 allowed for the counting of technology
grants to equate to the full-time equivalent of a police officer, that part of the money did not put
another body on the street like most people believed it would. And, in fact, questions have been
raised as to whether the COPS program's count of officers or even that of the *National Evaluation*
is correct. A Heritage Foundation study found that by 1998, only 39,617 officers had been hired
and that the way the COPS Office counted officers was suspicious.[128] Heritage Foundation researcher Muhlhausen gives the example that "COPS officials claim that the Spokane Police
Department had hired 56 new officers based on three COPS grants worth $4.2 million, but the
Spokane Police Department said that it had hired only 25 officers. Nevertheless, COPS officials
counted the 31 'missing' officers in the total number of additional officers it supposedly put on
the streets."[129] This problem of official number counts has continued to plague the COPS office,
and the larger the agency, the more discrepancies there tend to be. Additional research into this
discrepancy continues to find the same disparities.[130]

Another study by Muhlhausen also challenged the *National Evaluation's* limited claims that
COPS grants went to areas with either the highest crime rates or the highest murder rates.[131]
Although the authors do not look at the outcome of this, since theirs was a process evaluation,

TABLE 14.5 Full-time community policing officers in local police departments (by size of population served, United States, 2000)

Population served	Full-time community policing officers		
	Percentage of agencies using	Number of officers	Average number of officers
All sizes	66	102,598	12
1,000,000 or more	100	33,214	2,208
500,000 to 999,999	85	8,617	297
250,000 to 499,999	95	6,866	180
150,000 to 249,999	94	8,580	53
50,000 to 149,999	93	7,167	20
25,000 to 49,999	83	7,854	12
10,000 to 24,999	72	9,184	7
2,500 to 9,999	63	12,745	5
Less than 2,500	60	8,370	3

Source: U.S. Department of Justice, Bureau of Justice Statistics, *Local Police Departments, 2000*, Bulletin NCJ 196002 (Washington, D.C.: U.S. Department of Justice, October 2002), p. 15, table 32.

their inclusion of this would allow many to make the natural assumption that by channeling the grants to jurisdictions with the highest crime problems, it would have an impact on crime. Muhlhausen looked at the impact that the hiring grants had on crime and found no statistically measurable effect on violent crime and that most of the declining crime was attributed to social changes in minority communities and prison expansion. The greatest effect of the COPS program was found in the COPS funding that targeted specific problems in specific locations, such as gangs, juvenile youth crime, and domestic violence.[132] Muhlhausen concluded that "there are two possible explanations for the ineffectiveness of the COPS hiring and redeployment grants: 1) the actual number of officers 'added' to the street by these grants may be substantially less than the funding indicates, and 2) merely paying for the operational expense of law enforcement agencies without a clear crime-fighting objective is likely to be ineffective in reducing violent crime."[133] This has also been the finding of other independent researchers who have found that both the concepts of hiring more officers and community policing have probably had no influence on national rates of violent crime.[134]

Policy Change & Termination

Policy evaluation almost always creates a feedback cycle to either the agenda setting process or the policy formulation stages. This will cause the policy to change, ideally based on the evaluation, but often based upon politics. If the policy is seen as no longer being viable, then in extreme cases the policy will be terminated. Policy change will often take one of three forms, it will see incremental change, the enactment of new statutes that will change the policy, or major shifts in the public policy, usually as a result of political change. The VCCLEA Bill witnessed some interesting changes over the past ten years, changes that seemed to indicate it may have been moving toward policy termination (which the original bill had a sunset clause indicating the COPS Office would disband in 2000). However, incremental changes, news statutes, and major political shifts have dramatically changed the outlook of this bill.

In 2001, following the inauguration of President George W. Bush into the Office of the Presidency, the COPS program was being retooled to focus more heavily on school violence through an emphasis on school resource officers. The Bush administration did not want to be associated with a Clinton-era program, so it began retooling the COPS Office, which had been kept alive through the passage of the 2000 reauthorization bill. When the terrorist attacks of September 11, 2001 occurred, the Bush administration moved its emphasis entirely toward Homeland Security and the COPS Office became part of that major reemphasis of policy. Programs within the COPS Office emphasized "homeland security through community policing." While many felt that the two were symbiotic in nature, others felt the COPS Office just provided another funding means for the Bush Administration's "War on Terror." Throughout the Bush years (2001–2009), as the Department of Homeland Security appropriations rose, the administrations requests plummeted causing COPS Office appropriations fell. At its high in the late 1990s, the COPS Office was funded with over $1.4 billion. In 2004 through 2008, the Bush Administration asked for less than $100 million each fiscal year, and although Congress funded it at a higher level, appropriations still dropped below $600 million.[135] It appeared that the COPS Office was moving toward possible policy termination.

In 2008, however, Hillary Clinton, running for the Democratic nomination for the Presidency, played up her husband's COPS program and campaigned that if elected, she would reinvigorate the COPS program. Although she lost the nomination to Barack Obama, Obama picked up the same campaign promise and solidified it with the selection of Senator Joe Biden as his Vice-Presidential running mate. The campaign then employed the fact that Biden had helped to create the program and their opponent, Senator John McCain had voted against the COPS bill in 1994. As one of the original architects of the COPS bill was about to become the vice president of the United States there was little doubt the new administration would move to keep the COPS program alive.

In January of 2009, with the inauguration of Barack Obama as president, the new administration was facing a severe recession and quickly moved to pass the Economic Recovery and Reinvestment Act. This particular act appropriated an additional $1 Billion dollars for the COPS program and eliminated the state matching requirement, as well as the cap on grant awards, in order to push more money into the economy quickly. Not long after that, Representative Anthony Weiner (D-NY) introduced House Bill 1139— The COPS Improvement Act of 2009, which would authorize the COPS office $1.8 billion annually in appropriations through 2014. While the bill remains under consideration due to the numerous other bills (e.g., health care) taking up Congress's time, the bill has yet to pass the House. There is little doubt, however, that the Obama administration will continue to support the COPS program due to the legacy of the Clintons and Vice President Biden, keeping it alive and viable, at least through this administration.

Conclusion

This case study on the Violent Crime Control and Law Enforcement Act of 1994—especially the bill's centerpiece, the "100,000 Cops" initiative aimed at implementing and supporting community policing programs across the country—highlights the public policy process as it relates to crime policy in the United States. Understanding how crime was identified as a problem in the early 1990s and, more specifically, why community policing was seen as the solution demonstrates how problems are identified. Understanding how community policing became linked with the "100,000 Cops" program and how government came to entertain such a sweeping and costly policy allows us to understand more fully the agenda-setting process. Walking through how the act was crafted by Congress assists us in more fully comprehending how policies are often made and bills passed. Reviewing how the policy was ultimately implemented explains the powerful role of the bureaucracies in implementing public policy.

Analyzing the evaluations of the COPS program allows us to understand how policy evaluation is conducted. Assessing the concept of policy change and termination through the COPS program provides insight into how policies stay alive or eventually die. Finally, looking at the entire public process through this case study highlights how crime and the criminal justice system helps create public policy and how public policy impacts the criminal justice system.

Notes

1. N. E. Marion, *A History of Federal Crime Control Initiatives, 1960–1993* (Westport, Conn.: Praeger, 1994).

2. G. Cordner, "Elements of Community Policing," in *Policing Perspectives: An Anthology*, ed. L. K. Gaines and G. Cordner (Los Angeles: Roxbury Press, 1999), pp. 137–49.

3. W. M. Oliver, *Community-Oriented Policing: A Systemic Approach to Policing*, 3rd ed. (Upper Saddle River, N.J.: Prentice Hall, 2003).

4. W. M. Oliver, "The Third Generation of Community Policing: Moving through Innovation, Diffusion, and Institutionalization," *Police Quarterly* 3 (4, 2000): 367–88.

5. Oliver, *Community-Oriented Policing*.

6. Ibid.

7. As cited in T. Gest, *Crime and Politics* (New York: Oxford University Press, 2001), p. 168.

8. Ibid.

9. Christopher B. Daly, "Massachusetts Seen Near Return to Death Penalty," *Washington Post*, August 18, 1991, p. A4.

10. See Kathleen Hall Jamieson, *Dirty Politics: Deception, Distraction, and Democracy* (New York: Oxford University Press 1992; Darrell M. West, *Air Wars: Television Advertising in Election Campaigns 1952–1996*, 2nd ed. (Washington, D.C.: Congressional Quarterly Press, 1997).

11. Democratic National Convention, "1992 Democratic Party Platform," reprinted in *World Book Encyclopedia: American Reference Library*. CD-ROM (Orem, Utah: Western Standard, 1998).

12. Ibid.

13. Ibid.

14. Harry A. Chernoff, Christopher M. Kelly, and John R. Kroger, "The Politics of Crime," *Harvard Journal on Legislation* 33 (2, 1996): 527–79; Nancy E. Marion, "Symbolic Policies in Clinton's Crime Control Agenda," *Buffalo Criminal Law Review* 1 (1, 1997): 67–108; Jill Zuckman, "The President's Call to Serve Is Clear but Undefined," *Congressional Quarterly Weekly Report* 218 (1993): 51.

15. Ronald G. Shaiko, "Reverse Lobbying: Interest Group Mobilization from the White House and the Hill," in *Interest Group Politics*, 5th ed., ed. Allan J. Cigler and Burdett A. Loomis (Washington, D.C.: Congressional Quarterly Press, 1998), pp. 255–82, at 259–60.

16. Chernoff et al., "The Politics of Crime"; Ben J. Wattenberg, *Values Matter Most: How Democrats or Republicans or a Third Party Can Win and Renew the American Way of Life* (New York: Regnery Publishing, 1996), p. 4. Note: One of the death-row inmates is reported to have had an IQ in the 70s. See Katherine Beckett and Theodore Sasson, *The Politics of Injustice* (Thousand Oaks, Calif.: Pine Forge Press, 2000), p. 70.

17. Gwen Ifill, "Clinton, in Houston Speech, Assails Bush on Crime Issue," *New York Times*, July 24, 1992, p. A13.

18. Henry Scott Wallace, "Clinton's Real Plan on Crime," *National Law Journal* 12 (1992): 15.

19. Ifill, "Clinton, in Houston Speech, Assails Bush on Crime Issue"; Marion, *A History of Federal Crime Control Initiatives, 1960–1993*.

20. Marion, *A History of Federal Crime Control Initiatives, 1960–1993*.

21. Ifill, "Clinton, in Houston Speech, Assails Bush on Crime Issue."

22. Marion, "Symbolic Policies in Clinton's Crime Control Agenda."

23. Cited in Eva Bertram et al., *Drug War Politics: The Price of Denial* (Berkeley: University of California Press, 1996), p. 117.

24. Marion, "Symbolic Policies in Clinton's Crime Control Agenda," p. 71.

25. Chernoff et al., "The Politics of Crime," p. 543.

26. Ifill, "Clinton, in Houston Speech, Assails Bush on Crime Issue"; Edward Walsh, "Clinton Charges Bush Uses Crime Issue to Divide," *Washington Post*, July 24, 1992, p. A16.

27. Ann Devroy and Ruth Marcus, "Police Group Gives Bush Its Blessing: President Fought for Endorsement," *The Washington Post*, October 10, 1992, p. A1.

28. Chernoff et al., "The Politics of Crime," p. 543.

29. Bill Clinton and Al Gore, *Putting People First* (New York: Times Books, 1992).

30. Ifill, "Clinton, in Houston Speech, Assails Bush on Crime Issue"; Walsh, "Clinton Charges Bush Uses Crime Issue to Divide."

31. Raymond Michelowski, "Some Thoughts regarding the Impact of Clinton's Election on Crime and Justice Policy," *The Criminologist* 18 (3, 1993): 6.

32. Newsweek poll, March 19–20, 1992, gave Bush a 41 percent to 35 percent lead over Clinton on crime. A CBS/New York Times poll, May 6–8, 1992, gave Bush a 36 percent to 22 percent lead on law and order. An ABC News/Washington Post poll, May 8–11, 1992, gave Bush a 39 percent to 26 percent lead on crime. An ABC News/Washington Post poll, June 3–7, 1992, gave Bush a 32 percent to 21 percent lead on crime. A Gallup/Newsweek poll, July 9–10, 1992, showed Clinton leading Bush on crime 25 percent to 24 percent. A U.S. News and World Reports/Princeton Survey Research poll, August 6–9, 1992, demonstrated an equal tie of 38 percent each. A NBC News/Wall Street Journal poll, August 10–12, 1992, gave Clinton a lead over Bush, 33 percent to 25 percent. A Gallup poll, August 10–12, 1992, gave Clinton the lead 51 percent to 35 percent. An ABC News/Washington Post poll, October 4, 1992, gave Clinton the lead, 38 percent to 32 percent. A Times Mirror poll, October 8–11, 1992, showed Clinton leading 31 percent to 27 percent. A Gallup/USA Today/CNN poll, October 9–11, 1992, showed Clinton leading 39 percent to 34 percent. Finally, a Princeton Survey Research poll, October 20–22, 1992, showed Clinton leading 35 percent to 25 percent. All these polls are available on LEXIS. See also Chernoff et al., "The Politics of Crime," footnotes 93 and 94.

33. Chernoff et al., "The Politics of Crime," p. 544.

34. See James P. Pfiffner, *The Strategic Presidency: Hitting the Ground Running*, 2nd ed. revised. (Lawrence: University Press of Kansas, 1996).

35. Chernoff et al., "The Politics of Crime," p. 544.

36. Ibid.

37. Ibid., p. 545.

38. Ibid.

39. Robert DiClerico, *The American President*, 4th ed. (Englewood Cliffs, N.J.: Prentice Hall, 1995); Robert DiClerico, "Assessing Context and Character," *Society* 33 (6, 1996): 28–36; Richard E. Neustadt, *Presidential Power and the Modern Presidents* (New York: Free Press, 1990); Pfiffner, *The Strategic Presidency*.

40. DiClerico, "Assessing Context and Character," p. 28.

41. DiClerico, *The American President*; DiClerico, "Assessing Context and Character"; Neustadt, *Presidential Power and the Modern Presidents*; Pfiffner, *The Strategic Presidency*.

42. DiClerico, "Assessing Context and Character," p. 28.

43. Katherine Beckett, *Making Crime Pay: Law and Order in Contemporary American Politics* (New York: Oxford University Press, 1997); Katherine Beckett, "Setting the Public Agenda: Street Crime and Drug Use in American Politics," *Social Problems* 41 (3, 1994): 425–47; Beckett and Sasson, *The Politics of Injustice*; Bertram et al., *Drug War Politics*; Chernoff et al., "The Politics of Crime"; Marion, "Symbolic Policies in Clinton's Crime Control Agenda"; Michael Massing, *The Fix* (New York: Simon & Schuster, 1998); Tony G. Poveda, "Clinton, Crime, and the Justice Department," *Social Justice* 21 (3, 1996): 73–84.

44. DiClerico, "Assessing Context and Character"; William J. Clinton, *Public Papers of the Presidents of the United States-1993* (Washington, D.C.: U.S. Government Printing Office, 1996).

45. Chernoff et al., "The Politics of Crime," p. 545.

46. Marion, "Symbolic Policies in Clinton's Crime Control Agenda," pp. 73 and 74.

47. Chernoff et al., "The Politics of Crime," p. 545; National Archives and Records Administration, "Executive Orders Disposition Tables," available online at www.nara.gov/fedreg/eo.html (data downloaded October 19, 1999; see specifically January 1993 through July 1993).

48. William J. Clinton, "Address before a Joint Session of Congress on Administration Goals. February 17, 1993," in *Public Papers of the Presidents of the United States-1993*, p. 117.

49. William J. Clinton, "Remarks to Law Enforcement Organizations and an Exchange with Reporters. April 15, 1993," in *Public Papers of the Presidents of the United States-1993*, pp. 435–37.

50. William J. Clinton, "Remarks at the National Law Enforcement Officers Memorial Ceremony. May 13,

1993," in *Public Papers of the Presidents of the United States—1993*, pp. 654–56.

51. Morton Kondracke, "Hour Is Late, but Crime Bill Is Finally Coming," *Roll Call* July 8 1993, as cited in Chernoff et al., "The Politics of Crime," p. 545, footnote 103.

52. Chernoff et al., "The Politics of Crime," p. 545.

53. Ibid.

54. Ibid., p. 547.

55. The first nomination was for Zoe Baird, vice president and general counsel to Aetna Life and Casualty Insurance, and the second nomination was Kimba Woods, a judge of the U.S. District Court for the Southern District of New York.

56. Chernoff et al., "The Politics of Crime," p. 547; William J. Clinton, "Remarks on the Swearing-In of Attorney General Janet Reno," in *Public Papers of the Presidents of the United States-1993*, p. 279; Lord Windlesham, *Politics, Punishment, and Populism* (New York: Oxford University Press, 1998), p. 78.

57. Clinton, *Public Papers of the Presidents of the United States-1993*; Herb Kohl, "Response to 'The Politics of Crime,'" *Harvard Journal on Legislation* 33 (2, 1996): 527–79, at 581–84.

58. Chernoff et al., p. 548.

59. Interview with a senior White House official on January 16, 1996, as cited in Chernoff et al., "The Politics of Crime," pp. 548–49.

60. Chernoff et al., "The Politics of Crime," p. 549; DiClerico, "Assessing Context and Character."

61. Chernoff et al., "The Politics of Crime," p. 549; Lyn Ragsdale, *Vital Statistics on the Presidency: Washington to Clinton*, rev. ed. (Washington, D.C.: Congressional Quarterly Press, 1998), p. 214.

62. Poveda, "Clinton, Crime, and the Justice Department," p. 76.

63. Marion, "Symbolic Policies in Clinton's Crime Control Agenda."

64. Windlesham, *Politics, Punishment, and Populism*, p. 35.

65. Ibid., p. 31.

66. Poveda, "Clinton, Crime, and the Justice Department," pp. 73–84.

67. This is not unusual for incoming presidents to support previous legislative bills circulating in Congress because they generally have been worked out in committees, have reached their final stages, and provide for an instant "win" on the part of the president. See Paul C. Light, *The President's Agenda: Domestic Policy Choice from Kennedy to Reagan*, rev. ed. (Baltimore: The Johns Hopkins University Press, 1991), pp. 122–26.

68. William J. Clinton, "Remarks Announcing the Anti-Crime Initiative and an Exchange with Reporters. August 11, 1993," in *Public Papers of the Presidents of the United States-1993*, pp. 1360–63. For similar remarks, see Ifill, "Clinton, in Houston Speech, Assails Bush on Crime Issue."

69. Clinton, *Public Papers of the Presidents of the United States-1993*, p. 2241; Windlesham, *Politics, Punishment, and Populism*, pp. 32–33.

70. William J. Clinton, "The President's Radio Address. August 14, 1993," in *Public Papers of the Presidents of the United States-1993*, pp. 1379–80.

71. W. M. Oliver, *The Law and Order Presidency* (Upper Saddle River, N.J.: Prentice Hall, 2003).

72. Chernoff et al., "The Politics of Crime," p. 550.

73. For a comprehensive outline of the history of the Violent Crime Control and Law Enforcement Act of 1994 (HR 3355), see Congressional Information Service, *CIS Annual 1994* (Bethesda, Md.: Congressional Information Service, 1995), pp. 170–84; 103rd Congress, 2nd Session, "Violence Crime Control and Law Enforcement Act of 1994," *Congressional and Administrative News* (St. Paul, Minn.: West, 1995), pp. 1801–80; James Houston and William W. Parsons, *Criminal Justice and the Policy Process* (Chicago: Nelson Hall, 1998), pp. 77–82.

74. "Brooks, Biden Offer Crime Measures," *Congressional Quarterly Weekly Report*, September 25, 1994, p. 51. In the House, it was designated House Resolution 3131; in the Senate, it was Senate Bill 1488.

75. "Brooks, Biden Offer Crime Measures"; Marion, "Symbolic Policies in Clinton's Crime Control Agenda," p. 77; Windlesham, *Politics, Punishment, and Populism*, p. 32.

76. William J. Clinton, "The President's Radio Address. October 9, 1993," in *Public Papers of the Presidents of the United States-1993*, pp. 1721–22.

77. William J. Clinton, "The President's Radio Address. October 23, 1993," in *Public Papers of the Presidents of the United States-1993*, pp. 1811–12.

78. Chernoff et al., "The Politics of Crime," p. 551; Windlesham, *Politics, Punishment, and Populism*, pp. 35–36.

79. Windlesham, *Politics, Punishment, and Populism*, p. 36.

80. Chernoff et al., "The Politics of Crime," p. 554.

81. William J. Clinton, "Remarks on Signing Handgun Control Legislation. November 30, 1993," in *Public Papers of the Presidents of the United States-1993*, pp. 2079–81; Carol J. DeFrances and Steven K. Smith, "Federal-State Relations in Gun Control: The 1993

Brady Handgun Violence Prevention Act," *Publius: The Journal of Federalism* 24 (summer 1994): 69–82.

82. William J. Clinton, "Statement on Signing the International Parental Kidnapping Crime Act of 1993. December 2, 1993," in *Public Papers of the Presidents of the United States-1993*, p. 2093.

83. William J. Clinton, "Statement on Signing the National Child Protection Act of 1993. December 20, 1993," in *Public Papers of the Presidents of the United States-1993*, pp. 2192–93.

84. William J. Clinton, "The President's Radio Address. December 11, 1993," in *Public Papers of the Presidents of the United States-1993*, pp. 2154–55.

85. William J. Clinton, "Address Before a Joint Session of the Congress on the State of the Union. January 25, 1994," in *Public Papers of the Presidents of the United States-1994* (Washington, D.C.: U.S. Government Printing Office, 1995), pp. 126–35, specifically p. 133.

86. Chernoff et al., "The Politics of Crime," p. 557; Gwen Ifill, "Clinton Embraces Crime Measure, Ever so Vaguely," *New York Times*, February 21, 1994, p. A13. As cited in the Ifill article, White House Press Secretary Dee Dee Myers stated, "It is up to Congress to work out all the details" demonstrating a very hands-off approach to the crime legislation by President Clinton.

87. Chernoff et al., "The Politics of Crime," p. 557.

88. Clinton, *Public Papers of the Presidents of the United States-1994*, see pp. 658–60, "The President's Radio Address," April 9, 1994; pp. 701–2, "The President's Radio Address," April 16, 1994; pp. 766–67, "The President's Radio Address," April 23, 1994; pp. 1096–98, "The President's Radio Address," June 18, 1994; pp. 1258–59, "The President's Radio Address," July 16, 1994; and pp. 1340–41, "The President's Radio Address," July 30, 1994.

89. J. G. Gimpel, Fulfilling the Contract: The First One Hundred Days (Boston: Allyn & Bacon, 1996).

90. Ibid.

91. Congressional Quarterly, *Congressional Quarterly Weekly Report*, May 7, 1994.

92. Many of these were coordinated with the assistance of the White House and their "reverse lobbying" with the various interest groups representing the law enforcement community. See Shaiko, "Reverse Lobbying."

93. Ibid.

94. Windlesham, *Politics, Punishment, and Populism*, p. 96.

95. As Wolpe and Levine explain, "On the evening of August 12, at a rally at the National Association of Police Organizations meeting in Minneapolis, Clinton stood surrounded by uniformed officers and American flags as he blamed special interests for the House vote defeating the rule for floor consideration of HR 3355, as he attacked Republicans for playing politics with America's safety, and as he tapped widespread public support for a ban on assault weapons. The evening news pictures were vintage Reagan. Within a week, a *USA Today* poll showed that confidence in Clinton's handling of crime had bounced up to 42 percent from 29 percent just a month earlier." See Bruce C. Wolpe and Bertram J. Levine, *Lobbying Congress: How the System Works*, 2nd ed. (Washington, D.C.: Congressional Quarterly Press, 1996), p. 133.

96. Chernoff et al., "The Politics of Crime," p. 570, footnote 251; Shaiko, "Reverse Lobbying"; Windlesham, *Politics, Punishment, and Populism*, p. 96. According to Shaiko, Clinton was able to obtain support from the following interest groups: Fraternal Order of Police, National Association of Police Organizations, International Union of Police Associations, National Troopers Coalition, International Brotherhood of Police Officers, International Association of Chiefs of Police, Federal Law Enforcement Officers Association, National Organization of Black Law Enforcement Executives, National Sheriffs Association, Major City Police Chiefs Association, Police Executive Research Forum, and Police Foundation. The only association missing was the Police Benevolent Association, which would not support the crime bill because of its unhappiness with the Brady Bill and the assault weapons ban.

97. Chernoff et al., "The Politics of Crime," pp. 570–71.

98. Shaiko, "Reverse Lobbying," p. 261; Windlesham, *Politics, Punishment, and Populism*, pp. 100–102. According to Windlesham, "During the final stages of negotiation, a potential swing voter, Representative Susan Molinari (R-NY), pressed for a fundamental change in the judicial process. She wanted evidence of previous charges of sexual offenses to be admissible as evidence in court, even if the defendant had not been convicted of the offense.... Molinari had obtained an encouraging response from a surprising quarter. She has said that when she had talked to Clinton on the telephone, he had expressed his disappointment that two items had been dropped from the bill-the sexual predator notification provision and the provision that would make admissible in court, at the discretion of the judge, a defendant's prior charges of sexual offenses. According to Molinari, Clinton had said that he would try and get them back."

99. Chernoff et al., "The Politics of Crime," pp. 570–73; Windlesham, *Politics, Punishment, and Populism*, pp. 96–103.

100. Windlesham, *Politics, Punishment, and Populism*, p. 103.

101. DiClerico, "Assessing Context and Character."

102. William J. Clinton, "Remarks on Signing the Violent Crime Control and Law Enforcement Act of 1994. September 13, 1994," in *Public Papers of the Presidents of the United States-1994*, pp. 1539–41.

103. As cited in Gest, *Crime and Politics*, p. 183.

104. U.S. Department of Justice, *The Violent Crime Control and Law Enforcement Act of 1994: Briefing Book* (Washington, D.C.: U.S. Department of Justice, 1994).

105. J. E. Brann, Interview by author, Washington, D.C., December 20, 1996.

106. Ibid.

107. U.S. General Accounting Office, *Community Policing: Information on the "COPS on the Beat" Grant Program* (Washington, D.C.: U.S. General Accounting Office, 1995).

108. Ibid.

109. Ibid.

110. W. M. Oliver, *Community Policing: Training Needs Assessment* (Institute, W. Va.: West Virginia Regional Community Policing Institute, 1998).

111. U.S. General Accounting Office, *Community Policing*.

112. Ibid.; U.S. General Accounting Office, *Community Policing: Issues Related to the Design, Operation, and Management of the Grant Program* (Washington, D.C.: U.S. General Accounting Office, 1997).

113. Ibid.

114. Ibid.

115. National Public Radio, "Community Policing," *All Things Considered*, October 6, 1998.

116. Ibid.

117. U.S. General Accounting Office, *Community Policing: Issues Related to the Design, Operation, and Management of the Grant Program*.

118. U.S. General Accounting Office, *Community Policing: Information on the "COPS on the Beat" Grant Program*.

119. Associated Press, "Finding Promised Cops a Tough Task," *Parkersburg News*, October 29, 1996, p. 6B; A. G. Sharp, "Special Report: A Report Card on COPS," *Law and Order*, February 1999, pp. 76–80.

120. L. Sherman et al., *Preventing Crime: What Works, What Doesn't, What's Promising* (Washington, D.C.: Office of Justice Programs, 1997).

121. Ibid.

122. Ibid.

123. Ibid.

124. Sharp, "A Report Card on COPS."

125. J. A. Roth and J. F. Ryan, *National Evaluation of the COPS Program-Title 1 of the 1994 Crime Act* (Washington, D.C.: National Institute of Justice, 2000).

126. Ibid.

127. Ibid.

128. D. B. Muhlhausen, "More COPS Funding Will Not Mean More Cops and Less Crime," *Heritage Foundation Executive Memorandum*, No. 752 (Washington, D.C.: Heritage Foundation, 2001).

129. Ibid.

130. E. R. Maguire, J. B. Snipes, C. D. Uchida, and M. Townsend, "Counting Cops: Estimating the Number of Police Officers and Police Agencies in the USA," *Policing: An International Journal of Police Strategies and Management* 21 (1, 1998): 97–120.

131. D. B. Muhlhausen, "Do Community Oriented Policing Services Grants Affect Violent Crime Rates?" in *A Report of the Heritage Center for Data Analysis* (Washington, D.C.: Heritage Foundation, 2001).

132. Ibid.

133. Ibid.

134. J. E. Eck and E. R. Maguire, "Have Changes in Policing Reduced Violent Crime? An Assessment of the Evidence, in *The Crime Drop*, ed. A. Blumstein and J. Wallman (New York: Cambridge University Press, 2000), pp. 207–65.

135. N. James, "Community Oriented Policing Services (COPS): Background, Legislation, and Issues." CRS Report for Congress. January 15, 2008.

INDEX